D1234783

GOTTERDAMMERUNG 1945

1945

GERMANY'S LAST STAND IN THE EAST

GOTTERDAMMERUNG 1945

1945

GERMANY'S LAST STAND IN THE EAST

Russ Schneider

edited by Richard S. Warfield

EASTERN FRONT/WARFIELD BOOKS

Philomont, VA.

Copyright 1998
by
EASTERN FRONT/WARFIELD BOOKS INC.

ISBN 0-9655683-1-8
Printed in the United States of America

Published by
EASTERN FRONT/WARFIELD BOOKS INC.
36734 Pelham Ct
Philomont, VA. 20131 USA
(540) 338-1972
Fax (540) 338-1910
www.sonic.net/~bstone/eastfront
e-mail: efwb@erols.com

TABLE OF CONTENTS

PART IV—HUNGARY

PART V—EAST AND WEST PRUSSIA

PART VI—ALONG THE ODER

Maps

INTRODUCTION

East Versus West in 1945—The Last Blow in the West

The only German offensive on the Western Front in 1945 began just a few minutes before the year of 1944 came to a close. Artillery fire, preliminary scouting raids, and scattered air attacks had already commenced before midnight. The official starting date was January 1st.

The German objective was the city of Strasbourg and the American and French armies deployed in Alsace. SS Reichsfuhrer Heinrich Himmler, with no previous military experience, had been placed in nominal command of this operation, which the Germans christened Nordwind—North Wind.

German historians do not devote much attention to this battle, probably with good reason. At the time, the Western Allies looked on it as a much more serious business, but over the years this too has been obscured by the continuous fascination with the Battle of the Bulge, still in progress on January 1st in the Ardennes forests a hundred and fifty miles to the north. By this time the crisis stage of the Battle of the Bulge had already passed, but there remained a great deal of mopping up to do— that is to say countless small savage combats—which would consume most of this first month of the new year.

The German strategic objectives in launching yet another offensive, this time onto the plains of Alsace, were somewhat ambiguous. With his usual directness, Army Chief of Staff General Heinz Guderian declared the whole business to be a waste of time and resources. The Eastern Front was where the great catastrophe was looming. But Hitler was simply unwilling to accept the magnitude of the Russian threat, a threat that was both far more powerful and far more imminent than events in the West. The truth about Russian strength was so daunting that perhaps Hitler was incapable of making an objective appraisal of it, despite the vociferous complaints of Guderian. Hitler's tendency to retreat into a kind of vague and obstinate unreality whenever the facts did not suit his vision of events is all too well known.

In any case, Operation North Wind was unleashed out of the snow-covered hills and forests of the Vosges Mountains in northern Alsace. Terrain and weather conditions were similar to those found in the Ardennes forests further north. Some of the German assault units were fought to a standstill in the gloomy and narrow valleys of the hill country; others made progress down onto the plain below and were soon threatening Strasbourg.

The Germans were aware that American strength in this area had been depleted, with a number of divisions taken out of the line and sent to deal with the crisis in the Ardennes. From a tactical standpoint, it was a good place for a German attack. But the larger strategic picture was more muddled. What could this operation hope to accomplish, with forces even weaker than those deployed in the already-failed Ardennes gamble?

Daily records from Hitler's headquarters would seem to indicate that he had nothing more in mind than relieving some of the pressure against the German forces still fighting in the Ardennes. In hindsight, it is clear that by the beginning of January the surprise attack in the Ardennes had already run out of steam. But at the time, Hitler seemed to think that the Waffen SS panzer divisions still fighting around Bastogne and St. Vith might be able to resume the offensive, if the Western Allies were distracted by another offensive launched elsewhere. As far as can be ascertained, this was the only real motivation behind the launching of North Wind on January 1st.

But the consequences of this second attack were to be more far reaching than Hitler had anticipated, and for a few weeks it appeared that the Germans were about to reap a number of unexpected benefits. Almost immediately the American and French commanders in Alsace became embroiled in an enormous dispute over how to deal with this new German threat. Different military and political priorities were at the bottom of this argument, which eventually became so serious that it threatened to destroy any co-operation between the French and American armies.

The Free French 1st Division had only recently liberated the Alsatian capital of Strasbourg, after four years of German occupation. In French eyes, Strasbourg was not an ordinary city; it was the birthplace of "La Marseillaise" and for generations had been viewed as a symbol of national pride. Strasbourg and Alsace had not only been occupied by the Germans, but had actually been incorporated within the borders of the Third Reich as a new German province. Alsace had also been incorporated into the German nation for nearly fifty years after the Franco-Prussian War—a long and bitter memory for many Frenchmen.

The upshot of all this was that in January of 1945 the first thought of the French military command was to defend Strasbourg at all costs against the North Wind offensive. In their view, more than national pride was at stake. If the city were lost the civilian population would have to undergo yet another winter of occupation by the Nazi regime, a seriously demoralizing prospect.

But the American commanders in Alsace were less interested in these factors. For them, basic military priorities overrode political ones. The German advance threatened to cut off Strasbourg from the west and trap all its defenders in a huge pocket. In order to avert this danger the American commanders simply wanted to withdraw, abandoning Strasbourg and northern Alsace till the German attack lost its impetus.

From the local commanders on the spot, this dispute would rise all the way up the chain of command, finally setting Eisenhower and DeGaulle against each other. If Strasbourg were abandoned, DeGaulle threatened political repercussions which might seriously hamper the Allied war effort. Perhaps his most serious threat was to close down, either partially or in full, the French ports through which all the supplies for the Allied war effort in Europe were arriving. Whether DeGaulle would have gone through with this is hard to say, but the issue was threatening to turn into a political crisis.

Eisenhower, blessed with a talent for judiciously weighing up the different factors in tangled situations, finally gave in. This would be neither the first nor the last time DeGaulle would cause problems for the Allies, but at least in this instance Eisenhower seemed to sympathize with his grievances. Despite the loud objections of the American commanders in the field, he judged that the military situation in Alsace was not as serious as it appeared. After initially drawing up plans for a retreat, he rescinded these orders at the last moment. DeGaulle had won; Strasbourg would be defended.

Eisenhower and DeGaulle would be proved right. The Germans had already shot their bolt in the Ardennes; in Alsace, North Wind would also soon grind to a halt. Hitler's potential windfall of exploiting a rift in French-American relations came to nothing, due not only to Eisenhower's role as an arbiter but also to the inadequacy of German military strength in the field.

All that remained was the actual fighting. This was as savage as anything that took place further north around Bastogne, Malmédy, or St. Vith. Small Alsatian towns, French villages bearing German-sounding names like Hagenau and Wissembourg, were fought over grimly in the deep snows. The German strike force consisted of a motley collection of Army and Volksgrenadier divisions, along with parts of three SS divisions, but none of them were adequately equipped with armor. The appearance of a few of the new German King Tigers would sometimes lead to panic among the Allied defenders, but only small numbers of these vehicles were on hand. North Wind degenerated into bitter house-to-house fighting by the opposing infantrymen. The Germans never reached Strasbourg. The attack petered out by mid-January. Scattered but ferocious small-unit actions would last for another month. It was during these battles in Alsace that Audie Murphy won the Medal of Honor, mounting a knocked-out American tank destroyer in the midst of a German attack and using the radio to call in artillery fire directly on his own head. The enemy force was scattered.

But by this time it was the middle of February, and no one in the German High Command, neither Hitler, Himmler, Guderian, nor anyone else, had any interest in Alsace any longer. A battle that had led to major concern among the Western Allies would be viewed from the German side as only a small-scale offensive whose significance would be overshadowed almost instantly by the enormous drama about to unfold on the Eastern Front.

On January 12th the Russians had launched their great offensive across the Vistula River in Poland. It was an attack which overwhelmed two hundred miles of the German line at a single blow and which subsequently advanced two hundred miles in a matter of weeks, crossing the German frontier and heading straight for Berlin. The real drama of 1945 had begun, and this drama would take place almost entirely in the East. The Western Front, which had pre-occupied Hitler since the invasion of Normandy the preceding June, would be almost forgotten. The Soviets invading Germany from the east would be bent not only on the defeat of their hated enemy, but on mass-destruction and mass-slaughter of both soldiers and the civilian population.

Operation North Wind, as Guderian had seen all along, was

nothing more than a side-show, and scarcely even that. Once the Soviet Vistula Offensive had begun, there was no longer any debate over East versus West. Throughout eastern Germany the Third Reich would put up a ferocious last-ditch resistance that would continue until the final hours of the war, fighting against an enemy consumed by hatred, determined to avenge Nazi crimes in Russia and seemingly intent on exterminating the German nation. Battles fought on the Eastern Front in 1945 would constitute one of the most violent and all-consuming last stands in history.

That is the story of this book.

East Versus West in 1945—Deployment of the German Panzer Divisions

During the course of the war the German Army created nearly forty panzer divisions. In addition, about a dozen panzer divisions were formed by the Waffen SS. Even after the Normandy invasion, only six Army and five SS panzer divisions were ever deployed on the Western Front.

Of these, one Army and all five of the Waffen SS panzer divisions would be transferred back to the Eastern Front in late January of 1945. They would join nearly forty other Army and SS panzer divisions already in action against the Soviets. German panzer forces still fighting in the West would be reduced to the absolute minimum. Still in action on the Italian Front, not included among those mentioned above, would be only one panzer division, the 26th.

For the majority of German armored crews, the Eastern Front, the all-consuming struggle against the Soviet Union, was the only war they would ever know. Except for those divisions listed above and two others destroyed with Rommel's Afrika Korps, every German panzer division had been fighting on the Eastern Front since 1941 and would see exclusive service there until the end of the war. Hitler would use the panzer divisions in Russia in the manner of "fire brigades," shipping them back and forth for thousands of miles across that country in order to deal with crisis situations in every sector of the over-extended German front.

Among these units was the elite Grossdeutschland Division,

the Army's most powerful striking force. But in fact it would be difficult to single out elite units among the army's panzer divisions. Almost all could be said to have acquired that status; almost without exception, they had achieved remarkable combat records during long years of fighting in the East. The same was true for the Waffen SS panzer divisions. A somewhat higher proportion of these would fight in the West in 1944, but overall the Waffen SS armored crews also saw the great majority of their combat action on the Eastern Front. By February of 1945 only a single battalion of Waffen SS tanks would be left fighting in the West.

This focus on German armored divisions is not intended to denigrate the German infantry divisions. In fact the proportion of veteran infantry divisions that saw combat on the Eastern Front—and nowhere else—was even higher. But in World War Two the most critical striking power for any army resided in its armored formations. The Eastern Front had always formed the greatest drain on German resources; in 1945 almost every German tank would be fighting there in an attempt to hold back the Soviet deluge.

As for the infantry divisions, they always bore the brunt of tragedy, hardship, and violent death. The reader will see more than a few of these divisions go down almost to the last man in the story about to unfold. As for civilians in eastern Germany, the suffering they would undergo in 1945 would be almost beyond description.

There would remain scattered fighting on the Western Front in 1945, some of it quite violent. While the Americans fought mopping up actions in Alsace and the Ardennes and struggled on towards the Rhine, the British-Canadian armies would also suffer heavily attacking the Reichswald forest in northern Germany. But on any true scale of human suffering and human resources, these battles would be minuscule in comparison with the appalling struggle that began with the Soviet invasion of Germany's eastern frontiers. On this front the Third Reich would conduct a last stand as terrible as any ever seen.

Hitler's Wagnerian vision had reached its climax. The funeral pyre—*GOTTERDAMMERUNG*—was being lit in the East.

PART I
IN THE EAST

A group of men lurking at the forest's edge. Some wear steel helmets, most wear field caps with the long brims shadowing their faces. A motley collection of weapons among them—a few panzerfausts, a few of the new-model assault rifles with low-slung curved magazines. Shadows from naked tree limbs crisscross randomly over their bodies, like the jagged dazzle camouflage painted on the hulls of ships. They wear winter parkas, though as yet no snow has fallen on this lonely corner of the Baltic.

Tension, anxiety. Fear. They stare across a barren meadow that spreads out from the edge of the woods. Suddenly the first T-34 emerges from another patch of woods in the distance, roaring at high speed up the road. It is shocking how fast the Russians drive these vehicles, probably over thirty miles an hour. In the woods an onlooker's jaw drops, gaping, dumbfounded as he watches the approach of the tank.

A tremendous explosion. The T-34 stops dead, slewing around at right angles to the road, burning. Huge billows of smoke. A single man, Einzelkampfer, stands up down in the meadow, right next to the road embankment. Screened by blowing smoke, he runs to join his comrades waiting in the woods, still carrying the discharged panzerfaust in his right hand . . .

Quiet returns, apart from the crackle of flames. The explosion was so violent that the tank crew was killed instantly; the watchers in the woods hear no screams of burning men. But this was only the first probe, there will be more T-34s assembled down the road. The German grenadiers collect their nerves, waiting to see what happens next.

1

NO EXIT FROM COURLAND

Army Group North Fights with Its Back to the Sea

The war in the East can be broadly divided into two parts—the war fought on Russian soil, and the Soviet invasion of the German empire.

Paul Carell acknowledged this in his two-volume history of the Russian Front, HITLER MOVES EAST and SCORCHED EARTH. This is the terrible epic story of the war on Russian soil. The second volume concludes with the annihilation of the German Army Group Center in Byelorussia in July 1944. "The war in Russia was over; the battle for Germany had begun."

The preliminaries for the final disaster of 1945 began in the autumn of 1944. The most immediate threat to the German nation lay with the Soviet front along the Vistula River, still in Poland, and then northward to the border of East Prussia. In October the Russians ventured across this border and gained their first toehold on German soil. A swift counterattack by several elite units, including the Herman Goering Panzer Division and the Grossdeutschland Division, reclaimed the Prussian village of Nemmersdorf. The German grenadiers found a charnel house of atrocities and murdered civilians, the first sign of the terrible Russian vengeance that would fall upon Germany the following year.

There was bitter fighting in Prussia that autumn, with the Germans conducting several other counterattacks to drive the "Asiatic beasts" out of the few German villages they had captured. But in general the front in Prussia and along the Vistula remained static, almost quiescent. After their great victory in Byelorussia, the Soviets had reached the Vistula by the end of July; after establishing a few bridgeheads across the river, they made no determined effort to resume the offensive for the remainder of the year. The men of the newly formed IV SS Panzer Corps, comprising the Totenkopf and Wiking Divisions of the Waffen SS, would remember several months of brutal fighting in the so-called "Wet Triangle," at the confluence of the Vistula and

Narew Rivers, just north of Warsaw. But the Russians did not break through, and these battles had subsided by mid-October. A strange and peaceful interlude settled on the Vistula Front, the lull before the storm. The German soldiers were able to celebrate a quiet Christmas, that holiday which seems to evoke deeper sentiment in Germany than in any other nation.

The most violent Russian threat that autumn lay to the south, in Hungary. Rumania had been lost in August, with the Rumanians—up to then the Third Reich's most active military partner on the Eastern Front—switching sides overnight in the middle of a Russian offensive. The desertion of most of the Rumanian Army left huge gaps in the line which the neighboring German divisions had no hope of closing. A rout followed which was almost as complete as the destruction of Army Group Center in July. The Russian armored units stormed through the Carpathian passes and spilled down onto the plains of Hungary, another of Hitler's satellite allies, albeit a less active one than Rumania had been. Up to this point Budapest had been untouched by war, untouched by the air raids that had brought death and terror to so many other civilian populations in Europe. The natives of the Hungarian capital, living as close to a normal life as was possible anywhere in those days, had little time to react to this abrupt change in circumstances; the Russian spearheads were swift and soon threatened the city. By November Budapest was nearly surrounded; by December the ring was closed. All major German military operations on the Eastern Front were now focussed on breaking that ring and lifting the siege.

The most tangible sign of these efforts was the removal of the strongest German force along the Vistula Front and its transshipments to the Hungarian battleground. In late December the tough Wiking and Totenkopf men of IV SS Corps were pulled out of the "Wet Triangle," along with all their tanks and equipment, and put on board long trains headed southward. Thus the German Army High Command created a critical chink in the armor of its already thin Vistula defenses. This decision had not been made lightly. There are the usual accounts of Hitler arguing bitterly with his most recent appointment as Chief of Staff to the High Command, General Heinz Guderian, in Hitler's headquarters. Week by week these disagreements were to grow more violent; in the months to come onlookers at these meetings would be stunned by Guderian's outspokenness.

As of yet, however, Guderian did not express himself so forcefully. He made it known that he took a dim view of removing the strongest units from the Vistula; he knew that a Russian offensive here would only be a matter of time, and that the threat would be not to an ally's capital but to Berlin itself. On the other hand, he acknowledged that the situation in Hungary was very serious, entailing not only the possible loss of Budapest but of the Hungarian oilfields with which Hitler was to remain obsessed until the end of the war. "By deliberately taking a very grave risk on the rest of the Eastern Front, we have done everything possible to restore firm contact with Budapest."

Guderian was now in something of a quandary. Of course so was Hitler himself; so was anyone who had to decide how to cope with the seemingly insurmountable problems facing the Reich at the end of 1944. But Guderian would not allow his attention to be distracted from what he considered to be the main event—and this would take place on the Vistula. Reinforcements were sorely needed. In the West a powerful striking force had just been lost in the Ardennes battle, with more units now being squandered in an operation of dubious value in Alsace. Rather than being shored-up, the Vistula Front was being drained by the admittedly desperate situation in Hungary.[1]

Yet for Guderian there remained one obvious source of manpower, a source that was currently languishing in an obscure and far-off place.

This place was Courland.

Courland

We shall return soon enough to the main theaters of violence, but for the moment let us take a brief tour of this unfamiliar, indeed almost mysterious battlefield—certainly the least-known of all the combat zones of 1945. Here Guderian had at his disposal—or seemingly at his disposal—not just a few divisions, a corps or two, but an entire well-equipped army group of over twenty divisions. These were not any of the recently raised Volksturm battalions, consisting of the old, the sick, of pitiful young teenagers, all even more woefully equipped. Nor were they inexperienced garrison divisions who had spent the whole war idling away in Norway or in fortress towns along the Atlantic coast (though Guderian was interested in getting his hands on these men as well). On the contrary, the divisions currently isolated in Courland were among the most battle-proven in the German Army, with years of grim experience fighting the Russians. Among them were three panzer divisions; two SS divisions of Dutch and Danish volunteers who had shown themselves to be fanatical fighters; and among the Army formations, the East Prussian 11th Infantry Division, which had been praised several times in Wehrmacht communiqués as the best infantry division in the German military.

But first, where is Courland, and what were so many first-rate troops doing there so near the end of the war?

Courland in English—in German, Kurland. It is the name given to a small peninsula in Latvia jutting into the Baltic Sea. The Latvians call it Kurzeme, differentiating it from the more mainland part of the country, known as Vidzeme.

The German units here were veterans of the siege of Leningrad and the terrible battles in the swamps of the Volkhov River; veterans as well of the year-long cauldron battle at Demyansk in 1942. They were the remnants of the German Army Group North, a force which, in stark contrast to the shattered legions of Army Groups Center and South, had survived almost intact up to this late stage of the war.

Like all German forces in Russia, they had been on the retreat for most of 1944, but the Russians had not marshalled such overwhelming strength in the north as they had done in Byelorussia and Rumania. Still, the Soviets were far superior in numbers of men and heavy weapons, and they slowly pushed the Germans back—driving them out of old Russia at Pskov and Narva, harrying them back into the Baltic states of Estonia and Latvia, and finally bottling up the entire army group in the Courland peninsula in October of 1944. At this point Army Group North was cut off from all other German forces; the only communication with Germany, or anywhere else, was by sea.

They might have been extracted from this forlorn situation. For about a month in August and September a German counterattack from East Prussia, spearheaded by the Panther tanks of the Grossdeutschland Division, had created a land bridge to Courland, an escape corridor which might have allowed Army Group North to slip away and add its considerable fighting strength to the other fronts in Poland or Hungary. But Hitler's notorious obsession with holding onto conquered territory now came into play once again. Despite objections from Guderian that grew daily more vehement, he refused to allow Courland to be abandoned. By September the Soviets had shattered the tenuous landbridge and pushed Grossdeutschland back to the south. An entire Army Group—consisting initially of over 300,000 men—was to spend the remainder of the war defending this obscure Latvian peninsula.

At least the newsreels could show the German public, even while catastrophe approached their home cities, that German soldiers were still fighting and holding on somewhere on Soviet soil. And indeed, the fighting in Courland was as desperate as any that took place elsewhere in 1945.

It was the schizophrenic existence of the kind that had been seen in the trench warfare of World War One. Once a month, almost like clockwork, the Russians would mount a grand offensive, hurling themselves at the German line. After about ten days or two weeks the carnage would subside, and a monotonous, almost peaceful life in the trenches would resume for another few weeks, before the Russians tried again. Thus the Six Great Battles of Courland (Die Sechs Grosse Kurlandschlachten) took place at regular intervals—October, November, December of 1944; January, February, March of 1945.

The combat history of the 215th Infantry Division records that the Third Courland Battle was the most violent; it began on December 20th, 1944, focussing on the center of the German line near the town of Frauenberg.

On the morning of December 20th all hell broke loose. A three-hour drumfire barrage opened the third battle, the worst of the six fought in Courland. Fire and smoke enveloped the front of our division and that of our right-hand neighbor, the 205th Infantry Division. Our forward defense lines could not hold up against the onslaught of six Russian rifle divisions. Once again, as we had experienced so often in the past, the strength of the infantry companies melted away until only small battle groups remained. Bulwarks of resistance remained around the battalion and regimental command posts, as well as the anti-tank (PAK) and artillery emplacements holding out in the rear. Repeated counterattacks by grenadiers and assault guns (Sturmgeschutzen) blunted the force of the enemy attacks, leaving the Russians bled out and exhausted. Every hundred meters along the road to Frauenburg cost the Russians staggering casualties, yet our own division sacrificed the lives of many brave fighters in every patch of forest, in every bunker. There was never a position so toughly and bitterly defended, as here in Courland.

In the field hospitals the surgeons operated night and day, often three nights running without an hour's sleep. The wounded groaned in agony as the hospital trucks (Sankas) carried them out at night to the ships in Libau harbor, the only remaining link with Germany. On Christmas Eve there was a sudden calm. The Wehrmacht communique reported that the Baden-Wurttemberger 215th Infantry Division had repelled 111 enemy attacks of company strength or greater. So much bravery, so much suffering, so much tenacity, all in such a short period of time![2]

As mentioned above, the Russians uncharacteristically broke off the battle at Christmas, though it was only a brief hiatus. German soldiers mixed with Latvian civilians in the small churches scattered across the countryside to celebrate the holy season. It would have been an anxious time, full of longing and uncertainty. The Russians had taken their usual high losses without managing to breach the defenses, but there was no telling how long this would last. The German soldiers were stranded in this place, isolated hundreds of miles to the northeast of any other battlefront; they might have felt some kinship with the Japanese defenders of islands that were bypassed and left far behind the main American advance across the Pacific.

The Latvian civilians would have felt no more comfortable. The great majority of them were firmly anti-Soviet. Taking advantage of the collapse of Tsarist Russia and the initial weakness of the nascent Bolshevik state, the Latvians had declared themselves independent from Russia in 1920, as had Lithuania and Estonia. But the new nation had enjoyed a lifespan of only two decades before being annexed back into the Soviet Union in

1940, in a "peaceful" invasion reminiscent of Hitler's conquest of Czechoslovakia.

Almost all Latvians had deeply resented being forcibly absorbed back into the Russian state, even more so now that it was run by the Communist Party. With the onset of Hitler's attack upon the Soviet Union in 1941, they had greeted the Germans as liberators, feting the spearheads of Army Group North with gifts of flowers and emotional demonstrations in the streets. They would later find to their dismay that Hitler was not about to restore Latvia's independence, but as so-called ethnic Aryan cousins they had been treated much more tolerantly by the Nazi administrators than the Slavic population inside Russia and the Ukraine. They had raised two Latvian divisions to fight against the Soviets, one of which was still in the Courland trenches near Libau. If the Russians broke through, or if the Germans simply evacuated Army Group North by sea, what fate would then befall the civilian population? No one knew. Even if the Russians did not engage in the atrocities meted out to the German civilians in East Prussia, a return to life under the Communist dictatorship was viewed with loathing by nearly everyone.

Christmas night was cold, clear, starry. With the guns momentarily silent, the strains of "Stille Nacht" could be heard for long distances across the barren countryside. As yet there was no snow on the ground; for the Eastern Front, it had been an unusually mild winter, though the weather would turn more severe after the new year. Traditionally Latvia, like the other Baltic states, had stronger cultural ties to the West, with Germany, with Scandinavia; Russians had never been popular here. For generations there had been a large German population, many of them wealthy merchants and estate owners. They too had been resented by the native Latvians to some degree, but the Communist regime had been far more hated. Courland was a place of deep forests mingled with lonely fields and farmsteads, tidy rural communities that more resembled certain villages in Prussia or Pomerania than anything in Russia. The peninsula was barely a third of the size of the Florida peninsula in North America, with no point very far from the sea. During lulls in the fighting, German soldiers could be seen strolling among the dunes along the Baltic shoreline, gazing out to sea, no doubt wondering if they would ever leave this place.

For two days peace and calm lay across the land. Finally at dawn on December 26th the front around Frauenburg erupted with a barrage from thousands of guns. The battle was not over yet!

The Red Army attacked even more fiercely than before. The 93rd Infantry Division was only able to prevent a breakthrough with the help of the Heavy Machine Gun Battalion "Stettin." Once again the 4th and 12th Panzer Divisions formed the last available reserves. Colonel Kretschmar of the 12th Luftwaffe Field Division was hailed as "the breakwater in the storm." On the last day of the year the 19th SS Division stood firm against twenty seven enemy assaults.[3]

The great offensive finally ground to a halt on January 1st. Photographs show Latvian soldiers inspecting the hulks of knocked-out Soviet tanks in a dull, snowless landscape, naked trees in the distance. Many of them were Sherman tanks from the US, along with large numbers of the huge, nose-heavy new Russian tank destroyers.

These Latvians were members of the just-mentioned 19th SS Division. For several years SS Reichsfuhrer Himmler had been raising Waffen SS divisions of foreign volunteers to augment the ranks of his personal army. He had even compromised supposedly sacrosanct beliefs about racial purity by enlisting Muslims, Ukrainians, and Caucasian mountain tribesmen to the Nazi cause, though in propaganda terms this was invariably referred to as the anti-Bolshevik cause. All these groups had every reason to despise the Communist regime, particularly as the Russians had long been viewed as no more than colonial invaders of their lands. Thus they had few scruples about serving under the SS banner, and for obvious reasons they did not receive the same kind of racial indoctrination as did the purely German SS cadres.

The Latvian soldiers of 19th SS Division also fit this mold, though according to the Nazi theorists they were even more acceptable in racial terms, being part of the overall Germanic brotherhood of northern Europe. Originally the Latvian units had been commanded by German SS officers, whose more than occasionally arrogant and condescending attitudes had not sat well with these Baltic volunteers. Btu in the end the Latvians were allowed to elect their own officers (although the divisional commanders would remain German) and there followed a marked improvement in their fighting spirit.

For most of these men, keeping the Communists from returning to their homeland was their only concern; it was their only reason for fighting alongside the Germans, and it is doubtful that many of them particularly cared whether they served under the aegis of the Waffen SS or the regular army. On the other hand, there do exist some interesting accounts by German soldiers, indicating that at least some of these Baltic volunteers displayed a good deal of enthusiasm for Nazi ideals, parroting the views of their German overlords in the exaggerated and somewhat absurd fashion of colonial natives who sometimes seek to emulate the ways of their masters.

In a way, this is hardly a surprise, considering the long-standing cultural ties between Germany and the Baltic states. The same could be said of the Dutch and Danish SS volunteers who were also fighting in Courland; and certainly these men could not argue that their homelands were faced with imminent Soviet invasion. German infantrymen in particular were a little taken aback to find enthusiastic National Socialists among their Baltic comrades in arms, though perhaps such cases were fairly isolated, for on the whole there do not seem to be any accounts of wide-spread Nazi fanaticism among the Latvian divisions. Anti-Communism was the theme that united these men, with any other political credo running a distant second. Survivors from these Latvian units would carry on their fight even after the war was over; ongoing battles against partisan bands hidden deep in the Courland forests were reported by the Russians as late as 1947.

But in the meantime, during these early weeks of 1945, the Soviets would continue to hurl men and tanks against this nearly impervious defensive barrier, stretching across the peninsula from Libau in the west to the Bay of Riga in the east. The first snow had begun to fall, and by late January the fir trees and meadows were draped beneath a deep layer of white. The Fourth Battle of Courland erupted on January 24th and was fought in the kind of mid-winter conditions long familiar to the combatants of both sides, during previous grueling winters around Leningrad and Demyansk. The 215th Infantry Division history reports with just a hint of irony, "Once again our positions were buried under ice and snow—by now a tradition dear to our hearts."[4]

This time the men of the 215th did not bear the brunt of the Russian assault. Their neighbors on the right, the 205th Infantry Division, suffered more heavily, destroying 117 Soviet tanks in five days of close-combat in a gloomy fir forest known as the Gobaswald. Throughout the Courland battles the Russians would probe for different weak spots in the sixty-mile long defense line; on this occasion they mounted simultaneous offensives around Frauenburg in the center and near Libau by the coast. German reserves were stretched to the breaking point to meet these twin threats, with the panzer divisions once again taking on the unenviable role of "fire brigades." The 14th Panzer Division was sent into action in the Libau sector, coming head to head with a Russian bridgehead across a small stream known as the Vartaja River.

> A ghostly convoy comprising every type of vehicle—Panther tanks, Kubelwagens, prime movers, Ford, Opel, Renault, and Studebaker trucks, and still others—all loaded to capacity with weapons, ammunition, trenching gear, and every available fighting man moved out towards the battlefield.[5]

Once again a local Russian breakthrough was sealed off after days of desperate fighting. On the evening of the second day 14th Panzer Division regained the original trench line, leaving the hulks of 63 Russian tanks scattered across the snow-covered "clumps of fir and bushland." Many of these kills were scored by the attached Panzer Abteilung 510, which fielded the Tiger tanks that were the scourge of Soviet armor on every sector of the Eastern Front.

The fighting went on for five more days, back and forth across the Vartaja, until the Russian assaults again ran out of steam and the Fourth Battle of Courland came to an end. Number Five would begin soon enough, as per the monthly schedule, in the third week of February, with the same frenzied close-quarter combat in the snow, reaping the same fruitless harvest.

Part of the reason for the Russian lack of success was that Army Group North had enough men to man the trenches; they were not spread so thinly as they had been in the much vaster regions of mainland Russia in earlier years. Thus there were always a few units that could be held in the rear to form the critical mobile reserves. Having three panzer divisions close at hand—not to mention a Tiger tank battalion—could almost be considered a luxury, when compared with the German strength tables for other, much broader fronts elsewhere in the East. Panthers and Mk IVs were in relatively short supply, but the Sturmgeschutz, the ubiquitous all-purpose German tank destroyer, played a crucial role in breaking up Russian armored attacks.

Army Group North was also helped by having a line that ran to the sea at both ends; the Russians could not outflank them there. German artillery, though weak in numbers of cannon, more than compensated by delivering devastatingly accurate fire on enemy assembly positions; artillery intervention at critical moments was a decisive factor in all the Courland battles. When interrogated, Russian prisoners were heard cursing bitterly about the "damned German artillery." For the long-suffering soldiers of the Red Army, the Courland offensives were little more than pig-headed exercises in butchery little different from countless other battles they had experienced over the preceding four years.

The stress in the Courland trenches was not brought about by combat alone. The troglodyte warfare in the defensive works brought about its own kind of mental anguish, a bizarre and unnerving existence that has been vividly described by one of its survivors.

"Two hours on, two hours off."

Two hours on, two hours off. Day after day, week after week, month after month.

These are the duty rotations that Jan Montyn experienced in the Courland front line. It was a mostly quiet sector; the continuous Russian offensives must not have struck in this area, at least not during his time there. All the same, the life he remembers resembles a strange kind of nightmare. Two hours on, two hours off. Two hours spent on sentry duty peering out across the dreary landscape towards the Russian lines, down a hillside, with a few black stands of pine the only visible life. Then two hours spent in a cramped dugout only a few meters away, playing cards with his comrades, eating if the soup cannisters (Goulaschkanone) happened to arrive, daydreaming listlessly. Sleeping.

This was his only routine for months on end. Anyone who has ever done any kind of shift duty around the clock knows the way the passage of time gradually takes on a kind of unreality. It is difficult enough to adapt to four or six hour shifts, but at least a man's off-duty period is long enough to collect his thoughts a little bit, to attempt to relax, to actually get a decent sleep.

For the first few weeks Montyn had four hours off-duty for every two hours on, but then casualties and the shortage of manpower led to the unending two-hour rotation, which soon grew to be an especially unnatural strain on the nervous system. Without any prolonged opportunity to sleep, the difference between one day and the next almost disappears; Montyn's account sometimes reads like the dreamlike, disoriented mumblings of someone who has been awake continuously for weeks on end.

The scene is also very claustrophobic somehow, like life on a submarine. The two-hour rotation effectively keeps him confined to his small section of trench, alternating with the gloomy candlelit dugout. A few times during all these months he is allowed to visit a friend of his in a neighboring trench; just to be able to spend an hour or so in another muddy slit in the earth only thirty yards away seems almost like a holiday excursion. Or, perhaps more aptly, like a visit to another tiny submarine lost in the vast ocean of mud and darkness.

Most of the Courland campaign was fought in the long winter darkness of these high latitudes, as far north as the polar bear–frequented town of Churchill on Hudson's Bay in North America. Long periods of night alternated with a few murky hours of daylight, the same black pines standing down the hill every day, these trees forming the only distraction in the landscape but after a while also becoming a kind of idiotic fixation. There was nothing else to look at; the Russians a few hundred yards away were almost never visible.

His immediate commander is a Captain who lost an arm in North Africa; he might have spent the rest of the war convalescing, but bodies of any kind were running short in 1945. Montyn makes no mention of any other officers, and in general there seem to be few other people around. He is serving with an ad hoc naval unit that has been transferred to the ground war, Montyn's torpedo boat having been sunk in the Baltic a few months earlier. A few wounded infantry veterans like the Captain have been placed in command of these sailors and sundry other personnel, this small, non-descript collection of humanity seeming only to intensify the grey and faceless atmosphere. Montyn describes the kind of derangement that eventually takes hold of some soldiers in these conditions. Anything to break up the monotony, to break up this unnatural pattern of hours. "Trench fever"—the phrase originated in World War One, but the disorder is still easily recognizable in the dugouts of the Eastern Front during the next war.

One comrade demonstrates the favorite trick of exploding a grenade on top of his helmet. If you stand perfectly still the explosive force will go out horizontally and leave you unharmed. But this man is already a little unhinged, almost intentionally careless. He is chuckling foolishly to himself as he performs this little feat; the grenade topples off his helmet and blows him to pieces.

Another man decides to play a game of exposing his head to the view of the Russians below, winning small wagers of cigarettes from his more nervous comrades. Time after time nothing happens; it becomes rather amusing. Perhaps another one of those "undeclared truces" is in effect here, when soldiers in quiet sectors grow sick of shooting at each other and making life miserable to no purpose. But no one seems very sure of this. After all, sharpshooting can become another way to relieve the monotony. This childish little game goes on for days; then suddenly Montyn's comrade receives a bullet through the head and that is the end of it.

Then there are the sudden, random barrages that are always a feature of trench warfare, bringing about the daily wastage in casualties even when there is no other fighting. During these months Montyn will never see a Russian attack, nor take part in one himself, yet gradually more and more men are killed by this random fire until he despairs of ever escaping this place alive. The Germans have their own unique phrase for this kind of brief and unpredictable shelling—Feueruberfall. "Fire ambush" in English, but the literal translation is not entirely right. It conveys the idea of a cleverly set-up trap, and while the Germans occasionally also use it in this sense, it far more often refers to the kind of senseless and arbitrary periodic fire that falls God only knows where, blowing men to pieces while they are going about their daily routine.

German histories of the Courland campaign mention a kind of normal life being established after a while, between the big battles, with rest homes and cinemas being set up in the rear areas, visits for a good meal in the homes of hospitable Latvian civilians. Montyn never talks about any of these things. The only change is when he is occasionally sent back to the field kitchens in the rear to bring up the soup, each man shouldering the heavy soup cannister like a metal backpack. But so much for the outer world—it is only a short trip across an overcast, featureless terrain, made in darkness most of the time.

Eventually Montyn is able to escape this hopeless existence by the infantryman's most time-honored method, that is by receiving a serious wound. A shellburst—a typical "Feuerüberfall" landing at random—riddles him with shrapnel; after being operated on in the field hospital he is given a ticket home.

In the dismal conditions of the Eastern Front, fighting a war that seemed likely to end only in defeat—or perhaps even worse, never end at all—many German soldiers prized these kinds of "home wounds" as obsessively as did soldiers from other nations. It literally meant the difference between life and death, and the right kind of wound for a lucky soldier inspired among his comrades a cross between jealousy and awe. No doubt this was a perfectly appropriate sentiment for men to feel upon seeing one of their comrades about to escape back to the world of the living. It was an almost mystical rite of passage that in general became more meaningful the longer men had been at the front. Sometimes when men have undergone only a small dose of combat it is not enough to satisfy the strange male urge towards violent experience. But for men who had been fighting in Russia for years—for an eternity—such urges had long since been satisfied and vanished into the realm of utter meaninglessness.

Of course there was the other aspect to all this, embodied by men who had become addicted to combat, or at least to the strange world of comradeship and freedom from civilian drudgery that went along with it. And it was not at all uncommon for men to fall prey to both influences, yearning obsessively for the "million dollar wound," as the Americans called it, yet feeling empty and unsatisfied upon returning to the peace and safety of the homeland. The Germans had their own phrase for this kind of wound, which doctors in field hospitals would hear asked of them over and over again from the men they were attending: "Komme Ich damit nach Hause?" ("Am I hurt badly enough to get a ticket home?").

In the empty, seemingly meaningless wastelands of Russia

these questions were especially common; ideas of purpose, of fighting for a cause, tended gradually to disappear within this vast grim wilderness. In 1945, fighting on their own soil against an enemy bent not only on conquest but on vengeance and annihilation, many German soldiers would find their backbone once again, with ideas of purpose rekindled by the awful sights of their civilian kin being massacred by the Soviet invaders. But even in this context the desire for a "life-saving" wound could never be extinguished.

And Courland, of course, was not German soil; it was only another dreary and isolated stretch of the infinite Russian landscape, where men might still pray more than ever for the right kind of wound. And so Montyn was one of the lucky ones, a winner in that strange and feverish lottery; aching fiercely from the lacerations of shrapnel, yet relieved all the same, he was carried out by ambulance truck to the port of Libau, there to await a ship that would carry him back to Germany.

Yet at last by January and February more than just wounded men were being shipped home. Guderian's angry badgering, as well as the eruption of the Russian Vistula offensive, inclined Hitler to change his mind about Courland. Even he had to make some concessions to common sense, and to keep 300,000 men defending sixty miles of front in Latvia was nothing short of lunacy. But even now he could not entirely relinquish his strange obsessions about territory. Army Group North would continue to stay where it was, but a number of its divisions would be removed from the line and shipped out to reinforce the disaster zones in Poland and East Prussia.

These transfers happened in fits and starts. 4th Panzer and several infantry divisions were brought home in January, followed by 215th Infantry and the Danish and Dutch SS divisions in February. Other units would leave at other times. By the end of the war nearly a third of the Courland veterans would be brought back to defend the Reich. In truth they were better off where they were. They might have been trapped with their backs to the sea in this forgotten corner of Soviet territory, but at least the Courland army survived the war intact; the Russians never did manage to break through. Whereas almost every division that was shipped back to the Reich was ground to pieces in the final battles there.

But for the moment, every fighting man waiting for a ship in

Libau must have been relieved to be leaving this lonely and far-away peninsula. Even the last few hours spent assembling at the docks were filled with anxiety, for the port was under constant air attack by the Russians. Clouds of smoke rose unendingly above the old stone houses and the harbor cranes. From the ordinary Landser's point of view, the situation here had all the makings of another Stalingrad. He knew the news from home was not good, but he wanted to go home all the same. For most of these men the return home would end in an unmarked grave somewhere in eastern Germany.

For Jan Montyn a different ordeal was in the offing, an ordeal that would take place before he ever set foot in Germany again, a nightmarish fight for survival on the high seas of the Baltic. We will meet him again in a later chapter, on board one of the doomed transport ships.

In January Hitler decreed that Army Group North would be redesignated. These troops would now be known as Army Group Kurland. The title of Army Group North was transferred to the German forces fighting in East Prussia. In addition, Hitler approved a commemorative sleeveband that would be issued to the Courland defenders. Throughout the war the Germans had issued sleevebands or bronze shoulder shields to honor the veterans of various brutal campaigns, or at least those that had not ended in defeat. On the Eastern Front, almost all of these decorations referred to battles where German soldiers had held out for months on end against overwhelming odds—the Cholm shield, the Demyansk shield, the Kuban shield. The Courland battles fit this pattern. The simple white sleeveband, with **KURLAND** stitched in bold black lettering, would be the last German campaign award issued during the war. Most of the men would never receive it anyway, if any of them even cared at this late date. The situation everywhere was approaching total chaos, and these rather insignificant strips of cloth tended to remain crated up in various supply depots.

Also in January, there was another change in the status of Army Group Kurland. Its commander, General Ferdinand Schorner, was recalled by Hitler to take charge of one of the shattered army groups that had been thrown back from the Vistula River. Schorner was a strong, capable leader, a front-line fighter who had always been fiercely dedicated to the Nazi cause. Hitler needed men like him to stave off the crisis on German soil. He was an Army man, but over the months to come he was to develop a reputation for ruthlessness that would put any SS officer to shame.

The era which would see fifteen year old boys being strung up from lampposts was about to begin.

A gloomy cellar, dank blocks of stone carved a thousand years before. Hindenburg lamps—merely candlewicks in paraffin set inside a shell casing—send up thin curls of smoke and a flickering illumination. Vibrations from shellfire send light and shadow jangling across the walls. Sounds of gunfire and shouting can be heard from the castle courtyard—more like a large, empty compound—just outside. The crump of grenades. Occasionally the shock-light of a flare penetrates into the cellar.

A table, a radio operator listening with headphones. The powerful transmitter has been brought in from a command vehicle parked just outside. The small insignia painted on the front mudguard is an ancient Teutonic sunwheel. Symbol of SS Wiking. Next to the radio operator an SS Obersturmbannfuhrer stares into space, his features composed, his nerves tense.

"Try again," he says. *"Tell them we are almost out of ammunition."*

2

BUDAPEST MERRY-GO-ROUND

IV SS Corps Attempts to Raise the Siege

As we have seen, the IV SS Corps was pulled out of the Vistula Front at the end of December 1944, in order to form the spearhead of an attack to raise the siege of Budapest.

The Totenkopf Division first departed from their positions in the "Wet Triangle," where they had been on the defensive for nearly half a year; they were followed by Wiking a few days later. Some men of the Wiking Division expressed surprise that they were being pulled out of such a critical sector of the front. But the move proceeded smoothly. Neighboring army units extended their line to take over the SS positions without—as yet—being disturbed by the Russians.

The transport by rail of two well-equipped panzer divisions was a mammoth logistical operation. The Wiking combat history reports that its men and equipment were assembled at over fifty different train stations in the area between the "Wet Triangle" and Warsaw. Each division would require nearly one hundred trains to make the move south to Hungary. The clockwork efficiency of rail transport had been a major factor in German military success ever since the Franco-Prussian War. That so many trains could be routed smoothly in such a short period of time still seems a remarkable feat. One of the headaches peculiar to transporting German armor by rail was the loading and unloading of Tiger tanks. They were not a normal component of panzer divisions, being used almost exclusively in independent battalion-sized units. In 1944 the SS divisions followed the army in adopting this practice, detaching Tiger companies to form independent SS battalions. Totenkopf, however, was allowed to keep its Tiger company as part of the division's normal complement of panzers. Thus the Totenkopf tankers and work crews still had to deal with the difficulties posed by railroad transport of these vehicles. Both Tiger Is and Tiger IIs (King Tigers) were equipped with two sets of tracks. The normal tracks used in combat were too wide to allow passage through most of the railroad cuttings and tunnels in Europe. Thus these "battle tracks" had to be removed, always a laborious undertaking, and replaced by narrower "transport tracks" before the Tigers could be loaded onto the railroad flatbed cars. At journey's end this aggravating task would then be repeated in reverse. It was one of many examples of German technical expertise becoming overly complicated in practical situations.

Totenkopf originally had been equipped with fifteen Tiger Is for the Kursk offensive in the summer of 1943. Strength reports for the following year listed only five Tigers still operational, with no more being delivered by the factories at this time. (Production had switched to the Tiger II, which was used solely by the new independent battalions.) But as had been seen again and again on the Eastern Front, even a small number of Tigers could deal out a tremendous amount of punishment against Russian armor, and Totenkopf transport orders listed the heavy (or Tiger) company as being part of its long rail convoy. Wiking, on the other hand, even though another of the elite divisions of the Waffen SS, had never been equipped with Tigers; their flatbed cars carried only Panthers and Mk IVs.

But even with only five of the heavy tanks available (or possibly even fewer by December), IV SS Corps by no means lacked striking power for the coming offensive. The Mk IV, outfitted with armored side skirts since the Kursk battle, continued to be a reliable weapon; and the Panther was the equal to any Soviet tank in the field. The Germans, as always, were confident that their superior tactics and gunnery would provide a decisive edge in any armored engagement with the Russians.

The long trains of Waffen SS men rumbled across southern Poland. Many of them would have been routed through the industrial region of Kattowitz, and at some point they would have passed by the side-spur leading to the nearby Polish village of Oswiecim—or Auschwitz, as it was known in German. The existence of Auschwitz, as with all the other extermination camps, was a state secret; though how well this secret was actually kept hidden from German civilians and soldiers, especially Waffen SS soldiers, will be forever debated. At this time the Soviets were close at hand in southern Poland, and Himmler was already making preparations to raze Auschwitz to the ground, with the rather dim hope of erasing what had occurred in this monstrous place.

By now most of the Wiking and Totenkopf men would have had more than a general idea of what went on in these camps, though perhaps only a few of them would have heard of Auschwitz in particular. But the men on the long trains bound for Hungary would have passed by this evil side-spur without taking any notice of it; for obvious reasons, the route to the camp was not marked by any signs. Would they also have passed long strings of boxcars, sitting for hours or days on end along sidetracks next to the main line, boxcars packed to overflowing with Hungarian Jews destined for the Auschwitz furnaces?

About this one can only speculate. At a certain point in late 1944 the gas nozzles in the shower rooms were shut off, the horrible furnace fires were damped. Inmates at Auschwitz were marched off, with most of them shot or dying of starvation along the way, to other camps deeper inside Germany. The Hungarian Jews, for reasons which we shall see later, were the last major Jewish contingent in occupied Europe to be shipped to Auschwitz, and conceivably some of them could have still been arriving at this late date. Otherwise they too would have been sent marching off to other camps deeper inside Germany; possibly the corpses of some of those who had died along the way would have been visible on the roads alongside the tracks bearing the trainloads of Wiking and Totenkopf men.

The trains rumbled on into the Carpathian Mountains, taking the Jablunska Pass or Moravian Gate in eastern Slovakia. The Carpathian chain consists of low but steep-sided mountains that occasionally reach heights of six or seven thousand feet. The mountains form a great semi-circle around northern and eastern Hungary, with steep grassy meadows and forests of dense black fir climbing the slopes. The Germans had already conducted a grim fighting retreat through the eastern Carpathians in the summer of 1944, after the collapse of Army Group South in Rumania. The Red Army had followed at their heels all the way to Budapest.

At last the trains of IV SS Corps would pass through the mountains and descend to the plains of Hungary. Grey, desolate plains, still empty of snow. These steppes, comprising almost the entire Hungarian nation, were like a vast inland sea surrounded by mountains on all sides. This would be the fighting arena for the Wiking and Totenkopf Divisions until the end of the war.

The debarkation points were at various towns along the Danube River. From the nearest of them, Budapest lay only about forty miles away to the southeast. The Soviets were aware that the SS men had departed from the Vistula, but remained in the dark as to their eventual destination. The SS assembly areas along the south bank were small and well-concealed. The Budapest relief attack, coinciding with Operation North Wind on the Western Front, commenced on the night of January 1st.

The Germans were not in the habit of making night attacks with armor, when the lack of visibility could turn the advance of a tank column into an exercise in chaos. But the roads in Hungary were much better mapped and maintained than they had ever been in Russia. The element of surprise was judged to be more important than any other factor, and to this end there was no preliminary artillery barrage. Still, launching an offensive of this size in the dark was a serious gamble, almost without precedent on the Eastern Front. Only the enormous relative strength of the Soviet forces at this point in the war could have led the Germans to attempt something so risky.

22:30 hours, on the first evening of the new year. The night was cold, starlit, with puddles of ice in the roads and fields. The panzers moved out. And at least for the first few miles, the gamble paid off with high dividends. The Wiking spearheads routed the Russians from the town of Agostian, many of the Red Army men "fleeing from their beds in their undershorts." A thousand German and Hungarian prisoners were quickly freed within the town, but an ugly spectacle lay waiting beside the road leading to the east. Here the Wikings discovered "a number of Heer (Army) and Waffen SS soldiers who had broken out of Budapest . . . murdered in a ditch."[1]

The attack continued into the morning. At first light the renowned tank-busting Stukas of Hans Rudel's Immelman Geschwader roared overhead, coming in at low altitude and pumping 37mm shells into every visible target. The SS corps was reinforced by army units on both flanks—6th Panzer Division and Kampfgruppe Pape on Wiking's right; with the 96th and 711th Infantry Divisions on Totenkopf's left. The 96th had begun the offensive by making a surprise crossing of the Danube into the Russians' rear, reaching the south bank in 100 assault boats and storming the village of Sutto, thus clearing Totenkopf's axis of advance. The 711th was a garrison division that had only just been transferred to the East from the Netherlands; even though they had never faced the Russians before, they too would give a good account of themselves in the coming battle.

But after this encouraging start the advance quickly deteriorated. The south bank of the Danube in this area was dominated by a chain of densely wooded hills. In essence, it was one of the few regions in Hungary that was not suited to a quick armored breakthrough. General Wohler, the current commander of Army Group South, had chosen this starting point because of its close proximity to Budapest, counting on a surprise blow that would carry the SS panzers through the hills and down to the steppe country beyond before the Russians could recover. But it was not to be.

In Wiking's sector the Panthers and Mk IVs were jammed up along winding roads through steep valleys; along the way the Russians erected roadblocks where massed anti-tank guns put a number of the SS panzers out of action. Small battlegroups of Russian infantry descended from the hills to harass the flanks of the long vehicle columns. The German difficulties bore a disturbing resemblance to the problems faced by Jochen Peiper and the SS tankmen in the Ardennes only a month before: narrow winding roads, where every bend and intersection could be easily defended by small enemy forces. The Wikings pushed on. The Russians counterattacked with armored units; tank versus tank duels were fought at close range. The advance slowed to a crawl, marked by the shot-up hulks of Panthers and T-34s. The divisional commander, SS General Karl Ullrich, heatedly urged his battalion and regimental leaders to get going; in return he received equally short-tempered radio messages suggesting he come up to see the lay of the land for himself. He promptly did so, and after driving up to the point was heard to remark in disgust that the terrain was suitable only for mountain troops. Nevertheless he was under pressure from his own superiors at Corps HQ, and he could only tell the embattled tank crews to push on as best they could. By now, more level country lay only a few miles away, but to reach it the Wikings had to resort to towing their panzers with prime movers up the last remaining hills.

On January 4th the Wiking grenadiers of the Westland and Germania regiments broke out into open country near the town of Bicske. Swirling fog had descended on the battlefield. Most of the armored support was still stuck back in the hill country, with many tanks knocked out or else requiring retrieval and repair. Only a few were still on hand to support the grenadiers. For days the Russian air force had been competing with Rudel's Stukas in delivering devastating close-support fire. Even now low-level flights of Stor-moviks were constantly overhead, searching out any breaks in the fog and wreaking havoc on the over-extended SS units.

Beside the road to Bicske, an old Hungarian castle stood in a commanding position on top of a low hill. The Russians had set up more PAK fronts (anti-tank guns) here, raining down heavy fire through the fog on the Wiking armored vehicles. Leading the com-bined Kampfgruppe at Bicske was Obersturmbannfuhrer Fritz Darges, commander of the Wiking panzer regiment. He immedi-ately ordered an assault to clear the Russians from the hilltop, which succeeded in quick fashion and sent the staff of a Soviet corps headquarters fleeing from the castle. By now other grena-dier companies had fought their way into a cemetery on the out-skirts of the town, but were stalled under heavy small arms and mortar fire. Only a few Panthers were on hand.

The attack was nearly finished. In a last attempt to clear the Russians from Bicske, Darges sent in his five remaining Panthers. At first the dense fog concealed them from the murderous fire of the PAK fronts and the ever-present Stormoviks circling overhead, but halfway to the town the mist lifted at a most inopportune moment. The Panthers were crossing open terrain and almost instantly two were knocked out by anti-tank fire. The crews baled out and clambered onto the three surviving vehicles, which then lit smoke candles to cover their retreat back to the castle hill.

It was the end. Darges knew that any further sorties would only meet with the same results. Reluctantly he ordered the grena-diers to establish a defensive position within the castle walls. The Panthers remained in ambush position just outside. Before long the hilltop was surrounded by at least twenty T-34s. One had its turret blown off at close range by a 75mm Panther shell. The others then kept their distance, waiting for night to fall.

We now come to the scene described at the opening of this chapter. In the dark the Panthers were unable to pick out their targets and became vulnerable instead to infantry infiltration; they were pulled back inside the castle and laagered in the courtyard. The grenadiers took up the fight on the castle walls, repelling a Russian infantry assault at midnight in a series of fierce hand grenade duels.

Obersturmbannfuhrer Darges was faced with a dilemma. His tanks had only a few shells left. A breakout at dawn would probably be shot to pieces by the twenty T-34s still roaming outside. A breakout during the dark would probably degenerate into chaos. Surrender to the Russians was, as usual, out of the question. There was no physical contact with the rest of the division. Darges made his decision and radioed Wiking HQ that he would hold out on the hilltop until help arrived. If the defenders' ammunition was exhausted before then, he would fire a signal flare to indicate his men were breaking out on their own.

A nearly hopeless situation. The freezing night hours passed by, broken by intermittent Russian attacks upon the castle walls. In fact only three walls of this medieval ruin were still standing. The east side was open; the three Panthers still operational took up position there. One can only imagine the defenders' relief when a Wiking armored convoy broke through the Russian encirclement a few hours after midnight. Ammunition, fuel, and rations were brought in under fire; the wounded were taken out. But the battle around the Hegyks Estate, as the castle was known, raged on for days at close quarters. Heavy Stalin tanks were brought up to demolish the castle walls at close range; some were knocked out by handheld panzerfausts. Among the defenders were the Norwegian volunteers of SS Grenadier Battalion Norge, who had been surrounded with the Panther crewmen since the beginning. During the long and bloody years in the East, the Wiking Division had had large contingents of Scandinavian volunteers fighting alongside its German cadres. It was the first Waffen SS division to enlist other Europeans to the anti-Soviet cause, and it was to remain the most famous. The final battles in Hungary would be the culmination of four years of campaigning which had taken Wiking all the way to the southernmost foothills of the Caucasus and back again, the longest trek of any of the SS divisions.

In the meantime, advancing to the left of Wiking, Totenkopf had run into similar stiff resistance. Rather than struggling directly through the hill country, the Totenkopf armor skirted along the northern side of it, with the Danube River immediately on their left. But the road here was still narrow and congested and blocked by the riverside towns, with the Russians continually waiting in ambush. At Dunaalmas, hidden in garden plots and narrow alleys around the church, a squadron of T-34/85's took the Germans under fire from point blank range. All of this was happening in the confusing darkness of that first starry, icy night—Totenkopf like

Wiking had counted on the element of surprise, but they were to fare considerably worse than Wiking had done that first night at Agostian.

The commander of the Totenkopf Panther battalion, Sturm-bannfuhrer Erwin Meierdress, was studying the scene from the command cupola of his tank. He and his crew were killed instantly by a direct hit to the side of their turret fired from only five meters distance. Meierdress had hoped to race through the town and catch the Russians off-guard in a quick coup de main, a risky plan which cost him his life. He was one of the old guard who had been at Demyansk in 1942, fighting in the terrible winter battles there when Totenkopf was still only an infantry division. He had nearly died from wounds suffered while leading a small battle-group out of a Russian encirclement, a feat which won him the Knight's Cross. Recovering from his wounds, he subsequently went on to win the Oak Leaves, only to meet his end in this small village by the Danube River. Of Austrian descent, he was given a state funeral and buried in Vienna beside another Viennese hero of the Reich, fighter pilot Walter Nowotny.

The attack continued to be stalled for hours as point-blank duels raged between Panthers, Sturmgeschutzen, and T-34s in the pitch-black alleys around the church. Finally a reconnaissance patrol found a way around the town, along a narrow path that hugged the Danube shore. The Panthers moved out with grena-diers clinging to their decks, breaking into the clear just as the dawn light was beginning to spread over the river.

But this bitter fight would only be repeated over and over again in the days ahead, in other towns along the river. Totenkopf reached Sutto, which had already been cleared by the surprise river crossing of 96th Infantry Division. From here the infantrymen continued to forge eastward along the riverbank in the direction of Estregom; Totenkopf, however, now turned inland, trying to keep their attack abreast of Wiking's advance in the hills. Finally the town of Szambek was reached, about ten miles north of Bicske, and a link-up was made with a battalion of Wiking's Westland regiment.

But by now Totenkopf was as fought-out as Darges' Kampf-gruppe in the Hegyks castle. It was January 5th. Snow was beginning to fall on the brown hills. Desperate messages were coming in over the radio from the defenders of Buda-pest. The Russians were in control of most of the city and the besieged garrison was running out of ammunition and every other necessity, with thousands of wounded lying in the bombed-out cellars. IV SS Corps needed to try a new approach, and quickly.

There now follows a highly confusing chain of command decisions, which were ultimately to rout the SS relief attack all over the map. Close study of the situation still leads to only a certain stubborn obscurity. For the moment, let us back up a few days and turn to the highest command level at Fuhrer HQ, where an interesting and perhaps critical meeting took place between Hitler and Hans Rudel, apparently at some point during the first day or two of the offensive.

At this time Rudel's Stukas were flying continuous close-support missions in both the Wiking and Totenkopf sectors, dealing out the low-level cannon fire which had become the scourge of Russian tank columns. However, Rudel's memoirs suggest he himself was not with his squadron for these first few days, having been summoned to Fuhrer HQ to be awarded yet another in his long string of decorations, this time the unique Golden Oak Leaves with Diamonds to the Knight's Cross, a medal which no one other than Rudel would ever wear. But he had already spent many hours flying low-altitude missions over the Danube hill country during December, and the Wiking combat history reports an intriguing conversation between the Stuka pilot and Hitler about prospects for further advances across this difficult terrain.

Rudel does not give a word for word account, but summarizes the meetings as follows:

> The Fuhrer takes me over to the map table and tells me that the conference just concluded was regarding the situation at Budapest. I have just come from that sector, have I not? He recapitulates the reasons given to him for the not exactly satisfactory progress of the operation in the Budapest area, which had so far failed to link-up with the encircled city. I gather that weather, transport, and other difficulties have been offered as excuses, but no mention has been made of the blunders which we see every day on our sorties: the splitting-up of the panzer divisions and choice of poor terrain for the tank and infantry assaults.
>
> After a short pause the Fuhrer remarks, with a glance at his circle of advisors:

"You see, this is how I have been misled—who knows for how long?"

. . . With reference to the map he shows his willingness to regroup our forces for a fresh attempt to relieve Budapest. He asks me where I think would be the most favorable terrain for the panzers to attack. I give my opinion.[2]

If this account is accurate, then Hitler quickly took Rudel's advice. He often had more interest in the opinions of fighting men than in the views of his staff generals, especially when the man involved was a personal favorite of Hitler's, and destined to become the most highly decorated soldier in the history of the Third Reich. Unfortunately, the decisions now handed down through the various command levels become very difficult to follow. The relief attack was about to be ham-strung by a series of confusing and contradictory orders, ultimately resulting in the final holocaust in Budapest. Even upon close study, it is difficult to establish exactly who was responsible for the chaotic chain of events now set into play.

In any case, the main role in this bewildering next phase would fall to the Wiking Division, still holding on against fierce Russian counterattacks in the Bicske area. The bitter defense of the Hegyks castle had raged for days to no purpose; abruptly Wiking was ordered to abandon the place and move to a new start-line near the town of Estregom, which lay along the Danube, but was much closer to Budapest than the original jumping-off point of January 1st.

It might be deduced that this sudden transfer was made at Hitler's behest, following his conversation with Rudel; at least this is the implication left by the Wiking history. But subsequent events suggest that both Hitler and Rudel had something entirely different in mind. If so, then Wiking's move must have been ordered at the local level, perhaps by General Wohler or by IV SS Corps commander Herbert Gille.

In any case, Wiking made a fresh start from the Estregom area on January 11th and again met with great initial success. A broad valley, already partially cleared by the 711th Infantry Division, led southeast almost to the suburbs of Budapest. The going was made difficult by the fresh snowfall, but all the same the enemy was thrown back in confusion. The Russians, perhaps not expecting the Germans to shift the axis of attack so quickly, were again taken by surprise, and this time they did not recover. The Waffen SS men were elated; large hauls of prisoners and captured equipment were sent to the rear. After only two days the Wiking Panther columns reached open country, and now Budapest lay less than fifteen miles away. After nearly two years of disastrous setbacks on the Eastern Front, it appeared that the Germans were on the verge of a stunning counterblow.

What followed at this point was, by all accounts from the men in the field, quite incomprehensible.

The attack was stopped.

The church spires of the ancient Magyar capital were visible to the Wiking grenadiers at the head of the advance. During this second relief attempt more falling snow had mingled with weak sunshine; the city rose up in a black, snow-covered silhouette at the end of a snow-covered plain. It appeared to be only a stone's throw away. Russian resistance was disorganized. The sound of gunfire could be heard, but much of it came from the besieged garrison itself.

Nonetheless, the attack was stopped. The Wiking history lays the blame for this decision on the shoulders of General Wohler, commander of Army Group South. SS General Herbert Gille, one-time Wiking commander and now commanding general of IV SS Corps, made an impassioned plea for the attack to go on, but he was turned down. As the local commander in the field, Wohler had jurisdiction over IV SS Corps, but clearly Hitler had ultimate operational control over every military situation. If the decision was Wohler's, Hitler could easily have overturned it. He did not. Indeed, both Wohler and General Balck, another army group commander in Hungary, effectively passed the buck by telling Gille that the decision "had come down from higher levels." This does not seem in any way unlikely, given Hitler's style of command.

It is always easier to assess a difficult predicament in hindsight. At this moment the Russians were still on the offensive further south, coming ominously near to the Hungarian oilfields around Lake Balaton. But this segment of Army Group South's line was still holding out; there was no sign of imminent collapse. Nonetheless, the Budapest relief offensive was re-routed once again. This time the bewildered Waffen SS men were shuttled down to Lake Balaton and ordered to try again from there.

But what was Hitler's reason for doing this? He had always had his own idiosyncratic, often inscrutable way of looking at military situations. The conversation with Rudel comes back to mind. In his memoirs, Rudel does not indicate exactly where on the map he was pointing to when he advised Hitler to regroup the attack. But the most logical answer would be the Lake Balaton area, where the steppe country offered good tank terrain and the possibility of closer cooperation between the attacking SS divisions—in short, it was exactly the kind of situation Rudel had been arguing for.

But this conversation had allegedly taken place over a week earlier. Was Hitler not aware that in the meantime Wiking had already reached the outskirts of Budapest? None of the combat histories or other archives offers a clear answer to this question. Speculation would seem to lead only to confusion at the different command levels, with critical on-the-spot information possibly becoming lost somewhere between the HQs of Gille's corps, Wohler's army group, and Hitler's High Command. It seems fairly certain that Hitler had already issued orders to shift the attack to Lake Balaton before Wiking's successful thrust from Estregom. The real question then is, Why weren't these orders immediately countermanded, when he received news that the SS grenadiers were within view of the Budapest skyline? Or did General Wohler, who now seemed more interested in the Lake Balaton attack, somehow fail to pass this news along? These questions only give rise to a number of other theories about this decision, each possibly with its own merits; but unfortunately, for the moment any conclusive solution to this puzzle must remain a mystery.[3]

By any standards, it would have to rank as one of the more dumbfounding decisions of the war, certainly one of the more demoralizing. Within Budapest, civilians and soldiers alike knew that a relief column was only a few miles away. It is easy to speculate that most of them were never told about this latest change in plan; they could only guess among themselves why the sound of gunfire approaching from beyond the city limits should so suddenly cease.

Before shifting their attack once again, many of the Wiking grenadiers "drove to the health spa at Dogobeko to see the spires of Budapest with their own eyes."[4] It was a sight they would not behold again.

The Lake Balaton area was over fifty miles to the south. The new offensive (for the Wikings it was relief attempt number three) began on January 18th. The situation was beginning to develop its own perverse and maddening style. Once again both Wiking and Totenkopf made good initial progress. The SS armor was now reinforced by the King Tigers of the army's Panzer Abteilung 509. With the elan that perhaps only they were capable of at this point in the war, the SS grenadiers shouted, "On to Budapest!" ("Nach Budapest!" in German, which sounds somewhat less bombastic than the English translation.)[5]

But it was more than Waffen SS bravado which spurred them on. About half the German forces holding out inside the capital were other SS divisions, including many personal acquaintances of the men in the relief force. Coming from the south this time, they again fought nearly to the suburbs of the city; though no one reported seeing any church spires this time. Meanwhile, the Russians had had quite enough of this whole business. The overall commander of the Soviet forces in Hungary, Marshal R.Y. Malinovsky, could match even the strongest German panzer spearhead tank for tank, and the infantry divisions at his disposal vastly outnumbered the SS grenadiers supporting the armor. After retreating steadily for a week in mud and snow, the forces assembled by Malinovsky counterattacked in massive strength. The fog-wracked plains between Lake Balaton and Budapest were turned into an enormous tank graveyard, with hundreds of black patches in the snow marking the burnt-out hulks of both sides. As always, the Germans took the upper hand in these armored duels, but their vehicle strength was being rapidly whittled away. On January 25th, General Gille reported a total strength for his corps of 5 Mk IVs, 27 Panthers, 11 Tigers and King Tigers, and 7 Sturmgeschutzen. In normal circumstances, it was only enough to outfit a single panzer battalion; whereas the Russian reinforcements of T-34s and lend-lease Shermans seemed inexhaustible. Faced with this kind of opposition, IV SS Corps was thrown back, this time for good.

The saga outside the city walls had come to an end. Meanwhile the besieged garrison continued to fight on, entering its second month of desperate house-to-house combat, an epic bloodbath in a heavily built-up area that would become known in some quarters as the "Stalingrad of the Waffen SS."[6] But none of it really mattered anymore. Budapest was doomed.

From the Deutsche Wochenschau, January 1945. . . .

A Jagdpanther drives slowly through a village in Belgium. The commentator finishes the news from the Western Front.

A map of the Vistula Front appears on the flickering screen. A shot of some unidentified bend in the river. Then follows a chaotic mosaic of images, each barely a second long. German soldiers firing from dugouts and pillbox slits; a man crouches behind the shield of a panzerschreck, staggering from the backblast of the weapon as he launches the rocket. A T-34 burns among shattered trees. Another T-34 rolls forward, spewing oily fire from a hull-mounted flame thrower. Enormous shellbursts are filmed at very close range—the German cameramen risk their lives as frequently as the news teams of any other nation. The public will see perhaps a few bits of stock footage, but almost all of this is very real.

A loader drops shells into a mortar tube one after the other, at intervals of less than a second. A man barely able to walk, staggering with the help of a cane, follows his comrades out of a shattered dugout. Massed flights of Stormoviks roar overhead.

The commentator:

"Street fighting rages in hundreds of villages. Every house and copse of trees is bitterly fought over. The front is in flames for a thousand kilometers. Over the first five days of the offensive, the Soviets have lost a thousand tanks. There is no longer any day or night. The enemy is everywhere."

More: bare fields a few days earlier, now a light snow covers the ground. A tank-hunting Stuka wheels above this white landscape, passing over the trails of hundreds of Russian tanks.

The commentator:

"The white earth is blackened by craters and the burnt-out hulks of Soviet tanks, marking the end of their advance to the west.

"On the ground, the grenadiers in advanced positions crouch under the hail of shellfire, as well as heavy bombing by the Soviet air force. These days and weeks in the East bring unparalleled hardship, demanding the strongest hearts and strongest nerves. On the ground the unending savagery of the fighting rages on, with all weapons, with every passing hour."[1]

3

A DELUGE OF SHELLS

The Soviet Offensive Demolishes the German
Vistula Front

Hitler had his hands full. It is difficult to say whether his strange re-routing of the Budapest relief offensive simply ignored up-to-the-minute information, or if other factors were involved. Such a critical operation should have had his full attention, but at this moment he was still preoccupied by the dwindling German fortunes in the Ardennes battle in the west. Were there still enough forces on hand in Belgium to somehow renew the offensive? All of these pressing concerns may have affected his judgment; in the midst of all this, even more terrible news was relayed to his headquarters. On January 12th, the same day the Wiking men were actually within view of the Budapest skyline, the long-awaited Russian offensive on the Vistula burst with sledgehammer force against the German armies in Poland.

In 1941, just prior to his momentous undertaking in the East, Hitler had compared the Soviet Union to a rotting edifice. "One good kick at the front door and the whole structure will come tumbling down," he had said.[2]

This colorful description could just as easily have applied to the German Vistula Front four years later. Indeed, in trying to impress the dire nature of the situation upon Hitler, Guderian used an expression with different images but identical meaning: "Our defenses along the Vistula are no more substantial than a house of cards."[3] The German divisions were undermanned and dispersed over wide areas. Panzer divisions that should have been kept in reserve were stationed almost directly behind the front in order to plug the gaps in the line. Before they could be mobilized for a counterattack, many were inundated by Russian artillery fire. The Germans had nothing like the defenses in depth which the Soviets had employed with such success ever since the Kursk battle in 1943, with deep belts of mines and PAK batteries reaching back for miles behind the front.

Guderian was well aware of all these shortcomings. For months his intelligence chief, Reinhard von Gehlen, had been keeping him apprised not only of the weakness of the German positions but of the enormous Soviet buildup opposing them. Hitler had dismissed Gehlen's information out of hand as "the ravings of a lunatic."[4]

Hitler insisted on keeping a firm hold on one of his most persistent delusions. Despite all indications to the contrary, he continued to believe that the Russians were reaching the end of their reserves of manpower. Although the Soviet armies had mounted one successful offensive after another for almost two years, they continued to take casualties at a horrendous rate. The hulks of thousands upon thousands of destroyed T-34s littered the Soviet drive towards German soil. Even in these years of defeat and retreat, German soldiers in the East continued to be amazed by the quantities of blood shed by the Red Army.

It was true that by 1944 the Russians' profligate wasting of lives had begun to lead to shortages of experienced soldiers. Young teenagers and old men were often to be found in Red Army battalions. Civilians from the newly liberated areas of western Russia had been absorbed en masse into the armed forces, often without any military training. With typical Aryan prejudice, the Germans had been referring to the Soviet Union as a whole since 1941 as the homeland of the "Asiatic hordes"; by 1945, more and more soldiers from the remote eastern reaches of the Soviet empire were serving in the army. They had always been there, of course, but in the early years the army had been dominated by soldiers from the western or European regions of Russia. Now with so many of these men already dead, the numbers of Kazakhs, Uzbekis, Buryat Mongols and other Asians were proportionately greater, fighting against a European foe they had never seen before and perhaps had barely heard of, with their increased presence in the battle lines only serving to escalate German fears of having their nation destroyed by "Mongol hordes."

These Asian contingents were also composed of many teenagers and old men; while not suffering as badly as western Russia, the Siberian republics had still sent thousands of their best soldiers off to be slaughtered in the first years of the war. Many of the remnants of 1945, both European and Asian, did present a rather sorry and beleaguered appearance; poorly and hastily trained, they continued to die in enormous, mind-numbing numbers. While veteran Soviet units from the early years began to perform more effectively on the battlefield, more recent draftees were still sent forward in mass attacks with the usual attendant carnage. Many of these second-rate units were present along the Courland Front, this area being a less important target than Germany itself, which did much to account for the ongoing slaughter of Red Army men on that lonely battlefield.

The overall scale of casualties had also forced the Russians, albeit reluctantly, to draft large numbers of women into the armed forces. Most were used as signal or supply troops, or as medical attendants, but many were employed in combat as tank drivers, snipers, pilots, and so. It was the only instance in modern history—and perhaps ancient as well—in which such a high proportion of females had fought alongside their male comrades in arms. (Although popular myth has exaggerated the role of women in the Red Army to some degree; they still comprised only a small fraction of the fighting troops.)

Thus Hitler was not entirely wrong about Russia's dwindling manpower reserves. But essentially the hopes he placed on this situation were misguided. German losses on the Eastern Front, especially in 1944, had also been horrendous, and Germany's manpower crisis was now far more critical than the Soviets'. For all practical purposes, the Red Army's supply of blood and fresh bodies might as well have been inexhaustible. Still more critical, however, was the by now huge disparity in material resources between the two nations. The Soviets' staggering advantage in numbers of tanks, planes, and artillery pieces would really provide the decisive factor in crushing the German army in the final months of the war. Untouched by bombing or any other wartime distractions, the Russian factories beyond the Urals continued to churn out weapons at a staggering pace.

The Russian numerical superiority in heavy weapons of these kinds generally ranged anywhere from 5:1 to 10:1. The odds were worst in local areas targeted to be struck first in the upcoming offensive. Out of all the varieties of material power at their disposal, the Russians' most overwhelming advantage probably lay with their artillery arm. They tended to squander their superior numbers of tanks through poor tactics and communications on the battlefield, but the firepower and accuracy of their artillery grew more and more devastating as the war went on. The adage that the artillery is "the queen of the battlefield" has been ascribed to Napoleon, but the Soviet Union more than any other nation had taken up this tradition and made it a reality. The massed ranks of heavy cannon employed by the Russians in 1945 would be unequaled in the history of war, surpassing even the terrible concentrations of guns along the Western Front in World War One.

For most of the war, Soviet artillery had not been known for pinpoint accuracy. Modern systems of forward observation and fire adjustment were still at fairly primitive stages, at times non-existent. Soviet barrages would fall time after time on pre-deter-mined areas; for years the Germans had learned to adjust their defensive positions on the Eastern Front accordingly, so that the deluge of enemy shells was often not very effective, all too fre-quently landing on ground that was no longer occupied. Even when Russian gunners had the range, their shellfire tended to be dispersed across a wide area, rather than hammering specific targets within the barrage zone.

Due to their smaller numbers of cannon, the German appli-cation of artillery had of necessity been entirely the opposite. If it had not been, their armies in the East might have collapsed as early as 1942. There exist countless examples of Russian troops and armored concentrations on the verge of overwhelm-ingly thinly held German positions in every part of Russia, only to be destroyed at the last moment by the deadly accuracy of the German guns.

But the Germans never had enough of anything—tanks, planes, cannon, men. The Russians made up for their lack of accuracy by employing artillery en masse. By 1945 their field pieces were lined up wheel-to-wheel for miles behind the Vistula Front. It was an arrogant display unlike anything ever seen be-fore, these Soviet artillery parks, frequently set up without even the bother of camouflage in the open countryside. They had little to fear in the way of German retaliation. The Luftwaffe had long since disappeared from large areas of the Eastern Front. German artillerymen would agonize over the presence of so many inviting targets, yet they no longer had enough shells, let alone cannon, to deliver effective counterbattery fire on the Russian guns. Ger-man ammunition stocks were so low that in many cases firing was forbidden altogether; the precious shells were allowed to be used only when an enemy attack was underway.

Even from an organizational standpoint, the Russians used artillery differently from the Western nations. Theirs was the only army to employ entire divisions of artillery. A division in any of the world's armed forces will normally consist of from somewhere between 10,000 and 20,000 men; to have a unit of this size devoted entirely to the operation of heavy cannon is difficult to conceive of in terms of traditional military organizational tables. But for the Russians this seemed a natural enough evolution in their use of weaponry.

In essence, the Soviets simply did not have enough skilled observers and signalmen to provide for the normal dispersal of these personnel among regiments and battalions. Only by putting men with this kind of training at the disposal of a single divisional HQ were they able to conduct accurate barrage fire. From this central control point target information was relayed out to batteries stationed along different sections of the front. Mass still counted for more than precision, but even so German soldiers were to discover to their dismay that the accuracy of the Russian artillery had improved considerably from a few years earlier.

And so there they were, spread out for miles in the barren fields on the east bank of the Vistula, or packed into the several bridgeheads the Russians had established on the west bank. The massed gun barrels were lent an even more menacing appearance by the huge muzzle brakes peculiar to Russian artillery pieces of all sizes. The famed Katyushas or Stalin Organs were also present in large numbers. These artillery rockets were the scourge of German soldiers everywhere on the Eastern Front, for they carried a greater weight of explosive per projectile than any cannon shell.

In a certain sense, there is little to be said about the Vistula battle. It was over almost as soon as it started, involving little more than a rout that went on for two hundred miles to the banks of the Oder River, where the Russian spearheads were stopped by fuel and supply shortages as much as by German resistance.

But this would be little more than a strategic overview, meaningless to the men actually trapped on that hellish battlefield.

The Soviet offensive originated from three bridgeheads across the Vistula, all to the south of Warsaw—at Magnuszew, at Pulawy, and at Baranov/Sandomierz.[5] The armies of the 1st

Byelorussian Front under General Zhukov were to burst out from Pulawy and Magnuszew and meet in a pincer movement to trap the divisions of the German 9th Army defending this area, starting on January 14th.

But the first and most devastating blow would come from the southernmost and largest bridgehead at Baranov/Sandomierz, in the sector of 4th Panzer Army. Here, General Konev's 1st Ukrainian Front attacked on January 12th, raising the curtain, so to speak, on the entire Soviet operation in Poland and East Prussia.

Stationed in this area as part of 4th Panzer Army was the 20th Panzer Grenadier Division. For a time this unit was nearly trapped in a German bridgehead on the east bank of the Vistula, just to the south of Sandomierz.

Werner Adamczyk was a gunlayer in 20th Panzer Grenadier's artillery regiment. He had seen action on the Eastern Front since 1941, fighting in all parts of Russia from the Volkhov River in the far north to the steppes of the Ukraine. Anyone who had served for this length of time in the East had begun to develop a grim and cynical attitude about the war long before 1945. Adamczyk reports an amusing little ditty sung by his comrades as early as the fall of 1943, during the long and difficult retreat across the Ukraine:

Haben Sie schon ein Hitler Bild?
Danke nein,
Ich brauche kein
Denn habe Ich vom Stalin eins!

Have you got your Hitler picture yet?
Thanks no,
I won't be needing it,
'Cause I've already got one of Stalin![6]

This song was simply regarded as an example of front-line humor; no one was ever disciplined for singing it.

By January 1945 Adamczyk and his comrades had just finished a grueling retreat along the eastern slopes of the Carpathians, wending their way slowly northwestward until at last they arrived at the southern bend of the Vistula near Baranov/Sandomierz. By this time latrine gossip was not about WHETHER they would lose the war, but about what would happen WHEN they lost the war. If they even survived that far.

As with other memoirs of the Eastern Front, Adamczyk's account reaches a crescendo of violence in 1945. In the West, the war would wind down pathetically in these final months; in the East, Adamczyk describes an escalation of horror and fear that would not let up until the end.

As mentioned a moment ago, his division was for a time still fighting on the east bank of the Vistula in a dangerously exposed position. His memory for exact dates is not very clear, but this is not unusual among combat veterans engaged in the day-to-day confusion of events. It appears that this period of time was just prior to the opening of Konev's offensive on January 12th. The Russians were already conducting preliminary attacks against the east-bank bridgehead of 20th Pz. Gren., and Adamczyk reports a sense of mounting anxiety among his comrades, fearing that they would be trapped and wiped out with their backs to the river:

> Finally the day of reckoning had arrived. Ivan attacked with artillery and Stalin Organs, tanks and masses of infantry. Our own infantry called for a fire density we could not possibly attain. One command was overruling another. It became chaos. We just kept firing, following the commands at random . . . We thought we had really had it, yet there was a surprise in store. A good number of tanks had crossed the river, coming to our rescue.[7]

It turned out the tanks were from an SS division, an interesting observation, as no SS armor is reported serving with 4th Panzer Army at this time. Nonetheless, their counterattack bought time for Adamczyk's unit to retreat across a pontoon bridge to the west bank of the river. None of the SS tanks survived the battle.

> When I realized the sacrifice they had made, I burst out into tears. Later I learned they were part of an SS division, dedicated to die for Germany if necessary. Al-

though none of us liked the SS, because they were always favored when it came to supplies and weapons, we really felt grateful to them. They gave their lives to get us out of this mess.[8]

The identity (or mis-identification) of this SS unit is a mystery of the kind that crops up all too frequently in the memories of front-line veterans. Their ground-level descriptions of combat tend to be both more vivid and more confusing than broader historical accounts, but for certain obvious reasons, theirs was the only real view of the war. In any case, the reprieve bought by the sacrifice of the SS tanks was only temporary; the feeling of security offered by the west bank of the Vistula was only an illusion.

A few days later General Konev's general offensive began, and the men of 20th Pz. Gren. were caught in the deluge of shells delivered by the Russians' initial bombardment. German positions were simply buried beneath this mass of fire, with the defenders themselves buried beneath collapsed earth and timbers. HQ bunkers in the rear were obliterated along with the front-line trenches. Months earlier, Guderian had beseeched Hitler to establish a secondary defensive line out of the range of the Russian guns. Typically, Hitler had refused. Now the German line around Baranov/Sandomierz was simply blown away. Time after time during the earlier years, German soldiers had fought tenaciously from well dug-in defensive works, repelling wave after wave of Russian attackers and inflicting terrible carnage on the enemy. But now in the fourth year of the war the Russians had finally amassed a weight of shellfire that was too much to bear, especially when their improved fire-control systems made the guns so much more accurate than they had been in the past. Now all around the perimeter of the bridgehead the Red Army's first assault groups found only dead Germans, or Germans wandering in a daze, or Germans simply fleeing for their lives to the rear.

Adamczyk's account offers no contradiction to the Russians' first impressions:

As the morning light grew, the earth was turned upside down by the Russian artillery. We got a command to fire back, but we could not get out of our bunkers without being killed instantly, so dense was the rain of shells hitting our position . . . A flash of light emerged from the entrance of the bunker, followed by a terrible crush of compressed air. I thought that my lungs would burst . . . The entrance had collapsed and we were trapped in the bunker.[9]

Adamczyk and his comrades had to dig their way out, a long and arduous struggle that was made worse by their fears that they would all suffocate before they could free themselves. Meanwhile the great barrage continued, deafening them with its noise and making them wonder if it would not be simpler just to die where they were. During this time the first Russian assault groups were beginning to probe the ruins of the German defenses.

Along with their assault infantry, the Russians sent out special battalions of Stalin tanks to wipe out whatever pockets of German resistance still remained. Possibly they would have had little work to do after the artillery barrage. The battlefield lay almost invisible beneath the clouds of smoke that mingled with an already foggy and overcast sky. Snow had been falling on and off for several days, though much of the ground was blackened now by explosions and the churned-up trails of mud left by the tanks.

Still held in reserve, the masses of faster T-34s were waiting for the signal to advance through the first breaches in the line. It was their task to make the deep penetrations into enemy territory that would turn local success into a full-scale rout. The hours passed in the gently falling snow as Konev continued to keep them in check.

Meanwhile the Stalin tanks rumbled slowly through the killing zone, using their enormous 122mm cannon to blast away the sporadic German attempts to return fire. Even now in this Verdun-like crater field, there may have remained enough individual combatants, Einzelkampfer[10] to deliver some serious harm to the Russian machines. A single anti-tank gun remaining in action, a single handheld panzerfaust fired at close range—and a forty-ton Stalin would be blown to pieces or turned into a flaming pyre. However many of these Einzelkampfer were still fighting will probably remain forever unknown; there were too few survivors to tell any coherent tales later on. But after the smoke cleared there remained numerous graveyards of knocked-out Stalins, not only along the Vistula but on every battlefield of 1945. In appearance, these tanks had a disproportionately top-heavy shape that made them look even larger than they really were. The Stalin chassis was based on the KV model that had been in service since 1941, but the huge new cannon dominated the entire silhouette of the vehicle like the snout of some prehistoric beast. Graveyards of Stalin tanks resembled dinosaur graveyards. After the first week of combat on the Vistula, the German propaganda ministry reported the destruction of several thousand Soviet tanks—no doubt an excessively high figure. But false numbers sometimes portrayed a certain truth, for the Russians would continue to lose huge numbers of tanks in Poland and eastern Germany, no differently than in Russia itself.

Finally Konev unleashed the T-34s waiting to exploit the breakthrough. They advanced through the devastation along predetermined lanes that had been left untouched by the bombardment. The Russian co-ordination of artillery fire with the other combat arms was showing some improvement since 1941. In a scene that had been repeated many times during the war, the T-34s moved out at high speed with platoons of Russian infantry clinging to their decks. On this first day they would advance almost twenty miles. It was a pace they would maintain for weeks to come.

Adamczyk and his comrades would have no chance if left to fight on foot. Fortunately for them, their division had been upgraded to fully motorized status, a rarity among German units even in 1945. Three years earlier, he had watched his artillery pieces being pulled across Russia by teams of horses. Now men were frantically hitching the guns to trucks and half-tracks and roaring at full speed to the west to escape the all-consuming barrage. Adamczyk and his comrades had only barely managed to dig their way out of the collapsed dugout when they saw the rest of the artillery teams fleeing all around them. They gave chase through the rain of shells, with one of the men being blown to pieces after taking only a few steps. Adamczyk attempted to flag down a prime mover but it would not even reduce speed; he and his comrades jumped onto the running boards as it passed by.

The vehicle columns finally halted miles to the west, and the guns were set up again. But they would be on the move again before any of them could be fired. Adamczyk reports a strange interlude in a Polish farmhouse where he spent the first night of the retreat. Even in chaos a few hours of peace could pass by inexplicably. He and his friends entered the farmhouse to find a Polish family seated around a large table heaped up with tobacco leaves, nonchalantly rolling cigars. They offered the disheveled Germans a plentiful farm-style meal, of the kind city dwellers in the Reich could only dream about anymore. The Poles seemed entirely unaware of the Russian advance, or else were unperturbed by it. Russian soldiers had been told to exact whatever revenge they liked on German civilians, but to leave the Poles alone. This distinction often existed in theory more than in practice, especially in areas where German and Polish settlers were mixed together. The retreat continued early the next day, the fate of Adamczyk's hosts remaining unknown.

The Destruction of Panzer Abteilung 424

The dismal German response to the Soviet attack was perhaps best illustrated by the fate of one of the strongest armored units on the Vistula Front, Panzer Abteilung 424. To confuse enemy intelligence sources, the Germans had recently renumbered many of their Tiger tank battalions. For most of the war, 424 had been Panzer Abteilung 501. This unit had a far-flung history, originally seeing action in North Africa before being transferred to Russia. 501 was wiped out with the fall of Tunisia in 1943, then destroyed a second time during the Russian summer offensives of 1944. In late 1944 the unit was fully re-equipped with 45 new King Tigers and attached to the armored corps of General Walter Nehring, forming part of the mobile reserve of 4th Panzer Army along the upper Vistula.

A few weeks before Konev's offensive from the Baranov bridgehead, Panzer Abteilung 424 had been transferred to an assembly area only a few miles behind the front, a move which basically sealed the fate of this unit. The men were disturbed by this situation, recognizing that they might be overrun by a major Soviet attack before they could organize any effective counterattack, which was supposedly their role as 4th Panzer Army's most potent reserve force.

Unfortunately, their fears were to be fully realized. To make matters worse, the panzer crews were highly dissatisfied with the location of their new assembly area, which was in a series of large sand pits almost completely surrounded by marshy and water-logged terrain. Some men of 424 were so distressed by this site that they began circulating rumors of sabotage. This was unlikely; their predicament was almost certainly due to the inadequate strength of the German units positioned in the front lines. 424 had been moved this close to the front in order to provide an additional defensive bulwark. It was a fatal error, for it completely negated their far more meaningful capacity as a mobile reserve.

Things began to go wrong from the moment Konev launched his offensive on January 12th. The mammoth Soviet artillery barrage demolished German lines of communication. At dawn the Tiger crewmen could clearly see and hear the eruption of fire only a few miles away, yet they received no orders of any kind until noon, and even then they were merely put on standby alert.

The situation looked ominous, to say the least. Finally Major Saemisch, in command of 424, decided he could no longer wait for operational orders, and on his own initiative he led his King Tigers eastward towards the roar of battle around 1500 hours. Ironically, Saemisch's already powerful force had recently been strengthened by the addition of a number of the older Tiger Is. These tanks had belonged to Panzer Abteilung 509, but they had been handed over to 424 so that 509 could be re-equipped with King Tigers, pending their transfer to the Hungarian front. Thus Major Saemisch had at his disposal on January 12th a total of 52 Tiger Is and King Tigers, comprising probably the largest assemblage of Tiger tanks of any unit during the war. But this potentially lethal strike force wound up accomplishing almost nothing.

Even as Saemisch led his panzers into action, the early winter dusk was beginning to fall. A light snowfall adhered moistly to the muddy landscape. Any further advance during the night would inevitably result in large numbers of the heavy Tigers bogging down in the treacherous terrain. Saemisch drove on ahead in his Kubelwagen to the nearest divisional command post, desperately seeking to get a clear picture of the situation and above all to get firm orders. Hour after hour his tank crews waited in the dark, surrounded on all sides by the din of battle and the endless flickering of artillery fire. At one point the exhaust flames from a large column of Soviet tanks were sighted in the distance, eerily illuminating the lightly falling snowflakes. The Russians were heading directly for 424's fuel and supply depot, a highly unnerving development, and still the Tiger crews could do nothing. Finally Major Saemisch returned around midnight, bearing news that the divisional command post had been overrun. His orders were to attack and recapture it the following day. These orders would have been out-of-date from almost the moment they were issued, yet still 424 remained immobile as the night hours dragged by interminably.

The attack got underway at dawn and initially met with little resistance. The reason for this was simple: the Russian spearheads had already bypassed 424 the previous day. At this moment 4th Panzer Army's most powerful reserve force was operating in isolation deep in the Russian rear. At length another column of T-34s was encountered moving to the west and taken under fire. The King Tigers were deadly mobile fortresses, nearly impervious to enemy fire in any kind of tank versus tank duel on an open battlefield. The Russian armor was reduced to a smoking shambles, with 424 scoring 20 kills against no losses of their own. As was frequently the case in the elite panzer units, a single ace tank commander did the lion's share of the damage. In this instance the King Tiger of Lt. Oberbracht accounted for twelve of the enemy vehicles.

This was exactly the kind of all-out havoc the Tiger battalions were used to inflicting on Soviet armored attacks. But such a local success could count for nothing against the waves of T-34s that had already advanced ten or twenty miles to the west. 424 was in the position of an elephant trying to stamp out a swarm of army ants. In a sense, Major Saemisch's battalion was too strong for its own good. The Tigers were such powerful weapons that a single platoon or company could have probably dealt out as much punishment as Saemisch's unwieldy total of over 50 panzers. If 424 had been divided into two or three sub-units and stationed further to the rear, both standard practices on the Eastern Front, Konev's spearheads might have been blocked at several different points, delaying his attack considerably. Even this kind of deployment would probably have done no more than slow down the overwhelming power that the Soviets had assembled. But in their present situation, Saemisch's Tigers could not even accomplish that much.

The original attack was called off. There was no longer any point in trying to recapture a single command post when almost every division around the Baranov bridgehead had already been sent reeling in flight. The ironic German Landsers' adage of "attack to the rear, boys"—a phrase which had come into common parlance during the long years of retreat—now took on literal meaning for the King Tigers. Major Saemisch next received orders to turn southwest and attack the town of Lissow, which had been in the German rear only the day before. Rather than blocking the Russian advance, the panzers of 424 were following in its wake, a course that would lead to their destruction.

Ground conditions began to take their toll as both 56 ton Tiger Is and 68 ton King Tigers became bogged down in the snowy mud. Other tanks diverted to retrieve them also got stuck. Rather than have further recovery attempts degenerate into a complete fiasco, the remaining Tigers were sent onward. This was just as well, for almost immediately they encountered seven T-34s cresting a ridge within sight of the bogged-down vehicles. The Tigers still mobile destroyed all seven T-34s within minutes, again without loss to themselves. They then forged on towards Lissow, leaving the tanks trapped in the mud to fend for themselves.

Two of the bogged Tigers belonged to the platoon of Lt. Schroder, who had remained behind with the crews. Certainly by now the men must have begun to grasp the overall gravity of the situation. The odds of any of 424's tanks returning to pull them free seemed less and less likely. Schroder climbed down and waved over a small group of SPWs (half-tracks) which were also heading for Lissow. On board these vehicles he followed the main element of 424 into the town, hoping there would be enough of a lull in the fighting that a few other panzers could be brought back to help the stuck tanks before other Russian armored groups overran them.

There was a lull all right, but the scene that greeted Schroder in Lissow was the aftermath of a disaster. The Russians had already entered the town the previous day. They had received word that a large force of Tigers was operating in their rear and was headed for Lissow. An ambush was set up, with Stalins and PAK batteries concealed in alleys and buildings. Apparently Major Saemisch got the impression that the Russian armor had already passed through the town on its way west. This is only speculation, as he was killed just minutes later. In any case, the situation was not properly reconnoitered and the Tigers simply drove on into the town, there to be devastated at point-blank range by a hail of high-powered anti-tank fire from every direction.

German records of Tiger tank losses are usually very thorough, but due to the state of confusion produced by Konev's offensive, there is no exact tally of casualties from the debacle at Lissow. Sources indicate that almost the whole battalion was involved, less the half dozen or so tanks that had broken down or gotten stuck en route. This would suggest that as many as twenty, and possibly more, Tigers were destroyed in this one engagement. The scene in this small Polish village must have been the most hellish sort of free-for-all. For once, Soviet tank crews had the upper hand against their most hated nemesis. (Kill-to-loss ratios for both Tigers and King Tigers on the Eastern Front generally stood at an astounding 10:1.) Almost certainly this was the single greatest killing of Tiger tanks by Russian armor during the war.

Both adversaries effectively annihilated each other, to say nothing of reducing Lissow to a pile of smoking rubble. Accounts vary as to the fates of the individual crews. Lt. Oberbracht's King Tiger 111, already credited with 12 kills earlier in the day, had both its tracks shot off, either inside or just on the outskirts of town. He was credited with destroying seven more Russian tanks while sitting immobilized, before he was mortally wounded and his panzer shot to pieces. (In what must have been a madhouse, it is hard to imagine how anyone could have kept track of the exact number of Oberbracht's kills before he went down, but such are the statements on record.) Major Saemisch and numerous other commanders and crews were killed in the raging exchange of point-blank fire. King Tigers bogged down outside town, if they were still within range, added their firepower to the melee and were likewise hit in return. The aftermath of this inferno showed Tigers, Stalins, and anti-tank guns buried under rubble and twisted into every conceivable position, sometimes with cannon interlocked like the horns of beasts.

Apparently the Soviets were entirely wiped out or else driven off, for Lissow was in German hands by the time Lt. Schroder arrived with the half-tracks. But no matter their own losses; the Russians would have to count the near annihilation of a whole Tiger battalion as a unique victory.

Schroder received the dolorous news from one of the survivors of the battle. A few tank crewmen whose Tigers had been destroyed climbed into the Kubelwagen of the dead Major Sae-misch; others mounted the half-tracks and the few King Tigers that had survived the massacre, leaving the wrecks of friend and foe behind and heading on to the west. There is no account of the fate of the crews of the bogged-down tanks Schroder had left behind. Perhaps someone drove back to fetch them, as it seems unlikely their comrades would have left them to fall into the hands of the Russians. But they all had to move with haste now if they were to escape being cut off behind enemy lines. The few King Tigers and other vehicles made it to the nearest river, presumably the Nida, crossing over just before the arrival of the Soviets. From there they headed for Kielce, which had become the focal point for other units fleeing from the shattered lines around the Baranov bridgehead.

Three of 424's King Tigers had been sent by train to Kielce the preceding day, apparently the only ones not to participate in the engagement at Lissow. But the days were numbered for these vehicles as well. The long retreat had only just begun.[11]

Nehring's Cauldron Escapes to the West

The microcosm of battle represented by Werner Adamczyk's small team of artillerymen, as well as Panzer Abteilung 424, was part of a larger saga, generally referred to as "Nehring's wandering cauldron."

Cauldron battles (Kesselschlachten) had long been a pecu-liarly unpleasant feature of combat in Russia, referring to the many times when German soldiers had been surrounded and forced to fight their way to freedom against terrible odds. On one occasion, which Adamczyk remembered only too well, an entire German army had struggled for over a hundred miles through enemy-held territory to re-establish contact with the main defense line, during the spring of 1944. This had been Gen-eral Hube's "wandering cauldron." Now this situation was about to be played out once again.

General Walter Nehring commanded a corps whose main components were 16th and 17th Panzer Divisions. Many of his tanks had already been destroyed by the bombardment; others, sharing the same problem as 424, could not operate effectively because of the breakdown in communications. Those that survived the first day were too few to conduct any meaningful coun-terattack. By January 13th Nehring, a battle-hardened leader who had seen disaster before, both in Russia and North Africa, judged that survival and escape were the only issues that mat-tered. His corps was joined by the fleeing remnants of other divisions around the bridgehead, among which were 20th Pz. Gren. and the 72nd Infantry Division. These disorganized groups of survivors assembled around the town of Kielce. Most of them reported seeing long columns of Russian armor already bypass-ing them and headed for the west.

In the Vistula operation, the Soviet high command was more intent on exploiting the breakthrough and racing as quickly as possible towards the German frontier. The destruction of the Ger-man forces left behind was not a top priority. If it had been, the men of Nehring's cauldron, as well as the nameless survivors of other small pockets, would have been crushed without mercy. By keeping a close eye on the direction of the Russian spearheads, and aided by a strong dose of luck and cunning intuition, Nehring was able to lead his entire force out to the west. He sought to avoid combat and stay in between the main enemy thrusts. These survivors roamed for days through the snowy Polish countryside, moving mostly at night, hiding by day in patches of woodland, sending patrols into the few towns to ensure they were not already occupied by the enemy.

They came to the first natural barrier, the Pilica River. Un-known to them, the Soviet armor had already crossed it to the north and south, after locating fords to allow passage of the tanks where the ice was too thin to hold them. The T-34s had simply plunged in and plowed through dirty ice that reached up to their decks, emerging on the far side and continuing onward. This kind of reckless crossing method would have been unthinkable for the more temperamental German tanks, but the Russians had often taken advantage of the T-34's robust construction in situations like this. Even so they may have left a few vehicles behind at the bottom of the river, but they would not have allowed such normal wastage to delay their advance.

Some of Nehring's men found a country bridge which they attempted to reinforce with fallen timbers. The lighter vehicles crossed over. Finally two tanks were driven directly under the bridge to give support for the passage of the rest of the armor. Elsewhere the ice was thick enough to support a crossing, though just barely. Photos exist showing men of the 72nd Infantry Division testing the ice on the Pilica with metal prods. A thread of open water still lapped along the shoreline. The situation looked chancy, but eventually even the prime movers, which weighed almost as much as tanks, were driven across, towing the heavy field pieces behind them. Men on foot leapt over the shoreline crack of water and then walked slowly over to the other side. Everything was done in a reasonably calm fashion. The sun shone down weakly through a thin haze. There is an air of urgency but not panic in these photographs. It is always surprising to see the unhurried, step-by-step way in which things are done, even in desperate situations. The life of a combat soldier is like that—even under fire, a man can only run for a short ways before he tires and must simply begin walking again.

It was the veteran soldiers, the junior officers and NCOs, who by their example helped maintain an atmosphere of order and calm. Particularly in the 72nd Infantry Division, there were very few of these who had survived this far into the war. The 72nd had been seriously bled-out during the attack on the great Sevastapol fortress in the searing heat of July 1942. But the greatest disaster for this unit had occurred during the crossing of yet another ice-bound river, back in the steppes of the Ukraine only a year before the present retreat across the Pilica. The 72nd was one of several divisions that were nearly annihilated during the terrible breakout from the Cherkassy cauldron in February 1944. Many of the veterans had been drowned or machine-gunned by packs of T-34s while trying to flee across the treacherous thaw ice of the Gniloy Tikich River. It was one of the most nightmarish ordeals of a nightmarish war. No doubt some of the Cherkassy survivors were now reliving those moments as they gathered anxiously along the shores of the Pilica, waiting to see if the ice was thick enough to hold them; waiting to see too, if the packs of T-34s would suddenly appear on the riverbank at their backs, just as they had done the year before. But their luck was better this time, far better. The breakout from the Cherkassy cauldron had been an unforgettable horror; by comparison, General Nehring's cauldron was to lead a charmed existence.

It was fortunate that the wanderings of these men took them almost directly between Konev's thrust from the south and Zhukov's from the north; still more fortunate, that the Russians remained intent on driving to the west. The Soviet commanders had one strategic goal in mind—to reach the Oder River as quickly as possible, without allowing the Germans time to recover and set up another defensive line. Such intermediate lines did exist at various intervals across Poland, and the Soviet leaders were sorely troubled by them—until they reached these positions and discovered they were not manned. The entire German military presence had been directly behind the Vistula. There had been no reserves available for a defense-in-depth (though the presence of the Courland army group would have solved this problem handily) and Hitler had never believed in that kind of thing anyway, thinking it only encouraged the front-line troops to fall back more easily.

Occasionally Nehring's men engaged in brief firefights in villages where the Russians had set up flanking positions; occasionally they were taken under fire by columns of T-34s, but then the Russian tanks disappeared into the gloom, moving onward. Nehring remained intent on keeping the greater bulk of his force hidden from view as much as possible. By this time many of the vehicles had run out of fuel and were blown up or abandoned along woodland trails. The King Tigers with their enormous fuel consumption would have been among the first to go; only one or two were still kept operational with preciously doled out liters of gasoline. By this time, too, large numbers of civilian refugees had joined Nehring's men, bearing frightful tales of the Soviet massacres already underway.

The wandering cauldron covered 150 miles in ten days. By now its impetus was beginning to disintegrate; soldiers and civilians alike were exhausted, their nerves strung taut by the continual sightings of the Russians moving across the horizon. Radio contact was made with the Grossdeutschland Panzer Corps in the city of Lodz. The distance to Lodz was not far, and Nehring's staff officers urged him to take the shortest route via the main highway. But Nehring's instincts had guided them all this far, and he ordered a wide detour through yet another stretch of forest and empty heathland. Keep hidden, stay out of sight until the last possible moment . . .

Some of the other officers became exasperated with these lengthy meanderings, thinking their leader was confused and indecisive and declaring as much in accounts after the war, emphasizing their words with the vehemence of men who had been through a grueling experience where their lives had depended on someone making clear and correct decisions. Perhaps Nehring's decisions had not always been clear to his subordinates, but in the end they proved to be correct; the other officers might have acknowledged this afterwards, but perhaps they were still living in the bitter moments of arguments that had taken place during their trek. Such heated reminiscences among survivors of groups lost in the wilderness or on the open ocean are not uncommon; the same holds true for desperate men trying to escape from behind the lines of a ruthless enemy.

Nehring seems to have been guided by intuition and experience more than anything else; he was not aware that large Russian forces were in fact blocking the direct highway route to Lodz. From this city a few armored reconnaissance vehicles of Grossdeutschland were sent out along back roads to search for the wandering cauldron, and at last a link-up was made in a foggy wood near the Warthe River. The Grossdeutschland men guided the first of Nehring's people to the far bank and safety.

It was January 22nd. Von Saucken, the Grossdeutschland commander, greeted Nehring and informed him that his own corps in Lodz was nearly surrounded. Nehring listened to this news without visible emotion. The trek to the west was about to begin all over again, onward to the banks of the Oder. Werner Adamczyk marched on with the others, and on many days he saw Russian columns moving nearly abreast of them off in the distance, advancing deeper into Germany.

Stalin was a Georgian, born of a people whose way of life could oscillate unpredictably between festive gaiety, ruthlessness, and violence. Westerners might regard such stereotypes as merely exaggerated versions of Russian traits. But the Russians themselves might dismiss any such perceived similarities, generally regarding Georgians as untrustworthy sorts, if not outright criminals.

On one occasion a Soviet general became angry with one of Stalin's decisions; it had led to yet another disaster on the battlefield. The general was attending a late-night gathering at Stalin's villa outside Moscow and expressed his displeasure by picking up a whole roast pig from a buffet table and hurling it across the room. He then kicked the table over for good measure.

But it was a party after all, a few hours release from the endless stress of running the war, and the general's outburst did not seem to dampen anyone's spirits. Stalin took it in stride. Such a spontaneous display of feeling was only part of the atmosphere.

Perhaps only a Russian or a fellow Georgian could blow up like that without wondering if he would be punished later—exiled, imprisoned, shot. But people did tend to relax at these midnight get-togethers, and Stalin was no different. Perhaps it would be amusing to imagine the Soviet High Command planning the war over buffet tables laden with roast pigs—but in fact such festive occasions were all too rare, almost non-existent. All of them could count on their fingers the few fleeting hours they had had for such amusements during the war. Stalin chided the general for a moment, but that was all there was to it, and the drinking and eating went on until dawn.

The next day both of them were back at work as if nothing had happened, back to their endless round-the-clock routine, devising yet another plan that would somehow throw the Nazi bastards out of their country.

4

STALIN

Terror and Relaxation of Terror

The Russian thrust to the Oder would leave large German forces to its rear. There were numerous other disorganized, barely combat-worthy formations like Nehring's, fighting for their own survival and wandering all over Poland and East Prussia. These decimated units wandering in the rear areas did not constitute a serious menace, and the Russians had made no determined efforts to wipe them out.

The situation on the flanks was different though. By the end of January Zhukov's 1st Byelorussian Front had reached the Oder at a point only forty miles from Berlin. But arcing around Zhukov's spearheads, in a vast semi-circle extending to the northeast and southeast, remained a number of German armies that were still almost intact. The Germans remained in control of the Baltic shoreline all the way from the mouth of the Oder to Konigsberg in East Prussia, a distance of about three hundred miles. Already Konigsberg was under siege, and soon Danzig and numerous other Baltic ports would also be under siege. But to Stalin and the Stavka, the Soviet High Command, this three hundred mile exposed flank remained a source of danger and concern. Did the Germans still have enough strength to mount a counterattack from somewhere in this area, a strike that would cut right across the rear of Zhukov's spearheads already on the Oder?

In hindsight, this seems an exaggerated worry. But hindsight is always like that. The reality at the time was that Russian strength was nearly everywhere overwhelming, not only at the Oder but along the flanks as well. But in the fog of war, during endless late-night meetings in the Kremlin, Stalin and the Stavka had no way of knowing this for sure. During the long course of the war in the East, the Germans had been notorious for launching counterattacks at the worst possible moment, cutting across the path of a Russian advance and turning Soviet success into disaster almost overnight.

Stalin had a long memory, and his sleep was not made easier by the knowledge that he had been the driving force behind many of these doomed attacks earlier in the war. The Volkhov Offensive to free Leningrad in 1942 . . . what a debacle that had been. The Russians had ruptured the front of Army Group North to a depth of over fifty miles; but the German counterattacks finally managed to seal off the point of the initial breakthrough, and whole Russian armies were doomed to encirclement and starvation in the snow. General Vlasov, the commander in the field, had felt personally betrayed by Stalin's inept leadership and had gone over to the Germans. Even now in 1945 Vlasov was touring the cities of the Reich, trying to find support among Nazi leaders to raise an army of Russian POWs to fight against Stalin.

Still other examples of this kind of travesty would remain to cloud Stalin's thinking. After the great victory at Stalingrad the resurgent Soviet armies had driven the Germans back for hundreds of miles, harrying them all the way across southern Russia. But then another stunning counterattack by Waffen SS panzer divisions had slashed into their overextended flanks and cut several more armies to pieces. Now, when the war seemed nearly won, would not be a propitious moment for another setback of that kind.

The flank to the south was identical to that along the Baltic. For hundreds of miles through southern Poland and Silesia, the Germans still maintained coherent forces of unknown striking power.

Stalin had learned a thing or two from past mistakes; he was more adaptable than Hitler in this respect. As far as controlling the ultimate reins of power in his own domain, he was far more the absolute master of the Soviet empire than Hitler had ever been of the Third Reich. Stalin maintained a force of control and intimidation over the average Soviet citizen that Hitler, by and large, had never brought to bear against his fellow Germans (excepting, of course, German Jews). The aura of fear surrounding the SS and the Gestapo was far more terrifying to Jews and Slavs, to hostages rounded up in conquered nations, than it ever was to the typical German civilian, or for that matter to the typical German front-line soldier. Even during Hitler's regime Germany would maintain (at least within its own borders) some semblance of traditional legalities and due process. Hitler may have debased and perverted these traditions on many occasions, but they were never completely erased, and it seems that most German civilians did not live in fear that they would be.

Much of this had to do with Hitler's view of himself as a popular leader of his nation. He did not wish to be perceived by his own people as a tyrant or oppressor. How the rest of the world perceived him was, of course, an entirely different matter.

On the other hand, Stalin had never devoted quite the same kind of attention to his popular image, apart from draping his portrait from the sides of buildings or erecting busts of himself in town squares. The field of public relations had never really existed inside the Soviet Union. Propaganda, yes—in massive doses much more tightly censored and controlled than any of the news media inside Germany, but this kind of absolute control of information by the state could be called public relations only in the very loosest sense. Favorable propaganda about Stalin and the Communist system was always backed up by a vast web of coercion and intimidation. Political commissars and other elements of the NKVD, Stalin's secret police, were a continuous presence in every unit of the Red Army, down to the company and platoon level. There was never any kind of comparable system within the German Army.

Yet one thing that Stalin had learned, perhaps reluctantly, was that his army simply could not function effectively with such a network of terror and reprisal always lurking in its midst. It paralyzed the initiative of commanders in the field, particularly when they had to deal with an unexpected crisis in the form of a German counterattack. For the most part, Russian commanders were not allowed the flexibility to make on-the-spot decisions in an emergency. Again and again during the earlier phases of the war, fear of reprisals from above inhibited them from re-routing an attack when it was threatened from the rear; they showed little of the unique German talent for instantly re-arranging their troop dispositions, either to take advantage of an opportunity or to fend off disaster.

Part of this problem had to do with the Russians' traditionally more unwieldy manner of leading large armies in battle. But Stalin's appalling purges of the Red Army's officer corps in the 1930's had exacerbated these difficulties enormously; by the time of Hitler's invasion only a few years later the pall of terror within the army had barely begun to subside, if it had even subsided at all.

Coupled with fear was the inexperience of so many junior officers who had been promoted to replace the thousands of colonels and generals murdered during the purges. Under conditions like these, the Red Army tended to function as little more than a massive blunt instrument, with almost no ability to conduct intricate maneuvers or make swift decisions within the ongoing fog of battle.

All of these factors had led to the near-total destruction of the army during the first year of the war. Even during the miraculous period of recuperation which followed, Soviet military operations would remain cumbersome, generally inflexible affairs. This would remain so even during the era of great victories in 1944 and 1945. Because the movements of large units in the field remained so cumbersome, the success of any major Soviet operation depended on being well-planned in advance at the highest levels of command, that is to say by Stalin and the other key decision makers of the Stavka.

Fortunately, the ability of the Soviet High Command to envisage and carry out these massive strategic operations grew better and better as the war went on. Stalin always remained the final arbiter, but over time his decisions became less peremptory and he tended to carefully consider the advice of his best strategic planners. By the end of the war, and even long before, Stalin and the Stavka were working very much as a team—a situation which was exactly the opposite of Hitler's obsessive desire to run the German war machine almost entirely on his own, down to the smallest and most petty details.

In this respect, Hitler operated less like a dictator than a somewhat deranged artist who is forever obsessed with controlling every aspect of his own creations. Like many artists, either great or fraudulent, the idea of teamwork was generally foreign to him. He tolerated the input of his staff generals—even of those he respected—with only a certain ill-tempered reluctance. While not always interested in exercising absolute domination over the German people, he did tend to exercise these powers when it came to his own strange views about running the war.

Thus the renowned flexibility and on-the-spot initiative of German officers in the field became more and more hindered as the war went on, though even Hitler was not able to entirely inhibit these qualities. German small-unit tactics, at the level of battalion, company, or platoon, almost always displayed greater skill than those of their Russian opponents. But on the higher strategic level Stalin and the Stavka had developed a rational, carefully thought-out approach to operations which continually outwitted Hitler's method of strange and frequently unworkable inspirations.

Meanwhile, at the local level of the units in the field, Stalin gradually relaxed the power, and above all the threat of instant retaliation, wielded by the commissars and the NKVD. Perhaps he sensed a certain risk to his own absolute authority in doing this, but with his army on the verge of utter destruction earlier in the war he had had little choice. He did not have Hitler's pretensions towards being a great military genius, and at some point he must have realized that changes were necessary if the Red Army were to function with any kind of efficiency. Thus gradually the network of terror which Stalin had instituted in the 30's was withdrawn, at least to some degree. A regimental or divisional commander felt somewhat freer to make decisions on the battlefield, without being distracted by fears of instant demotion to the enlisted ranks, or, of course, being placed in front of a firing squad.

Nonetheless, all these changes merely served to make a monstrous system somewhat more manageable. Throughout the war, Red Army commanders were governed by fear more than their German counterparts; only in 1945, with Hitler verging more and more towards rage and hysteria, did this situation also start to prevail in the German army. But essentially Stalin learned to adapt when he had to; above all, he had learned to curb his paranoid and ruthless tendencies enough so that he did not continually ham-string the efforts of his best men—men like Zhukov, Konev, Khrushchev and Chuikov, and the Stavka advisors whose names remain obscure even today. These men were allowed to speak their minds more and more as the war went on, and Stalin developed a better capacity for listening to their advice—thus going in completely the opposite direction from Hitler, almost as if the two great dictators were on board ships passing each other in the darkness, sailing inexorably towards opposing poles of fate. Stalin might berate his generals, shame them, intimidate them, cashier them, execute any number of them; but ultimately he also managed to listen to them. It was only sensible, after all, and Stalin was a sensible man. He knew that any final decision was still his to make.

The Decision—Berlin or the Flanks?

Most of the failed Soviet offensives from earlier in the war had stemmed from this problem of overextended flanks, particularly if the breach in the German line was only along a narrow front. The offensive would find itself funneled through a small bottleneck, inviting a German counterattack which more often than not would be successful, cutting off the Russian spearheads from their supply trains and ensuring their demise. Vlasov's offensive against Leningrad in 1942 had been the classic example of this kind of mistake, but it was far from the only one.

By 1945 Stalin and his Stavka advisors had made a great deal of progress towards solving these problems. The previous year had in fact seen a nearly uninterrupted string of Soviet victories. Each offensive had been made along a broad sector of the front; the Germans had been pushed back uniformly all across Russia. For the most part, Stavka had allowed no extended flanks or inviting bottlenecks to present themselves. Of course, these operational aims were aided immensely by the Soviets' great numerical advantage in manpower and, above all, in heavy weapons of all kinds. Normally to attack along a broad front is to invite a war of attrition, of gains measured in yards rather than miles, as had occurred in World War One. But the Germans no longer had the material resources to withstand attacks on such a massive scale, especially when their defensive lines in Russia were so vastly overextended. The result was that one front collapsed after another. By year's end Hitler's armies had been expelled from every square inch of Soviet territory, save for the tiny thumb of the Courland Peninsula.

But now what? The just-completed Vistula offensive had also been conducted along a broad front, to be sure, obtaining the same huge gains as had been seen the previous year. But Stalin could not have looked at a map of this operation without being perturbed by those long flanks to the north and south.

At the end of January Berlin lay almost within his grasp. Should he strike now, and simply disregard the German forces still along the Baltic and in Silesia?

It was certainly tempting. At this point, accounts of both Stalin's and General Zhukov's thinking about continuing the offensive straight into Berlin vary widely. The most widely-held conception has Zhukov arguing strongly in favor of it. His 1st

Byelorussian Front had reached the Oder River at several points between the cities of Frankfurt and Kustrin, only forty miles from Hitler's capital; reconnaissance patrols sent over to the west bank had found almost no German defenses in place. Although Zhukov's armies were weary after their headlong race across Poland, they were by no means exhausted, and on the whole their casualties had been light. The popular view has Zhukov worrying that any pause to regroup and re-supply would only allow the Germans the critical time they needed to bring up re-inforcements and block the river crossings. Furthermore, the Oder was still frozen over and offered no barrier to Russian tanks; this was a great advantage that would be squandered if an early thaw melted the ice.

Above all, any delay imposed by diverting forces to clear up the flanks in Silesia and along the Baltic would be far too time-consuming. Berlin was ripe for the taking—take it!

So much for the popular view of Zhukov, Stalin's most am-bitious and successful general. Arguments such as these would have made a great deal of sense, but they did not entirely reflect the facts. The reality of the situation was more complicated than this, presenting problems of which Zhukov was well aware. Be-fore he could resume the drive on Berlin he first had to get sub-stantial forces, especially armored forces, across the river—and almost immediately it became clear that this task would be much more difficult than it had first appeared.

In essence, the Soviets ran into bad luck at this critical mo-ment. When they first arrived on the east bank of the Oder, the river ice was indeed frozen solid. But within 48 hours weather conditions began to change drastically; temperatures rose, rain fell, and the ice began to melt. Even if Zhukov had acted imme-diately, without consulting Stalin, it is doubtful that he could have gotten enough men and tanks across the river during this short time to resume the offensive. Only the most advanced Russian spearheads had actually reached the Oder, and at widely scat-tered points; the bulk of Zhukov's armies were following not far behind, but by the time they too were in position to cross the damage had already been done—the thaw had begun.

The initial spearheads had not sat idly by; during this exas-perating, fleeting period of a day or two when the ice was still firm some of Zhukov's forces did get across and establish several bridgeheads on the west bank. But they were not strong enough to strike for Berlin on their own, and now there remained the maddening problem of how to get the rest of the army across the river—which by now had turned into a jumble of drifting ice, stretches of open water, stretches of ice that were still firm merging unpredictably with other stretches that were treacherously weak.

It was the worst possible situation, for under such chaotic, rapidly changing conditions the Soviets also found it difficult to build pontoon bridges or use ferries to send supplies across. They did try all of these things, but in the end the battle for the Oder bridgeheads was destined to be a long, drawn-out affair, as we shall see in greater detail in a later chapter.

In any case, the widely held notion that Zhukov wished to push on towards Berlin with all possible speed, only to be overruled by an excessively cautious Stalin, is too simplistic. It is quite possible, even likely, that a debate of this kind did take place between these two men—but the dramatic change in weather conditions would have made any such discussion academic almost immediately.

It was true that Stalin had other concerns besides Zhukov's thrust on Berlin. And these concerns may have led him into a more cautious frame of mind, especially now that the opportunity to quickly cross the Oder had been lost.

While conferring with the Stavka in the Kremlin, Stalin's eye would have wandered across the entire map of eastern Germany. His attention would be drawn to the long and potentially dangerous flanks of the Soviet invasion—especially to the northern flank along the Baltic. Already Soviet intelligence was picking up rumors of a new German army group being massed near the Baltic coast in Pomerania, an army group that consisted in large part of Waffen SS panzer divisions. Years after the event, we have become used to thinking of many of Hitler's divisions in 1945 as "existing only on paper," hollow armies that were hopelessly outmanned and outgunned. But at the time, Stalin could only have wondered.

He might have been haunted by past failures, failures that had occurred years before in Russian steppes and forests. One could never underestimate the Germans' ability to strike back, and strike back hard, even now in the Third Reich's dying convulsions.

Or perhaps especially now, Stalin decided. For almost three months to come the Soviets would remain poised on the Oder

River, but would not strike. These messy loose ends along the flanks would have to be cleared up first. Berlin would be spared, the war would go on, leading to months on end of some of the bloodiest fighting either Russians or Germans had ever seen.[1]

Scenes from the Deutsche Wochenschau, July 21, 1944. . . .

Major Otto Remer is shown addressing his men, a special Grossdeutschland security detachment assigned to guard duties in Berlin.

It is the day after the assassination attempt against Hitler in his Wolf's Lair headquarters in East Prussia. The commentator reports that Remer and his men have just performed a critical service for the nation, suppressing the conspirators' simultaneous coup d'etat attempt against Nazi government leaders inside Berlin. The decisive action taken by Major Remer was instrumental in shattering the coup and restoring order.

He now gives a brief speech to his men, who are gathered before him on a dusty parade ground in the capital. Remer stands on a podium in front of a German flag, the national flag that bears both the swastika and the German cross, speaking into a microphone with loud, urgent, tautly enunciated phrases:

"On this date, we have become political soldiers. Our political mission is the following:

"Security! Defense of our German fatherland! Defense of our National Socialist ideals! We are to carry out, under any and all conditions, this political mission, from this date forward and forevermore!"

The security detachment, the Grossdeutschland Wacht Battalion, then marches past Remer, goosestepping with strict precision, flanked by officers and NCOs bearing ceremonial swords. Major Remer holds his right arm out rigidly in the Fuhrer salute that from this day forward will replace the normal military salute in every unit of the German army. The commentator announces that for his action Hitler has instantly promoted Remer to full colonel.

At the end of the year he will be promoted again, to general, and will be given command of one of the newly raised Grossdeutschland Corps divisions, destined to fight until the last day of the war on the Eastern Front.[1]

GROSSDEUTSCHLAND

The Army Within the Army

Stalin's intelligence sources were quite correct. Already Hitler and Guderian were desperately trying to assemble the forces to deliver the kind of counterattack that had been so successful in the past. Presently we shall witness another of their epic shouting matches regarding how best to go about doing this. The most likely staging area seemed obvious to them both: somewhere on the Baltic flank between Stargard and the port of Stettin at the mouth of the Oder. At least on the map, the Russians appeared to be most dangerously over-extended here; and a sufficiently violent strike would not have to cover any great distance to cut across Zhukov's rear.

But various other details would set Guderian and Hitler against each other again, culminating in at least one meeting in which their aides would have to physically separate them.

Before elaborating further on this battle of wills at Fuhrer HQ, let us return to the lower level of operations, as seen by the units in the field.

The Grossdeutschland Panzer Corps, along with General Nehring's men, had continued to retreat towards the west from the vicinity of Lodz. By February 1st, this rather substantial force had managed to fight its way almost intact back into German-held territory on the west bank of the upper Oder, about 150 miles southeast of Berlin. Almost immediately they were thrown into local counterattacks against several small bridgeheads the Soviets had established along this stretch of the river, around the town of Steinau. This was General Konev's area of operations, and his 1st Ukrainian Front would contine to exert so much pressure here that none of the German forces in this region could be made available to strike at Zhukov further north.

In fact this small corner of Silesia between the Oder and Neisse Rivers would become the single most closely contested area of German soil until the end of the war. The small cities in this region would change hands on numerous occasions, with a few still being liberated by German panzer columns even after the fall of Berlin. Grossdeutschland units would play a very active role in many of these battles.

The Grossdeutschland Corps was an interesting formation; by 1945 it had developed into a highly complex and at times rather confusing organization. In many ways Grossdeutschland was like a separate army within the army, in the same sense as the Waffen SS, though without being burdened by the political and moral stigma attached to Himmler's SS soldiers.

Like a number of Himmler's early Waffen SS units (notably the Leibstandarte), Grossdeutschland had entered the war against Russia as only a regimental-strength unit, a showcase formation for the German army. In 1942 the regiment was upgraded to divisional strength; referred to in military tables as a panzer grenadier unit, it was in fact fully equipped with tanks as any panzer division, and was employed in the same "fire brigade" role as the panzer divisions were, constantly shuttling about to every crisis sector on the Eastern Front.

We first saw the Grossdeutschland Division (or GD) in this book leading the counterattack to make contact with Army Group North in Courland in the late summer of 1944. Since then they had been fighting in the vicinity of Memel and Konigsberg in East Prussia. In the autumn Hitler had decided to expand Grossdeutschland to a full panzer corps. This decision would be only the first step of a frantic era of still further expansion during the final months of the war.

Normally a corps is composed of two or three divisions fighting under a corps HQ staff in a particular sector of the front. Yet by the end of the war five armored divisions were fighting the Russians under the Grossdeutschland banner, often widely separated from each other across every battlefield in eastern Germany. For reference, they are listed as follows:

Grossdeutschland Panzer Grenadier Division
Fuhrer Panzer Grenadier Division
Fuhrer Begleit Panzer Division
Brandenburg Panzer Grenadier Division
Kurmark Panzer Grenadier Division

For the historian this is a rather fortuitous circumstance, as the combat record of each of these divisions becomes a microcosm for almost every one of the final agonizing battles in the East.

At this time the original Grossdeutschland Division—the parent division, as it were—was still fighting in East Prussia south of Konigsberg. Over the next few months the Russians would slowly drive it into the sea. One of the confusing aspects of this period was that this division was now fighting alongside the Herman Goering Panzergrenadier Division, with both controlled by the HQ staff of the Herman Goering Corps.

Meanwhile, the HQ staff of the Grossdeutschland Panzer Corps had been assigned to take control of the Brandenburg Division and the Herman Goering Panzer Division (the second of the two Hermann Goering armored units). These two divisions were then rushed south from East Prussia to counter the Soviet offensive across the Vistula. It was this corps formation under General Von Saucken that had detrained at Lodz in the midst of a rout, barely holding its positions long enough to shepherd the men in Nehring's cauldron to safety, before undertaking the long retreat to the upper Oder.

Essentially, the HQ staff for both Herman Goering Panzer Corps and Grossdeutschland Panzer Corps had simply traded two of their component divisions to each other—though the reasons behind this rather confusing exchange remain obscure. In any case, we are left with the irony of the original Grossdeutschland Division fighting under a Luftwaffe corps HQ for the remainder of the war.

During these same chaotic weeks in late January and early February, other Grossdeutschland Corps formations—some of them expanded to divisional strength almost overnight—were being despatched to other critical sectors. Panzer Grenadier Division Kurmark was hastily brought up to strength outside Berlin and rushed to the nearby Oder bend only forty miles away, where Zhukov's reconnaissance patrols were still finding only half-occupied defensive positions. The arrival of Kurmark marked the beginning of hasty German attempts to shore up the Oder defenses before Zhukov's tanks could advance any further.

Finally, two brigade-strength Grossdeutschland Corps formations were recalled from the Western Front. They too were hastily re-equipped and expanded to become the Fuhrer Begleit (Escort) Division and the Fuhrer Grenadier Division—with the former commanded by the same Otto Remer who had been only a major in Berlin six months before. For the moment they were being kept in reserve as part of the mysterious army group on the Baltic flank that had Stalin so concerned, that same army group which Hitler and Guderian were trying to assemble between Stettin and Stargard, with the aim of blasting a hole into Zhukov's northern flank.

The last real hope of driving the Russians away from Berlin lay with this operation. Perhaps by this time it was not even a realistic hope. But it was the only chance remaining, and—at least on paper—it bore the hallmarks of other German counterattacks which had savaged Russian offensives in the past.

It was christened Unternehmen Sonnenwende.

In spite of all their disagreements, Guderian was one of the few generals Hitler felt comfortable with in man to man conversations. At least earlier in the war, many of these talks were informal, taking place at the end of Hitler's lengthy conferences, after his other generals and advisors had been ushered out of the room. Sometimes they would talk about nothing in particular; once or twice Hitler would admit he should have taken Guderian's advice about some issue they had earlier disagreed on.

Guderian had become used to this atmosphere of mutual frankness. It only contributed to the vehemence with which he expressed his opinions in 1945, opinions to which Hitler reacted with an equally violent outspokenness. The other generals of the High Command were becoming unnerved, even embarrassed, by these outbursts between the two men, almost as if they were being forced to witness a violent domestic quarrel between a married couple. And, not unlike married couples, Guderian and Hitler would frequently shout at each other with blind fury and then calm down almost instantly, as if to give the appearance that nothing untoward had occurred.

They disagreed about which fronts most urgently needed reinforcing, inevitably at the expense of other fronts. Guderian would not let up about Courland. That an entire army group was being wasted in a remote and worthless area of the Soviet Union infuriated him so much that he brought up this issue every time he saw Hitler.

"Those men must be brought home to defend Berlin," he said over and over again.

Hitler had never had much tolerance for this kind of contrariness and finally he exploded, ranting that he was as great a patriot as Guderian and that he knew better than anyone what was best for the nation. But unlike other generals, Guderian simply did not know when to back down. At length Hermann Goering took him by the arm and led him from the conference room, offering him a cup of tea to help calm him down. Guderian and Hitler seethed in separate rooms for a while. Then the conference continued.

6

HITLER AND GUDERIAN

Mann Gegen Mann

From the opening pages of this account we have mentioned Hitler and Guderian, always in the same breath, as if these two men have become inseparable somehow. Like Siamese twins. Or, in a curious way, like spouses engaged in an endless domestic conflict.

Guderian was unique among German generals, for a number of reasons—but above all for his extraordinary relationship with Hitler during the final months of the war.

No other German leader—neither from the ranks of the Army nor the Waffen SS, nor from any branch of the Nazi political hierarchy—ever stood up to Hitler in quite the way Guderian did. No other general throughout the course of the war was so persistent and so vehement, never backing down, never cowed into silence by Hitler's explosive bursts of temper.

That Guderian had the inner fortitude to persist month after month in these highly emotional conferences was remarkable enough. But perhaps still more remarkable was Hitler's putting up with such a tenacious, indeed competing, personality for as long as he did.

Guderian is well known as a leading figure in the German military machine, yet history has still not done full justice to the intensity of this clash of personalities in 1945. The history of the Third Reich shows nothing that really compares to it. There are countless examples of Hitler berating other generals, bending them to his will, firing any who refused to bend and replacing them with more acquiescent types—this is in essence the stereotype of Hitler as a military leader that has come down to us over the decades.

Yet his dealings with Guderian were markedly different. To be sure, the famous temper tantrums and deranged accusations were still an ongoing part of Hitler's temperament—even reaching new heights with Guderian—but there was another element which had been missing from his dealings with almost all his other subordinates in the Army High Command. This was, quite simply, the element of respect.

How did Guderian achieve this unusual status?

One of the driving forces in Hitler's soul was his belief in the power of personality—especially, of course, his own—it was a kind of inner vision he had carried with him throughout his rise to power. This was more important to him than it was, say, to Stalin—who tended to operate in the shadows, using fear as his primary instrument of persuasion. We must then consider the force of Guderian's personality, a force strong enough to command Hitler's respect, strong enough even to compete with Hitler's authority—without ultimately threatening it.

This would entail a very delicate, delicate yet firm, combination of personal qualities, especially when given Hitler's increasingly paranoid frame of mind as the war went on.

Other generals had earned Hitler's respect, and perhaps more importantly, his trust. But these tended to be men with a firm belief in the Nazi vision of the world—men like Walter Model, like Ferdinand Schorner, like SS General Sepp Dietrich. They were all frontline generals, fighting men who visited Fuhrer HQ only on occasion. Hitler trusted them to the extent that they could at times disobey his orders in the field without fear of reprisal; yet none of them ever argued with him so vociferously about matters of grand strategy, none of them ever confronted him on an almost daily basis the way Guderian did.

Most of Hitler's headquarters staff—the generals of the High Command—had become little more than yes-men as the war dragged on. The highest ranking of them, Wilhelm Keitel, had long been no more than a puppet who gave his rubber-stamp of approval to Hitler's operational plans. Then there were others who were not quite so acquiescent, but who had learned over the years that opposing Hitler's will was akin to butting one's head against a stone wall.

In private, generals like Alfred Jodl and Kurt Zeitzler would have serious reservations about many of Hitler's plans, but over time they kept these thoughts more and more to themselves. Zeitzler, to his credit, did offer to resign rather than accept Hitler's continued bullying, but he was never as stubborn and vehement as Guderian would later prove to be. Eventually Hitler simply fired Zeitzler; Jodl, however, would remain along with Keitel until the war's end. Above all, these men had learned that even though they might discuss matters of strategy with the Fuhrer, disagree with him, bring alternate plans to his attention, they simply did not have the emotional stamina to stand up to him on any long-term basis. Dealing with Hitler, even in co-operative terms, was always an exhausting business that tended to drain those around him, both mentally and physically. Only an agreeable woodenhead like Keitel could have served Hitler's side throughout the war without being severely affected by this stress.

It cannot be said that most of them became mindless instruments of his will; rather, they simply became worn out. Or, to be more precise, most of them succumbed to his will because they understood that complete emotional exhaustion was the only other alternative. Either that, or removal from their posts.

Guderian, on the other hand, simply did not have the emotional make-up to surrender to Hitler's will. He paid the price— high blood pressure, heart trouble, the same kind of exhausting stress that other generals had avoided—but he refused to back down. This was the kind of man that Hitler tolerated daily by his side for the final year of the war.

Guderian was a latecomer to Hitler's HQ. He was named chief of staff to the Army High Command, replacing Kurt Zeitzler, only after the failed attempt against Hitler's life in July 1944. Years earlier he had been a front-line general, achieving great success as a panzer leader both in France in 1940 and later on in Russia. This was always Guderian's greatest claim to fame, and it has remained the basis for his reputation even up to the present day. He was both the principal architect and the most well-known commander in the field of the early panzer armies, the embodiment of the blitzkrieg style of war.

His career had nearly come to a premature end in the disastrous winter of 1941. The debacle in front of Moscow had led Hitler to clean house on the Eastern Front, sacking a number of Army and Army group commanders. Among them was Guderian, who on his own initiative had pulled back parts of his 2nd Panzer Army in order to avoid being overrun by the Russians. This was done in direct disobedience of Hitler's "stand firm" orders. Guderian was not alone in taking this kind of action, but he was one of only two cashiered generals whose careers were not destroyed. (The other, General von Rundstedt, did not participate in the Battle of Moscow, but ordered the same kind of retreat along his front in southern Russia.) Instead, Guderian's removal from front-line command would only lead to more important positions of authority later on.

Less than a year later, he was named Superintendent of Armored Production and Design. This was a key post, for the German panzer forces were in need of serious revamping. The early model panzers which had been in action since 1939 were being consistently out-performed by the Russian T-34. Guderian, working closely with Albert Speer, would oversee the design and production of two new armored vehicles that would hopefully achieve the quest for combat supremacy—the Panther and the Tiger I.

Hitler as always was highly interested in technical matters of this kind and was in frequent contact with Guderian. Especially in the spring of 1943, on the eve of the Kursk offensive, the urgent question of how soon the Panther tank would become available obliged Guderian to make numerous visits to Fuhrer HQ. At these conferences he expressed his views as firmly as if he were already a member of the Army High Command, debating the pros and cons of the upcoming offensive with Hitler and the other staff generals. There were a number of design problems with the Panther that needed solving before rushing it into production. That was Guderian's purview, but he did not stop with that; he argued against any large-scale operation in the East in 1943, declaring that such a move would squander the available armored reserves. He proposed a defensive posture on the Russian Front that would buy time for mass-production of the new models, rather than throwing them into combat in small numbers and, especially in the case of the Panther, still with serious teething troubles.

With characteristic bluntness he summarized the entire situation in a single sentence: "No one in the rest of the world cares whether we take Kursk or not."[1]

For once Hitler was troubled by his own doubts, but he ordered the attack to proceed. Operation Citadel, the greatest armored clash in history, began on July 5, 1943. All of Guderian's objections were shown to be valid—in particular the Panther's debut on the battlefield was a fiasco—but probably even he could not have foreseen the extent of the disasters that followed. The Battle of Kursk, in and of itself, was a standoff, a ferocious week-long contest of attrition that left the field littered with the smoking hulks of thousands of Russian and German armored vehicles.

But the loss of so many tanks was much more critical to the Germans. The Russians had already amassed the huge reserves of armor which Guderian and Speer had been striving to achieve for the Reich; Stalin was able to brush aside the losses suffered at Kursk and launch massive counterattacks in every sector of central and southern Russia.

In the great duel between the two dictators, this was the beginning of the end for Hitler. From a morale and propaganda standpoint, the loss of the 6th Army at Stalingrad the previous winter had been a terrible shock, but it was only after Kursk that the German armies in Russia were pushed into irrevocable retreat, a retreat that would never really come to an end until May of 1945.

Guderian could only return to the drawing board and continue to gear up German tank production as best he could. The Panther's design problems were largely solved, and it went on to serve as one of the most potent armored vehicles of the war. He saw comparatively little of Hitler until a year later, when the Fuhrer somehow emerged alive from the explosion of an assassin's bomb at his Wolf's Lair headquarters in East Prussia.

All of a sudden Guderian was named as the army's new chief of staff. It was not an obvious choice—he had had no experience at this level of command. Previously when Hitler had become dissatisfied with one chief of staff he had looked for a replacement among the other generals in the High Command. But Hitler had finally reached the end of his tether with these men. For one thing, a number of them were involved in the plot against his life and would soon be hanging by their necks from piano wire.

He needed someone he could trust. The Allies had landed in Normandy and the Russians were everywhere on the offensive; the Third Reich had reached the crisis point. He might have looked for someone more openly devoted to the National Socialist cause. Considering the shock of betrayal he had just undergone, it is surprising that he didn't. Guderian had never been among the ranks of the hard-line fanatics; his was a lesser voice even among the more moderate supporters of the regime, men which included such capable generals as Erich von Manstein and Albert Kesselring. Nor had he ever shown himself to be particularly co-operative; he had been fired for insubordination only three years before. Since then he had given no indication that his independence of mind was any less than it had ever been. Other generals, in particular von Manstein, were known to voice strong opinions about military operations—but none were as blunt, nor as volatile and persistent, as Guderian. In many respects he must rank as among the least likely of choices to run the Army High Command at this point in the war.

In the days following the explosion at the Wolf's Lair, Hitler was suffering from shock, from hearing loss, raging headaches, dizziness, serious nerve damage; his right arm was nearly paralyzed. But on the whole he made a remarkably swift recovery for a man who could have easily been blown to pieces. He immediately decided that General Zeitzler, though not implicated in the bomb plot, was no longer adequate to deal with the kinds of crises now facing the Third Reich. Hitler's first choice to replace him as Army Chief of Staff was the rather obscure General Buhle, perhaps with the idea that Buhle would be a more co-operative sort of man. But this decision came to nothing only a few hours after Hitler announced it; Buhle had been wounded by the explosion and it would take him weeks to recover his health.

Hitler then took a completely opposite tack and designated the superbly competent but volatile Guderian as "interim" Chief of Staff. But this "interim" proviso did not last long. Even after recovering from his injuries Buhle was dropped from consideration, and Guderian now took center stage and remained there, playing a role almost as dominant as that of Hitler himself until the final month of the war.

It was never an easy relationship. But Hitler must have foreseen this. With his own great energy beginning to fail him, he needed someone who could compensate, someone with both the talent and the enormous energy required to turn the Eastern Front around. One of the peculiarities of Hitler's command structure was that the Army High Command (OKH) had been devoted solely to the war against Russia since 1941. The rather less-demanding war in the West had become the responsibility of the War Ministry, or Armed Forces High Command (OKW), run by the team of Keitel and Jodl, both of them amenable generals and devoted National Socialists.

During the autumn of 1944, Hitler was primarily occupied with matters on the Western Front, making plans for the Ardennes offensive, moving his personal headquarters to Ziegenberg, only a few miles from the Belgian frontier. Previously his personal military command post had always been in the East, at Vinnitsa in the Ukraine or at the Wolf's Lair at Rastenburg in East Prussia. But his relatively short tenure on the Western Front came to an end in January 1945; the news of Stalin's breakthrough on the Vistula brought him back to Berlin. The mysterious forest compound of the Wolf's Lair was gone now, overrun by the Russians; for years it had been the site of Hitler's great operational planning conferences, as well as the place where a bomb had nearly ended his life. From now on he would run the war from a bunker hidden deep within the cellars of the Reichskanzellerei in Berlin, emerging only rarely into the open air.

Once again the struggle against the Bolshevik hordes would have his full attention; in a certain sense, it had always been that way. Guderian, the man he had chosen to carry this fight to the end, would plead with him, speak frankly with him, argue with him, rage at him—in effect stand up to him almost as an equal—in a way that no other general had ever done before.

Already several issues had set them against each other: the removal of the SS corps from the Vistula Front, the lost army group languishing in Courland, above all the dire reality of the entire situation in the East. Now, with Zhukov only forty miles from Berlin, it was time to strike back—perhaps the last time. Operation Sonnenwende, the counteroffensive aimed at Zhukov's Baltic flank, was set for February 15th, 1945. An able commander was needed to take charge of the new army group that would unleash this blow. Guderian would find that his choice for this task was radically different from Hitler's. Their partnership was about to enter its stormiest phase.

PART II
POMERANIA

The staff car travelled at high speed along the autobahn. Days earlier, the highway had been jammed with convoys of reinforcements headed east to participate in the coming offensive. But now the attack was well underway, and the autobahn was deserted. The general urged his driver to make good time; he was in a hurry to get back to the front.

The general was also exhausted. He had been awake for nearly forty eight hours. Unfortunately, so had his driver. They had driven from the Stargard area all the way back to Berlin so the general could confer with Hitler about the progress of the attack. An enormous rigamarole—the aggravation of having to make this long drive at the height of the offensive only intensified the general's fatigue. As usual the conference with Hitler had dragged on and on, with the Fuhrer rambling endlessly about one thing or another. The general had not been able to leave the Reichskanzellerei until four in the morning. He needed to rest, and tried to nap in the car while his driver negotiated the blacked-out, bombed-out streets of Berlin. The capital, or the ruins of it, lay in eerie pre-dawn silence. At length the car left the vast urban sprawl behind and sped along the lonely autobahn leading east back to the Oder.

At times strangely balmy gusts of air filtered in through the vents. The winter had arrived late and now seemed to be leaving early. The highway was treacherous: patches of firm ice, melting ice, puddles of water. The powerful twin headlights cut through the blackness; the general's need for haste allowed him to dispense with the regulations requiring the use of dim lights only. The scene was ghostly.

On several occasions the driver swerved alarmingly. Finally he told the general he could not go on; he was falling asleep at the wheel. The general had barely managed a few snatches of sleep, but he switched seats and took over without complaint. Every hour that he remained away from the front could be crucial. The car sped on.

There were no witnesses to the accident. Probably it took place just before daylight. The car skidded off the pavement. It was found the next morning wrapped around a tree. The general's driver was dead. In the driver's seat General Wenck still clung to life with a fractured skull, mumbling something about drifting off in his sleep.

Fifty miles further east, across the River Oder, the great counterattack continued.

SONNENWENDE

11th SS Army Counterattacks from Stargard

The day before the offensive, Goering put in an appearance at the troops' assembly positions outside Stargard. Brigadefuhrer Leon DeGrelle, commander of the Wallonian SS Division, reports:

> Goering came to visit the advanced positions in the capacity of an enthusiast—not without some daring. He made a big hit with our soldiers, whom he addressed with a truculent geniality. He was quite voluminous, covered in layers of coats of an astonishing yellow-brown, and looked like an enormous wet-nurse dressed up as a Serbian general. He drew forth from his bosom cigars as big as baby bottles.
>
> Everyone stocked up from this illustrious source.[1]

By this time Goering was no more than a shadow, a ghost, although a fat and rather jovial ghost. Technically he was still Hitler's successor, but few people—certainly not him—took this very seriously anymore. His power had been ebbing away for several years. He was frequently absent from the operational conferences at Fuhrer HQ; even his title as head of the Luftwaffe was largely ceremonial by now.

He spent most of his time at his great hunting lodge of Karinhall, in the deep pine forests and moorlands north of Berlin. Wounded as a fighter pilot in WWI, then brutally beaten by an anarchist mob after the war, he had used morphine to ease the pain and had gradually become addicted to the drug over the long course of the years. Some of those closest to him insist he had beaten this habit before World War Two, and that reports of his bacchanalian lifestyle, both in Germany and abroad, were greatly exaggerated. All the same, during the final years he isolated himself more and more at Karinhall, drinking, eating, wearing fantastic costumes, entertaining cronies, and generally removing himself from the day-to-day realities of the war.

But it cannot be said that Goering retreated into a fantasy world. He simply retreated. Deep down, he seemed to have as clear an intuition as anyone about what the end for all of them was going to be, sooner or later. He simply refused to take it seriously anymore; his ironic, half-rueful and half-belligerent, coarsely joking manner would stay with him all the way to the prisoners' dock at Nuremburg.

He was probably the only Nazi leader to have any real rapport with ordinary soldiers. His performance on the eve of the Stargard counterattack—the so-called Operation Sonnenwende—was pure Goering. His visits to the troops, who were not above poking fun at him, seemed to offer them some strange human release in the midst of their final hardships.

". . . visiting in the capacity of an enthusiast." Leon DeGrelle could not have phrased it better, for by now Goering had no other meaningful function. After mingling with the assault formations on the eve of the attack, he returned to Karinhall in his enormous, bizarrely colored overcoat, fully aware that the Russians might show up at his doorstep before too much longer. "I wonder if we'll have to burn this old shack down," he commented to an aide. He would rarely be seen in public again before facing his judges after the war.

It was SS Reichsfuhrer Heinrich Himmler who delivered the more typically vainglorious pronouncement to the troops. The attack was scheduled to go forward at dawn on February 15th. Brigadefuhrer DeGrelle's memoirs record the following words from the SS leader:

> Himmler addressed a dazzling proclamation to the troops, in which he repeated forcefully, "Forward! Forward through the mud! Forward through the snow! Forward by day! Forward by night! Forward to free the soil of the Reich!"[2]

It was the usual bombast. In fact DeGrelle's version of this speech is somewhat misleading, for Himmler did not give it in person. It was simply delivered to the front lines and read aloud by various lower level commanders. DeGrelle was an ardent believer in the National Socialist cause, who for years had gloried in all the insane violence of the fighting on the Eastern Front. He relates Himmler's exhortations without a trace of sarcasm, though perhaps a number of his comrades gathering for the attack might have had somewhat different reactions. Even among the Waffen SS troops, Himmler had never been regarded with great enthusiasm. But whatever their personal feelings about the man, they must have realized that at least the urgency in his speech was justified. After all these years, the Russian hordes were here, here in the heart of Germany, ruthlessly murdering civilian refugees by the thousands and tens of thousands. These facts would have everything to do with the German soldiers' willingness to fight on to the very end, regardless of whatever faith they might still have in people like Himmler or anyone else in the upper levels of their mad government.

Along with Hermann Goering, other leading personalities were to put in an appearance at Stargard. Guderian was there too, making whatever practical last-minute arrangements he could. Himmler, as he had been in Alsace during Operation Nordwind, was in nominal overall command of the Stargard operation—much to Guderian's disgust. Guderian also had a good rapport with the front-line soldiers, but for the moment he was preoccupied with ironing out the final details with the real commanders of the attack. Himmler was no more than a figurehead who had no concept of military operations, and whose headquarters were so far behind the front that he was almost unreachable by the front-line generals. In a way Guderian must have been relieved to know this, for it would make Himmler less prone to meddle with the real business at hand, which would be conducted by the two men he had come to see, General Walther Wenck and SS General Felix Steiner.

But even with Himmler safely out of the way, Guderian was beginning to show all the signs of severe stress. He had won his most recent battle with Hitler, insisting for hours at Fuhrer HQ a few days earlier that someone—anyone—other than Himmler be given actual operational control over the attack. Guderian's choice was Wenck, a highly capable man who at the time was Guderian's chief assistant at Army High Command.

Hitler had exploded. For years he had had to deal with obstinate generals, but no one had ever had such gall as this Guderian fellow—proposing his own assistant in place of the leader of the SS. It was embarrassing, not least of all because Himmler was standing right there in the room with them, too mortified to utter a word. "Die treue Heinrich"—loyal Heinrich, as Hitler had always called Himmler with a certain conde- scension. Strange, loyal Heinrich, that puny, chinless, bespecta- cled man, who looked as though he had never quite developed into full human form—the grand master of the SS empire. Guderian had more than once described him to friends and as- sociates as being like a man from another planet. Now he simply ignored Himmler as if he were not even present in the room, doggedly repeating his request for Wenck over and over again, wearing down Hitler with the same tenacious, monotonous style that Hitler had used to wear down others in the past.

At this meeting Guderian's tactic was stubbornness rather than anger; he tried to remain calm, determined only that he would hold his ground, for hours if need be, until he got what he wanted. Hitler provided the theatrics, furiously declaring that Himmler was man enough for the job, pacing back and forth in the Reichskan- zellerei office, delivering tirades to the four walls with bulging eyes, every so often striding up to Guderian to hurl incomprehensible accusations in his face. Guderian returned Hitler's gaze unflinch- ingly. There was more than patience in his calm; there was also a great store of determination and rage, rage which he held stonily in check but which must have been unnervingly visible to Hitler between his bouts of shouting.

All the post-war stereotypes of Hitler as a kind of crazed screamer, flecks of spittle forming at the corners of his mouth, temples nearly bursting with anger—all of these images derive almost solely from his meetings with Guderian during the last months of the war. He had never been like this before. In public he had always been an impassioned orator, but it was an artful passion that skillfully combined other elements of wit, cunning, and bold directness. During the war years he had used scorn more than anger to intimidate his other generals; never had he so completely lost control of himself like this.

It could not be said that in Guderian he had met his match. Hitler would never dream of acknowledging such a thing. But he had met a kind of unyielding rock, a force of personality which deep down Hitler could not help but respect.

He vented his spleen for several hours, raging on and on. At last his mood calmed almost instantaneously. Some of the old orator's guile returned to him, though perhaps it was mixed with exhaustion this time. Dramatically he lowered his voice, shrugged his shoulders indifferently, and addressed Himmler in a perfectly matter of fact tone of voice, as if he had been speaking that way all along,

"All right then, Himmler, Wenck will join you tonight. The attack begins on February 15th."

Himmler said nothing, perhaps nodded his head slightly.

Hitler quietly sat down at his desk and said to Guderian,

"General, the Army High Command has won the battle today. Thank you for coming."[3]

He smiled imperturbably.

Later General Wenck duly reported to Himmler's Army Group Vistula headquarters at Prenzlau, about fifty miles north of Berlin. Wenck observed that this was no place from which to conduct a battle. For one thing, it was on the wrong side of the Oder River, closer to Berlin than to Stargard. Himmler gave out a few meek and perfunctory comments, complaining that he was really not feeling very well. Wenck quickly departed, driving to the east bank of the Oder where he could take charge of the armies now entrusted to him. This force, the newly-created Army Group Vistula, was still nominally commanded by Himmler, but at this moment General Wenck was its real leader.

Guderian met up with him at Stargard, where at last they could talk a little sense without outside interference. Guderian looked haggard and ill. Rather than appearing gratified that he had won his point with Hitler, he was worn-out; his large frame seemed alternately to be nearly bulging with stress, then sinking into itself.

Fortunately Wenck had the skill and energy to carry on while his chief stood on the verge of exhaustion. As the de facto commander of Army Group Vistula, he was now responsible for a motley collection of forces that reached along the Baltic shore from Stettin on the Oder to Danzig at the mouth of the Vistula. Many of these units were in disarray, having already been heavily engaged for weeks along Zhukov's northern flank. Many had lost a lot of men and almost all their vehicles, their stocks of ammunition dwindling to critical levels. Few of these divisions were capable of conducting any offensive action.

Thus the actual striking force that Wenck and Guderian had assembled was smaller than they would have desired, consisting solely of the hastily scraped together panzer divisions of SS General Felix Steiner's 11th SS Army. This "army" was actually closer to an overblown corps of nine divisions, most of them seriously under-strength; but they were still mostly first-class fighting units, and they disposed of nearly 300 tanks and assault guns among them.

Along the battle line around Stargard from west to east, they were:

SS Panzer Division Frundsberg
Panzer Division Holstein
Wallonian SS Division
SS Polizei Division
Langemarck SS Division
Nederland SS Division
SS Panzergrenadier Division Nordland
Fuhrer Begleit Division
Fuhrer Grenadier Division

A few miles to the west of Stargard lay a large, serene body of water known as Lake Madue. The lake would anchor the western flank of the attack. Panzer Division Holstein and SS Frundsberg would strike south from here along the lakeshore. This thrust would be parallelled in the center by the SS Polizei Division and Leon DeGrelle's Wallonian SS Division, attacking directly south from Stargard. A more easterly force would attempt to recapture the town of Arnswalde, which had just been surrounded by the Soviets, about twenty miles southeast of Stargard. The units assigned to this task were SS Nordland and SS Nederland (the Danish and Dutch volunteers who had just been shipped back from Courland), as well as two of the elite Grossdeutschland formations, the Fuhrer Begleit Division and the Fuhrer Grenadier Division.

In immediate command of these units was SS General Felix Steiner, a well-organized and highly motivated man who could not have provided a greater contrast to the remote and ineffectual SS Reichsfuhrer. Wenck and Guderian knew they could work

with him. He had been the famed Wiking Division's original commander in 1941, and his attitude towards all the foreign SS volunteers under his control was highly empathetic. (Indeed, if not
for the driving force provided by Steiner earlier in the war, the
so-called SS "European Volunteer" program might never have
gotten off the ground.) He sympathized with the cultural and
linguistic difficulties faced by soldiers of different nations serving
in a highly-demanding, and at times intolerant, foreign army, be
it either the Wehrmacht or the Waffen SS. Steiner was a big,
square-set bull of a man, another in a long line of skilled and
aggressive German front-line generals.

Even more than Wenck and Guderian, he was brimming with
enthusiasm for this new operation. He summoned Brigadefuhrer
DeGrelle to Panke, a village outside Stargard, to lay out the tactical assignments for the SS Wallonian Division. DeGrelle recalls
Steiner as being exultant, declaring, "This year we will be on the
Dnepr again!"[4] cheerfully slapping the Wallonian commander on
the back.

They were old cronies, Steiner and DeGrelle, having fought
together during the bitter retreat from northern Russia to Courland
in 1944. Leon DeGrelle was another one of these foreign anti-
Bolshevik crusaders, a Belgian who had formed his own fascist
party, the Rexists, before the war. The Wallonian (or Walloon)
volunteers were French-speaking Belgians who had fought as
an independent regiment alongside the Wiking Division for much
of the Russian campaign. DeGrelle had discarded his prominent
political position and enlisted as a private in this unit, originally
organized by the German army before being absorbed into the
Waffen SS in 1943. He had risen through the ranks to command
what was now a full division (though in truth its manpower was
considerably less than that). A full account of DeGrelle's experiences on the Eastern Front would read as an unending catalog
of horror, sacrifice, and unbelievable bravery. In addition, though
technically not a member of the National Socialist Party, he was
in many respects the prototypically arrogant, perversely idealistic
Nazi. Not a complimentary description, to be sure, but DeGrelle
was a highly controversial figure. We will leave further discussion
of this subject for a little bit later.

For the moment, let us follow DeGrelle and his men as Operation Sonnenwende begins in the wet winter fields of Pomerania.

Stargard—Brallentin—Lindenberg

The attack had been organized in great haste, and some of the panzer units were not ready to meet the 5 AM start time. DeGrelle drove up to the forward positions in his Kubelwagen and noted with dismay that the tanks were still gassing up and assembling into assault formations, frittering away the precious element of surprise. German factories would continue to turn out large numbers of armored vehicles until the end of the war, but stocks of other essentials, notably gasoline and shells, were abysmally low, leading to every manner of confusion, delay, and inadequate make-shift arrangements.

Once again there was no preliminary barrage—the lack of ammunition probably weighing equally with the hoped-for element of surprise—and the panzers did not get going until late in the morning. DeGrelle observed their progress from a machine gun nest as they advanced south from Stargard. The village of Brallentin, which he thought could have been stormed immediately at dawn, was not captured until two in the afternoon. The Russians as usual had great numbers of anti-tank guns, set up with interlocking fields of fire for a depth of several miles. These PAK fronts were more effective than Soviet tanks when it came to absorbing a German armored thrust and wearing down its momentum.

"Several of our tanks burned, looking like flowering fruit trees, before reaching the woods covering the opposite slope."[5]

More than other memoirists, DeGrelle had a gift for vivid description. One can picture the countless tiny flames flickering within the dark silhouette of a tank, indeed like clumps of bright fruit within the dark mass of a tree, immediately before the vehicle erupts into a single sheet of fire.

But the armored battalions took their losses and kept going. DeGrelle was more dissatisfied with the infantry, which was slow to keep up. These men didn't have "the health, the vigor, the faith, the technical training of the victors of the first two summers. The outstanding noncoms of 1941 and 1942 were no longer there to lead the newcomers."[6]

It was true. So many thousands of dead veterans were scattered the length and breadth of Russia. The NCOs had always formed the backbone of the small-unit assault groups which had so skillfully advanced across the battlefields of the past. Skill, experience, initiative—all were in short supply, residing in the few surviving NCOs and junior officers. For every fanatical teenage product of the Hitler Youth fighting in 1945, there were many other youngsters who were simply confused and overwhelmed by the shock of battle. Both the Waffen SS and the army suffered from this problem.

The assault groups advancing on Brallentin were part of the SS Polizei Division. DeGrelle refers to them as "the Reich" division, but his memory is faulty. (He did not set his experiences on paper until many years later, as an unrepentant exile living in Franco's Spain.) At this time the Das Reich Division, if that was who he had in mind, was still licking its wounds in western Germany after the Ardennes offensive, pending transfer to the Hungarian battleground. The SS Polizei Division was an infantry formation that had only recently been supplemented by a panzer battalion. Unlike the more renowned Waffen SS divisions, they did not have a great deal of experience coordinating an armored attack with infantry support. DeGrelle watched as the half-tracks carrying the grenadiers lagged behind the tanks, discharging their cargoes of foot soldiers too soon, leaving them under fire in the flat wet fields.

DeGrelle departed to see to the progress of his own command, the Wallonian SS. This was not a motorized formation; thus General Steiner had assigned them to set up a stationary position on the flank to screen Polizei's advance. The Walloons had already moved out under cover of darkness, and by late morning they were firmly established on a long ridge just to the west of Brallentin, immediately overlooking the tiny hamlet of Lindenberg. They did not see much action on this first day, the Russians being kept busy by the dogged forward progress of Polizei's armor. These Belgians would not have long to wait, however, before their turn came.

The Walloon position stretched for about a mile from north to south, facing west towards Lake Madue. They were already familiar with this ridge, having captured it a week earlier in a local attack that had gone off half-cocked in other sectors. The Walloons had thus been obliged to evacuate this position only a day later.

Now they were back again, manning the same trenches and firing pits they had dug a week before, as well as hastily digging new ones. Comrades who had been killed here during that first engagement were still lying about in the mud, beginning to stink as the days grew gradually warmer. Now, during these relatively quiet hours, there was time to bury them.

It was a nasty position, as they already knew only too well. The ridge dropped off steeply to the north and west; to the south it dwindled away into marshland. As a defensive position this was all well and good, but on the other hand it was the only high ground for miles around, a small and isolated stretch of elevation which invited encirclement. To their rear, to the north and east, supplies and reinforcements would have to come across a wide-open muddy plain which stretched for several miles to the next patch of woodland around Brallentin.

DeGrelle's men waited, through the day, on through the night. Sounds of battle were audible all around them. To the west they could hear the sharp cracks of tank cannon as Holstein and SS Frundsberg advanced along the shore of Lake Madue. Behind them they could hear a continuous roar as SS Polizei maintained its advance, growing fainter as the tanks fought their way south-ward. DeGrelle drove back during the night to confer again with Steiner, receiving word that Polizei had captured two other vil-lages south of Brallentin.

The next step of the plan called for Polizei to turn west and the Lake Madue force to turn east, hopefully to link up later that night or at worst on the day following. With the armored spear-heads joining up to the south, the Russians would then be trapped in a cauldron between Lake Madue to the west and the Walloons on the Lindenberg Ridge to the east.

Within the ever-present racket of gunfire the Walloons could hear the roar of motorized columns and the unmistakable rumble of heavy tanks moving in front of their ridge. After losing entire armies to German encirclement earlier in the war, the Soviets had made it a consistent practice to evacuate any developing "cauldron" before the ring closed shut around them. Keeping this tactic in mind, the Walloons expected the Soviet columns passing in front of them to be moving southward as they tried to escape the trap. But quite the opposite was taking place. The Russians seemed to be moving more men and tanks northward into the cauldron.

In the overall scheme of things, this was all for the better. If large Soviet forces were trapped and annihilated, then Son-nenwende had a chance of succeeding. But for the Walloons holding out on the ridge, this unexpected development was a very ominous sign. The low ground in front of them was swarming with Russian infantry, assault artillery, and tanks, none of which gave any indications of retreating. Even worse, the muddy plain to their rear was also being overrun. As dawn broke on the 17th, the Walloons saw they were cut off.

Arnswalde—Nantikow—Liebenow

Meanwhile, the more easterly forces of Sonnenwende were making good progress towards the besieged town of Arnswalde. SS Nordland had only just returned from Courland a week earlier, leaving all its tanks and assault guns behind to be doled out among the other defenders of the beleaguered peninsula. Nordland's main striking force was the Panzer Battalion Herman von Salza, which was hastily sent to the armor depot at Grafenwohr to be re-equipped with new Panthers and Sturmgeschutzen. They returned to the parent division near Stargard just in time for the attack. The Russians were caught off guard by the appearance of these tanks, and on the first day SS Nordland covered most of the ten-mile distance to Arnswalde.

It was intended that Nordland would be reinforced by an additional panzer battalion, consisting of the King Tigers of SS Abteilung 503. This would have given the Scandinavians the striking power of a fully-equipped panzer division and constituted a far more serious menace to the Russians.

Unfortunately, the powerful King Tigers were in urgent demand everywhere; half the SS battalion was shipped to Danzig before the offensive. The other half had remained under the jurisdiction of Steiner's 11th SS Army, but their strength too was whittled away by local engagements before Sonnenwende got underway. This was the problem everywhere in 1945—powerful units were needed to stem the Russian advance in every sector of the front, almost always at the expense of building up the necessary reserves to make any kind of decisive counterattack.

A few of the King Tigers had been at Arnswalde when the Russians surrounded the town in early February. The remainder, stationed around Stargard, had attempted to break through in a local counterattack on February 8th (the same date as the Walloons' first abortive attempt to occupy the Lindenberg Ridge).

Advancing with only five King Tigers, plus a few assault guns provided by Herman von Salza, the SS panzer crews displayed tremendous courage, running a gauntlet of fire from Stalins and T-34s that, as usual, seemed to be lurking behind every house. Every King Tiger was put out of action; many of the crews were killed or badly wounded in hand-to-hand combat with Russian foot soldiers climbing onto the tanks. The SS tankmen failed to break through to their comrades surrounded in Arnswalde. They never really had a prayer of doing so.

These preliminary engagements were every bit as savage as the fighting during Sonnenwende itself. The result was that none of the King Tigers were available to take part in the offensive. The only good that came from all this was that they might have inflicted enough harm on the Russians to ensure Nordland's relatively quick advance on February 16th; the Scandinavians had forced their way into Arnswalde by early evening.

The first arrivals in the town, however, were the German grenadiers of a battalion from the neighboring Fuhrer Begleit Division. These troops were among the army's elite combat soldiers, and their attack into Arnswalde was conducted with considerable daring. Advancing in only ten thinly armored SPWs (half-tracks), the battalion found the Arnswalde road blocked by felled trees and other obstacles. Captain Georg Storck was badly wounded by small arms fire from the Russian defenders. His executive officer, Captain Hubert Schulte, took over and led the convoy out into the wet fields, continuing at full speed alongside the road. The countryside was rapidly becoming muddy from the rising temperatures, but the lighter-weight SPWs succeeded in breaking through the surprised pockets of enemy resistance without bogging down.

The whole operation was done in lightning-style, with all guns firing continuously and not a single halt to scout the terrain. Schulte's convoy entered Arnswalde along the Muhlenstrasse and finally pulled up in the main square. They were greeted with the usual delirious relief by the besieged defenders and especially by the civilian population. Most of these Pomeranian refugees would make it to safety across the Oder River, barely escaping the Soviet terror that was laying waste to so many other towns.

But a small Kampfgruppe like Schulte's could not have lifted the siege by itself. Only with the arrival of the SS Nordland spearheads later in the day was Arnswalde made fully secure. The few SS King Tigers that had been with the besieged garrison also added their firepower to keep the relief corridor open. Schulte received the Knight's Cross for this feat, while the wounded Captain Storck was recommended for the Oak Leaves. (Interestingly, Storck's paperwork became lost in a bureaucratic muddle during the war's final days; it was not until 1978 that the Knight's Cross Awards Committee, by now only a semi-official organization, notified him that he had been awarded the Oak Leaves to the Knight's Cross.)

Meanwhile the main body of the Fuhrer Begleit Division was engaged east of Arnswalde around the villages of Reetz and Nantikow, along with its sister unit the Fuhrer Grenadier Division. Only a few weeks earlier, both these formations had been re-called from the Ardennes front around Bastogne and St. Vith. They had been heavily engaged in the Battle of the Bulge from its inception all the way to the final American mopping-up op-erations in mid-January. Almost all their armor had been lost in the snowy hills of eastern Belgium. Many of the tanks had sur-vived the fighting intact, only to be blown up for lack of fuel during the retreat. The twin formations were then upgraded from brigades to full division—though in reality this change in status existed only on paper—and given a few weeks to rest and re-equip before the Stargard offensive. This was the thankless role of these "fire-brigade" type units. Most of these men must have been half-crazed from exhaustion—a few weeks of rest would have been no more than a blink of an eye among these endless counterattacks on both the Western and Eastern Fronts. (Imme-diately before the Battle of the Bulge, they had been fighting the Russians in East Prussia.) But as elite fighters, their morale seems not to have suffered. Even Operation Sonnenwende was only another short step along the frenzied path to final destruc-tion. Only a few days later both Fuhrer Begleit and Fuhrer Grena-dier would be boarding the railroad cars once again, this time to participate in a counterattack in the Oder-Neisse triangle in Silesia. Before war's end both divisions would be shipped all over Germany and Austria.

For almost all the elite armored divisions, 1945 was not so much a last stand, with the German defenders bitterly holding out until the Russians overwhelmed them. Rather, it was a time of chaotic movement all over the map, shuttling almost non-stop from one threatened area to another, day after day, week after week, month after month. To the historian or interested observer, the months of 1945 seem to pass almost in a rush, leading up to the final inevitable disaster in Berlin. But for the men fighting the Russians day after day, the winter and spring of this year must have seemed like an eternity.

But Sonnenwende was not quite finished yet; let us return to developments in Pomerania. While Schulte's Fuhrer Begleit Kampfgruppe was storming into Arnswalde, the assault gun detachment of Fuhrer Grenadier, under Captain Gottfried Tornau, reached its first-day objective of Nantikow. Here as elsewhere the Russians had been caught flat-footed, and Tornau's Sturmgeschutzen were able to push on to the next village of Liebenow a few miles further south. But here the advance stalled in the face of mounting Soviet resistance.

The German units in every sector of Sonnenwende were simply too weak to exploit these first surprise blows. There were no reserves available to rush through the few gaps breached in Zhukov's flank. Almost all the divisions involved in the attack had been hastily re-equipped with armor to replace the tanks lost in earlier battles. Despite Albert Speer's Herculean efforts to increase factory production, the delivery of new tanks remained spasmodic. Each of the Sonnenwende panzer or panzergrenadier divisions had at most a battalion of Panthers or Mark IVs, and even these units were probably short-handed. Much of the shortfall was made up by companies of Sturmgeschutzen such as those commanded by Captain Tornau.

The German newsreels of 1945 would show columns of Sturmgeschutzen and Hetzers moving through German towns more frequently than actual tanks. These vehicles were hampered by the lack of a rotating turret, but their crews still managed to outperform their Russian counterparts. Used as a stopgap measure whenever some kind of armored vehicle was required, they did remarkably well, both in Russia and in every phase of the last battles in Germany. During the course of the war, the Sturmgeschutzen alone was responsible for more enemy tank kills than all other German armored models combined.

With their low profiles, these assault guns (or tank destroyers—as the war progressed the Germans tended to use these terms interchangeably) were especially dangerous in defense or ambush positions. Having advanced from Nantikow to Liebenow, the

Sturmgeschutzen of Captain Tornau were quickly forced to switch from offensive to defensive tactics. It was only on this first day that the Russians were caught off-guard. Zhukov still had enormous reserves of tanks stationed in depth south of the battlefield, and in the coming days they counterattacked all along the line from Liebenow to Lake Madue.

Fighting from well-camouflaged ambush positions, Tornau's battalion racked up an impressive number of kills around Liebenow, holding back the waves of Soviet armor until February 18th. Tornau won the Knight's Cross for this "defensive success" (Abwehrerfolg— a phrase seen more and more in German communiqués later in the war), but the very nature of the phrase indicated that the eastern arm of Operation Sonnenwende had lost its impetus. Possibly the Germans might have held on longer in these few recaptured villages, but, as already mentioned, Fuhrer Begleit and Fuhrer Grenadier were pulled out of the line to carry the fight somewhere else. So it went. Within days Arnswalde and all the other ruined Pomeranian villages were in Russian hands again.

Last Stand of the Walloons on the Lindenberg Ridge

The story was much the same over by Lake Madue. The Walloons on the Lindenberg Ridge were about to undergo martyrdom in the name of their peculiar anti-Bolshevik crusade.

As dawn broke on the 17th, the ridge was taken under fire by large numbers of Stalin tanks. The Walloons had no armor or artillery support, only a few anti-tank guns which were quickly targeted and put out of action. DeGrelle was maddened by the lack of armored reserves, but there were simply none available. Even one or two Sturmgeschutzen would have been a priceless help, but the nearest German armor was with SS Polizei ten miles to the south, trying desperately to close the pincers that would encircle the Russians in the cauldron.

The Soviets in front of Lindenberg were not distracted by these events elsewhere. The ridge was covered with a dense pine forest, which for a while served to keep the tanks at bay. But under such sustained and concentrated fire the woods were simply blown to pieces. They had already been half-wrecked during the fighting a week earlier, and by now the whole ridge was becoming a barren crater-field, full of toothpick-like stumps and flattened timbers. The Walloons were left to defend themselves with panzerfausts as the Stalins rolled in through the shattered trees.

The Belgians were shelled mercilessly in their primitive dugouts and firing pits. Time and again an einzelkampfer would leave these dubious shelters and crawl through the blasted timber until he got within a hundred feet of one of the huge Stalins. That was the panzerfaust rocket's maximum range for accuracy. Probably he would try to get even closer, or position himself so the tank would move closer to him. It was really not that difficult to sneak up on a tank, whose field of vision was always rather limited. But there were always other tanks in support, there were always Russian infantrymen raking the whole area with small arms fire.

DeGrelle reports that the Stalins countered these tactics by simply staying out of range at the base of the ridge. They were still close enough to devastate the whole area with their 122mm cannon. One Walloon junior officer stubbornly kept on crawling forward. He was hit twice and covered with blood, probably already dying. At last he got close enough to let off a shot, but it was only a glancing blow. The Stalins' machine guns promptly finished him off.

This was close combat, Eastern Front style, grim and harrowing. These daring—some would say insane—man versus tank duels had been a staple of the war from the very beginning. For a long time both German and Russian infantrymen would have to climb right onto the tank itself to attach magnetic mines or other explosive devices. With the advent of the panzerfaust rocket-launcher it still remained a perilous game. Even if successful, the einzelkampfer would betray his position by the stream of fiery gases let off by his weapon. Time and again he would be gunned down before he managed to retreat to a safer area. As these grueling hours went on, the Walloons on the Lindenberg Ridge were slowly being wiped out.

DeGrelle could only listen to reports of the fighting over the radio. He was in the rear at his divisional HQ, and spent most of the day trying to put together some reinforcements for the defenders of the ridge. He still had a few of his Walloon companies in reserve, but to get to Lindenberg they had to cross several miles of wide-open, boggy fields which were already being raked by Soviet fire. The reserves were cut up on the open ground; few ever made it to the ridge. Likewise, the wounded could only be brought out with great difficulty. Stalin tanks were constantly roaming back and forth in these rear areas. On one of his trips back to Stargard, DeGrelle even found a Stalin blocking the road right in front of his Kubelwagen, miles inside the German lines. Fortunately for him an einzelkampfer was already stalking the armored beast, destroying it with a rocket fired from a roadside thicket as it advanced on DeGrelle's car.

The Walloon commander stopped to inspect the hulk, finding a letter in the wallet of one of the dead Russian crewmen.

"These last few days I've crushed lots of Fritzes under my treads. Soon the Red Flag will be flying over Berlin. Then we can all go back to our villages."[7]

The only heavy weapons available to DeGrelle were two armored flak trains which General Steiner had somehow managed to commandeer. He sent them as far south as they could go before the tracks were cut, giving the Walloons whatever fire support they could. These trains bristled with guns, especially the deadly 88mms, and provided some much-needed assistance; but they were too far to the rear and the Soviets around the ridge simply had too many tanks. The trains were blanketed with fire from Stalin Organ rocket launchers and eventually had to withdraw before the tracks were destroyed behind them.

Steiner had kept DeGrelle apprised of the pincer movement still in progress further south. Apparently the gap between the SS Polizei spearheads and the Holstein/SS Frundsberg group was now only a few miles wide. Throughout the 17th they struggled to close the gap and shut the Russians in the cauldron. But they were too weak and the Soviets were too strong. It was as simple as that. Stalins roaming everywhere. The even deadlier PAK fronts set up in ambush positions everywhere. A few Stukas roared overhead to blast the Russian positions, but it was not enough. The battle continued into the night, but hopes for success were growing dim. Even if the German tanks managed to shut the trap, they might well be too weak to hold the Russians within the cauldron.

The Walloons on the ridge held their positions throughout the day, on into the night. By the following morning, February 18th, the end was near. A Lieutenant Capelle was now in command of the survivors; calmly he delivered reports to DeGrelle at regular intervals over the radio. The Stalins were now roaming back and forth over the ridge, crushing men beneath their tracks, breaking the Walloons up into isolated pockets of resistance. The last report came in at three in the afternoon. Capelle said he had only seventy men left. Then there was no more radio contact.

Later that night two wounded and exhausted men were found by a patrol near Brallentin. Apparently they were the sole Walloon survivors from the ridge. They said that four of them had set out to escape across the muddy fields, but two had succumbed to their wounds somewhere along the way. They said that rather than be taken prisoner, Lieutenant Capelle had blown his brains out with a pistol while the Russians were swarming around his command post.

The last stand of the Walloons at Lindenberg was lauded by a Wehrmacht communiqué a few days later. These Belgian volunteers had not always had such a reputation for valor. In the early days in the East, a German officer had studied them as they marched towards the front somewhere on the Russian steppes. He commented, "Good fellows, but they look too soft for this line of work."

Indeed, they may have looked that way at first glance. But it was a patently false observation. The Walloons, like the Dutch, like the Danish and Norwegians, like the Latvians and the Finns, like the Spaniards of the famed Blue Division, all more than held their own alongside the German formations in Russia. Hitler had personally invited DeGrelle to his headquarters on a number of occasions, and this was by no means a mere propaganda concession to the foreign volunteers. Hitler is reported to have looked upon DeGrelle almost like a son, saying he wished he had more men like him fighting in his own army.

The Missing Attack

After only three days of fighting, Sonnenwende was over. For all the fierce debate and frantic arrangements that had preceded it, it had been a rather meager affair. The German armored pincers south of Lindenberg failed to link up. Within days the Soviets recovered all the territory they had given up, excepting only the insignificant village of Brallentin just outside Stargard.

Some observers have pointed to General Wenck's nearly fatal car accident as one of the factors that crippled German success.

The reader will recall that Hitler had summoned him to Berlin while the attack was in full swing. This was on February 17th, the first day of the Walloons' terrrible ordeal at Lindenberg, the same day Tornau's assault guns were beating off Russian counterattacks at Liebenow.

It was during the early morning hours of the 18th that the exhausted Wenck left Fuhrer HQ in Berlin to return to the front, finally falling asleep at the wheel and veering off the lonely autobahn into a tree. Guderian especially was crushed by this news. It was not just that Sonnenwende had lost its commander in the field. Wenck had previously been Guderian's chief assistant for many months, and the two had developed a close personal relationship.

But it is debatable that Wenck's safe return to the battle would have had much effect on its outcome. Possibly as the effective commander of Army Group Vistula, he could have marshaled some reinforcements for Steiner's 11th SS Army to keep the attack going. But Wenck had few other units at his disposal that could have made a difference, and certainly not panzer units.

Even if the German armor in the Lake Madue area had succeeded in shutting the Russians inside a cauldron, it would have been an insignificant victory, no more than a short-lived local triumph. Possibly the Russians would have broken out of the cauldron anyway, and even if they hadn't, Zhukov still had more than enough forces in reserve to blunt any further southward progress of the German attack.

It had been hoped that Sonnenwende would be the decisive counterblow that would sow panic and disorder in Zhukov's rear, unhinging his entire forward line along the Oder. In this respect it was a total failure.

A few observations are in order. From a purely tactical point of view, the Stargard operation was curiously managed. The astute reader will have noticed that in reality two separate battles took place, each developing in an almost entirely unrelated fashion to the other. The cauldron battle that took place just east of Lake Madue provided some moments of hope and excitement, but it had no real effect on the other main thrust further to the east around Arnswalde and Liebenow. Especially with regard to the small German forces available, a single more coordinated blow might have been more effective.

But to criticize German generalship in this regard would probably be inappropriate. Clearly it was intended that the two separate thrusts would link up at some point further south. The striking units simply never got that far. The lack of any armored reserves was critical. If one or two more panzer divisions had been on hand, thrown in during the crucial hours when the first spearheads had begun to run out of steam, the Soviets would have been put in a much more alarming position.

But of course they were not on hand. One could say that the situation at Stargard was no different from anywhere else in 1945. The Germans with too few tanks, too few men; the Russians with far too many of both.

Even so, Sonnenwende was the only real opportunity to drive Zhukov away from Berlin, and Guderian especially knew that more could have been done if Hitler had allowed it. Guderian's stubbornness had got him the commander he wanted in General Wenck, but in other respects Hitler had remained unyielding.

The whole business in Courland remained a lame compromise. All Guderian's clamoring had only succeeded in bringing a few divisions back to Germany, and all of their armor had been left behind in Latvia. Panzer Abteilung 510, a unit which still had almost its full complement of Tiger tanks, would have been a very potent addition to the Sonnenwende force, but it was still in Courland. Hitler did not order it shipped home until the middle of March, far too late to have any effect on anything.

Guderian was also dismayed for another reason. The whole Stargard operation had been only half the attack he had originally envisaged. To explain this we must return to the heated debates taking place at Fuhrer HQ in the days just preceding the offensive. Originally both he and Hitler had intended another attack to be launched simultaneously from the south, from the area of the Oder bend at Kustrin. If this attack had struck north to meet the Stargard force striking south, Zhukov's entire front along the Oder would have been encircled in a cauldron far larger than the paltry affair that developed near Lake Madue.

But where were the troops and tanks that would make up this southern pincer arm? They were available, and Guderian knew it. Most of the 6th SS Army which had attacked in the Ardennes in December had been withdrawn by early January. To be sure, they had lost much of their armor, but since then there had been enough time to rest and re-equip them at their depots in western Germany. This army, under SS General Sepp Dietrich, contained some of the most powerful units still remaining in the German order of battle, including SS Leibstandarte, SS Das Reich, and SS Hitler Jugend.

Guderian insisted that they should be sent to Kustrin on the Oder to make up this southern pincer arm. If this had been done, they would have constituted an even more powerful force than Steiner's army at Stargard.

But Hitler had other plans in mind for Sepp Dietrich's army. He wanted to send them to Hungary. Guderian was flabbergasted. Courland . . . Hungary . . . what about the Reich itself, what about the Oder front only forty miles from Berlin? Such a move, with Wiking and Totenkopf already engaged around Lake Balaton, would mean that all the best Waffen SS panzer divisions would be fighting hundreds of miles to the south in Hungary.

Hitler had blithely replied that the oil fields were in Hungary, and what would Guderian do if they were lost and he found he no longer had any fuel for his tanks?

Hitler's head for industrial production figures, which he often manipulated to suit his wishes, had Guderian at a loss. Hitler has often been depicted as being addle-brained for sending such strong forces to Hungary, but more recently some historians have conceded that his point may have been well-founded. Refineries within Germany were frantically producing synthetic fuel, but even today it is not clear just how large these reserves were. The Allied bombing campaign was wreaking havoc on German industry, and front-line tank crews knew better than anyone that on-hand fuel stocks were dwindling to pathetic levels. Panzers in both east and west were literally being gassed up one gallon at a time. The same was true for fighter planes over German skies. Speer's industrial re-organization had led to a many-fold increase in fighter production, but now there was no fuel to fly them with.

But Guderian was operating on another plane of vision. Instinctively he knew that the end was near, and for the moment nothing was more important than driving the Russians away from Berlin. There were already enough forces in Hungary to keep the Russians away from the oil fields for a while longer.

Hitler would not be swayed. Until the last possible moment, he would not acknowledge that the Third Reich was finished. It has been said that even by 1945 he was still fighting a kind of "Seven Years War." In other words, he clung to desperate, no doubt deluded, hopes that somehow Germany would be able to fight on through the months and years ahead; and if so, then the Hungarian oil refineries would be more critical than even the defense of the capital. His great vision at this point was that somehow, some way, the Soviets and the western Allies would have a serious falling-out which would save the Reich from being crushed between them. He continued to refer to one of his idols, Frederick the Great, whose Prussian empire in the 18th century had been spared at the last moment by just such a falling-out within the European coalition allied against him.

Frederick the Great had become a kind of talisman in Hitler's thinking. In hindsight, all this seems no more than idle daydreaming, grasping at straws. Hitler did get his wish, of course, but the advent of the Cold War simply came too late for him. He was not the only Nazi leader who saw the Allied-Soviet conflict coming, but none of them seemed to really grasp just how utterly the Third Reich was feared and hated, and that any later disputes among the Allies would only take place upon the ashes of Hitler's empire.

And so all of this cloudy thinking leads back, step by step, to the failure of Sepp Dietrich's 6th SS Army to materialize on Zhukov's southern flank. By the time of the Stargard operation, Guderian knew they would not be available, which may account for his exhausted and deflated appearance when he met with Wenck and Steiner on the eve of the attack.

Leon DeGrelle's memoirs suggest that both he and Steiner believed all along that the pincer striking to meet them from the south was still part of the plan. Steiner's exuberant back-slapping episode with DeGrelle would certainly be hard to explain otherwise. Clearly Guderian would have told Wenck of the real situation; probably Steiner was informed too, though perhaps not till Sonnenwende was already underway.

Still, this half-cocked offensive in Pomerania was not entirely without effect. Stalin had already been worried about the long Baltic flank in this area. As brief as it had been, Sonnenwende still showed the striking power of German armor rearing its ugly head, and Stalin could not be sure that other such counterattacks into his rear were not in the offing. Zhukov's ideas about marching straight into Berlin had already been tabled for several weeks; now, the Berlin attack would be delayed for two more months.

During this time all Soviet energies would be devoted to driving the Germans on the northern flank into the sea, while simultaneously driving the forces on the southern flank into the mountains of Czechoslovakia. Total, uninterrupted war would be waged on all these fronts throughout the spring, combat as bitter and bloody as anything that had been seen in the earlier years in Russia.

SS Foreign Volunteers; Leon DeGrelle

A few final remarks about Sonnenwende. It had the distinction of being the only major German attack during the war to comprise such a large number of the foreign volunteer units. Besides SS Nordland and SS Wallonian, the Langemarck and Nederland SS Divisions had also been present. The former were Flemish-speaking Belgians who had been positioned to secure the flanks of the Arnswalde thrust. The latter were Dutch volunteers who had been shipped from Courland at the same time as SS Nordland. They were intended to play a more prominent role in the attack, but a Soviet submarine sank one of the division's transport ships in the Baltic, leaving only a weakened force to be deployed at Stargard.

There was no particular reason for assembling so many of these foreign units at this critical time. They simply happened to be available, and it was widely recognized that their fighting spirit was equal to that of German troops, and perhaps even better. These volunteers very much ressembled a crusading army, after all, with all the strange ardor that that entailed; something which could not be said of the war-weary draftees of the average German infantry division. Due to their intense anti-Communist credo, all of these formations had been promised by Hitler that they would be used to fight only against the Soviets. They were never to be deployed on the Western Front. With a few minor exceptions, this promise was kept.

Almost half the German strike force around Stargard was composed of these foreign units. Post-war historians, particularly those from the Allied nations, have tended to belittle this crusading army as comprising mostly fascist cranks and other malcontents, traitors to their native lands. Undoubtedly there is some truth to this, but it is equally true that the Finns, the Latvians, and the Spaniards of the Blue Division, were widely viewed as heroes by their countrymen, engaged in the same kind of anti-Communist struggle that would consume American soldiers in the decades to come.

Not all the foreign SS units received this kind of admiration, however. The Danes and Norwegians of SS Nordland were not viewed in this same heroic light after the war, but neither did their countrymen take severe reprisals against them. The motives of the volunteers may have been looked on suspiciously by many, but they were not universally condemned as traitors. The same could not be said, however, of the Dutch and Belgian volunteers. These two nations had suffered much more heavily under the Nazi occupation, and feelings against those who had volunteered for Hitler's armies were much more bitter. Many of DeGrelle's Walloons, for example, were imprisoned by the Belgian government under abusive conditions for lengthy periods after the war. Reprisals were taken against members of DeGrelle's family, and he himself was forced to take refuge in Spain.

As with many situations involving vengeance, there was a certain amount of unfairness and excessive harshness in all this. It has been established beyond any doubt that a fairly large proportion of the Belgians and the Dutch volunteered for these foreign units simply to escape doing forced labor in German factories. It was perhaps not an attractive choice, but there are more than a few accounts of men who simply found life working in German factories unbearable, and who were willing to take almost any option to escape. Indeed, this is another reason why Western historians have declined to take this crusading army as seriously as they might. Leon DeGrelle, perhaps unwittingly, paints a vivid picture of this situation in his memoirs. In 1944 he had toured factories inside Germany, inducing about 800 Belgian workers to enlist in his cause—but only after having to encourage them with a number of "lengthy harangues."[8]

But it should be said that among disgruntled workers there were also large cadres of fiercely anti-Communist volunteers. More than a few of them were also quite sympathetic to National Socialism and to fascist movements in general. More to the point, and especially in the case of the Wallonian SS, they were usually tremendous fighters.

By 1945 even DeGrelle was becoming a little more realistic. With his division nearly destroyed around Stargard, German authorities delivered him several hundred more of these factory workers as replacements. After so much horror and bloodshed, DeGrelle wanted only firmly committed volunteers. Discovering that all these men had been coerced into joining him, he simply arranged for their demobilization and had them sent home. (One wonders if such a benign gesture could really be put into effect, however. How were these men going to get back to Belgium through the ruins of Germany, wearing German uniforms, with the military police hanging deserters at every street corner? Some may have made it home safely—stranger things were happening—but DeGrelle does not elaborate on this point.)

Despite all the peculiar and varied circumstances surrounding his compatriots, DeGrelle himself does not invite a whole lot of sympathy. Before, during, and long after the war, he remained an unabashed admirer of Adolf Hitler. If he had any anti-Semitic tendencies, he does not give voice to them in his memoirs. But neither does he make any effort to condemn the Holocaust or the Nazi leaders responsible for it. He mentions, rather off-handedly, that the brutal occupation policies in the conquered areas of Russia were foolish and counterproductive—but he noticeably abstains from condemning them for simple humanitarian reasons.

No evidence has ever come to light that Walloon units were guilty of war crimes. DeGrelle was one of these high-minded idealists who lived in an abstract world of honor and glory, who tended to avoid looking at life on a fundamentally human level. "Noble" and "chivalrous" sacrifices for the cause are mentioned so frequently in his account that the whole campaign on the Eastern Front takes on a kind of absurd knightly glamor. Indeed, some of the more down-to-earth crusaders who served with him described him as being a bit of a bore. DeGrelle himself lends substances to this view, for he rarely identifies his fellow soldiers as individuals, and almost never engages in any kind of conversation or normal camaraderie with them. (Unless, of course, they are discussing the "cause," or one of them has just performed some exceptionally heroic deed.)

In all these respects, DeGrelle shows the kind of basic character flaws that contaminated the Nazi party in particular and fascist movements in general.

But after all this has been said, it should be pointed out that his memoir, CAMPAIGN IN RUSSIA, is a classic of its kind, and not just as an example of the fascist point of view. Simply as a work of literature, DeGrelle's book is unmatched in many respects. He had an extraordinary gift for descriptive language. His pictures of the Russian countryside and of all the small details of life in the East—as experienced both by soldiers and civilians—are so vivid that they seem almost to emerge in color on the page, while other memoirists simply write in black and white.

The horror of combat on the Eastern Front, as well as the suffering caused by the brutal climate, are depicted with equal vividness. DeGrelle tends not to react to these agonies with quite the same revulsion that other people might experience, but he has no trouble describing them. In the end, it cannot be denied that his book has its own kind of deeply poetic force. One of the enduring truisms that followed the collapse of the Third Reich was that its moral bankruptcy also entailed aesthetic bankruptcy. In other words, the fascist empires were intrinsically incapable of producing any great works of art. The accepted canon of great German books about the war tends to include only those with a clearly anti-fascist, humanitarian vein. But uncomfortable as it may seem, DeGrelle's book, taken on its own merits, must be considered an exception to this rule.

The men were falling out from frostbite. The weather was not that cold, but they had been fighting around the clock for days in the snowy countryside and exposure was taking its toll. The German commander was killed and his replacement, a certain Adolf Ax, was an incompetent with little sympathy for the Latvian soldiers.

They were barely able to keep pace with the Soviet advance, threatened with encirclement day after day. One of the Latvian regimental commanders, Sturmbannfuhrer Janums, was ordered to set up a rear guard to give the division time to retreat. Before he could deploy his men a Soviet barrage descended on the road with unusual accuracy and horrifying effect. Shattered vehicles and the corpses of men and horses were thrown everywhere; buildings went up in flames in the night darkness, illuminating the area for Soviet machine gun fire which began to come in from every direction.

The survivors fled along the road, mingling with enormous crowds of refugees. They had not yet reached the next village when Russian tanks surged in unopposed from the west, continuing the massacre. Escape routes to the west had been cut off; the only path left lay to the north, towards the Baltic. But the Russian tanks were about to block this route as well. Janums' regiment used panzerfausts and handheld charges to throw them back in a battle lasting eleven hours, clearing the retreat road once again. But scarcely had they accomplished this than Soviet tanks blocked the road at another point further north. The Latvians were nearly dead from exhaustion; every time they broke out of one encirclement they were encircled yet again. This time every available man from the entire division was thrown in to re-open the road.

8

VILLAGES, REFUGEES, CHAOS

The Long Trek of 5th Jaegers and 15th Latvian SS;
Short-lived Existence of SS Charlemagne

A glance at the map will show that Sonnenwende took place in only a very small area of the 300 mile long Baltic flank. Steiner's 11th SS Army was the only coherent force in this sector of Army Group Vistula; the Baltic front was in a shambles everywhere else. Among the Pomeranian lakes and forests east of Stargard, scores of bled-out German divisions or miscellaneous smaller units were fighting day after day in engagements that would not be dignified with the names of major battles.

Only a few of these units had motorized transport. The horse-drawn wagons of the soldiers would frequently mingle with the long horse-drawn columns of civilian refugees fleeing from East and West Prussia, jamming the country roads of these regions. Soviet tanks would often overtake these slow floods of humanity and run amok, crushing soldiers, men, women, children, horses, wagons, everything beneath their treads, leaving trails of bloody slush and mud and dismembered body parts all over the landscape of eastern Germany. The dead Stalin tank crewman outside Stargard who had written about "crushing lots of Fritzes beneath my treads" was not just using colorful language; it was a quite literal description of the day-to-day actions of Russian tankmen.

The depleted German divisions or scattered foreign units would constantly deploy around the small villages on the path of retreat, setting up one rear-guard position after another while buying time for the civilians to escape.

While the Soviet Vistula offensive had utterly routed the German armies in central and southern Poland, their advance along the lower Vistula towards the Baltic Sea had proceeded much more slowly, bleeding both attackers and defenders day by day, mile by mile.

The 35th Infantry Division, the 252nd Infantry Division, and the 5th Jaeger Division had taken over the positions occupied by IV SS Corps after its transfer south to Hungary. Their front was along the Narew River down to its juncture with the Vistula, just north of Warsaw. The great Soviet offensive of January 12–14th had pushed them back to the northwest, with their line of retreat generally following the Vistula in the direction of Danzig. This was not a rout but a slow, grueling retreat, in which every passing day saw some kind of savage small-unit combat.

The history of the 252nd Infantry Division reports:

> From the onset of the Russian attack against the Narew bridgehead on January 14th, the regiments took severe losses. The fighting was very bitter, yet the development of the overall situation soon obliged us to retreat with some haste to the north, through snow and cold weather, with inadequate supplies of gasoline and ammunition.
>
> During the night of January 25–26th we retreated across the Vistula [to the west bank], and immediately became involved in heavy fighting around the Russian bridgehead at Neunhuber. On February 16th the retreat began again, northward through the Tucheler Heide (Moors), with days of uninterrupted combat. For the most part the retreat was conducted in short steps; the troops, never fully disengaged from the enemy, had no rest whatsoever. On March 9th, in the area north of Schoneck, the regiments were loaded onto trucks and transported to the nearly undefended west side of Danzig, which was already under attack by packs of Soviet tanks.[1]

This is an all too brief summary of nearly two months of desperate, uninterrupted fighting, a far different picture from the great rout that had taken place from the Vistula to the Oder.

The history of the 15th SS Division paints a similar picture. This was the Latvian unit which had been shipped back from Courland in late 1944, in order to undergo training and re-equipping in the supposedly peaceful West Prussian countryside south of Danzig. By January the Latvians were still woefully short of heavy weapons and other kinds of basic equipment. Even panzerfausts, which were hastily being delivered by the thousands to every conceivable unit in the East, were in short supply when the Russians attacked across the Vistula. Nonetheless, the Latvians were immediately ordered to leave their training barracks and establish a position along the Vistula-Oder Canal near the West Prussian town of Bromberg.

There then followed a two-month long ordeal similar to that described by 252nd Infantry Division, with the retreat to the northwest conducted in slow steps, alternating with bloody defensive stands around a seemingly endless succession of small Prussian and Pomeranian towns: Immerhein, Nakel, Flatow, Belgard, Schlochau, Hammerstein, Cammin, Horst, Dievenow, and still others. Defensive stands alternated with local counterattacks to drive the Russians away from the path of retreat, counterattacks to clear commanding heights or critical road junctions, to break out of Russian encirclements on at least three occasions, always with dwindling supplies of ammunition. At one point the artillery units had only forty shells left with which to support the entire division.

For a brief time the Latvians fought beside the French volunteers of the SS Charlemagne Division, one of the oddest and least effective of all the foreign SS units. Most foreign volunteer divisions presented a firmly united anti-Communist front; SS Charlemagne, while equally anti-Communist, was composed of a number of bickering and disruptive factions.

Charlemagne was one of the last foreign units raised by the Waffen SS, not seeing action as a complete division until 1945, though several of its cadres had been fighting on the Russian Front for two years already. The first of these, the LVF (Legion Voluntaire Française) was a unit recruited by the Vichy government from French army officers and others who wanted to fight Bolshevism. It was not organized by the Waffen SS and owed allegiance strictly to Vichy's Marshal Petain. The next cadre was called the "Storm Brigade," composed largely of younger men and teenagers whose fascist and pro-German leanings were much more pronounced. These two groups, divided essentially between nationalistic French officers and pro-German fascists, developed a certain degree of mutual antipathy when they were thrown together in late 1944 to form the basis of the Charlemagne Division.

This situation was made still more complicated by the arrival of the third and largest cadre. This last group came almost entirely from the ranks of the Milice, the Vichy secret police who had relentlessly persecuted groups of the French Resistance in what by 1944 had become nearly a civil war in central and southern France. Fiercely anti-Communist, the Milice perceived the resistance bands, many of them Communist-led, to be threats to France rather than allies to the British and Americans. In fact it was an extremely tangled and vicious situation, full of ambushes, betrayal, and confused loyalties, which cannot be effectively summarized in a few sentences. Many members of the Milice were no better than gangsters and bullies; to some degree, the same could be said of resistance bands operated by the Maquis. Those fighting out of genuine conviction on one side or the other only added to the confusion.

The upshot of all this was that the Milice fully collaborated with the Germans in suppressing the resistance, and with the Allied liberation of France in 1944 they all became marked men. Wishing to escape the vengeance of their countrymen, they found they had very few options, none of them attractive. They did not consider themselves pro-German, and in typically Gallic fashion they often adopted the viewpoint that the Germans had been collaborating with them rather than the other way around. Sadly, many Frenchmen whose relatives had been shot by Milice or German firing squads could not appreciate the nuances of this reasoning. In late 1944 great numbers of the Milice found themselves fleeing the country along with the retreating German armies. They were then offered the opportunity to fill out the ranks of the SS Charlemagne Division, which they accepted only with the greatest reluctance. Almost immediately they were at odds with the pro-German "Storm Brigade" cadre, whose militarized Prussian demeanor contrasted markedly with the more informal, freebooter mentality of the Milice.

Almost lost in this strange mix of factions were the only elements they had in common: a deep loathing for Communists and Jews. The German commander of SS Charlemagne, General Krukenberg, kept wondering what he was going to do with all these "screwy Frenchmen."

The answer was—not very much. The fact is that the formative history of Charlemagne makes for more interesting reading than their performance on the battlefield. Hastily organized and poorly equipped, they were thrown into the Pomeranian battles to fight for a cause that was already lost.

Detraining around the central Pomeranian town of Hammerstein in late February, the division almost completely disintegrated in the face of the first Russian attack, with many of the disgruntled Milice "volunteers" deserting outright. 15th Latvian SS, now retreating through this area, had far more combat experience in Russia and an equally superior fighting spirit. Their combat history reports that the French volunteers were "prone to panic," and indeed surviving battlegroups of SS Charlemagne would continue to leave the Latvian units in the lurch on other occasions during the long retreat. At least the Latvians were able to benefit by gathering up the weapons left behind by the fleeing Frenchmen. A few of these small French battlegroups put up a stiff resistance for a few days in other Pomeranian villages, but then they too simply vanished in disorder into the forests; with this the two- or three-week combat history of the Charlemagne Division had come to an end.

The Latvians, however, kept their cohesion and continued week after week fighting and retreating, fighting and retreating. Elsewhere in Pomerania they fought beside the 5th Jaeger Division, and frequently they were combined with miscellaneous German units, ad hoc battlegroups known only by the names of their commanders: Kampfgruppe, Jarmens, Kampfgruppe Ziegler, Kampfgruppe Joachim, Kampfgruppe Harmel.

The scene described at the beginning of this chapter took place along the road from Jastrow to Flederborn, two obscure Pomeranian towns, during the first days of February. Yet it would only be repeated over and over again throughout all that month and into the next. Adolf Ax, the new German divisional commander, was an incompetent leader who blamed the Latvians for every developing crisis. Sturmbannfuhrer Janums and the other Latvian regimental officers were frequently forced to take operational control into their own hands to keep the division from being overrun. Since the days of the Czars the Latvians had been known as good fighters, serving Czarist Russia in World War One and now fighting against Communist Russia at the close of World War Two. After breaking out of the trap along the Flederborn road they got their only breathing pause of the retreat, moving north to Krummensee and setting up defensive positions behind the Dobrinka Stream. Yet after resting for only a few days they were marched off to counter a Russian threat at Camin, making a grueling trek on foot through thawing weather and deep mud.

Janums' regiment was surrounded at Camin and after several days was nearly wiped out. He ignored orders from divisional headquarters to hold out to the last man and ordered a breakout on his own, regaining contact with the rest of the division after a bloody march back to the Dobrinka Stream. The incompetent Ax was replaced as divisional commander by SS Oberfuhrer Karl Burk, who continued to treat the Latvians with disdain until he observed their tenacious fighting abilities for himself; he then reconsidered his opinion. Along the Dobrinka Stream 15th Latvian SS Division waited for the final Soviet offensive to clear Army Group Vistula out of Pomerania, which began on February 23rd. But again the Soviets were unable to completely rout the defenders; the retreat towards the Baltic Sea continued with agonizing slowness and high casualties for both sides.

These were the endless, unknown, often unrecorded combats of February and March 1945. Rather than falling back on Danzig, the Latvians and 5th Jaegers retreated further to the northwest towards the Pomeranian port of Kolberg. In many places the Russians had already reached the sea ahead of the horse-drawn or foot-marching defenders. Kolberg and Danzig were under siege. Other cities throughout the East which had resisted the initial Soviet advance were also under siege: Konigsberg, Graudenz, Posen, Breslau. A number of these cities would hold out for months to come, engaging in epic yet depressingly similar struggles, agonizing battles which varied only in certain details from one to the other. The Latvians escaped being encircled at Kolberg, reaching the Baltic coast just to the west of that city and then retreating further west along the shore during the first week of March.

All along this narrow path, the Soviets threatened to push the defenders into the sea. In fact in some places the Soviet forward units were already on the sea and had to be thrown back in order to keep the line of retreat open. The Latvian divisional history describes the dismal scene along the beaches between the Baltic coastal villages of Horst and Dievenow:

> There was a constant flow of troops and refugees
> along the seashore on the evening of March 11th, under
> continuous shelling by the enemy. By dawn of March

12th the flow of humanity had subsided and the beaches presented a horrendous sight. The entire coast was littered with destroyed and abandoned motor vehicles, wagons, corpses and horses.[2]

A German witness presents a near identical, though perhaps still more horrific, account of the shoreline retreat path:

> Never had I seen so many bodies—civilians, German and Russian soldiers—but especially the Russians in great heaps, lying this way and that and on top of each other. Between the corpses were strewn dead horses, the overturned carts of the refugees, bogged-down military transport, burnt-out cars, weapons, and equipment.
> It was depressing enough to see the soldiers, who had had nothing to eat for days and were totally exhausted, but the faces of the women were indescribable. I saw mothers cast their infants into the sea because they could carry them no further.[3]

The last substantial, or at least coherent, German unit in this area was the 5th Jaeger Division. The jaegers had achieved fame earlier in the war for their leading role in lifting the siege of Demyansk in northern Russia. Their combat ordeal in 1945 would be every bit as severe, though not so well known. The path of their retreat during these terrible months had probably been longer than that of almost any other German division. They had been stationed alongside 252nd Infantry Division in the Narew bridgehead in January, but eventually the paths of these two units had diverged, with the jaegers undertaking a much longer trek further to the west.

Now they formed the last line of resistance between the Russians and the Baltic beaches west of Kolberg. These defenses were in no way continuous, as much of the division had already broken up into small battlegroups, many of which had wandered through the coastal pine forests for days without food. By March 12th they were wedged right up against the sea, subjected to devastating artillery fire, frequently engaging in hand-to-hand skirmishes with Russian assault groups trying to infiltrate the narrow retreat corridor right along the beach. The jaegers and the Latvians, who were also famished and utterly exhausted by this point, were finally bottled up inside the small seaside resort town of Dievenow.

This was the end of the line in Pomerania. There could be no further retreat by land. Dievenow lay beside the Oder Haff, the great bay of brackish water where the Oder River flowed into the sea. Much of this bay was occupied by two large islands. The most westerly was Usedom, until recently the site of the German V-2 rocket launches outside the village of Peenemunde. The more easterly, or nearer, island was Wollin, separated from the defenders of Dievenow by only a narrow tidal channel. There was also a large bridge leading across to the island, which for days had been packed with refugees fleeing to the west, under constant Soviet air attack. Now the Russian artillery was close enough to bring the bridge under fire. (Some accounts mention a ferry rather than a bridge. Possibly both were in use.)

By evening of March 12th Dievenow was evacuated. The 5th Jaegers crossed the bridge over to Wollin. The last defenders to cross were the Latvians; when the last of them had made it to the far side the bridge was blown by German engineers.

Though lying only a few hundred yards offshore, the island of Wollin was safe for the time being. The Soviet forces on the mainland now turned south towards Stettin, the great port at the mouth of the Oder.

DeGrelle had a hundred and fifty men left and no tanks. Stargard had just fallen and they were ordered to defend the next village. The place was indefensible but the Walloons dug in and erected barriers in the streets. Soviet T-34s attacked in packs of tens and twenties. DeGrelle positioned a few anti-tank guns at the entrance to the village and waited till the Russians approached to point-blank range. The PAK batteries fired. "Under this tornado of iron the Reds' tanks withdrew to shelter in an oak grove, then started blasting at the town from there. The houses fell in on my staff officers and signalmen."

The muddy fields were covered with wounded Walloon soldiers, overrun by the Russian tanks before they could take shelter in the village. The few survivors watched in helpless rage as the Russian infantry came up behind the T-34s, swinging trenching spades to crush in the skulls of the wounded men. One man tried to wave a white handkerchief but his skull was smashed in like the others.

By nightfall DeGrelle had only fifteen men left. The rest were dead or scattered. They pulled out of the village and headed for the edge of the dark Augustenwalde forest. Russian tanks switched on their headlights and hounded them every step of the way. The temperature began to drop and thick snowflakes drifted down among the firs.

9

AFTERMATH OF SONNENWENDE

Retreat from Stargard to Stettin

Leon DeGrelle's Walloons were also undergoing this same kind of exhausting day-to-day combat. This had been the pattern before the Stargard offensive and it remained exactly the same for weeks afterwards. For almost all of these men, the few days of Operation Sonnenwende were almost indistinguishable from the blur of days and weeks which followed. They were all equally violent, equally costly in terms of bloodshed and fatigue, and to the infantryman fighting the ground war this was all that really mattered. Sonnenwende may have been a major battle, but perhaps the historian would recognize it as such more than the average fighting man, whose ground's eye view saw only the same kind of violence and exhaustion continuing on and on.

All the armored units were gone now. When it was realized that the Sonnenwende attack would not succeed, the tanks and assault guns were simply called back and shipped off to other places. SS Polizei, along with a few King Tigers of SS Panzer Abteilung 503 that had been repaired, were sent to Danzig, arriving just in time to be encircled by the Soviet spearheads there. Fuhrer Begleit and Fuhrer Grenadier were sent to Field Marshal Schorner's army group on the southern, or upper, Oder in Silesia, there to fight alongside several of their sister units from the Grossdeutschland Corps. The two panzer divisions of the Lake Madue force, Holstein and SS Frundsberg, were sent north in a vain attempt to keep the Russians from driving the German forces along the Oder Haff into the sea, fighting in the same coastal areas as the 5th Jaegers and the Latvian division.

It was in a mood of disillusionment, mixed no doubt with a certain degree of resignation, that DeGrelle saw his men left to fight on around Stargard after all these armored units had simply disappeared. He comments on conditions during the last week of February:

> An extremely stringent order forbade me, like all the divisional commanders of the Pomeranian front, to use no more than six shells a day, or ten, depending on the caliber of the weapons. In the case of a Soviet attack our cannon would fire for a few minutes, and then would have to be silent for the rest of the day.
>
> The troops, cut to pieces by incredible machine gun fire, had to endure the blows of enemy troops that were almost at full strength and surrounded by tanks five times, ten times, or twenty times as numerous as ours.[1]

The fighting during these days was as bitter as anything these men had experienced during the war. It is a tribute to their tenacity that the Russians did not take Stargard until March 3rd, more than two weeks after Sonnenwende had fizzled out. Even after this the fighting simply continued without pause. SS Nordland, SS Nederland, the Walloons, and a few German infantry divisions were pushed back mile by mile towards Stettin on the Oder. During all this time, DeGrelle reports only one almost absurd incident in which there was any German armored support whatsoever. His frantic pleas for help just prior to the fall of Stargard managed to pry four MK IV tanks loose from some higher authority. Two of these tanks were diverted elsewhere and never arrived on the scene; the remaining two were supplied with only four shells apiece. In any case they too were recalled before they could go into action with DeGrelle's men.

From Stargard the Walloons spent several nightmarish days retreating through the Augustenwalde forest, the remains of the division nearly disintegrating in the dense woods while Russian tank convoys roared through on the only main road.

> Several tanks rushed at our position behind a barrier across the forest road. We sacrificed the last panzerfaust we had left. We were hit right back. A shell killed one of my men and wounded another.
>
> I had to make every effort to regroup my soldiers, who had been driven under the pines. My driver dragged

the wounded man and the dead one over to my Kubel-wagen, which was hidden in a thicket. I rejoined them, firing as I ran. The entire forest was alive with gunfire. We drove on until we reached a village in a large clear-ing.[2]

Exhaustion brought about its own kind of strange humor. Finally DeGrelle and a few of his men reported to a German corps headquarters at the northern end of the forest, less than ten miles from Stettin. The woods were even denser here and for the moment there seemed to be no Russian troops in the vicinity. The corps HQ was in a farmhouse well-stocked with poultry, and the Walloons and the German staff officers sat down to enjoy a rare feast.

Every few minutes the field telephone would ring with re-ports of Russian tanks bearing down from every direction. The famished men simply laughed nonchalantly and went on with their meal. Gunfire began to strike the walls of the farmhouse, which only prompted another outburst of laughter and half-crazed raillery. A Walloon officer, a major in the Belgian army before the war, commented dryly, "Oh well, the men are just killing more chickens, ha ha."[3]

DeGrelle replied that they must be killing chickens with tanks. Soviet T-34s had arrived and were shelling and machine-gunning everything in sight. A few cars and trucks belonging to the headquarters staff were parked outside the farmhouse. Ger-mans and Walloons quickly fled the building and climbed into the vehicles, the last men having to cling to the roofs and running boards. They sped off along the muddy forest roads, skidding so violently on the slick surface that the men on the roof were continually falling off and having to climb back on again.

Thus they barely made it into Altdamm, a suburban town on the east bank of the Oder across from Stettin. It was March 8th.

The Altdamm Bridgehead

The so-called Altdamm Bridgehead, on the east bank of the Oder, would hold out for another two weeks. The surrounding terrain was heavily wooded and broken up by the marshes around the Oder Haff. These factors, along with the muddy conditions brought about by the early spring weather, hindered the Russian armored attacks for a while. After the brutal push up from Stargard, Zhukov spent several days re-organizing his mobile units. But in the meantime the Russians had already reached the Oder just south of Altdamm, and they busied themselves during this interlude by setting up hundreds of artillery batteries, which proceeded to devastate the entire bridgehead.

It was a highly compressed area, and after a few days hardly any buildings were left standing. No place was safe. Command posts were shelled, bodies of dead soldiers littered the streets. German counterbattery fire was immediately targeted and silenced by the overwhelming Soviet barrages that remained one of the singular nightmares of 1945. The field hospital, with much assistance provided by Red Cross volunteers, was wisely left unmarked, as such an inviting insignia would only bring down Russian fire. The Germans had ignored the guidelines of the Geneva Convention since the beginning of Operation Barbarossa, and it was widely known that the Russians in return had no sympathy for buildings or vehicles marked with the red cross. In any case, this was a moot point in Altdamm. The large building housing the wounded was reduced to rubble by the same shellfire that blanketed every other square yard of the bridgehead. Those who were not killed instantly were buried alive under tons of brick and timber. Their cries from deep beneath all the collapsed masonry could be heard for days afterwards.

After the terrible flight through the Augustenwalde Forest, DeGrelle had managed to regroup the survivors of his division, but they still numbered only 600 men. He organized them into a single assault battalion which was then sent into the center of the German line around the Altdamm airport. In immediate command of this battalion was a certain Major Dierickx. He was

> . . . an extraordinary man who had come from the virgin forests of the Congo to the snows of the steppes. His kepi hanging on the nape of his neck, in the fashion of the pioneers, he was the bravest of the brave, a kind of Captain Conan from Katanga.[4]

This passage is typical of DeGrelle's heroic prose style, though in fairness it should be said that most of the men he singles out were probably very much as he describes them. Acts of incredible valor were commonplace everywhere in 1945. But just as frequent were the instances of men losing their nerve under the relentless pounding, who saw no future in fighting to the end for a hopeless cause and who simply took to their heels.

Indeed, most of these men had no future at all, for the reign of terror implemented against deserters was now well underway. Young men and young boys who had been reduced to a state of shock by the shelling or other horrors were soon dangling from lampposts at every street corner. The army's field police, along with miscellaneous roving squads of SS men, pursued these poor souls relentlessly, stringing them up or shooting them without trial. Many an innocent man who had simply become separated from his unit in the confusion of battle met his end in the same way. Couriers carrying messages back and forth between the forward lines and the various command posts also had to run the gauntlet of these packs of hangmen; the orders they carried had to be very explicit, or they too might find themselves dangling from ropes.

The distended corpses were superfluously identified by placards draped around their necks. Coward. Deserter. A traitor to his homeland. And so on. So were German boys identified in 1945, just as civilian hostages and partisans had been identified on gallows trees throughout Russia during the preceding years.

The shelling went on and on. It was impossible to move anywhere during the day, and even at night flares illuminated the bridgehead, bringing down more fire on any movement spotted in the blasted streets. The roof of DeGrelle's command post was split asunder by a shell which then buried itself in the foundations without exploding. It was far from his first miraculous escape from death on the Eastern Front. Some people led charmed lives, and he was one of them. At the airport Major Dierickx had an observation post in the ruined terminal tower. Beyond the runways strewn with wrecked planes, there was a clear view of Soviet tanks lined up in their assembly positions, waiting for the moment when Zhukov decided to renew the attack. The massed artillery batteries, just as they had been along the Vistula, were also lined up in plain view, though shrouded much of the time by gunsmoke wafting around the many hundreds of barrels.

The defenders, crouching in trenches and shellholes with only their eyes raised above ground level, frequently received ghastly facial wounds by the shrapnel flying everywhere. "They would run up to my little command post with a monstrous bloody hole instead of a jawbone. Often their tongues would still be panting, feverishly pink and hanging from the wound."[5]

At last on March 21st the order was given to abandon the bridgehead. The Russians had begun a number of probing attacks, but it was the artillery fire more than anything else which made the situation untenable. In overall command of the Stettin/Altdamm region was General Hasso von Manteuffel, a dapper, angular-faced little man who was widely respected both by soldiers and senior commanders for his hard-headed, practical approach to military situations. He had previously commanded a number of panzer divisions, including 7th Panzer and Grossdeutschland, fighting on both the Western and Eastern Fronts. Both Hitler and Guderian urged him to maintain the Altdamm bridgehead till the last possible moment. But in the meantime Manteuffel's last panzer units, the remnants of Holstein and SS Frundsberg, were ordered out and transported to other threatened sectors of eastern Germany. The remaining defenders in Altdamm were by now reduced to skeleton battalions, skeleton platoons. On the evening of March 20th, Manteuffel telephoned Hitler and declared bluntly, "Either withdraw everyone to safety on the west bank of the Oder tonight, or they will all be lost."[6]

Von Manteuffel was another front-line commander with a reputation as a fighter, one of those few remaining generals whose judgment Hitler trusted. The order to evacuate the bridgehead was carried out that same night. German batteries around Stettin on the west bank unleashed a rare barrage of shells to cover the defenders' escape.

The railroad bridge and the concrete autobahn bridge had already been blown up by German engineers during the preceding days. There remained only the older bridge that connected Altdamm with the heart of Stettin. But the numbers of the defenders had been so greatly reduced by this time that the withdrawal across this single artery was carried out in a reasonably calm and orderly fashion. Stettin was one of the great ports of Germany, and the rusting hulks of freighters and naval craft were scattered throughout the harbor and the approaches to the Oder Haff. Until the beginning of March, Stettin had been one of the main reception points for thousands of refugees fleeing by ship from East Prussia. Now all the water approaches were covered by Russian batteries. The refugee convoys on the Baltic Sea would have to run a longer gauntlet of Soviet submarine patrols till they reached other ports further west.

Meanwhile, the last of the defenders crossed the bridge over to Stettin, with the salt tang of the sea carrying through the night air, replacing the stench of cordite and rotting flesh that had been with them for weeks on end. Perhaps there was some point of pride for these foreign volunteer units in being the very last ones across. Perhaps it was just coincidence. Or perhaps various German units would make the same claims. In any case, DeGrelle reports that his Walloons, by now numbering only a few hundred souls, were the last to leave Altdamm, just as the Latvians had been the last to cross over from Dievenow to Wollin a week earlier.

The bridge dated from the previous century, with much fine stonework and ornate ironwork in its high towers. The retreating men marched beneath three greenish corpses dangling from a steel beam, deserters left hanging there days before by the field police. When the last man reached the far side the bridge was blown.

After the dust had settled, it was seen that the three deserters still remained strung up from the wreckage, turning slowly in the aftershocks of the explosion.

PART III
SILESIA

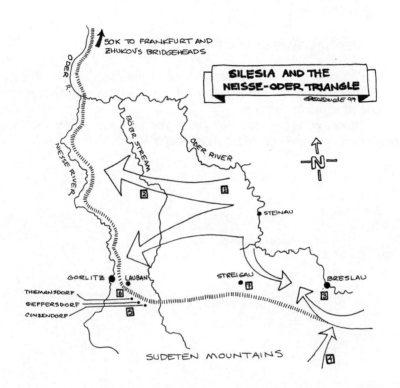

SILESIA AND THE NEISSE-ODER TRIANGLE

ⒼⒺⓇⓄⓊⒼⓁⒺ 99

SOK TO FRANKFURT AND ZHUKOV'S BRIDGEHEADS

ODER R.

BOBR STREAM

ODER RIVER

NEISSE RIVER

N

STEINAU

GORLITZ   LAUBAN

THIEMANSDORF
SIEFFERSDORF
CUNZENDORF

STREIGAU

BRESLAU

SUDETEN MOUNTAINS

|||||||||| EXTENT OF SOVIET ADVANCE ON
MARCH 2, EVE OF LAUBAN OFFENSIVE

1 KONEV'S 4th TANK ARMY & THIRD GUARDS,
TANK ARMY ADVANCE TO THE NEISSE, FEB 8-24

2 GERMAN COUNTERATTACK AT
BOBR STREAM, FEB. 14-17

3 5th GUARDS ARMY ENCIRCLES
BRESLAU, FEB. 10-15

4 RELIEF ATTACK AGAINST BRESLAU
BY 8th PZ. AND 19th PZ,
BROKEN OFF FEB. 12

5 LOCAL ENGAGEMENTS OF 8th PZ,
FEB. 18-23 PRIOR TO LAUBAN ATTACK

6 COUNTERATTACK BY 6 GERMAN PANZER
DIVISIONS LIBERATES LAUBAN, MAR 2-5

7 STRIEGAU LIBERATED BY GERMAN
208th INF. DIV, MARCH 9-14

Outside Steinau we saw the first sign of a new and harsher policy. Two old infantrymen had been hanged, from separate telephone poles. On their breasts were cardboard signs, with these words written in red letters:

Too cowardly to defend the Fatherland!

We stopped for a moment to look at the two of them. They were hanging there in the middle of the marketplace, swinging like pendulums in the wind.

"I know what this means," the Legionnaire said. "The army's beginning to break up. Most wars end this way."[1]

—*Sven Hassel*

10

THE HANGMAN TAKES COMMAND

Schorner's Reign in Silesia

His motto was "Strength through Fear." Visitors to his headquarters could see these words on a small wooden plaque sitting on his desk. He easily managed to live up to this adage. Neither Hitler nor Himmler was as ruthless a National Socialist as General Ferdinand Schorner.

In his diaries Propaganda Minister Joseph Goebbels describes Schorner almost with a certain fondness, as one die-hard speaking about another:

> In particular, he has taken a grip on the so-called "professional stragglers," by which he means men who continually disappear in critical situations and head for the rear on some pretext or other. His method with such types is fairly brutal; he hangs them on the nearest tree with a placard announcing: "I am a deserter who has failed to defend German women and children."[2]

In mid-January of 1945, Hitler had recalled General Schorner from his post as commander of Army Group North in Courland. His hangman-style of leadership had not been so evident on the besieged Latvian peninsula. After three major battles, with three more still to come, the German defenses were holding firm; thus there was no need to deal with any panic-stricken mobs of deserters by hanging the lot of them. Besides, where was a deserter going to go in this small corner of Latvia, with the Russians on one side and the sea on every other side?

But with Schorner's new posting, as commander of the German Army Group A in Silesia, his brutal style came into play immediately. Army Group A was a shattered force. Moving in parallel along the southern flank of Zhukov's thrust towards Berlin, General Konev's First Ukrainian Front had driven it back for two hundred miles from the Vistula to the upper Oder. Stragglers, deserters, disorganized mobs of soldiers, wandering cauldrons large or small, were all trying to make it back into German-held territory on the west bank of the Oder. Upon reaching safety, many of these men succumbed to the temptation to just keep on going, fleeing to their homes or simply disappearing into the towns and small cities of the Silesian countryside.

With his own peculiar stentorian gusto, Schorner tracked these men down mercilessly. Soon they were dangling by their necks from trees, from balconies, from lampposts. Soldiers found wandering in the rear areas without valid transport orders became his especial prey. Thus some of the placards draped around their necks were almost amusing in an unintentional sort of way:

> *I am a Yellow-Bellied Swine Who Disobeyed the Orders of his Transport Leader.*
> *I am a Coward without a Valid Pass.*

And so on. Most, of course, were simply identified as deserters or traitors, the same in Silesia as in the Altdamm bridgehead, as in Danzig, as in Konigsberg. The terror of the field police was rampant everywhere on the Eastern Front; Schorner by no means had a monopoly on this kind of activity. But he rose head and shoulders above all other field commanders in his thoroughness and determination in carrying it out.

Generals elsewhere tended to concentrate on more purely military matters. In fact many of them never issued any orders to hang or shoot suspected deserters without trial. The military police more frequently did this on their own initiative, with the tacit encouragement of civilian Nazi governors or district leaders who were trying to impress the higher leadership with their own fanatical resolve.

But Schorner made this kind of judicial terror his first order of business, leaving many of the details of planning military operations to his staff officers. He would take his car and tour the rear areas in person, coming across his victims in a random fashion that only heightened the atmosphere of dread and uncertainty. There was never even a pretense of a trial. Any man found without proper papers would likely be hung or shot within minutes. Naturally, with this kind of example to encourage them, the military police worked night and day when Schorner was not personally on the scene.

But he did not confine himself merely to the hangman's role. He was another man who had a reputation as a front-line general, one of those who liked to mingle with his troops and by his presence instill morale and fighting spirit. This was a quality he had put to good use in the past. Whatever a general's talents as a strategist or tactician, his example as a leader among the enlisted ranks was perhaps equally important. The men tended to fight better when these high authorities came in person to witness their hardships in the trenches, to chat with them for a few moments, pat them on the back, share their food. The force of personality again came into play here, for the troops could tell instinctively when a general was doing this only reluctantly, just for show; and when he was doing it cheerfully as a regular part of his duties. Schorner definitely fell into the latter category. But he had always been known as a strict disciplinarian, and whatever fighting spirit he instilled in his men was always backed by a large degree of intimidation.

The German Army in World War Two had an unusually strong emphasis on highly visible styles of leadership and rapport with the lower ranks. This rapport could take different forms, but it was important that it be displayed in some fashion. Schorner had developed a kind of grandfatherly, yet very strict approach. For comparison one might look to General Walter Model, another army group commander who liked to lead from the front, whose style with the enlisted men tended to be positive and empathetic. Model drove his officers very hard, often causing them a great deal of aggravation; but to the Landsers fighting in the trenches he was always a welcome sight.

It is doubtful, however, that Schorner's visits to the front were ever quite so welcome. This would have been so even before he fully unleashed his appetite for brutality in Silesia in 1945. He was a large, square-shouldered, silver-haired, bespectacled man who had once been a schoolteacher. Photographs taken of him during the war still suggest the kind of man who was used to ruling a classroom with an iron hand, projecting the image of a strict yet concerned father figure. In his own mind this attitude of concern may have been genuine, but it seems likely that most soldiers saw it as only a veneer that barely concealed the iron fist behind it.

There is a telling photograph of Schorner inspecting soldiers of the Grossdeutschland Division in 1944. His commanding presence is easily discerned; he towers over most of the men and tends to lean forward as he speaks to each of them personally. Soldiers standing a foot or two away seem to instinctively draw back, or else hold themselves rigidly still. None of them are relaxed or smiling, as they often are in photographs or newsreels of General Model. The only one smiling in this picture is Schorner, and this same expression appears on his face in many other photographs. One could say it is almost a smug expression, yet his presence is so commanding and quietly confident that 'smug' is not quite the right word. It is rather the calmly smiling mask of brutality, and of the man's untroubled belief in the righteousness of brutality.

In short, General Schorner was a frightening individual.

Differences in personality aside, both Schorner and Model typified the school of men who were leaders more than planners. These personal qualities became ever more important during the later years of the war, when the days of planning great strategic conquests were over, and the days of encouraging men to fight to their utmost in grueling defensive battles had arrived. To this end, Hitler had used both Schorner and Model almost in the manner of "one-man fire brigades," sending them all over the Eastern Front to take command of endangered sectors, wherever backbone and resolve were needed. Model had at one time or another commanded almost every Army Group in Russia, although he was sent to the Western Front in 1944 and finished the way by committing suicide when surrounded by American troops in April of 1945. Meanwhile Schorner remained on the Eastern Front, an arena which clearly suited his ruthless style. Before taking over in Silesia, he had commanded Army Groups in Courland and earlier in the Ukraine. His vigorous National Socialist beliefs were greatly admired by Hitler, though his ruthlessness was probably admired still more. Perhaps one might say that ultimately these two qualities were one and the same.

But Schorner got things done, and that was really the bottom line. It must be admitted that he inspired confidence as well as fear. As mentioned in an earlier chapter, the region between the Neisse and Oder Rivers under his command was to become the site of the last successful German counterattacks in 1945. German panzer divisions were continuously striking back at the Russian forces in Silesia until the last days of the war. Breslau, the great industrial city of this region, was taken under siege by the Russians in February, but continued to hold out month after month; and continued to hold out for days even after Hitler was dead and Berlin had fallen.

The Bobr Stream

A few days after his arrival in late January, Schorner's Army Group A in Silesia was redesignated Army Group Center, corresponding to the renaming of the other army groups in Courland and East Prussia. His most important formations were 4th Panzer and 17th Armies, both heavily engaged in the Oder-Neisse triangle west of Breslau. The besieged forces inside Breslau were also under Schorner's command, with instructions delivered via radio or occasionally by staff officers flying in on a Fieseler Storch.

Army Group Center also included 1st Panzer Army fighting further to the southeast, in the hill country of the Polish-Slovakian border. For the time being, Schorner was less concerned with the operations of this force; he left day-to-day matters to be carried out by General Heinrici, 1st Panzer's commander.

Schorner's main preoccupation was to contain, and hopefully to destroy, the Soviet bridgeheads across the upper Oder in the areas of 17th Army and 4th Panzer Army. His opponent, General Konev, was intent on breaking out of these bridgeheads in the direction of the Neisse River further to the west. This contest would not be decided until after two months of armored battles that see-sawed back and forth between the two rivers. The area would become the single largest tank graveyard on German soil.

A number of separate forces were to be consolidated on Schorner's front, arriving from different areas in different states of battle-worthiness. At the beginning of February, the divisions of General Nehring's "roving cauldron," which had combined with General von Saucken's Grossdeutschland Corps, finally ended their long retreat from the Vistula, crossing to the west bank of the Oder at the town of Glogau. Many of these divisions were more or less intact, but the men were exhausted. Nevertheless Schorner threw them into an immediate counterattack against the nearby Soviet bridgehead at Steinau.

Over the next few weeks, the Fuhrer Begleit and Fuhrer

Grenadier Divisions, which we last saw in Pomerania during Operation Sonnenwende, would also arrive on the scene. Other units, including the 8th and 20th Panzer Divisions, would be sent to Schorner's command from the Hungarian theater.

Movements back and forth, to and from Hungary during these final months constituted a mad round-robin of command decisions. At the same time that Hitler was preparing to send Sepp Dietrich's elite Waffen SS divisions into Hungary, 8th and 20th Panzer were recalled from that front to reinforce Schorner's army group in Silesia. The German rail network in 1945 was as busy as it had ever been.

Once all these disparate units had been assembled, Schorner intended to launch a major counterattack. But as these divisions kept arriving at different times, he was not able to put together a cohesive and powerful force until the end of February. Konev was not about to sit still waiting for this to happen. On February 8th he ordered the 3rd and 4th Tank Armies to break out of the Oder bridgehead at Steinau and attack westward to the Neisse. At Ohlau, another Soviet bridgehead further to the south, 5th Tank Army would also attack to complete the siege ring around Breslau. The Germans were forced to deal with the same kind of dilemma they had faced at Stargard before the opening of Sonnenwende: while trying to assemble panzer units for their own counterattack, they had to release some forces to deal with Konev's new offensive.

At this time most of the divisions mentioned on the preceding page had yet to arrive in Silesia. Schorner's strongest units on February 8th were the two corps of Generals Nehring and von Saucken that had retreated from the Vistula. It is a credit to these two men that the divisions under their command were still combat-worthy at all after such a grueling march. Nehring's men had already been diverted a few days earlier to attack the Steinau bridgehead, though little had come of this and the attack was terminated before Konev unleashed his own offensive.

For about a week the Russian tank columns advanced steadily, and by mid-February they reached the east bank of the Neisse River. On February 14th Schorner ordered a counterattack against Konev's 4th Tank Army, whose long flanks reached back to the Oder. The 16th and 17th Panzer Divisions of Nehring's corps struck the north flank, while von Saucken's Grossdeutschland Corps struck from the south.

A massive three-day tank battle developed, the first of many between the Oder and Neisse. The units under von Saucken's command were the Brandenberg Panzer Grenadier Division and the Herman Goering Panzer Division. The latter was not a Grossdeutschland unit, but it had been attached to von Saucken's corps since January and was probably the strongest division to survive the retreat from the Vistula. Herman Goering had a large contingent of Panther tanks, which scored a high proportion of the armor kills in this battle.

Brandenberg was a less well-equipped force at this time. One of its two tank battalions had already been wiped out the year before. The remaining battalion had been transferred away to form the nucleus of the Kurmark Panzer Grenadier Division, one of the newly-raised Grossdeutschland units, which was currently holding the line against Zhukov's armies near Kustrin on the lower Oder. But Brandenberg was not one of the "paper" divsions that existed in 1945. It retained a small but potent tank force with several mixed companies of Panthers and Mk IVs, known as Kampfgruppe von Wietersheim, after its commander Walter von Wietersheim. Brandenberg also fielded a battalion of Sturmgeschutzen.

Fighting together, Brandenberg and Herman Goering still formed a powerful force. Fending off this armored threat from the south, while simultaneously dealing with Nehring's two panzer divisions coming from the north, the Soviet 4th Tank Army nearly met with disaster. But as had happpened around Lake Madue in Pomerania, the two German thrusts were not strong enough to join up and trap the Russians in a cauldron. Both Nehring and von Saucken were attacking with understrength panzer units; they had already lost too many tanks during the long retreat from the Vistula. If they had been at full-strength, 4th Tank Army very likely would have been wiped out. But this is only another of the what-might-have-beens of 1945.

As always, the Russians had the on-hand reinforcements that the Germans lacked. Konev diverted his 3rd Guards Tank Army from the siege of Breslau to help restore the situation, and by February 19th the German armored pincers had been driven back. A major battle had just been fought, though history has failed to give it a name, a not unusual situation during the endless flux of combat in 1945. The focus of the fighting had been around a small watercourse known as the Bobr Stream, about halfway between the Oder and Neisse. Wrecked Stalins and T-34s were spread about the countryside for miles, along with smaller numbers of Panthers, Mk IVs and Sturmgeschutzen.

Dramatic as this engagement had been, it was still not the major counterstrike Schorner had in mind. Konev's offensive from the Oder bridgeheads had simply forced him to play his cards sooner than he would have wished. But fortunately for Schorner, he now had other strong cards in his hand, as more panzer divisions began to arrive in Silesia from the other fronts. Konev's forces had reached the Neisse River, but at considerable cost, and Schorner now had a few weeks to prepare a stronger and more decisive counterattack.

The train steams slowly forward at fifteen miles per hour, the flatcars laden with armored vehicles. Normally two locomotives are coupled together to pull so much weight, but here only one is available. Strafing attacks by the Western Allies have punished German railway traffic as severely as their high altitude bombers have punished German industry. Destroyed locomotives number in the thousands.

At least here in Silesia there is less danger from the sky, for the Red Air Force tends to concentrate its sorties over the battlefield in direct support of the Red Army. Riding on the flatcars, the panzer crews stand nonchalantly beside their vehicles—mostly Mk IVs and Sturmgeschutzen—smoking, talking amongst themselves, sometimes waving at civilians standing beside the tracks. They wear the black panzer uniforms that are more often associated with the SS, and on the whole they are a surprisingly cheerful-looking group, grinning cockily with their hands in their pockets, nodding down at attractive women in villages they pass through.

They are an elite in the same sense as jet fighter pilots will be in the century's later wars, and they have much the same demeanor. An aura of confidence and perhaps even exhilaration lingers about them, and the fact that the German war effort is facing disaster seems to have strangely little effect on their expressions. As they approach the combat zone they will become more business—like maybe—but they are one of the few warrior castes to carry themselves in such jaunty fashion in 1945.

Of course the tank crews form only a fraction of a panzer division's manpower. The grenadiers who serve as their supporting infantry wear much the same haggard expressions as infantrymen everywhere.

11

JOURNEYS BY RAIL
Travels of 8th Panzer Division

8th Panzer Division would play a leading role in this next phase of Schorner's Silesian campaign. It was far from a fresh unit, having been heavily engaged along the Hron River on the Hungarian Front in January, but of course there were no completely fresh units available to the Third Reich any longer. The reader may wish to place these January battles in context with IV SS Corps' Budapest relief attack. Technically, the Hron River was in Slovakia, flowing into the Danube from the north, opposite the town of Estregom. Estregom had been the jumping-off point for the thrust by SS Wiking on January 11th that had so nearly succeeded in reaching Budapest, before being called back in a series of bewildering command decisions.

Thus 8th Panzer's sector had been to the north of the SS attack, on the other side of the Danube River. For much of its length, the Hron flowed through the foothills of the Carpathian Mountains. The Soviets had made only slow progress through this difficult terrain, a factor which allowed for the transfer of 8th Panzer to Silesia in February.

For about ten days 8th Panzer and 20th Panzer, another armored unit transferred from the Hron River sector, had fought under the command of General Heinrici's 1st Panzer Army in southwestern Silesia, still some distance removed from the Oder-Neisse battleground. The 20th Panzer Division would remain under Heinrici's command around the towns of Olmutz and Ratibor. 8th Panzer, however, was soon on the move again, leaving Heinrici's zone of operations after ten days of combat to join the forces Schorner was assembling in the more critical Oder-Neisse sector. The reader can hardly be blamed if a certain bewilderment results from trying to keep track of all these movements from one front to another. Like so many other panzer divisions, the 8th seemed to spend as much time travelling the railroads in 1945 as it did actually fighting. It is hard not to think of the little Dutch boy running along the dyke, trying to plug one leak after another with his finger.

8th Panzer finally arrived in the Oder-Neisse sector on February 12th, disembarking in the town of Striegau about twenty miles west of Breslau. But like Nehring's and von Saucken's two corps their strength was to be sapped by several preliminary engagements. The first was an abortive attack to raise the siege of Breslau, in conjunction with 19th Panzer Division. This attack made progress for a few days, but was called off due to the Soviet 4th Tank Army's dangerous advance to the Neisse River, which culminated in the great armored battle around the Bobr Stream. Other huge Soviet forces were also advancing at this time. The 5th Guards Tank Army had just broken out of the Ohlau bridgehead south of Breslau, attacking to the northwest directly across 8th Panzer's line of advance, effectively sealing off Breslau from any further relief attempts.

8th Panzer succeeded only in recapturing a few insignificant German villages, which would only be lost again a few days later. The tank crews and grenadiers found the usual ghastly signs of Soviet occupation: raped and murdered women, murdered men and boys, as well as desecration of buildings, statues, monuments, any visible sign at all of German culture. In the village of Blucher-Ruh, they came across a curious example of this kind of defilement. Oberleutnant Kleyboldt, commander of one of the panzer companies, recalled:

> During one of these days we came across the grave of the Prussian "Marshal Forward" of the War of Liberation, Field Marshal Blucher. The neighboring town had borne the name of Blucher-Ruh [Blucher's Resting Place] for many years. The grave lay in a little park with the park attendant's house nearby. Inside the vault the coffin had been broken open, and the uniformed corpse of the field marshal lay sprawled beside it. Most of the uniform had been stripped away, the epaulettes cut off, decorations and buttons strewn all over the floor. We saw with revulsion that several of his fingers had been hacked off—they must have had rings on them. In the corner of the vault the "Asiatics" had vomited all over the floor, while in the other corner lay empty vodka bottles and the bloody remains of slaughtered chickens.[1]

Courland: Generaloberst Karl Hilpert, the last commander of Army Group Kurland.

Courland: Officers and men of the Latvian 19th SS Division. (Warfield)

Courland: *Armored cars and halftracks of the 14th Panzer Division during a counterattack during the 4th Battle of Courland in late January 1945. (Warfield)*

Courland: *Knights Cross with Oakleaves winner Josef "Sepp" Brandner of Stug.Abt. 912 with his late model Stug III G, January 1945. (Warfield)*

Courland: German infantry switch postions, February 1945.

Courland: January 1945, German reserves concentrate for a counterattack near Frauenberg.

Courland: *Winter camouflaged German infantry advance across a snow covered field.*

Courland: *An 88mm Pak 43 L/71 anti-tank gun in position to repel Soviet tank attacks. Note the Pz IV H's in the background.*

Kurland cuff title issued to veterans of the campaign.

Courland: Wounded from the 4th Battle of Courland are transported in horse drawn wagons to the port of Libau for evacuation, January 1945. (Warfield)

Budapest: Soviet troops of the 3rd Ukrainian Front in devastated Budapest.

Budapest: *Crewmen of the 5th SS Panzer Regiment, 5th SS Panzer Division "Wiking" load ammo and supplies into a surviving Panther D during the relief of Budapest. (Warfield)*

Vistula Front: *Heavy artillery battery of 150mm sFH 18 howitzers during the winter of 1945. Werner Adamcyzk spent his entire time on the Eastern Front as a gunlayer with the 20th Motorized Artillery Battalion of the 20th Panzergrenadier Division in a heavy artillery battery like this one. (Warfield)*

Vistula Front: *A series of photos showing vehicles, artillery, and infantry from 172nd Artillery Regiment and 266th Infantry Regiment of the 72nd Infantry Division crossing the ice covered Pilica River in January 1945. This unit was part of "Nehrings Wandering Pocket."*

Silesia: A victim of Field Marshal Schorner's travels behind the lines. The placard reads, "He who fights, may die. He who betrays the fatherland, must die. We must die." (Warfield)

Silesia: A group of "deserters" hanging from lamposts. This placard reads, "I collaborated with the Bolshevist party."

Silesia: *Field Marshal Schorner and Hitler in the Fuhrerbunker.*

Silesia: *Soviet machine gunners during fierce house to house fighting in Breslau. (Warfield)*

Silesia: *Gauleiter of Lower Silesia Karl Hanke swears in Volksurm units in Breslau. Hanke fled Silesia with Schorner in his Fiesler Storch only to be captured and shot by Czech partisans. Note the armband of the man closest to the camera. (Warfield)*

Silesia: *German grenadiers and Foreign volunteers move through Neustadt in mid-March 1945. These volunteers are unidentified but appear to be wearing helmets of Czech origin.*

Silesia: Foreign volunteers in house to house fighting in Neustadt, March 1945.

Silesia: German grenadiers withdraw near Jagendorf.

Silesia: A rare action photograph showing an Einzelkampfer destroying Russian T 34/85's with panzerfausts. Small Kampfgruppes of infantry formed to hunt Soviet armor were very successful.

Silesia: Another rare photo showing a grenadier of the 8th Panzer Division stalking Russian armor with a panzerfaust. The blast of the panzerfaust can be seen at the base of the tree at right.

Silesia:
Oberleutenant Telz
of 3./Panzer
Aufklarung
Abteilung of the
8th Panzer
Division.

Silesia: *Sd Kfz 251 halftrack of Panzergrenadier Regiment 28 of the 8th Panzer Division in Cunzendorf.*

After withdrawing from Breslau, 8th Panzer had a breathing pause (Verschnaufpause) for a few days, a chance for the men to rest while work crews repaired the vehicles. The passage of these three or four days seems an almost insignificant span of time, yet it is remarkable how frequently German divisional histories mention such "breathing pauses" during the course of the war between 1941 and 1945. Short as they were, seeming hardly more than a kind of long weekend, these periods of respite from the fighting were clearly important to morale. The wonder is that the men could maintain their fighting spirit after only three days of rest. Obviously they had little choice in the matter, and after four years they must have become used to this relentless tempo of fighting and resting. But it is not difficult to imagine the kind of mental exhaustion—perhaps after a time hardly distinguishable from physical exhaustion—that must have ultimately possessed so many of these men over these years.

In any case, 8th Panzer's constant shuttling by train over eastern Europe had come to an end. Schorner's long awaited counterattack would involve 8th Panzer in three weeks of continuous fighting on the Oder-Neisse battleground, with day after day of tank duels that differed not at all from the armored battles that had taken place on the steppes of Russia.

Men of 8th Panzer Division; Tank versus Infantry Casualties

Before becoming swept up in this next episode of the death agonies of the Third Reich, it might be of interest to become acquainted with some of the personalities serving in the 8th Panzer Division.

Like every division in the Wehrmacht, this unit had fought under a number of commanders during the war. Currently, 8th Panzer was led by Oberst (Colonel) Heinz Hax. At this late stage in the war it was not uncommon for divisions to be commanded by colonels rather than general officers. Hax was still a younger man in his thirties, but his youthfulness was not uncommon either. Youth and rapid battlefield promotions were widespread among German divisional commanders later in the war. Hax would be promoted to general before the end, still before the age of forty.

Other divisions that fought alongside 8th Panzer during these months would have even more youthful commanders. The Fuhrer Begleit Division, now also arriving in this part of Silesia, was led by General Remer, a man in his early thirties who could have been mistaken for an infantry captain. Less than a year before, as commander of a Grossdeutschland security unit in Berlin, he had been instrumental in helping to suppress the coup d'etat attempt that had followed Hitler's near-assassination. Only a major at this time, Remer's promotion to general had followed rapidly.

Most of these types of commanders were short on years but long on battlefield experience. Hax had been a staff officer serving with a corps headquarters earlier in the war, but since that time he had seen a great deal of combat as the commander of a panzer grenadier regiment in the 11th Panzer Division. He had been posted to the 8th Panzer Division in January of 1945, destined to be its last commanding officer.

One of the junior officers of 8th Panzer was Oberleutnant Wiswedel, who had the distinction of experiencing front-line combat in the East from the first day of the war to the last, a kind of eternity compressed into four years. The title of his memoir, "Gekampft und uberlebt" (I Fought and I Survived), tersely expresses the gist of his experiences. How fate can select a few men to survive so many encounters with violence and death is hard to understand. In raw statistical terms, there will be those few who survive after millions of their comrades in Russia have been killed. But numbers and statistics do not equate with actual experience, and the few men who experienced survival over these four years must have felt many strange thoughts passing through their heads.

One of the curiosities of the war in the East was the relative survival rates for tank crews as opposed to infantrymen. The Landsers fighting on the ground always got the worst of things, but even with their higher casualty rates, they often bore no envy whatsoever for their comrades fighting in armored vehicles. A tank always drew enemy fire more than any other target, and for the infantryman the idea of burning to death inside a steel hull, or being mangled beyond recognition by armor-piercing shot ricocheting back and forth inside a tank compartment, was too dreadful to contemplate. Otto Carius, who served in an obsolete Czech 38(t) tank in 1941 before moving on to a Tiger battalion later in the war, observed that "a proper infantryman, who had already been at the front for a while, could not be talked into climbing inside a tank, even by threat of force."[2]

Tank crewmen who had been burned alive presented one of war's most dreadful and alien spectacles. All too often they would flee out of their burning vehicles, writhing on the ground nearby as their death agonies consumed them, screaming like a species of creature from another planet. An edifying sight for any infantryman who happened to be watching. There exist photographs of tankmen who are simply unrecognizable as human beings. The corpses still bear arms and legs, even a head. But the head has been turned into a solid mass of congealed ash, expanded by heat pressure until it resembles some bulbous insectoid parody of a human skull.

Heat and flame would also do strange things to other parts of the body. Photos show Russian crewmen who have crawled out of the escape hatches of their vehicle, only to expire on the rear deck. The legs of these corpses are stretched out to almost twice their normal length, like the legs of mosquitoes or water bugs.

Earlier in the war, during 1941 and 1942, German crews were serving in inferior panzer models which were much more vulnerable to enemy fire. The infantryman's dread of being inside a tank was probably quite justified. But with the advent of the Panther and Tiger models in 1943, this situation changed drastically. From this point on, the survival rates for tank crews were immensely better than for infantrymen. It was almost as if tank crews were fighting a different war altogether. Anyone who doubts this has only to read the matter-of-fact, almost prosaic memoirs of a tankman like Otto Carius, and compare them with the far more horrific, nightmarish accounts written by infantrymen. This is by no means a denigration of the experiences of German panzer crews. Carius' account contains plenty of fear, stress, and hardship, not to mention battle deaths. But it still can hardly compare with the almost surreal atmosphere of anguish and horror found in the infantry accounts of Guy Sajer (THE FORGOTTEN SOLDIER) and Willy Heinrich (THE CROSS OF IRON), to name just two outstanding examples. Even Leon DeGrelle, whose tone can hardly be considered anti-war, frequently overwhelms the reader with his descriptions of the savagery of infantry combat in the East.

But for armored crews, the course of the war changed markedly in 1943. A Panther tank, even when disabled by enemy fire, was rugged enough that its crew could usually bale out and live to fight another day. The Tiger tank, compared with any other armored vehicle of any nation, was nearly invulnerable. German records are so complete that the fate of almost every single Tiger engaged in combat is ascertainable. Probably more than half of those that were lost were blown up by their own crews to prevent capture by the enemy. In many instances the crew was able to escape alive from a battle-damaged Tiger, and many of these vehicles were retrieved and repaired by German work crews.

Though not surrounded by quite the aura of mystery as the jet fighters or V-2 rockets, the Tiger tanks were "wonder weapons" in every sense of that oft-heard phrase. If they had been produced in numbers even remotely comparable to US Shermans or Soviet T-34s, the course of the war might have been very different. Possibly only the overwhelming Allied superiority in ground-attack aircraft could have prevented large numbers of Tigers from ruling every battlefield in both East and West. Especially on the Eastern Front, both Panthers and Tigers wrought havoc on Soviet armor, racking up kills almost like pinball scores. Kill to loss ratios of nearly 10:1 remained the norm throughout the last two years of the war. There are many well-documented accounts of a platoon of three or four Tigers or Panthers destroying twenty or more Soviet tanks in a single engagement, without suffering any loss to themselves.

The most effective Soviet countermeasures were the large-scale use of PAK fronts, or batteries of anti-tank guns, and the massive deployment of ground-attack aircraft, particularly the famous Stormovik. These two kinds of weapons took a much higher toll of German armored vehicles than did Soviet tanks.

Russian tanks like the T-34 and Josef Stalin, as well as the many variants of tank destroyers, were all good fighting vehicles, but crew training and battlefield tactics remained inferior throughout the war. After the horrendous defeats of 1941, the Russians did make progress in these two areas, but they were never able to effectively compete with their German counterparts. Even by 1945, when the Germans were finally beginning to suffer from a shortage of well-trained crews, Soviet armored casualties remained enormous. Their armored breakthroughs succeeded mostly by sheer weight of numbers, simply bypassing isolated squadrons of German tanks and terrrorizing the undermanned defensive lines of the German infantry.

Thus, even during these final battles in 1945, German tank crews stood a much better chance of surviving the war than their infantry comrades. Even older vehicles like the Mk IV, which were still being produced in greater numbers than Tigers, had good battlefield survivability. The same was true for the Sturm-geschutzen and other kinds of tank destroyers, whose low pro-files and ambush tactics allowed them to escape combat intact again and again.

Tank crews did take their losses, and in doing so frequently died horrible deaths. But perhaps an infantryman in 1945 would not have been so reluctant to step inside a tank if he had really understood how much poorer his own chances of survival were. It is hard to say. There were no good options available to anyone in those days, Germans and Russians alike.

We began this lengthy aside with reference to Lt. Wiswedel, one of these survivors of a German panzer division. Yet Wiswedel did not serve as a member of a tank crew. A panzer division comprised only a single tank regiment; the other two regiments consisted of motorized infantry, or panzer grenadiers. These men were typically carried into battle aboard armored halftracks (SPWs), either fighting on board these vehicles or dismounting and seeking cover when an objective was reached. Wiswedel served with this kind of unit, providing the infantry support with-out which tanks could not operate effectively. But their casualty rates were corrrespondingly higher, and the tone of Wiswedel's memoir reflects this. His account is not as graphic as Guy Sajer's or Willy Heinrich's, nor Leon DeGrelle's. His prose is more in the matter-of-fact mode typical of armored veterans, but it conveys an underlying mood of grimness and fatalism that grows stronger as the war goes on.

In mid-1944, he returned to his unit after convalescing from battle wounds. Wiswedel had nearly bled to death from an awful belly wound received in some obscure Russian village. The pain was so unbearable that he thought it would kill him before the bleeding did. It took him nearly a year to recover. In a lengthy passage in his book, he enquires about comrades he has not seen for all this time. The man he is questioning recites a depressing list of friends who have been killed or badly wounded during Wiswedel's absence.

Moving on to the fighting in 1945, he gives a good description of the small tricks learned by experienced halftrack crews to increase their odds of surviving:

> A number of incidents served to illustrate the difference between the older veterans and the new men, who needed to gain experience, though much of this experience was only acquired at the cost of their own blood. Even during a breathing pause in the battle, the "old men" of the crew would never dismount from the vehicle unless directly ordered to do so. Nothing is to be seen of the entire crew, except for a single man attending the weapon for security, who will barely raise his head above the armored sidewall of the vehicle. In my company, the veterans knew that we had never experienced a direct hit on a vehicle from artillery or mortar fire. As long as we knew that the enemy had no armor-piercing weapons nearby, we could relax inside the vehicle with a feeling of almost complete security, something which the "old men" treasured more than anything else.[3]

To illustrate this point, he describes an occasion when his SPWs were bringing wounded men back to the field hospitals in the rear areas. After unloading the casualties, the halftracks would return to the combat zone, but somewhere along the way one of the veteran crews parked to catch a few minutes of rest, the breathing pause Wiswedel mentions above. Even behind the front, they were still within range of Russian artillery fire. Wiswedel's point is that the "old men" knew that the chances of a direct hit were very slim, and so felt safe holed up inside their halftrack, whereas inexperienced men tended to abandon their vehicles under shellfire to seek shelter in buildings or trenches. During these few moments they would be vulnerable to shrapnel, and apparently a number of them became casualties in this manner.

Another of 8th Panzer's veteran SPW commanders was Hauptman Sell, who led the division's reconnaissance battalion and would be awarded the Knight's Cross for actions during the Oder-Neisse battles in February and March of 1945. Lt. Wiswedel describes an operational meeting with Sell; the scene is still on the Hungarian front in January of 1945, but it provides a good example of the thought processes of an experienced and aggressive leader.

The Russians were momentarily on the retreat, and Sell was considering how best to take advantage of this situation. Several previous frontal attacks had resulted only in failure and more casualties. Now Sell tells Wiswedel that he intends to make a flanking movement into the Russians' rear, catching them off-guard while their retreat was in "mid-step" (Hervortreten). He goes on to say:

> I have no desire to have one or two of my best vehicle crews shot up at the next village crossroads. We're not going into this confounded hornet's nest again today. For the moment we'll set up a secure perimeter and get a few hours rest. We badly need it. If I know the Russians, they will pull back their rear guard, along with their PAKs, during the night.[4]

Sell's flanking movement was intended for dawn the next day. He was hoping that by this time the Russians would have withdrawn the anti-tank nests which always constituted the most serious menace to German armor. He intended to strike for Niregyhaza, a village on the Russian path of retreat, and surprise them before they could set up new defensive positions.

Wiswedel describes Sell as "a very large man, almost a head taller than the rest of us, and none of us is exactly small. He gives the impression that his large frame is going to burst the walls of the tiny kitchen in this Hungarian farmhouse. For his age, he has an extraordinarily calm and serious demeanor, yet such an appearance among battle-hardened soldiers is not uncommon during the final years of the war. If at times his headstrong temper gets the better of him, and he is intent on doing the impossible, then the company adjutant has to work hard to hold him in check. On the other hand, we all recognize that in general he gives a good deal of prudent consideration to any situation, and above all takes pains to see that his men are not thrown recklessly into a mission."[5]

It is an interesting picture of seemingly contradictory personality traits—prudence, gravity, yet also fiery determination. All the same, Hauptman Sell seems fully believable as an experienced leader of men, who has already gained long years' of insight into different combat situations. In 1945 he is still only 26 years of age, though inwardly he is much older. This, as Wiswedel observes, is not uncommon for men who have fought on the Eastern Front since the early days.

Defense of Cunzendorf

In the photo gallery of 8th Panzer personnel, the divisional history indicates that no photograph of Hauptman Sell is available. In place of his portrait there is a postcard showing a drawing of a Sd. Kfz. 251 halftrack roaring into combat with all guns blazing—a fairly typical example of German war art, full of martial elan. Fortunately, it seems that the caption next to this postcard is mistaken. The divisional history does contain a photograph of Sell on a preceding page. It is not a portrait shot; rather it shows him in conference with a group of his fellow officers, planning to seize and subsequently defend the small Silesian village of Cunzendorf during these February battles in the Oder-Neisse region.

The engagement around Cunzendorf took place immediately after the three day breathing pause mentioned a few pages previously. The fighting here and in the neighboring villages of Seiffersdorf and Thiemendorf formed the opening phase of three weeks of uninterrupted combat that centered around the Silesian city of Lauban, one of the key points in the Oder-Neisse battleground. Lauban was to be the first objective of General Schorner's upcoming counterattack. But the battles in these small outlying villages would keep 8th Panzer fully occupied for almost two weeks, before Lauban itself could be approached.

Cunzendorf was defended by only a small detachment from Hauptman Sell's reconnaissance battalion. In a larger context, the four days of combat that took place here from February 18-22nd were not highly significant, but an interesting set of circumstances merits further attention, allowing a unique view of a small-unit action in 1945.

On hand to record the events at Cunzendorf were several journalists and photographers from the *Berliner Illustrierte Zeitung* (Berlin Times Illustrated), the equivalent of a newspaper's Sunday magazine section. The group picture of Hauptman Sell conferring with his other officers was the first in a remarkable series of shots which provide a mosaic of the upcoming four days of combat. This first shot in the B.I.Z. series appears to be taken in the den or library of an abandoned German house. Books fill the floor-to-ceiling shelves along one wall. Seven attentive, sober-looking German officers are gathered around a table in the foreground, discussing the plan to occupy Cunzendorf. Typically, German captions identifying figures in a group picture are not always very clear; from the placement of the caption, Hauptman Sell could be one of two men. The largest man seems to be the figure sitting with his back to the camera; judging from the description provided earlier by Lt. Wiswedel, this must be Sell. His facial features are not visible, but both his head and shoulders appear to be broader than those of anyone else in the room.

The remaining photos in the series are all action shots of the fighting around Cunzendorf. Government archives are full of millions of individual combat pictures, but photographs taken in a sequence covering several days are rarer, and these can give a more substantial and interesting view of how a combat engagement develops. After the group operational meeting shown in the library, there is a shot of 8th Panzer men, both mounted in halftracks and marching on foot, crossing a country bridge over a small stream, moving out in the direction of Cunzendorf. A close-up shows the crew of a halftrack exactly as Lt. Wiswedel describes them, with barely the rims of their helmets raised enough to peer over the armored sidewall. An officer is standing up to give directions to some other vehicles following behind, but he will not remain exposed for more than a moment. He carries an MP40 submachine gun and has a stick grenade crammed into his belt. The other men hidden in the fighting compartment carry their own individual weapons. The halftrack's main armament consists of two MG 42 heavy machine guns, extremely potent automatic weapons whose high rate of fire made them much feared by soldiers of all the Allied nations. German halftracks were outfitted with all kinds of different weapons, ranging from stubby infantry cannon to anti-tank guns to heavy mortars, but the variant armed with two heavy machine guns was the most common.

These little armored landships became the homes of the German panzer grenadiers. They could not withstand a direct hit from an anti-tank shell, but they were secure against shrapnel bursts and smaller caliber weapons and in a rapid advance could induce lightly armed infantrymen to flee their positions. They formed an integral part of the German concept of mobile warfare and were the first true armored personnel carriers, allowing supporting infantry (as the grenadiers essentially were) to keep pace with advancing tanks. Or, as was often the case in 1945, to conduct local attacks on their own. Neither the Soviets nor the Western Allies had any real equivalents to these vehicles. The American standard halftrack was so thinly armored that it was next to useless in actual combat, and in effect was no more than a semi-tracked supply vehicle. The Russians never deployed any useful armored personnel carriers, though experience fighting the Germans prompted their development after the war.

Later photos in the B.I.Z. sequence show two other armored vehicles escorting the reconnaissance detachment. One is an obsolete Mk II tank, useful only for scouting purposes at this point in the war. (The more modern Panthers and Mk IVs would be found in 8th Panzer's tank regiment, which at this moment was engaged in other Silesian villages just a few miles away.) Shown alongside the Mk II is a second vehicle, a Hetzer tank destroyer, a much more useful weapon capable of knocking out Russian tanks. The Hetzer was first produced in mid-1944, but was not seen in significant numbers until 1945. German newsreels of the period frequently show Hetzers moving through German villages to meet the Soviet advance. They were diminutive vehicles, based on the obsolete Czech 38(t) tank, but they had been re-fitted with sloped armor and upgunned to carry a 75mm cannon. Used from ambush positions, they were as dangerous to Soviet tanks as the more familiar Sturmgeschutz. The Hetzer was in fact so small that it is hard to imagine how the four-man crew could fit inside it. Such cramped quarters were clearly highly uncomfortable for their occupants, but the Hetzer's agility and tiny silhouette were put to good use in combat.

From the ensemble of photographs one gets a good feel for the terrain and kinds of villages in this part of Germany. It is clear that the Silesian countryside has been left almost untouched by Allied bombing raids. The houses and other buildings are handsome, quaint-looking structures of white plaster with dark wooden beams, somewhat in the manner of the English Tudor style. How little of this beautiful village architecture was to remain standing after the fighting in 1945 . . . The terrain consists of rolling hills sparsely covered by copses of bare winter trees. The snow has melted from the ground and the afternoon sun casts a pleasant

glow as the German grenadiers advance cautiously into Cunzendorf. Altogether it is a very peaceful looking scene.

Not for long, however.

Next shot—scouts in the hilly woods in front of the village
report the approach of Soviet tanks.

Next shot—soldiers in Cunzendorf run to take cover in buildings and alleys, while the Hetzer takes up a firing position on the
main street. Even this scene just moments before the shooting
starts has a strangely quiet and tranquil look to it. Combat in
reality never has quite the frantic pace one imagines. Soldiers
simply do not have the stamina to run around in a frenzy for hours
at a time. Some men run for cover, while others merely walk. A
few remain standing in the street trying to get a look at whatever
is coming. The same low winter sun continues to shine calmly
over these hours. In some ways, a firefight will have the same
slow curious pace as a baseball game, with moments of intense
activity broken up by longer pauses of waiting, peering out of
windows to see where the enemy is going to move next, or crawling through trees meter by meter to get within range of a good
panzerfaust shot. There is always some kind of shooting going
on, making a continuous racket, but on the whole there is only
intermittent movement, with men walking in a kind of cautious
half-stoop more often than actually running.

On the Eastern Front this slow yet anxious, almost dream-like
tempo could turn into a raging nightmare within moments. Of all
the combatants fighting in Europe in World War Two, the Russians
were the least shy about making headlong assaults that would
result in the berserk fury of hand-to-hand combat, with men clawing at each other with knives, spades, rifle butts, fists. The German
grenadiers are only too well aware of what will ensue if the Russian
infantry manages to break into their positions.

The captions to the B.I.Z. photographs do not provide
enough detail to tell us if this is what happened, or if the Russian
attack was broken up at longer range. But another source picks
up the story at this point, giving a fuller account of what happened in Cunzendorf. This source is the March 1945 issue of
the divisional newspaper of 8th Panzer, known as Die Wurfel
(The Die). On the front page there is a little graphic of a tumbling
dice cube, with faces showing three and five thus adding up to
eight, one infers. Directly underneath is the headline:

156

Ein Heiss Umkampftes Strassenkreuz
(A Hotly Contested Crossroads)

Over the last few days, the Cunzendorf-Lowen-burg crossroads has become the grave of still more Bolshevik panzers.

In the first light of dawn, Oberleutnant Teltz and four men of the reconnaissance battalion suddenly spotted five Bolshevik tanks and a battalion of infantry preparing to attack. Two of the tanks were destroyed with panzer-fausts. A third was knocked out by one of our self-pro-pelled tank destroyers. The two surviving tanks broke off their attack and fled. [No doubt this was the Hetzer shown in the B.I.Z. photgraphs.] The infantry battalion was taken under fire by all weapons and driven back after suffering heavy casualties. Every subsequent at-tempt by the Bolsheviks to pass over the crossroads and enter Cunzendorf met with a similar fate. Three days of these useless efforts cost the Soviets a total of 18 tanks. The brave men of the reconnaissance battalion turned the area into a veritable armored graveyard, a dire warning to the enemy against any future break-through attempts.

With their success, the recon soldiers make it known once again that it is not materiel which decides the battle, but rather the man, who stands firm and mas-ters the enemy at the critical moment.[6]

The leading role in this news item was played by Oblt. Teltz, who was also present in the group photograph with Hauptman Sell at the beginning of the B.I.Z. series. The final photograph in the series shows Oblt. Teltz standing in the middle of the wrecked village street four days later, apparently after the fighting has died down. His face bears the exhausted, half-crazed expression that one frequently sees in pictures taken immediately after prolonged combat action. Teltz has his left arm raised to give some kind of signal; he has been wounded in the hand, which is wrapped in bandages. The caption to this B.I.Z. photo declares that 38 Soviet tanks were destroyed, as opposed to the 18 mentioned in the divisional news story. Either figure is plausible, though the latter seems more likely. It amounts to quite a lot of wrecked armor, in any case, especially if one considers that almost all of it was probably destroyed by panzerfausts.

Other shots near the end of the B.I.Z. series show the quaint buildings of Cunzendorf, which appear wholly untouched in the opening photographs, reduced to ruins after the four days of fighting. Scattered in the rubble are the hulks of Soviet T-34/85 tanks and tank destroyers. One remarkable photo shows the exact instant when a T-34 on a hillside just outside the village is struck by a panzerfaust rocket. The German einzelkampfer is also clearly visible, sheltered behind a tall tree, with the gases released by his rocket launcher rising in a thick plume into the winter air.

After the battle, Oblt. Teltz and several of his men were awarded the Tank Destruction Badge (Panzer Vernichtung Abzeichen), an award given only in the case of a tank being destroyed by a single infantryman or grenadier. These man versus tank contests were the apotheosis of the German tradition of the "einzelkampfer." Ground soldiers who had personally destroyed a number of Russian tanks could be seen wearing as many as seven of these special badges on the right-hand sleeves of their uniforms, lined up from cuff to shoulder almost like the kill-tallies painted under the cockpits of fighter planes.

Soldiers with such a high number of personal tank kills were rare indeed. They tended to be regarded with awe by their comrades, perhaps even a little fear. Such brave fellows clearly had a maniacal streak in them; it went without saying.

But in 1945 thousands of more ordinary German soldiers could be seen sporting at least one or two of these badges on their sleeves. This was the era in which nearly every other man was equipped with a panzerfaust. Not just grizzled and slightly deranged veterans, but also terrified youngsters fresh out of the Hitler Youth, were using these rockets to knock out Stalins and T-34s in 1945.

The panzerfaust has never received full credit as being probably the war's most deadly handheld weapon. It was a rather silly looking device, consisting of no more than a thin metal tube with a bulb-shaped rocket fixed to one end. Altogether, it resembled more than a little a metallic version of an ordinary plunger used to unclog drains.

But the panzerfaust had one great advantage over other simi-

lar types of handheld rocket launchers. Both the American bazooka and its German counterpart, the panzerschreck, were
larger, more sophisticated weapons, which could fire rockets over
a longer range than the panzerfaust. But both these weapons had
to be operated by two men, a gunner and a loader. It was much
more difficult for a two-man team to get within firing range of a
tank, than for a single man sneaking up alone. This factor was
what really gave the panzerfaust its decisive edge as a killing
weapon. There do exist accounts of American soldiers crawling
forward with a bazooka after it had already been loaded, but such
instances were highly uncommon. The bazooka weighed more
than the panzerfaust and was more awkward to carry. The same
was true for the panzerschreck, which was even heavier than the
bazooka. In terms of actual damage done to enemy armored vehicles, neither of these more sophisticated weapons could hold
a candle to the panzerfaust.

Seiffersdorf and Thiemansdorf

The defense of Cunzendorf by Hauptman Sell's reconnaissance battalion was carried out in order to set up a blocking
position that would screen the flank of the division, which was
currently engaged in a costly, village-by-village advance in the
direction of Lauban, a small city which had just been encircled
by the Soviets. The main body of 8th Panzer, notably the tank
regiment, advanced to within a few miles of Lauban on February
20th, but became bogged down in heavy combat around the
villages of Seiffersdorf and Thiemendorf.

Along the approaches to Seiffersdorf, the countryside once
again appeared deceptively peaceful. Major von Lossow, commander of Panzer Regiment 10 (8th Panzer's tank regiment), recalled the scene just before the first Russian tanks came into
view at 1300 hours on February 20th:

> The warming weather made the day seem like early
> spring. The pleasant Silesian countryside had the char-
> acter of rolling foothills, with scattered pastures showing
> signs of fresh greenery. No gunfire or cries of battle could
> be heard. Everything was calm. A man would never sus-

pect that in the houses of a tiny hamlet only a few hundred meters away, the enemy was going about his infernal business.[7]

Then the first Soviet tank was spotted off to the right, a Stalin with infantry riding on its deck. It backed into a ravine and disappeared before it could be taken under fire.

The terrain grew hillier and more wooded as Panzer Regiment 10 approached Seiffersdorf. The tanks regrouped before attacking the town. The panzer regiment consisted of two battalions—I. Battalion equipped with Panthers, and II. Battalion equipped with Mk IVs. Both battalions had been brought up to full strength in Hungary in late 1944, the first time since 1941 that 8th Panzer Division had received a full complement of armor. But they had seen a lot of action since the previous fall and their numbers would surely have dwindled considerably by the time of these Oder-Neisse battles.

Apart from the reconnaissance detachment fighting at the Cunzendorf, Oberst Hax would employ the full weight of his division for this attack. He called forward his two panzer grenadier regiments to screen his tank battalions.

Pz. Gren. Rgt. 98 was assigned to set up a security line to the left, or west, of Seiffersdorf, where a number of Soviet tanks with mounted infantry had been spotted. Pz. Gren. Rgt. 28 was assigned to board the Mk IVs of II. Battalion and ride directly into the town in a frontal attack. The Panthers of I. Battalion were sent over a high elevation, marked as Hill 480, to the right, or east, of the town. From there they would continue on in a wide encircling maneuver entirely around Seiffersdorf.

II. Battalion's Mk IVs drew the first enemy fire, from PAK nests hidden on the outskirts of the town. The men of Pz. Gren. Rgt. 28 could not have looked favorably on having to ride the tanks directly into this hail of Russian anti-tank fire. They would crouch behind the spaced armored skirts fitted around the turrets of the Mk IVs, yet they would still feel highly exposed.

Concentrated fire from all guns succeeded in wiping out the PAK batteries, and the panzers and grenadiers stormed on into the town. But they were not able to expel the Russians with this first assault. There followed hours of fierce house-to-house combat. In the narrow village streets the grenadiers riding the tanks were exposed to fire from every direction; they quickly dismounted and took whatever cover they could find among the houses, beginning the grim business of clearing out the Russians in close-quarters fighting.

Meanwhile the Panthers of I. Battalion had crossed over Hill 480 and encircled Seiffersdorf in a counterclockwise maneuver. The first Stalin tank was spotted next to a millhouse and quickly knocked out. I. Battalion then linked up with the grenadiers of Pz. Gren. Rgt. 98, who had established a defensive line to the west of town. It was in this area that most of the Soviet armor had been spotted before the attack. The sudden arrival of German Panthers from an unexpected direction played the usual havoc with the Russians. By day's end 28 Soviet tanks had been destroyed. Many were caught by surprise at the end of I. Battalion's encirclement maneuver. The rest were knocked out later in the day as they attempted to attack back into Seiffersdorf, where house-to-house fighting still raged, only to be ambushed by I. Battalion's Panthers lying in wait outside the town.

By nightfall Pz. Gren. Rgt. 28 and the Mk IVs of II. Battalion had finally cleared the last pockets of resistance inside the town. A battalion of grenadiers was then detached to storm the next village of Thiemensdorf, this time mounted on the more familiar SPWs. It was probably too ambitious an assignment after the exertions of the day. The SPWs became lost in the dark, and wound up having to fight their way through a number of Russian positions before regaining contact with the division the next morning.

The divisional history does not give a casualty report for this engagement. Conceivably the 28 Russian tanks could have been destroyed without loss to Panzer Regiment 10. We have seen before that such enormous kill-to-loss ratios were not unusual. But it is not clear if this was also the case around Seiffersdorf.

Over the next several days, until the night of February 23rd, 8th Panzer continued its slow and brutal advance towards Lauban, managing barely a few miles of further progress. T-34s held commanding fields of fire over the main road leading into the city, and on one occasion two Panthers were knocked out in quick succession. Both Major von Lossow, commander of Panzer Regiment 10, and Hauptman Kruger, commander of II. Battalion, were badly wounded during these days.

The Soviets had by now nearly wiped out the small German garrison that had been holding on inside Lauban. Outside the city, 8th Panzer was coming under increasingly heavy counter-attacks and was finally forced onto the defensive.

More punch was needed if the Russians were to be thrown out of the city. Already 8th Panzer had been engaged in two costly battle actions in the Oder-Neisse sector: first, the aborted relief attempt against Breslau, and then a week of exhausting combat in the villages outside Lauban. But at last, at the end of February, the additional panzer divisions arrived on the scene to give General Schorner the striking power he needed. Instead of nibbling at the Russians in costly minor engagements, a series of more decisive blows was about to be struck.

Only five Panthers remain to lead the attack. There is a brief exchange of fire with a Russian security patrol at the edge of the woods.

The Russians are driven off and the Panthers surge over a steep earthen wall without further resistance. In the hilly terrain south of the Hennig industrial park they use machine-gun fire to wipe out an enemy PAK crew trying to pull their gun into position.

As the first Panther nears Hennig it draws flanking fire from a T-34 on the Lauban road. Two Panthers are quickly hit. Soon more T-34s move up until the German armored group is hemmed in on three sides. The Russians counterattack and by late afternoon the small force of Panthers is driven back past Hennig. The first attempt to re-open the Lauban road has stalled. In the evening the division receives orders from 17th Army to refrain from further attacks. Reinforcements are on the way.

12

LAUBAN

A Rare German Success in 1945

General Schorner, inclined as he was to lead his armies through intimidation, National Socialist ardor, and the sheer presence of his imposing personality, probably left the details of planning the Lauban attack to his staff officers and to the commander of XXIV Corps, General Walter Nehring.

For his skilful leadership during the retreat from the Vistula, as well as the part played by his corps during the armor battle around the Bobr Stream, Nehring was charged with direct control over the Lauban operation. Nehring's corps was part of 17th Army, whose zone of operations included Lauban and Breslau and which was currently the most powerful of the three armies in Schorner's Army Group Center. 17th Army commander General Schulz had been taken ill, and so for the time being Nehring was effectively in control of this entire formation.

At the end of February Nehring had at his disposal a total of six panzer divisions: Fuhrer Begleit, Fuhrer Grenadier, 8th Panzer, 16th Panzer, 17th Panzer, and 19th Panzer. All of these divisions had been in continuous action since January (or even earlier), fighting on every front from Belgium to the Vistula to Stargard to Hungary. Their tank regiments were understrength, their men suffering from battle fatigue.

But the morale of these troops was still fairly good, at least after Schorner had ruthlessly weeded out the bad elements. Soviet atrocities served to unite the German soldiers fighting in the East. That the war was probably lost was now a secondary issue. The driving motivation for anyone fighting to the bitter end was to keep the Russians at bay for as long as possible, to buy time for civilian refugees to escape to the west, in short to do anything possible to prevent the German population in the eastern provinces from being massacred wholesale.

Understrength or not, six panzer divisions still amounted to a considerable force. At this time, it was probably the most potent armored group still fighting on German soil, with as many tanks assembled in this small corner of Silesia as on the entire Western Front. (Naturally, the Waffen SS divisions sent to Hungary at Hitler's behest were stronger still.) The importance of recapturing Lauban was two-fold: it would be the first step towards eventually raising the siege of Breslau, and it would also secure railroad communication to the Carpathian hill country—rich with many of the Third Reich's last natural resource—to the south of Breslau.

Nehring planned a pincer attack around Lauban, scheduled for March 2nd. 8th Panzer and Fuhrer Begleit would advance north from the Thiemansdorf-Seiffersdorf area. 19th Panzer and Fuhrer Grenadier would assemble northwest of Lauban and attack eastward. These two converging forces would then link up east of the city.

Nehring was able to hold 16th and 17th Panzer Divisions in reserve, one of the few instances when this was possible in 1945. This time the attack would not fail if the initial spearheads ran out of steam.

The vehicle strength of 8th Panzer on the eve of this battle shows that Nehring needed every additional division he could get. On March 1st, 8th Panzer had an operational total of only six Panthers and fourteen Mk IVs. The grenadier regiments were in better shape, with 100 SPWs and armored cars still available. The artillery detachment was nearest to full strength, with 33 Hummel and Wespe mobile guns and a battery of six 88mm cannon towed by prime movers.

8th Panzer had seen the most continuous action during February; thus it seems likely that the other divisions had more tanks available, though perhaps not by any substantial margin. Additional support was provided by Panzer Brigade 103. A number of these armored brigades had been created since 1944. In general they fielded a strong force of Panthers or Mk IVs, but lacked all the additional support personnel of a normal panzer division. Such a brigade, even fighting at reduced strength, could provide a powerful punch, but the total number of vehicles available to Panzer Brigade 103 at this time is not known. As with many other German panzer units, it is possible that this formation fielded as many Sturmgeschutzen and Hetzers as actual tanks.

Once again, a surprise night attack was a key factor in the German plan. After a short but violent barrage, the panzers roared off into the darkness in the waning hours of March 2nd. 8th Panzer stormed into Thiemansdorf, the target of the grenadiers' abortive attack ten days earlier. This time around brought much better results. In a scene reminiscent of SS Wiking's night attack against Agostian on January 1st, the Russians were caught completely off guard, with many of their tanks parked "as if they were sleeping."[1] The six Panthers of Major Schmidt's I. Battalion shot up every Stalin or T-34 they could see, then pressed on ahead to the north. German pioneers and panzer grenadiers were momentarily left behind to mop up the panicked Soviet garrison in Thiemandorf, which they did in prompt fashion, destroying still more enemy tanks in close-quarters fighting.

The attack from the northwest of Lauban by 19th Panzer and Fuhrer Grenadier met with equal success. Both northern and southern spearheads forged on steadily as darkness gave way to dawn on March 3rd. Throughout the course of the day disorganized packs of Russian tanks were shot up and bypassed. Unlike the cauldron battle around Lake Madue the month before, the Russians saw prudence as the better side of valor and began to withdraw their forces from the Lauban area. It was as well that they did. This time the German spearheads succeeded in linking up east of the city, when the first elements of 8th Panzer made contact with the Fuhrer Grenadier Division on March 4th. The Soviet forces that had not managed to get out of Lauban were mopped up by Panzer Brigade 103 and the 6th Infantry Division after another day of house-to-house combat inside the city.

The Fuhrer Begleit Division, which had been positioned on the right, or eastern, flank of 8th Panzer, had the most difficult going during the attack. Their own right flank was open and here, furthest to the east of Lauban, Russian resistance was stiffer, not pulling back in disorganized flight as it was closer to the city. General Nehring called up 16th Panzer Division to keep progress going in this area. On March 5th Fuhrer Begleit under General Remer pulled abreast of the forward elements of 8th Panzer, thus firmly securing the eastern wall of the German cauldron.

This attack constituted the first real success by any German forces in 1945. Unlike the few Pomeranian towns recaptured and then quickly lost again during Operation Sonnenwende, Lauban would remain in German hands until late April. Prompt Soviet attempts to evacuate the cauldron had resulted in an unusually small number of prisoners being captured, only several hundred men. (One thinks back to the great cauldron battles in Russia in 1941, when Soviet prisoners had totaled in the hundreds of thousands.) But over 150 Soviet tanks had been destroyed east of the city, at a loss of only ten German panzers, and for the moment the German tank crews and grenadiers could bask in the faint glow of one last success before war's end.

The six Panthers of 8th Panzer's I. Battalion had alone accounted for 31 enemy tanks destroyed. Hauptman's Sell's reconnaissance battalion, which had so recently received full media coverage during the fighting at Cunzendorf, made a major contribution by driving the Russians out of the village of Maureck, thus securing the initial link-up between 8th Panzer and the Fuhrer Grenadier Division. Sell was awarded the Knight's Cross for his leadership in this action.

Schorner and Goebbels Preside at a Victory Parade

Most of the credit for this victory should have gone to General Nehring. General Schorner was not publicity-shy, however, and he arranged to give a victory speech in the Lauban town square, accompanied by the illustrious propaganda minister, Dr. Joseph Goebbels.

Goebbels was delighted, not only with this rare military success, but also with the opportunity to leave the gloomy rubble of Berlin for a few days. His diaries reflect the tone of a harrassed man unexpectedly taken away from his worries to go for a pleasant drive in the country:

> On leaving the ruins of Berlin, one enters a region apparently untouched by war. A man becomes elated to see the countryside and breathe fresh air again.[2]

The sky was hard and clear, full of bright sunshine. The fields, showing the first signs of spring greenery a few days earlier, now gleamed under a light frost as a short period of colder weather returned. It must have been quite a stimulating drive for Goebbels, who had been obliged to spend far too much time of late sharing Hitler's mole-like quarters in the bunker under the

Reichskanzellerei. Living conditions in the bunker were claustrophobic and unnerving; Goebbels' craving for fresh air would have been genuine indeed.

He met with Schorner in Goerlitz, a short distance west of Lauban, in the early afternoon of March 8th. From here they drove in Schorner's large touring car to the victory parade he had arranged in the Lauban town square.

An occasion like this would inevitably be covered by the film crews of the Deutsche Wochenschau, the German weekly newsreel. The autobahn between the two cities is shown littered with the hulks of Soviet tanks. The Reich highway system much resembles its direct descendant, the American interstate network. There is something eerie about seeing these burnt-out Russian T-34s straddling the smooth ribbons of concrete, with an overpass in the distance similar to countless such structures in Ohio or Michigan.

The troops assembled in the town square are only a small contingent; no more can be spared from the battlelines outside the city. The newsreel tries to lend a positive tone to the proceedings, but it cannot hide the grim reality of shattered buildings, another German town nearly razed to the ground after weeks of combat.

The soldiers summoned to the square are from the Fuhrer Grenadier Division, an elite Grossdeutschland unit full of healthy and capable young men. Yet we can see their strange and disturbed expressions, almost a kind of awe, as they gaze about at so much destruction in a city that was untouched by war as recently as a month before. As yet, there are no shots of sadistically mutilated civilians, though clearly such sights must be preying on the minds of these soldiers as well.

Goebbels arrives, wearing the long leather coat favored by so many generals and Nazi government leaders. He has never before been so close to a combat zone, and he seems a little cowed by the impressive bearing of these Grossdeutschland troops, who nonetheless wear the grim shock of battle on their own expressions. Goebbels marches stiffly before them, meeting their stares, his face strangely rigid, his right arm upraised in an equally rigid Fuhrer salute.

The leader of this Fuhrer Grenadier contingent is a striking-looking young man, a junior officer of some kind. He salutes Goebbels with an exquisite ramrod precision that would be the envy of any British sergeant major. Yet he also has the lean, blade-like facial features and mask-like stare common to so many officers of the Waffen-SS. This man is an army officer, but there can be no doubt that he is also a young fanatic of the cause; none of his fellow soldiers standing nearby can match the intensity of his gaze. Doubtless he has been chosen to preside over this ceremonial parade because of these very qualities.

He looks much like the stereotypical die-hard German soldier. But the curious thing is that men with such smooth and rigid stares are almost never to be seen in 1945. He is the exception, not the rule. After so much terrible combat and bloodshed, the faces of German soldiers often appear as unguarded mirrors of their souls; almost all of them appear more distinctly human, idiosyncratic, and emotionally complex than their predecessors in the confident armies of a few years earlier. The Deutsche Wochenschau of 1945 is a veritable portrait gallery of arresting human faces. Never before has the German soldier, even the Waffen SS soldier, looked so distinctively individual, each stamped with the unique circumstances of his own emotional journey through these years. Words such as these cannot really do justice to this strange human tableau; the interested reader would be advised to view some of these late-war newsreels for himself.

By and large, it cannot be said that these are the expressions of defeated men, even though they are staring defeat in the face. Most of them simply appear dazed, lost in unfathomable ruminations. They convey the paradox of men so battle-hardened as to be inured to horror, yet illuminated by an inner light of bewilderment, terror, stress, strange humor, and some deeper mystery unique to each of them, yet shared by all.

American soldiers fighting in Western Europe could hardly display this kind of variety. They were individuals, to be sure, confident of this fact in their typically American fashion. Yet almost all American GIs were united by their common distaste for the war, by the weary and business-like manner with which they went about this obnoxious foreign ordeal that had dragged them all out of their homes an ocean away. The faces of countless GIs displayed these common feelings, which were basically quite simple and down-to-earth, lending them all a certain unity of expression.

The German experience was much more complicated than

this. It goes without saying that many German soldiers were equally, if not more, war-weary. But in the service of their depraved government they had trod upon moral ground which at times must have seemed to tremble beneath their feet; each man's different awareness of this journey, mixed with feelings of guilt or innocence, callousness or sympathy, or just plain chaotic non-comprehension, must have leant a unique expression to his features.

And now they were faced, not only with defeat, but with a terrible wave of vengeance from their Russian enemies that would be unmatched in modern times.

And so Goebbels addresses these men with his own fiery oratical style. He is a good speaker, trained in the theater during his younger days, though not endowed with Hitler's more mysterious and deeply charismatic gifts. But at this time Goebbels is nearly alone in carrying the burden of speaking to both German soldiers and the civilian population. He is the only Nazi leader to be seen much in public anymore, touring the different provinces of the Reich, delivering his impassioned message of resolve to the end. Hitler at this point is hardly capable of speaking in public; he is a sick and prematurely aged man who is totally absorbed by his round-the-clock routine of running the war, a routine so exhausting that there are times when he looks nearly used-up as a man. By and large, Hitler vanishes from the newsreels and public speaking halls in 1945; his place as the visible leader of the German people is taken, however effectively, by Goebbels.

The newsreel continues. In Lauban, Goebbels awards the Iron Cross to a sixteen-year old boy who looks closer to twelve. The Reich is now drafting children like him into the armed forces, though it seems unlikely in this instance that this lad is serving officially with the Fuhrer Grenadier Division. These soldiers comprise one of the last truly elite army units, and they mostly look the part. Probably the boy has been merely adopted into this unit. The commentary indicates that he was employed as a messenger during the battle.

After the parade formation has been dismissed, Schorner and Goebbels take a tour of the battlefield. Though the weather has turned colder, Schorner is not wearing a coat. An ordinary dress tunic is stretched tautly over his muscular frame. We see a few shots of Goebbels inspecting a battery of Hummel self-propelled guns, still firing at the Russians while he looks on.

From here, Goebbels is scheduled to drive back to Goerlitz, where he is due to give an important speech to an anxious civilian population.

Goebbels Speaks in Goerlitz

During the previous autumn in East Prussia, German farmers had been found nailed upside-down to barn doors in the form of an inverted crucifixion. The rage of the Soviet invaders had inspired many examples of such demented creativity.

Men had been beaten, forced to watch the gang-rapes of their wives and daughters, after which their wives and daughters were killed before their eyes. Perhaps mercifully, the men were then also killed.

More than anything it was rape, though accompanied by an incredible frenzy of blood lust as often as not.

Was there any doubt about showing scenes such as these in the German newsreels? Possibly. There was a genuine threat that the civilian population would be thrown into a mass panic. Invaders from another world could not have inspired such terror. Nazi governors in the eastern provinces had already been responsible, some would say criminally responsible, for keeping the facts about the Soviet advance from the public. They had been frequently admonished from Berlin to prevent the spread of any kind of defeatist rumors. Many of these gauleiters had impeded the flight of refugees, refusing to allow regions under their control to be evacuated, barring civilians access to trains heading west.

Of course, it was impossible to disguise the reality of what was going on. Millions of refugees were already streaming westward, bearing tales of horror. Some gauleiters, afflicted by their consciences, ignored warnings about defeatist activity and did what they could to help their fellow citizens. In general, the German soldiers did everything possible to buy more time for the refugees to escape. Frequently, German military commanders came into conflict with other, more arrogant gauleiters who refused to provide any assistance for this mass exodus.

Awful scenes of murder from the East Prussian village of Nemmersdorf had already been shown on the newsreels the previous October. It had been hoped to stiffen the resolve of the German public against the Bolshevik menace. It was not intended to inspire massive flight, and in the fall of 1944 this had not occurred.

But all that was months ago now. The dam had burst and the flood had swept in.

The newsreel crews had been present with Goebbels and Schorner, filming the ruins of recaptured Lauban, filming the ordinary soldiers assembled there, who had been caught staring at their surroundings almost in a state of shock.

This scene was followed by a far grislier sequence. The images were no more hideous than those from Nemmersdorf the previous autumn. But these sights were no longer from a distant frontier town. The horrors were now being filmed in the heart of Germany.

There were shots of civilians from the areas of Silesia around Lauban, people beaten so badly that in death they resembled grotesque parodies of human beings. Their final expressions of agony were almost gargoyle-like. Many had puckered-looking bullet holes in the middles of their foreheads. Dead women lay with their skirts pulled above their heads. Dead children. A woman was shown lying in the mud with a heavy chain wrapped around her neck. She had been dragged to death behind a Soviet tank. The pain of such a death would be almost unimaginable, abrading the skin like fire; to be burned alive would be preferable to this.

From Lauban Dr. Goebbels drove to Goerlitz, a Saxon town that bordered Silesia on the west bank of the Neisse River. At this time the Soviet advance was only twenty miles away. The Russians had just been driven back from Lauban, but only a short distance further to the north they were lodged firmly along the Neisse, and in places had established bridgeheads in towns across the river, towns very similar to Goerlitz.

Goebbels addressed the public in the town hall, probably on the night of March 8th or 9th. He gave his usual fiery and histrionic speech. An orator is an actor, and he was not as good an actor as Hitler. But few people were. Hitler always interwove his more impassioned remarks with quieter moments of hypnotic subtlety.

Goebbels started quietly, but then rose steadily to a furious crescendo. It was a cruder display of feeling, seeming somehow artful and insincere—the work of a politician—even though, at least on this night, his message was probably as sincere as any he would ever deliver:

> I have seen the horrors committed by the Bolshevik monsters with my own eyes. We must all rise as one, as in God's service, to expel these Asiatics from Europe.[3]

It was Hitler who had originally cultivated the Nazi disdain for organized religion. But he had never really pressed the issue, and the majority of German civilians had simply ignored this aspect of his cult. Other Nazi leaders, like Goebbels in this case, were quite willing to call upon God's assistance in the hour of need.

The newsreel crews were here as well, showing Goebbels' habitual speaker's gesture of clenching his fist and flipping it up and down as he talked, as if he were slowly shaking a pair of dice. Shots of people in the audience show expressions ranging from worry, consternation, to an almost paralytic fright. Fear was the common denominator. It could hardly have been otherwise.

Yet as Goebbels concluded his speech he was greeted by a highly emotional outburst of applause that could not have been faked or orchestrated. It was like a momentary, cathartic release from the atmosphere of terror that seemed to grip them all. Even to the end they wanted to believe, believe that they and the rest of Germany would somehow be spared.

Goebbels might have advised them all to flee for their lives while they still had a chance, to flee for the sake of their children's lives. He did not do so. Nor did he warn them against it, however.

The civilians had no way of knowing it, but Goerlitz was to be spared the fate of places like Striegau, a small Silesian town which we shall visit momentarily. The Soviets did not capture Goerlitz until late April, by which time much of their insane blood lust had spent itself. There would still be countless rapes, but the orgy of murder and torture would begin to abate. Just how much consolation could be found in this is hard to say.

Striegau

Generals Schorner and Nehring were not content merely to hold onto Lauban, which was little more than a large rural town. Schorner still wished to raise the siege of Breslau, now entering its second month of encirclement. The success and above all the negligible casualties sustained in the Lauban operation, once sufficient striking forces had been assembled, encouraged the German commanders to believe that more ambitious attacks were now possible.

Since the long advance from the Vistula, the Soviets had made only negligible further progress. From its source in Slovakia to its mouth at Stettin, the Oder River line was holding firm. The only exception was Konev's breakthrough to the Neisse in mid-February, but now the German defenses behind that river seemed to have stabilized as well. Meanwhile, just to the south, 17th Army was still operating east of the Neisse, and Schorner and Nehring lost no time in striking another blow in this area.

Striegau, about fifty miles east of Lauban, was the last important town before Breslau. As soon as he had concluded his little propaganda tour with Goebbels, Schorner sent two of Nehring's panzer divisions to take Striegau.

But what of the other four panzer divisions which had ensured success at Lauban?

It was the same old story. Crisis situations elsewhere dragged them away before Schorner could follow up his victory with any really meaningful gains. The Fuhrer Grenadier Division was sent back to Stettin, in the region they had just come from, to help thwart any Russian attacks against this important port. This division was destined to be the greatest rail traveller in 1945. A few weeks later they would be shipped south again, to the critical area around Kustrin where Zhukov's armies had forged a bridgehead across the Oder only forty miles from Berlin. After a short, horribly unsuccessful counterattack against Kustrin (which we shall see in a later chapter) Fuhrer Grenadier would be shipped all the way to Austria to shore up the defenses of Vienna, where this division would at last finish the war. It would be quite an itinerary for men who had started the year attacking American paratroopers outside Bastogne.

Even more critical was the situation in the area of General Heinrici's 1st Panzer Army in the Slovakian hill country. Konev had withdrawn one of his tank armies from the Oder-Neisse triangle to support a new offensive in this southernmost region of Silesia.

Conceivably General Schorner could have simply ignored the threat to this out-of-the-way area, leaving General Heinrici to fend for himself and continuing to keep his panzer divisions together to attack Breslau. Breslau, after all, was by far the most important German city in Silesia. A determined effort to raise the siege would have caused some serious disruption to the plans of the Soviet High Command. But when the final defense of their nation consisted of little more than an endless "firedrill," German generals can hardly be blamed for making hasty command decisions. Unfortunately, the numerous little hill towns along the front of Heinrici's 1st Panzer Army contained many of the last natural resources available to the Reich, including rich deposits of coal and natural gas.

Schorner felt he had no choice. He had already ordered the abandonment of Kattowitz, the most important industrial city in Heinrici's sector, immediately upon taking command of Army Group Center in late January. Hitler had not been pleased with this decision; only his respect for Schorner's abilities had kept him from overruling it. Schorner had given up Kattowitz in order to consolidate his forces before they were overrun in the wake of the Vistula Offensive. But now to surrender any more of this resource-rich region to the Soviets would be as crippling to the German war machine as the loss of the Hungarian oil fields. Schorner immediately sent 8th, 16th, and 17th Panzer Divisions to defend this area against Konev's new offensive, thus effectively throwing away the last hope to recapture Breslau.

The 8th Panzer history records:

"We had barely had time to bury our dead from the fighting around Seiffersdorf . . . than the division was moved off again to another front."[4]

The first train steamed out to Heinrici's command on March 9th, only a day after Schorner's victory parade at Lauban. 8th Panzer had already spent almost two weeks fighting with 1st Panzer Army at the beginning of February; now they were back again, and would conduct a long fighting retreat through these Slovakian hills until the end of the war.

Oberst Hax received a message of encouragement from General Schorner:

I have had several opportunities to visit the rear areas of your division and have been pleased with the prevailing atmosphere of order and discipline. I extend to the men of the division my especial recognition. With divisions like this a man can drag the devil straight out of hell.[5]

It was the typical fighting bluster from Schorner. Good warriors received a hearty pat on the back, while weaklings were simply executed. There is something about Schorner's personal style which reminds one of General George Patton, another man about whom many good and bad things have been said. Schorner's hint about visiting the rear areas of 8th Panzer, even when couched in a positive vein, would not have gone unnoticed either. But at least few, if any, of 8th Panzer's soldiers were strung up from trees by Schorner's roaming hangmen.

And so the fighting for this division simply went on and on, in major battles or minor, a blur of violent days no different from those experienced by DeGrelle's Walloons after Sonnenwende.

Instead of a grand relief attempt against Breslau, Schorner had to content himself with using his two remaining armored units, 19th Panzer and Fuhrer Begleit, to recapture Striegau, which was really only another medium-sized dot on the map.

The clear and frosty weather Goebbels had enjoyed on his drive out from Berlin had turned colder and gloomier. The attack on Striegau was another savage, sparsely documented affair, fought much of the time in a driving snowstorm. The men of General Remer's Fuhrer Begleit were every bit as tough and driven as the men of the Fuhrer Grenadier contingent that had so recently impressed Joseph Goebbels. The two panzer divisions were deployed outside Striegau, duelling with the ever-present packs of Russian armor; the actual liberators of the town were German landsers from the 337th Regiment of the 208th Infantry Division. At first an SS Division had been slated to make the infantry attack, but the Army Corps Commander (which would have been Nehring, though it is not entirely clear if he was the party in question) insisted that an Army unit lead the actual assault to free Striegau. The SS Division was one of the late war ad-hoc formations thrown together by Himmler, the soldiers in this particular unit being mostly ethnic Germans from Hungary and the Banat. Their commander acquiesced to the army change in plan, allowing 337th Regiment to take over his division's positions, as well as carry the burden of the house to house combat inside Striegau. Finally after a bitter five-day fight, the Russians again attempted to withdraw from the trap, but this time panic broke out and the German mobile units were able to conclude the battle by mowing down large numbers of fleeing Soviet troops.

And so another small city passed back into German hands. It was an entirely meaningless success, in light of events looming in the not-too-distant future. Schorner had shot his bolt. In doing so he had accomplished about as much as could be reasonably hoped for—but this amounted to no more than retaking a small corridor of land at the southern base of the Oder-Neisse battleground.

On the heights along the west bank of the Oder, overlooking Breslau which lay just across the river, the most advanced positions of 17th Army had a clear view of the battle raging inside the city. Smoke rose everywhere, explosions erupted in dense patterns, tumbling whole city blocks. At night the German soldiers on the Oder heights, known locally as the Zobtenberg Hills, could see enormous columns of Soviet vehicles moving along the autobahn with headlights blazing unconcernedly.

The recent victories of Schorner's and Nehring's panzer divisions had been no more than pin-pricks in the overall Soviet scheme of things, events which the Soviet High Command seems barely to have noticed. General Konev could hardly have been alarmed, considering his withdrawal of an entire tank army from this sector to send against Heinrici further to the southeast.

The Germans' long defensive stand on the Oder was no more than an illusion. The Russians were doing little more than clearing up loose ends during this time, and all the while forces of gigantic proportions were being built up in Zhukov's front along the lower Oder opposite Berlin.

But there remained another month of terrible fighting throughout the East before the door to the capital would finally be kicked in. Civilian refugees would continue to flee, or else wander in circles hopelessly trapped behind the Russian lines. Even to this day the slaughter of civilians in eastern Germany in 1945 has not been fully recognized for what it really was. It was nothing short of a spontaneous mass orgy of murder conducted by an invading army without precedent in European history. Russian commentators make no apology whatsoever for these events, perhaps understandably so. Vengeance often increases in geometric proportion to the original grievances, and Nazi barbarism in Russia had caused an immense accumulation of grief.

The German liberators of Striegau were treated to a close examination of this ten-fold retaliation. Apparently the atrocities committed in this town were of an exceptionally ghastly nature. Civilian survivors were found wandering around quite literally out of their minds. German soldiers responded by beating Russian prisoners to death with spades and rifle butts. One of them declared, "After Striegau there was no looking back, there was no question of giving quarter anymore."[6]

First a German soldier entered the farmhouse in the middle of the night. He was nearly delirious, saying his regiment had been massacred. He told his tale and then collapsed in a corner, falling dead asleep.

The farmer looked out the window at the snow falling heavily through the darkness. He knew some of the local party bosses and decided to telephone them. The people in the area had to be warned, had to be told to flee immediately.

He picked up the phone but had to wait a few minutes for the call to be put through. The first Russians burst into the farmhouse and shot him dead with the receiver still in his hand. Their captain looked at the German soldier still asleep in the corner; he yanked the man's head up by the hair and slit his throat, then emptied his pistol into the corpse for good measure. The search for women and loot began.

In the village square, gathered around a huge bonfire, Red Army soldiers listened as a commissar read aloud from one of the murderous propaganda leaflets penned by Comrade Ehrenburg.

In another house nearby, a family named Haupt was routed out of bed. Haupt and his wife were forced to watch while the Russians ripped the nightshirts off their eighteen and twelve year old daughters and began raping them on the parlor room floor.

The twelve year old girl was first. Haupt watched in shock, muttering gibberish to himself. A Russian officer finished with the little girl and then began on the older daughter. Haupt attacked him. He managed to throw the officer against a wall before being shot by the other Russians in the room. He was still alive and the officer dragged him out of the house by his hair, out into the snow, dumping him in the yard, where two more of his soldiers proceeded to cut off Haupt's genitals.

They released him and he stumbled off through the snowfall and the darkness, shrieking interminably out there.

Back inside the house a Russian soldier went upstairs and found another child, a one year old infant, sleeping on a bed. The child was uncovered and he laid a blanket over it, then sat quietly beside it and stared into space while Haupt's screams continued outside and his daughters' screams continued from the floor below.[1]

13

HORROR

A Tour of Striegau

About a week after the 208th Infantry Division recaptured Striegau on March 14th, German government agencies began compiling a report on what the Russians had left behind. Officials went from house to house, documenting their findings at every address. The following items are excerpted from their report.

No. 12 Pilgrimshainer Strasse.
Three dead women, one child, gas poisoning, suicide. In front of the house, several male bodies, dead from gunshot wounds.

Corner of Wilhelmstrasse and Zigarstrasse (Baker's shop).
Three old women with lower bodies uncovered, signs of being raped, shot dead. In the attic, an old man, his body strung up from a beam with his head hanging down.

No. 5 Zigarstrasse.
In the basement, an old couple, shot, their eyes gouged out. Hanging by their necks in the attic, two old women, a middle-aged woman, a girl of about twenty, a girl of about ten. All showing signs of rape.

Under the monastery church, near the basement door.
The naked body of a girl, about fourteen years old, apparently dead from starvation after being locked inside.

Wilhelmstrasse, on the property of Master Saddler Kretschmer.
Herr and Frau Kretschmer committed suicide by hanging themselves from the crossbeam of a window.

No. 8 Bahnhofstrasse (Bookshop).

In the first-floor flat, the body of a sixty-year old man hung from the doorhandle. Lying on the floor, two middle-aged women, dead from gunshot wounds, signs of sadistic rape. On the sofa, a thirteen year old boy, shot dead. Lying in a bed, the uncovered corpse of a sixteen year old girl, shot dead, violated with a broomstick.

Bahnhofstrasse.
In Frau H.'s flat, the bodies of Frau H. and her daughter found lying in bed. Frau H. had slashed her wrists, but had killed her daughter beforehand by throttling her with a knotted towel. Apparently she could not bear the thought of her daughter being raped.

No. 2 Thomasstrasse.
Lying in the gutter, the body of a boy about fourteen years old, crushed flat by heavy vehicles, also shot through the nape of the neck.

Pilgrimshainer Strasse, property not named.
The nude body of a young girl, violated with a wooden stick.

Gasworks, in the flat of the gas supervisor, demolished by shellfire.
Under the rubble lay the half-dressed body of a woman, gunshot wounds to her mouth, breasts and buttocks lacerated by sadistic sexual assault.

Near the Evangelical Church.
An SS man, his throat slit.

Gasworks, in the flat of the pipeline supervisor.
Lying on the sofa, a woman partially undressed, two gunshot wounds through her mouth, her brains clinging to the wall.

Corner of Guntherstrasse and Bahnhofstrasse.
In the broken glass and china of a crockery shop, the body of an old woman, shot dead, clothes torn and smeared with blood. Around her lay many white china plaques with the inscription, "Here rests with God . . ."[2]

The report goes on listing such individual cases for several more pages. After this there follow a few paragraphs of commentary about these events. Some excerpts:

> It was not until March 20th, 1945 [a week after the German recapture of the town] that the first 148 victims of this bloody frenzy could be buried . . .
> Adding other victims discovered later, the total of murdered civilians came to nearly 200. A Polish female doctor certified the most frequent causes of death as being "asphyxiated," "throttled," "beaten to death," "shot to death."[3]

Soviet troops had been engaged in such berserk acts all over the invaded provinces of Germany. The report notes that the findings in Striegau were exceptionally horrible. In an addendum, there is a partial explanation for what happened in this town.

Apparently the Russians in Striegau had captured an immense stock of hard liquor from Herr K.'s Rye-Whiskey Distillery. They had occupied the village for four weeks before being driven out again, and during this time they were continually drunk, so much so that they were several deaths from alcohol poisoning. The area of the main square was blanketed with the stench of alcohol fumes. Russian soldiers washed their boots in buckets full of sparkling wine. Every day, the garrisons of other villages from around the area would requisition whole wagon-loads of alcohol from Striegau.

As brutal as many of the rapes and murders were, civilians were also killed unintentionally. Many Russians were so stupefied with drink that they would fire their weapons accidentally, causing casualties among their own men and hapless civilian bystanders.

The owner of the liquor distillery, identified only as Herr K., was seen as being partially to blame. (An curious assessment of guilt in a German document.) The report notes that Herr K. had fled the town before the arrival of the Russians on February 13th. In its strange tone of reprimanding an irresponsible citizen, the report suggests that Herr K. had had plenty of time to pour his stocks into the gutters before the Russians entered the town.

Millions of leaflets fluttered down through the air over Silesia, over East Prussia and Pomerania, dropped by the Red Air Force. Usually these propaganda messages were intended for the eyes of the enemy, to demoralize him and induce him to surrender. This time, however, the leaflets were spilled down into the Russian lines, bearing exhortations for the soldiers of the Red Army, signed by Stalin himself. The leaflets said:

Soldiers of the Red Army! Kill the Germans! Kill all Germans! There can be no innocent fascists, from the very oldest to the as yet unborn. Kill! Kill! Kill![1]

This brief message had been composed by Ilya Ehrenburg, a poet who was responsible for much of the late-war Soviet propaganda. Usually his outpourings were a little more imaginative than the terse sentences shown above. He became famous for his bloodthirsty ravings, enraged calls for revenge against the German beasts who had committed such horrible crimes on Russian soil. Perhaps never before in modern history, and perhaps even in ancient history, had a government leader so overtly and unapologetically exhorted his soldiers to murder the entire people of the enemy.

After the war some historians would describe Ehrenburg's tirades as a sick and racist form of propaganda—as if they were merely some Soviet counterpart to Nazi propaganda about Bolshevik subhumans. Perhaps many Russians would have been puzzled by this attitude. All Ehrenburg was doing was calling for—crying out for—vengeance. Vengeance! Vengeance!

After all the horrors of the Nazi invasion, what could be more natural than that?

14

THE RUSSIANS

The Nightmare of Nazi Occupation; Mysteries of
Life in the Red Army

In a way, it is difficult to seek an explanation for the Russian
acts of depravity in Germany. The reason for this is paradoxical:
the basic explanation, that it was all a matter of revenge, is so
obvious that it becomes difficult to look any further. Anyone attempting to make a deeper analysis of these events could be
accused of making a very simple matter unnecessarily complicated. The desire for vengeance and the explosions of rage that
follow upon this desire are among the most fundamental, though
unpleasant, aspects of human nature.

But every situation, every historical drama, is different. To
outsiders, the Russians have always been a mysterious people.
While in broader terms it is not difficult to understand their actions in 1945, the specific motives twisting and turning inside
their tormented souls are harder for an outsider to see—to see
through the Russians' own eyes, as it were.

The author is not an authority on Russian culture. Even so,
some of the causes of Russian behavior in this era, when scrutinized closely, can be made fairly evident. Other causes can be
derived from speculation based on conditions of life inside the
Soviet Union during these nightmarish years.

Sources

Before making any kind of commentary on the psyche of the
Russian soldier at the end of World War Two, one basic problem must
be addressed. Very simply, archives, source material, and eyewitness
reports from the Russian side of the war are not there—the sum total
of these most basic forms of evidence amounts to a kind of void.

The reader may wonder why almost all of this book is told
from the German point of view. The answer, or at least one an-

swer, is the wealth of every imaginable kind of source material to be found in Germany. German military records are very detailed, and in the strict sense of such issues as casualties suffered and casualties inflicted, they tend to be remarkably accurate. The Germans have always been sticklers for these kinds of details, even when amassing reports of their own criminal activities. For example, the demented travels of the SS Einsatzgruppen through the rear areas of Russia are quite well documented. The Stroop Report, detailing the slaughter of Polish civilians during the Warsaw Uprising, is the very model of German thoroughness. Even more than the cold numbers found in official records, the eye-witness reports and memoirs written by German soldiers offer an enormously detailed and variegated look at every aspect of the war. German eyewitnesses clearly emerge as individuals, whether sympathetic or repellent.

The same is not true for reports coming from the Soviet Union. All too often, casualty figures showing German and Russian losses are so far off the mark that they seem to have been made up from thin air. Russian reports for the Battle of Kursk, for example, indicate the total losses of German tanks and aircraft to be far higher than the numbers actually fielded by the Germans at the start of the battle. This kind of highly "approximate" reporting was simply a standard Soviet practice. The USSR was a bureaucratic state, but it was not a MODERN bureaucratic state; Soviet methods of accounting and records-keeping were as chaotic as the Germans' were organized. (The Germans tended to be over-organized, a fact which in itself hampered efficiency in certain curious ways.) This kind of numbers-juggling was not restricted to the Soviet military; it was a practice that could be seen in almost every aspect of Soviet society. The Russians' deeply ingrained tendencies of secretiveness and censorship merely served to make their record-keeping even more impenetrable. In a sense, one might gather that the compiling of raw numbers has never been a highly-prized cultural tradition in Russia, an outlook quite the opposite from the obsessive data gathering that one sees not only in Germany but in other Western societies. The only clear facts that one can really infer from Russian documents are whether battles were won or lost. Perhaps there is something to be said for this, when one looks at the overwhelming flood of numbers and statistics churned out by modern Western nations.

In any case, the lack of accurate statistical reporting from

Russia would not be so important, if it were at least compensated for by memoirs and eye-witness accounts. These are always the most telling documents of any historical situation, especially if they are accumulated in such large numbers that a realistic over-all picture can be formed, regardless of the biases or misleading statements of a few individuals.

But this kind of evidence is also lacking, and herein lies the reason for why it is so difficult to see any clear aspect of this terrible war through Russian eyes.

At this point, it should be said that in fact there are a great number of eye-witness accounts available from Soviet archives. Russians have also written novels and memoirs about the war, authored by men who took part in the fighting. But if this is so, does it not contradict everything just said above about the lack of such material?

The answer is no, it does not. Russian eye-witness accounts form one of the most troubling aspects of trying to understand the events that took place between 1941 and 1945. Unlike Russian statistical data, the problem with these eye-witness reports is not that they are inaccurate. Especially when giving evidence for German atrocities against Russian civilians, many of these accounts are believable and compelling—in fact every bit as believable as the German report about Russian atrocities in Striegau.

The real problem is that there is something missing from Russian eye-witness accounts, especially from the accounts of front-line soldiers who took part in so many of these horrendous battles. What then is this missing element, and why is it missing to begin with?

This is one of the most critical questions for any student of the war, and it is a question that can probably only be discussed and contemplated, rather than clearly answered. But before finishing this line of thought, let us first go into some of the more specific areas of Russian behavior during the war.

Drunkenness

One of the early Viking rulers of Russia declared, "It is not possible to endure living in this country without strong drink."[2]

Russia has long had the world's foremost tradition of high alcohol consumption. Neither Irish nor Germans, Americans,

French, or Australians, all with their own fondness for alcohol, can compare with the Russians when it comes to drinking to excess. Alcohol is a leading component of many Asian cultures as well. In their heyday as well as in the present, the Mongols have been notorious consumers of strong drink. During the Middle Ages, Mongol invasions influenced Russian society in many ways, most of them negative. But the steppe hordes did not pass along their fondness for strong beverages—simply because this fondness had already been deeply ingrained in Russian culture for centuries.

The episode at Striegau encapsulate many of the horrifying scenes of 1945. Russians who had already whetted their appetite for revenge by memories of German crimes simply lost all their inhibitions under the influence of alcohol.

One of the problems with alcohol in Russian culture was its irregular availability, due to that country's eternally wretched system of distributing consumer goods and the necessities of daily life. Alcohol was manufactured everywhere, in the remotest villages, and was always closer at hand than say, new shovels or boots or sewing needles. But it was still not regularly available on a day-to-day basis, and thus no moderate tradition of consuming a satisfactory amount of drink with daily meals ever developed. A tradition such as this at least serves to regulate even fairly heavy consumption, as is seen in France and Germany and other countries.

In short, the Russians are among the world's most hideous binge drinkers. The Russian custom of never opening a bottle of vodka without draining it to the last drop can be quite unnerving to Western visitors. No less so is the custom of drinking not for merriment, for the sensation of being pleasantly drunk or even heavily drunk, but for the goal of becoming absolutely stupefied with drink on a routine basis.

In these respects, there is really no other comparable culture in the world.

Small glass vials of vodka had long been part of the ration kit for Russian soldiers. But these supplies were quickly consumed and never replaced according to any regular or predictable pattern. Especially earlier in the war, there were countless episodes of large quantities of vodka being made available just before an attack, in order to numb the soldiers' sensibilities about being sent forward en masse to almost certain death.

When the Russians invaded Germany in 1945, they discovered in village after village an amazing variety of goods which to them were simply unknown luxuries. The idea that the meanest German worker possessed such items as decent beds to sleep in, clocks, radios, silverware, paper, pens, household tools, matches, good clothes, linens, was dumbfounding to these invaders. Most importantly, every village and every city had large and easily accessible stocks of alcohol. The atrocities of 1945 were carred out in the fog of one of history's most epic drunken binges.

For years the soldiers of the Red Army had suffered not just from the cruelties of the German invaders, but from the brutal discipline, hardships, and privations of life within their own armed forces. Discipline especially was loosened once German territory was entered, and years of suffering and pent-up frustration resulted in a nearly spontaneous mass-orgy of drunken mayhem. The genie had at last been let out of its lamp, Pandora's box had been opened, and the outcome was truly astounding. Many Russian officers were shocked and dismayed by what they saw, but far more succumbed to the same temptations and became just as drunk and deranged as the enlisted men.

In circumstances like these it became nearly impossible to discipline anyone; in effect, the Red Army's notoriously strict system of discipline simply collapsed. Upper level commanders feared their armies might lose their fighting effectiveness before the Nazi beast was hammered down once and for all. (In fact a number of Soviet commentators have pointed to this collapse of discipline as being an important factor in the Russians' failure to capture Berlin more quickly in 1945.) In Silesia, General Konev took extremely harsh disciplinary action against numerous unit commanders for failing to restrain their soldiers; these men were demoted and sentenced to penal battalions, their names published on a long list subsequently distributed to other commanders for their own edification. But even when faced with these kinds of threats, most officers proved utterly incapable of curtailing the madness that now seemed to infect every battalion and company in the Red Army.

Russian soldiers attacked German women in a demented drunken rage. Any German men that stood in the way were usually killed instantly. Drunkenness enhanced black memories of relatives killed in the most ruthless ways during the German occupation of Russia; drunkenness enhanced black motives of revenge which now took shape in twisted and cunning varieties of the most sadistic torture.

As the Striegau report illustrates, Russian troops garrisoning German villages could go for weeks on end in a continual state of drunkenness. Every so often one of these men might emerge from his alcoholic frenzy, sober up, and look about himself. Even with memories of Nazi barbarism still fresh in his mind, he might be deeply ashamed by what he saw, signs of so many depraved acts being committed by his comrades and himself. Of course by then it was too late. He might repent of his filthy behavior and offer some act of kindness to a German civilian, in the form of a loaf of bread or perhaps momentary protection from the cruel acts of his drunken brethren. Reports of such paradoxical behavior were not uncommon, though they had little effect on the prevailing atmosphere of murder, rape, and hatred.

Such a momentarily sobered soldier might start drinking again a few hours later, and repeat the whole mad cycle all over again.

He might be tormented by urges of decency towards innocent civilians, yet also tormented by opposing urges of vengeance for his equally innocent murdered relatives in Russia, and perhaps tormented more than anything else by the urge to free himself from all the suffering of these years and get stark raving drunk for as long as possible, and in the meantime rape as many women as possible.

Vengeance

Revenge is often cyclical in nature, taking on the aspect of a vicious circle that grows larger and more all-consuming. This pattern was sadly apparent in the Russo-German War.

The German Army of 1941 did not descend on the Soviet Union with the intention of slaughtering Russian civilians. German soldiers were pleased to be greeted as liberators, welcomed with gifts of flowers, of bread and salt, in many regions of western Russia. One of the great themes of Nazi propaganda, that the Slavic peoples were subhuman, or untermenschen, was simply not taken very seriously by great numbers of German soldiers. There might also have been many thousands who did take this theme seriously, but such beliefs did not entail the wholesale extermination of the Russian populace.

All the same, it took only a short period of time for German brutality to rear its head.

This brutality took several distinct forms, each of which encouraged the Russians' desire for ultimate revenge.

The callous behavior of Nazi civilian administrators in the occupied rear areas of Russia is all too well known, and need not be discussed in great detail here. These men were advocates of all the most repellent aspects of the Nazi cult, including the untermenschen theme, which was far more real to them than to the typical front-line soldier. Civilians were soon obliged, under penalty of death, to live under the most obnoxious restrictions. People were dragooned into massive and brutal labor projects, always with inadequate supplies of food. Families were split up, and as the war went on more and more able-bodied men and women were deported to work in German factories and farms, in situations little different from slavery. German promises to abolish the detested agricultural communes and return land to individual farmers were almost never fulfilled. On the contrary, the Germans saw that the commune system made it easier to oversee and confiscate food supplies for their hungry armies; thus it was in their own interest to keep the system in place.

None of these measures was drastically different from many of the cruel acts perpetrated under Stalin's regime. But one can only imagine the sense of anguish and betrayal felt by these civilians who had looked—indeed looked quite desperately—for the German invasion to bring some kind of liberating, progressive changes to their lives. Nothing of the kind happened. Betrayal, disappointment, frustration, already simmering for decades, now began to seethe. (See addendum on pg. 546 for additional comments.)

Centuries of the most savage kind of oppression under the Mongols had had the effect of making Russians paranoid in the extreme about invading armies. In Western Europe, armies for centuries had routinely crossed back and forth over national borders. These transgressions were never welcome, but they were largely seen as an ongoing part of human affairs; armies in Western Europe did not normally threaten civilians with slavery or extermination. If the German occupiers in Russia had behaved more humanely, Russian paranoia might have abated. But instead it was exacerbated till it became a terrible fear of extermination at German hands which tended to unite the entire country. Nothing could have provoked these fears more than the awful travels of the SS Einsatzgruppen. These few battalion-sized units were miniscule in comparison with the huge overall numbers of German armed forces, yet their infamous deeds magnified the aura of German cruelty beyond all redemption. The Einsatzgruppen were tasked to liquidate commissars and anyone else who might fit under the broad category of potential subversives. Yet history has shown that this was more or less a smokescreen; more than anything else, the Einsatzgruppen were interested in killing Soviet Jews, which they did in numbers reaching to the hundreds of thousands.

Herein lies a certain irony. Russia has had a long history of virulent anti-Semitism. As recently as the years of the Communist Revolution and the civil war which followed it, Jews in the Ukraine were subjected to the most sickening massacres, large-scale orgiastic pogroms which ultimately resulted in death totals comparable to the ghastly tallies put up by the SS Einsatzgruppen twenty years later. It became a standard practice for the SS units to be assisted in their murders by anti-Semitic groups of Ukrainians, Byelorussians, Lithuanians, Latvians, and others.

All the same, the trail of slaughter was appalling, and countless thousands of more open-minded Russians viewed it with horror. The untermenschen propaganda suddenly became absolutely real, even to civilians who might have been treated tolerantly by German soldiers. For if the Germans were capable of so coldly exterminating the Jews, did it not seem possible that the equally despised Slavic peoples could be next? Indeed it did seem possible, even likely.

The treatment of Russian prisoners of war also served to fulfill these paranoid visions. They were routinely starved to death in enormous barren compounds, provided with supplies of food so inadequate as to be beneath contempt. Cannibalism flourished. Death totals ran in the millions. Some German apologists take issue with this situation, pointing to the great logistical difficulties posed by trying to supply their own armies with food in the depths of Russia. No one had expected to feed and care for such incredibly large numbers of Russian prisoners, at least two million by the end of 1941 alone. But the element of truth in these objections cannot disguise the overwhelming, and above all purposeful, neglect of these prisoners. Finding ways to feed them all would have been difficult, it is true, but in fact almost no attempt was made to feed them in the first place.

Some men escaped from these places, bearing their hellish

tales. Listeners could only think that if this was not a war of extermination, then what was?

Another irony: many men escaped these camps, but not to return to the unconquered areas of the mother country. Thousands of them fled starvation in the camps by enlisting as Hiwis (Hilfswillige) in the German army. These "voluntary helpers" were attached to almost every German army unit in Russia, performing various menial chores, assisting with cooking and above all with the arduous tasks of keeping the front-line units supplied. Some, if they were found to be trustworthy, were even armed to fight against their fellow countrymen. For obvious reasons, these Hiwis tended to have divided loyalties. But many were so grateful to be delivered from life in the camps that they looked on the ordinary German soldiers as saviours, serving them with surprising faithfulness. For one thing, their treatment in the German army was better in almost every respect than their earlier treatment in the brutal ranks of their own army. The food was better and the officers and noncoms did not beat them. They were not threatened with death or imprisonment at the slightest transgression. They were not sent out in suicidal waves against German artillery and machine guns. By and large, they found life among German soldiers to be more humane than life in the Red Army.

On the other hand, they could hardly forget the horrors of the German camps they had fled from in the first place. The shadow of Nazi terror was still there, even amidst the strange comradeship offered by ordinary German Landsers. The desertion rate among Hiwis was high. It was an uneasy relationship at best.

Partisan Warfare—Madness and Counter-Madness

All of the German atrocities discussed to this point—abuse and murder of civilians, starvation of prisoners—have been in the form of clear-cut provocations. They could not be described as being part of a vicious circle of revenge, with both parties being guilty to some extent. The Germans alone bore responsibility for these crimes.

But there was another aspect of German brutality in Russia that was more complicated, resulting in hundreds of thousands of civilian deaths, involving not only the inexcusable acts of Nazi administrators and SS death squads, but also the regular ranks of the German army. In this case the cycle of vengeance revolved over and over and over again, fanning enraged emotional fires that perhaps more than anything else would carry all the way back to Germany in 1945.

The situation in question here is the partisan warfare that raged continuously behind German lines. Nowhere in western Europe was there an underground resistance movement even remotely as violent and determined as the Russian partisan movement. Yugoslavia was the only occupied nation that could rank with the USSR in fielding these civilian armies. The ruthless, highly emotional nature of this kind of fighting resulted in the most spectacular massacres of Russian civilians, atrocities that were separate from the highly-focussed SS campaign against the Jews.

One German soldier wrote home that the worst thing about life in Russia was the snipers, which were everywhere. He did not mean snipers in the front lines, though they were present there as well. What he was referring to was the impossibility of moving anywhere in the rear areas without being shot at at any time. For all their military power, the Germans had almost no control over the vast interior regions of Russia. German troops garrisoned towns, roads, and railway lines, with varying degress of control; all other areas of the immense Russian wilderness became a kind of no-man's land, alternately mastered either by the partisans or by the constant German drives to eliminate the partisans.

It was in this arena that the typical Russian civilian faced the full unforgiving weight of German brutality. Russian cries of revenge for the murders of innocent loved ones originated more than anywhere else in the cruel excesses of this partisan war.

In this situation, at least, it can be clearly stated that the Germans were provoked to a large degree, and provoked over and over again.

It has often been said that partisans operating in the rear areas were given specific instructions—either by Stalin or by his minions in the NKVD—to commit cruel acts against unwary German soldiers. The logic behind this sadism was clear: the Germans would inevitably retaliate against the civilian population, thus serving to poison any potential bonds of friendliness or tolerance between these two groups. The last thing Stalin wanted was a civilian population in occupied Russia that was more well-disposed towards the Germans than towards himself.

No documents bearing these kinds of specific instructions have ever come to light, though much anecdotal evidence suggests they were a reality. It seems in no way unlikely that partisans did receive this kind of encouragement from Moscow. On the other hand, German soldiers captured by the Russians were obscenely tortured from the very first days of the war, with their mutilated corpses being left to be discovered later by their comrades. One must then consider the alternative possibility, that many partisan atrocities were simply spontaneous acts of cruelty that needed no prompting from Stalin or anyone else.

German soldiers were found who had been set on fire and strung up from trees. Many were simply mutilated with knives, their genitals hacked off and shoved down their throats. German heads were cut off and furtively assembled in grotesque rows at some village crossroads, there to be discovered by patrols the following day. In winter naked soldiers were doused with water until they froze solid, their torturers manipulating their right arms so they would freeze in the position of giving a Fuhrer salute. These amusing mannequins would then be positioned along a nearby road, there to greet the next German convoy to pass by. One creative partisan leader punished a civilian informer by cutting open the man's belly while he was still alive, then looping his intestines around and around a tree.

The German front-line soldiers involved in day-to-day combat in the trenches did not regularly experience this kind of thing. As a whole, their recollections of the war do not indicate frequent encounters with such horrors. Life in the combat zone was already bad enough. But a small dose of this kind of bestiality can go a long way, and partisan depredations were by no means rare occurrences. Regardless of the more lurid forms of torture, the prospect of simply being shot at from any direction at any time in the rear areas was enough to stretch German nerves to the breaking point.

The Germans responded to these activities in typically German fashion. Their grim methods of retaliation took the form of massive overkill. The extreme measures they took to deal with any kind of partisan or subversive activity tends to separate the Germans from other nations who have faced similar problems in various other modern wars.

The guerrilla fighting in Vietnam, for example, bore a great deal of similarity to the partisan warfare in Russia, particularly in terms of the unending nervous stress faced by American soldiers who could be shot at in any area at any time. Atrocious retaliatory measures against civilians were very much the same in both these wars. The massacre at My Lai was the direct result of emotional stress reaching the breaking point for American soldiers combating guerrilla warfare. It has been said that My Lai was far from the only instance of this kind of massacre—a claim which, even without specific evidence, seems fairly credible. French soldiers fighting in Indochina and Algeria were guilty of the same kind of behavior, as were Russians fighting in Afghanistan in later decades.

There are some German historians who would suggest that the Germany military in occupied Russia was faced with this same kind of emotional stress, and simply reacted in the same unfortunate fashion. They would claim that the racist Nazi world-view had very little to do with the horrors of partisan warfare in Russia. In some respects, it is hard to deny the truth of such claims. But in other respects, it is hard to ignore the German habit of routinely responding to these kinds of grievances with murderous and overwhelming force, making it a matter of standard practice to execute civilian hostages by the hundreds and by the thousands.

Russian villages in areas of partisan activity were routinely razed to the ground. If the German commander in the area were in enough of a rage, the inhabitants of the village could be burned alive inside these same buildings. German machine gunners would be positioned to mow down anyone attempting to flee. Civilians suspected of partisan activity were frequently executed on the spot. When the partisans proved impossible to catch, innocent hostages would be executed, hundreds at a time, either by hanging or firing squads.

Historians who suggest that these kinds of reprisals were not inherently related to the Nazi creed would be quite correct. Long before the rise of Adolph Hitler, the German military had had a tradition of responding with ruthless force to any signs of partisan warfare. A minimal degree of partisan activity in Belgium in World War One resulted in German executions of hundreds of civilian hostages, a display of Teutonic overkill which caught the attention of the world and did much to cast Germany, in many ways unfairly, in the villain's role in this conflict.

The full story of the partisan war in Russia may never be told. German military archives are much less explicit about specific actions taken during anti-partisan drives, than they are with regard to combat actions at the front. Memoirs of individual soldiers also become unaccountably vague when discussing the fight against the partisans. A number of grisly anecdotes stand out, but one is left with the impression that far more has been left unsaid.

The number of civilians killed during this atrocious secret war may never be known either, but estimates in the millions are probably not exaggerated. The hastily-dug graves of all these victims were discovered by the Russians during the great offensives of 1944, when the German invaders were at last expelled from Russian soil. These murders may not have been the result of a deliberate Nazi program of extermination, but probably more than any other living thing they inflamed Russian desires for vengeance, an exceedingly pitiless vengeance.

Further Remarks on Russian Memoirs and Eye-Witness Accounts

Any discussion of these topics would be aided immensely by the "missing element" mentioned earlier—that of Russian eye-witness reports.

The accounts of individual Red Army soldiers from the war do exist—but frustratingly, these accounts almost always bear the strange quality of being both there and not-there. Whether due to Communist censorship or to other factors more inherently related to Russian society, most combat reports from the Soviet side tend to be written in stilted, rather impersonal language, which makes it difficult to get a real grasp of these men as human beings. While many of the combat episodes described seem to be factually accurate, the tone of these accounts is often bland and unemotional, or else inflated with a tedious deadweight of heroic and patriotic phrases. There is little of the vividness, the pervasive climate of terror, stress, and physical hardship, that emerges over and over again from the memories of German soldiers.

There are some accounts of Nazi atrocities against Russian civilians which are both vivid and horrifying—but sadly, this vividness seems almost never to extend to the experiences of Red Army soldiers actually engaged in combat. One could read dozens upon dozens of Soviet battle accounts, written either by state propagandists or by men who participated in the fighting, and never once get any real impression of the horrendous casualties suffered by the Red Army during World War Two.

The cumulative effect of all this is a kind of mysterious opacity. One gets certain glimpses of how Russian soldiers lived and died, how they talked and what they felt, but in such superficial ways that one is left with the impression of an enormous gap existing between the written words and the real events.

There are few, if any, accounts—either in the form of state publications or private memoirs—which even begin to describe the orgy of murder and rape on German soil in 1945. This subject is less than vague; it is almost as if it never existed. Of course the Soviet Union is not the only nation to minimize, or even ignore, atrocities perpetrated by its own soldiers. But at least in the more intimate world of individual memoirs, some descriptions of this climate of insanity will usually emerge, be it only in the form of hints or dark suggestions. If one looks hard enough, one can find enough German accounts of German cruelty during the war—but any such corresponding accounts written by Russians about Russian behavior are almost non-existent.

Perhaps this lack is not surprising, given the climate of censorship and ideological conformity within the Soviet state, especially under Stalin. But the Russians had endured so many terrible provocations during the Nazi invasion of their country, that one might expect at least some mention of the equally terrible vengeance they later exacted upon their enemies on German soil. Russian behavior in eastern Germany in 1945 may have been appalling, but conceivably the state propaganda machine could have presented it in the light of an understandable explosion of rage against Nazi barbarism—a kind of grim moral fable, if you will.

But Soviet accounts do not take this approach either. They in fact take no approach at all—any discussion of Red Army atrocities in 1945 is apparently strictly taboo. Almost the only written evidence that does exist are the ravings of Ilya Ehrenburg. Some Soviet generals do mention the crazed drunken behavior of their soldiers, in terms of a falling-off in discipline and fighting effectiveness—but these accounts never graphically describe the true extent of the horrors endured by German civilians. Perhaps it was all too terrible for the Soviets to own up to, regardless of earlier Nazi atrocities on Russian soil.

Even memoirs and novels written by Russian combatants long after the war, even long after Stalin's death, do very little to lift this veil of opacity. The novels of Konstantin Simonov, Vassily Grossman, Anatoly Rybalkov—who all experienced the war first-hand—have generally been hailed by Western critics as being important works of literature about life in the Red Army on the Eastern Front. But Western critics have the bad habit of over-praising many works to come out of the Soviet Union—almost as if, because these books deal with such serious subjects, they must also be taken seriously as both works of literature and as authentic documents about the Soviet experience.

In reality, any close examination of these books would tend to suggest the opposite. While they do present an insider's view of life in the Red Army, they are not particularly well-written—and above all they do not graphically portray the anguish and brutality of the war on the Eastern Front. I must admit that I do not really understand the reasons for this; other factors besides state censorship seem to be involved, but what these other factors might be remains strangely elusive.

Rybalkov's books were published not only after the death of Stalin but after the collapse of Communism—yet his descriptions of the war against Nazi Germany remain as bland and sketchy as anything published in earlier decades. Grossman, like Alexander Solzhenitsyn, has been justly praised for exposing the evils of the Stalinist regime, but he is unimpressive when it comes to exposing the reality of combat as seen through Russian eyes. Simonov's DAYS AND NIGHTS, a lengthy account of Red Army soldiers during the Battle of Stalingrad, where Simonov himself was present as a war correspondent, is a strangely uninvolving book. In contrast to the horrors so graphically described by German survivors, its dullness—even uneventfulness—seems almost surreal.

Perhaps this opacity is related in some ways to the suffering and privations endured by the Russian people throughout their history, engendering a stoic and fatalistic outlook which might seem alien to Western readers. As if all the horrors of the war were only matter-of-fact occurrences within the context of other terrible events that had gone on for decades and centuries. But such blanket generalizations are almost always distorted and unfair, and in the end they do not even begin to offer an adequate explanation for what is really an overwhelming void. Some authorities point out that great numbers of Soviet soldiers were illiterate or semi-literate peasants, many of whom did not even speak Russian, which may in some measure account for the paucity of first-hand accounts. Perhaps so, but this explanation also seems dubious; illiteracy did not permeate the entire Red Army.

Perhaps someday there will be a great Russian book about the war—whether a novel, memoir, or work of history hardly matters—but such a work has yet to surface. Yet sometimes it seems equally likely that this disturbing void will remain unchanged—a hole and a silence set at the very heart of all the lore about this terrible conflict.

These few paragraphs can only scratch the surface of this perplexing subject. But it is an important subject, which will perhaps someday be more fully investigated by students of Russia and Russian literature, if not by the Russian people themselves.

Two More German Reports from 1945

Account of Medical Officer Major Jaenecke

In late January Major Jaenecke was sent to Graudenz on the Vistula; it was one of the few cities along that river still in German hands. Along the way he encountered endless columns of refugees fleeing from East Prussia, most of them stupefied with cold, misery, and fear, walking slowly, or else sitting silently in farm carts pulled by slowly walking draft animals.

As a doctor he interrupted his journey many times to attend to sick or injured people. A man hailed him and brought him to a farm cart standing in the middle of a snowy field. The man and his wife had been captured by a Russian tank crew a few days before. The woman now lay at the bottom of the cart, bleeding uncontrollably from her vagina. Jaenecke had performed many difficult operations in freezing conditions during his years on the Russian Front. An icy wind was blowing; the woman's clothes were filthy and soaked with blood. Her pulse was almost gone and Jaenecke doubted anything could be done for her. He gave her two injections and then attempted a tamponnade of the uterus.

As he did this the husband, who had a broken arm and looked very sick, related in a monotone how they had finally escaped. His wife had not begun bleeding until a day or so later. Before then, while the tank crew and perhaps fifteen other soldiers were raping her, the husband had been forced to hold up a lantern so the Russians could see her face and body. At one point he dropped the lantern, and that was when one of them had clubbed him and broken his arm. He was then forced to pick up the lantern again with his other arm, holding the light over his wife until the Russians had finished with her.

After Jaenecke finished the operation he walked back to his truck and headed on towards Graudenz. The woman had already lost too much blood; he doubted he had been able to save her. When he finally reached Graudenz, after this and many similar incidents, he filed a report about what he had seen. It concluded with the following paragraphs, which—especially coming from a German—offer an unusual degree of insight into the unspeakable acts of those days. I have italicized certain phrases for emphasis.

The things I heard from the refugees during those final days sound so incredible that people living in more peaceful times will probably not believe them. There are still human beings who do such things—who find an incomprehensible pleasure in raping the same woman over and over, dozens and dozens of times, even while other women standing nearby are left untouched. *THERE IS A PERVERSE HATRED BEHIND THIS WHICH CANNOT BE EXPLAINED BY PHRASES ABOUT BOLSHEVISM, OR THE SO-CALLED ASIATIC MENTALITY, OR BY THE ASSERTION THAT THE RUSSIAN SOLDIERS HAVE ALWAYS CONSIDERED THE WOMEN OF THE CONQUERED AS THEIR BOOTY.* I was in Poland in 1939 when the Russians moved in [dividing that nation with the Germans] and I did not see a single woman being molested.

This shows the frightful power of propaganda. Goebbels once planted in the masses of our soldiers the notion that the Russians were Bolshevist subhumans. God knows our men are not by nature cruel. But that notion was drilled into them until many of them believed it. How else could German soldiers have stood by in 1941 while Russian prisoners of war literally died like flies, by the tens of thousands? And Goebbels' opponents in Moscow—what pictures must they have painted of us Germans, to unleash this flood of murder and rape?[3]

There is an awful, almost unbearable kind of human understanding in these words. Compared with all the accounts that have come out of Auschwitz and other such places, there exist almost no accounts of the German camps in Russia where millions of Soviet prisoners were routinely starved to death. Yet it is clear that Major Jaenecke was present at some of those camps, probably in a futile attempt to provide medical assistance to those thousands "dying like flies."

There can be no doubt that the ravings of the Soviet propagandist Ilya Ehrenburg did encourage Russian soldiers in their mad, murderous rampages—stripping them of their inhibitions every bit as much as the influence of alcohol. It is Ehrenburg that Major Jaenecke is referring to when he speaks of Goebbels' opponents in Moscow. But even Jaenecke's words, insightful as they are in attempting to compare two hideous systems of propaganda, still leave out the most terrible motivation of all—that of vengeance.

Account of Frau Hanisch

Frau Hanisch fled from Breslau at the end of January, just before the Russians besieged that city. Once she passed a group of about twenty Russian soldiers waiting in line to rape an old German woman, who looked to be about seventy. It was clear that the old woman was already dead, but this fact did not seem to deter the soldiers' lust. They all remained lined up with great eagerness, each awaiting his turn to satisfy himself upon her corpse.

Sometimes even Soviet officers, when coming across this kind of behavior, had to turn away in revulsion. Frau Hanisch said it was the most horrible thing she had ever seen.

Frau Hanisch wrote about these sights in a letter to her mother dated January 29, 1945, which was mailed from the town of Striegau. This would have been only a few days before the Russians reached Striegau and began the massacres described in the previous chapter. Whether Frau Hanisch was still present in the town at that time is not known.[4]

PART IV
HUNGARY

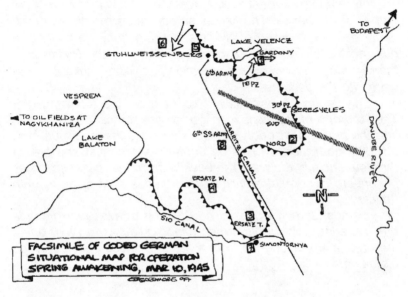

TO
BUDAPEST

LAKE VELENCZ

6 STUHLWEISSENBERG 5 GARDONY 1

6ᵗʰ ARMY

1ˢᵗ PZ

VESPREM

3ᵈ PZ BEREGYELES

TO OIL FIELDS AT
NAGYKHANIZA

SUD

LAKE
BALATON

6ᵗʰ SS ARMY
8 NORD 2

SARROTZE CANAL

DANUBE RIVER

ERSATZ W.
4

N

SIO CANAL

3
ERSATZ T.

7 SIMONTORNYA

**FACSIMILE OF CODED GERMAN
SITUATIONAL MAP FOR OPERATION
SPRING AWAKENING, MAR. 10, 1945**
CBLACKMORE 97

🔺🔺🔺🔺 GERMAN LINES ON MAR. 10

▨▨▨▨ OPERATIONAL BOUNDRY
BETWEEN SS & ARMY TROOPS

1 KAMPFGRUPPE BRADEL ADVANCES
TO GARDONY, MAR. 11

2 NORTH & SOUTH DIVISIONS
(SS DAS REICH & SS HOENSTAUFEN)

3 TOTENKOPF REPLACEMENT
DETATCHMENT (SS HITLER JUGEND)

4 WIKING REPLACEMENT DETATCHMENT
(SS LEIBSTANDARTE)

5 SS WIKING DIVISION

6 SOVIET COUNTER OFFENSIVE
BEGINNING MAR. 15

7 GERMAN BRIDGEHEAD ACROSS
SIO CANAL, MAR. 11-15

8 NOTE: PRESENCE OF 6ᵗʰ
SS ARMY NOT INDICATED
ON GERMAN MAPS

Street fighting continues into the night. First Maier, the cook, spots movement in the house across the way and hoses it down with a flamethrower. But the Russians continue to bring up heavy weapons and position them in windows and doorways. Now it is Jonas who fires a panzerfaust over there, blowing off an entire corner of the house. The flames spread more rapidly and suddenly they see a group of civilians crawling from the coal cellar out into the street. The SS men keep firing at the Russians in the burning windows overhead while the civilians make their escape into the darkness.

The fighting subsides until about noon the following day. Then a group of Russians manages to get across the street and into the house next door. The SS men fire a machine gun from the bathroom. Jonas picks up another panzerfaust and fires it through a hole in the wall. The backfire from the rocket scorches his uniform. The explosion next door sends dust flying in both houses.

Flames, screaming . . . The SS men throw every grenade they have into the rubble. When things quiet down Wolff offers the crew a sip of cognac from a flask he keeps stashed inside his gas mask.

15

STALINGRAD BY THE DANUBE

To the Bitter End in Budapest

Pest had fallen on January 18th. Only pontoon bridges remained intact across the Danube. Then they too were blown up as the survivors of this holocaust retreated into Buda to make their last stand.

By this time SS Wiking had already retreated from the northern suburbs, the closest that any of the German relief attempts would get to the city. But January 18th also marked the beginning of the third and final relief attempt by IV SS Corps, coming from the south this time, from the area of Lake Balaton. False rays of hope would continue to cheer and torment the minds of the desperate garrison.

Buda was the administrative seat of the capital. Massive government buildings and old royal palaces rose up in blocks and tiers on the slopes of Castle Hill, the highest ground in the city. Smoke rose incessantly from its looming walls. From the streets below, Castle Hill resembled a volcano, the majestic, shell-blasted buildings recalling some scene from Pompeii just before the black cloud of Vesuvius destroyed it forever. Budapest had lain under such a pall of smoke for over a month, with still another month of fighting to go. Stalin Organs unleashed their rockets with their peculiar firing pattern resembling quick successive digits of shrieking flame, destroying whole buildings at a time, sometimes whole blocks. The Red Air Force was overhead hour after hour, flying in at rooftop level through the columns of smoke and hot updrafts, releasing arsenals of close-support munitions, including phosphorus bombs.

Phosphorus—that cousin of napalm, surely one of the vilest weapons to emerge from World War Two. It burned horribly, and burning people could not escape by plunging into the waters of the Danube. Phosphorus had the peculiar property of clinging to the skin and re-igniting when coming back into contact with the air, even after immersion. Victims who survived phosphorus burns would present one of the war's most horrible sights—even days later the skin on the faces could be pulled away like molten wax, the unquenched inner fire still continuing to eat at the living flesh. Perhaps the dead were luckier. The dead victims of this foul chemical would be so shrivelled up and mummified that in all likelihood they would be scarcely noticeable amongst all the debris and dark smoke and other bodies more whole.

The defenders had a substantial number of 4-barrelled 20mm flak guns belonging to the Feldhernhalle Panzergrenadier Division and the 8th SS Cavalry Division. They added to the hail of metal flying around above the city, downing Soviet aircraft but also posing a threat to the JU-52s attempting to bring in supplies to the tiny landing strip that remained in the one-square mile area held by the defenders. Frequently the JU-52s had to resort to parachute drops which all too often fell into no-man's land, fought over as both sides tried to retrieve whatever precious cargo was in the supply bombs. (Powdered chocolate? Toilet paper? Shells? Medicine? Boxes of Iron Crosses?)

The 20mm flak was called the "machine-gun cannon" and was equally deadly against ground targets, particularly attacking infantry. The peculiar quick-firing thudding of this gun had long been one of the most familiar sounds of combat on the Eastern Front, along with the blurring noise of the MG 42 machine gun with its tremendous rate of fire. It was almost impossible for the Russians to attack along city streets through such an intense and concentrated storm of metal. Instead they took to the houses and advanced from one house to the next by blasting through the walls.

The defenders also resorted to this tactic, as a means of communicating between housing blocks without having to enter the streets. Hellish hand-to-hand combat would take place when the two sides met in these "hole in the wall" encounters, particularly in the large residential sectors of Pest before it fell. Hand grenades, machine pistols, and razor-sharp spades were the weapons of these mad indoor skirmishes. "The combined fire power of five Schmeisser machine pistols in such an enclosed space had to be seen to be believed," wrote Heinz Landau.[1] Other weapons used inside apartment blocks had an equally magnified effect. The defenders liked to fire panzerfausts through these holes in the walls, wiping out an entire roomful of Russians with one shot. Unfortunately the release of rockets gases in such a confined space also had a tendency to burn the defenders; it was difficult to know where to stand to get out of the way. The lucky ones escaped with only scorched uniforms, though some were burned more severely. Everyone had minor burn wounds on his hands from randomly brushing against hot gun barrels at all hours of the day and night.

The air was filled with the powdery acrid smell of volatilized brick, which at least served to absorb some of the more hideous odors of rotting flesh. All the normal battlefield smells would become more concentrated in this dense urban terrain—cordite, smoke, gasoline, burning rubber, a hundred other vaguely toxic materials also burning, burning flesh, rotting flesh, excrement. A stench to fill the nostrils and lungs as if men were fighting at the bottom of a refuse heap that had been smoldering for months. Which, in effect, was very much what Budapest had become.

Stalingrad stands out in human memory as the greatest urban battle of the war, the epitome of depraved combat within the skeletal wrecks of buildings, yet Budapest was its equal in every respect. These two cities formed the war's grimmest examples of prolonged house-to-house combat, going on month after month.

Warsaw had been nearly razed to the ground during the uprising of the Polish resistance in the late summer of 1944, but much of that battle had been more in the nature of a mass-slaughter: over 100,000 dead Polish civilians against only a few thousand German casualties. Stalingrad and Budapest were the sites of the most tenacious close-quarter melees between two well-armed adversaries. German soldiers who managed to survive—and there was not very many—would repeat time after time that the fighting in Budapest was as ferocious as anything they ever saw.

Only a few months earlier, German soldiers arriving in Budapest had been amazed to see civilian life proceeding as if there were no war. Hungarians filled the theaters and cafes, restaurants were stocked with food and drink, women strolled the streets in fur coats. Motor traffic moving along the streets and avenues contributed to the atmosphere of busy, unconcerned urban normalcy. Civilians wandered through all the shops during the Christmas season, even after the Russians had surrounded the city.

Budapest had lived on in a kind of dream world during the

war years. It had been subjected to only a few token air raids. There was no rationing; farm produce from the rich Hungarian steppes was always plentiful. The Hungarian government under the prudent Admiral Horthy had never made more than a token gesture of military support for Hitler's war in Russia. After a number of Hungarian divisions were wiped out outside Stalingrad, Horthy withdrew almost all his remaining fighting units from Russia, effectively taking Hungary out of the war in 1943. No doubt it was a wise move, but unwisely the civilian population simply went on about its daily affairs as if this reprieve would last forever. Perhaps it is only natural for people to cling to the semblance of normalcy for as long as possible.

Hitler, distressed by Horthy's lackadaisical attitude towards the Bolshevik menace, had sent German troops in to occupy Hungary in March of 1944, but even then the Hungarians were still technically allies in the Axis partnership, and the ordinary lives of civilians were in no way constricted as they were elsewhere in German-occupied Europe.

In the fall of 1944 Hitler had gone a step further, sending in his ace commando-cum-troublemaker Otto Skorzeny to instigate a coup that deposed Admiral Horthy, replacing his government with the crackpot and virulently anti-Semitic fascist regime of the Hungarian Arrowcross Party. A Jewish population which previously had lived in an island of safety in the middle of Nazi-occupied Europe was now subjected to a reign of terror at the hands of their own countrymen. A brief but horrible era had begun. Thugs wearing the green Arrowcross armband rivalled concentration camp guards in their ruthless persecution and murder of Hungary's Jews. (Assisted, it must be said, by many of Adolf Eichmann's German SS teams. Eichmann had long wanted to get his hands on the Hungarian Jews, who up to now had remained so irritatingly out of reach.)

But for everyone else in Budapest, life continued to go on more or less normally. Even after the Russians invaded the country in late 1944, there was no mass flight of civilian refugees to the west. People seemed to hope, naively, that somehow they would not be sucked into the maelstrom of destruction. At worst, the German-backed Arrowcross government would be thrown out by the Russians, and then hopefully the Russians would just keep their war moving on towards the German border, leaving Hungary and Budapest to recuperate with minimal damage.

Instead, Budapest became a Dante-esque hell, with at least half the civilian population trapped within the city limits as the siege raged on.

The Defenders—an SS Motley Crew

The defenders were made up of a strange combination of military forces and nationalities. The German army was mainly represented by the Feldhernhalle Division and the 13th Panzer Division. (Ironically, Feldhernhalle had been created from the surviving cadres of 60th Panzergrenadier Division, which had been wiped out at Stalingrad two years earlier.) Waffen SS units were also present in large numbers, perhaps fate's way of compensating for the absence of any Waffen SS troops during the Stalingrad disaster. Out of almost 20,000 SS men, less than two hundred would ever escape from Budapest.

Most of these SS men belonged either to the 8th SS Cavalry Division Florian Geyer or the 22nd SS Cavalry Division Maria Theresa. Together they formed the IX SS Mountain Corps under SS General Pfeffer-Wildenbruch, who was also in overall command of the Budapest garrison. (The reference to "mountain" troops was completely meaningless; for some reason, German units were often designated by these kinds of misnomers.) The SS Polizei Division, formed early in the war from ordinary policemen who in most cases had been drafted into the Waffen SS, also had a few battalions in Budapest, though the main body of this unit would be found in Pomerania as part of Operation Sonnenwende.

The two SS cavalry divisions both contained large contingents of foreigners, primarily ethnic Germans from Rumania, Hungary, and the Banat farming region of Yugoslavia. They spoke German with their peculiar accents or often barely spoke the language at all. Maria Theresa in particular was really a Hungarian Army (Honved) unit that had been co-opted into the Waffen SS, staffed with only a few German officers and NCOs. The rest of the officers and almost all the enlisted men were Hungarians of German descent who originally had been slated to be drafted into the Honved, or Hungarian Armed Forces. A treaty had been arranged with Admiral Horthy before he was deposed from power, which had allowed these men to be transferred to this nominally German SS division.

In reality, Maria Theresa was more of a Hungarian version of one of the "foreign volunteer" divisions, along the lines of SS Nordland, SS Nederland, or the Wallonian SS of Leon DeGrelle. But the comparison is still not exact, for almost all of the men of Maria Theresa were conscripts rather than volunteers; the treaty signed by Horthy and Hitler had not given them any choice about which unit, or even which nationality, they would serve under. Normally, this awkward combination of circumstances would not have boded well for the fighting morale of these men. Other foreign SS units which had been built around cadres of sometimes unenthusiastic conscripts, notably in Yugoslavia, had had poor fighting records, with the troops often taking out their displeasure at being dragooned into the SS war machine by conducting massacres and frightful vendettas against civilian fellow countrymen. (As always in the Balkans, these bloody feuds were carried out against countrymen of different ethnic backgrounds—Croat versus Serb, Muslim versus Serb, etc etc—leading in no small degree to the hatreds and cycles of revenge that still plague the Balkans today.)

But Maria Theresa, despite these handicaps, would turn out to be a determined fighting force. The men had no illusions that the Russian invasion of Hungary would somehow be benign, simply passing through on the road to Germany. Russian atrocities against civilians, though not reaching the epidemic proportions seen in Silesia and East Prussia, were already being widely reported. The men of Maria Theresa had an excellent rapport with their fellow countrymen and were one of the mainstays of the defense of Budapest. Basically, they were fighting to keep a murderous and deranged-seeming foreign invader from overrunning their country; in this respect, they had much in common with the Latvian and Estonian SS units fighting the Russians in the Baltic states. They were equipped almost exclusively with weapons "borrowed" from the Hungarian army, some of which, notably the Zrinyi tank destroyer, were put to very good use during the siege.

So much for the ostensibly German military presence in Budapest. The remainder of the garrison, that is to say more than half, consisted of the regular Hungarian army units of the Honved. Here, fighting morale varied considerably, with the result that German troops could never be sure if Honved units fighting at their side could be relied upon or not. Their record during the early days of the campaign in Russia had been poor. In 1941, Admiral Horthy had been more or less coerced by Hitler, in the form of vague but potent threats, into joining his attack on the Soviet Union. The Hungarians had never had any real basis for a quarrel with the Russians, and their combat performance had reflected this. For the soldiers of the Honved, it had been a strange war indeed. After taking heavy losses in Russia for the first two years, they had been almost completely withdrawn from the campaign by Horthy, returning to the deceptively peaceful environment of their native land in 1943. Only a token presence had remained inside Russia, and these troops were used almost exclusively for security or anti-partisan duties.

But now the war had returned, returned with a vengeance, and this time the Hungarian army was fighting in defense of its homeland. This brought mixed results. Some units were poorly trained and had no enthusiasm for fighting a war which they believed the Germans had forced onto their country; many of these men deserted to the Russians, and a few Hungarian Communist units were formed. Others wound up being forcibly incorporated into the Red Army; others were simply imprisoned or shot by the notoriously capricious Russians.

But scattered throughout the surviving divisions of the Honved were thousands of fiercely anti-Communist soldiers. These men would fight as hard as the Germans or the Hungarian-Germans during the siege of Budapest, though as a whole their units tended to lack cohesion and discipline.

Finally, there were the militia bands of the Arrowcross Party, small in number (only several thousand) but ferocious in battle. They took equal pride in acts of courage against the Russians and acts of sadism against the Jews. They were completely ungovernable, as the Arrowcross leader Ferenc Szelasi had already fled Budapest in November when the siege began. His thugs subsequently wandered the city, looting Jewish dwellings, pulling Jews out of housing blocks marked with the yellow star and shooting them with great displays of vicious delight, then toppling their bodies into the Danube.

It was a hideous situation, rife with irony. Adolf Eichmann, the SS scourge of the Jews of occupied Europe, had been forced to abandon his mission of extermination upon the arrival of the

Russians; he had fled the city along with Szelasi. The Arrowcross depredations became so sickening that the SS garrison commander Pfeffer-Wildenbruch finally decided to take measures to protect the Jews. A wholesome irony indeed. These measures consisted mainly of placing a protective guard at the entrances to the two large Jewish ghettos on the Pest side of the river. Budapest thus witnessed some of the strangest scenes of the entire Jewish tragedy during the war, in which Waffen SS soldiers sometimes forcibly intervened to keep Arrowcross lynch mobs from going about their ugly business. Even bizarre spectacles such as this had their own curious sub-plots: photos exist showing SS soldiers and Arrowcross militiamen chatting amiably at the guard stations around the ghettos. Despite their temporary role as protectors, it is clear that not all the SS men were greatly perturbed by the Arrowcross reign of terror.

In any case, with the fall of Pest on January 18th, the pogrom atmosphere disappeared. Thousands of Jews had been shot, tortured, or otherwise murdered, but over 100,000 still survived inside their ghettos (which had also served to protect them somewhat from the savage combat raging everywhere else) to be liberated by the Russians. Despite their own traditions of anti-Semitism, the Soviets sympathized, at least officially, with the plight of the Jews, and for the most part spared them from the kinds of drunken atrocities they were perpetrating against other Hungarian civilians. It was not uncommon for the Red Army to perform acts of cruelty with one hand and acts of benevolence with the other, for the Russians also issued supplies of bread and other staples to the starving citizens of Pest.

Meanwhile the fight to the end continued in Buda on the west bank of the Danube, dominated by the grim smoking elevation of Castle Hill. In vaults and tunnels beneath these heights, thousands of wounded men lay in dank confined misery. Inside a tunnel next to the railroad station, a passenger train was serving as a hospital for other wounded men. On January 29th the battle log for Pfeffer-Wildenbruch's IX SS Corps reported that the wounded men would soon outnumber men fit for duty.

Above ground, every available artillery piece was set up on Castle Hill, dominating the Russian approaches to the defensive cordon, by now less than one square mile in area. For weeks a number of 88 mm flak guns had been keeping Russian tanks at bay with their deadly combination of power and accuracy. Shells for these weapons were at a premium, a top priority on the list of supplies being flown in or parachuted by the JU-52s. A landing strip had been created at the Budapest racetrack some weeks earlier, but by late January it lay in a kind of no-man's land completely exposed to Russian fire. Work was underway to construct another landing strip, though by this time the defensive perimeter was so constricted that it too would almost surely be under continuous shellfire when, or if, it was ever finished. Red Army units overran this new site for a few hours on January 19th, before being thrown back in a counterattack by parts of SS Maria Theresa.

Needless to say, almost all supplies at this point were arriving by the haphazard method of parachute drop. The dominating terrain of Castle Hill provided a good aiming point for the pilots, but many supply bombs still fell into Russian hands or into the Danube. Silk parachute canopies became tangled up with the bobbing corpses of Jews and other dead floating in the river. At the beginning of February the river froze over, with the dead imbedded in the ice or sprawled on top of it.

As they had been during their fruitless efforts to keep Stalingrad supplied, so the JU-52s were also shot down in large numbers over Budapest. These missions were becoming more and more suicidal, with two or three planes being shot down out of flights of ten or twelve almost every day. Night drops were attempted to reduce these casualties, but the planes still had to fly in at low altitude, silhouetted against the backdrop of flames over the city and passing through clouds of Soviet anti-aircraft fire.

Finally the stocks of artillery shells were exhausted. The crews of the 88mms and the other field pieces abandoned their guns to fight as infantry. A gunner from the artillery regiment of SS Florian Geyer reported that his field piece was down to an allotment of six shells per day, though under the circumstances this might almost be considered an abundance. Armored vehicles could no longer maneuver in the steep, rubble-clogged streets around Castle Hill; these crews were also forced to fight as infantry. Some tanks remained in use as stationary strong points, but they drew volumes of enemy fire as soon as they were spotted and were soon put out of action, or else simply abandoned by men who found it safer to fight from the chaotic shelter of the surrounding rubble.

Food supplies were also becoming critical, though they would not reach the levels of mass-starvation seen at Stalingrad. The Russians were not inclined to wait and starve the Budapest defenders into submission. The way things were going, ammunition stocks would be used up before the food.

Account of Heinz Landau

One of the SS defenders was an ethnic German from the Siebenbergen region of Rumania, Heinz Landau, who has left a vivid but in some ways rather baffling account of his participation in the siege.

In fact, his entire wartime career was rather peculiar and merits some background explanation. If nothing else, it illustrates the strange tangle of conflicting loyalties, ethnic hatreds, and different military roles taken on by Eastern Europeans of German descent.

The German community in Rumania—Landau refers to them as Saxons—had been placed in what they considered an unjust situation following the widespread gerrymandering of national borders after World War One. Though these Saxons had never been part of the German nation, they had never been part of Rumania either, until Siebenbergen was annexed by that country in 1919. Previously, this region had been part of the Austro-Hungarian empire, and in reality it had been allowed to function almost autonomously, a kind of semi-independent German state that had existed for several hundred years in the hills of Transylvania.

The Saxons had deeply resented their sudden assimilation into the Rumanian nation. It was not so much a matter of persecution at the hands of a new overlord, as the flourishing of a deep ethnic antagonism brought about by the mixing of two cultures that had previously existed separately. More specifically, the largely autonomous lifestyle enjoyed by the Saxons was now hindered by the introduction of Rumanian laws, Rumanian government officials, and Rumanian settlers.

Basically, these two groups of people simply did not like each other. Landau minces no words in this respect, describing Rumanians as "dirty, malodorous, greasy-haired, nose-picking low-lifes who enjoy hanging around at places of ill repute." The

Saxons were a prosperous, orderly community—typical of German enclaves elsewhere in the world—and the Rumanians were regarded as little more than a rabble of peasants. The reader is left to wonder how the Rumanians viewed the Saxons, but it is not hard to infer strong feelings of German cultural arrogance from Landau's account, no matter how legitimate the grievances of his people. To be fair, he does report having some Rumanian friends—no doubt from the better classes of gentry—and this climate of mutual dislike may never have degenerated into more serious forms of persecution. Regardless of the unwanted intrusions by the Rumanian government, the Saxons continued to live as prosperously as before.

Ironically, it was Rumania's Axis partnership with Hitler's Germany that served to heighten the antagonism of the Saxons. They had hoped for Hitler to pressure the government of Marshal Antonescu into granting independence to Siebenbergen, or else simply to seize the region by force. The Saxons' wishes were ignored. Hitler was satisfied that German troops were allowed to enter Rumania, and especially that the Reich now had exclusive access to the oilfields at Ploesti. He had no wish to upset this agreeable situation by concerning himself with the political problems of a few thousand ethnic Germans. He had a good working relationship with Marshal Antonescu, a hardline fascist dictator with dreams of aggrandizement that Hitler would have understood only too well. (In this respect he was the exact opposite of Hungary's Admiral Horthy.) With Antonescu firmly dragging his nation along, willingly or not, Rumania would become Germany's most important ally in the war against the Soviet Union.

Even before the advent of Operation Barbarossa, the Saxons were beginning to show signs of resistance to Antonescu's rule. Above all they were determined not to be drafted into the Rumanian army, a primitive and brutal force that much resembled the Russian army. There was a deep division between officers and enlisted men, with the lower ranks frequently disciplined by beatings from officers and NCOs. Young Saxons commonly evaded the draft by disappearing into the Transylvanian mountains, or, as in Landau's case, by surreptitiously joining one of the German units that were now stationed throughout the country.

Landau was thus serving unofficially with a Luftwaffe anti-aircraft battery in Ploesti when the invasion of the Soviet Union commenced in June of 1941. Within days his German commander informed him that the unit would be transferred to some sector of the Russian Front. Surprisingly, considering the normal German regard for regulations, Landau was allowed to accompany them in his entirely unofficial status as a foreign national. He was far from the only one to take this course. Thousands of other Saxons attached themselves to German units in order to avoid serving in the army of their own country.

In one respect, the end result of all this was academic— these men were still going to have to fight in the savage and all-consuming campaign in the East. Landau saw little action in 1941; his Luftwaffe battery did not have much to shoot at after the Russian air force was all but swept from the skies during the initial weeks of the invasion. But this period of inactivity would be more than compensated for by the years of madness that were to follow.

In December, he received the dismaying news that Antonescu had protested vehemently to Hitler about the thousands of Saxons who had chosen to don German rather than Rumanian uniforms. Hitler consistently took an amenable stance towards this fellow dictator who was willing to provide so many of his own troops for the Russian Front meatgrinder. An agreement was reached whereby all Saxon troops would be dismissed from their adopted German units, in essence returning them to the jurisdiction of Antonescu's armed forces.

"I was sick with apprehension. I would never submit to the Rumanians!"[2]

Thus did Heniz Landau express his sentiments, while immediately casting about for some new loophole to extricate himself from Rumanian service. He quickly found one.

Antonescu had granted SS Reichsfuhrer Himmler the right to recruit ethnic Germans for the ranks of the Waffen SS. Perhaps for some Saxons this was not an attractive alternative, but Landau found it an agreeable solution. He had been impressed by Waffen SS units he had seen in Russia and enlisted in their ranks without hesitation. Now, at last, he was officially a member of the German armed forces, and would remain so until the end.

It was at this point that the nightmare of fighting on the Eastern Front fully revealed itself. Momentarily we will move on to the more specific horrors of Landau's days in Budapest in

1945, but it must be said that his Waffen SS experiences in Russia were filled with hellish ordeals from beginning to end. He was posted to the 2nd SS Cavalry Brigade, a unit which would eventually become part of the 8th SS Cavalry Division Florian Geyer, ultimately destined for extinction in the ruins of Budapest.

Landau's first taste of real combat came in the horrible winter of 1941/1942. Like so many German soldiers, he found the severity of the Russian climate to be almost beyond description. His most telling observation was that thousands of men who survived this frozen agony were so broken in spirit that they spent the rest of the war institutionalized in mental hospitals.

Next came anti-partisan duties in the summer of 1942. The SS cavalry brigades had already become notorious for atrocities committed in the hinterland of occupied Russia. Landau makes only scant mention of this, in the vein of many other Germans who prefer not to go into great detail when recalling partisan warfare. He indicates that he was present at a lot of executions of Russian civilians, by either hanging or firing squad. He also says that the stress of this kind of guerrilla fighting in the rear areas, where a man could be shot at, stabbed, or grenaded by unknown enemies in civilian garb at any time, was worse than being at the front. He describes the consequently vile mood of his SS comrades as follows:

> Soon our nerves were raw, our customary cool, orderly and disciplined behavior turned to raw hatred. Eye for eye, tooth for tooth; the bloodbath was now in full swing. We soon buried an alarming number of comrades, in most cases never sure where the shot had come from.[3]

Landau himself barely escaped being buried somewhere in partisan country. After a wild chase on horseback, he became involved in a frenzied hand-to-hand skirmish with partisans wearing tattered Russian uniforms. He reports killing one or more of these men, receiving in return a bayonet thrust to his gut which left his intestines spilling from a gaping wound.

After recovering in hospital, he was posted back to the strange peace and quiet of occupied Western Europe, where German soldiers at this point in the war were almost never troubled by any kind of violent underground resistance. In December of 1942 he was transferred to the Wiking SS Division and sent back to Russia, where he became swept up in another winter of brutal combat. But we have already drifted rather far afield in tracing Landau's career. Readers curious for further details are referred to his memoir GOODBYE TRANSYLVANIA, certainly one of the more grisly accounts of the campaign in the East. In fairness to Landau, his tale bears little resemblance to the perverted glamor and glory found in Leon DeGrelle's memoirs. Landau's toughness and bitterness, his sarcastic soldier's slang, his cool tone that often abruptly changes into barely controlled rage and grief, all show a more human aspect of human nature.

And so at last we find him in the hell of Budapest in 1945. It is here that we encounter some of the more baffling elements of his story. He had made a brief, rather uneventful appearance in the Battle of the Bulge in the closing days of 1944. Budapest was already surrounded by the Russians at this time, so Landau could not have been trapped there at the beginning of the siege.

He reports fighting his way into the city with an unidentified SS unit sometime during January of 1945, even though no official reports exist of any German units breaking INTO the siege ring from outside.

This is brought up not to call Landau's veracity into account; as mentioned in earlier chapters, the memories of combat veterans are sometimes riddled with these perplexing anomalies. Like DeGrelle and Werner Adamcyk, he did not set his experiences on paper till many years after the war. One longs for a clearer explanation of exactly how he did get into Budapest, but the grotesque vividness of his memories leave no doubt that he was there.

Inside Budapest, sometime in January of 1945:

> I clearly remember kneeling amongst the massacred corpses of our soldiers, hacked to pieces in a frenzy of bloodlust, and typical Russian custom, always their genitals cut off and stuffed into their mouths. Women of all ages were ravished, their vaginas slashed open to the umbilicus and the heads, face first, of the men and boys pushed inside, in some cases while still alive. There were the bodies of small children and babies, their remains literally smeared on the walls, and

to crown it all these sub-humans then defecated all over the bodies. I knelt, vomiting, the pain in my stomach worse than ever, and I prayed like I never had before in my life.

"Almighty God, let us push back these animals, let us wipe them off the face of the earth or, failing that, let them loose on the Western Allies, let THEM experience what it is like fighting these people."[4]

A few hours after coming across these spectacles, Landau and his men found some Russian prisoners being guarded by Hungarian gendarmes. The SS soldiers promptly marched the prisoners over to the nearest scene of Soviet butchery and shot each one of them through the head.

This is possibly the single most grotesque passage I have ever come across in any memoir of the war. It was not written until the mid-1980s, and it seems to have emerged from decades of pent-up horror and rage. Few, if any, German memoirs from the immediate post-war decades can match the nearly demented passion of these paragraphs. Judging from other accounts that have also been written more recently, one might suspect that it has taken all these decades for German survivors—and especially Waffen SS survivors—to even begin to speak freely about some of the events they witnessed on the Eastern Front.

Like so many of the defenders, Landau quickly became an adept "panzer-knacker" (tank-buster) with the panzerfaust. If none of these rocket launchers were handy, men would roll grenades down the gun barrels of tanks, or plant a variety of mines or hollow-charge explosives onto the hulls or under the turrets. Veterans of the Eastern Front already had years of practice with this kind of thing. Heavily built-up urban areas were notoriously dangerous fighting grounds for armored vehicles. It was too easy for an Einzelkampfer to sneak up close through the myriad of ruins, and countless windows above the street offered ideal ambush positions for men armed with panzerfausts. But the Russians had great quantities of tanks, and they were not shy about using them inside the city. (Landau reports seeing only two German tanks during the siege, though there were a number of self-propelled guns, most likely Hetzers, Sturmgeschutzen, and Zrinyi's.)

He describes waiting beside a window with panzerfaust at the ready, watching a Russian tank emerge from a side alley, then turn to advance cautiously along the main street. It was agonizing to wait for the enemy to approach to within the panzerfaust's limited firing range, but an old veteran would have gotten used to this, waiting patiently in a kind of dead emotionless calm. He could not help his adrenalin from racing, but he would be familiar with the whole feeling, not allowing it to distract him.

On the floor beside Landau lay a pile of grenades, plus several other panzerfausts. It was good to have a few spares, and the handheld rockets were almost the only weapons available in large quantities anymore. If his first shot missed or glanced off, the stream of fire would instantly betray his position, but if he remained calm he could pick up the next firing tube by his feet and get off a second shot before enemy fire blasted him out of his lair.

The tank continued to crawl forward, gun barrel swivelling ominously back and forth as the Russian commander scanned the seemingly infinite number of hiding places from which a rocket could be fired. No escorting infantry were visible, and in reality the tank was far more vulnerable than Landau by his window. Possibly the Russians were sending this first vehicle out as bait to see where the German fire would come from.

But apparently Landau had already been spotted. A hole half as large as his body suddenly opened in the wall only inches from where he knelt, matched instantaneously by another hole in the wall behind him. Paralyzed by shock, he could only listen dumbly as the enemy shell exploded somewhere deep in the interior of the building. A deep rumbling roar, sending out vibrations, bringing down plaster dust from the ceiling and launching other dust up from the floor . . . all this sent him into a paroxysm of choking, made worse by the fact that he had been scarcely breathing for several minutes. Now his surprise caused him to gulp down more dust-clogged air.

Another shell shrieked past only inches from his face; this time the only hole was in the wall behind him. The shell must have come right in through the open window.

Enough. He had to get out. Instinctively he knew the tank commander could not have spotted him through his narrow viewing slit; the Reds must have set up a forward observation post somewhere along the street.

Landau doesn't say whether it was the tank or some other artillery piece that fired on him, but his recollections tend to be like that—intensely vivid stretches with occasional details lost in a blur.

He and his comrades evacuated the building in a hurry, spilling out the back way into a maze of dank alleys and dreary garden plots, splashing through pools of refuse and melted snow. Their training and experience instantly took over. "Our boys had perfected the use of panzerfausts and hand grenades in the street fighting to a fine art."[5] One detachment was sent to comb the neighboring buildings for the enemy forward observer, while Landau and half a dozen men made an end run through the back alleys, trying to work their way past and then behind the tank on the main street.

They were in for a surprise, but then so were the Russians.

They emerged onto a perpendicular alley, the one from which the tank had first emerged onto the main street. From here they could follow around behind it and attack it from the rear. They knew this whole area, holding out here for days already. The buildings on either side of the alley were demolished, great piles of brick and stone dust and chunks of masonry spilled everywhere across the pavement.

But the way back out to the main street was blocked off. Not by debris. Three more Russian tanks were standing by in the alley, and the infantry escort was here too. But thank God they were distracted, all of them clustered at the end of the alley and peering out at the progress of the first tank. Landau and his men took them all from behind. Again the murderous effect of half a dozen Schmeissers firing in a confined area . . .

The infantry were obliterated or driven off in less than a minute, the tank crews scarcely able to see what was happening from inside their iron coffins. Now they were easy prey, the first two knocked out within seconds. How? Landau doesn't remember, or doesn't say . . . the blur of fighting at close-quarters. Perhaps some of his men were still carrying panzerfausts; otherwise it would have been done with grenades. The third tank roared off, trying to escape, he remembers it bursting into flames for no apparent reason as it emerged onto the main street, he didn't see it get hit, but now it too was a smoking pyre.

The SS men raced on past the wrecks, still intent on getting the first tank. The frenzy of the hunt. But the first one had disappeared somewhere. Landau especially wanted to destroy it; in the core of his body he could still feel those shells shrieking past within inches of his face.

But now another development. Landau's half-dozen men scurried back through the alleys again, meeting up with the other men who had been sent to comb the buildings. An excited looking younger recruit told him the Russians had moved into the building where the SS men had been holding out a half hour before.

A crazy merry-go-round, men armed to the teeth chasing each other in circles . . .

Landau calmed the younger man and got him to explain the picture in detail. Some of the Reds were still watching from the back garden, the rest had gone inside, storming up the stairs, no doubt expecting to find the SS men cornered up there somewhere.

From past experience Landau knew how to deal with this. Upon finding the building abandoned the Russians would throw caution to the winds and set themselves to looting. The splendors of bourgeois civilization, even in the demolished hulk of a city, exerted a mad temptation which they never seemed able to resist. Even in the dismal wilderness back in Russia it had been like that—how many times had Soviet attacks broken into German positions somewhere in those snowy wastelands, only to lose all impetus as the Ivans stumbled across bottles of cognac, boxes of chocolate, cheese, other little treats mailed out by the Landsers' families back in Germany? For years the Landsers had perfected the tactic of the immediate shock counterattack, even with only a handful of men; time after time they would burst back into their positions to find the Russians lost in the pleasures of drinking or eating whatever strange delicacies they had discovered, many of them already incapacitated with drink if the timing was right.

Landau led his men back in a rush, overwhelming the few Russians standing guard in the garden before they could warn their comrades inside. A rifle was useless in this kind of melee; if a man didn't have a Schmeisser he would wade in with a razor-honed trenching spade.

The ones inside the building were alerted, and there were

too many of them. From the upper floors they poured down the stairs in a mad rush that overwhelmed Landau's men. Dead bodies lay on the stairs, in the ground floor room, draped around the back door, scattered out in the garden. A scene identical to so many that had taken place in Stalingrad . . . With their wild bull's rush twenty or thirty Russians managed to get away, leaving about the same number of dead behind.

Landau's group had seven killed, frightening losses for a small unit to incur in only a few minutes time. Among them was Lutz, the recruit who had briefed him on the situation only moments earlier. Coming to his senses after the murderous brawl, Landau found himself covered with scratches, cuts, bruises; suddenly he realized he had been kicked in the balls and hunkered down in pain. Dully he looked about at Russian corpses still clutching the loot they had tried to abscond with. One of them had tried to carry off a grandfather clock and lay dead with his arms wrapped tightly around it. "God, how I had come to despise these people," thought Landau.[6]

The festivities were not over. The Russian observers, who had still not been located, were quick to notice that the evacuated building was now swarming with SS men again. Howitzers and heavy mortars lobbed in shells that threatened to bring down the entire block. The Germans fled, having to leave their dead behind, something they hated to do when the Russians with their taste for mutilation were close by.

Landau's men nearly ran headlong into a Russian flamethrower team that had been sent in to mop up after the destruction. Horror . . . But an SS man spotted them first and mowed them down before Landau's people could be incinerated. He writes:

> The thought of a narrow escape from getting fried alive was not a cheery one, but by then it had become second nature to most of us to make fun of everything, and someone yelled, "They'll be disappointed to find their roast has escaped them!"[7]

Ha ha. They were exhausted and their nerves were strung taut, but it was amusing all the same. Days and nights, days and nights. Buildings, alleys, rooms, roofs, doorways, stairwells—in this maze of ruined structures they lost all track of time, the days blended together. A day could last an eternity while a week cold pass in a blur. Little wonder that a man would have a poor memory for dates when thinking back on this forty years later. The food situation was bad but the men were more obsessed with tobacco, the only substance that could calm their nerves for a few moments. The ration was down to three cigarettes a day. They would search shattered apartments or dead bodies for cigarettes the way the Russians would look for loot. "Whatever else we could 'organize' ourselves was religiously shared."[8]

Landau comes across as a very tough character, more because of his tone of voice than anything he specifically says. Photos of him show a small-framed, rather delicately handsome young man (much more youthful-seeming than the grim and prematurely aged voice that speaks in his book). But this delicate appearance is belied by a sly, almost impertinent expression that is present in almost every picture in his family album. It is clear that the man behind this face has seen a few things, quite a few . . . There is also a kind of unflappable directness in his gaze, the look of a man who is rarely backed down by anything, though he has clearly learned to view just about everything through a sardonic eye.

All in all, he has a livelier expression than one tends to see in photographs of German soldiers. Perhaps it has to do with his East European background, or maybe it is just the way he is. Photos of human faces tend to suggest a lot of things without ever revealing anything definite. You have to know the man to really fill in the details.

It is interesting that in his account he almost never speaks about fear. Some German memoirs are like that, coming across with a rather cold tone—but Landau's tone is anything but cold. German tankmen and fighter pilots often give accounts that resemble sporting competitions or hunting trips. They are rarely so crass as to actually say as much, but inevitably the impression leaks through their descriptions. Soldiers of other nations would paint kill marks on their planes or tanks, but none were so obsessed as the Germans with keeping exact counts of these tallies, celebrating them with champagne and toasts towards a hoped-for Knight's Cross.

All these men knew fear, but they kept their cool about it. Stuka pilot Hans Rudel, Messerschmitt ace Erich Hartmann,

Focke Wulf ace Walter Nowotny, Tiger tank commanders Otto Carius and Michael Wittman, Waffen SS panzer leaders Jochen Peiper and Kurt Meyer, the SS commando Otto Skorzeny, were all very cool characters indeed, as laconic and imperturbable as any Old West gunfighter out of myth or Hollywood.

They were all elite combat soldiers, and such an attitude goes with the territory of the elite. Many of them had the intensely focused, almost single-minded outlook on both war and life that is sometimes seen in star athletes, often more or less oblivious to the more complex political realities swirling around them, sometimes even downright obtuse. Hans Rudel had been a champion skier and ski jumper before the war, Hartmann a glider pilot, Skorzeny a fencer with a duelling scar.

They were not entirely without a sense of humor—Jochen Peiper especially was a rather amusing fellow—but above all they exuded an almost magnetic sense of confidence and calm.

But none of this really seems to apply to Heinz Landau, though he does display some of these traits. During the war he was shuttled around between a number of Waffen SS units, some elite forces like the Wiking Division, others more ad hoc or run of the mill. On the whole he does not seem to attach much importance to what unit he was serving with. And he had too much of a personal stake in the political turmoil of his native region of Siebenbergen to ever display the kind of cool detachment evinced by some of these men. More than that, he had simply seen too much horror.

Fighting mostly as an infantryman, he was much more closely exposed to the sickening and grisly face of the war than pilots or tank crews generally were. The most famous infantry accounts tend to convey an aura of horror and revulsion that grows stronger as the war goes on; fear as well becomes slowly more magnified and debilitating.

This is what makes the absence of fear in Landau's book so noticeable. Perhaps he simply neglects to mention it. Perhaps years of horror and stress serve to exaggerate fear in some men, while others more or less become inured to it, an emotion cauterized by so much exposure to death.

But one shouldn't neglect the obvious—Landau did, after all, spend nearly the entire war serving in the Waffen SS. The hard-bitten, almost mercenary atmosphere in many of these units probably had a lot to do with the strange absence of fear in his account.

In other reports Waffen SS soldiers do talk about fear—describe how it could grow so pervasive as to become mentally crippling. But without a doubt, such reports from the Waffen SS are far less common than those from the regular army. There are plenty of SS accounts that show the other side of these feelings—describing men who developed an exhilarating lust for combat, who found an intense satisfaction in fighting shoulder to shoulder with comrades who shared their tough and prideful outlook. Certainly these stereotypes did not fit all, nor perhaps even most, Waffen SS soldiers—but they did have a strong basis in reality. Landau himself never really seems exhilarated by combat; perhaps "crazed" would be a better word.

Landau's off-hand, sometimes almost flippant tone, mixed with the unflinchingly graphic way he describes so much madness and bloodshed, calls to mind more than anything else the voice of Sven Hassel, who served on the Eastern Front in a German penal regiment.

Hassel's books almost burst at the seams with their peculiar mix of sardonicism, outrage, numbness, vulgar humor, and utter disgust. Underlying all of Sven Hassel's accounts is his hatred for the Nazi regime; being an SS man, Landau has little to say about this subject. He mentions in one place that men in his unit with deep-set Nazi ideals were often made fun of—they were jokingly nicknamed "the Nazis," the way other men were given other nicknames. In another place he comes across a wretched group of Jews performing forced labor to build an SS training camp. "The only crime these unfortunate people ever committed was their accident of birth."[9]

Landau does have a lot of hatred in him, but he saves almost all of it for the Russians and Rumanians. He is not entirely blind to German faults, especially German arrogance, but he is too fond of the supposedly saving graces of German culture to be overly critical of it. It is interesting that his dislike for the Rumanians while growing up blends almost seamlessly into an identical hatred for the Russians, a people he had never had any contact with before the war. It was a nuisance having the Rumanians as allies; after they switched sides and joined the Russians in August of 1944, Landau was able to lump both these nationalities together, and from here on his hatred assumed almost pathological dimensions.

He describes climbing aboard a German self-propelled gun,

a Marder III, while trying to escape from a Russian armored attack that had overrun his machine gun position. Suddenly a number of German tanks appeared and the Marder turned around and joined them in a counterattack, plowing forward and grinding Russian soldiers beneath its tracks.

> I looked down at the mangled flesh and bone, bits of khaki and blue colored rags, among them the odd field-grey uniform from days and weeks past and suddenly realized I was actually elated, glad to see all these dead Russkies, wanting to kill, kill, kill. God, I thought, I'm really going around the bend.[10]

This passage comes from a confused period of time either in 1943 or 1944. By the time of Budapest in 1945, Landau's loathing had become permanently rooted in his psyche. But he was not alone in his crazed desire to kill as many Russians as possible. His sentiments are echoed almost exactly by Peter Neumann, another Waffen SS man who at this time was fighting with the SS Wiking Division outside of Budapest. Neumann grimly relates enduring a terrible barrage of Stalin Organs and artillery fire in some Hungarian village, waiting for the Russian infantry to attack:

> And here we are, waiting impatiently for them . . . a sort of cold anger makes us grind our teeth. Our fingers close around our guns. Our hands grip our grenades more tightly . . . We have one dream left, and in order to make it come true, I believe we would willingly lay down our lives. It is to kill Russians, to destroy thousands and thousands of Russians like so many poisonous insects. To see Russian blood spurting in all directions. To drown in a lake of Russian blood.[11]

Neumann was the author of perhaps one of the most famous Waffen SS memoirs, THE BLACK MARCH, in which he relates not only the long and terrible journey of SS Wiking through Russia and Hungary, but also the kind of training and indoctrination received at SS officer-candidate schools. The latter is a subject which most SS memoirs do not touch on in any great detail. But

Neumann's account makes it very clear that he did not learn to hate Russians or any other kind of Slavic untermensch by listening to dull and rambling lectures at an SS school. Neumann, like Landau in this respect, learned to hate Russians entirely from his experiences fighting them on the battlefield.

Neither he nor Landau was oblivious to German atrocities committed inside Russia. Neumann himself was present at a horrendous massacre of a village of Ukrainian peasants. In sadly typical fashion, his enraged SS comrades were retaliating against the villagers after they had found several of their men burned to death by partisans nearby. Neumann actually tried to prevent this slaughter, but he was a young and untried officer at the time and his men simply ignored him.

But Neumann makes no attempt to portray himself as any kind of angel of mercy. He was simply inexperienced at this time, still sensitive to feelings of horror and injustice at the murder of innocents. That was in 1941. By 1945, he had by his own admission worked himself into a nearly psychotic state, even more dehumanized than Landau, bent at war's end on the single goal of "drowning in a lake of Russian blood."

Some German veterans, much more so if they served in the army instead of the Waffen SS, tend to recount the sickening behavior of Russians in battle (and especially after a battle) as being the inevitable byproduct of revenge, an absolute explosion of revenge. This is not to say that army Landsers never became enraged by Russian cruelty, especially at Striegau and any number of other Silesian or Prussian villages. But the frame of mind of people like Neumann and Landau seems to present a particular case of psychic overload. They had reached a point where they no longer had any interest in Russian grievances, even if brought about largely by their own SS brutality. Both these men were aware of this logic, but simply did not care anymore. The mad, drunken orgiastic nature of Russian atrocities, the fiendish creativity displayed in their sick and hilarious, endlessly inventive methods of torture and mutilation, obviously served to warp the minds of some Germans beyond all redemption.

Somehow one does not find any of this very surprising, in what had been from the very beginning a war of mutual extermination.

But perhaps Landau and Neumann would take issue with the idea that the Russians were motivated solely by revenge.

Clearly that was part of it, but something about the basic character of the soldiers in the Red Army struck an even deeper and
more terrible chord. The Soviet soldiers appeared to have been
so brutalized by the cruel nature of servitude in their own army,
by the callousness with which their officers sent them to certain
death in mass attacks, or coldly executed them when such attacks failed, that after a certain point they became almost completely dehumanized—achieving a psychotic state that more
than equalled the mindsets of anyone like Landau or Neumann.

Is all this only a vile, unfairly biased stereotype, based on
the overheated reminiscences of a few SS men?

No, obviously there is a great deal of truth in such a description. But what is really lacking, as mentioned in an earlier
chapter, is any kind of compensating point of view from the Russian side. One cannot describe the Germans, even members of
the Waffen SS, solely by resorting to stereotypes and caricatures
of "the evil Nazi," even though the evidence of history has shown
that these stereotypes did have a firm basis in reality. But reality
is always more complicated than that, and the wealth of memoirs
and anecdotes from the German side allows any truly interested
party to see the Germans as they really were, for good or bad,
for everything in between. Guilty or not, brutal or not, racist or
not, they emerge for the most part as recognizable human beings. This is exactly what is missing from all these descriptions
of the Russians as no more than a horde of depraved animals.

The mystery of the Red Army will remain, filled in only by
bits and pieces of conflicting evidence that tantalize without ever
producing a clear picture. But in its way, this void is as much a
part of the Russo-German epic as the volumes of recollections
left behind by German soldiers.

One final question, perhaps relevant, perhaps not: as fellow
soldiers in the SS Wiking Division for much of the war, did Landau
and Neumann ever know each other? Perhaps only God will ever
know.

The Breakout

The end was in sight. It had been in sight for weeks, ever
since the failure of the third and final relief attempt by IV SS
Corps. Naturally Hitler had ordered the Budapest garrison to fight

to the last man. Then, as he had done on several other occasions in the years after the Stalingrad disaster, he began to have second thoughts, waffling for a number of critical days, until it was finally too late to save the besieged troops.

Budapest commander Pfeffer-Wildenbruch had sent out a steady flow of radio messages requesting permission for the surviving garrison to make a break for freedom. On February 9th, he received the vague but encouraging reply that his request was being given "positive consideration" at Fuhrer HQ in Berlin. Pfeffer-Wildenbruch waited for a more definite answer. When none was forthcoming by February 11th, he took matters into his own hands and transmitted the decisive message to Hitler and the Army High Command:

> Ammunition is at an end, provisions are finished. To remain further in Buda can only result in an unconditional surrender or a hopeless struggle to the end. I intend to relocate with my troops from Buda and seek to establish a new base for further operations.[12]

"Relocate" is certainly a euphemistic sounding phrase, but its meaning was unmistakable—the breakout attempt was on. Pfeffer-Wildenbruch, as well as the various divisional commanders serving in his IX SS Mountain Corps, knew very well that the chances of success were almost nil. The defenders were jammed into a tiny area, and the Soviets had already driven their own positions up onto the slopes of Castle Hill.

The hill with its tiers of massively constructed government buildings was like a fortress; conceivably Pfeffer-Wildenbruch's troops could have held out for quite some time to come if they hadn't run out of food and ammunition. But they had, and the strength of the position they had held for so long—like a stone and concrete Mount Suribachi rising above the Danube—was now a moot point. Incredibly, strength reports for IX SS Corps still listed almost 50,000 German and Hungarian troops fighting inside a perimeter of less than one square mile.

The breakout would be led by battle groups from the two strongest remaining units, 8th SS Cavalry Division Florian Geyer and the army's Feldherrnhalle Division. The two respective commanders, SS Brigadefuhrer Joachim Rumohr and General Major

Schmidhuber, spent the last remaining hours in a mood of care-free resignation at the Florian Geyer command post, drinking schnapps with a number of other high-ranking officers. The doom-laden atmosphere was nonchalant and relaxed; they all knew that soon the months of worry and stress would come to an end, one way or another, most likely permanently. A courier arrived in the room and Rumohr invited him to join in:

"Come and drink up, my boy. As soon as we leave here we'll be heading straight into the shit."[13]

He was right. Almost all of those present would be dead before the next sunrise.

The breakout was scheduled for 2000 hours on February 11th. The Russians knew it was coming, allegedly tipped off by an informer, though Pfeffer-Wildenbruch's last radio message had been rather careless to say the least. The actual breakout was not set for the "onset of darkness" as the message had indicated, but for three hours later. It is highly unlikely, however, that this short delay would have been long enough to put the Russians off their guard.

In fact they could hardly have asked for a better plan to finally reduce this maddening Axis stronghold. Assembling for the breakout, the defenders were no longer squirreled away in the bunkers, cellars, and massively reinforced buildings where the Russians had been unable to get at them. The rubble-choked streets on top of the hill were jammed with men waiting tensely for the count-down. The element of surprise might at least have given them a chance to storm through the first Russian positions, but this had been lost.

The enemy was fully prepared and unleashed a hurricane of fire at the first indication that the breakout was underway. Stalin Organs and heavy artillery pieces fired from almost point blank range; now Castle Hill had literally become a volcano of smoke and volatilized debris pluming upwards for thousands of feet. The great majority of the besieged men were wiped out in the streets by this terrible barrage. The Budapest breakout would rival the infamous Cherkassy breakout, which had taken place in the Ukraine exactly a year earlier, for producing the greatest slaughter of German soldiers within a few-hour period. There would never be an exact count of the death-toll for the night of February 11th but the figure was probably somewhere between twenty and thirty thousand.

The initial assault groups of Florian Geyer and Feldhernhalle broke into the Russian defenses but were stopped cold by the deluge of return fire. Behind them, the masses of men waiting to rush through the hoped-for breaks in the siege ring began to panic as the attack stalled and the artillery and rocket shells descended on them like rain. Those not immediately obliterated broke into small groups and scattered in all directions. Many simply retreated to the cellars and dugouts to wait out the metal-storm, where they were smoked out dazed and half-mad by Soviet mopping-up operations the following day. Feldherrnhalle commander General Schmidhuber was killed by blast or shrapnel within the first minutes of the ordeal. SS Florian Geyer commander Joachim Rumohr and SS Maria Theresa commander August Zehender reportedly escaped from Castle Hill, but both were wounded and subsequently shot themselves to avoid capture somewhere in the Buda suburbs. Both these men had served with the original Waffen SS cavalry brigades during 1941 and 1942; Zehender especially was a ruthless character who had personally led a number of savage anti-partisan drives in Russia.

At first Pfeffer-Wildenbruch remained behind with his staff at corps headquarters, in an attempt to coordinate the different phases of the breakout. In the light of the stampede that occurred, this was clearly a useless enterprise, but it probably saved him from becoming a victim of the initial slaughter. Attempting to escape some time later, he was wounded and captured; he would spend the next ten years in a Soviet prison camp.

Apparently the units scheduled for later breakout waves or rearguard actions had better luck. They were still in sheltered positions when the bombardment came down. A follow-up group from the Feldherrnhalle Division succeeded in fighting its way out of the city by dawn, reaching the relative safety of a region of dense woods and tangled ravines near the suburb of Budakesci. Once out in the country this band of originally about 600 men actually had a chance, with about half this number surviving to reach German lines two days later. (Almost certainly most of those who failed to make it were killed before getting out of the city.) Other small groups experienced similar fates. Obersturmfuhrer Harry Phoenix, despite being severely wounded, led a few dozen Florian Geyer men to safety, reporting that once outside the city they were able to sneak across country without any particular difficulty.

About 5,000 Germans and Hungarians reportedly escaped from Castle Hill, only to be rounded up and killed or captured over the next few days. By February 14th less than a thousand men were still roaming free in small groups in Soviet territory between Budapest and the German lines. Almost all of them were headed for the Pils Mountains, a small range of wooded hills northwest of the city. German aerial reconnaissance spotted some of these men, and a short relief corridor was punched out about three miles beyond the main lines in order to help bring them in. The Feldherrnhalle battlegroup came through here, followed by other miscellaneous bands of survivors. The grand total of escapees from the Budapest cauldron numbered 785 men. Waffen SS survivors numbered only 170. The total strength of the garrison at the beginning of the siege had been over 70,000.

Soviet archives have never published any Russian casualty figures for this battle. This is not a serious omission, as Soviet casualty reports from the war generally seem to be little more than wild guesses anyway. But clearly the siege consumed enormous quantities of lives. In terms of blood shed during actual combat, it may have been worse than Stalingrad, where the fighting had actually died down after the Russians surrounded that city in November 1942. Most of the men of Von Paulus' 6th Army inside Stalingrad died from starvation or in Russian captivity after the surrender. If one excludes urban battles on Russian soil, Budapest clearly emerges as the bloodiest struggle for a city in European history.

The crews of the Deutsche Wochenschau were present when the few survivors came through the German lines in the snow-covered Pils Mountains. The filmed portrait gallery of German faces in 1945 was never more striking than this. The escaped men were gaunt, disheveled, haggard, bearded, giving out a powerful impression of still being in the grip of prolonged shock.

Some wore the blocky splinter camouflage of the army on their parkas, others the more subtle dappled camo of the Waffen SS. Some looked as though they could barely stand, others unable to walk were being carried on the backs of comrades. Probably the most striking thing was the way these men were smiling—they appeared to be in almost an ecstasy of relief, hardly able to believe their good fortune at escaping alive. Some were chattering continually from nervous excitement, while others simply stared at their surroundings in a daze. They had made it out of there, by God they had made it out of there alive . . .

In these pictures their souls seemed nearly to emerge from within themselves, settling visibly on the gaunt outer planes of their faces. More than anything they resembled a group of people who had been lost and starving for months in the wilderness without hope of rescue, or the survivors of a disaster at sea who had drifted on the ocean for a similar length of time.

The newsreel mentioned their heroic escape, but neglected to disclose just how few in number they really were.

And what of Heinz Landau? How did he get out?

He gives no indication that he was with any of these last breakout groups. Numerous reports suggest that small parties of men had been escaping from Budapest throughout the course of the siege—the reader may remember that SS Wiking found a number of these men murdered in a ditch outside Agostian on January 1st. But Landau's account of getting out of the city is as puzzling as his account of getting into it. He reports that his unit, whatever unit that was, was withdrawn before the final disaster on February 11th. There are no accounts of units being withdrawn from the siege, even if it were physically possible to do so. Perhaps he was involved in some earlier breakout attempt, but it is hard to make sense of this or any other theory. His memoir consistently alternates between scenes of terrible clarity and passages of mystifying vagueness.

After Budapest he continued to fight in Hungary with the Wiking Division, and one gets the unsettling impression that he had been with Wiking during this whole period of time. But this seems impossible; no Wiking units were actually trapped inside Budapest. Or were they?

I find myself unable to make sense of these anomalies and can only wonder how they might be reconciled. Landau's memories of the siege are so vivid that it seems unlikely they could have been invented, or confused from some other place.

Yet we will see that he did participate in another nightmarish urban battle in 1945, the very last battle, in Berlin.

Could these two great cities, Berlin and Budapest, have become confused in the recollections of a seventy year old man? An intriguing possibility—but upon close study this idea becomes no more satisfying than any of the others. Perhaps Landau could clear this up if he is still alive. Otherwise it will remain another of the war's unanswered questions.

Towards the end of the offensive the mud actually begins to dry out a little. But many of the trapped vehicles still cannot be freed. The earth continues to grip the wheels and running boards like concrete that has firmly set. And so these trucks, tanks, half-tracks, and Kubelwagens line the roads of the retreat, like fossils partially dug up beneath the late winter skies.

16

MUD

The Final Ride of the SS Panzer Divisions

One authority has declared that Sonnenwende came as near to being a "planned fiasco" as the war would produce.[1] When one compares the original possibilities of this operation with the final results, that assessment is hard to argue with. The reader will remember that the critical southern pincer arm of the Sonnenwende attack never materialized. Guderian had envisaged using Sepp Dietrich's 6th SS Army to strike north from Kustrin-on-Oder, hopefully to link up with Felix Steiner's 11th SS Army striking south from Stargard.

Instead Hitler sent Dietrich's divisions off to Hungary, there to take part in an offensive which would become no less of a planned fiasco than Sonnenwende. The code name for this operation was Fruhlingserwachen—Spring Awakening. Dietrich's 6th SS Army was the single most powerful formation of its size remaining in the German order of battle. Its core units were four Waffen SS panzer divisions—Leibstandarte, Das Reich, Hohenstaufen, and Hitler Jugend. Their panzer regiments and support formations were as close to full strength as any German armored units still in existence. As in other Waffen SS divisions, heavy casualties throughout the war years had forced Heinrich Himmler to use conscripts to replace many of the original volunteers, but a hard core of such dedicated veterans still remained.

Fruhlingserwachen was planned for the first week of March, nearly a month after the Hungarian capital had fallen to the Russians. In essence it was little more than a replay of the third Budapest relief attack by IV SS Corps in late January, when Herbert Gille's Wiking and Totenkopf SS Divisions had struck east from the landbridge between Lake Balaton and Lake Velencz. Now the task of Dietrich's far stronger army would be much the same, though the recapture of Budapest was no longer listed as an immediate objective. In fact the overall operational purpose of this offensive was rather obscure. Hitler's instructions to Dietrich, in conferences including Army Group South commander General Wohler and 6th Army Commander General Balck, were to clear all the Russian forces from the west bank of the Danube. It was a rather formidable proposition, as the Soviets now occupied an enormous stretch of territory west of that river.

But one is left to wonder what purpose would be served by such a major expenditure of German resources. Spring Awakening would be a huge operation, involving far more men and tanks than Sonnenwende or any other German counterattack in 1945. Dietrich's Waffen SS divisions would be matched by a force of nearly equal size from the neighboring 6th Army of General Balck. Clearly Hitler was still preoccupied with the protection of the oilfields at Nagykhaniza. The attack he had in mind, if successful, would create a large enough buffer zone between the oil and the Soviets to allow him some peace of mind about this issue.

This was a useful goal, but would it be worth the inevitable cost in troops and materiel, resources that were urgently needed to thwart Zhukov's buildup on the lower Oder?

In fact this debate had already been settled a month earlier, for good or ill. Guderian's large personal reserve of stubbornness and resolve had been temporarily exhausted by the heated arguments over the dispositions for Sonnenwende in February. His implacable dislike for Himmler, especially in his incompetent capacity as commander of Army Group Vistula, had finally worn down Hitler and led to General Wenck being placed in de facto command of these forces. But Hitler had remained unyielding with regard to the equally critical issue of what to do with Sepp Dietrich's powerful SS divisions. They were going to Hungary and that was that. Throughout the weeks following Guderian had remained distressed by this decision, but the nervous energy required for another facedown with Hitler was momentarily played out. Guderian would regather his stamina, eventually leading him to still more violent confrontations with the Fuhrer, but by that time Operation Spring Awakening would have already run its brief and sorry course.

Hitler had the bad habit of using his best SS divisions as if they were an infinitely renewable resource. Perversely, the remarkable fighting records of these units had only served to encourage him in this view. He tended to ignore the inevitable cost in attrition brought about by prolonged combat. The manic shuttling around of Wiking and Totenkopf back in January had been a perfect illustration of this; each of the succeeding relief attacks against Budapest had been conducted by men that were becoming more and more exhausted, with Hitler meanwhile seeming to think that the energies of his SS soldiers could be revived sheerly by willpower and wishful thinking. Clearly, few other of the world's elite combat forces could have done as much to turn this wishful thinking into reality. Three separate attacks against a powerful enemy in less than a month's time must be considered, in retrospect, a remarkable display of stamina by the Wiking and Totenkopf men. But in the end it had all come to nothing. Even worse, Wiking and Totenkopf were now so burnt-out that they were no longer capable of offensive operations. Instead of providing additional striking power to Spring Awakening, they were forced to watch from the sidelines, settled into defensive positions on the flanks of Dietrich's attack.

Still Hitler persisted in using his remaining SS divisions up to and beyond the limits of their capabilities. Even before the main blow of Fruhlingserwachen was scheduled to fall between the Hungarian lakes, he detached Hitler Jugend and part of Leibstandarte from Dietrich's army to conduct a preliminary, and entirely separate, operation. Not only did he want his SS panzers to clear out the Soviets from the west bank of the Danube, he also wanted them to clear the enemy from the Hron River bridgehead to the north of the Danube in Slovakia. A tall order indeed.

The Hron River Attack

The merry go round continued along the German rail network. 8th Panzer Division had been fighting along the Hron River back in January, before being shipped to General Schorner's army group in Silesia. In fact 8th Panzer had already achieved a fair amount of success in this area, forcing the Russians to retreat back towards the river and keeping them confined to their bridgehead west of the Hron. Shortly after 8th Panzer's departure for Silesia, SS Leibstandarte and Hitler Jugend were transferred in to finish up the job.

The country to the west of the Hron changed quickly from steep Carpathian foothills to a rolling plain that led all the way to Vienna. The suitability of this terrain for a rapid Soviet armored advance was what concerned Hitler about this area. Some authorities suggest that he was also perturbed by the sudden vulnerability of his native Austria, at the expense of other, even more threatened regions elsewhere in Germany. In any case, it cannot really be argued that the destruction of the Hron River bridgehead was a *NECESSARY* precondition for the success of the main attack towards the Danube a hundred miles further south. It was rather another illustration of Hitler's tendency to use the SS divisions to deal with everything and anything, especially within an unrealistically short time-frame.

He had made it clear to both Dietrich and Guderian that once the Soviets had been expelled from the Hron River area, *AND* from the west bank of the Danube, he would then transfer 6th SS Army to the lower Oder front to deal with the forces General Zhukov was marshaling against Berlin. Guderian especially might have been appeased by such an arrangement, except for one small problem—he would have instantly realized that such a grandiose plan, involving the incessant re-use of limited forces, was no more than a fantasy. But for the time being he refrained from saying as much. For the moment, it would be enough simply to achieve some success with these attacks in Hungary.

Sepp Dietrich as well was not prone to illusions of grandeur. He was a tough, pragmatic man who had never pretended to possess any keen insight into matters of strategy and tactics. He exemplified the egalitarian model of the Waffen SS, in which the class distinction between officers and enlisted men was considerably more relaxed than in the Germany army, or for that matter than in the world's other armies. He was another general who saw himself as a leader more than a planner, and his deeply ingrained sense of loyalty and comradeship towards his men made him more respected than someone like the ruthless Schorner. For Dietrich, it would have been unthinkable to enforce discipline with roving squads of hangmen behind the lines. Of course, the SS soldiers had never needed that kind of encouragement anyway. But Dietrich was the kind of man who would probably have resigned before resorting to such methods, especially on the grand scale employed by Schorner. He had been a member of the Nazi party from its earliest days, but his brand of fanaticism, if that term can properly be applied to him, was more subdued than Schorner's. He was not a highly articulate person, and his deepest

views about Hitler's aims and National Socialism can only be sur-
mised, as he left little of his thoughts on record. It was clear that
by 1945 he had seen more than enough of the war, and that by
this point his loyalties were directed more towards his own men
than towards the Fuhrer or even, perhaps, the fate of the nation.
The Waffen SS was a strange brotherhood, and Dietrich was its
foremost family member. It may be too much to call him a sympathetic character, especially in light of his involvement in the
brutal early days of the party, but ultimately he comes across as
less repellent than many of his colleagues in the SS and the army.

He rarely argued with orders. On occasion, if he found them
to be unrealistic, he simply ignored them. Debate was not his
forte. For the moment he merely followed Hitler's scheme, detaching 1st SS Corps with Hitler Jugend and Leibstandarte to
make their attack against the Hron River, starting on February
17th.

Hitler Jugend struck the main blow, as Leibstandarte was
only present with an armored kampfgruppe. Misty weather prevailed over the battlefield, swirling among the vineyards scattered
across this region. With their customary elan the SS grenadiers
drove forward through stiff Russian resistance, supported by
Hitler Jugend's panzer regiment, which had been fully re-
equipped with over eighty Panthers and Mk IVs after the Battle
of the Bulge. At this time three panzer divisions of the regular
army put together could not have fielded so may tanks.

During the night of the 17th, Hitler Jugend was counterattacked by Soviet armor, but this resulted in high enemy tank
losses and effectively opened the way for a further advance by
the SS troops the following day. The enemy was kept off balance
by the armored kampfgruppe of SS Leibstandarte, operating
near the Danube on HJ's right, which made the best gains of all
during the first days of the operation. This was not surprising, in
light of the fact that part of this kampfgruppe consisted of the
King Tigers of SS Panzer Abteilung 501, a unit which had always
been closely associated with the Leibstandarte.

It was clear that the Soviets had not expected a major attack
in this area, and by the 20th their bridgehead had been reduced
to only a small wedge of land angled between the Hron and the
Danube. Their resistance continued to intensify, however, and
HJ was shifted to the left to force through the stalled attack of
the neighboring 211th Volksgrenadier Division, requiring another

four days to break through a heavily defended railroad embankment between the towns of Bart and Beny. The fighting here was exceptionally brutal, with the usual deadly array of Soviet PAK batteries lined up behind the embankment. Combined forces of armored cars, SPWs, and panzers finally succeeded in expelling the Soviets on the 24th, thus fully clearing the bridgehead and bringing the operation to a close. It had been a complete success, but casualties had been severe, especially among officers and NCOs, as was so often the case with Waffen SS attacks.

But there was no opportunity to recuperate or receive replacements. HJ, along with the Leibstandarte kampgruppe, was immediately shipped south to play their roles upon the main stage of Fruhlingserwachen, between the Hungarian lakes. Here the rest of Dietrich's 6th SS Army—Das Reich, Hohenstaufen, and the main elements of Leibstandarte—was already in position for the offensive.

The SS divisions were deployed by the shore of Lake Balaton, forming the southern spearhead. Just to the north, around the shore of Lake Velencz, was the other striking arm, composed of the panzer divisions of General Balck's 6th Army. The great attack was scheduled to begin on the night of March 5th.

Personnel of SS Hitler Jugend

Even before the action along the Hron River, the Hitler Jugend (Hitler Youth) Division had become something of a hybrid force. This unusual unit had been created from cadres of Hitler Youth groups, with enlisted ranks consisting almost entirely of 17 and 18 year old boys. They had fought with fanatical ardor in Normandy the year before; it was their first combat experience, and it had very nearly been their last. Most of these young teenagers had been killed leading the initial counterattacks against the Allied beachhead, driving old Mk IVs with the names of their girlfriends—Paula, Gudrun, Ilse—painted on the turrets. They were killed by the terrible offshore naval bombardments of the American battleships, by the relentless air attacks, by weeks on end of tank versus tank engagements with Montgomery's British and Canadian armored divisions. During training these boys had become imbued with the normal reckless abandon of Waffen SS tactics and simply stepped it up a notch, with the result that HJ took the highest losses of any German unit in Normandy.

It was a strangely moving situation. Any fighting unit will have a fair amount of men under the age of twenty, but when the enlisted ranks are composed 100% of boys 18 years old or younger, it presents an evocative and disturbing spectacle. They had grown up with every aspect of their lives influenced by National Socialist propaganda, and the faces of some of them did bear the smiling, thug-like expressions of the more vicious followers of that cult. But it is clear that the ardor that radiates with almost embarrassing intensity from most of these faces in photos and newsreels is the ardor of youth more than any other thing—the ardor of youth who have been given a cause, any cause, and then kept segregated from the influences of any more hard-bitten or cynical veterans.

Composed, ostensibly, of a majority of 18 year olds, most of the Hitler Jugend soldiers in Normandy looked even younger than that. Without the offsetting presence of older men, they presented as a group the image of a boy scout troop suddenly thrown into a life-or-death crusade, and embracing it with all the strange emotional forces of the very young. Allied soldiers would send Hitler Jugend prisoners back to the German lines, with notices pinned to their backs saying they would not make war on children. Allied soldiers also occasionally murdered Hitler Jugend prisoners in a blind fury, part of a vicious circle of reprisals in which the highstrung SS youths had also murdered Allied prisoners.

But the Hitler Jugend that fought in Normandy was not the same Hitler Jugend that fought in Hungary during the war's final months. The teenagers who had not been killed in France were later killed in the Ardennes around Bastogne. Whoever had survived to fight the Russians at war's end was supplemented by other personnel scraped together from army units, even naval and Luftwaffe units, often with little training in ground warfare. By this time many of the officers of HJ were also recent transfers from the army. The leadership provided by Waffen SS veterans Franz Witt and Kurt Meyer was gone; Witt was killed in Normandy and Meyer wounded and captured there. But despite all these debilitating factors, HJ continued to fight as well as any other Waffen SS division in 1945. They would be one of the few units to make any real headway in the upcoming offensive.

The Making of a Fiasco

The delay caused by the reduction of the Hron River bridge-head would lead to a critical problem for Operation Spring Awakening. By the beginning of March the spring thaw had set in on the steppe country around Lake Balaton. Several feet below the surface, the ground was still frozen; everything above this level was transformed into a wretched morass that would take weeks to drain away. Spring thaw conditions in Russia had never been any worse than this, and the Germans had learned long ago that operations in the muddy season tended to be exercises in futility.

The offensive might as well have been aborted, but there was never room for this kind of thinking in Hitler's mindset. By now everything pointed towards a debacle. It has been said that the unexpected thaw caught the Germans by surprise, but in fact warming conditions in March should have surprised no one. Even in Russia, muddy weather at this time of year was not uncommon, and Hungary's climate was by no means as severe. Hitler's bouts of strategic inspiration had always been flawed by a tendency to ignore the logistical realities of weather and terrain.

To make matters worse, the Russians' lack of preparation along the Hron River had been more than offset by their construction of a deeply echeloned defensive system between Lake Balaton and Lake Velancz. Either through inspired guesswork or accurate intelligence sources (most likely the latter), the Russians knew the Germans were planning to come through this area. Throughout the war, the Russian intelligence network had been much more active and successful than its German counterpart, relying on an enormous web of spies and informers with Communist (or at least anti-Nazi) sympathies. Though Soviet small-unit tactics on the battlefield remained primitive and costly, their high command's strategic interpretation of German plans was highly sophisticated and frequently right on the mark. Dietrich's SS divisions were about to advance right into yet another Eastern Front meatgrinder, from which only scattered and retreating battle-groups would survive.

Ironically, Hitler had ordered excessive security precautions in the vain hope that Fruhlingserwachen would catch the Russians by surprise. All of the SS divisions were travelling under false identities. Rail transport documents listed Hitler Jugend and Leib-

standarte as replacement detachments for the Wiking and Totenkopf Divisions. Das Reich and Hohenstaufen were travelling under
the odd designations of "North" and "South" Divisions, two units
which had originally been cavalry divisions but which now no
longer even existed. German battle maps, even after the offensive
had already begun, continued to use these false designations,
which offer a confusing tangle of misinformation to any student
of this affair. (Possibly this is one reason why Fruhlingserwachen
remains the most obscure major operation of the war.)

The SS troops had also been ordered to remove the deco-
rative cuffbands which identified their units—although some accounts indicate that Dietrich thought this order was frivolous and
did not bother to pass it along to his men. Even preliminary reconnaissance of the Russian positions had been curtailed, for fear
that captured soldiers would betray the presence of the SS strike-
force. Thus Dietrich's soldiers had almost no foreknowledge of
the defenses they were up against.

This mania for secrecy had been stunningly effective in the
Ardennes attack three months earlier, with the American forces
in Belgium being taken completely by surprise. In Hungary these
security measures, as well as every other part of the German plan,
would backfire dismally.

The preliminary attack against the Hron bridgehead had undoubtedly tipped the Soviets off to the presence of additional SS
forces in Hungary. Soviet records, as usual, do not reveal whether
their intelligence was fully aware of the presence of Dietrich's other
two divisions. To some degree, the deep defensive lines between
the Hungarian lakes were only a preliminary measure for the Russians' own upcoming grand offensive, which in a strategic or operational sense would outmaneuver the Germans brilliantly.

We will see how this unfolded shortly. For the moment, let
us turn to the pre-dawn hours of March 5th, when the SS divisions
were moving up to their start lines for the attack through a sea of
mud.

Assistance Requested from the German Navy

Most of the SS units were forced to make a long approach
march, as much as ten miles, just to reach their jumping-off
points. Trucks carrying the assault units had dropped them off

that far to the rear to keep the Soviets from being alerted by the noise of excessive motorized traffic. But probably the trucks would not have been able to come any further through the mud in any case. The armored units had the same problem, bogging down continuously through the night and falling far behind the infantry.

Obersturmbannfuhrer Jochen Peiper, in command of SS Leibstandarte's panzer regiment, was so exasperated by the mud that he declared the attack should be made by U-Boats instead of tanks.[2] Other accounts mention soldiers jokingly requesting assistance from the German navy to carry them across the waterlogged terrain, though perhaps these are only apocryphal remarks stemming from Peiper's sarcastic comment.[3] In interviews after the war, Peiper also related that the mud was so deep that some of the fuel tanks of his panzers became contaminated with water, requiring men to dive underneath them like frogmen to open drain valves to take care of the problem.

Three months earlier Peiper had been at the head of the SS panzers advancing along the winding, hilly Belgian roads during the Battle of the Bulge. The narrow roads and winter conditions had caused him a number of headaches then. But now the situation in Hungary was worse than bad; it was almost farcical, and Peiper began to fall back on his familiar brand of black humor to keep from despairing.

The attack was scheduled to start at dawn, and as dawn broke on March 5th the infantry, who were themselves exhausted from their long approach march, saw that the tanks had still not struggled forward to support them. So the infantry advanced alone. A light snow was falling now, but the flakes were moist and heavy and only added to the filthy conditions.

Mud-spattered SS grenadiers slogged in to grapple with the first of as many as five successive Soviet trench systems. Their only support came from the lighter weight SPWs and armored cars; the heavy tanks were still laboring far behind. As a result, infantry casualties were very heavy throughout the first day. HJ's two panzer grenadier regiments became stalled in the Russians' outlying positions at Odin-Puszta, unable to push on until HJ's panzer battalion finally arrived on the scene at dawn of the day following, March 6th. The other SS divisions were faced with identical problems all along the line. As was their custom, the Soviets had laid deep belts of mines along every possible approach route—roads, low ridge lines, any artery at all that was elevated above the impassable quagmire of the surrounding fields. Pioneer units and even the crews of individual tanks worked to clear the mines. Any panzer that veered off these elevated causeways onto the open steppe threatened to bog down immediately; many sank in up to their hulls, impossible for recovery vehicles to retrieve.

Photographs of the terrain in this area bear an ominous resemblance to scenes from the mud-hell of Passchendaele in 1917, a name that will be forever connected to images of British infantry being massacred as they advanced through thigh-deep filth and shellholes overflowing with liquid slime. Only the armored mobility of the German units allowed them to avoid, just barely, an identical fate in Hungary in 1945. In particular it was the mobile tactics of the grenadiers aboard the armored cars and SPWs which kept them from becoming hopelessly stalled. Even so, the slim gains of the first day were giving every indication that the attack would degenerate completely. Only the late arrival of the heavy tanks provided the impetus needed to break through the Soviet defenses.

Progress improved over the following days, with the various armored elements finally beginning to operate in a more coordinated fashion. On the left of Dietrich's 6th SS Army, elements of General Balck's 6th Army were advancing along the southern shore of Lake Velencz. Here the army's 1st and 3rd Panzer Divisions, supported by the King Tigers of Panzer Abteilung 509, were conducting their own grim struggle through the morass. The results were the same: the panzergrenadiers in their light-weight halftracks surged ahead until they were stalled by Russian defensive fire, then had to hold on while the tanks labored forward to catch up with them.

One company of 509's King Tigers had been slated to make a combined-arms strike with the panzer regiment and grenadiers of 1st Panzer Division, with all these elements forming Kampfgruppe Bradel—named after the commander of 1st Panzer's panzergrenadier regiment.

Once again the tanks were nowhere near their start lines in time for the dawn attack. About half had bogged down on the approach march during the night. The only vehicle capable of towing a King Tiger was another King Tiger; hours were wasted on these recovery attempts, some of which were successful, but at least three of the 68 ton tanks remained hopelessly stuck. The company was not fully assembled and ready to attack until later in the morning, by which time Oberst Bradel's grenadiers had already gone ahead without them, plowing through the mud in their SPWs into the teeth of the enemy fire.

Bradel's men had taken the first objective, the town of Seregyeles, by noon, but they were unable to prevent the Soviets from destroying several critical bridges over the many canals that crisscrossed this region. A number of Stalin tanks were still operating in Bradel's rear, some of them dug in on ridge-top positions, waiting for the long-delayed German armor. A heavy exchange of fire began as the King Tigers finally came into range. Within minutes four Stalins were knocked out without loss to the Germans.

The Panther tanks of 1st Panzer Division had a more difficult time; their 75 mm cannon were outranged by the 122 mms of the Stalins, and their approach was stalled by the intense enemy fire from a distance of 2000 meters. The Panthers recorded a few hits but could not penetrate the enemy's armor plate at that range. Firing from a stable, dug-in platform, the Soviet tank gunnery was more accurate than usual. Rather than advance further into a potential killing zone, the Panthers requested assistance from 509. Two King Tigers were detached and they quickly disposed of two more of the troublesome Stalins along the commanding ridgeline.

Yet there were further delays while pioneer units, assisted by Bradel's grenadiers, worked frantically to repair two railroad bridges en route to the grenadiers' advanced position at Seregyeles. It was not until the following day that the tanks were able to reach the town. This only gave the Soviets more time to consolidate their defenses.

The bridges had been repaired in great haste and threatened to collapse under the weight of other armored elements of 1st and 3rd Panzer Divisions that were following behind Bradel's spearhead. Further repairs had to be made, using up three more critical days. This was blitzkrieg in extreme slow motion.

The attack got underway again on the 10th, with all of 509's tank companies finally operating together. A total of 26 King Tigers, along with assorted Panthers from the two panzer divisions, provided enough firepower for Kampfgruppe Bradel to force its way into Gardony on the 11th. This was a picturesque town on the south shore of Lake Velencz, with vineyards sloping gently down to the placid winter-blue waters of the lake, a sharp contrast in scenery to the liquefied mud of the steppe country spreading beyond.

The attack crawled forward, eastward again into the morass. There must have been a certain ignominious sense of deja-vu for all these tank crews and grenadiers. Both 509 and 1st Panzer Division had crossed this same area as part of the final Budapest relief attack six weeks before. Then the ground had been frozen and the tanks had made steady progress all the way to the Danube, before being driven back by Malinovsky's counterattack. This misguided March offensive would not even cover half that distance. The Germans slogged on through the mud, doubtless passing numerous burnt-out wrecks from those earlier battles littered across the landscape.

The end came in the form of a steel wall of Soviet ISU-122 tank destroyers, dug in along a ridgeline somewhere east of Gardony. A long distance slugging match ensued while German pioneers worked to clear deep belts of mines leading up to the ridge. Unable to advance, the King Tigers fired from stationary positions in open country, receiving a withering hail of armor-piercing shot in return. The Tigers' thick plate deflected strikes by the dozen, but three became so shot-up that they had to be written off as total losses, abandoned by their crews.

This engagement between two stationary, evenly-matched rows of heavy tanks and tank destroyers must have resembled two 18th century ships of the line hurling all-out broadsides at each other. There were 24 ISU-122s dug in along the ridge; after hours of deafening noise and concussion, all 24 were destroyed. Of the remaining King Tigers, only two were still under power, driving up onto the ridge among the twisted iron remains of their enemy. Apart from the three total losses, about twenty other King Tigers were so badly shot-up as to require extensive repairs before resuming the advance.

But the advance was over. Bradel's grenadiers followed the two King Tigers still mobile up onto the ridge, setting up a hedgehog defensive position. The staff of 1st Panzer Division wanted to continue the attack, but 509's commander, Major Konig, declared his battalion was finished for the time being. It was March 14th. Mechanics worked around the clock to repair the damaged tanks, and remarkably twenty of them were made combat-ready again by the 18th. But by that time Spring Awakening was over. The Russians had just launched their own massive offensive to the north of Lake Velencz, sweeping entirely around the lake in less than two days and threatening to cut across the rear of the German spearheads. It was an operational masterpiece, comparable to the counterattacks that had cut off Von Paulus' 6th Army at Stalingrad in 1942 and driven the Germans in disarray from the Kursk bulge in 1943. Panzer Abteilung 509's next action would take place deep in the German rear, trying to fend off disaster.

Let us return briefly to Seep Dietrich's 6th SS Army operating to the right of the army's panzer divisions. Immediately to the right, the vaunted armored power of SS Das Reich and SS Hohenstaufen (as the mysteriously designated "North" and "South" divisions) had accomplished almost nothing, achieving the smallest gains of the entire offensive. The approach routes of their armor had been plagued by the longest delays, and their infantry/grenadiers had suffered accordingly out in the muddy wastelands. It was probably the most futile combat episode experienced by either of these divisions. Blame it on the weather. The excuse was quite legitimate. When Das Reich's armor finally advanced, the SS Panthers contributed a respectable number of tank kills, but they had met with so many delays that the offensive had already run its course by this time.

Further to the right, Hitler Jugend and Leibstandarte had made the best progress, helped considerably by the fact that the road network was somewhat better in their sector. After breaching the initial Soviet defenses around Odin-Puszta, battle groups of armored cars, SPWs, and tanks raced hell for leather down the roads, taking their losses from Russian PAK batteries and bursting right on through.

The Russians reacted with a disorganized series of retreats and counterattacks, practically the only instance in Fruhlingserwachen where the enemy showed any sign of confusion. The Russians attempted in vain to establish another defensive position in front of the town of Simorntaya on the Sio Canal. Hitler Jugend's panzergrenadiers got there first, crossing the canal and establishing a bridgehead on the south bank on March 11th.

They had covered more than twenty miles in five days, but casualties during this reckless thrust had been extremely heavy. The tactic of moving rapidly along the elevated roadways had resulted in large numbers of halftracks and armored cars being shot up along the route. The bridges across the Sio Canal at Simorntaya formed a bottleneck that the by now exhausted HJ grenadiers were unable to enlarge. Instead they spent the next three days repelling Soviet counterattacks against their south bank bridgehead. Elements of the Leibstandarte relieved them on March 15th. On the same day, the Soviet counteroffensive erupted north of Lake Velencz.

The Hungarian Front Disintegrates

The German line just to the north of Lake Velencz was held by the burnt-out remnants of SS Wiking and SS Totenkopf. Next in line to the north was the Hungarian 3rd Army. The dispirited and poorly armed Hungarians simply evaporated under the weight of the Soviet attack, which effectively split the entire German front in Hungary asunder. Hitler should have known better than to rely on his allies to defend his flank. The Germans had made this same mistake before, when the Soviets had overwhelmed a series of underequipped Rumanian, Italian, and Hungarian armies all along the overextended flanks at Stalingrad. By March 16th the Soviets had already bypassed Stuhlweissenberg, to the west of Lake Velencz, and were threatening to seal off the entire land corridor between Lakes Velencz and Balaton. The question now was whether Dietrich's 6th SS Army and Balck's 6th Army would meet the same fate as the original 6th Army at Stalingrad.

The Army and SS troops were in possession of nothing but several hundred square miles of mud and swamp. For once, Hitler decided not to defend this misbegotten area to the last man. Dietrich's and Balck's armies were allowed to retreat, though these orders came in the guise of a "transfer" to defend the area north of Stuhlweissenberg where the Russians had broken through.

All the SS divisions, as well as 1st Panzer, 3rd Panzer, Tiger Abteilung 509, and the other supporting Army units, began to pull back through the dismal countryside in the direction of Stuhlweissenberg. Packs of Russian T-34s, better able to negotiate the soggy ground, followed in close pursuit. 509's King Tigers set up blocking positions on several occasions, buying time for Bradel's 1st Panzer kampfgruppe to escape to the west. These actions led to the end of 509 as a fighting force. Only a few King Tigers were destroyed by enemy fire. As the retreat turned into a rout, fourteen tanks had to be destroyed by their own crews for lack of fuel. Less than half a dozen remained to be mounted onto railroad cars heading west for the Austrian border.

The SS divisions were also moving west in full scale retreat, leaving countless vehicles abandoned along the roads. Hitler Jugend, nearly finished as a fighting force, was ordered to take over Totenkopf's sector north of Stuhlweissenberg, after Totenkopf's battle-weary units failed to hold the line. HJ was no more capable of holding on than Totenkopf; the retreat continued.

Defending Stuhlweissenberg proper, SS Wiking was outflanked to the north and nearly surrounded. Hitler regarded this city as the critical linchpin necessary to keep the retreat route open between Lakes Velencz and Balaton. Wiking was therefore ordered to hold to the last man.

But both SS troopers and SS generals were beginning to reach the end of their tether as far as devotion to the Fuhrer was concerned. After so many years of struggle and bloodshed, Wiking commander Karl Ullrich was not about to let his division be annihilated at Hitler's behest. On his own initiative he ordered his men to break out to the west. At this moment SS Hohenstaufen was withdrawing just to the south of Stuhlweissenberg. Hohenstaufen commander Sylvester Stadler abetted Ullrich's disobedience by ordering his men to link up with Wiking and establish a corridor through which Wiking could escape. Thus Hohenstaufen performed a greater service during the retreat than it had done during the actual offensive. Throughout the war army officers had been cashiered for displaying this kind of disobedience. Both Ullrich and Stadler risked the same fate, but once again Hitler's favorites were effectively granted dispensation; neither removal from their posts nor even a reprimand awaited these two men.

The Cuffband Incident

Instead a rather more curious episode now occurred, of which several conflicting versions exist.

Version number one:

General Wohler, commander of Army Group South, drove up to the forward areas to see just how bad the situation really was. At this time, probably around March 15th, the orders for a general retreat had not been issued yet. He encountered a Ne-belwerfer rocket battery of SS Leibstandarte, towed by a truck and headed for the rear. Wohler demanded an explanation for their flight and was told that the truck had broken down and become separated from its unit; the SS men were now trying to catch up with it.

Wohler took this to mean that Leibstandarte had begun a general retreat. He concluded that if even the SS men were taking to their heels, then Dietrich's offensive—still supposedly under-way at this point—would have to be called off. In any case this was the rationale Wohler used in a phone call to Guderian later in the day. In essence, Wohler was calling to say he had sus-pended Fruhlingserwachen on his own authority.

Possibly he did run across this retreating Leibstandarte bat-tery, but for him to justify a full-scale withdrawal on the basis of this one incident is hardly credible. Obviously it was the over-whelming danger posed by the Russian counteroffensive which had led him to call off Fruhlingserwachen. For Wohler to do this without Hitler's approval required a good deal of nerve, and pos-sibly he began berating the SS divisions during the course of his conversation with Guderian simply as a way of shifting the blame for his own decision.

If so, then the ploy succeeded. Rather than overruling Wo-hler, Hitler apparently agreed that the offensive would have to be discontinued in order to meet the Soviet threat. Hitler then vented his disgust with the whole situation by declaring that Diet-rich's SS divisions had failed him and ordering all members of Leibstandarte, Das Reich, Hohenstaufen, and Totkenkopf to be stripped of their honorary unit cuffbands. (These famous cuff-bands, by the way, were merely black strips of cloth worn around the lower forearm outside the uniform, with the name of the di-vision sewn-in bold silver script. The army's Grossdeutschland Division had a similar cuffband, which sometimes caused men from this formation to be mistaken for Waffen SS soldiers.)

It was a ridiculous and quite unjustified display of pique, typical of Hitler's mood during these days. Possibly it was only a momentary tantrum that Hitler himself did not take seriously for long. There are different accounts of Sepp Dietrich's reaction to this. In one he considered the whole matter an absurd mis-understanding, so frivolous that he did not even bother to feel insulted; he simply disregarded the "cuffband order" as if it had never been issued. Another source indicates he was genuinely offended by this insult to his soldiers, voicing his feelings with quite colorful language. For years the Waffen SS divisions had battled through every kind of hell, carrying out one brutal operation after another in accordance with their great leader's commands. Dietrich sent a staff officer to Hitler's headquarters to defend the performance of his men. Hitler apparently regretted his tirade and apologized.[4]

Version number two:

General Balck, commander of 6th Army, whose panzer divisions had been operating to the left of Dietrich's 6th SS Army, drove up to the forward areas to see just how bad the situation really was. In this version, it seems that the general retreat had already begun. Balck, who evidently bore a grudge against the Waffen SS for its favored status, encountered some retreating units from SS Hohenstaufen. He immediately paid a visit to that division's headquarters and got into a violent argument with Hohenstaufen's commander, Sylvester Stadler.

Stadler was another hard character with a face that looked chiselled from bone. (A look at any number of photo histories would show that such features were not uncommon among Waffen SS officers.) He defended his men, using the same kind of language his chief Dietrich would have used, and declared that whomever Balck had encountered must have belonged to some other SS division. Stadler must have appeared more than a little threatening. For his part, Balck was a dour, heavy-set, highly decorated soldier who would not easily have backed down in this kind of confrontation. The conversation between these two men would surely have been quite interesting to listen to, with the long inter-service feud between the army and the Waffen SS finally coming to a head, aggravated still further by the disastrous military situation at the time. Balck subsequently reported this incident to his own chief General Wohler, but for no apparent reason shifted the blame from Hohenstaufen men to Leibstandarte men.[5]

From this point, the two versions begin to coincide. Upon hearing from General Balck, or else seeing the situation for himself, General Wohler called Guderian and said that if Leibstandarte was on the retreat then how could the rest of the army be blamed for pulling back. Hitler flew into a rage and ordered Dietrich's men to be stripped of their honorary cuffbands.

No doubt still other versions of this bewildering affair also exist. The only things known for certain are that Wohler did order the retreat on his own authority (though possibly he then lost his nerve and began shifting the blame around); and that Hitler did issue the notorious cuffband order.

The interesting thing about this whole situation is that the direct disobedience of Stadler and Wiking commander Karl Ullrich, in conducting the breakout from Stuhlweissenberg, appears to have gone entirely unnoticed. Perhaps this says a little about the chaos of those days, not only at the front but at Hitler's headquarters. Ironically, the men of SS Wiking, since they had not taken part in Dietrich's attack, were not included in Hitler's cuffband order. (One might then ask why Totenkopf—which like Wiking had not been part of the attack—was included in Hitler's order, while Hitler Jugend was left out. Conceivably there was a reason for this, but it is more tempting to think this was just another senseless element of the whole matter.)

Along with anger, frustration, and despair, there is more than a faint hint of farce in this business. But disaster was sweeping away any elements of comedy. There remains one final scene to be recounted, however.

Peiper and the Latrine Bucket

The men of 6th SS Army quickly got the word about being stripped of their cuffbands. Many would not have been wearing them at all; in combat most men had on the SS camo blouses and the cuffbands would most likely have been stuffed in their pockets. In any case the SS troopers were not amused by Hitler's humiliating order. Jochen Peiper, in command of a group of Leibstandarte's few remaining tanks, gathered his men around him somewhere on the filthy steppe and had them toss all their cuffbands into a helmet that had been used as a latrine bucket, joking that Hitler would be pleased to receive this token of their loyalty. Apparently he was so angry that he intended in all seriousness to send this splendid gift to Hitler personally, but a few of his men finally persuaded him it would not be wise.

"Tell him it's from Goetz von Berlichingen," said Peiper.

This was a standard German military wisecrack, an inside joke which translated to, "Kiss my ass." The heroic von Berlichingen had made just such an uncouth remark several hundred years before, in response to receiving similarly humiliating orders from his superiors.

This scene with Peiper and his men has achieved legendary status; it is also widely believed never to have occurred. Yet it may actually have happened in just the manner described above, for Peiper himself related this story in interviews after the war. He talked at length wit John Toland, author of the book THE LAST 100 DAYS, and there seems little reason to believe he would have made up such an incident.[6] A lot of confusion may have stemmed from the fact that Toland used a pseudonym for Peiper in his book, identifying him as Sturmbannfuhrer Fritz Hagen. Obviously Toland was acquiescing to Peiper's own wishes to keep his identity a secret, the reason for which would be quite clear to those familiar with Peiper's untimely death in 1976. (Peiper's murder in a French village was the final act in a long and bizarre series of events. We will touch further on this in the epilog to this book.)

In any case, as a symbolic act, Peiper's gesture has stayed alive in soldiers' memories. Certainly it is not hard to imagine him resorting to such a stunt. He had fought the entire war with his own brand of grim hilarity. Leading the Leibstandarte panzer group during the Battle of the Bulge, he took several American officers prisoner for a time. One of them later reported being surprised to find Peiper a rather relaxed and humorous fellow. Commanding the spearhead of a desperate attack which was rapidly running out of steam, Peiper was actually under tremendous stress at this time, but such conditions seemed to bring out this kind of humor in him. There are reports that immediately after the Battle of the Bulge he was mentally exhausted and experienced a kind of momentary nervous breakdown; but if so, then he and his quick-witted tongue had recovered by the time of the March offensive in Hungary.

During the earlier years of the war in Russia, he had been given the nickname "Blowtorch" Peiper, and his unit called the "Blowtorch" battalion. Placed on trial for war-crimes immediately after the German surrender (he had been accused of perpetrating the Malmedy massacre in the Ardennes), Peiper had declared this nickname to be nothing but a joke. His American interrogators were convinced that it referred to arson and other brutal SS methods used to wipe out Russian villages during the campaign in the

East. Peiper said that the blowtorch was commonly used to heat up engines that had frozen solid in the Russian winters, as well as to boil water and perform any number of other chores that required instant heating. Like soldiers everywhere, his men developed their own humorous jargon, saying "we'll torch it" whenever given any kind of task to carry out.

Perhaps Peiper was not being entirely frank here. Somehow it is easy to imagine that his men also used this expression in combat; the fighting in Russia tended to be rather insane, after all. After the war, some Waffen SS men were not above giving rather far-fetched excuses for acts of atrocity (the wholesale massacre of the French village of Oradour-sur-Glane in 1944 comes to mind) but Peiper's claim that "Blowtorch" was only a joking nickname rings true somehow. He did have that kind of hardbitten comical streak in him. Did his men "torch" any number of Russian villages in the midst of battle? Probably so, just as did almost every other Army and SS unit in Russia. Peiper admitted this was just the reality of combat—Russian villages tended to burn because they were built of wood and thatch that ignited when men were shooting at them from all directions.

Such discussions tend to reach a point of splitting hairs after a while. One might remember that American officers were known to have nicknames such as "Blood and Guts" and "Fireball."

In the end it is only fitting that Peiper would be associated with this latrine bucket episode. And fitting also, that this scene should take place on the quagmire of the Hungarian steppe, so reminiscent of the endless muddy desolation of Russia where the had fought for so many years.

While venting their anger with obscene jokes about throwing medals and cuff-bands into a shit-filled helmet, perhaps they also spent a few minutes joking about GROFARZ, as their leader Adolph Hitler was mockingly nicknamed by both Waffen SS and Army soldiers during the later years of the war. It was nothing but soldiers' humor, though the nickname was being uttered more and more with a tone of contempt. The Germans have long had a passion for acronyms. GROFARZ—it stood for Grosste Fuhrer aller Zeit—The Greatest Leader of All Time. Just the sound of the word brings a chuckle to one's lips. And so there they were, the dishonored SS soldiers sitting around in the mud, having a good laugh about the magnificent GROFARZ.

Where were they exactly? God only knows. Peiper told Toland after the war that his panzers had advanced to within twenty miles of the Danube, and it was here that he received the word about the cuffbands—in other words just at the moment when the general retreat was about to begin. Being ordered to retreat after having advanced so far through this filthy morass only heightened Peiper's disgust. But if one looks at the actual route of Leibstandarte's attack during Spring Awakening, it seems doubtful that Peiper could have advanced as far as he said he did. Perhaps he was exaggerating, or simply making a general kind of statement which Toland took literally. For one sees on the map that the thrust of Leibstandarte's initial advance towards the Sio Canal was not anywhere near the Danube. It was on March 15th that Leibstandarte relieved Hitler Jugend in their bridgehead south of the Sio Canal. Conceivably Peiper could have broken out of this bridgehead and led his panzers in a last-gasp rush towards the Danube, but if so his movements were not recorded on any German battle maps at the time.

In any case, these kinds of exact details were becoming less and less relevant. Peiper and his last surviving tanks were out there somewhere in the mud, far ahead of the rest of his division and the rest of Dietrich's army, and now they were going to have to turn around and recross all of that terrain to escape being trapped by the Russians.

Spring came early that year. The trees lining the retreat roads were already showing sprouts of green. The mud in the fields remained the same.

Account of Ernst Barkmann; Peiper Lectures New Arrivals

Although not covering as much distance, the German retreat from Hungary into Austria was every bit as chaotic as the rout from the Vistula to the Oder two months before. The SS units broke up into small battle groups. Or to put it another way, all that remained of the typical SS unit was a small battlegroup. Tanks were continually in danger running out of fuel; thus every effort was made to assemble the remaining armored units and ship them by rail to the approaches of Vienna, where hopefully a new defensive line could be established.

SS Das Reich had fallen back to the Hungarian town of

Vesprem, with the Soviet armor columns following close behind. Tanks and supporting units were loaded onto railroad cars, while one company of Panthers under Ernst Barkmann set up a defensive cordon to guard this time-consuming operation.

The majority of the division barely managed to escape, steaming northwest in the direction of Vienna. When Barkmann's rear guard company assembled at the train station to be shipped out, they received word that Russian tanks were now blocking the tracks outside of Vesprem. Well, that was it. They were on their own now, and Barkmann's ten Panthers had almost no fuel remaining.

Barkmann was a resourceful fellow, as well as one of Das Reich's leading tank killers. He led his company to a nearby airfield and employed a combination of threats and persuasion to commandeer enough fuel for his tanks to keep going. An unidentified armored group of the Army was also trying to gas up here. Barkmann reported to this unit and was ordered to participate in a counterattack that night. He does not mention whether any of the army crews resented still having to hold the line while Das Reich had already escaped to freedom. Probably the situation was too confused for anyone to have a clear grasp of the overall picture.

Barkmann lost two Panthers that night; according to him the Army unit was wiped out completely. The SS company then headed west on its own, fording a river, crossing the same railroad tracks along which their divisional comrades had escaped the day before. The area was still swarming with Russian armor. Barkmann and his men would surely have been done for, had they not had the good fortune to make contact with rear guard elements of SS Leibstandarte.

Jochen Peiper was in command of what was left of Leibstandarte's panzer regiment—only ten vehicles, Panthers and Mk IVs, possibly one or two King Tigers. Peiper's eyes lit up when he saw that Barkmann had eight almost fully gassed up Panthers.

Not bothering to waste time on preliminaries, he got right to the point.

"I've got a lot of crews who've lost their tanks, so they'll be taking over your vehicles."

"I see," said Barkmann. "So my men are supposed to fight as infantry and walk all the way home?"

"Well, you can come with us, of course," said Peiper. "But my men will be needing those tanks."

Peiper outranked Barkmann by a considerable margin, an Obersturmbannfuhrer speaking to a Scharfuhrer; the army equivalent would be a full colonel giving orders to a staff sergeant. But the Waffen SS veterans, especially after six years of war, were not overly impressed by rank.

Barkmann eyed Peiper coolly.

"Aus die Traum," he said. "You must be dreaming."

Peiper shrugged and spent a few moments delivering a pompous and spirited lecture.

"Have it your way then. Usually I treat my guests more cordially, but we'll dispense with any pleasantries. If you want to fight with us you'll have to show you're up to it. My boys are as tough as they get. If you don't hold your own, they'll be taking over your tanks very quickly."[7]

Peiper managed to say all this with a straight face, but some of his men were grinning crookedly and laughing to themselves. Others were too dirty and worn out to have any reaction; they simply stared at the proceedings. Finally Peiper himself broke into a faint grin. One of Barkmann's men shook his head and nudged Barkmann in the arm.

Barkmann's men kept their tanks. They joined Peiper's group in an insane retreat to the Austrian border. One rear guard action followed another, always without infantry support. Fighting in isolation, the entire group could have been ambushed and wiped out at any time. But in some ways the Soviets were less dangerous, or at least less careful, in the course of their all-out pursuit of a broken enemy. Peiper's tanks no longer had to face the masses of dug-in Stalins, ISU-122s and PAK fronts that had broken up the German offensive a few days earlier. Now the Soviet armored columns were constantly on the move. Initially the retreat passed through the wooded hills of the Bakony Forest, now erupting with strangely idyllic greenery as spring seemed to arrive overnight. Peiper kept his vehicles on hilltops during the day, watching the Russian columns pass along the valley roads below, beating off any squadrons of T-34s that might be detached to attack them.

They descended from the hills onto the plains around the Raba River in western Hungary. In night marches they fought right through towns occupied by the enemy, rejoining other retreating German units, losing contact again, rejoining them again, fighting more rearguard actions.

Nine T-34s caught up with Peiper's group at dawn one day, while the SS tanks were retreating in column along a main road. The Soviets roared out onto the fields to the left and right, taking the Germans under fire from every direction. Although showing reckless courage, the Russians tended not to shoot very accurately during these fast-moving melees. Engaging in tank duels from a moving platform was a tactic they had never mastered. The T-34s were shot up one after the other. In either rage or frustration, one of the Soviet tanks headed straight for the main road and got into the midst of Peiper's column. It rammed into one Panther with a tremendous crash; following right behind, Barkmann's Panther fired at point-blank range and blasted the T-34's turret off its hull.

The rammed Panther must have been disabled at the least, though Barkmann doesn't mention its fate.

Each succeeding day brought similar actions. Disabled Panthers were taken under tow or abandoned. Ultimately Barkmann had to abandon and then blow up his own battle-damaged tank in the midst of another firefight.

He does not indicate how many vehicles survived to cross the Austrian frontier. While Leibstandarte fought a delaying action in the Vienna woods, Barkmann and his men finally caught up with Das Reich, positioned right along the border. His superiors told him that his Panther company had long since been given up for dead. "Written off," in the German soldiers' parlance. It was March 28th, 1945.

Years later Peiper told Toland that throughout the course of this retreat his crews had destroyed 125 Soviet tanks. In other phases of the war this figure would not be hard to believe, but with Peiper's small group being so low on fuel and shells, it seems possible that this was just another exaggerated or generalized statement. Ernst Barkmann's account does not give the impression of over 100 enemy tanks being knocked out. Individuals reminiscing after the war tend not to be as exact with numbers as German official records. On the other hand, anything was possible during those days, as German tank crews had shown again and again.

The Cost of Fruhlingserwachen

Of all the elite Waffen SS panzer divisions, only Frundsberg was still fighting in Germany. Most of the other SS divisions engaged along the lower Oder on the approaches to Berlin were less well-equipped foreign volunteer units.

Of Leibstandarte, Das Reich, Totenkopf, Wiking, Hohenstaufen, and Hitler Jugend, almost nothing remained. Small battlegroups gathered in the hills and forests outside Vienna or along the shores of the Neusiedler Lake nearby. Each panzer regiment had only a handful of tanks.

There was nothing left of 6th SS Army, or IV SS Corps, to ship to the Oder Front against Zhukov. Hitler had thrown his favorites into the meatgrinder once too often, and now they were finished, effectively out of the war. They would fight on around and inside Vienna, but it would not be another prolonged bloodbath like Budapest. Short, bitter, violent—the defense of Vienna by the SS would be as useless as the defense of Berlin by the remaining German forces there.

From the Soviet point of view, Operation Fruhlingserwachen had been the perfect trap. The most powerful panzer divisions remaining in both the army and the Waffen SS had been drawn into the mudfields, the mine belts and the dug-in Soviet armored groups between Lake Velencz and Lake Balaton. The Hungarian army to the north had been scattered so quickly by the Russian counteroffensive that it might as well never have existed. True, the Soviet spearheads did not quite manage to seal off the land corridor between the two lakes; almost all of the German units managed to escape through the narrow bottleneck between Vesprem and Stuhl-weissenberg, or else westward along the north shore of Lake Balaton.

But it didn't matter. The retreating units were shattered and might as well have been erased from the German order of battle. The Soviet response to the German offensive had turned into one of the war's most successful operations of deception and counter-maneuver. 6th SS Panzer Army, Germany's most powerful remaining armored formation, had been thrown away without accomplishing anything. Hitler's entire purpose for conducting this strange offensive had completely backfired. Rather than creating a wide buffer zone between the Soviets and the critical oil fields, the attack had degenerated into a rout which would lead the Soviets into the oil fields almost unopposed. The vast oil reserves at Nagykanisza fell into Soviet hands in the last days of March.

The Germans had begun Fruhlingserwachen with about as many men and armored vehicles as they had used in the Ardennes offensive. Clearly Hitler had hoped to repeat the success—or at least the initial success—of the Belgian operation. He needed to secure the Hungarian oilfields and he needed to buy time— time for all the SS panzer divisions to move up to Berlin after they had driven the Soviets in Hungary back to the Danube. From a strategic point of view it all made sense, as much sense as many of the successful fast-moving operations conducted earlier in the war.

But the enemy was infinitely stronger and more experienced than he had been in the early years. Hitler continued to ignore this fact up to the very end. Likewise he continued to ignore the terrible cost in attrition and exhaustion brought about by throwing his SS divisions into one major offensive after another, re-using them until they were used up.

What would have happened if Hitler had aborted Fruhlingserwachen altogether and shipped 6th SS Army, while it was still intact, to the Oder front? Probably he would have just thrown them into another fruitless counterattack against Zhukov's forces. Hitler and his compulsive supply of nervous energy seemed unable to abide the idea of establishing a static, deeply echeloned defensive system. Possibly such a tactic, combined with the deployment of Dietrich's army along the Oder, might have held off Zhukov's forces for a considerable length of time.

Time enough, perhaps, to allow the Western Allies to reach Berlin before the Soviets did.

Seen in this light, the Fruhlingserwachen debacle might be considered as one of the decisive battles in history. But such thinking is necessarily based on a good deal of speculation. And to speculate about alternative possibilities for a military situation that had degenerated into chaos and unreality is probably a vain endeavor.

PART V
EAST AND WEST PRUSSIA

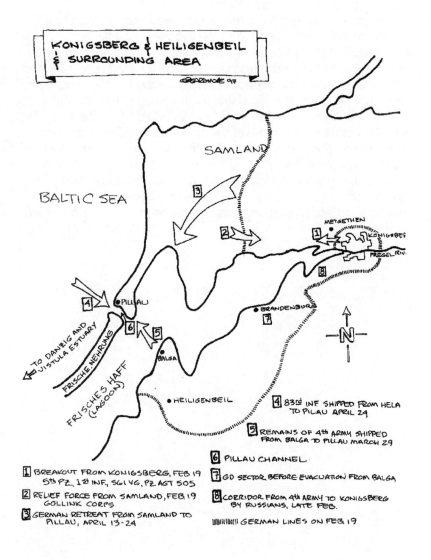

KONIGSBERG & HEILIGENBEIL
& SURROUNDING AREA

GREARDMORE 97

SAMLAND

BALTIC SEA

METGETHEN

KONIGSBERG

PREGEL RIV.

1

2

3

8

BRANDENBURG

7

N

PILLAU

4

6

5

TO DANZIG AND
VISTULA ESTUARY

FRISCHE NEHRUNG

FRISCHES HAFF
(LAGOON)

BALGA

HEILIGENBEIL

4 83RD INF SHIPPED FROM HELA
TO PILAU APRIL 24

5 REMAINS OF 4TH ARMY SHIPPED
FROM BALGA TO PILLAU MARCH 29

1 BREAKOUT FROM KONIGSBERG, FEB 19
5TH PZ, 1ST INF, 561 VG, PZ AGT 505

2 RELIEF FORCE FROM SAMLAND, FEB 19
GOLLNIK CORPS

3 GERMAN RETREAT FROM SAMLAND TO
PILLAU, APRIL 13-24

6 PILLAU CHANNEL

7 GD SECTOR BEFORE EVACUATION FROM BALGA

8 CORRIDOR FROM 4TH ARMY TO KONIGSBERG
BY RUSSIANS, LATE FEB.

|||||||||||| GERMAN LINES ON FEB 19

A heavy layer of snow still covers the Prussian landscape. The division, less one regiment left behind to defend Fortress Graudenz, continues its slow northward retreat through the moorlands of the Tucheler Heide.

A counterattack by a few Sturmgeschutzen, supported by an 88mm flak battery firing from the railroad embankment at Leutmannsdorf, destroys six T-34s and forces the Soviets to momentarily break off their relentless pursuit. The men in Leutmannsdorf use up all their ammunition and have to abandon the village, but for almost a week the Russians do not resume the advance.

Three days later the division is still holding in the next defensive position, around Neukirch. February 25th is a Sunday. The observation post in the church tower broadcasts "Day of Rest" through loudspeakers, the report carrying far and wide through the winter stillness. Within the church below, one of the grenadiers begins to play the organ—the deep tones of this music carrying far across the empty moorlands, lasting for many hours.

17

FORTRESS GRAUDENZ

257th Infantry Regiment Takes Its Turn to Die

83rd Infantry Division was shipped from Courland to West Prussia in November of 1944. They were one of the first units to be transferred out of that remote corner of Latvia.

Their timing was good. The Vistula Front was still quiet, and the Landsers of the 83rd were granted home leave. It was a rare occurrence this late in the war. "What a welcome surprise," exclaims the divisional history.[1]

Most of the veterans were from the Hamburg area, where the 83rd had been raised. So they travelled to this region of northwest Germany and were able to spend Christmas with their families there. In the meantime 7,000 replacements were shipped to the division's new base at Thorn in West Prussia. This was a very large number to be absorbed into one division. But the 83rd had left a large number of graves behind in Russia.

The new men left a lot to be desired. There were a lot of barely fit specimens who would not have qualified for the draft in the early years. There were wounded men still not fully recovered from their wounds. The majority of the replacements were poorly trained teenagers or "alte Knochen" (old bones—older men in their thirties and forties). After an inspection by the division's medical staff, 10% of the new arrivals were declared unfit for duty and sent back to the replacement depots.

The Reich was reaching the end of its manpower reserves. Every combat unit on the Eastern and Western Front was experiencing the same kinds of problems. During these days every manner of re-organization and personnel reshuffling was resorted to. Naval and Luftwaffe personnel were combed out to replenish the ground forces. During the months to come the 83rd would incorporate policemen and railroad workers on an ad hoc basis. These men would fight well, as the end neared.

In the winter of 1942/43, the 83rd's 277th Infantry Regiment had been wiped out to the last man during the siege of Velikiye

Luki. It had been a horrible battle, largely unnoticed by the rest of the nation, which had been preoccupied by the Stalingrad catastrophe at that time. But the veterans of the 83rd remembered. In honor of this unit, a new 277th Infantry Regiment was established at Thorn in January of 1945.

The 83rd was the "W/W" Division, with these two initials symbolizing the division's epic winter battles in the obscure Russian towns of Velizh and Velikiye Luki (Welish and Welikiye Luki in German). Both those names were already years old in the soldiers' memories; the more recent fighting in 1944 had been almost as bad, the grim retreat through northern Russia and Latvia that had finally ended in the Courland Peninsula, where the 83rd had taken heavy casualties during the Russians' first grand offensive there. But now the immediate future would involve these long-suffering infantrymen in more terrible battles still. Out of all the German divisions that were wiped-out or nearly wiped-out in 1945, the fate of the 83rd was to be one of the most tragic.

The veterans returned from their home-leave at the beginning of January. The division was slated to move to East Prussia, where the Russians had been making their first murderous forays across the German frontier since the autumn of 1944. The Landsers were actually en route to this area when the Soviet Vistula Offensive tore the Eastern Front apart. The 83rd was immediately called back to Thorn, finding upon their return here that the Russian spearheads were only a few miles away. All of this happened so quickly that some elements of the division were still in transit to East Prussia and never returned to the parent formation.

The brutal fighting retreat began. The Soviet drive north to the Baltic was much more fiercely contested than their drive west to the Oder. The Russians had deployed relatively weaker forces here, while the Germans, in light of their hard-fought defense of the frontier since the previous fall, were relatively stronger. While only two armies—the 9th and 4th Panzer—had been stationed behind the Vistula, there were three in East and West Prussia: 2nd Army, 3rd Panzer Army, and 4th Army.

2nd Army, deployed furthest to the west, was the weakest of the three, and it was in this sector that the Russians made their best initial gains towards the Baltic. Even so, the German retreat here was anything but a rout. Every village was bitterly contested, at least for a few days, until the Soviets managed to push the defenders back another few miles to the next village.

The weather was snowy and bitterly cold. The winter, relatively mild elsewhere in eastern Europe, paid a brutal visit to the two Prussian provinces in January and February. The frozen miseries of the weather added a great deal to the thousandfold other miseries of the refugees fleeing this area.

83rd Infantry Division retreated with the rest of 2nd Army, falling back from Thorn in the general direction of Graudenz. Their path parallelled that of several divisions we mentioned briefly in an earlier chapter—252nd Infantry Division, 35th Infantry Division, 5th Jaeger Division, 15th Latvian SS Division. The Jaegers and the Latvians were driven west of the Vistula, eventually to be decimated in the coastal regions of Pomerania. The other units of 2nd Army continued to fall back towards the north, still in West Prussia.

After two weeks of fighting in snowy villages and hamlets, the 83rd fell back upon the larger town of Graudenz, a picturesque old place on the east bank of the Vistula. From cellar foundations built right along the river, sheer walls of old stone masonry rose up for several hundred feet to the levels of buildings and churches situated on the highest part of the river bank. Thus the riverside part of town resembled a cliff wall constructed of medieval blocks of stone, with massive buttresses flaring out at intervals. But this fortress-like appearance was misleading. From the landward side, Graudenz was no more than another old Prussian town.

Whether by design or by fate, the regiments of the 83rd were to develop a cruel tradition of fighting to the last man by war's end. At Velikiye Luki the 277th had gone down. At Graudenz in 1945, it would be the turn of 257th Infantry Regiment to fight to the last.

For the first two weeks of February, the entire division was still engaged here. Contact with other German units was tenuous at best. To the east there was no one except the Russians. To the west, across the Vistula, there was only intermittent contact with the neighboring 252nd Infantry Division. The ice on the river was still frozen solid and the Russians had been able to cross over, pushing relentlessly to the north along both banks. Yet their further progress would be stymied throughout the month of February by the defenders of Graudenz.

One battalion of the 83rd had been sent across the river to establish a bridgehead on the west bank, and it was in this area that the action was heaviest for the first two weeks. If the Russians broke through here they could simply bypass Graudenz and leave the garrison to die. As they so often did, the Germans considered offense to be the best defense, and this west bank battalion went over to the attack as soon as the first Russian elements appeared. The enemy was caught by surprise and the battalion was able to clear out the woods along the west bank for a distance of several miles. It was a startling achievement, considering that this unit had only about fifty "old hands" among several hundred inexperienced recruits and ex-navy men.

But somehow it never seemed that difficult to catch the Russians off guard, at least at first. The enemy almost seemed to employ the tactic of sacrificing their advance units, simply to test the German strength. The battalion was now assigned to maintain contact with the neighboring 252nd Infantry Division, which was being heavily punished and pushed further to the north and west. Combat raged for days around the Andreas Forest House, with the German battalion doggedly attacking in the face of heavy machine gun fire. The Russians abandoned the forest house, then recaptured it. The dead of both sides lay in the snow all through the woods. The battalion counterattacked again with only fifty men still fit for action. It was a bloody failure. Finally the division sent another battalion over to the west bank, and with the highly fortuitous arrival of six Sturmgeschutzen the Russians in the Andreas Forest House were wiped out after a three-hour firefight. "The brave defenders—Siberians—did not budge an inch and fought to the last man."[2]

By this time Major Beneke's battalion, the first to go over to the west bank, had only 45 men remaining.

But the bridgehead had to be held; it provided the only link with other German forces. All of the east bank of the river outside Graudenz was now in Soviet hands. The divisional commander needed every available man just to defend the town, but he had no choice but to send more reinforcements over to the west bank. The entire 257th Infantry Regiment now took up positions there.

The bridgehead was ringed by low hills manned by Russian observation posts. They had a clear view of anything that moved below and directed ceaseless artillery strikes against the supply columns crossing the bridge from Graudenz. At length it was only possible to supply the bridgehead at night. The

Silesia: *A Hetzer tank destroyer and Panzer II F of the Panzer Aufklarung Abteilung move to contact with Russian armor.*

Silesia: *Panzergrenadiers of Panzergrenadier Regiment 28 advance in support of the Hetzer.*

Silesia: Burning Soviet SU 85 tank destroyer in Cunzendorf.

Silesia: Panzer II F of the Panzer Aufklarung Abteilung in outskirts of Cunzendorf. It is rare to find a Panzer II still operational in February 1945.

Silesia: Goebbels meets with Field Marshal Schorner in Lauban after its recapture, March 1945.

Silesia: Goebbels reviews the assembled troops.

Silesia: Goebbels addresses the troops in Lauban.

Hungary: Sepp Dietrich Commander of the 6th SS Panzer Army. *(Wilson)*

Hungary: Heinz Landau on right photographed in February 1945.

Hungary: Hungarian Zrinyi II tank destroyer. This successful vehicle was armed with a 105mm 40/43.M. Mavag howitzer. (Warfield)

Hungary: *Soviet sub-machine gunners fight their way through the outskirts of Budapest. (Warfield)*

Hungary: *Soviet engineers built this pontoon bridge across the Danube in Budapest. (Warfield)*

Hungary: SS
Oberscharfuhrer Ernst
Barkmann of the 2nd SS
Panzer Division "Das Reich."
Knights Cross awarded August
8th, 1944. (Wilson)

Hungary: Soldiers of the Red Army march through liberated Budapest. (Warfield)

East Prussia: Russian and German soldiers talk after the surrender of Graudenz on March 6th, 1945. (Warfield)

East Prussia: A Kampfgruppe of the RAD (Reichsarbeitsdienst – Labor Service) in action.

German forces were too weak to take possession of the commanding hills.

The fate of 257th Infantry Regiment was sealed not by the Russians but by the German High Command. Hitler had designated Graudenz as a fortress city, falling into the same luckless category as Posen and Konigsberg, Budapest and Breslau. The term "fortress city" had nothing to do with fortifications or actual defensive strength. It was simply a phrase that Hitler had coined out of thin air, with the stipulation that the garrison would hold out without retreating and fight to the last man. "Bis zum letzen Patrone," as the Landsers would say. To the last cartridge.

Thus the men of the 83rd were cheered considerably, when they received word from 2nd Army on February 15th that they were to evacuate Graudenz and withdraw to the north. What a relief it must have been for the fighting men to hear this news. Had Hitler changed his mind, rescinded the fortress decree? No one knew or cared. There were still a number of Volksturm units garrisoning the town, as well as a so-called "Replacement Brigade" of the Herman Goering Corps. Perhaps these poor bastards would still be ordered to hold out to the last man. In these days a man could see the shape of his own good fortune outlined by the awful fate of someone else not so lucky.

But then later that night further instructions were radioed in from 2nd Army. The 83rd was still pulling out, but one of its regiments was ordered to stay behind at Graudenz. This was 257th Infantry Regiment. The divisional commander, General Heun, was heartsick at this news and made repeated requests to have the orders changed. All to no avail. More than heartsick, the mood of the men of this abandoned, and now obviously doomed, regiment can only be imagined.

The orders were of that capricious and cruelly arbitrary nature that seemingly only the "rarefied higher headquarters swine" would ever understand. They were destined to leave everyone with bitter feelings. For not only the 83rd was affected. The Herman Goering Replacement Brigade was also split in half, with one regiment ordered to withdraw and the other ordered to fight on in Graudenz beside 257th Infantry Regiment.

By this time it was almost too late for anyone to escape. The only route out of town started from the west bank bridgehead and followed a narrow road leading north, right next to the Vistula River. The withdrawal took place as scheduled during the night of February 16th, but only a few hours later the Russians finally managed to block the road for good. The lucky regiments escaped to the north in the direction of Danzig and the Tucheler Heide (Moor). Those left behind to continue the defense of Graudenz were now completely isolated.

For a few days 257th Infantry Regiment remained in position on the west bank, repelling Russian tank attacks that frequently penetrated right up to the river. But the bridgehead no longer served any purpose. With Soviet assaults intensifying against the city proper on the east bank, the regiment was pulled back across the river to help man the walls, fighting beside the Volksturm and the second regiment of the Herman Goering Replacement Brigade.

The withdrawal into the city was a close thing. Russian artillery fire had destroyed the main bridge several days before; the only other crossing was a wooden pontoon bridge built by the engineers. By now the ice had begun to melt and the cracked and upheaved floes drifting down the river threatened to sweep away the makeshift bridge. The regiment managed to cross over under heavy fire, but Russian assault units were right on their heels and the whole structure had to be destroyed immediately. For some reason no demolition charges had been prepared; instead the bridge was doused with gasoline and set afire. But the damnable wooden pontoons were so soaked through from melting ice that they burned very slowly. A few courageous Russians stormed onto the bridge and tried to put out the flames. In fact they succeeded in doing so, but only after the structure had been too badly damaged to bear the weight of vehicles.

The Soviets switched the weight of their assaults to the east bank. The siege entered its last phase, nearly three weeks of frightful house-to-house combat inside the town, differing only in scale from the tremendous urban violence that had just come to an end at Budapest.

Again holes were blown through walls and cellars to make passageways for the combatants of both sides, with the same terrible skirmishes taking place at these indoor intersections. Much of Graudenz had already been honeycombed below-ground earlier in the war, passages leading from one housing block to another that had been designed originally to help civilians escape from collapsed buildings during air raids. But the air raids had never come to this part of West Prussia, though now Russian Stormoviks were overhead hour after hour. Instead the underground passages were used by the Russians to infiltrate the German defenses. Frequently they were guided through the maze by Polish civilians who had lived in Graudenz during the war years. There was a certain irony in this, for the Poles and Russians were ancient enemies, and any alliance between them during these last months of the war would be fleeting at best. But since 1939 the Poles had learned to hate the Germans far more.

Graudenz was located in one of these gerrymandered areas that had been ceded to the new nation of Poland after World War One, even though the city had been primarily German for hundreds of years. During all these generations Poles and Germans had co-existed more or less peacefully, apart from the usual forms of ethnic antagonism. After annexation back into the Reich in 1939, relations between the two peoples had deteriorated drastically with the advent of brutal Nazi repression.

And so embittered Polish civilians were now in the position of leading Russian storm battalions through the underground tunnels in 1945, or pointing out likely German strong points above ground. Yet for others the sense of loyalty remained confused, the contempt for the familiar mixed with the dread of the unknown. Some Poles remained in the cellars with the German civilians, falling back block by block as the garrison retreated.

The terror of the civilians was augmented by a lack of water, as the city's mains had ceased to function. People jammed into the cellars began to go mad with thirst. Water was only available from a few broken mains out in the streets, which were surrounded by the bodies of thirst-crazed human beings who had been shot down by Russian snipers. The corpses did not deter others dying of thirst, who were shot down in their turn as they emerged into the open to fetch water. Other people ate handfuls of grimy, cordite-blackened snow, which only made their thirst worse than before. The defenders were crowded underground along with the town's population, and the distress of the civilians became so unbearable that the soldiers could hardly concentrate on fighting.

Very few German combatants survived to tell tales of these battles.

"Slowly, from street to street, from block to block, house to house, the city was rolled up from south to north. Men fought with bayonets and hand grenades in the murky darkness of the brick kilns inside the brewery. How many were killed in this street and house to house fighting can never be known for sure."[3]

By March 5th the defenders had been broken up into isolated pockets. The fortress commandant, General Fricke, granted each small unit freedom of action—essentially meaning they had permission to break out, if they could. But it was hopeless. One battalion of the Hermann Goering regiment tried to escape to the north; they were wiped out except for a small group of stragglers, whom the Russians killed or captured out in the countryside a few days later.

The only men from 257th Infantry Regiment to escape were five pioneers led by a seventeen year old corporal, who set off down the river in a rubber boat, dodging ice floes and Russian fire. A heavy snowfall camouflaged their passage along the water. About fifty other men who tried the same escape route never made it. The Russians got wind of what was going on and machine-gunned everyone else at the moment they were putting their boats into the water. The dead were swept down the Vistula or lay sprawled beneath the soaring riverside walls of the city. The five who got away eventually arrived at Danzig at the mouth of the river, half-frozen, bearing terrible tales.

The rest of the garrison surrendered on March 8th. They were marched off to spend years of captivity inside the Soviet Union, a destination from which few German soldiers ever returned. The siege of this insignificant West Prussian town had lasted nearly six weeks. The bodies of dead civilians lay everywhere, as if felled by a plague.

And yet, for the other regiments of 83rd Infantry Division who had been withdrawn three weeks earlier, the mad ordeal of 1945 was only just beginning.

Alarm battalions are formed to fill in gaps in the decimated front lines. These units consist of men scraped together from anywhere—clerks, signalmen, wounded men. Many have never been in combat before.

They are issued panzerfausts and thrown against the Russian tanks. Three Stalins are advancing. Two are hit and destroyed by the hand-held rockets. The third accelerates and keeps rumbling forward until it is only thirty yards away. Sajer grabs a panzerfaust, but he is blinded by the exhaust gases from another panzerfaust fired by a comrade. By the time he regains his sight the tank is driving past only a few feet away. Tracks and road wheels caked with mud fill his field of vision. He is screaming with terror and he hears other screams all around him.

The Stalin drives onward until it disappears in the midst of a huge explosion. An instant later he sees the tank lifted bodily into the air, then falling and disappearing again within an impenetrable cloud of smoke. Sajer looks around for some kind of solid object, thinking he has been blinded again, but he can see nothing except smoke and flames.

VERHEIZEN

Trapped Against the Baltic

The 215th Infantry Division left Courland in February, shipping out of Libau and debarking a few days later in Gotenhafen. This was a relatively new city that had been expanded after World War One to provide a home base for the fleet of the new nation of Poland. It had been Gdynia in those days, before the German fleet moved in in 1939. Now it was Gotenhafen, grown up to become a sister city to the great port of Danzig lying only a few miles to the south.

Like almost every division that had fought in Russia, the 215th had undergone an odyssey since 1941. It had borne the initial brunt of the Russians' great midwinter attack across the Volkhov River in 1942. There had followed months of terrible fighting in the frozen Volkhov swamps, after which subzero temperatures rose and released clouds of mosquitoes in those hellish humid forests. Then came nearly a year spent in the siege lines in a "quiet" sector on the west side of Leningrad, hard by the waters of the Gulf of Finland. Then transfer to the more violent sector on the east side of the siege ring, between Lake Ladoga and the Ssyinyavino Hills—the Third Battle of Lake Ladoga in the late summer of 1943.

Then the long retreat from Leningrad to the Lake of Peipus in January of 1944, barely escaping annihilation along with the rest of Army Group North. Pskov, the Velikaya River. Then Latvia in the summer of 1944, countless small towns in Latvia, facing a Red Army whose force had become unstoppable. Then finally retreat into the Courland peninsula in the fall of 1944, the last German redoubt in the East.

The First Courland Battle in October. The Second Courland Battle in November. The third in December. The fourth in January. Before war's end the Russians would make two more grand offensives against the German lines. But 215th Infantry Division was shipped back to Germany in late February of 1945. The men were pleased to escape from that remote and doomed battlefield.

Even in midwinter, the cruise across the Baltic was almost pleasant. The seas were mild. There was danger from Soviet submarines, the infantrymen had probably seen too much by now and simply ignored this threat. Let the sailors worry about it. They played the accordion on deck, they played cards, they smoked, they drank real German beer dispensed by the ship's commissary. Much of the voyage was sunny and many men simply sat on deck staring into space. There is nothing quite like a sea cruise to alleviate years of stress and privation.

A few days later the men walked down the gangways onto the docks of Gotenhafen, under skies that were still sunny and mild. Perhaps large numbers of them, up to this point, had wondered if they would ever set foot on German soil again.

Within a month of this date, almost all of these men would be dead on German soil.

Another division shipped from Courland to Gotenhafen at this same time was 32nd Infantry Division. They had fought in the epic cauldron battle at Demyansk in 1942.

Both the 215th and 32nd were immediately moved south of Danzig to take up part of 2nd Army's defensive positions on the moorlands of the Tucheler Heide. Here they hoped to hold back the Russian armies which had blasted across the Vistula and Narew Rivers back in January. At this time the main body of 83rd Infantry Division was also engaged in these moorlands, while the remainder of the doomed garrison continued to hold out at Graudenz.

The Soviet drive north to Danzig and the Baltic had been a secondary operation to the main drive to the Oder. German and Russian forces in both East and West Prussia were somewhat more evenly matched. The Germans were pushed back towards the Baltic, but the retreat was slow and savagely fought.

At the end of February 1945, 215th Infantry Division confronted its destiny near Konitz on the Tucheler Heide. A pair of veteran divisions from Courland [referring also to 32nd Infantry Division] attempted to hold back the great flood of the Soviet advance. But the enemy merely probed our defenses, then turned to our flanks and broke through the positions of the neighboring Volksturm battalions. Day after day we held on to our positions, but night after night we had to retreat

from ten to fifteen miles, as the Russians were continually advancing on our flanks.[1]

It was a brutal trek. The distance was relatively short, but the days and weeks were long, filled with blood and one defensive stand after another. By mid-March the 215th had been forced all the way back to Gotenhafen. Already Danzig was on the verge of being overrun and obliterated. Gotenhafen would soon meet an identical fate. Over a million refugees and wounded soldiers crowded the twin ports, under constant shellfire and air attack. Day after day ships overflowing with civilians sailed out into the Baltic, hoping to reach safety in Denmark or the ports of western Germany.

This hellish period in the winter and spring of 1945 was the finest hour for the German Navy and merchant marine. The sea-borne rescue of millions of terrified refugees was the largest operation of its kind in history. This period also saw the worst disasters at sea in history. Merchant ships and converted passenger liners would carry 5,000, 6,000, as many as 7,000 civilians and soldiers at a time; several of these vessels were sunk by Russian submarines, with the loss of almost everyone on board. As tragedies on the high seas, these incidents would be without equal.

But in fact there were only a few such episodes. In 1945 the German Navy re-enacted the miracle of Dunkirk on a tenfold larger scale, beneath the guns of an enemy set not only on victory but on mass-slaughter. By war's end over ninety percent of the refugee ships would manage to bring their human cargoes to safety in the west.

But the men of 215th Infantry Division would never make it to these safe havens. The soldiers of this and most of the other German divisions would remain trapped in and around Goten-hafen, enduring slaughter day after day while the civilians escaped.

In the front lines ammunition was running out; shells for the artillery were already gone. Supply and artillery units were combed out ["ausgekammt"] and sent to the front lines as alarm-battalions. Soldiers not trained for infantry combat merely served as target practice for Russian tanks. In the jargon of the Landsers, the useless slaughter resulting from these actions was described by a single phrase—"Verheizen." Into the flames.[2]

Gotenhafen, what was left of it, fell on March 26th. The German divisions retreated to Oxhoft, a wide barren plateau along the coast just a few miles to the north. Tens of thousands of men were crammed onto this bleak elevation, probably a third of them lying wounded in the hospital tents. Many of the remainder were either without weapons or the ammunition to fire them with. Massed Soviet artillery parks vaporized every structure still standing on this plateau from one end to the other. If Leon DeGrelle had been here, he would have witnessed the same awesome barrages that he had experienced in the Altdamm Bridgehead on the lower Oder.

Still the surviving fighting men refused to be cornered. In the first days of April naval ferries evacuated almost every German unit on Oxhoft, landing right on the beach at the foot of the high plateau. Almost the entire operation was conducted during the night hours in order to elude the Soviet artillery and air attacks. As the last ferries pulled away in the dawn light of the final day, a few despairing bands of men were observed running back and forth beneath the cliffs. Perhaps they were part of a rear guard unit, perhaps they had gotten lost somehow, but they had not made it to the beaches in time. They made only a few half-hearted attempts at waving and signalling; they seemed to realize that no one would be coming back for them now.

At least they would not be alone. Thousands of wounded men had been left behind up on the plateau, along with a few brave doctors, either brave or conscience-bound to their chosen profession. Usually the Russians, when faced with such a large number of prisoners, did not murder them all outright. The abandoned men could only hope that this would be so.

The naval ferries headed for the only dry land remaining, the long thread of the Hela peninsula that jutted into the Baltic to the east. A few small resorts and vacation homes lined the beaches, a few small fishing settlements; but on the whole there were only empty dunes. At the very tip lay the tiny port of Hela; that was where the ferries were going, a journey of about twenty miles from Oxhoft across Danzig Bay. From here, larger ships, most of them anchored out in the bay, would continue to evacuate civilians and wounded men to the west.

The 215th Infantry Division was dissolved, its few surviving fighting men parcelled out to reinforce 32nd Infantry Division. The headquarters staff of the 215th was shipped out from Hela—lucky devils—headed for safety and reassignment somewhere in the west. "The divisional commander was deeply moved as he bade farewell to the remains of this division which had fought so bravely."[3] This was General Frankewitz. He and his staff had been ordered to return to Berlin, there to take over a newly formed and untrained division, which would soon be wiped out in the final battle for the capital of the Reich.

The 215th had been one of so many army units to rely almost entirely on horse-drawn transport from the beginning of the war to the end. "Die treue Camerade." "Die Treue Begleiter." (Our true friends. Our true companions.) Phrases like these become almost cliches in the histories of German infantry divisions. Horses were as much a part of the German soldiers' lives on the Eastern Front as they had been for the soldiers of Napoleon's armies. "Half-starving and dying of thirst," the horses of the 215th had all been shot by their keepers on the Oxhoft plateau, before the final crossing over to the Hela peninsula. The Soviets climbing up to the plateau would find as many dead horses as dead soldiers.[4]

The surviving infantrymen, now attached to 32nd Infantry Division, were assembled into a bedraggled force designated as Kampfgruppe Herb, named after the commander of one of the 215th's former regiments. These men were not destined to stay in Hela for very long—almost as soon as they arrived here they were shipped out again. Were they sailing out to the west, following their divisional commander to safety?

"Aus die Traume," as Panther commander Ernst Barkmann might have said at about this same time in Hungary.

Only in their dreams.

The sea voyage for Kampfgruppe Herb was very short, only a matter of hours. More of a day's excursion than a voyage. Herb's men, together with the rest of 32nd Infantry Division, left Hela on the same naval ferries in which they had arrived from Oxhoft—the flat, barge-like vessels nicknamed "sea-snakes" by both sailors and Landsers. But they were sailing towards the east, not the west. They crossed forty miles of open sea and then disembarked at the port of Pillau, a resort town near Konigsberg that was nearly a mirror image of Hela, the place they had just left. Not only that—the terrible fighting still going on around Konigsberg was also nearly a mirror image of the awful, backs-to-the-sea ordeal they had just endured around Danzig and Gotenhafen. Rather than sailing to freedom in the west, Kampfgruppe Herb marched off to the trenches around Konigsberg, there to face the last Soviet offensive against that city. What hell.

"Do you see them?"
"Ja, Bix."

BIX AND THE JAGDPANTHERS

Tank-killing Ace of 4th Panzer Division

As usual, there are too many stories to tell, not only from this region but from everywhere else. Let us recount a few more episodes from the fighting outside Danzig and Gotenhafen in February and March.

4th Panzer Division had been shipped from Courland to West Prussia in late 1944, along with 83rd Infantry Division. Like a number of other units, these two divisions were resting, reorganizing, and receiving much needed replacements when the Russian Vistula offensive began in January.

By the beginning of March, 4th Panzer had retreated through the Tucheler Heide to positions around Prussian Stargard (not to be confused with Stargard in Pomerania), only a few miles southwest of Danzig. The Russians had already reached the Baltic coast at numerous points in Pomerania, cutting off West and East Prussia from the rest of Germany. Thousands of refugees who had been fleeing west towards the Oder now found their escape route blocked by the Red Army; they had no choice but to turn around and fall back on Danzig and Gotenhafen. The roads around these cities were jammed with civilians milling in confusion, constantly obstructing the movements of the military units trying to establish defensive positions.

Serving in 4th Panzer Division was Oberfeldwebel Hermann Bix, one of the army's leading tank killers. He had gone into Russia in a Mk III in 1941, scoring only a few kills in this undergunned tank. By 1944 he was commanding a Panther and had destroyed over fifty Russian tanks in a six month period during the summer and fall. During this time he was wounded twice and had two Panthers shot out from under him. On the last occasion, during the First Courland Battle in October, his Panther had received a direct hit from a Stalin Organ rocket. How any of his crew survived this blast was beyond comprehension, but four of them did, though they all had to be hospitalized with severe concussions.

Bix recalled feeling as if his skull plates were about to give way from the inside out. He also recalled the inhuman screams of the one crew member who had not survived the blast. The explosive power of these rockets was so great that it created a void in the atmosphere immediately around the point of impact, sucking the air out of men's lungs and expanding their chest cavities almost to the bursting point. Perhaps this was what had happened to his dead comrade. But Bix didn't know if it was possible to scream or not when your lungs were sucked out.

He might have spent months recovering from this ordeal, psychologically as well as physically, but instead he returned to his unit after only a short stay in the field hospital. 1944 had been a bad year. 1945 would be no better.

By March, 4th Panzer had only a handful of Panthers left. Somehow the division found itself in possession of six Jagdpanthers that had been intended for some other unit. German factories were still turning out new armored vehicles, but they never seemed to arrive at the front in more than small parcels. Bix was given command of this platoon of tank destroyers, though after spending so much time in a Panther he continued to refer to them as tanks. At first his crew felt uncomfortable fighting in a vehicle that had no rotating turret. In its fixed mantlet the cannon had only a limited traverse from left to right. But the gun was a long 88mm, the same weapon that armed the King Tiger, and for penetrating power and accuracy it was without equal.

The smooth unbroken slope of the Jagdpanther's armor tended to deflect even the heaviest caliber enemy shells, and its low, even silhouette made it difficult to spot. In short it was the ideal ambush vehicle, the best tank destroyer produced by any side during the war.

It had a strangely beautiful appearance, with the long slope of the forward armor lending it an illusion of being slightly jacked-up at the rear end, like a massive hot rod encased in sleek armor. Less than 400 were ever built, with most not entering service until the end of the war. It was a somewhat mysterious weapon, rarely seen in photographs or newsreels. Bix and his crew became acclimated to it in a short time, then put it to work.

The Russians had just captured Prussian Stargard. Bix took three Jagdpanthers to block any further enemy advance towards Danzig. The tank destroyers shelled the Russians in the village, buying time for the German infantry to retreat. Patches of snow still lay scattered across the ground. The winter had been a short one; further to the south it had also been fairly mild. But blizzards had swept across all of Prussia during January and February. It was starting to get warmer now, but one last storm had hit only a few days earlier. Now the snow was melting slowly. Bix positioned the Jagdpanther behind a large compost heap next to some farm buildings. The faint warmth issuing from the refuse brought a slight blur to the air. Hopefully it might blur the lines of his vehicle as well, to the eyes of any enemy observers in the village.

The other two Jagdpanthers had already shot off almost all their ammunition. Bix ordered them to pull back out of range for the time being.

Ahead of him and to the right lay the village. Beyond lay a range of the low hills that crowded the coastal areas behind Danzig and Gotenhafen. He was in an unnerving position, as it was impossible to get a good view of his surroundings from inside the vehicle. Tanks would be easy for him to spot, but the Russian infantry inside the village might easily infiltrate unseen. They had their ways of killing armored vehicles just as the German infantry did. Bix would crack the hatch every so often and peer about, but he was reluctant to make even this much movement. Winter stillness filled the air.

He was relieved to see a small group of men on foot approach the Jagdpanther, Germans. The infantry had already pulled back; these people turned out to be tank crews from 4th Panzer whose vehicles had been destroyed. He had no idea what they were doing here, but the officer in charge was acquainted with Bix and offered to set up a defensive perimeter and keep an eye out for any Russians approaching with Molotov cocktails, magnetic charges, or the like.

Much better. Bix lowered the hatch and set himself to scanning the hills beyond the village through the periscope, where the Soviet armor would have to come through.

Presently two silhouettes appeared over the nearest crest. Not T-34s, not Stalins. They were American tanks, lend-lease Shermans. Bix spoke in the silence.

"1200 meters."

His gunner put his forehead against the rubberized guard around the optical sight. He was used to the excellent accuracy of the Panther's long 75mm. He would find that the Jagdpanther's long 88mm was more accurate still.

The first shot blew one of the tracks off the leading Sherman. It stopped dead. The second shot transformed the tank into a torch.

The second Sherman halted, fired. The shot ripped through the still air near the compost heap.

Bix's gunner traversed the long cannon by a few degrees. He fired again.

In an instant the second Sherman was spewing flame and smoke alongside the first one. Two pyres. None of the crews escaped.

Sherman tanks were inadequately armored and they ran on high-octane aviation fuel. It was a fairly dreadful combination. The Russians hated them. On the Western Front, British crews using Shermans derisively called them "Ronsons," after the cigarette lighter. Because they burned. American crews also took to using this unhappy nickname. What the Russian crews called them has not been recorded.

Time passed. Bix peered through the periscope. The Third Reich was being torn asunder. Behind the compost heap somewhere between Danzig and Prussian Stargard, all was still.

Two more Shermans appeared, veering around the outskirts of the village. How had they gotten so close? Maybe they'd been lurking in there the whole time. Already they'd driven right past the Jagdpanther's flank, and the tank destroyer had no rotating turret to track them with.

But the Russians still didn't know where Bix was. It is surprising how swiftly a 50 ton vehicle can turn on opposing treads. Bix's driver would have had to get used to performing this maneuver on an instant's notice, but it was still no different from driving a tank. The Jagdpanther turned left 90 degrees and fired. The Shermans were passing only 100 yards away. The first was holed in the side; in all likelihood, at point blank range, the armor-piercing shell would have gone entirely through the enemy vehicle. It erupted in flames. The second Sherman reacted instantly and turned to fire. Bix's gunner and loader were swifter. Their second shot torched the Russian before it could get off a shot. Two more "Ronsons" were burning. A few crewmen managed to bale out this time. They were gunned down by the men on foot who had set up a perimeter around Bix's vehicle.

The Russians tactics had been sensible enough, in their peculiar way. Twice now they had sent out two tanks, one to draw the German's fire and the other to kill the German vehicle after it revealed its position. But the reaction time of the Soviet crews was simply not fast enough; typically a German gunner could get off twice as many shots over a given time period as his adversary, and do it more accurately.

But meanwhile there remained the threat of the infantry still inside the village. Now more Russian foot soldiers were coming down from the hills and entering the houses. The dozen or so German tank crewmen who had been covering Bix's vehicle began to get nervous and pulled back. At this point Bix would have liked to do the same. The Ivans must have spotted his position by now. Bix radioed his commander, requesting either new orders or assistance.

"What about Dehmer and Pollerd?" came the reply.

These were the two Jagdpanther commanders Bix had told to pull back earlier.

"They're low on ammunition. Pollerd's also got engine damage."

Bix's commander told him to hold his position. The retreating German infantry needed time to set up new defensive works before the Russian resumed the attack.

Bix did not argue. He was not pleased, but nor was he overly perturbed. In four years he had had as many tanks shot out from under him; he had been wounded time and again; he had seen his crew members die inside vehicles from which he had escaped; he had seen a comrade with his arm ripped off by an enemy shell being hauled out of a wrecked Panther and borne screaming to the rear. There was nothing to think about anymore. His nerves would respond unconsciously like a normal bodily function; if his nerve were ever to give out on him, it probably would have already done so long ago.

He scanned the hills. Now the Russians were setting up anti-tank guns there. The accuracy of the Soviet PAK batteries was much better than that of their tank gunners.

"See them?" said Bix to his gunner.

"Ja, Bix."

The Jagdpanther fired, high explosive this time. Splinters of wood on the hilltop were sent cartwheeling into the air. It was a trick; the Russian guns were dummies made of wood, set up to draw fire so the German vehicle would be located.

Now what? The Ivans were cunning but also more than a little pigheaded. They promptly rolled two more guns into position. Were they real ones this time or more decoys? To hell with it.

Bix ordered his driver to back away from the compost heap and find a new position. Still they were not fired on. It seemed hardly possible that the Russians had not seen them yet, especially with the two Shermans still burning only a hundred yards away. But the atmosphere of strange inactivity persisted.

Over the course of several hours four Russian tanks had been burnt-out, along with a number of hapless footsoldiers killed next to their dummy guns, sent to their deaths as decoys by their commanders. But these incidents had been only momentary interruptions in the prevailing stillness of a winter day. When tanks are fighting in motion with motors roaring there is nothing louder. When a crew stands by for hours in ambush, never sure if they have been spotted yet, there is nothing quieter.

The Jagdpanther backed up a short distance into a new firing position. The crew began another indefinite period of waiting. At least now they were further away from the enemy infantry, who still posed the greatest potential threat, the greatest source of tension.

After a while more vehicles appeared coming over the hills, a long column this time. Tanks in front, followed by trucks carrying infantry. The tanks were T-34s.

So at last the Russians had decided to get on the move again. Perhaps they had spotted Bix pulling back and concluded that he was gone from the area. There was no way to know. But no need to worry about it any longer either. The long harsh waiting silence was replaced by a few moments of roaring panic.

"The leading T-34 first," said Bix.

His gunner fired. The shot went wide, striking a tree. The tree collapsed onto the first T-34, which promptly veered off into a ditch. Nothing like a little luck. The rear deck of the Russian tilted up high and blocked the road, jamming the vehicles behind it. They were following too close together to get out of each other's way. Some left the road and likewise became stuck in the ditch. Others rotated their cannon like the antennae of insects frantically feeling for prey, firing all over the place. Most were shooting in entirely the wrong direction, at the earth mounds marking the trench lines outside the village, the positions abandoned by the German infantry hours ago.

A tank cannon is no more than an enormous rifle. Bix's gunner picked off one T-34 after another like a sniper. The Soviets began rotating their turrets the other way and firing in Bix's direction, still without seeing exactly where he was. Explosions blanketed the landscape. Russian crews scrambled to get out of knocked-out vehicles. Flames from burning T-34s spread to others jammed up close behind; within minutes the entire column was a mass of stinking flame. A few T-34s emerged from the fire. At last one spotted the Jagdpanther and delivered a shot which ricocheted screaming off the sloped forward armor. The long 88mm blew one of the tracks off the advancing Russian. The next shot blew its turret off, sending it soaring into the air like multi-ton debris picked up by a tornado.

The German crew was soaked with adrenalin-sweat. Bix looked around wildly for other tanks, couldn't spot any. "All right, now get the trucks," he said.

But his gunner said there were only two shells remaining. Bix was almost glad to hear this. Enough of this madness. He told his driver to pull out and head back for the German lines.

On the way to the rear Bix spotted a lone T-34 lurking in another village. How the devil had he gotten there? But what could you expect, with only a single Jagdpanther holding a whole sector of the front . . . The driver slammed on the brakes, opposed the treads, turned 90 degrees. The maneuver should have consumed only two or three seconds; it was actually much swifter than tracking with a rotating turret. But they had driven into a mud slick and the treads were flailing away while only turning the Jagdpanther very slowly. The Russian too seemed to have got himself out of position in the mud, unable to bring his gun to bear. Bix's vehicle spewed mud out in all directions, turning, turning, until at last facing the T-34. From a distance of eighty yards the 88mm spoke; the T-34 was hit and became a mass of flames.

Bix's crew had one shell left. They drove on back towards the rear.

An Aborted Attack

Sixteen Soviet tanks destroyed outside Prussian Stargard, not to mention stalling the enemy advance for at least another day.

One day closer to the end.

Kleschkau—another little village west of Danzig. The Russians had just taken it. An assault group of 4th Panzer's grenadiers was sent in to take it back. Counterattack. A miserable and depressing chore. A small group of men, no longer with any support from heavy weapons, were to be sent in against an enemy that outnumbered them, defending a heavily fortified position. House-to-house combat was always an exercise in hysteria.

Once again Bix's Jagdpanther was positioned outside the village to cover the approach routes of Soviet armor.

The major in charge of the grenadiers approached the tank destroyer to talk with Bix. It was a grim conversation. He asked if Bix could advance with his men to give them fire support. The grenadiers no longer had any SPWs; they were simply a small band of footsoldiers, tasked for another shoestring assault.

Bix said he had his orders. If he left his position to roll into the village, Russian tanks could easily skirt around and keep right on going towards Danzig.

The major merely nodded with an expression of hopeless resignation. Bix reconsidered. If no Russian tanks appeared, he would be left sitting idly by, watching the footsoldiers go in to be slaughtered.

"Never mind," he told the major. "Give the word and we'll go."

A strange brightness illuminated the major's face. Half his men were probably about to be killed anyway, but he could not hide his gratitude. The situation had improved from hopeless to bad.

The Jagdpanther moved forward with the grenadiers flanked on either side. The approach to the village was open terrain, the dull bare ground of late winter. Soviet machine guns opened up from the houses. The Germans took casualties. The long 88mm took the enemy nests under fire. A high explosive shell pierced the wall of one of the houses, blew up inside. The windows erupted outward.

The Germans made it into the first houses. The hellish melee began now. Several times the Jagdpanther was struck by the weird dull ping of an anti-tank rifle. This was a crude handheld weapon of a caliber no larger than a machine gun, but with an extremely long barrel. It was incapable of piercing the Jagdpanther's armor, but it was deadly accurate. At such close range a good marksman could send one of these rifle shells through an armored vehicle's narrow viewing slits, penetrating the small rectangle of armored glass and planting itself right in the eye of a German driver or gun aimer.

Alert to this danger, Bix's radio operator fired the bow machine gun at every possible hiding place, madly hosing the entire area. No way to know if he had hit anything.

"Just keep going," said Bix. "Just keep going."

They drove on into the center of the village. Houses on every side. This was the most dangerous place for an armored vehicle to be. The grenadiers followed behind, swarming among the houses, tossing grenades into the windows and doorways, killing and being killed. Wild crosswinds of small caliber metal were flying in every direction.

In the midst of all this Bix's radioman received word that Russian tanks had broken through in some other sector of the front, headed straight for Danzig. The Germans had no tanks left in that area, no anti-tank guns, nothing.

Bix got on the radio.

"We're heavily engaged in Kleschkau. The grenadiers are fighting to clear out the town. If we pull back I don't know if they'll be able to hold on here."

The voice speaking through the headphones was adamant. Bix was to return to the depot and proceed with two other Jagdpanthers to the threatened area.

"This is an emergency situation. Do it now," said the voice.

Where wasn't it an emergency situation? Just send the two vehicles at the depot, thought Bix. The voice had broken off contact. Bix tried to get through again but there was no response. He cracked the commander's hatch, looking around for the major leading the grenadiers. But it was a madhouse out there, no telling where he would be. If Bix got out of his vehicle to look for the man he would probably be shot down in seconds.

"All right, do as they say," he told his driver.

The Jagdpanther began pulling back. The grenadiers did not like the looks of this hasty retreat; now they began withdrawing from the village as well. Discipline was not what it had once been.

Another officer, a lieutenant, came running over to the vehicle, shouting up at Bix. Bix tried to explain the situation, but it was difficult to make himself heard over all the noise. The lieutenant stared up with sullen disbelief. His men were beginning to flee back down the main street.

"Are the Ivans coming with tanks?" shouted the lieutenant.

"Not here! Some other sector! I've got orders to move over there!"

The lieutenant looked up with disgust, looked around at his men with disgust. Bix didn't know if he'd been able to make himself understood. The lieutenant had been running alongside the vehicle all this time; he gave up and the Jagdpanther left him behind.

"Shit," said Bix. He lowered the hatch. Before shutting it he saw some of the grenadiers scrambling up onto the rear deck and bow plate, trying to catch a ride out of this place. A dangerous maneuver, trying to jump on a tank in motion. They would have been safer inside the houses. They were clinging like rats all over the vehicle when it was bracketed by a cluster of mortar shells. Men screamed and fell, riddled by shrapnel, some falling off to be crushed to death beneath the treads. The survivors jumped off and fled for shelter into the nearest houses.

"Christ," said Bix.

They drove back to the depot.

His commanding officer, a Lieutenant Tautorus, was waiting there in a state of visible excitement. He explained the new assignment in more detail. Bix was not impressed. He liked Tautorus well enough, but for the moment he absorbed his instructions with a somewhat blank expression. He had his pride, which now took the form of suppressed anger; the scene back at the village had looked like cowardice and it gnawed at him.

At length he interrupted Tautorus by spewing out a few curses. For a moment Tautorus kept right on chattering, sounding as if they were all on the verge of being driven into the sea. Then he calmed down a bit. Bix exhaled, gradually calming down also.

"Very good, Herr Leutnant. We'll leave right away."

Bix found Igels and Schwaffert, the other two Jagdpanther commanders detailed for the mission, and told them what Tautorus had told him. The sun was going down and they would have to make a night march. That should bring them to the new sector in plenty of time, if they didn't get lost along the way. During the years in Russia the Soviets had been fond of making night attacks. Now in Germany they showed less inclination towards that kind of thing, probably inhibited by drunkenness or sleeping off drunkenness or other preoccupations.

Their destination was a large Prussian estate, dominated by a hill known as the Totenkopf—the Skull, or Death's Head.

Action atop Skull Hill

A windy March darkness settled across the land. Snow blew crosswise through the dark, across the road. The road was clogged with refugees in despair, exhausted, hungry, cold. In the dark they were as silent and downtrodden as a defeated army. Some of them would have been on the move for several months, retreating on foot or in their pathetic farm wagons all the way from the East Prussian frontiers. Their escape to the west had been blocked and they had been forced to turn around, heading eastward again towards the ports of Danzig and Gotenhafen. Rescue ships awaited them there, but there were never enough ships to carry everyone away, and these miserable civilians would find that scenes of bribery, panic, wailing, and treachery also awaited them there on the bombed-out docks of those ports.

For the moment they simply moved on numbly through the snow-blowing dark. Many of them would have already witnessed unspeakable scenes that would scald their memories forever. Initial days of terror and uncertainty back in January would have given way to the dull monotony of their trek, their fears not disappearing but settling deep down inside them.

During these months they would have been attacked by Soviet aircraft and tanks, the ordinary weapons of modern battle, leaving an indescribable mutilated shambles of the plodding and defenseless refugee columns, with always a few civilians managing to escape somehow and keep on going, reduced to a state of almost speechless fear.

Soviet tanks driving like bulldozers right through the middle of a group of civilian wagons, pasting the bloody remains of men, women, and children to their metal treads, treads revolving around and around and leaving long trails of blood and flesh through the snow. It was real. Nightmares were real. It was all real.

Then of course there were the madly hilarious escapades of the soldiers of the Red Army whenever they entered a village, bringing that peculiar Russian atmosphere of drunkenness, rape, torture, and murder.

Perhaps most of these refugees would have heard word of such scenes but not actually witnessed them. That was why they were fleeing, after all. But inevitably some would have witnessed these things with their own eyes, marching through the snowy dark along with the others.

Unexpected Outcome of Hitler's Warmaking

In a way, Hitler had been wise to declare war on the United States in December of 1941, only a few days after Pearl Harbor. From a military standpoint, it was perhaps the most inexcusably foolish thing he had ever done—ranking, perhaps, with his invasion of the Soviet Union earlier that same year.

But at least the conquest of Russia was part of Hitler's vision, whatever that vision really was. To declare war on the United States had seemed entirely pointless.

And yet, without the arrival of the Americans, the British could not have built up the strength to invade the European continent for another fifty years, if even then. Without the Americans, there would have been no coalition of Western Allies marching into Germany in 1945. In other words, the entire German nation would have been at the mercy of the Russian invaders. Without the offsetting presence of the Americans, the British, and the French advancing almost unhindered into western Germany, it is quite possible that the Russians in their righteous frenzy of vengeance and hate would have razed the entire German nation to the ground, leaving nothing but ashes and bones for a hundred years.

It is true that without the threat of the Americans, Hitler could have mustered the entire strength of his nation against the Soviet Union, without distractions from the West. But even then it might not have been enough. From the very instant that it began, at 3 AM Berlin time on June 22, 1941, the war against the Soviet Union had consumed the vast majority of German military resources. This situation had remained unchanged ever since, right up to these final, unbelievably violent months in 1945, and what had come of it all?

The Russians had run amok on German soil. Centuries earlier, the Mongols of Genghis Khan had obliterated civilizations in the Middle East that had existed for over a thousand years, effectively erasing them from the historical list of nations. The Russians, if they had had a mind to do so, and they were giving every indication that they did, could have done much the same thing to the German nation in 1945.

Hitler's wisdom was inscrutable; and so perhaps it was just as well that he had declared war on the Americans back in 1941.

The Russo-German War was by far the greatest and most terrible conflict between two nations in human history. It is one of history's peculiar ironies that this fact has been obscured by all the other violence scattered around the globe during World War Two.

In any case, Hitler's wisdom did not extend to the terrified refugees of East and West Prussia, of Silesia and Pomerania. No Americans or other western Allies were coming to save these people from the Russian invaders.

Bix meanwhile was having trouble advancing in the darkness along these jammed-up roads. The refugees showed no inclination to get out of the way of his three vehicles, and why should they? Many of them were as fed up with the German military as they were afraid of the Russians. In the darkness and the snow carried along by the wind, Bix's Jagdpanthers were simply three more vehicles competing for space among thousands of others on the roadway.

A few times Bix drove out into the fields to get around the crowds. But this was too time-consuming, and there was the danger of bogging down in the mud. Finally he gave orders to keep to the road and force the civilians to get out of the way. Exactly how he accomplished this without running them down is not explained by the chronicler of these events. Anyone who has ever tried to drive a vehicle through a crowd of people, at any pace faster than a walk, is left to wonder about this. The chronicler relates that the refugees cursed at him as he drove by.

It seems likely that he would have been advancing in the

opposite direction from these streams of people; they were flee-ing from the Russians, and he was heading towards the Rus-sians. But in the chaos of that night it would be impossible to say for sure which direction all these different groups were mov-ing in. The Russians had broken through almost everywhere by this time.

The ten-mile drive to the threatened area took hours. These were only country roads, unlit, poorly mapped. Several times Bix had to stop at crossroads to ascertain which direction to take. With Lt. Tautorus' help he had drawn his own map. Occasionally there were signposts by the roads but just as often there were none. It would not have been that difficult to drive into the Rus-sian lines.

At length the refugee columns disappeared and the three vehicles entered the strange midnight quiet of the combat zone. They found the old Prussian estate surmounted by the Skull Hill. They were met by a few guides sent out by the German unit that was holding here. Bix dismounted and followed these men on foot into the darkness, leaving the three vehicles to await his return. He actually felt unburdened somewhat, after leaving the civilians and their misery behind, after finally managing to find this place. They crawled through a cellar window into one of the buildings of the estate. There was gunfire now, the Russians seeming to be firing from every direction, though aimless and desultory in the night. Every so often a spray of bullets raked the building, which appeared to be some kind of distillery or wine cellar.

Down in the cellar the German defenders were gathered. No matter how much he had seen of the war, an experienced tank killer like Bix would have been in a somewhat different mood from that of the filthy German infantrymen here, underarmed, trapped, outnumbered, unnerved by a grim laconic sense of hopelessness.

The major in command tersely expressed this feeling with a few sentences:

"This is my fighting force. Early in the morning I will go into battle with these men and you are to support me. How many tanks do you have?"

Bix told him. The major indicated the positions of the Soviet tanks on a diagram of the estate. A few minutes later the guides led Bix out of the building and back through the darkness.

One of the guides remained with the Jagdpanthers to lead them to their firing position. This was on the top of the Skull Hill, which was a long low ridge flanked by scattered groups of firs and bare deciduous trees. The path leading up into the dark was meant for farm carts, but Bix's vehicles were able to negotiate it.

The major in the distillery had said that a German quadruple, flak gun was positioned up here, though there had been no con-tact with these men since the preceding day. The hill commanded the entire area and why the Russians had not captured it as their first order of business was anybody's guess. Indeed, it was pos-sible by now that they had captured it . . .

But when the Jagdpanthers were finally hailed it was by German sentries, from the crew of the flak battery. Bix's guide had gone on ahead to make sure the tank destroyers were not mistaken for Soviet vehicles and fired upon.

It was dawn now. Leaden skies, a few light flurries of snow carried in a dull breeze. The various buildings of the estate came into view below. Bix had to be oriented again as to which building held the few German defenders. There were a few farm fields down there, though much of the estate was parkland, no doubt some old Prussian Junker's domain, with geometric patterns of trees in groves or lining a few dirt roads. The Russian tanks were scattered everywhere down there, blurry shapes in the early twi-light. There was still scattered gunfire but it seemed to have nothing to do with the motionless tanks. At dawn they seemed as somnolent and inert as the landscape itself. Almost as if they were not there at all. Bix stared down at them until he could begin to make out the white numbers painted on their turrets.

Some were out in the open. Most were parked close to the walls of various large and small buildings, barns, other structures.

Bix, along with Igels and Schwafferts in their two vehicles, backed up a short distance into a reverse-slope position, so that only their long cannon protruded beyond the ridgeline. The Rus-sians below gave no sign of being disturbed by the noise of other armored vehicles moving in the area.

What followed next was almost an anti-climax. The German tank gunners were used to their own sharpshooting skills. They were used to the scenes that unfolded whenever the Russians were caught off guard like this. Generally, in tank or tank de-stroyer units, there was one commander and one crew that did the lion's share of the killing. This was not part of the basic design of panzer tactics; it just seemed to work out that way, in the manner of star athletes whose greater skill carries the rest of the team along. This analogy with athletic competition might seem irksome or trivial, in light of the slaughter about to unfold, if not for the fact that the moment-by-moment skills required to use a tank to kill other tanks did tend to follow this pattern. Bix was recognized as the ace killer among this group of three vehicles.

A half-hour later, when it was all over, they counted nineteen Soviet wrecks scattered across the snowy parks below. Bix and his gunner had killed eleven. Igels and Schwafferts had divided the other eight between them. One of Bix's shells had holed two tanks simultaneously, parked side by side next to a barn.

Trained gunnery, coupled with the pinpoint accuracy of the long 88mm's, had done it all. The Russian vehicles not destroyed where they sat had driven off across the estate in all directions. Moving targets were hard to hit but the best sharpshooters could do it. In the frenzy a few T-34s might have escaped being hit, but if so they had left the area.

In the confusion a few of them had driven right into trees or stone walls. Some were burning, but most were not. They had simply been ripped apart by armor-piercing shot and now sat motionless and dead, as inert and somnolent and obscure as they had appeared at first light a half-hour before.

All in all the random collection of T-34s scattered across the snow now displayed its own inscrutable geometric pattern, next to and among the more orderly patterns of the park trees.

During this time the three Jagdpanthers on the Skull Hill had not even been fired on. This lack of resistance would not have hurt the accuracy of the German gunners.

In a way, there is something almost tedious about describing such a magnificent display of skill, in the midst of a military situation that was hopeless and doomed, where scenes of pain and despair far outnumbered scenes of any other kind.

The Russians too took their losses on their march into Germany, at the end of this insane and idiotic war.

In the distillery building down below, or whatever building it was, the German defenders erupted in jubilation out into the snow, entirely heedless of any Russian tankmen who might still be lurking on foot with pistols or submachine guns. But no one fired at them. The surviving Russians had either fled or were too terrified to reveal their presence.

Bix led his tank destroyers back down the hill. The infantry major thanked him profusely, removing his Iron Cross and offering it to Bix, to Igels, to Schwafferts, to their crewmen, to anyone who would take it. None of them did; they stood around smiling, staring around at things, talking with the foot soldiers.

The infantrymen were mostly beaming crazily, chattering the way men do when their nerves are shot, or else looking about without a word, but mostly smiling. It was the same fixed and disbelieving smile, maybe, of the few men who had escaped from Budapest. By God, they had just escaped from almost certain death. They could feel it aching in their facial muscles, this unfamiliar expression, this incredible relief.

They might all be dead by tomorrow. But for the moment that seemed as remote as some date a hundred years away. For the moment they were alive, and the Russians had all been driven off. Their surroundings, the sky, the snow, the earth, did not look too bad all of a sudden. The junked Soviet vehicles out in the distance were less noticeable than the calm air against their faces.

The last days of March at Oxhoft . . .

7th Panzer is holding the south slope of the plateau. Word arrives that Russian tanks have broken through the lines of SS Polizei on the west slope. The panzer crews are ordered to counterattack and restore the situation.

Every remaining armored vehicle is assembled. Three Panthers, a handful of Sturmgeschutzen, a somewhat larger number of half-tracks. Ammunition is doled out—a few shells each for the tanks and assault guns, a few hundred rounds of ammunition for the heavy MGs on the half-tracks.

Then every last vehicle goes in to the attack in a single armored wedge, surging out of their assembly positions in a forest and heading straight for the Russian lines. It is an impressive sight, the division's last all-out armored assault of the war. But with such a severe shortage of ammunition the attack does not last long. The Panthers and Sturmgeschutzen destroy thirteen Stalins before they run out of shells.

Throughout the battle, some of the SS Polizei soldiers are seen still running in panic for the rear. Infuriated by this lack of support, the grenadiers from 7th Panzer begin machine-gunning them as they flee.

LESS HEROIC ADVENTURES
Paul von Ruhland and 7th Panzer Division

Herman Bix was awarded the Knight's Cross on March 22, 1945, only a few days before the fall of Danzig. In less than a month he had destroyed 75 enemy tanks in the West Prussian battles.

The Germans would continue to award men with the Knight's Cross, or various other decorations, up until the final hours of the war, through normal bureaucratic channels that typically involved a good deal of paperwork. This process continued even after Hitler had committed suicide in the bunker beneath the Reichskanzlei.

Bix's accomplishments were unusual, though there were other German tank commanders with similar high numbers of kills. To put this in perspective, it might be noted that the idea of a "tank ace" or "tank killer" simply did not exist in the British or American armies. Sherman or Churchill tanks were not adequate weapons for destroying German tanks, at least not in large numbers. It is doubtful that any single Western commander or crew killed as many as ten German tanks during the war. On the whole, morale in British and American armored units was not high; they did not function as an elite branch of the armed forces, the way the German panzer units did. Like the infantry, they did their jobs in a more or less grim and business-like manner, occasionally prone to panic, but more often simply working stoically to suppress their fears of being burned alive inside their "Ronsons."

Russian archives report a few Russian tank crews with high numbers of kills—say twenty or thirty. Whether these reports can be believed is impossible to say.

These episodes of heroism and skill show only one side of the picture. Other members of panzer divisions have left far different accounts, in which there were no days of destroying ten or fifteen Russian tanks at a time, but days of confusion, fear, disintegration, and the endless fight for survival.

Paul von Ruhland fought with 7th Panzer Division in the same areas of West Prussia where Bix's 4th Panzer Division was engaged. Like Lt. Wiswedel and Hauptman Sell, whom we met in Silesia, von Ruhland was a panzer grenadier who went into combat aboard an SPW (halftrack).

As a rule, these crews would divide their time between fighting inside their vehicles and fighting on foot; often they were detailed to defend trench systems and fox holes no differently from regular infantry. By 1945, with more and more vehicles being lost, more and more SPW crews (and also tank crews) were having to fight as infantry because there was no alternative.

Panzer divisions fighting in East and West Prussia were not constantly shipped all over the German rail network as they were in Pomerania, Silesia, and Hungary. Prussia was cut off, as isolated from the rest of Germany as the Courland Front in Latvia. For this reason, also, few replacement vehicles were received from the factories. They cold have been shipped in to Danzig or Konigsberg, but at this point armored vehicles were too few and too precious and Hitler did not wish to see them sent to the bottom of the Baltic by Soviet submarines.

The German armored units in Prussia gradually lost almost all their vehicles until they were effectively reduced to infantry divisions.

From von Ruhland's account, it is clear that he was neither a hero nor a coward; he was not skilled or resourceful; he was not particularly stoic. He fought only to survive.

He is not a very good writer and his story is often so confusing that it becomes a blur, shifting back and forth in time without warning. But this kind of chaotic and unvarnished document still has its own authenticity and in its way is as valuable as any other. Almost all his combat experience took place during the last year of the war. But that was plenty.

He fought with 7th Panzer in the Baltic states of Lithuania and Latvia in 1944, though his division was shipped back to Germany instead of retreating into the Courland peninsula. He says that the subsequent fighting in East and West Prussia in 1945 was the worst that he saw.

His memoir is almost bereft of dates, place names or the names of fellow soldiers. They were simply anonymous comrades sharing his misery, fear, and dim hopes of living through it all. Battles that clearly took place in Prussia in 1945 are followed, at least in his story, by other incidents that seem to have occurred in the Baltic states in 1944. These are not related in the manner of flashbacks; the different incidents are simply set down in helter-skelter fashion. Obviously von Ruhland's memory has become as jangled and twisted by his experiences as the memories of some of the other veterans in this book—probably more so.

His story conveys its own peculiar flavor of the chaos and mental exhaustion induced by months of combat. It becomes a blur of frightening incidents and anecdotes. Here are some:

Daily living conditions on the Eastern Front meant constant battles with lice and other vermin. Von Ruhland developed a skin disease which plagued him for months, eventually becoming so bad that he had to be hospitalized back in Germany.

Upon recovering his health, he was slated to return to 7th Panzer. A troop train was leaving for the front, but due to a mix-up von Ruhland was not on it. He was lucky. The train ran afoul of a surprise Russian offensive and almost everyone on it was killed or captured. (Almost certainly it was destroyed during the opening phases of the Vistula-Narew Offensive in January.)

Von Ruhland shipped out with another group of replacements, taking the sea route this time and disembarking in Konigsberg in East Prussia. He almost never mentions dates, but this must have been sometime early in 1945.

The countryside in East Prussia was not as vast as what he remembered from the Soviet Union, but it was full of deep forests, primitive, empty, and disturbing.

For some reason, his comrades began to regard him as a lucky fellow, a good luck charm. He really had no idea why. Men said they felt safer being near him. This curious status seemed to irk one of his commanding officers, who flew into a rage one day and began berating him: "Who do you think you are?" Von Ruhland had no answer and could only shrug. The officer refused to ever speak to him again. The stress of those days was making men irrational.

One day his unit was manning some trenches in these East

Prussian forests when a Russian armored attack overwhelmed them. They had to flee for their lives. They had left their SPWs parked in a forest clearing some distance behind the trench line and were unable to recover them.

Some hours later, after the Russian tanks had passed through, they went back to search for their vehicles. The SPWs were still parked in the clearing, apparently undamaged. But it was a trap. Russian machine gunners were hiding inside the crew compartments; as von Ruhland and his comrades approached the Russians opened fire and killed half a dozen men, driving the rest back into the forest.

They were running short of weapons of every kind, especially heavy weapons. During a counterattack they captured a Russian anti-tank gun and decided to put it to use. The Germans called these guns "Ratsch-booms," because the crack of the shot was followed almost instantaneously by the sound of the explosion against the target. Von Ruhland and his comrades did not know how to operate this weapon and spent some time figuring out how to adjust it. They miscalculated. Their first shot plowed into the ground only a few feet in front of them, nearly killing them all. They eventually got the hang of the piece and began firing it on the Russians, before having to abandon it in another retreat.

Another counterattack, foot soldiers supported by a single Sturmgeschutz. This time it was the German vehicle that fired short, sending a shell straight into the German infantry. It exploded a few feet from von Ruhland and sent shrapnel flying into his scalp. But it was only a superficial gash. He saw the twisted piece of metal lying beside him and picked it up, still hot to the touch.

Another counterattack, foot soldiers supported by Panther tanks this time, some of the few that remained. He was in a foxhole with another man, frantically signalling to the nearest tank so that it would not run over them. But the Panther kept coming, its crew unable to see them. He wanted to flee but the Russians were machine-gunning everything that moved. He and the other man crouched down as deep as they could get. The 45 ton Panther rolled right over them. He was buried alive. The other man somehow struggled free and then dug him out, all the while under enemy fire.

Fortunately the Panther was knocked out by a Russian shell only a few feet away, thus screening them somewhat from the hail of bullets. The tank crew baled out and joined von Ruhland and his friend in the remains of the collapsed foxhole, jammed into the tiny space like sardines in a can. The Panther commander apologized for burying the two infantrymen alive. He and his crew were covered with minor burn wounds.

After a while the gunfire subsided and the tankers went back to their vehicle, discovering it was still drivable. The battle went on.

Perhaps von Ruhland's comrades had good reason to think he was lucky.

He never volunteered for anything, as it was too dangerous. But one of the forward observers was killed and his commander ordered him to go up and take the man's place. Everyone was dead from exhaustion, day and night, all the time. In a way trying to stay awake in a foxhole was a worse ordeal than combat. Night fell in the forward position. He couldn't stand it anymore and finally fell asleep. He was jolted awake by the sound of his commander approaching to check on him. He fired his weapon to show he was awake, but the officer wasn't deceived and screamed at him for quite a while.

Regrettably he was promoted to sergeant, perhaps due to his reputation for luck. He had no desire to be an NCO, as any position of leadership only increased the chances of being killed. He cut the sergeant's stripes off his uniform so as to be less conspicuous to Russian snipers. He had been awarded the Iron Cross, both first and second class, but threw these medals away, thinking that if he was captured the Russians would treat him less brutally.

Casualties were so heavy that for a time he was placed in command of his company, much to his annoyance. He says that many men prayed to be wounded so they could be evacuated. They talked about it openly.

Elsewhere he describes men being evacuated, but only as corpses. The dead wagon, an SPW modified for this duty, drove back and forth during these Prussian battles. The corpses would be assembled at the front lines, then loaded onto the dead wagon under cover of darkness, before being driven back for burial in the rear areas. A few times von Ruhland was detailed to assist with this chore, tossing the dead into the crew compartment of the SPW, among them the bodies of men he had known. He reports that he had little reaction to this grim business: "I had become so used to this that nothing seemed to bother me."

From the deep forests of East Prussia 7th Panzer retreated to the somewhat more populated areas of West Prussia. Von Ruhland mentions falling back on Danzig and Gotenhafen, one of the few instances where he identifies places by name.

A shell exploded in a tree and a man standing beside him was shredded, drenching von Ruhland with his blood. The man was still breathing and the crew hauled him inside the SPW to carry him to the rear. Machine gun fire struck a tree von Ruhland was leaning against; he ran and jumped aboard the SPW as it moved off.

One of the track pins sheared off. The crew rigged up another one, only a makeshift job. The other SPWs were retreating and had already left them far behind, and now the Russian tanks came into view again. They drove off at high speed, the repaired track wobbling loosely all the way, threatening to come off at any time. He doesn't say if the wounded man survived.

The Oxhoft plateau, north of Gotenhafen. 7th Panzer was up on this miserable barren space, along with 215th and 32nd Infantry Divisions, along with 83rd Infantry Division and many other units. Von Ruhland saw the heavy cruiser Prinz Eugen steaming calmly a few miles offshore, shelling the Russian positions. The big naval guns were almost all that stood between the German ground forces and annihilation. It was neither the first nor the last time that the German heavy ships provided this crucial support.

All kinds of other units, or bits and pieces of them, were surrounded at Oxhoft. The 4th SS Polizei Division was there, transferred to the Danzig front after their brief appearance at Stargard in Operation Sonnenwende. It may have been soldiers from SS Polizei who were fighting alongside von Ruhland's unit one day. They broke and fled to the rear and von Ruhland's men machine gunned them in disgust.

He identifies them only as Waffen SS soldiers. Possibly they were from another, ad hoc SS unit.

The few remaining heavy weapons were set up on the plateau, providing a paltry response to the horrible curtain of Soviet artillery fire. Some of the last SPWs were mounted with Nebelwerfer rockets—the German equivalent to the Stalin Organ—slung along the sides of the vehicles in odd-looking wooden firing crates. But the rockets were true weapons of mass destruction, almost as good as the Prinz Eugen's guns firing from offshore. Von Ruhland speaks fondly of the Nebelwerfers, saying they were nicknamed "Holle Gerate"—Hell Devices. (I have no reason to doubt this, though I have never seen this phrase used elsewhere.) Fired at night they were a spectacular sight, raining fireballs down on the Russian siege ring.

But the rockets, like every other form of ammunition, were used up quickly.

The commanding general of 7th Panzer was in despair. During one of the last nights in Oxhoft he addressed some of the men just behind the forward lines:

"Comrades, what have we done to deserve the terrible ordeal of this war?"

But he then offered a note of hope. Orders had just come in: 7th Panzer was to be shipped out to the Western Front. They would evacuate Oxhoft by naval ferries, crossing over to the Hela peninsula, where troop ships were waiting to carry them all back to western Germany.

According to von Ruhland, the general had made many requests in the past to have his division transferred to the Western Front. "We deserved a change." A man could just as easily be killed in action against the British and Americans. But a man could also secretly (or perhaps not so secretly) hope to be taken prisoner by the Western Allies. The gnawing fear of being taken prisoner by the Russians was one of the peculiar psychological ordeals of the Eastern Front:

> . . . on the Eastern Front, we would have everything to fear. Our signal unit once tuned in to an enemy wavelength and listened to a broadcast in which they announced that every soldier from 7th Panzer Division

who was captured alive would be sent for eighteen years of hard labor in Siberia. No one would be able to survive such an ordeal.

We were told of terrible cruelties committed by the Russians. In some cases German prisoners were tied by the legs between two Russian tanks and as they moved apart the prisoner's body was torn in two. I don't know if this actually did occur, or if it was merely a scare tactic used by our side in order to avoid being taken prisoner at any cost. Such and other cruel tactics were used on both sides.[1]

But as mentioned in an earlier chapter, the German forces holding out on the Oxhoft Plateau, including the remains of 7th Panzer, were able to escape at the last moment. Protected by the guns of the warships, the naval ferries or "sea snakes" carried them the twenty miles across Danzig Bay to Hela. This peninsula, like Wollin Island at the mouth of the Oder, was separated from the mainland by a narrow channel of water. The Russians could easily have attacked across it, but for the time being they chose not to. The pitiful remains of the German divisions at Hela actually spent the last month of the war resting and re-fitting in the expectation of being shipped to other operations elsewhere. Despite all indications, there was no way to know for sure that the end was only a few weeks away. For all the soldiers knew, the war might still drag on for years, just as it had done inside Russia. The men relaxed on the narrow beaches in the warming April sun, a strange interlude of peace by the seashore at the very end of everything.

Sadly there remained one catch to this much-deserved respite. Fighting still raged around Konigsberg, at the other end of Danzig Bay. The men on Hela were shipped out by rotation, one division or battlegroup at a time, to be slaughtered around Konigsberg and its port of Pillau all during the month of April. The decimated survivors would then be shipped back to Hela, always aboard the everpresent "sea snakes", and another unit would be sent over. Kampfgruppe Herb of the dissolved 215th Infantry Division, whom we saw being ferried over to Konigsberg only a day after stepping ashore at Hela, was shipped back in the last week of April, a shattered group of only a few hundred men.

Next in rotation was the 83rd Infantry Division, ferried over from Hela to Pillau on April 24th. The great stone lighthouse at the end of the channel mole at Pillau was like a beacon of doom. The 83rd, whose 277th Infantry Regiment had fought to the last man in Velikiye Luki in 1942, whose 257th Infantry Regiment had fought to the last man at Graudenz in 1945, would never return from this place.

The situation was different for Paul von Ruhland and the men of 7th Panzer. Their commanding general had not deceived them about their transfer to the west. A few days after arriving at Hela, the tank crews and panzer grenadiers (who had no vehicles left whatsoever) were ordered to board the great luxury liners moored at Hela, now converted to troop transports. They were going to escape, they were going to get away to the west. The ships were jammed with thousands of troops and civilians. A hospital ship full of wounded, marked with the red cross, was bombed over and over again, the Soviet pilots seeming to enjoy targeting this big red and white bull's eye. It began to list so badly that it was sent ahead of the rest of the convoy, hoping to reach safety in the west. Apparently it succeeded.

The remaining troop transports followed the next day, steaming west into the Baltic in fine April weather.

Soviet submarines only rarely attacked these seemingly inviting targets, but this voyage was to be an exception. One of the transports, carrying large numbers of 7th Panzer men, was torpedoed and sunk, going to the bottom with almost everyone on board. These disasters at sea were among the least known and most horrible episodes of the war. Although von Ruhland doesn't mention it by name, the torpedoed ship was almost certainly the Goya, whose fate we shall presently explore in more detail.

On board another ship in the convoy, Paul von Ruhland escaped to the port of Swinemunde in the west.

The commander of 7th Panzer, who had delivered that unusual and impassioned speech on the Oxhoft plateau, was General Maus. He was not a whiner. During the retreat to Gotenhafen and Oxhoft he had several times led counterattacks in person, firing a machine gun on board one of the SPWs. During a reconnaissance patrol in the last days on the plateau, his vehicle was struck by heavy artillery and Maus had his leg blown off. He was evacuated to western Germany several weeks ahead of the rest of his division.

Hitler awarded him the Diamonds to the Knight's Cross, the Third Reich's ultimate decoration, worn by only a handful of men. The Diamonds followed Maus' earlier reception of the Swords, the Oak Leaves, and the Knight's Cross itself, awarded over his preceding years on the Eastern Front.

The only combatant in the Third Reich to receive a higher honor was Stuka pilot Hans Rudel, who received the Diamonds and Oak Leaves in Gold, an award designed exclusively for him.

Even before General Maus, 7th Panzer had had a long line of famous commanders, starting with Erwin Rommel in 1940, later including Hasso von Manteuffel. All German panzer divisions were elite units, but the 7th was one of the most famous, nicknamed the Gespenster (Ghost) Division. 7th Panzer's tanks had come the closest of any panzer division to reaching Moscow in December 1941, during that first terrible winter.

The chaotic, blood-soaked and entirely unheroic memoirs of panzer grenadier Paul von Ruhland provide an interesting counterpoint to the official combat history of this division.

The Dunes at the Mouth of the Vistula

Herman Bix and the 4th Panzer Division were not among those who retreated via Gotenhafen, Oxhoft and Hela. The Russians reached the Baltic shore between Danzig and Gotenhafen in mid-March, thus splitting 2nd Army in half. The German units east of this point, including 4th Panzer Division, fell back on Danzig, but they were too shattered and disorganized to put up much of a defense in that city. They retreated further east into the scrubby sand dunes at the mouth of the Vistula River.

The divisions retreating north to Oxhoft had had it bad enough, but those retreating from Danzig to the Vistula estuary passed through many scenes straight out of hell. One of the most sickening atrocities was committed not by the Russians but by the field police and SS Sonderkommandos. Unlike General Schorner's somewhat more organized reign of terror in Silesia, the on-the-spot executions in Danzig took place largely without control from any higher authority. Both the governor of West Prussia, Albert Forster (one of the few Nazi governors who showed concern for the refugees) and the highest-ranking military leader, General von Saucken, had their last headquarters in Gotenhafen, and thus could exercise no control over these brutal bands of men who now roamed the streets of Danzig, meting out justice on their own initiative.[2]

For the SS Sonderkommandos in Danzig, the idea of administering justice was only an excuse for their murderous reprisals. At this point they were imbued with a kind of mad dog mentality, motivated by irrational feelings of rage and vengeance, by a sense of their own impending doom as they saw the Third Reich collapsing all around them. Jurgen Thorwald, who after the war published the first in-depth account of the German catastrophe in 1945, wrote:

> The men in these Sonderkommandos—excepting, perhaps, a few hopeless fools—had lost all illusions about their work. The claim that they punished cowardice, that they were serving their country, was a mere pretext. They all knew they were doomed, and raged with the fury and ruthlessness of cornered rats. Their victims dangled on trees adorned with signs: "I did not obey my transport commander," "I was too yellow to fight," "I am a deserter," and the like.[3]

The single most egregious "special purpose" action carried out by these men was the mass-hanging of a group of fifteen and sixteen year old boys during the final days of the siege of Danzig in late March. These boys had just been drafted a few days earlier by a Luftwaffe unit that was now fighting as an infantry force. The commander had granted these youngsters, who were all locals, permission to make a last visit to their parents inside the city, before they were thrown into the hopeless last-ditch battles against the Russians. The SS Sonderkommandos found these teenagers wandering through the town and executed every one of them for desertion, stringing them up by their necks from trees the entire length of the Hindenburgallee, one of Danzig's main thoroughfares. The hanged youngsters formed a kind of perverted victory procession, with their grotesquely distended bodies taking the place of the heroic statues that would normally line such triumphant avenues, either in ancient Rome or Nazi Germany. The inane, dementedly correct placards of justice were draped around their necks as always.

Many refugees and soldiers fleeing from Danzig would have passed beside this wretched spectacle, with one hanged youngster after another staring down at them for the entire length of the street. A dispatch rider from 4th Panzer, Robert Poensgen, had to drive his motorcycle back into Danzig to inform rear elements of the division that the retreat to the Vistula estuary was now underway. Upon driving back to catch up with the main body of the division, just east of the city, he came upon a ghastly column of fleeing soldiers and civilians. The following description can only be considered typical of the kinds of scenes that had been taking place everywhere in eastern Germany for over two months now:

> For kilometers on end the road was totally jammed with vehicles drawn up three and four abreast—gasoline trucks, ammunition trucks, ambulances, teams of wagons and horses. It was impossible to move forward or back. Russian fighter-bombers now arrived in wave after wave, dropping bombs into that unprotected, inextricable mass. This is what hell must be like. Ammunition exploded, and burning gasoline sprayed over the dead, over the wounded and the living, over men and horses. It looked like a heap of scrap metal flaming in a blast furnace of huge dimensions. It was the worst thing I had ever seen in all my years of active service—and I tell you I had already seen a lot.[4]

This hideous frenzy was followed by a much calmer, though still macabre, procession later that night. 4th Panzer's commander, General Betzel, was killed by shellfire on March 26th. His flag-draped coffin was carried aboard a Kubelwagen at the head of a long funeral procession, bearing the dead general out of Danzig on a moonlit night, leaving the flames of the city behind and laying him to rest somewhere in the marsh and dune country at the mouth of the Vistula.

On March 27th German engineers blew up a number of dykes along the river, flooding all the approaches to this small area of raised ground right at the river's mouth. German soldiers and civilians, among them Herman Bix, would remain isolated on this inhospitable clump of sand until the end of the war. Dune grass and marsh reeds grew everywhere and the shelterless sky arched overhead. There was barely enough food to avert starvation, even with naval ships continuing to bring in supplies and evacuate refugees and wounded men. The Red Air Force bombed the place day after day and there was no shelter anywhere. The divisions isolated on the Hela peninsula across the bay had it easy compared to this. Many men, enfeebled from going for weeks without adequate food, exhausted by the nonstop aerial bombardments, were so weak that they had to be carried from their trenches and foxholes in the dunes out to the rescue vessels waiting along the beach.

Around Balga the muddy, shell-cratered fields abruptly drop away in steep cliffs down to a narrow thread of beach. The last survivors of Grossdeutschland and a few other units are dug in at the edge of the sandy cliffs, their backs to the water, their few remaining heavy weapons aimed inland in anticipation of the final Russian offensive.

From time to time shells from enormous artillery rifles roar over their heads to land on the Russian positions. These barrages are a godsend, overturning Stalins and T-34s like dead leaves, devastating the Russians' own heavy artillery batteries. The firing comes from the German pocket battleships Lutzow and Admiral Scheer, cruising thirty miles away in the open Baltic.

Without these naval guns the Grossdeutschland men would probably have been driven into the sea by now. The soldiers are profoundly grateful and a few times small groups of them are driven out in naval launches to the battleships, where they mingle with the sailors and express heartfelt messages of thanks. These short visits help the morale of the exhausted and desperate Landsers. The big ships are the last visible symbols of German power, a stark contrast to the pathetically outnumbered groups of men still holding out on the shore.

21

REDUCING THE TUMOR
Grossdeutschland and the Heiligenbeil Cauldron

In addition to the mirror-image charnel houses of Danzig/Gotenhafen and Konigsberg, facing each other across Danzig Bay, there was a third large combat zone in Prussia.

This region was held by the German 4th Army and centered around the small town of Heiligenbeil, about halfway between the larger port cities. Here the German defenders were not backed up against the Baltic proper, but against a large salt-water lagoon known as the Frisches Haff. This wide, stagnant, brackish, rather unappealing body of water was separated from the open sea by a narrow tidal strand called the Frische Nehrung, a long desolate peninsula that stretched all the way from the Vistula estuary to Konigsberg's port of Pillau.

The weather had been severe in January and thousands of refugees had fled the Heiligenbeil area by crossing the frozen surface of the lagoon over to the Frische Nehrung. They then retreated further west along the narrow, uninhabited sands of the Nehrung in the direction of Danzig. When Danzig fell in late March the refugees became trapped on this tiny thread of land, without food, with little water, without shelter. It was a thoroughly miserable situation, little different from that of the people trapped in the sand dunes at the mouth of the Vistula.

After fleeing to the west for so long, many refugees turned around and headed east along the Frische Nehrung, back towards Pillau and Konigsberg, which still had not fallen to the Russians. Frequently they met up with other refugees who were still fleeing to the west from those cities. Pillau and Konigsberg had seemed like death traps; to be forced to turn around and head back in that direction must have been the occasion for much despair among these wretched people. Many simply gave up and camped for months along these slender dunes, praying for ships to take them off, slowly starving, descending into fits of madness and despondency.

Meanwhile, across the dreary lagoon of the Frisches Haff, 4th Army was fighting to its death in the so-called Heiligenbeil Cauldron. At the beginning of the year this had been one of the strongest and best-equipped armies on the Eastern Front. Even after the departure of the Grossdeutschland Corps to southern Poland at the beginning of the Vistula Offensive in January, 4th Army remained a powerful force. Well into February the Russians had made very little progress in reducing this area, which protruded southward like a huge tumor from the shores of the Frisches Haff.

The Battle of the Heiligenbeil Cauldron was one of the bloodiest and hardest-fought of the war, though in the midst of so many other terrible events it has lapsed into almost total obscurity.

It was here that the famed Grossdeutschland Division was nearly wiped out, though only after putting up a savage resistance from mid-January to the last days of March. The headquarters staff of Grossdeutschland Corps, under General von Saucken, had been sent south with the Brandenburg and Hermann Goering Panzer Divisions, escaping the inferno at Heiligenbeil only to be caught up in the long retreat from the Vistula to the Oder. But the parent division, the unit which had provided the original cadres for all the other far-flung Grossdeutschland divisions (Brandenberg, Fuhrer Begleit, Fuhrer Grenadier, Kurmark) remained behind in East Prussia.

For most of the long campaign in Russia, Grossdeutschland had been the most powerfully equipped division in the German Army. At any given time, depending on the flux of losses and replacements, it would have had more tanks than the typical panzer division, including its own company of Tiger tanks, a luxury granted to no other army division. These were always Tiger Is, but in fact the early model Tigers were as powerful as the later King Tigers, and probably could have remained in service for another ten years without becoming obsolete. A number of Grossdeutschland Tigers had survived years of combat in the East and continued to take their deadly toll in 1945, along with strong contingents of Panthers, Mk IVs, Sturmgeschutzen, and many other models of tank destroyers and self-propelled artillery.

4th Army also comprised 24th Panzer Division and the second of the Hermann Goering armored divisions, along with a number of veteran infantry divisions. While Zhukov's and Konev's armies had advanced hundreds of miles to the Oder by the end of January, the Russians in this part of East Prussia had barely dented 4th Army's defensive positions.

The Army commander, General Hossbach, had wanted to take this powerful force and break out to the west, where his divisions might have greatly disrupted the Russian thrusts to the Baltic in Pomerania and West Prussia. Hitler, as usual, ordered 4th Army to stand where it was. Hossbach was a strong-willed individual and at the end of January he attacked towards the west anyway, pretending that he had not received Hitler's orders and throwing the Russians back in confusion during a week of terrible battles in the snow, fought mostly by tough veteran Landsers from the 170th Infantry Division. Hitler was enraged. Even Guderian was angered by this arrant disobedience. Hossbach was cashiered, replaced by a more amenable general, and the attack to the west was called off.

Now the real mayhem around Heiligenbeil began. There was no place to retreat to. With their backs to the broad lagoon, the German divisions here put up as prolonged and bitter a defensive stand as any that took place in 1945. The Russians attacked with tanks, the Germans counterattacked with tanks. Attrition favored the Russians, and slowly the huge tumor, the cauldron, was reduced—but by only a few yards or a few miles at a time.

Hundreds of skirmishes were fought in the drifting blizzards of January and February, with troops garbed in white snow capes patrolling a landscape that looked little different from the Russian steppes. The east wind howled as it had howled years before at Rzhev and along the Donets and the Dnepr. The long and complex history of the Grossdeutschland Division has been published in English up to the end of 1944; the original German editions that cover 1945 are long out of print, making it difficult to get a clear picture of these final battles. But a few published photo albums of GD also contain fragments of daily battle logs from these days, as well as brief reports of actions by men who won the Knight's Cross. From these scattered sources it is possible to piece together a picture of the months of combat around Heiligenbeil. Sadly, the most famous source of information about GD's years in the East, Guy Sajer's THE FORGOTTEN SOLDIER, does not provide details about these battles. Sajer was separated from the main body of the unit in 1945, and wound up fighting with another unit around Danzig and Gotenhafen. He gives a hellish account of his time there, but we have already heard such accounts from other veterans of those areas.

Knight's Cross Actions in the Heiligenbeil Cauldron, GD Division

Obert Wolfgang Heeseman, commander of Panzer Grenadier Regiment GD:

GD had established two thin security lines in the deep, snow-covered fir forests of East Prussia around Passenheim. These lines were not built-up defensive positions but only thin screens of outposts and patrols.

Without strong defensive works, the German tactics relied on immediate counterattacks by small battlegroups—a dashing, brutal, costly and uniquely German style of warfare. On January 28th, Russian forces in the strength of several regiments easily slipped through the first of these security lines, held by elements of GD's panzer grenadier regiment. The enemy's timing was good, for almost all the regiment's vehicles were immbolized due to lack of fuel. Oberst Heeseman counterattacked anyway, finding the fuel to operate two flakpanzers and leading a group of only 15 men into the snowy woods.

Close-quarters combat raged for hours in the dense firs near the Gastenau Forest House, where Heeseman had had his HQ. His 15 men formed an island of resistance in the middle of the Russian advance, repelling three attacks, frequently resorting to hand-to-hand combat. The flakpanzers were in all probability late-model "Whirlwinds," each armed with a quadruple set of 20mm guns, the "machine-gun cannon" that we referred to at Budapest. No German weapon could send out a heavier and faster-flying wall of metal; the effect against the Soviet infantry must have been awful to behold. Later 300 enemy dead were counted in the snow.

Heeseman's men were exhausted, dazed with fear and endless surges of adrenalin. With a courage borne perhaps by a kind of combat-dementia he now led them in yet another counterattack, exchanging fire with Russian positions scattered throughout the forest. Finally as dusk fell he managed to lead his small group (the Knight's Cross citation alternately refers either to 15 or 25 men) back to GD's main lines. The Soviet advance had been stalled and GD was able to shore up its defenses and hold out around Passenheim for several days until the next enemy thrust.

Heeseman was awarded the Knight's Cross posthumously on February 17th, ten days after he was killed leading yet another counterattack on February 6th.

Leutnant Hans Thiessen:

In mid-February the cauldron still covered a wide area, but the perimeter was slowly contracting. Around the village of Bartenstein, about twenty miles southeast of Heiligenbeil, GD held out for about a week before being pushed back again. Russian pursuit was blunted time and again by the 88mm flak battery commanded by Lt. Thiessen. At length all the 88mm shells were expended. Thiessen's gunners continued to hold their positions as the Russians broke in and overwhelmed them in hand to hand combat, wiping out Thiessen and his soldiers to the last man.

Thiessen was awarded the Knight's Cross posthumously on May 9th, 1945, the last day of the war.

Hauptman Hans Bock:

GD was engaged on the eastern perimeter of the cauldron. In late January and early February an armored battlegroup under Hauptman Bock, a mixed group of vehicles that included a few captured T-34s, attacked eastward along the shore of the Frisches Haff. The objective was to link up with the German forces holding on around Konigsberg. Bock's attack succeeded in opening up a corridor along the shore of the lagoon, destroying 68 Russian tanks while shepherding refugees to safety who had fled from the Konigsberg area.

It was a rather pointless exercise, however. Konigsberg was under siege, and 4th Army in the Heiligenbeil Cauldron was also effectively under siege. To establish land communications between these two areas really accomplished nothing. In any case, a few weeks later the Russians advanced to the lagoon again and the corridor was severed.

Bock was awarded the Knight's Cross on May 2nd, 1945.

Hauptman Horst Warschnauer:

Warschnauer had already won the Knight's Cross in 1942, leading an engineer detachment into a deep complex of Russian bunkers in the Rzhev area of Army Group Center.

In late February of 1945, GD was still established hard by the lagoon on the eastern flank of the cauldron, around the village of Brandenburg. Russian pressure grew stronger by the day. GD continued to counterattack. Hauptman Warschnauer and his engineers stormed a village identified only as M., then continued to advance towards the heights above the town. The Russians were dug in with heavy weapons and the attack stalled. Warschnauer boarded his unit's only remaining SPW and drove straight up the hill, firing the vehicle's machine gun while standing upright and waving and shouting at his men to move forward. They responded and overran the hill in a mad charge. The crest was littered with Russian and German dead. Warschnauer and his men held the position; he was awarded the Oak Leaves to the Knight's Cross on February 24th, 1945.

Combat Log of 2nd Battery, I Battalion, Panzer Artillery Regiment GD:

The men of this battery operated Wespe self-propelled guns. These were a form of mobile heavy artillery, firing 105mm howitzers from a thinly armored open compartment mounted on a tracked chassis. They were not intended for tank versus tank combat, but rather to provide fast-moving artillery support. In this role they were highly-prized vehicles, and GD was well-equipped with them. (Other batteries operated the Hummel, a similar vehicle fitted with a 150mm howitzer.)

The log of 2nd Battery indicates the beginning of the great Russian offensive on January 14th, falling against this unit in the town of Fraschnitz on the Polish/East Prussian border. Daily entries for the rest of January consist of only the names of one East Prussian town after another, during the slow and bitter retreat as the cauldron gradually took shape.

The entry for January 26th:

"Tiefensee. (All vehicles blown up by their crews.)"[1]

No doubt they were out of fuel.

The entire month of February and the first half of March was spent in the area around Brandenburg. The log records a Russian offensive in this area from February 21st to 26th, followed by a counterattack by GD infantry and armor on March 4th, along the autobahn towards Konigsberg. (Presumably this was a follow-up attack to Hauptman Bock's operation the month before.) One would assume that many or all of these Wespe crews were now fighting as infantry.

It is clear that the Germans were forced to fiercely defend the Heiligenbeil Cauldron right from the start. But another reason for its prolonged existence was that the Russians had not yet amassed overwhelming force around its perimeter; operations further west along the Oder in Pomerania and Silesia consumed most of STAVKA's energy during this time. Closer at hand, the Soviets made several preliminary assaults against Konigsberg before turning their full attention to 4th Army.

All this changed on March 13th. Marshal Chernyakovski assembled seven armies around Heiligenbeil and began an offensive intended to drive the defenders into the waters of the Frisches Haff.

2nd Battery's entry for March 14th tersely summarizes the overwhelming force of this onslaught:

"Grand offensive against Brandenburg (enormous losses, 104 of our tanks knocked out, night battle tank versus tank)."[2]

This entry, if correct, is stunning. Without corroborating evidence, I would tend to think the figure of 104 tanks must be exaggerated. But if the tally is accurate, this night battle around Brandenberg would rank closely with the wild melee at Prokhorovka—the climax of the Kursk battle in 1943—as one of the costliest and most savage armored engagements of the war. No other instance comes to mind in which the Germans lost 104 vehicles in a single night. This would mean that almost the entire vehicle strength of GD was wiped out in a single blow.

Conceivably this entry refers not just to GD but also to the other panzer divisions engaged in the cauldron. It also seems possible, even likely, that a large number of these vehicles were not knocked-out, but abandoned and destroyed by their crews. But even so, the grand total makes a startling figure.

The cauldron was now doomed. But there was no immediate collapse. The town of Heiligenbeil was abandoned in a rain of phosphorus shells, the evil cousins of napalm. German soldiers not burned to death escaped "with their waterproof capes singed and melting."[3] The Germans' last stand took place on a tiny wart of land jutting into the lagoon, around the waterside village of Balga. Though there were still a few days of light flurries, the deep snow across the land had all melted by now. The battlefield was covered with mud and torn-up shell craters, littered with the wrecks of vehicles from both sides. Here as elsewhere, Soviet air attacks and artillery barrages were relentless. Many of the German positions during these last days were in steep bluffs directly above the beach, where the defenders dug into the sandy soil and huddled like moles. Naval ferries came in daily to take out the wounded.

2nd Battery's entry for March 9th:

"Renzegut (terrible losses, 108 men killed, only 21 survivors)."

Entry for March 27th:

"We are the last battery to be ferried out. Crossing made from Balga to Pillau." (Added in a handwritten scrawl after the typed entry: "The last three Wespes were blown up by their crews.")[4]

This seems to contradict the entry for January 26th, stating that all the battery's vehicles were blown up then. It is doubtful that GD or any other unit in the cauldron ever received any replacement vehicles. Probably 2nd Battery was loaned a few more Wespes from some other GD unit after January 26th.

Two months of combat ended with a whimper. The Russians did not contest the final German evacuation of Balga. The last ferries, "sea snakes" again, pulled out on March 29th. The skies were leaden and the wind was still, another light snow flurry drifting quietly down on the water. But at least the overcast kept the Russian air force away from the beachhead till the evacuation was finished. This did not include the men of 562nd Volksgrenadier Division, whose commander volunteered to defend the tiny perimeter around Balga to the end. It was a terrible fate for these men, but their sacrifice allowed the rest of 4th Army to be evacuated.

The defense of the Heiligenbeil Cauldron had cost GD as many casualties (and probably more) as any of the division's earlier battles in Russia. But once again, the survivors' escape across the water was only an illusion. The naval ferries were not carrying the exhausted and shell-shocked men out to troop transports steaming for the west. Rather, they were headed for Konigsberg's port city of Pillau, only twenty miles away across the lagoon.

Like Kampfgruppe Herb and 32nd Infantry Division, like 83rd Infantry Division, which had found only a brief respite at Hela, all the surviving divisions from the Heiligenbeil Cauldron were shipped over to the hell's-gate of Pillau, past the stone lighthouse of the channel, disembarking there and marching to the trenches around Konigsberg, heading into one final battle from which almost none of these men would ever return.

Sometimes there were short features about the Helferinnen in the newsreels, showing attractive young women at teletype machines or operating telephone exchanges. Their uniform was a fetching ensemble of short jacket, blouse, dark skirt, topped off with a jaunty little cap. They would be shown touring the Eiffel Tower during off-duty hours, or perhaps the Acropolis in Athens, then donning bathing suits and enjoying themselves in the warm waters of the Mediterranean. There were thousands of these women performing clerical duties everywhere in Germany and occupied Europe, including Russia, releasing men from these jobs so they could be sent to the combat divisions.

A group of Helferinnen was on board the Gustloff. Every square foot of space was already occupied by refugees and wounded soldiers, so the young women were obliged to bed down at the bottom of the drained indoor swimming pool, seven decks below the water line. They accepted these quarters with good humor. The deck all around the edge of the pool was already crowded with wounded men, who flirted with the girls and exchanged lewd remarks. The atmosphere of crisis seemed to relax sexual tension, at least between men and women fighting on the same side. The girls reacted to all this with good humor as well. The whole area recalled some strange off-kilter re-enactment of a scene from the baths of ancient Rome—laughing maidens in a pool, except there was no water in it; surrounded by hundreds of ogling men who lounged on stretchers instead of divans, who wore blood-crusted bandages instead of togas. Strangely, there was a tile mural all along one wall, depicting just such a scene of naked nymphs frolicking in an ancient bath.

The first torpedo struck the bow of the Gustloff. The second, following almost instantly, struck amidships and exploded on the pool deck.

22

HELL AND HIGH WATER

Disasters at Sea

The German surface fleet had spent most of the war in a state of demoralizing frustration. After the sinking of the Bismarck in 1941, Hitler had been reluctant to let any of his heavy ships venture out into the open seas. For the next several years, the battleships, pocket battleships, and heavy cruisers were confined to ports in Germany or kept hidden deep within the fjords along the Norwegian coast.

Both Hitler and his admirals envisioned using the heavy ships in Norway as raiders that would destroy the Allied convoys steaming across the Arctic Ocean to the Russian ports of Murmansk and Archangel. But Hitler's paranoia about losing any more heavy ships continually tied the navy's hands, and eventually admirals and captains became infected with his anxiety, fearing Hitler's wrath if any of their vessels were sunk during sea battles. On only two occasions did the German surface fleets venture out from its Norwegian lairs to attack the Allied convoys, in December of 1942 and again in December of 1943.

Both were embarrassing fiascos. Though outgunned and outnumbered, British light cruisers and destroyers managed to confuse and scatter the German ships, and in both instances the convoys were able to escape unharmed to the Russian ports. The German commanders on the scene acted with extreme tentativeness, as if they could feel the presence of Hitler glaring over their shoulders.

The first battle in 1942 had been more in the nature of a non-event, with only minimal losses inflicted on both sides. The German admiralty was humiliated; Hitler ignored his own shortcomings in this affair and accused the navy of cowardice and incompetence. The second battle the following year was more aggressively fought, but the severe Arctic weather and the superior seamanship of the British brought the same results. The convoy escaped unharmed. The German battleship Scharnhorst was damaged in a running engagement with British cruisers. Reduced to a speed of a few knots, the Scharnhorst was unable to make it back to port before the British battleship Duke of York arrived on the scene. Nearly dead in the water, the Scharnhorst put up a tremendous fight before being sunk with the loss of nearly everyone on board.

German naval officers could at least feel gratified that some of the stigma of cowardice had been erased. But the surface fleet would never again venture into the open waters of the Atlantic or the Arctic. The sinking of the Scharnhorst signalled the last ship versus ship engagement of the war.

Ironically, it was the period of great Russian offensives on land beginning in the summer of 1944 that allowed the navy a chance to redeem itself.

The brief German counterattack from East Prussia to Courland in August of 1944 was continually supported by the big guns of the naval vessels lying just offshore in the Baltic. Likewise, when Army Group North was bottled up in Courland, German battleships lying off Libau harbor devastated Russian armored concentrations during the First Courland Battle in October.

These offshore bombardments had none of the glamor of a naval battle on the high seas, but they served a far more important purpose. The big naval rifles were vastly more powerful than the largest standard field guns used by the army. Even a near-miss from an 11 or 12 inch shell threw out a blast that could overturn Russian tanks like toys. The Russian tendency to use massed concentrations of tanks and artillery pieces invited obliteration by German naval guns on many occasions. The German stranglehold on the Normandy beaches in June and July of 1944 had been devastated by the Allied battleships lying offshore. Throughout 1944 and on into 1945, Russian forces advancing along the Baltic coast would face the same kind of destruction from the German surface fleet.

During 1944-45, the German Navy fired more shells against the Russian army than it had fired during all the preceding years of the war. The firing was so intense and so continuous that the rifling grooves inside the big barrels became worn smooth; each of the warships had to return to the dockyards at Kiel to have its guns re-rifled at one time or another. In any case it was frequently necessary to return to the ports in western Germany just to replenish ammunition stocks after all the shells had been fired off. Thousands of refugees were carried along on these return voyages; the civilians were much safer aboard the naval vessels than on the slow and critically overloaded transport ships. As soon as they could be restocked with shells the heavy ships would steam back to the eastern Baltic to begin another cycle of bombardment against the Russians. In addition to the battleships and cruisers, numerous destroyers added the not inconsiderable weight of their 5 inch batteries, ranging only a mile or two offshore to fire at every available target.

We have seen the heavy cruiser Prinz Eugen steaming offshore from Gotenhafen, hurling 8 inch shells against the Russian siege ring around the Oxhoft plateau. The ground shook for miles around and every building trembled in its foundations with each incoming salvo.

The GD Division and the rest of 4th Army trapped around Heiligenbeil were supported by the 11 inch batteries of the Lutzow and Admiral Scheer, twin pocket battleships. The big guns had a range of almost thirty miles. Cruising in the Baltic off the sandspit of the Frische Nehrung, the ships sent salvoes rocketing entirely over the lagoon of the Frisches Haff to land on Soviet assembly positions, expertly pinpointed by forward observers stationed on shore. Without this kind of support, 4th Army would probably have been hurled into the lagoon long before the last ferries left Balga on March 29th.

As naval opponents, the Soviets could not compare with the British. Most of the Russian Baltic Fleet had been sunk in 1941, wiped out by German aircraft, submarines, and mines during a single disastrous voyage from Tallinn in Estonia to the safe haven of Leningrad. The few capital ships that survived this debacle would never again venture into the open sea. The German naval presence in the Baltic in 1945 would be uncontested by the Russian surface fleet.

Nor did Russian naval aircraft and submarines make an impressive showing. Soviet pilots, poorly trained in the tactics of bombing ships at sea, showed little inclination to brave the clouds of anti-aircraft fire thrown out by the German warships. The training of Soviet submarine crews was also primitive by Western standards. The Russians had a large fleet of submarines, which could have posed the same deadly threat to German convoys in the Baltic as the U-boats did to Allied convoys in the Atlantic. But with the exception of a few tragic incidents, this threat never really materialized. No Russian torpedoes ever came close to striking the German capital ships.

The same was true for the vast majority of the slow and defenseless merchant ships and converted liners. Hundreds of thousands of refugees who might otherwise have been lost at sea made it safely to ports in the west. Thus a slaughter of almost inconceivable proportions was averted, the scale of which might be guessed at from the few instances when Russian torpedoes did strike home. For in these several isolated cases, the results were truly horrendous.

The Wilhelm Gustloff Goes Down

January 30th 1945—port of Gotenhafen. Snow was falling heavily on Danzig Bay. The Soviet advance against Danzig and Gotenhafen was still over a month away, but the ports were already jammed with terrified refugees trying to escape. The great Russian offensive from the Vistula had begun two weeks before, and mass panic had broken out among the civilians of the eastern provinces.

Wealthy citizens offered fantastic bribes to port officials to ensure a place on any ship heading west. Women and children were granted first priority, resulting in families being broken up as husbands were left behind on the docks. The regulations were capricious—sometimes husbands were allowed to accompany their families, other times not. Some women smuggled their husbands aboard in steamer trunks, though even to bring on extra luggage of this kind would require a hefty bribe. Mothers carrying babies or small children were at the head of the passenger lists. There were instances of women stealing babies from the arms of sleeping, exhausted mothers so that they could secure passage on a ship.

Many of the refugees had already trekked for hundreds of miles in frozen misery across East Prussia. Yet the madhouse of panic and human treachery swirling around the docks became the climax rather than the end of their nightmares. Every available vessel, from the great liners to the smallest minesweepers and fishing trawlers, was pressed into emergency service, and still there was not enough space on board for all those trying to flee.

Soviet air raids on these jam-packed port cities probably killed as many civilians as did the soldiers of the Red Army during their murderous sprees across the inland countryside.

All during January 29th and on into the 30th, refugees were loaded onto four old liners—the Hansa, the Deutschland, the Hamburg, and the Wilhelm Gustloff—which had been kept moored in ports as barracks ships during the war years. Each vessel would ultimately carry between six and seven thousand people. All were civilians, except for small groups of wounded men and a contingent of two thousand submarine cadets from the U-boat training schools at Danzig and Gotenhafen.

None of the liners had been at sea for years. Shortly after departure on the afternoon of the 30th, the Hansa developed engine trouble off the Hela peninsula and the convoy was delayed for some hours in the choppy waters of Danzig Bay. But the captain of the Wilhelm Gustloff made the fateful decision to leave the other vessels behind and head out alone into the Baltic. The naval commander of the convoy, on board a small corvette, urged the Gustloff's captain to stay with the escort vessels around the other three liners. With the Hansa already damaged, this would have meant a slow and nerve-wracking voyage. The captain of the Gustloff decided to press on at full speed. With luck he could reach port at Kolberg or Swinemunde sometime the following day.

The naval commander detached a single minesweeper to escort the Gustloff. Both left the main body of the convoy behind during the early evening of the 30th, disappearing into roaring winds and high seas, into blackness and snow.

The Baltic is a treacherous body of water, shallow and sandy-bottomed, with characteristics more like the Great Lakes of North America than the open oceans of the world. Ocean waves can be higher, but they tend to roll in even and predictable patterns as they travel for thousands of miles. If one likens the movement of waves to a traffic pattern, one might say that ocean waves have plenty of space in which to maneuver, with even the giant swells rolling along in a somewhat coherent and organized fashion.

A violent storm on a narrow inland sea, such as the Baltic or one of the American Great Lakes, has none of these characteristics. Bound by land on all sides, the water does not have enough space to develop long and evenly rolling swells. Instead, waves swirl and buffet into each other with a mad turbulence that during the most violent weather resembles a witch's cauldron. Large freighters on the Great Lakes which might have ridden out the worst ocean storms have been broken in half by this chaotic pounding. The force of water in these land-bound seas is so unpredictable that the exact cause of many of these sinkings has never been determined.

The Baltic shares this reputation for treachery. On many days the water will be as smooth as sheet glass, with scarcely a ripple lapping along the shore. But not during a winter storm.

It was intended that the convoy would cross the shallower waters only a few miles off the coast of West Prussia and Pomerania, as Soviet submarines generally kept to deeper waters. But the Gustloff had a deeper draft than any of the other vessels and was obliged to stay about twentyfive miles offshore. The violence of the weather increased the danger of running aground.

The first torpedo struck at about 2100 hours on the night of the 30th. Within seconds the big liner was hit by two more. All lights below deck were extinguished. Panic broke out immediately. Civilians were packed into every cabin, hold, and gangway. Countless passengers were trampled to death in the mad surge to reach the upper decks. Terrible scenes were played out as people clawed at each other in the darkness, fighting to gain access to the ladders leading upwards. Some armed with pistols tried to shoot their way to safety. All emergency instructions were forgotten or ignored. Crew members trying to stem the panic were themselves overwhelmed and trampled.

The second torpedo had struck amidships in the area of the pool deck. The young Hilferinnen quartered on the floor of the pool would have stood hardly a chance of struggling up to the main deck from so deep within the bowels of the ship. But it hardly mattered. Already all of them were either dead from the explosion or else on the verge of death, screaming in their final agony. The pool had become a ghastly pile of maimed and crushed young women, with the wall-length tile mural of naked nymphs collapsing on top of them. Wounded soldiers, now either dead or far more hideously wounded, also lay entangled among them. Blood an inch deep poured out the drains at the bottom of the pool. As the emergency lights came on a few crewmen made their way into the pool area from nearby regions of the ship. The sights that met their eyes sickened them so much that they quickly left.

Civilians who reached the outer hatches and doorways found themselves emerging into a freezing gale. The lifeboats were crusted with ice inches thick. Before the boats could be lowered, ice had to be broken off the lines and winches. Crewmen trying to perform these tasks were swept aside by the maddened crowds. Only a few boats were lowered without mishap. Others were simply dropped headlong into the sea, spilling their occupants with the violence of the jolt. Others were lowered unevenly from their lines until they dangled at steep angles halfway down the hull of the ship, spilling out all who could not hold on. Even boats that somehow stayed afloat were smashed against the hull by the cauldron of the waves. Adding to the tragedy was the dismal fact that many of the lifeboats were lacking their oars, a bureaucratic oversight bound up in the long inactive years the Gustloff had spent anchored in port. Unable to pull away from the ship, the people in the boats could only pray to be borne off by the current. But many were capsized or battered against the ship's hull.

The terrible bedlam lasted for about half an hour. The ship was listing to port at an angle of 25 degrees; to those struggling in panic, this would have seemed nearly vertical.

But the Gustloff did not go down. The crew managed to seal off the bulkheads surrounding the torpedoed areas. Pumps began to operate. A few lights began to come on again, then more and more. The terror of the first few minutes began to die down. The upper deck became mostly deserted once again; the howling cold was unbearable and people descended back to the warmth below decks, there to wait and pray, sitting in shocked, frozen, exhausted silence among the bodies of those who had been shot or trampled. Mothers who could not find their children wept in hysteria or in unconsolable silence.

The screams of those clinging to capsized lifeboats out in the raging waters went unheard.

The captain radioed for help. The escorting minesweeper had vanished into the storm and could not be contacted. But a naval ferry was in the area and within a remarkably short period of time, by around 2200 hours, it had responded to the distress call and pulled abreast of the Gustloff. But this only led to further scenes of carnage.

The swirling waves battered the ferry against the Gustloff's hull. The waters were so chaotic that it was impossible to time a jump from the liner's deck to the ferry rocking uncontrollably below. Some people made it, while others were crushed to death between the two vessels.

Trying to board the ferry now seemed the worst of two evils. The majority of the passengers remained below decks, praying that the Gustloff would somehow make it to the nearest port. Several thousand of them were crowded onto the glass-walled promenade deck just beneath the main deck. Far below, the sealed-off bulkheads now gave way. Perhaps it was stress induced by the torpedo strikes. Just as likely, the crippled ship could no longer endure the violence of the storm. It began to capsize.

Those on the promenade deck were pressed against the glass windows, through which they could now see the raging waves rising towards their faces. Part of the ship's crew was standing guard here, armed with rifles to prevent any more stampedes out to the main deck. Already, while the lifeboats were still being lowered, they had been forced to fire into the crowds to prevent the boats from being overloaded and swamped. But now the boats were gone and the end was near; the captain gave orders that it was now every man for himself, crew and passengers both. An enormous wave crashed against the windows of the promenade deck; panic broke out once again and some of the armed passengers began shooting; the sailors responded by firing back, and a hideous calm settled over the crowd for the last time. The sailors, sickened by their own attempts to keep order, now left their posts and ascended to the main deck to escape. Some of the crowd followed them out, but thousands remained trapped on the promenade deck while the ship continued to roll, until finally the windows passed beneath the surface of the water. Then the glass burst and the sea poured in.

For about a minute the Gustloff remained afloat at nearly a right angle. Then it went down, taking all those still on board.

The Admiral Hipper and the T-36

The heavy cruiser Admiral Hipper was steaming west that night, headed for Kiel to take on more ammunition for another tour of bombardment off the coast of East Prussia. The Hipper was also loaded with refugees who would ultimately reach safe haven. The captain received the Gustloff's distress signal and sped to the scene, well aware of the target his vessel presented to any submarines still lurking nearby. He increased this danger by ordering the cruiser's searchlights turned on to guide the lifeboats to the Hipper. But in the raging seas it was nearly impossible for the frozen survivors from the Gustloff to climb the boarding nets up the high sides of a large warship; smaller vessels with lower decks were far better suited to rescue operations. Some of the Hipper's crew crawled down to assist people out of the lifeboats, but the whole operation was painstakingly slow and only small numbers of people were being hauled aboard. The captain knew that the Hipper was in mortal danger, sitting dead in the water with lights ablaze; he was already carrying several thousand refugees whose lives were endangered with every passing second. Now smaller vessels were beginning to arrive on the scene and he ordered the Hipper to leave the area at full steam.

The Wehrmacht communique noted only that the Hipper fled the area to escape submarine attack; the courageous, though largely futile, efforts of the captain to help the Gustloff's survivors were not mentioned.

Rescue operations were left to the T-36, a large torpedo boat nearly the size of a destroyer, which had been escorting the Hipper. As the cruiser departed the scene, lookouts on board the T-36 could see distress signals rising from the Gustloff in the distance. The smaller vessel came up astern of the sinking liner, shortly after the arrival of the naval ferry at 2200 hours. The crew watched the futile rescue operation in the freezing witches' cauldron, the passengers being crushed between the buffeting hulls of the Gustloff and the ferry. There are few spectacles in nature more awesome than a large ship in distress in raging seas. Great marine vessels have their own enormity, which even in quiet waters can be unnerving to an onlooker on a small craft nearby. Something about their massiveness and scale disturbs some unknown instinct inside the puny human observer. Divers exploring wrecks lying in stillness on the sea floor have experienced this same sensation—a kind of scalp-prickling giddiness, akin to the sensation of standing too close to the railing at the top of a tall building.

To witness a large ship about to go down in a howling storm magnifies this feeling considerably.

But seamen would be in their element, even on a night like this, and they would set themselves to doing whatever they could.

Before the T-36 could take further action the Gustloff went down, its distress siren shrieking, huge fountains of steam erupting from the inundated boilers, before all sounds were extinguished as the vessel slid beneath the waters. The crew threw lines to people tossing in the waves. Many were too weak to hang on as the sailors dragged them in, and they disappeared in the darkness. Some crewmen left the T-36 to help people in lifeboats and life rafts, tying lines around them so they could be pulled onto the ship. Others began roping liferafts together so they would not be scattered by the waves.

The T-36 was already crowded with more than two hundred refugees from Danzig, and sonar revealed that the Russian submarine was still nearby. The captain attempted to minimize the target he presented by facing his bow towards the sub. Rescue operations continued. Presently sonar picked up another submarine, both of them now circling only a few miles away. The seamen displayed great courage as they left their own vessel to assist more than five hundred half-frozen souls off the lifeboats onto the deck of the T-36. The captain was now faced with a terrible decision, of the kind that only sea captains generally ever face—the same dilemma the captain of the Hipper had faced a short time earlier. Two torpedoes were sighted that just missed his vessel, one passing by on each side of the ship. There were now close to eight hundred souls on board, and a third torpedo might doom them all. Yet there were still unknown numbers of people waiting out on the liferafts, including members of his own crew who had gone out to help rope them together.

The captain of the T-36 gave orders to leave the danger area at full steam. Survivors who had not yet been pulled aboard were left to die. Members of his own crew who were out there with them were left to die. Almost none of the remaining lifeboats and rafts would survive the storm. The few found by other rescue vessels the next day contained only passengers who had been frozen to death, literally welded to their seats beneath layers of ice.

By his action Captain Hering of the T-36 brought over five hundred survivors of the Gustloff to safety, along with the several hundred refugees originally on board. All were transferred to a hospital ship moored off the Baltic island of Ruege the following day. Another torpedo boat, the Lowe, picked up several hundred more survivors and also brought them to the hospital ship.

In all, 950 people survived the torpedoing of the Gustloff. About 5,000 others either went down with the ship or drowned or froze to death out in the terrible waters. To this date it was the worst loss of life in the annals of the sea.

The Loss of the General Steuben

The Steuben was another old luxury liner, somewhat smaller than the Gustloff. By early February it had already made one voyage carrying refugees and wounded from East Prussia to the west. On February 8th it returned to Konigsberg's port of Pillau to take on another shipload of humanity.

At this time the scene at Pillau was more desperate and ghastly than at Gotenhafen or Danzig. Konigsberg was surrounded and the Russian forces nearest to the port were only about ten miles away. The refugees were well aware of this and were frantic to escape. The rural areas outlying from Konigsberg had already seen some of the worst massacres of civilians by Soviet soldiers.

Pillau was attacked from the air and shelled by artillery. Trucks drove back and forth picking dead civilians off the crowded streets. Many refugees could not bear to wait for the arrival of a ship, or to have to fight their way on board if one did arrive. They took ferries from Pillau across to the sandspit of the Frische Nehrung, from where they intended to trek west towards Danzig. These people were destined for a long and futile odyssey. Some would reach Danzig and Gotenhafen, only to be trapped there as they had been trapped at Pillau. Others would remain stranded for months on the sandspit, freezing to death, starving, strafed by Russian planes. Ultimately, when Danzig fell, they would find themselves turning around and heading back to Pillau, a charnel-house that would hold out against Russian attacks until the end of April.

In this numbing miasma of ruin and despair there intruded occasional scenes of strange fantasy. Well into February the lagoon of the Frisches Haff remained covered with ice, though it was full of treacherous soft spots that would grow wider and more treacherous as the thaw progressed. Refugees plodded across the ice just as they plodded along the sandspit that bordered it, or rode in their farm carts behind plodding draft animals. Then suddenly a sail would be seen sweeping across the ice, moving so swiftly and smoothly that it seemed like the visitation of something supernatural. What could this be? A large cart, built almost like a boat, set up on runners and sliding across the ice under full sail. It looked like a boat, perhaps it originally had been a boat of some kind. The wind was not strong but all the same the strange craft moved with an almost unnatural swiftness. There and then gone. The refugees trekking on foot, their thoughts deeply wrapped up in the dullness of fear or horror, could scarcely make sense of what they saw, and then it was gone anyway. No doubt the sailing craft carried clever people whose ingenuity had not been benumbed by scenes of horror and murder. They seemed to be escaping not into the west but into some storybook realm.

The General Steuben lay docked at Pillau through February 8th and 9th. Wounded men were given first priority, and with the battlefront so nearby there were over two thousand of these to be carried aboard. About a thousand refugees were then allowed to follow. The figure is an estimate; exact tallies of passengers were no longer being kept. Harbor personnel were preoccupied with trying to prevent riots from breaking out on the docks.

The Steuben steamed out at 1530 hours on the 9th, about an hour before dusk. She was escorted by several old minesweepers that had been pressed into emergency service. One of them, the T-196, was strafed by Soviet aircraft. A few refugees on board were killed. The Russian planes then disappeared into the growing darkness. The pilots of the Red Air Force were never eager to attack the heavy cruisers and battleships, but smaller vessels were strafed constantly all over the Baltic.

The planes posed another danger though. They would have reported the location and direction of the Steuben and word would be relayed to patrolling submarines.

Snow was falling. It grew dark. Yet on this night the Baltic showed none of the viciousness that had hindered rescue operations around the Gustloff ten days earlier. There was no wind. Snow fell quietly. The frigid sea was calm.

A single torpedo struck starboard almost at the stroke of midnight. The Steuben's location was very near to where the

Gustloff had gone down. She might have passed over the grave of the other ship.

The Steuben went down more quickly than its predecessor. Within minutes the bow was underwater and the sea was washing around the forward funnel. There was time to lower only a few lifeboats onto the calm water.

But the ship sank so quickly that most of her passengers barely had a chance to realize what was happening. Great numbers of wounded men were only semi-conscious, contentedly dazed after receiving their first hot meal in weeks, lying in the clean and pleasant warmth of the ship after escaping from the awful conditions at Pillau. The Steuben must have seemed like salvation, a kind of heaven. They would go down with it to the bottom of the sea.

Many of the refugees had also been in bad physical shape at Pillau. By midnight, almost all would have been lying in exhausted sleep below decks, gliding easily over the calm waters.

For about half an hour the Steuben seemed to stabilize, God only knew how, with the bow submerged and the stern suspended high above the water. Rescue operations continued, even though most of the passengers were now trapped or drowned in the sunken bow and mid-ship compartments. Of those who had escaped to the afterdeck, many were reluctant to make the leap to the liferafts scattered on the water below.

At about 0100 hours the bow suddenly lurched down and the ship began to plummet. The stern rose higher and higher. Horrible screams carried across the windless sea. Now that it was too late scores of people jumped from the stern rail. Some fell into the huge exposed propeller blades and were mangled. The screaming reached a mind-numbing crescendo as the stern stood near the vertical. The Steuben went down like a rock, sucking hundreds of people into the depths who had been floating nearby.

By dawn the escort vessels had rescued three hundred souls, pulled from lifeboats or fished out of the water. Many were already dead from exposure, or died on deck shortly thereafter.

The Steuben carried over three thousand people to the bottom, settling in the sand at the bottom of the Baltic a few miles from the wreck of the Gustloff.

342

The Goya Goes Down

The Goya was a much smaller vessel, not a liner but a cargo ship. The Gustloff had displaced 25,000 tons, the General Steuben 17,500. The Goya displaced only 5,000 tons.

It was mid-April and the constant air raids had gradually reduced Hela to rubble. The devastation was not as bad as at Pillau across the bay, but it was bad enough. During this strange "vacation" in the month of April, German soldiers continued to be bombed and strafed, but at least the Red Army had made no serious attempt to attack the long peninsula.

Port facilities at Hela were not large enough to accommodate all the rescue ships. Larger vessels were at anchor in the bay just offshore. While some of the "sea snake" ferries continued to carry luckless soldiers over to die around Pillau and Konigsberg, others carried civilians from the docks out to the steamers.

The weather was mild and sunny now. The Goya was one of a convoy of eight ships. The ferries were shuttling continuously back and forth across the harbor waters. At noon on April 16th Russian planes came over, Stormovik fighter-bombers. They had big triangular tails like meat axes and for years the Landsers had nicknamed them "Schlachtern" (Butchers), because they butchered everything in their path. Heavily armed and armored, they were the Soviets' most destructive aircraft. The Soviets also favored American lend-lease A-20 ground attack bombers, known as Bostons or Havocs, for many of these late-war shipping raids.

A bomb fell on a refugee-laden ferry that had just tied up alongside the Goya. There were many old people on board, as well as a number of women and children, about 100 souls in all. The blast did not sink the ferry, but as it pulled away from the Goya its decks were awash with blood and blood streamed over the low gunwales into the bay.

The Stormoviks disappeared and the ferries kept coming, all throughout the afternoon, on into the evening. For months ships had been leaving port overloaded with passengers, but the number of people packed into the Goya was nearly obscene. About 7,000, as many as had been on the Wilhelm Gustloff, were packed into the cargo holds of a freighter only one fifth the Gustloff's size. Large, dark holds intended for bearing freight were crowded wall to wall with humanity, like convicts aboard a prison ship. Still the ferries continued to come until the captain, more than a little unnerved, declared he could take no more on board.

The same scenes were repeated among the other seven ships of the convoy.

According to the divisional history, the surviving men of 7th Panzer had departed Hela in four ships the previous day, April 15th. The divisional history also states that the convoy made port in the west at Swinemunde without incident. This contradicts Paul von Ruhland's statement that one of the 7th Panzer ships was lost with almost everyone on board.

Almost certainly he was referring to the convoy that departed the following day, April 16th. Some of 7th Panzer's soldiers had had to wait to leave with this day's convoy, some of them on board the Goya.

The convoy weighed anchor at 1900 hours, just at sunset. The weather was breezy but otherwise beautiful. A few minutes earlier another Soviet air raid had been driven off by anti-aircraft fire, downing one plane and leaving the ships unharmed. A single minesweeper formed a rather pathetic escort at the head of the convoy. The Goya was in the most vulnerable position, far out on the starboard, or seaward, side of the other vessels.

At midnight the convoy was sixty miles off the Pomeranian port of Stolp. This was the favorite hunting ground for Russian submarines. The Gustloff and Steuben had gone down here, though closer to shore. Why these eight freighters were passing through deeper and more dangerous waters has not been explained. They were heading not to a German port but to Copenhagen in Denmark, and the most direct route would have taken them across this deeper region of the Baltic. On the other hand, it would not have been that far out of the way to take a safer route closer to the German coast. Another factor may have been the fact that, since the loss of the General Steuben, there had not been another major sinking in over two months. Despite the two great tragedies just recounted, Russian submarine activity had been strangely insignificant throughout 1945.

Shortly after midnight the Goya was struck by two torpedoes and sank within minutes. The passengers crammed into the dark holds set up a hideous screaming and swarmed like rats to get up to the main deck. The ship went down so quickly that few ever made it. Even the terrible scenes from the Gustloff and the

Steuben could hardly compare with this. Seawater poured into the holds and once again shots rang out as people tried to fight their way abovedecks.

But at least this time it was all over in a matter of minutes. The Goya disappeared.

A few hundred survivors were scattered on the water. There had been no time to drop the lifeboats and there were only a few liferafts floating about. In mid-April the water was still cold enough to kill.

A Lt. Brinkmann of 7th Panzer had been on deck when the torpedoes hit. As the Goya went down he climbed up to the bridge; when the bridge was awash a wave swept him overboard. He found a liferaft and struggled onto it with four other soldiers.

People floated all around, most without lifebelts, clinging to debris or swimming helplessly. For a time Brinkmann heard a woman screaming insanely in the dark, carrying above all other noise. This seemed to initiate a frenzied cacophony of shouts, curses, and screams the like of which Brinkmann had never heard before. People cursed Hitler in the most obscene terms imaginable. They cursed the Nazi party, they cursed anyone they could think of. They cursed Erich Koch, the swinish gauleiter of East Prussia who months earlier had blocked the flight of refugees to the west, declaring that the province under his rule would not succumb to panic and defeatism.

Brinkmann was already half-maddened by all he had experienced with 7th Panzer during the endless bloody retreat from East Prussia to Gotenhafen to the Oxhoft plateau to Hela. He had seen terrible things on the battlefield and done terrible things himself. He felt his will to live ebbing away and as the uproar of screaming went on and on he drew his pistol with the idea of killing himself.

Perhaps he did not realize at first that much of this screaming came from swimmers fighting with other swimmers to gain possession of the few rafts and bits of floating debris. Then after a while there were swimmers around his own raft and they struggled like demons to pull Brinkmann and the four men with him into the water and take their places. One man was dragged off and went under. Brinkmann used a piece of driftwood as a club to beat at other swimmers trying to claw their way onto the tiny boat. No sins he had committed in combat would equal this. But in delirium all judgement of human conduct was suspended.

This sickening eternity came to an end only an hour later. Brinkmann, nearly speechless from horror and fatigue and cold, was picked up by a rescue vessel.

To this date the sinking of the Wilhelm Gustloff had been history's worst sea disaster. The sinking of the Goya surpassed it. Nearly seven thousand people went down. 170 were rescued. By a curious coincidence, this figure was identical to the number of SS survivors reported to have escaped from the inferno at Budapest.

But among scenes of endless horror the notion of coincidence, along with all kinds of other notions and ideas about the nature of things, tends to lose any meaning.

Still, it might be said that the doomed ship Goya bore a not inappropriate name. The Spanish painter Goya was renowned for his portraits of members of the Spanish royal court during the early 1800s. But he also had a darker side. He was one of the first great artists to depict the horror of war in the depraved and nightmarish style that war really deserves. He also did a curious series of paintings depicting the Titans, the primeval forebears of the ancient Greek gods. The most powerful of these paintings shows the Titan Cronos devouring his own son, blood gushing from his greedy mouth, his son's arm thrust halfway down his throat.

The loss of these three ships later became known as "the three great sinkings." About a dozen other smaller vessels were sunk in the Baltic by submarines and mines during these months.

Soldiers from a Volksgrenadier division have set up positions in the country estate of the swine Erich Koch. The men make themselves at home, bedding down on the costly furniture, helping themselves to liquor and whatever provisions they can find. It is a nice place, and they feel no guilt about indulging in these small luxuries, as the Soviets are shelling and machine gunning the estate every day and the grenadiers are hard-pressed to defend it.

A delegation arrives from Gauleiter Koch to complain about the mess being made of his country home. The major in command of the grenadiers listens with as much patience as he can muster.

Koch's men swiftly depart for the safety of the rear, but then the gauleiter despatches them to pay another visit a few days later. This time they are outraged to find one of Koch's dress uniforms being worn by a statue of the goddess Diana in the main entrance hall. The grenadiers find all this quite amusing. The party underlings of Gauleiter Koch deliver a good deal of threats and cursing before the major orders his men to throw them out, hoping he has seen the last of these fools.[1]

23

KONIGSBERG AND PILLAU

Reduction of the East Prussian Fortress

The siege of Konigsberg went through several peculiar phases.

3rd Panzer Army was responsible for this region of East Prussia, and during the first days of the great January offensive the Russians made little headway against bitter resistance in heavy snowstorms.

Many of the German units here were composed of veterans from Courland, with long years of experience fighting in northern Russia. Two of the infantry divisions, the 1st and 61st, had been raised in East Prussia before the war and comprised many natives of that province. After years of fighting around Leningrad and the Volkhov River, they were now defending their home corner of Germany, and they did so tenaciously.

It took two weeks for the 3rd Baltic Front under Marshal Vassilievski to advance through fifty miles of snow-covered forest to the outskirts of Konigsberg. By January 27th the Germans were bled out and reeling in confusion, ready for the knockout blow. But the Russians were also hurting, with the soldiers of 3rd Baltic Front suffering the heaviest casualties of the entire Vistula-Narew-East Prussian operation. After the hard fighting east of Konigsberg, there remained no coherent German defense within the city itself. By now 3rd Panzer Army had been dissolved, with its headquarters staff shipped out to the west to lead a new 3rd Panzer Army at the mouth of the Oder, part of Himmler's Army Group Vistula. On the evening of January 28th, a squadron of Russian tanks probed the defensive ring and actually broke through into the city streets. If the Russians had followed up with strong supporting forces, Konigsberg might have fallen that same night, but they were momentarily too exhausted to do so.

Fighting on their own, the small force of Stalins and new model T-34/85s did not fare well in this built-up urban area, especially in the dark. For a while they roamed almost unopposed along the broad avenues, their crews perplexed by the lack of resistance, seeming uncertain about what to do next. Basically they were conducting a reconnaissance in force, and they had not expected to break right into the heart of the city. A German Sturmgeschutz battalion was despatched to the scene to avert what appeared to be an impending crisis. The assault gun crews were up to the task, even though their unit had been reduced to a strength of six vehicles.

The city lay in snow-covered darkness, the lights extinguished on all the thoroughfares. More familiar with the area, the Germans advanced through the blackness and caught the disoriented Soviets unawares. Illuminating rounds from the Sturmgeschutzen showed the Russian tanks jammed-up in their notoriously easy to hit columns. Eight T-34s and Stalins were knocked out almost at once, and by the end of the night a total of thirty had been destroyed. For almost three months these hulks would remain the only Soviet vehicles to have made it inside the city walls.

The Russians fell back to regroup.

Possibly further concerted efforts could have succeeded in overrunning the city. The Russians were uncertain of the exact strength of the German defenses. Konigsberg was surrounded by a ring of 19th century forts built during the Bismarck era, solid and ominous-looking structures with walls of thick masonry, much like the great World War One forts around the French city of Verdun. To take them by frontal assault might have resulted in a bloodbath, if the Germans had adequately manned them and armed them with heavy weapons. But the gun crews had only small supplies of shells, and the garrisons were made up of a motley collection of veteran soldiers and poorly armed Volksturm battalions, whose untrained grenadiers ranged in age from fifteen to sixty.

On the Western Front, the Volksturm units were generally depicted as pathetic and ridiculous, prone to surrendering en masse after either a token resistance or none at all. But in the East the story was different. Some of these units simply melted away before the Soviet advance, an understandable occurrence in instances when they had almost no weapons to fight with. But elsewhere they fought with great tenacity, standing shoulder to shoulder with the veteran Landsers of the army, who frequently expressed praise for the courage of these teenagers and old men. Ad hoc units of railroad workers, longshoremen, and policemen also strengthened German resistance in the East, filling gaps in the line as best they could, and their efforts were a far cry from the feeble and unenthusiastic defense put up by similar units in the West.

Especially when armed with the panzerfaust, a weapon that an untrained combatant could learn to operate very quickly, these people's battalions could pose a formidable danger. In addition, their fighting morale tended to be at its best when they were deployed in built-up urban areas (which also happened to be their home towns). In a large city there would be myriad forms of shelter from the terrifying Russian bombardments and armored assaults—the twin elements of combat which were most unnerving to the inexperienced soldier. Both Breslau and Konigsberg, the two great German siege cities of 1945, relied heavily on the fortitude of these untrained civilians. Without them, both cities would have fallen much sooner than they did.

Teenagers especially took to the panzerfaust with enthusiasm. It imbued them with the fever of the hunt, and with the ability to kill Russian tanks single-handedly they were not so prone to the demoralizing feeling of being little more than cannon fodder. In Konigsberg teenage boys sometimes had an appetite for stalking Russian tanks which old and bitter veterans had lost years before. The Soviets continued to probe at different points around the Konigsberg perimeter, and the surprisingly inspired resistance put up by these rag-tag Volksturm units indicated that the city would not fall without a major offensive effort.

To some extent the Soviets were fooled by this initial show of resistance, along with the deceptively strong appearance of the ring of forts. The defenders were still critically outmanned and undergunned. But Konigsberg was now isolated and could no longer be considered a major strategic target. Its time would come. In the meantime the Russians settled down into an elaborate siege ring of earthworks and trenches outside the city, conducting their usual massive buildup of artillery pieces, movements which were clearly visible to the defenders manning the ancient medieval walls.

There followed a strangely uneventful interlude that lasted for over two months. In a way, the situation was similar to the one that prevailed in Berlin, with the citizens of the capital maintaining a shadowy semblance of normal life for months while the Russians stood ready to strike only forty miles away.

At first there had been a mad stampede of refugees trying to get from Konigsberg to its port at Pillau, before the Russians cut off this escape route. The gauleiter of East Prussia, the swine Erich Koch, had done everything in his power to censor the news of the Soviet advance and keep the citizens in ignorance of their fate, declaring to one and all that his domain was in no danger. When the refugees pouring in from the eastern frontier made it clear that the Russians might arrive at any moment, Koch boarded his own personal train and headed for Pillau, where he took up residence in the town's best hotel and continued to interfere with the military defense of Konigsberg by issuing orders to his Nazi henchmen still inside the city. When the Russians began bombing Pillau, Koch moved his headquarters over to a village on the Frische Nehrung, setting up residence in a house surrounded by barbed wire and SS guards.

At the end of January the Soviets reached the Frisches Haff between Pillau and Konigsberg, blocking the refugees' escape. Thousands of civilians remained unaware of this development until it was too late. One train jammed to capacity left the suburban farming village of Metgethen, steaming along the route to Pillau for only a short distance before the tracks were blocked by Russian tanks. Red Army soldiers boarded the train and had a splendid time raping the female passengers and murdering all the others, dumping bodies out the windows and leaving them to lie for months beside the tracks, frozen lumps in the snow. The screams of the women carried far through the night, audible to the men of broken German units scattered throughout the countryside.

Another train that had left Konigsberg was stopped by German stragglers, who informed the engineers that the tracks were now blocked. The train was forced to back up all the way to Konigsberg station, discharging its carloads of humanity, who now dispersed into the city to wait out the siege.

And so the shadow life went on during the months of winter and early spring. The tram lines began to operate again, gas and water mains were repaired, stores re-opened, cinemas ran their nightly film showings. Romance flourished between soldiers and young women, eager for a taste of life before the ax finally fell. None knew when this would be. The multiple German command agencies kept everyone in a state of confusion. Konigsberg had been designated a fortress city by Hitler, a sure sign that all the inhabitants and defenders had been written off. But the designated fortress commander, General Otto Lasch, refused to accept the situation as hopeless. He organized work crews to shore up the forts and the city's medieval walls, barricading streets with tram cars filled with debris, assembling stragglers from shattered units into coherent fighting forces. Lasch operated with the independence of a captain running his own ship, but he was continually running afoul of Gauleiter Koch's henchmen and occasionally of Koch himself, who would fly in by Fieseler Storch to meddle, threaten, and intimidate.

Koch was a leading figure in the hierarchy of the Nazi Party, determined not to cede an iota of power over his East Prussian domain. He had direct communication with Hitler and Himmler and used this leverage to threaten military commanders with removal from their posts. His influence had played a significant role in Hitler's decision to cashier General Hossbach, the recalcitrant commander of 4th Army, as well as Hossbach's immediate superior General Reinhardt.

General Lasch, however, refused to be intimidated, apparently unconcerned as to whether he would meet the same fate as the other generals. His attitude combined fatalism and pragmatism; essentially, he went about doing his job as best he could, ignoring the grim fact that it was probably all an exercise in futility. Koch had instructed his deputies to maintain firm control over the city's still fairly substantial depots of food and ammunition; for the most part, Lasch simply ignored these men and took what he needed, disbursing supplies to his soldiers and to the hungry civilians, patiently enduring furious interviews with Koch whenever this arrant coward bothered to fly in from the outside.

Koch was also technically in command of all the Volksturm units that provided so much of the city's defense. To Lasch, this division of military control was not only insufferable but unworkable, and he personally toured the Volksturm units, meeting with their commanders, determining which of them could be relied on to conduct a coordinated defense and which of them were party stooges faithful to Koch. The latter he simply dismissed from his plans, keeping them in the dark about operational matters as a further means of holding Koch and his underlings at arm's length. Lasch was helped considerably in these compli-cated dealings by the fact that Koch's prolonged absences made his cowardice more and more apparent to those still inside the siege ring.

Lasch knew that in spite of all his preparations, any last-ditch defense of the city would be doomed from the start. When-ever the Russians decided they were ready to mount a serious attack, the end would come quickly. He therefore set about plan-ning an operation that would break through the siege ring on the west side of Konigsberg and re-establish contact with Pillau. Such an attack, he reasoned, might only be temporarily success-ful, but at least it would provide the refugees still trapped inside the city with one last chance to escape to the port.

The Breakout to Pillau

Plans for this attack were made in secret, lest Koch be tempted to intimidate other military commanders and disrupt the whole operation. Lasch not only had to deal with the gauleiter, but also with the commanders of the German forces still fighting outside Konigsberg around Pillau and the Samland, a large rural area that jutted into the Baltic to the west of the city.

General Lothar Rendulic, who had replaced Reinhardt as commander of Army Group North in East Prussia, was a dedi-cated Nazi frequently called upon by Hitler to take command of troublesome situations.[2] Though General Lasch had independent control of the defense of Konigsberg, he was subordinate to Ren-dulic and would have to rely on his cooperation if the siege ring were to be broken. Fortunately, Rendulic was not entirely of the same ilk as his brutal Nazi colleague in Silesia, General Schorner. He had a subtler and, at least on occasion, more humane ap-proach to things, better able to accept the realities of Lasch's desperate position in Konigsberg. If thousands more civilians were not to be massacred an escape corridor to Pillau would have to be re-opened, and Rendulic agreed to conduct an attack from the Samland that would link up with Lasch's divisions when they broke out of the city.

The only catch to this operation was that Lasch was still under orders from Hitler to defend Konigsberg to the last man. He could not simply take all his forces and evacuate the city;

this meant that he would only be able to use a limited number of his units to conduct the attack to the west.

Lasch made a bold decision, in keeping with the independent style he had displayed since his arrival. Essentially he stripped the city's defenses to the bone, leaving only token garrisons along the walls and inside the forts, making sure that the strike force for the attack would be as strong as possible. If the Russians chose this moment to make their final assault, then all would be lost. Lasch could hardly be characterized as a gambler; rather, he based his decision on a pragmatic assessment of the best course of action to take in a desperate situation. Of course this decision was still a gamble—he accepted this fact and proceeded.

Rendulic had agreed to Lasch's breakout with the proviso that it include only 1st Infantry Division and a few elements of 5th Panzer Division. Almost certainly Rendulic was thinking of Hitler's reaction should larger forces be used, which might lead the Fuhrer to believe that the attack was no more than a ruse to evacuate Fortress Konigsberg.

Lasch however had no intention of leading this attack in a half-baked fashion. Along with 1st Infantry, he assembled all of 5th Panzer and threw in 561st Volksgrenadier Division for good measure. (The Volksgrenadier divisions were more in the nature of national guard units, not to be confused with the barely trained men of the Volkssturm.) He did not notify Rendulic of this last-minute change, but did inform General Gollnick, a corps commander serving under Rendulic whose divisions were to link up with Lasch's force from the Samland area. Gollnick could only reply that Lasch must take full responsibility for this action.

Lasch said,

> "Only a full-blooded commitment will help, and I am willing to answer for it. The life and death of the garrison and the civilian population hangs on the success or failure of this attack."[3]

The breakout took place on the night of February 19th. The ground was soft from a brief period of warmer weather, forcing the vehicles of 5th Panzer to advance along the roads and railroad embankments. The ancient veterans of 1st Infantry Division put out flanking units in the mud and slush of the surrounding fields. The 1st had been raised in Konigsberg and most of its soldiers hailed from rural areas in East Prussia, returning to their home counties in 1945 to engage in a struggle to the death after long years of fighting in northern Russia.

By this time 5th Panzer was only slightly better equipped than an infantry division, having lost most of its vehicles during the initial fierce battles on the eastern frontier in mid-January. The only available armored support was provided by five Tiger Is and King Tigers from the attached Panzer Abteilung 505, which had also lost almost all of its tanks in the frontier battles. Lastly there was also an indefinite number of SPWs and Sturmgeschutzen. All in all, it was an inadequate force that could barely hope to accomplish anything; just to break through the Russian lines required a clever bit of subterfuge.

Many of the soldiers from this part of East Prussia could speak Russian fluently. Before the war inter-marriage from both sides of the border had not been uncommon. A crew of these Russian-speakers manned a captured T-34 at the head of 5th Panzer's paltry armored column.

Racing boldly into the night with headlights blazing, with much shouting and fanfare, the crew cried out in panic that a large German armored force was right on their heels. This demented gamble paid off in the way that all-or-nothing gambles frequently do: the Russians were completely fooled and soldiers began abandoning their forward positions in wild disorder. German participants gave the standard comic relief account of "Russians fleeing from their beds in their underwear."[4] One begins to get the impression that the Soviets were sleeping more deeply than usual during these nights of 1945, being confident of victory and having to contend with so many drunken celebrations and other fleshly activities.

The five Tigers followed the T-34 almost unopposed to the village of Metgethen, scene of the massacre on board the refugee train three weeks earlier. The train was still there and the dead were still there, lying in the passenger cars or thrown outside, sprawled and preserved in frozen contortions of agony and silent screams, of every conceivable variation of rape and mutilation.

Immediately the East Prussians of 1st Infantry Division began painting white-washed slogans on the sides of the cars:

Revenge! Revenge for Metgethen!

The Germans were now caught up in a merciless frenzy, just as they would be after discovering the horrors at Striegau in Silesia. This was perhaps just as well, for only superhuman efforts over the next few days would prevent the Soviets from regaining their composure and crushing the German attack.

General Gollnick's divisions advancing from the Samland did not rely on any such ruses, with the result that the Russians recovered more quickly here and put up a ferocious defense. But every German soldier in East Prussia had seen terrible and inspirational sights. A few nearly deranged civilians led some Landsers to a large bomb crater. They said the Russians had herded thirty or forty refugees from a nearby village into the crater and then blown them all up with high explosives. Bits and pieces of these bodies were still visible, scattered throughout the area.

Gollnick's and Lasch's forces linked up during the waning daylight hours of February 20th. The escape corridor to Pillau was now open again, but who knew for how long? Russian units were still milling in confusion all over the countryside, but it would not take long for their enormous material edge in tanks, artillery, and ground attack aircraft to come into play.

The German flank on the right, or north, was dominated by a hill at the Regitten Farm that had a commanding view of the breakthrough corridor. Parts of 1st Infantry Division were stationed at the farm, which changed hands six times during February 20th in hand-to-hand melees as berserk as any seen during the war. The German unit here, Kampfgruppe Malotka, comprised both 1st Infantry veterans and teenagers of the Hitler Youth; by nightfall on the 20th this group of about 400 men had lost nearly 50 killed and over 300 wounded.

The five Tigers of Panzer Abteilung 505 that had spearheaded the breakout were sent up to the Regitten Farm to provide support. In addition to their heavy firepower, another ruse was in order here. The tank crews had captured some Soviet signal flares. The Red Air Force arrived in strength on the afternoon of the 21st, with Stormovik "Butchers" and A-20 Havocs bombing the area around the hilltop farm. But the Soviet pilots were deceived by the signal flares fired from the German position, leaving it untouched while several times dropping their loads on the Russians nearby. The enemy was demoralized and now, with the Tigers on the scene, the decimated survivors of

Kampfgruppe Malotka were able to maintain possession of the hill.

Even this close to the end of the war, the Russians remained faithful to their practice of setting up deeply echeloned defensive positions behind their main lines. More than anything else, this meant endless ranks of well-camouflaged PAK batteries, the anti-tank guns that German panzer crews feared more than Stalins or T-34s. General Gollnick's force coming from the Samland was spearheaded by another handful of Tigers, in this case from Panzer Abteilung 511. Before having its numerical designation changed to 511 a few weeks earlier, this unit had been known as Panzer Abteilung 502, the oldest and most experienced Tiger battalion in the army, which had seen uninterrupted service on the Eastern Front in northern Russia since late 1942.

The tank crews of 511 still fielded the older Tiger Is, but these vehicles remained just as deadly as King Tigers. They narrowly escaped destruction when a Stalin Organ rocket salvo landed in their assembly area at the beginning of the attack, but once underway they proved nearly unstoppable. Several times, while fighting to link-up with Lasch's force, these tanks were placed in do-or-die situations in which they were forced to charge massed Soviet anti-tank batteries like bulls. Only Tiger tanks could have endured such a deluge of fire without being annihilated. Many were shot to pieces, but amazingly none were completely knocked out. In the confusion some were even hit by German anti-tank guns. One by one by the Soviet nests were approached under fire, taken in the flank and then rolled up in bulldozer-like maneuvers.

Between them, Panzer Abteilungs 505 and 511 probably fielded no more than twenty Tigers and King Tigers. Without them the breakthrough, and especially the subsequent defense of its landward flank, would probably not have succeeded.

On February 26th the Wehrmacht communique declared that the corridor from Konigsberg to Pillau had been made fully secure. The Russians, more than a little exasperated, went over to the defensive for the time being. 3rd Baltic Front's commander, Marshal Vassilievski, had been killed by artillery fire the week before during a tour of the siege lines around Konigsberg. His successor, Marshal Chernyakovski, began shifting many of his divisions over to the Heiligenbeil Cauldron to crush the German 4th Army in that sector. These tumorous pockets of German resistance were becoming a great nuisance. If they could not be wiped out in simultaneous operations, they wold have to be reduced one by one.

Thus, while the fighting around Heiligenbeil reached its crescendo during March, quiet suddenly prevailed over the Konigsberg and Samland areas. A kind of unnerving silence would last here for another six weeks. As on the Hela peninsula, the Landsers and the Tiger crews were able to repair their vehicles and refresh themselves in another curious interval of peace and relaxation before the end came.

At the end of March the Konigsberg and Samland front was reinforced by the divisions of 4th Army, which had just been evacuated from the Heiligenbeil Cauldron. But these units were no more than wrecks. General Muller, a rather woodenheaded fellow who had been given command of 4th Army after the cashiered General Hossbach, sent 10,000 wounded men to reinforce General Lasch's divisions at Fortress Konigsberg. Many of them were soul-blasted and physical wrecks; many of them were so badly wounded they could not stand up on their own. Lasch sent all these men back to Pillau to be evacuated to western Germany.

Such actions caught the attention of the swine Koch, who again flew in to Konigsberg to inform Lasch that in light of such displays of defeatism he was asking Hitler to remove him from his post. Lasch could not have been very disappointed. But by now Hitler was harassed by a thousand worries and the transfer was never effected. Lasch would remain to the end in this doomed citadel.

Koch found the amenable and rather dim-witted General Muller more to his liking. The lull in the siege of Konigsberg prompted both these men to inane delusions of grandeur about prospects for the future. Before his tenure as gauleiter of East Prussia, Koch had served as the chief Nazi administrator for the occupied Ukraine. His brutal and unflappably racist regime had done more than anything to alienate Russian civilians forever from their so-called liberators. Yet now in April of 1945 Koch was confiding jovially to General Muller—in a scene reminiscent of SS General Steiner's backslapping episode with Leon DeGrelle at Stargard—that he had been the master of the eastern lands in the past and one day he would be their master again.

Not to be outdone, Muller paid a visit to General Lasch to announce a forthcoming offensive that would sweep the Russians out of East Prussia and throw them back into the Baltic States. It would have been out of character for Lasch to laugh. Instead he merely asked Muller where he would find the fresh divisions to carry out such a scheme. Muller, who had seen nearly his entire 4th Army torn to pieces around Heiligenbeil, admitted that he was not sure yet, but he was certain that final victory would still be theirs' in due time. He again reminded Lasch to be prepared to be stripped of his command very soon. With that the interview concluded.

Lasch's desperate breakout attack in February had paid off to the extent that about 100,000 more refugees were able to escape to Pillau. Strangely though, many civilians now seemed to prefer to remain inside Konigsberg, perhaps lulled into a sense of security against their better instincts by the cessation of the Russian attacks. The familiar is usually preferable to the unknown. Stories were rife about the overcrowding and corruption at the Pillau docks, about the inadequate numbers of rescue ships, about the frightful deaths of the passengers aboard the Wilhelm Gustloff and the General Steuben. People would remember the grisly fate of the trainload of civilians surprised by the Russians outside Metgethen at the end of January. Another Soviet offensive might sever the escape corridor at any time, and no doubt any refugees caught fleeing to Pillau at that moment would meet the same end.

All of these factors, combined with a normal human tendency towards inertia, served to keep a large civilian population inside the illusory safety of the fortress city. With the creature comforts of normal life being re-established to some degree, people sank numbly into a familiar day-to-day routine. All the city's young women seemed to seek out the company of the soldiers, guided by deep instincts that overruled other instincts. The weather grew warmer. Flowers bloomed in March, and a few weeks later small leaves started to show on smoke-blackened trees.

It was not until April that the Soviets felt satisfied that they had amassed the requisite number of artillery pieces, Stalin Organs, tanks, and aircraft. The Heiligenbeil tumor had just been erased; Konigsberg was next.

We will not labor in detail over the fate of a city that would differ little from that of Budapest or Altdamm, Danzig or Breslau. Here as elsewhere the Russians solved their problems with massed artillery parks, along with the airborne equivalent provided by ground attack bombers. For four days, starting on April 6th, the city was inundated by fire. Konigsberg, having perhaps the oldest and most medieval character of the major German cities, was tumbled into ruin. The outlying forts became deathtraps full of asphyxiating gases, the defenders rendered nearly prostrate by the endless concussions reverberating through the thick masonry. Finally most of the 19th century forts collapsed under the weight of 20th century shells.

The main Soviet assault continued until April 10th, tanks and infantry blasting the streets while the curtain of artillery fire still roared overhead. General Lasch ignored Hitler's fight-to-the-last-man edict and agreed to meet with Soviet emissaries on the 10th to arrange surrender terms. Continued resistance would only entail more useless bloodshed among soldiers and civilians. "I feel it is my duty to put an end to this horror," said Lasch simply.[5]

A few fanatics from an SS police battalion continued to hold out inside one of the city's many medieval bastions along the Pregel River. The Russians busied themselves with exterminating these men while in another part of town Lasch went over the terms of capitulation.

The swine Koch received word of the city's surrender at his safe haven on the Frische Nehrung. He informed Fuhrer HQ that his adamant intention of resisting to the end had been betrayed by the cowardly General Lasch. Then Koch promptly made arrangements to have a ship made ready to transport himself and his family to the west using falsified documents. They made it safely to western Germany where Koch became a farmer outside of Hamburg. The Allies finally caught up with Koch and he was arrested by the British in May 1949 and extradited to Poland in February 1950 to stand trial for war crimes. Koch was accused of the murder of four million Russians and some 400,000 Poles. During his trial in 1958 and 1959 Koch, now a broken down, emaciated old man, argued passionately for his innocence between fits of coughing. Koch claimed the crimes of the Polish communists were much worse than his own but his lengthy diatribes were not successful and as he was pulled to his feet he received a double verdict of guilt. In the first verdict the Polish judge ordered Koch to make a symbolic payment of one zloty (the equivalent of four cents) to a Polish farmer whose entire family was wiped under Koch's brutal rule. The second verdict was death for Koch but this was later commuted to life imprisonment because under Polish law prisoners in ill health, like Koch, are not allowed to be executed. Sources differ on the date of Koch's death stating he died in prison in either 1987 or 1993.[6] *{It is the editors belief that the 1987 date is correct. RSW}*

Yard by Yard to the Sea

Konigsberg was obliterated. The civilian population underwent the same ordeal of horror that was being repeated everywhere else in eastern Germany. After the war this city and its surrounding area would be incorporated into the Soviet Union, and so it has remained up to this very day, even after the collapse of Communism and the secession of the other Soviet republics. Now known as Kalliningrad, the former city of Konigsberg has been largely re-populated by Russian settlers; it is the capital of a small Russian enclave by the Baltic, separated from the motherland by the new independent nation of Lithuania.

On April 13th 1945, with Konigsberg finally taken, the Russians set about obliterating the last remaining German resistance in the Samland and Pillau.

We refer again to the combat log of 2nd Battery, II Battalion, in the Grossdeutschland Division's Panzer Artillery Regiment. The reader will recall that these men, the erstwhile crews of Wespe self-propelled guns, had escaped destruction around Heiligenbeil only to be ferried over to the Konigsberg area. After the fall of the city, the last decimated Grossdeutschland units were holding positions in the fields and sandy pine-covered hills of the Samland. 2nd Battery's log entry for April 13th reads simply:

13.IV.1945. vernichtender russ. Angriff beginnt im Samland.

April 13th, 1945. The Russians have began an offensive of annihilation in the Samland.[7]

Such phrases were not part of the normal German military jargon. But these were not normal days.

Later entries in the combat log, as well as sources from other units, indicate that this last Russian offensive was assisted by members of the Free Germany Committee. There were German soldiers who had been captured in Russia years before, subsequently persuaded by various legitimate or underhanded means to join the Russians in overthrowing Hitler's depraved empire. Some of these men, like their leader General Seydlitz, had grown to loathe the Nazi cancer and followed their own consciences in assisting with its extermination. The Soviets did make some genuine efforts towards re-educating (as opposed to simply brainwashing) these men, enlightening them about the shocking extent of Nazi criminality on Russian soil. But others who joined this movement had more than likely been broken by the simpler expedient of starvation and despair in Russian POW camps. The history of the Free Germany Committee is a complex subject which deserves further attention from historians. Needless to say, however, these men were not popular with the exhausted survivors of GD, 1st Infantry, 5th Panzer, 32nd Infantry, 58th Infantry, 170th Infantry, and other wrecked units holding out in the Samland. The Russians most frequently used the so-called turncoats to send false messages over the German radio channels, luring the defenders into ambushes, ordering them to retreat or send troops to the wrong sectors, and generally adding to the already confused state of command.

It took two weeks for the Russians to push down the long southwestern neck of the Samland to Pillau. The Germans threw up one defensive barrier after another, and Soviet gains were no more than a few hundred yards a day. On some days they made no headway whatsoever. It was the inferno of Heiligenbeil all over again, yet compressed into an even smaller area, flanked by beaches and salt water on both sides—the Baltic to the left, the Frisches Haff to the right. The fighting took on the insane, exhausting, yard-by-yard character that was currently being seen halfway across the world in the last Japanese redoubts in the Pacific, places such as Iwo Jima and Okinawa.

An idea of the tenacity of the German resistance against overwhelming odds can be seen in the actions of a single Tiger crew. From the beginning of the final offensive against the Samland on April 13th, the Soviets had lost over 100 tanks and tank destroyers to the bare handful of vehicles operated by Panzer Abteilung 511. By now this battalion fielded only a single under-strength company of perhaps ten Tigers, with a second company equipped with a similar number of Hetzers. The latter unit fared badly; the Hetzers were too thinly armored to withstand the constant firestorm from both the air and the ground, and within days all but two of these midget-sized tank destroyers had been knocked out.

As always, the Tigers endured. The lion's share of tank kills was recorded by the crew of Oberfeldwebel Kerscher in an old Tiger I; Kerscher's feats would rival those of Herman Bix in his Jagdpanther outside Danzig. By April 20th the Germans were holding onto an old man-made barrier called "the curtain," a sandy embankment that ran right across the Pillau neck from one beach to the other. Over the next several days Kerscher's Tiger destroyed over twenty Soviet tanks that were trying to over-run this position. At times he was reinforced by two Hetzers, a single Mk IV, and two other Tigers—yet eventually all of these vehicles were either destroyed or so badly damaged that they had to withdraw. There were long hours at a stretch when Kerscher's Tiger was the only heavy weapon preventing the massed Soviet armored assaults from driving right over "the curtain."

Even before his defensive stand here, Kerscher had destroyed over thirty Russian tanks in the preceding week; by now his vehicle had been hit so many times that it was little more than a mobile scrap heap. Only constant maintenance by work crews sent up between the Russian attacks enabled him to stay at his position behind "the curtain." Finally the combination of artillery fire and armor-piercing shot so badly damaged the Tiger's fuel tanks that gasoline leaked out and flooded the floor of the fighting compartment. The crew opened the vents to drain the fuel away, but with all the fumes and residue the tank was no more than a bomb waiting to go off. They did not need to be hit; just firing their own weapon might do the job. Nevertheless Kerscher and his crew stayed in position, firing shell after shell till yet another Soviet tank column was beaten off.

Only after the two Tigers damaged earlier had been repaired at Pillau and sent back to the front was Kerscher able to withdraw. Seemingly for hours the crew had scarcely breathed, waiting for their tank to blow sky high. Back in Pillau, the fuel tanks and other damage had scarcely been repaired when Kerscher was again sent up to "the curtain." The two Tigers that had relieved him had been knocked out. Alone, he and his crew held their position until April 23rd, when at last the tank was so badly shot-up it was no longer combat-worthy. The Russians overran "the curtain."

A dense forest of scraggly coastal pines was the only remaining terrain feature outside Pillau. The few remaining German armored vehicles were useless here; they had no clear field of fire through the tangled thickets. The decimated German infantry divisions fought on in the woods for about another day, enduring a deluge of artillery fire and aerial bombardment and engaging the Russian assault infantry in hand-to-hand combat. Then one final defensive position was set up just behind the forest, only a mile from Pillau.

As for Kerscher, he had personally destroyed over fifty Russian tanks in a period of only ten days. Even Herman Bix had not accomplished so much in such a short time. It is doubtful that any tank commander of any nation ever has equalled this performance. Kerscher was almost single-handedly responsible for delaying the Soviet offensive for a number of critical days.

But the end was near, very near. Deemed beyond repair, Kerscher's Tiger was blown up at the work shop in Pillau to prevent capture. He and his crew were ferried over to the Frische Nehrung, along with 511's last surviving Tiger.

By April 24th it was just about over. Bit by bit the blasted defenders were being ferried across the mile-wide channel from Pillau to the Frische Nehrung. The combat log of 2nd Battery, GD, reads:

> April 24th, 1945. Ferry across to the Mole [on the Nehrung side of the channel] during the night under the heaviest fire. A rain of burning phosphorus. Out of 35,000 men, only 7,000 reached the other side.[8]

This was a horrendous debacle. Yet it is hard to pin down for certain exactly when this terrible flight across the channel took place. A state of chaos will tend to bring about contradictory sources of information. The combat log seems to suggest that 28,000 men were lost during the ferry operation, but more detailed sources contradict this picture. Undoubtedly these casualty figures also refer to men who were killed during the final battles outside Pillau, before the last survivors were ferried out. And even these men were not the very last to go. For it was also on the night of April 24th that 83rd Infantry Division was shipped over from Hela to Pillau on its last mission of the war.

Last Ferry to Pillau—the Martyrdom of 83rd Infantry Division

By late April the Landsers of 83rd Infantry Division had been on the Hela peninsula for almost three weeks. After leaving 257th Infantry Regiment behind at Graudenz, the 83rd was reinforced by another regiment from a dissolved division. A few units were deployed to fend off desultory Russian attacks, more in the nature of probes, at the base of the peninsula. But for the most part this time period was marked by peace, sunshine, calm. So the divisional history reports. Other sources indicate the peninsula was under constant air attack, though probably most of these raids would have been focussed on the actual town of Hela. Air raids or not, the Landsers of the 83rd must have felt surrounded by a deafening silence during these weeks, in comparison to the battles they had just experienced at Gotenhafen and Oxhoft.

Then death cast its final shadow. On April 24th the division was assembled at Hela port to be ferried over to Pillau. The transfer across the bay took place during the still night hours. Sometime during the early hours of the 25th the "sea snakes" motored quietly past the stone lighthouse, clearly silhouetted in the starlight, that stood guard over the channel leading to Pillau harbor.

These men of the 83rd should never have been sent on this final mission. It was a "Himmelfahrt" in the truest and most dismal sense of that old Landsers' phrase: a journey to heaven. The English translation has a sunnier connotation that is inappropriate. "Suicide mission" more aptly conveys the meaning of this phrase.

The divisional history reports:

Not a single man crossing over to Pillau and an

unknown fate on the night of the 24th believed either in a good end for himself or victory of any kind. But that the entire division, in a period of only 48 hours, would be destroyed and utterly torn to pieces, would stand out as one of the most overwhelming experiences of the entire war for the few who survived this inferno.[9]

The ferries landed the 83rd in Pillau harbor without incident. The night was deceptively quiet as the Landsers marched through the stinking ruins of the town, heading for the trenches only about a mile away. (This clearly contradicts 2nd Battery's log entry, stating that GD and other survivors were ferried over to the Nehrung on the night of the 24th, beneath a "rain of phosphorus shells." Conceivably the log entry is referring only in general terms to events that took place over the course of several days.)

The units about to be relieved by 83rd Infantry Division were not divisions anymore, they were not even regiments or battlegroups. They were simply various handfuls of men, belonging to Grossdeutschland and a few other shattered divisions. Of Grossdeutschland, almost nothing remained except for the headquarters staff. There were no men left to command. From the beginning of the Russian offensive in January to this date in late April, GD had suffered nearly 100% casualties. 32nd Infantry Division, which now included Kampfgruppe Herb and the dissolved 58th Infantry Division, was still a ruined force by April 24th. But all these men were lucky. At the final moment they had been granted a reprieve—they were about to be relieved by the just arriving regiments of the 83rd. They handed over their trenches and defensive works in the dunes to the new men, uninterrupted by Russian fire in pre-dawn stillness. They marched like ghosts back to the harbor, where the ferries were waiting to ship them back to Hela or across the channel to the Frische Nehrung. The final nightmare at Pillau was left for the 83rd to experience on its own.

The new men took up their positions in the dunes among shell craters, dead bodies, wrecked vehicles, shattered pine trees, and blasted barbed wire entanglements. There was no armored support left; there was no artillery support left. The 83rd had had to leave its own artillery regiment behind at Hela. The

Landsers would fight their last fight with only rifles, machine guns, hand grenades, and panzerfausts, outnumbered nearly ten to one and facing tanks and heavy artillery. The dark hours passed by. By the time the Landsers had fully manned their new positions it was almost dawn. They had very little time to wait, to ready themselves. In the early morning hours the massed Soviet forces packed into this two-mile wide neck of land set about dealing the death blow.

It was a strange and unenviable fate for this division. One might imagine the Japanese sending a fresh division across the Pacific to Iwo Jima, to somehow reverse the situation on that island, only two days before the US Marine Corps burned out the last defenders of that place.

For that was all the time they had remaining. Two days, 48 hours. This final act deserves to be recounted in detail. We will save it for the end of this book.

PART VI
ALONG THE ODER

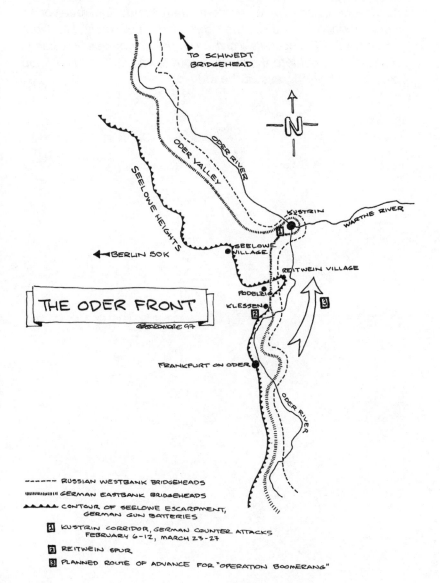

TO SCHWEDT
BRIDGEHEAD

N

ODER VALLEY

ODER RIVER

SEELOWE HEIGHTS

KUSTRIN

WARTHE RIVER

1

SEELOWE
VILLAGE

REITWEIN VILLAGE

◄ BERLIN 50 K

PODELZIG

3

KLESSEN

THE ODER FRONT

GEARDMORE 97

2

FRANKFURT ON ODER

ODER RIVER

------ RUSSIAN WESTBANK BRIDGEHEADS

GERMAN EASTBANK BRIDGEHEADS

CONTOUR OF SEELOWE ESCARPMENT,
GERMAN GUN BATTERIES

1 KUSTRIN CORRIDOR, GERMAN COUNTER ATTACKS
FEBRUARY 6-12, MARCH 23-27

2 REITWEIN SPUR

3 PLANNED ROUTE OF ADVANCE FOR "OPERATION BOOMERANG"

The squadron ready room is in a small wooden building. Winter sunlight spills through the window. The telephone rings. The orderly listens for a moment, then hands the receiver to Rudel. Rudel listens also, then gives a hurried reply. His flight suit resembles the overalls a civilian worker might wear. He hangs up and rushes out into the sunlight, out towards the Stukas lined up on the smooth grass of the airfield.

24

RUDEL

The Stukas Fly Above Every Battlefield

After receiving his latest medal and offering Hitler some suggestions for attacking across the Hungarian terrain, Hans Rudel flew back to his Stuka squadron on that battleground. They had been fighting in Hungary since the previous fall and were more dreaded by Soviet armored crews than Tiger tanks. By this time, in January of 1945, Rudel had destroyed over 450 Soviet tanks with the long 37mm cannon slung under his gull-winged plane, in a period of less than two years. He was something of a one-man army and Hitler's near-reverence for his achievements is not hard to understand.

Hitler hated to see his best men go down. Too many funerals for glorious men were bad for the nation. It is hard to say if Hitler was more worried about the morale of the population at large, or if there was some personal superstitious streak in him that caused him to fret about these men. In any case, he forbade Rudel to fly any more combat missions.

A strange decision—to take a one-man army like Rudel and put him up on a pedestal, removing him from the fighting at the very time when his nation most needed him. One thinks again of Hitler's strangely theatrical view of his own mission for the Third Reich. For a man who held such power in his hands, Hitler was very much given to his own kind of hero-worship. He admired Leon DeGrelle for exactly this reason, and it probably had much to do with his peculiar choice of Heinz Guderian to run the Army High Command so late in the war. Guderian was the best fighting man that Germany possessed, and Hitler, with his own ability to judge the talents of others, knew this very well. Of course Guderian's greatest strength was his ability to combine strategic vision and enormous energy with an unshakeable pragmatism that refused to tolerate illusions. Very few generals have ever possessed both these qualities to the highly balanced degree that Guderian did. The latter quality especially could only intrude exasperatingly upon Hitler's murky visions of things. Yet for all this, Hitler seemed strangely drawn to Guderian as a man.

With Rudel there were no such complications. He was a hero in the mode of Siegfried or some other warrior in Wagner's epic music-dramas. In Wagner's Ring Cycle it was Siegfried's death, and not the slaughter of armies containing millions of men, that signalled the end of everything—Gotterdammerung, the Twilight of the Gods. For all his love of Wagner's music, Hitler was probably not so lost in his inner world as to take this analogy literally. But clearly the thought of Hans Rudel being killed at this time played strange games with Hitler's nerves—perhaps it was no more than superstition, but whatever the reason, the only way he could calm these nagging thoughts was by forbidding Rudel to fly anymore. He would be promoted to group captain, confining him to a desk job.

He had informed Rudel of this decision before his return to Hungary, during the same high-level conference in which he invited the Stuka pilot to express his opinions about the terrain conditions there. It was also at this conference that Rudel received the highest decoration ever awarded to a German soldier—the Golden Oak Leaves to the Knight's Cross with Diamonds and Swords. It was a unique medal, the only one ever made.

In one hand Rudel held the black velvet-lined medal case. "The many lights in the room made the diamonds sparkle in a blaze of prismatic colors." With his other hand he found himself shaking hands with Hitler, with the Fuhrer's eyes staring directly into his. Rudel was in a "semi-daze," but upon being informed of the decisive news he collected his wits immediately. He declared,

"Mein Fuhrer, I cannot accept the decoration and the promotion if I am not allowed to go on flying with my wing."

For a moment Hitler was taken aback. His expression became grave. Then his face lightened and he smiled faintly.

"All right, you may go on flying," was all he said. Almost in spite of himself his smile broadened further, as if he could not help but be pleased with Rudel. And it was true, he had every reason to be. But this was only the first step in a curious fencing duel that would go on for the remainder of the war. Within days Hitler would change his mind, and during the remaining months he would order Rudel to stop flying on at least six more occasions. Rudel would disobey every time.[1]

* * *

Within days of the Russian offensive across the Vistula, their spearheads were at the gates of Rudel's home province of Silesia. Rudel immediately requested that his squadron be transferred to that area. Some writers have commented on the remarkable "pull" with higher authorities possessed by a man who was only a junior colonel in the Luftwaffe. A few days later his squadron was ordered to fly to General Schorner's command in Silesia. Possibly this had as much to do with the threat posed by the Red Army's invasion as Rudel's string-pulling. Or possibly not.

Rudel's first missions in this area gave him an excellent aerial view of the rout of the German armies. Russian tanks were reported to be 25 miles east of Tschenstochau, near the Polish-Silesian border. He was also instructed to be on the lookout for the armored units of 16th and 17th Panzer Divisions, the nucleus of General Nehring's "roaming cauldron," which for the past ten days had been retreating from the Vistula. Flying over Tschenstochau, Rudel saw columns of tanks moving through the town and assumed they must be from Nehring's divisions, still withdrawing from the Russians. But the tanks bore an unnerving resemblance to T-34s. He was unable to believe the Soviets had come so far so quickly; only when foot soldiers riding on the tanks began shooting at him with tommy guns did he realize his suspicions were correct. But even as he banked into his approach run Rudel was harassed by the worry that he might be firing on his own men; such cases of mistaken identity from the ground or the air were all too common, as were the tragic results that usually followed. Even if the tanks were T-34s they might have been captured and put to use by the Germans—but such captured vehicles were always painted over with over-size crosses and swastikas to avoid being strafed by German planes.

No, they were Russians all right, and the Ivan foot soldiers were continuing to take pot shots at him with their distinctively shaped submachine guns. Moving through the town's narrow streets, the tanks made difficult targets; the Stuka's approach was also hindered by the high trolley cables suspended between buildings. Rudel was further concerned that an all-out strafing attack might kill German civilians still in Tschenstochau. (Perhaps he was not yet aware of the grisly fate being meted out by the Russians to those same civilians.) He reasoned that more Russian columns would be following this spearhead in the open country to the east and ordered his squadron to head off in that direction.

Rudel was right. The snowy plains east of the city were swarming with Russian armor and now the Stukas swept in for the kill, leaving a dozen or so smoking hulks to blacken the ground.

But of General Nehring's lost panzer divisions he found not a trace—not surprisingly, as almost all of Nehring's tanks had probably been abandoned for lack of fuel by then.

During these days over Silesia in late January Rudel admits to the secret passion of many ace pilots and panzer commanders—that killing Russian tanks had long been a kind of sport for him and his men. To be sure, it was a dangerous sport. Rudel had already been shot down many times on the Eastern Front, and while he had escaped alive each time, many of his fellow pilots had flown out and never returned. Throughout the war German pilots would fly astronomical numbers of sorties, and their survival rate was not nearly as good as that of the armored killers crewing Panthers and Tigers. But sport was sport, and flying over the Eastern Front and seeing hundreds of Russian tanks moving below inevitably brought out the fever of the hunt. There was some kind of primitive instinct involved in all this; why try to deny it? What terrible satisfaction there was in swooping down on a T-34 or Stalin from the rear, pumping half a dozen 37mm shells into the vulnerable engine deck and watching the vehicle's gasoline tanks erupt in a flaming pyre. Especially for a marksman like Rudel, the surge of adrenalin that went with all this could become irresistible.

But along with such a straightforward confession, he avows that far more is at stake in 1945 and the passion of the hunt becomes secondary. He is determined to do everything he can to keep the Soviets from overrunning his home corner of Germany. His fellow pilots, hailing from whatever German provinces, feel the same urgency. Rudel's personal toll of blasted Russian tanks continues to rise, soon passing five hundred.

Suddenly Rudel was summoned to Karinhall, Hermann Goering's "old shack" in the forests north of Berlin. The place was large but had a rustic interior—wood paneling, plank furniture set before a small fieldstone fireplace, hunting trophies lining the walls. The Luftwaffe Reichsmarshal had bad news. Hitler had absolutely forbidden Rudel to fly anymore, but didn't have the heart to tell him to his face. So Goering, not very pleased at being the go-between in this matter, had been stuck with the job of telling the Reich's most decorated hero to stand down. A few weeks earlier he had been rather amused to see Rudel defy the Fuhrer over this flying business. As an ex-pilot himself, Goering had understood Rudel's attitude and found it stimulating in the midst of these dismal weeks. Nowadays he was only a costumed swashbuckler, but as a fighter pilot in World War I he had possessed much the same hell-bent-for-leather outlook as Rudel.

In truth Rudel's personality was much more serious and single-minded than the Reichsmarshal's, which did not make Goering's task any easier. He informed Rudel bluntly that he did not intend to be caught in the middle of this situation; he was to stop flying combat missions as of this moment and that was that.

Rudel listened in silence. Goering tried to remain agreeable, spending a few minutes asking Rudel about the situation in Silesia, but the atmosphere did not grow any more relaxed. The Stuka pilot left Karinhall and flew back to his squadron later in the day, still without the slightest intention of obeying the Fuhrer's order.

Bad weather in Silesia—snow squalls, fog. By now the Russians had reached the Oder River. Rudel's nerves were becoming a little frayed by his blind disobedience of his supreme commander, but he refused to remain grounded. He camouflaged his activities by not personally recording his continued tank-kills; they were passed off anonymously as "group kills," a phrase resorted to in chaotic situations when it was unclear which pilots had destroyed which targets. But now the higher authorities wanted to know why Rudel's wing suddenly had such a high number of these "group kills." Rudel could not think of a suitable answer and simply shelved these inquiries. Finally a general happened to pass by the airfield one day and saw Rudel flying in from a mission. The aviator declared that he was merely tutoring a younger pilot on a training run. It was arrant nonsense which deceived no one. Again he was summoned to Karinhall. Goering, obliged to bear Hitler's message a second time, made no pretense of geniality. He could not make the orders any more explicit, so he simply repeated them in an angry voice. Rudel listened in silence again, flew back to his squadron again, and began flying in combat again.

His wing was ordered to transfer to Pomerania. All of this mad shuttling about, flying back and forth between Berlin and Karinhall and different sectors of the front, was taking place in the last two weeks of January. Now SS Reichsfuhrer Himmler wanted Rudel's Stuka pilots to shore up his rapidly disintegrating Army Group Vistula. This was still two weeks before the Sonnenwende counterattack and the whole front in Pomerania was in a shambles.

News of the transfer threw General Schorner into a fury. He demanded that Rudel's pilots remain in Silesia and refused to authorize the move to Himmler's front. Besides being bluff, brutal, and belligerent, Schorner was more than a little crafty; it seems almost certain that he knew, or at least guessed, that Rudel was still flying—for his tank-killing abilities were worth as much as the rest of his pilots put together. Schorner could not have cared less about Hitler's grounding edict; to him the Stuka tank-busters were invaluable weapons and he wanted them to stay in Silesia to support his army group. Schorner was probably the last man in the German army to have any superstitious qualms about sacrificing heroes; if the Stukas could remain on his front and he could pretend not to know that Rudel was still leading them in person, then so much the better.

By this time Rudel and his men were already flying to Pomerania, but first had to make a stopover at Frankfurt-on-Oder due to the abominable weather conditions. Schorner phoned him at the airfield there and ordered him not to proceed any further until he had had it out with the Fuhrer.

"What am I supposed to do down here?" shouted Schorner. "Hold the front with nothing but rifles?"[2]

Rudel was becoming a little dazed by this convoluted drama. But Frankfurt was snowed in, so he remained there for the rest of the day, waiting to hear the results of Schorner's phone call to Hitler. At this time Frankfurt was almost in the front lines. The city lay on the west bank of the Oder; across the river on the east bank a German bridgehead was being rapidly hemmed in by the advance of Zhukov's armies. The airfield would soon lie within range of Soviet artillery. Rudel waited by the telephone.

Some Comments on the German Armaments Industry

A few reflections are in order here. In the impersonal immensity of modern warfare, it is remarkable to think that a single combat soldier could make such a difference in the outcome of events. True, Rudel's destruction of over 500 enemy tanks was an astounding total; none of his fellow pilots could even begin to compete with this number. It would have been interesting to see Rudel in a fighter plane, competing with the likes of Hartmann, Gunther Rall, or Walter Nowotny—for at least the top fighter aces had a certain rivalry among themselves. As a Stuka ground-attack pilot, Rudel stood alone; he had no peers.

But how do the accomplishments of a single man translate into any real effect on the course of the war? We have already seen the effect a single panzer commander could have on the outcome of a battle, but it is also clear that the actions of Herman Bix or Kerscher did no more than delay the Soviets for a day or two in a local area. But General Schorner was not the kind of man to be interested in numbers of kills simply for their own sake; obviously, he saw Rudel as playing a vital role in the defense of his front. Stukas could respond far more quickly than German tanks to a Soviet armored threat and inflict greater damage within a time span of a few minutes. After returning to base to re-fuel and re-arm, they could immediately fly off to some other threatened sector, a great advantage during these days when the Russian armored columns seemed to be everywhere at once.

And even if Rudel had given in and remained grounded, the other pilots in his wing could still inflict considerable damage. But this brings us to another issue, having to do with the highly curious nature of the German armaments industry during World War Two. The problem lay not just with Rudel himself, with every German army group commander vying for the use of his personal skills. Underlying the deeds of a single war-hero was the fact that there were simply not enough of these Stuka tank-busting aircraft to go around. Schorner might not have been so upset by the departure of Rudel's wing if other squadrons of these aircraft had been available to take their place.

But they were not. And this was a long-standing problem in the German military machine; it did not just rear its head at the end of the war when everything was going to pieces.

Solely from the point of view of running a war effectively,

the Germans' greatest problem—save perhaps for Hitler's tendencies to take on too many enemies at once—was their failure to fully grasp and implement the techniques of mass production. Unit for unit, their military machines tended to be either the finest or among the finest in the world. The sophistication of their late-war armored vehicles was years ahead of anything produced by other nations. But the manufacture of these vehicles was a very complicated process; the high degree of craftsmanship involved in building Panther or Tiger tanks made them innately unsuited to the techniques of mass production. It has been said that the genius of German armament design was more suited to a kind of extremely sophisticated "cottage industry." This "cottage industry" approach is all very well in the field of producing sensitive musical instruments—or other highly specialized scientific equipment for that matter—but leaves much to be desired in the field of waging all-out war across half the globe.

The Germans could never compete with the monumental scale of Soviet arms production. This fact was so depressing to Hitler that throughout the war he stubbornly refused to accept it as reality. It was the one drawback which more than anything threatened to destine all his plans for the scrap heap. (In the midst of on-going pigheadedness Hitler also tended to vacillate; there are records of conversations in which he did frankly admit, at least in private, to the colossal scale of his enemies' arsenals.) Perhaps the worst aspect of all this was that mass production did not necessarily entail inferior quality. Late war Soviet tanks were good weapons, robust and simple, though they had serious deficiencies in gunnery optics and communications equipment. On battlefields covering thousands of square miles, it was impossible for the great German weapons to be everywhere at once; whereas the Soviets never had the slightest difficulty in coping with this problem.

On the other side of the world the Americans had the capacity, as it were, to enjoy the best of everything. They were already the pioneers in the techniques of mass-production; and except in the field of armored vehicles, their weapon designs were as technologically advanced as the Germans'.

If one were to set aside the more ambiguous areas of moral bankruptcy and diplomatic and strategic errors, and focus solely on fighting capacity, then one could say that these flaws in efficiently combining design with mass-production were what lost Germany the war.

Albert Speer, the Reichsminister for Armament Production, grasped this problem more clearly than anyone. Essentially his difficulties were twofold. The first problem, as already mentioned, was the German love for fine machinery, overly sophisticated and time-consuming to manufacture. The second problem lay with Hitler's strange directives to the armaments industry earlier in the war; apparently intoxicated by the rapidity of his victories, he actually scaled down the Reich's war industries, thinking that peace and final German victory would soon be his.

This move may have been understandable in light of the lightning conquests of Poland and France, but even as late as 1942, faced with the world's most powerful industrial nations among his enemies, Hitler did not have the Third Reich's economy running on a full war-time basis. Only by 1943, thanks largely to the urgent recommendations of Albert Speer, did the war industries begin to gear-up and re-organize in terms of mass-production of weapons—and by 1943 it was already too late.

Even later in the war German designers remained somewhat hampered by their own brilliance, continuing to draw up excessively complicated types of weapons. (On the few occasions when they did hit upon a weapon that was both effective and easy to manufacture, such as the panzerfaust or the MG 42 machine gun, the results were outstanding.)

In the field of aircraft design and production, the Germans achieved a better medium—though here as well they could not compete with the staggering totals turned out by the Allied nations. But both the ME 109 and the FW 190, for example, were excellent weapons that were simple enough to be produced in large numbers. The ME 109, due mainly to its extraordinarily long combat career, was actually produced in larger numbers than any other aircraft of any nation. But in aircraft design the Germans were prone to another miscalculation about how to most efficiently maximize production.

The German military had the tendency to use the same aircraft models in all kinds of different combat roles. The result was that many of their planes were produced in a bewildering number of variants, which in effect meant that there were never enough aircraft available for any specific combat task. (The Americans also adopted this practice, but with their larger industrial base they could mass-produce as many variants of an individual aircraft as they wanted to.) The FW 190, for example, was both an excellent fighter and ground-attack plane, and it was desperately needed to fulfill both these roles—to attack Allied bombers over German skies, and to attack Russian ground formations on the Eastern Front. But there were never enough FW 190s to effectively carry out both these tasks.

The Stuka was also called upon to perform multiple roles later in the war. It was now too slow to carry out its original mission as a high-level dive bomber, but as a low-level attack aircraft on the Eastern Front it was as feared and deadly as its Russian counterpart, the Stormovik. And especially when outfitted with a pair of 37mm underwing cannon, it became an aerial version of the Tiger tank, capable of wreaking havoc on Soviet armored attacks.

But perversely, relatively few of this tank-busting Stuka variant were ever produced. Most were still carrying bombs or smaller caliber cannon, used against enemy infantry or fortifications in a more traditional ground-support role. Thus we come to the situation in 1945, when Hans Rudel's wing of 30 or so aircraft comprised the Luftwaffe's only available formation of Stuka tank-destroyers.

This kind of strange, piecemeal availability of crucial weapons systems was a source of endless aggravation to German commanders later in the war. Enough Stukas were still available that hundreds could have been fitted with these anti-tank cannon, but instead Rudel and his precious few pilots had to perform this role on every front, shuttled about everywhere like an aerial "fire brigade."

This was the context for Schorner's rage when he learned that Himmler was about to take Rudel's wing away from him. In a personal sense, Schorner was a far more intimidating authority figure than Himmler, whose own disposition was meek and non-confrontational. Thus could an army general openly vituperate against the supposedly fearsome SS Reichsfuhrer; Guderian had done exactly the same thing. But in the overall hierarchy Himmler was still the more powerful man.

What was said during Schorner's phone call to Hitler has not been recorded. The upshot was that later that same day Rudel received orders to continue flying to Himmler's army group in Pomerania. From Frankfurt Rudel and his planes took off into the ongoing snowfall, making a risky landing in pitch darkness a few hours later at their new airfield.

In the Wake of the Teutonic Knights

Beneath his bland exterior, Himmler also possessed a certain talent for subterfuge and getting things done by whatever means necessary. Like Schorner, he probably guessed or knew that Rudel was still flying in combat; during a meeting to brief the Stuka pilot on the situation in Pomerania, he made not the slightest reference to Hitler's grounding order. Himmler at least had enough modesty to recognize that he had no real talent for military command, but to have Rudel's potent weapons system at his disposal could go a long way towards alleviating these shortcomings. Himmler seemed to view himself as a kind of inspirational figurehead, as if his mere presence at the head of an army group would put more backbone and resolve into his soldiers. Hitler also seemed to have had this in mind when he nominated the SS Reichsfuhrer for this job. But if so, then both men considerably overestimated the average infantryman's respect for Himmler. The brief history of Army Group Vistula would be considerably less impressive than that of Schorner's Army Group Center in Silesia.

But Rudel and his pilots continued to make their own contributions, which were not inconsiderable. They flew sorties nonstop from dawn to dusk in terrible weather, leaving burnt-out Soviet armor wherever they found it along the long Baltic flank. Strangely, considering all their experience with winters in Russia, they were constantly hampered during these days by the feed mechanisms on their cannon icing up. Rudel reports several times having to destroy a tank with a single shell; then his guns jammed, leaving him in the maddening predicament of having to fly home while dozens of targets still surged forward on the ground below. "The day could have been three times as long and still there wouldn't have been enough time to fly as many missions as were needed."[3]

He mentions the Stukas bearing the ancient emblem of the Teutonic Knights painted on their fuselages. To him this was only an appropriate patriotic symbol, for the Teutonic Knights had waged their own centuries-long wars against the Eastern hordes during the Middle Ages. But those old Germanic orders had also carried out barbaric campaigns of extermination, retribution, and ruthless expansion against the Slavic peoples in eastern Europe during that by-gone era, parallelling in many ways Hitler's campaigns across this same territory during the 1940s. (One of the most effective propaganda films ever made, Sergei Eisenstein's ALEXANDER NEVSKY, depicted the cruelty of the Teutonic Knights during their medieval invasion of Russia. The images he put on the screen bore an incredible similarity to later popular images of Nazi ruthlessness. Perhaps the most remarkable thing about Eisenstein's film was that it was made before the war—a visionary work as much as a Soviet propaganda film.)

It must be said that Rudel had the same narrow-minded, one might almost say obtuse, attitude about all this as did many other Germans. He viewed himself and his countrymen as fighting to save their culture from the invasion of a horde of blood-thirsty barbarians, not bothering to reckon with the German invasion that had provoked these "hordes" in the first place.

By this time most German soldiers, even those fighting with instinctive desperation to keep their women from being raped and their children from being murdered, knew very well what had brought the Red Army to the gates of their homeland. They continued to fight not with the instinct of righteousness but with the deeper instinct of trying to save themselves and their kinfolk.

When writing about his exploits during the earlier years deep inside Russia, Rudel devotes very little space to discussing political issues—practically no space at all, in fact. He comes across little differently from thousands of other soldiers who had simply found themselves sucked into this terrible war, fighting, fighting, fighting, too lost in the middle of it all to think coherently about anything. He does not display any of Leon DeGrelle's arrogance or high-handed idealism, that peculiar blindness that all fascists seem to have with regard to their own callousness.

But when writing about events on German soil in 1945, Rudel suddenly leaves us with passages that could have come straight from DeGrelle's own hand:

> We are no more than a boulder, a small obstruction but unable to stem the tide. The devil is now gambling for Germany, for all Europe. Invaluable forces are bleeding to death, the last bastion of the world is crumbling

under the assaults of Red Asia. Stubborn refusal to accept this fate and the knowledge that "this must not happen" keep us going. I would not like to have to reproach myself for having failed to do everything within my power till the eleventh hour to stave off the appalling, menacing specter of defeat. I know that every young German thinks as I do.

But the Red hordes are devastating our country and we must fight on. . . . It is our plain duty also to the destiny which has placed us geographically in the heart of Europe and which we have obeyed for centuries: to be the bulwark of Europe against the East. Whether or not Europe understands or likes this role which fate has thrust upon us, or whether her attitude is one of fatal indifference or even of hostility, does not alter by one iota our European duty.[4]

It is not that uncommon for soldiers to develop attitudes that are one-sided, blinded by passion, even downright hypocritical, when they are thrust into the position of defending their homeland from utter destruction. There were many who thought as Rudel did, and still do today; there are also many non-Germans who can sympathize with these thoughts. But in the end Rudel comes across more self-righteously than many of his countrymen; even after all these years, there is a peculiar Germanic blindness to his tone which is still hard to stomach. In a way it is easier to sympathize with the deranged fury of men like Heinz Landau or Peter Neumann, wanting to "drown in a lake of Russian blood"; at least their sentiments make few pretensions about rationality or righteousness.

In any case Rudel's actions spoke louder than his words, and in that light it is easier to sympathize with him. By the end of the war his efforts to drive the enemy away from German soil would reach almost superhuman lengths. It is hard not to admire his love for his nation, if only because there was something entirely concrete about this love. There was nothing abstract or idealistic about his patriotism. He saw German soil, villages, trees, fields, men, women, being violated, and he reacted to it— blindly maybe, but at least this blindness was based on something real.

He would not only continue to defy every order from Hitler,

he would continue to fly until the war's final hour while suffering excruciating pain from the unhealed stump of a leg that had been blown off by Russian anti-aircraft fire.

But we are getting ahead of events—and there is not that much further to go.

They never see the sun come up. The valley floor is almost always cloaked with fog at dawn, lasting for several hours into the early morning. Sometimes the high ground atop the spur is above the fog, and the Kurmark grenadiers stationed up there can look down as if from a mountaintop upon a layer of cloud. But the spur is not that high, and more frequently it too will be as shrouded in mist as the valley floor below.

Then as the sun rises higher the mist will burn away. It is a daily phenomenon. The battlefield will be revealed. Flat brown fields. Craters. Wreckage. The shelling will begin.

25

DEATH VALLEY

Deadlock on the Oder

Himmler's Army Group Vistula was also responsible for the Brandenburg area, south of Pomerania—that is to say, the critical eastern approaches to Berlin itself. The two key cities in this region were Frankfurt—where Rudel had touched down a few days earlier—and Kustrin, both of them historic fortresses on the Oder River. Prussian soldiers had fought against the Russians and later against Napoleon's armies on this ground during the 18th and 19th centuries.

By now, at the beginning of February, Zhukov's 1st Byelorussian Front had forged two bridgeheads on the west bank of the Oder, one just north of Kustrin, the other between Kustrin and Frankfurt. Alternately, the mostly SS garrison holding out inside Kustrin formed a German bridgehead on the east bank of the river, standing like an island in the middle of Zhukov's armies. To the south, there was another German bridgehead on the east bank across the river from Frankfurt. (The reader is advised to refer to map #4 when attempting to follow the upcoming battles along the Oder. As mentioned earlier with regard to the Vistula offensive, the alternating German and Soviet bridgeheads along the river can be quite confusing.)

When they first arrived at the end of January, Zhukov's forces along this stretch of the Oder faced almost no opposition, as described briefly in the first section of this book. In particular there were no panzer formations in this area—a strange development in light of its close proximity to the German capital. But all the German tanks were either in Hungary, or undergoing repair and refurbishment in the West after the Ardennes battle, or being assembled from different points in preparation for Sonnenwende further north.

This was a period of crisis; the fate of Berlin was at stake. There was very little standing between Zhukov's tanks and the Fuhrer bunker beneath the Reichskanzellerei. But the situation for the Russians also had its disadvantages at this point. Bridge-heads were innately vulnerable positions; this fact was irrelevant so long as the Oder remained frozen, but if the ice thawed—as indeed it would over the next few days—all the Soviet forces on the west bank would be cut off from their supply trains. Zhukov's forces were exhausted from their headlong rush across Poland and eastern Germany, even though they had not encountered much resistance along the way. Every major military operation has its own distinctive goals, and almost invariably the impetus of an operation tends to diminish once these goals have been achieved. The objective of the Vistula operation had not been Berlin—in their wildest dreams the Soviet commanders could hardly have been that optimistic—but the Oder, and the Russians were probably surprised that they had gotten even this far in such a short period of time.

But now what? One operation had just been successfully completed; decisions had to be made about new operations. Communications between Stalin and Zhukov indicate that there was a brief period at the end of January in which they discussed immediately launching a new offensive against Berlin, scheduled to get underway by mid-February. But for a number of reasons these plans were tabled almost as soon as they were drawn up.

Zhukov's supply trains were strung out across the breadth of Poland, entailing the same kinds of logistical difficulties the Americans had faced after their race across France in 1944. Winter conditions alternating between mud and snow compounded these supply problems. The Red Air Force found that newly cap-tured airfields in Poland were frequently seas of mud and slush, severely curtailing the Soviets' up-to-then enormous air superi-ority.

Normally, all these factors would point towards a period of consolidation and re-supply—quite simply, a breathing space—before a military commander would feel inclined to strike the next major blow.

On the other hand, Berlin was so close, so damnably close, and there appeared to be very little German opposition standing in front of it. In some ways, and especially from a psychological point of view, Zhukov's (and by extension Stalin's) situation closely parallelled the one the Germans had faced in front of Moscow in the winter of 1941. Hitler's armies had also come within a stone's throw of their enemy's capital, after an arduous late-autumn offensive that had brought every German Landser to the brink of physical and mental collapse. But Moscow itself, and not some intermediate river barrier, had been the goal of that offensive, and for Hitler the temptation to just keep on going across those final miles, those final yards and inches, had been too great to resist. The leading elements of the German Army Group Center had fought their way into the suburbs, they had made it to the outermost stations of Moscow's urban tramcar network.

And then, of course, came the catastrophe. The Russian armies, brilliantly husbanded by Zhukov, had struck back along the German flanks, driving back Army Group Center for over a hundred miles and nearly destroying it in the process.

But despite these similarities, the Russians facing Berlin in 1945 were much stronger than the Germans had been in December of 1941. They were not coping with a Russian winter of unimaginable severity. Zhukov's troops were fatigued, his vehicles in need of overhaul, his supplies lagging behind the front lines—but on the whole his army was quite intact, and certainly nowhere near the limits of human endurance, as the Landsers had been in 1941.

As usual, all of this is clearer in hindsight. Especially the strength of the enemy is clearer in hindsight, and it is only in retrospect that we can see the one factor where the two situations were not parallel at all: the Germans no longer had the resources to mount a decisive counterattack into the Russian flanks. But Zhukov had no way of knowing this for sure, whereas he had quite vivid memories of what his own counterattack had done to the Germans in front of Moscow (or at Stalingrad, where the same kind of situation had been largely repeated). And of course Stalin, the man behind the man, had equally vivid memories of those days.

Finally there remained the problem of the Oder River, which was essentially a problem of timing. When would the thaw begin? If the ice were to remain frozen solid, then a continued drive on Berlin might not have been overly reckless. But if Zhukov immediately resumed the offensive and the ice melted behind him, his spearheads would be isolated far to the west of the river, extremely vulnerable to even a weakened German army.

The Soviets had not captured any bridges. It was true that they could build pontoon bridges in no time at all, but it was risky to mount an offensive across these fragile arteries. Not only were they vulnerable to German air attack, but they could be wrecked by drifting ice set loose by the thaw.

In essence, just to maintain the two limited bridgeheads on the west bank was a risky business. Zhukov was inclined to consolidate and massively re-inforce these bridgeheads, both to defend against German counterattacks and to build up his own forces until their striking power was comparable to that which had opened the Vistula offensive. Then he would be ready to go for Berlin.

This scenario basically followed the same pattern with which Zhukov had won so many battles in the past. Why meddle with success? Zhukov was an extremely confident general, but his confidence was not based on a talent for sudden improvisations but on a habit of dealing only from overwhelming strength when the time was ripe. That was his way of doing things, and he was the man in charge, a man who brooked little dissension from either his subordinates or his peers. Only Stalin had the power to say otherwise, and Stalin seems to have shared much of Zhukov's thinking; as the war had progressed, he had shown the wise tendency to let successful generals run operations in the ways that had brought them success in the first place.

The Nuts and Bolts of Getting Across the Oder

The strength of the ice varied from day to day, from mile-post to milepost along the river. These varying and unpredictable conditions caused Zhukov endless headaches. At times the ice could hold tanks, other times not. The Soviets built pontoon bridges to ensure a more regular flow of traffic. If drifting ice damaged them, they could be repaired or rebuilt, but such delays only further impeded Zhukov's efforts to get his armies across the river.

Nonetheless, more and more Russian troops and material were gradually packed into the small bridgeheads on the west bank. Compressed into such small areas, they made excellent targets. The Luftwaffe now made a rare operational resurgence, effectively its last of the war, taking advantage of the momentary absence of the Red Air Force and using the proximity of concrete airfields around Berlin to strafe and bomb the bridgeheads from dawn to dusk. German soldiers were cheered by the constant presence of their own planes overhead at long last.

Other measures: Hitler ordered flak batteries throughout Germany to be stripped of their 88mm guns. These were then set up by the hundreds in the low hills ringing the bridgeheads, creating almost overnight a gigantic anti-tank barrier between Zhukov and Berlin. The 88mm's had always been good anti-air-craft guns, but they had never been as effective as German fighter attacks when it came to shooting down Allied bombers in large numbers. But as anti-tank cannon the 88mm's were un-surpassed for accuracy and hitting power. Lobbing high explo-sive shells, they could also be used with devastating effect against enemy troop concentrations. It might be wondered if their predominant deployment in anti-aircraft batteries for most of the war had been a misuse of this deadly gun. Like most other German weapons, they had always been in relatively short supply on the Eastern Front. No more, however. The concentration of 88mm's in a purely ground-support role around Zhukov's Oder bridgeheads was the largest of the war.

But these cannon could still hardly make up for the dearth of trained troops and panzer divisions, and during the critical first days of February the 88mm's had not yet arrived on the Oder front. The first Soviet crossings had taken place in the area north of Kustrin on January 31st, followed by other crossings just south of Kustrin on February 1st. At this precise moment the German defenses along this stretch of the river were, quite literally, non-existent. The only unit in position in this area was the so-called Raegenar Division, a motley force named after Gen-eral Adolph Raegenar.

This unit may be considered the epitome of the "division in name only" of 1945, consisting of a pathetic mixture of Volksturm and RAD (Reichsarbeitdienst—the paramilitary construction corps) battalions. General Raegenar established his headquar-ters at the village of Podelzig, on a high and soon to be notorious spur of land that thrust into the Oder Valley along the west bank. An idea of the ad hoc nature of this "division" may be gathered from the fact that Raegenar had no staff officers and no com-munications equipment. The latter problem was solved initially by resorting to the civilian telephone network. As for staff officers, Raegenar recruited them from local estate owners, so-called "re-servists" who had last seen combat in World War One. For the most part these elderly soldiers responded with alacrity to Raegenar's summons, if only to help defend their property from the oncoming Soviets.

In all, it was a nearly laughable collection of troops to be found defending the last approaches to Berlin. They had no artillery or other heavy weapons.

This situation was to change very quickly, however. Over the next few days there developed a frantic race against time, as Hitler and Guderian brought in other units from all over Germany to bottle up Zhukov's bridgeheads. This race was won by the Germans by the narrowest of margins, with a major—indeed, decisive—assist from the weather gods. The winter was far from over, but the first Soviet attempts to get across the river were drastically hindered by the sudden thaw, combined with several days of heavy rainfall. Consequently the river was in a chaotic state of flux—in places it was a jumble of shifting ice floes, in places there were stretches of open water, while in other places the ice was still frozen solid. Even in the latter instance the Russians were faced with uncertainty—the ice was firm enough for infantry to cross over but not tanks or artillery. A few T-34s that tried to cross plunged through the ice and carried their crews to the bottom of the river; a few made it to the far side; and a few others were ferried across via intermittent stretches of open water. But even the ferries were frequently rendered unusable by the jumbled ice flowing downstream.

It was these exasperating weather conditions, more than any other factor, that basically brought Zhukov's armies to a halt along the Oder. Problems of supply, of German threats along the flanks, might be dealt with somehow—but there was no dealing with the force of nature.

In Berlin news of this thaw was hailed as a kind of divine intervention. Under the circumstances, it did not seem a far-fetched idea.

The Russians took a more pragmatic view, colored no doubt by their life-long experiences with the vagaries of weather inside their own country. A Russian colonel and infantryman, both serving with Zhukov's forces outside Kustrin, were standing at the bank of the Oder on one of the first days of February, listening to the enormous rifle-like cracks of the ice as it broke up during the first hours of the thaw. The infantryman shook his head, shrugging resignedly and saying to the colonel,

"What's to be done, Comrade Colonel? You can't fight Mother Nature."[1]

The result of this divine or climatic intervention was that the few Russian bridgeheads already on the west bank were very tenuous indeed. Despite every effort, Zhukov could get only a handful of tanks across the river to support them. If the Germans had had stronger forces on hand than General Raegenar's harlequin band of old men and construction laborers, the haphazard Soviet crossing attempts could have been severely threatened. But by the time sufficient German reinforcements reached the bluffs over the Oder Valley it was too late; the Soviets' bridgeheads, though still weak, were there to stay.

Over the next several weeks the weather turned colder again, firming up the ice in a number of places and allowing the Russian armored columns to get across the river. But by this time, that is by mid-February, it was now too late for the Russians—the German defenses, especially the hundreds of deadly 88mm guns, were then well-established on the bluffs above the west bank, ensuring that General Zhukov would have no chance to conduct an immediate breakout towards Berlin.

These were the conditions that led to over two months of stalemate on the Oder front. Over this time the two opposing armies became deadlocked in a situation reminiscent of the trench warfare of World War One. Most historical accounts—with the admirable exception of Tony LeTissier's classic book ZHUKOV AT THE ODER—pay scant heed to this period, generally giving the impression of a lull in combat operations, especially on the part of the Russians. Zhukov is usually depicted as biding his time over these months, gradually building up his forces inside the bridgeheads while waiting for the massive flank operations in Pomerania and Silesia to be completed.

But the reality of the situation was far more complicated—and far more violent—and does much to explain why it was not until mid-April that Zhukov was finally able to launch the massive assault on Berlin that would end the war.

The weather conditions that favored the Germans at the critical moment have already been mentioned. In addition, the terrain of the Oder Valley between Frankfurt and Kustrin was favorable to the defenders in almost every respect.

The river valley on the west bank was flat and nearly devoid of cover for a depth of four or five miles. The Soviet bridgeheads were confined to this area.

The western side of this naked and marshy plain terminated abruptly in the steep bluffs of the Seelowe Heights, a natural barrier generally between 150 and 200 feet high that walled off the entire river valley between Frankfurt and Kustrin. This was the area held by the Germans—or, to be more precise, by the 9th Army of General Busse, a force which had been nearly destroyed during the Vistula offensive but which was now being rebuilt with extreme haste.

Thus every Soviet movement on the plain below was clearly visible to German artillery observers and ground attack aircraft. By the end of the first week of February Hitler's order to ship every available 88mm flak battery to the Seelowe Heights had been carried out, resulting in a constant rain of barrage fire that caused enormous casualties among the Russian infantry massed below. This was the last occasion of the war in which the Germans were able to amass such a concentration of heavy guns, and it was a far cry from their paltry artillery response during the Vistula debacle. Even now the Germans were hindered to some degree by ammunition shortages, though the Russian soldiers cowering in the crater fields below may have been surprised to learn this. By this time the inadequate stocks of artillery shells had led to crisis on every German front in the East and the West; but supplies for the guns along the Seelowe Heights had the highest priority, and here at least the Germans were able to achieve a density of barrage fire that had not been seen anywhere else over the last several years.

Far from being ready to resume the offensive on Berlin, the Russians had all they could do just to sustain their bridgeheads under these relentless bombardments.

The entire layout of this battlefield, as well as the progress of the battle itself, bore a striking resemblance to another brutal campaign more familiar to Western readers: the battle of Anzio on the Italian coast early in 1944.

In January of 1944 American and British troops under General Lucas had made a surprise sea landing at Anzio-Nettuno, only a day's march south of Rome, with the intention of catching the German forces off guard and quickly breaking out to capture the Italian capital. The Allies were deployed across a small beachhead in a marshy, canal-transected area that was flat as a tabletop—much like the flat Oder Valley, which was also cut through by numerous dykes and canals. The Anzio beachhead was overlooked on all sides by the foothills of the Appenine Mountains only a few miles distant. Again there was a race against time narrowly won by the Germans, who rushed in troops to occupy the previously undefended heights above the Anzio plain. Rather than the weather, excessive Allied caution in the form of General Lucas' reluctance to quickly expand the beachhead ensured that a violent stalemate lasting nearly six months was to follow.

In the case of the Oder bridgeheads, General Zhukov was also criticized after the war (by none other than General Chuikov, the hero of Stalingrad and one of Zhukov's subordinate commanders in 1945) for excessive caution in failing to immediately resume the attack on Berlin. But a realistic examination of Zhukov's difficulties in establishing the Oder crossings during the thaw would seem to render much of this criticism invalid, or at least highly debatable.

Once the opposing armies had come to grips with each other the same kind of deadlock ensued on both battlefields. The Allies on the fire-swept Anzio plain proved incapable of forcing their way through the surrounding hills to take Rome. The Soviets faced the same difficulties in forcing their way over the Seelowe Heights, the last natural barrier on the road to Berlin. For their part, the Germans in both instances were not satisfied merely to defend the commanding high ground. At Anzio they counterattacked again and again until high casualties reduced both sides to a state of exhaustion. The canals and fortress-like stone farmhouses along the Italian coastal plain became the sites for savage combat at close quarters. From the Seelowe Heights in 1945 they also counterattacked throughout the entire month of February, battling furiously with Zhukov's troops for possession of ancient stone farmhouses and canal banks scattered across the valley floor below.

These counterattacks began from the moment additional divisions arrived to bolster General Raegenar's handful of troops. The 21st Panzer and 25th Panzer Grenadier Divisions were summoned from the Western Front, going into action as soon as they debarked at train stations near the Oder during the first days of February. 21st Panzer was one of the few German armored formations never to have seen action against the Russians. Their war had started with Rommel in North Africa, and many of these veterans still bore the crossed palm trees shoulder patch of the Deutches Afrika Korps. 21st Panzer had been one of the first divisions to attack the Allied beachhead at Normandy the preceding June; now they were faced with the same thankless task against Zhukov.

One sees again the same pattern of frenetic but usually fruitless counterattacks with ever-diminishing forces against the Russian invaders. The precarious nature of Zhukov's toeholds on the west bank—especially his inability to get tanks and artillery across the river during the first days of February—made it inevitable that the Germans would attempt to crush the bridgeheads as quickly as possible. Yet throughout the war on the Eastern Front the Russians had proven extremely difficult to dislodge, once they had established even a tentative bridgehead in enemy territory. Their defense of the Oder crossings was to display this same kind of tenacity.

For an entire week, from February 6th to 12th, 21st Panzer under General Hans von Luck attacked Soviet infantry formations in the sector of the west bank across from Fortress Kustrin—an area soon to be known as the Kustrin Corridor. With only a handful of tanks available, the Soviets again resorted to batteries of anti-tank guns covering every approach route to stymie von Luck's Panthers and Mk IV's. In a few places the Russians were thrown nearly back to the river, and 21st Panzer did manage to open and then keep open the narrow corridor leading to the bridge over to Kustrin on the east bank.

But the German attacks were hindered by the same days of pouring rain that were hastening the thaw of the ice and adding to Zhukov's logistical headaches. Much of the valley floor was turned into a quagmire during this period; rainfall was followed by snow flurries and then rain again. After six days of heavy casualties and only marginal success in this abominable weather, Hitler transferred 21st Panzer to General Schorner's command in Silesia on February 13th.

By this point Busse's 9th Army might have been well-advised to go over to the defensive. It was clear that the Russians were not about to be driven off the west bank, and by mid-February Soviet tanks were crossing over in substantial numbers in places where the ice was still firm, or else via the pontoon bridges being hastily erected everywhere. But there remained one dominant terrain feature on the west bank that was fought over again and again throughout February and into March. This was the Reitwein Spur, a long shell-blasted phallus of high ground that jutted north-eastward from the Seelowe Heights, stretching across the valley floor for a distance of several miles before terminating only a stone's throw from the banks of the Oder.

The importance of this ridge was clear to both sides. It commanded the entire valley floor to the north and to the south. It was on this high ground, in the village of Podelzig, that General Raegenar had established his headquarters in the opening phase of the battle. Unfortunately, Raegenar's ad hoc units had been too weak to prevent the Soviets from taking possession of the very eastern tip of this spur on February 2nd. During the two months that followed, this eastern tip of the Reitwein Spur would remain the only area of high ground in Soviet hands. Russian artillery observers here would have a commanding view of any German counterattacks developing on the northern valley floor towards Kustrin. While 21st Panzer was struggling towards Kustrin in the driving rain, other German units were arriving to reinforce Raegenar's men and throw the Russians off the Reitwein Spur. It was the beginning of a horrendous struggle.

Bloody Ridge

Thus far we have examined the fate of all the Grossdeutschland Corps divisions in 1945, with the exception of the very last formation to fight under the Grossdeutschland banner— the Kurmark Panzer Grenadier Division. Kurmark was commanded by General Willi Langkeit, who in earlier years had led the original Grossdeutschland Division's panzer regiment in campaigns all over the Soviet Union. Having barely finished training at Cottbus, only about thirty miles from the Oder front, this brand-new and well-equipped unit was sent into action on and around the Reitwein Spur on February 4th. The brief history of the Kurmark Division was to be closely tied to the battles that seesawed back and forth along this awful ridge.

Initially General Raegenar was loaned the use of Kurmark's two panzer battalions, during his first attempts to throw the Russians off the high ground. These two armored formations would not be able to negotiate the steep and wooded terrain on top of the Reitwein Spur itself. Instead, the Panthers of I. Battalion deployed on the valley floor along the northern flank of the spur, while the Hetzers of II. Battalion deployed along the southern flank. Their mission would be to advance towards the Oder and link up at the spur's eastern tip, thus surrounding the as yet relatively weak Russian detachments clinging to the heights. Meanwhile Raegenar's ad hoc battalions were to advance eastward from Podelzig and make a frontal assault directly along the crest of the spur.

Raegenar's Volksturm and RAD infantry moved out during the night of February 3rd-4th, attacking in alternating drizzles of rain, sleet, and snow that added greatly to the ensuing hours of mayhem and confusion on the broken ground atop the heights. They ran headlong into an attack by Russian infantry trying to expand their own precarious foothold on the spur. Both forces became hopelessly entangled in a series of wild melees in the dark. One of Raegenar's battalions made it to within 500 yards of the actual village of Reitwein—which lay on lower ground at the eastern base of the spur—before furious Soviet resistance and mortar fire forced the Germans to dig in. This was the closest any German unit would come to clearing the spur during the two-month deadlock to come.

As for the two Kurmark armored formations, II. Battalion advancing along the southern flank came the closest to reaching its objective. While the infantry battle raged on the heights above and to the left, the Hetzers of II. Battalion were able to quickly traverse the valley floor, initially meeting only sporadic enemy resistance. The diminutive tank destroyers made it almost to the bank of the Oder before being stopped by fierce opposition from a Russian battalion entrenched in front of one of Zhukov's crossing points, which was given critical support by Soviet heavy artillery firing from the east bank.

While regrouping for a second attempt to push the Soviets into the river, II. Battalion suddenly found itself outflanked along the valley floor to the south. Another Russian force had swung around the battalion's right flank and was threatening to take the Germans in the rear at the village of Klessin. The Hetzers were forced to withdraw almost to their start lines along the southern contour of the ridge. From here they moved against the Russian flanking force at Klessin and succeeded in wiping it out; but unfortunately this local victory had no relevance to the original objective of the attack.

Meanwhile Kurmark's strongest force, the Panther-equipped I. Battalion, was stymied at the western approaches to Reitwein village by a wall of Soviet anti-tank nests. Kurmark's Panthers were painted with an odd-looking camouflage pattern of green, white, and brown zebra stripes, perhaps with the idea of blending among the columns of bare trees that lined the roads in the Oder Valley. Roads flanked by a narrow row of trees were a common sight throughout western Europe, and in the Oder Valley these trees were almost the only terrain features higher than a man's head. Next to them the naked and marshy fields spread to all horizons. German panzer crews had mixed ideas about the effectiveness of camouflage paint—many of them regarded it as a waste of time—but German tanks continued to be more intricately camouflaged than those of other nations. In any case these strange looking Panthers were easily spotted by the Russian PAK gunners, and by late afternoon I. Battalion's attack had come to a standstill. In trying to hold this open ground the Panthers would only incur more casualties, and so they too withdrew back to their start lines.

Thus 24 hours after their first combat action, both Kurmark panzer battalions had been forced back to their assembly positions. The following day, February 5th, the Russian infantry along the crest of the Reitwein Spur resumed their attack against Raegenar's bedraggled formations, throwing them back almost to their own start lines at Podelzig. One Panther company was detached to give fire support to Raegenar's men, enabling them to dig in and establish a defensive line that cut right across the center of the ridge from north to south. Here the front would remain until April, the two sides locked together on the spur and subjecting each other to such continuous barrage fire that some older veterans were reminded of the hellish terrain they had seen around Verdun and Fort Douamont some thirty years before.

General Raegenar's men experienced only the beginning of this ordeal. These poorly trained units had acquitted themselves well during a week of heavy fighting; they were now withdrawn from the spur and Raegenar's ragtag division was dissolved, the various battalions being dispersed within the somewhat less dangerous sector around Frankfurt to the south. The Volksturmers and construction laborers were relieved by the remaining elements of Kurmark, with General Langkeit's panzer grenadier regiment and other support arms rejoining the armored battalions already deployed around the spur. With all the divisional elements now assembled together, Kurmark would fight on atop the heights and along the valley floor on either side until it was nearly wiped out over the coming weeks.

The names of tiny villages clinging to the lower slopes of the Reitwein Spur were soon to become as notorious as the spur itself—Wuhden, Klessin, Lebus, Mallnow. During early March a Kurmark battalion at Wuhden on the south slope was surrounded for over a week. Hitler rather preposterously designated this miserable hamlet a "fortress city," ordering the defenders to hold out while supplies were haphazardly dropped from the air. General Langkeit was yet another German commander who displayed courage and independence in the face of Hitler's edicts. He sent in a few Panthers to rescue the grenadiers holding out in "Fortress Wuhden," then withdrew them all to safety a few days later. Clearly Langkeit cared not a whit about the displeasure of any higher authorities. To cover for this action he simply issued an order of the day stating that Wuhden was still in German hands. Originally over 400 men had defended the place; only 80 escaped to reach Kurmark's main line, still atop the spur a mile to the west. All the wounded had to be left behind for the Soviets to dispose of as they pleased.

Langkeit could easily have paid with his head for such blatant disobedience. He was lucky. Four days later, on March 12th, Hitler rescinded the "fortress" order, apparently unaware that Langkeit had already abandoned Wuhden to the enemy. There followed a pleasant irony among the entire grimness of those days—every man that had escaped from Wuhden was decorated and given fourteen days leave of absence from the front.

General Langkeit also stood up for his soldiers on several other occasions. Ill-trained and elderly Volksturm battalions continued to be fed into the line; several of them were assigned to Kurmark's sector, which included not only the Reitwein Spur but also a lengthy stretch extending almost to Frankfurt in the south. One such unit was equipped only with Italian rifles, for which there were almost no cartridges. These men broke and fled in the face of a small-scale local attack; 9th Army commander General Busse ordered that the Volksturm major in charge be court-martialed and shot. Langkeit simply disregarded this order, giving

East Prussia: *German soldiers killed in a Soviet attack.*

East Prussia: *Elderly men of the Volksturm man a trench awaiting a Russian attack. Their wounded leader exhorts them to build their morale.*

East Prussia: Heavily armed men of the Volksturm. (Warfield)

East Prussia: Young boys even found their way into uniforms to defend the Fatherland. (Warfield)

East Prussia: More children and young boys in the service of the Third Reich. Note the Hetzer tank destroyers in the background.

East Prussia: Sd. Kfz. 251/10 halftrack advances past a destroyed Soviet truck column on an East Prussian road. (Warfield)

East Prussia: *Two examples of Siebel ferries and "Sea Snake" ferries employed in the Baltic for resupply and evacuation. (Warfield)*

East Prussia: *German grenadiers with panzerfausts and teller mines move into a new position, February-March 1945. (Warfield)*

East Prussia: *Tiger I crews and infantry examine abandoned refugee carts and wagons overrun by the Soviets outside of Danzig.*

East Prussia: *Soviet IS II heavy tank in Danzig. The tank commander fires a 12.7mm DshK heavy machine gun at infantry targets.*

East Prussia: *Soviet T 34/85's in Heiligenbeil after the city's capture on March 25th, 1945.*

East Prussia: *The last photo of the liner Wilhelm Gustloff in Gofenhafen before her final voyage. (Warfield)*

East Prussia: *Final photo of the General Steuben at Pillau prior to her last voyage. (Warfield)*

East Prussia: *The freighter Goya at Memel. (Warfield)*

East Prussia:
German soldiers being evacuated. A large majority of the men evacuated are wounded.

East Prussia: *Refugees waiting to board a transport in the harbor of Danzig. (Warfield)*

East Prussia: *German transports in the roadstead off of Hela, April 1945. (Warfield)*

East Prussia:
*General Lasch
the last Commander
of Fortress Konigsberg.*

East Prussia: *A Kampfgruppe of heavily armed grenadiers of the 1st East Prussian Infantry Division on the road between Methgethen and Warthen. (Warfield)*

East Prussia: *ISU 152 heavy tank destroyers involved in the encirclement of Konigsberg. (Warfield)*

East Prussia: *ISU 122 heavy tank destroyers in street fighting in Konigsberg early April 1945. (Warfield)*

East Prussia: *Newly recruited members of the Volksturm being issued weapons. (Warfield)*

East Prussia: *Soviet Guards troops of the 3rd White Russian Front in Konigsberg, April 8th, 1945.*

East Prussia: *Konigsberg — aftermath of the battle.*

East Prussia: *Marching off into Hell! German officers, men and Volksturm personnel being led into captivity. Few of these men would ever return.*

East Prussia: *A great series of photos taken in the aftermath of a Soviet air raid at Pillau on April 20th, 1945. Note the 20mm Fla SL MG 141/20 Drilling flak; an unusual shipboard mounting not commonly seen on Kriegsmarine vessels. (Warfield)*

Oder Front: *Late model Sd. Kfz. 7 halftrack tows an 88mm Flak 36 into position on the Seelowe Heights.*

Oder Front: *Unusually camouflaged late model Panther G's. These vehicles are believed to be from I. Battalion of the Panzer Regiment of Panzergrenadier Division Kurmark. Photo taken near Kustrin in February 1945.*

Oder Front: *Grand Admiral Karl Donitz inspecting Naval Infantry units on the Oder Front, March 1945.*

Oder Front: *Foreign Minister Ribbentrop observing Soviet positions from a trench on the Oder Front.*

the man a reprimand and then sending him and his soldiers back to the trenches.

Langkeit also refused to comply with the draconian orders regarding deserters, issued by Heinrich Himmler from his far-removed Army Group Vistula headquarters at Prenzlau. There were to be no hangings or shootings of deserters in Kurmark's sector of the front. But elsewhere in the rear areas of 9th Army the victims of these drumhead court-martials were dismally visible, hanging from the bare trees that lined the roads from the Oder Valley up to the Seelowe Heights. The ubiquitous and humiliating cardboard placards were draped around their black necks as always.

Apparently General Busse did not share Langkeit's disdain for Himmler's decree. Busse was another hard-headed general; like Schorner, he displayed an unforgiving attitude towards men who had lost their nerve in combat. Busse did not possess Schorner's strange inspirational ferocity, but he was equally determined not to see any men wandering around at loose ends in his rear areas. Any who were seen wandering around were then seen dangling from tree limbs only moments later.

The German field police who carried out these executions were universally recognizable by the large, crescent-shaped metal breastplates hanging by chains from around their necks. Wearing these devices, they called to mind some curious hybrid between normal German infantrymen and legionnaires from ancient Rome. Curious, also, that they wore such highly visible insignia around their necks—just as their executed victims did with their printed cardboard placards. How despised these military policemen must have been by frightened Landsers—who nicknamed them "headhunters"—during these ugly periods of the war.

The field police had to deal not only with deserters but also with infiltrators from the "Free Germany Committee," more commonly called the "Seydlitz Army" by the Landsers. These "turncoats," mentioned earlier during the German death throes in the East Prussian battles, would be used more and more by the Soviets as the war drew to a close. If captured, they would sometimes be shot by their former comrades in the infantry before the field police had a chance to hang them. A few telling anecdotes from the battles in the Oder Valley suggest that many of these "Seydlitz" men had been forced into a truly hopeless position. While it seems clear that some of them actively and perhaps even eagerly assisted the Soviets, others performed this role with considerably less enthusiasm. The price of freedom from Soviet prisoner camps would have been the torment of guilt and self-loathing—not only to be attacking their former comrades, but to have to witness first-hand the nightmare of Soviet atrocities on German soil.

They were identifiable (God only knows why) by red, black, and white insignia on their arms or chests. Forced by their new overlords to attack German positions on the Reitwein Spur or elsewhere in the Oder Valley, they would sometimes cry out pathetically for help from the defenders. "Help me, comrade, help me," a wounded Seydlitz man moaned upon being discovered by one German grenadier, who was surprised to hear his attacker beseeching him in his own language.[2] In some ways the Landsers were also tormented by the dilemma of the Seydlitz men; while generally holding the turncoats in contempt, they were sometimes reluctant to take personal vengeance against them or to turn them over to the field police. Many of the older Landsers especially would have remembered the horrors of the war inside Russia and may have been able to imagine themselves in the turncoats' situation. The fate of the wounded man described above would perhaps have been instructive, but he died in agony before the German grenadier could decide what to do with him.

Meanwhile, the Russians of General Vlasov's Liberation Army (in reality a force smaller than a division) were fighting in the Oder Valley alongside the Germans. Before now Vlasov's men had been mostly assigned to garrison duty along the French coast, or to anti-partisan operations against Tito's forces in Yugoslavia. These final battles around Kustrin would mark their first major deployment against their own former comrades in arms in the Red Army. The Russians' attitude towards the Vlasov Army would be less complex than the Landsers' attitude towards Seydlitz's men. After the war they would all be rounded up and shot, thousands at a time, in non-stop executions lasting for several days.

The Last Day with Two Legs

We have not finished with Hans Rudel's exploits along the Oder front. After a week of flying missions in Pomerania, his Stukas were diverted to targets along the critical stretch of the

Oder between Frankfurt and Kustrin. All of 9th Army's counterattacks against the Soviet bridgeheads in February were supported hour after hour by Rudel and his men. In addition to the Stukas, swarms of FW 190 fighter-bombers and miscellaneous other aircraft were overhead. While the Red Air Force was hampered by the primitive mud-soaked fields in Poland, German pilots were taking off and landing non-stop from Templehof and other concrete runways around Berlin. But neither did they confine themselves to these all-weather fields. Dramatic scenes from the Deutsche Wochenschau in February show bomb-carrying ME 109s and late model FW 190Ds—with their distinctively elongated noses—taxiing in quagmire conditions on fields just behind the Oder front, their wheels sending up fountains of mud and slush as they accelerated for the take-off.

But it was Rudel's Stukas that provided the most significant aerial presence over the Oder bridgeheads. His superiors wanted him to target pontoon bridges to disrupt Russian supply traffic. Rudel thought this a waste of time, mainly because many of these bridges were only dummies made of planks set down on the ice, designed to draw German planes into anti-aircraft killing zones. He had seen these tricks before in Russia, along the Don and the Donets and the Dnepr. Meanwhile he was seeing many Russian tanks crossing right over the ice without the use of bridges.

So Rudel wanted to stick to his forte of blasting tanks wherever he found them, or else attacking other genuine targets such as troop formations or ammunition depots.

February 9th, 1945—Rudel's last day with two legs. Already he had been flying for over two months with one leg encased in a plaster cast. He had been badly wounded in Hungary in November, almost bleeding to death before crash-landing behind German lines in a nearly blacked-out state. He did not fully recover his senses until he came to on the operating table. It seems typical of Rudel that in his memoirs he only mentions this incident at the time it occurred; over the following months he makes no reference to it whatsoever, basically giving the reader the impression that the wound has healed. He says nothing about flying with a plaster cast during all this time, nor about visiting Hitler and Goering with the thing still encased around his leg. Perhaps the Fuhrer's concern for his survival was a little more understandable after all.

Now on this wintry day in February he flies over the small Oder town of Lebus, less than a mile from the Reitwein Spur. There is a pontoon bridge here, a real one and not a dummy. But he still wants to go after tanks. The Soviets have countered the German air attacks by setting up enormous numbers of flak batteries, not only along the river but everywhere inside the bridgeheads. The anti-aircraft fire is as dense as anything Rudel has ever seen. With a slow, low-level aircraft like the Stuka, these sorties are beginning to look like suicide missions. Elsewhere on the Eastern Front, Rudel has always made it his practice to attack Russian tanks when they are moving across open country, separated from the protection of these murderous flak screens. The Stuka has long been obsolete in all but its tank-killing role, slow and unmaneuverable and a sitting duck for any kind of massed fire from the ground.

He knows, with his arrogant contempt for any orders that do not jibe with his own experience, that normally he would flatly refuse any command to attack targets as well-protected as these. He may be arrogant, but he knows what he is doing. This time, however, the situation is different. With the Russians established across the Oder only forty miles from Berlin, he feels duty-bound to attack regardless of his normal practices. He spots a group of Stalins and T-34s parked beside some buildings outside Lebus, on a bluff sloping up from the river. He begins his descent.

He is alone, save for the rear gunner who must stoically accompany him on all these missions. There are other Stuka pilots flying with him today, but he knows they are too inexperienced to deal with this particular devil. If they make their normal flat-out strafing runs, they will be shot to pieces by the flak. If they try to take evasive action, they will not be able to fire accurately on the Russian tanks. Rudel does not want to throw his men away. He radios them to circle overhead at higher altitude, using harassing fire from that range that will hopefully disrupt the aim of the flak gunners.

This is already his fourth sortie of the day. His Stuka has been hit on every flight; the last time out his plane was so badly damaged that he had to switch to another one. Since early morning he has destroyed twelve Russian tanks outside Lebus; now he is overhead again, ready to kill more. At 2500 feet, just above the maximum altitude of the enemy fire, he begins a screaming dive, weaving and jinking as soon as he descends into range.

"Trust to luck," he thinks.[3]

Luck may help him survive (as he reflects that he should already have been in his grave a dozen times by now), but it will not help him kill Stalin tanks. He is a world-class athlete, and he needs every ounce of his skill to bring his weaving, nearly ver-tically-diving aircraft under control for a fraction of a second—just long enough to level out and take accurate aim at a Stalin, pump two or three shells into its vital organs, then veer off again. He is only able to bring off this mad stunt-flying "thanks to my manifold experience and somnambulistic assurance."[4]

Climbing up to 2500 feet again, he sees that he has failed to hit the damn thing, or at least hit it with a killing shot. The Stalin won't burn; he is obsessed with seeing it set on fire. One of his guns has jammed; now a warning light comes on to tell him the other one only has one shell left.

He spends his last few moments in the air listening to inner voices debate the pros and cons of continuing this lunacy. It takes a long time for the slow bomber to get back up to 2500 feet to begin another dive, and his thoughts speak to him with wild urgency the whole time.

Only one shell left . . . it would be idiocy to risk his life just to get off one more shot.

Yes, but how many times in the past has he killed a tank with just one shot? A lot of times.

But this would be tank number thirteen for the day. Bad, bad, bad. He can't remember ever being superstitious before, but now the feeling grips his skull like a vise.

Best to let Rudel tell the rest. The heated inner dialog con-tinues, one side of his self speaking to another:

> Perhaps it requires just this one shot to stop the tank from rolling on through Germany.
>
> Rolling on through Germany sounds much too melodramatic! A lot more Russian tanks are going to roll on through Germany if you bungle it now, and you will bungle it, you may depend on that. It is madness to go down again to that level for the sake of a single shot. Sheer lunacy!
>
> You will say next that I will bungle it because it is

the thirteenth. Superstitious nonsense! You have one round left, so stop wasting your breath and get on with it![5]

And so he dives again. The same wild and steep maneuvering. He levels out, fires. The Stalin burns. Ha! The tank erupts in gouts of oily flame. Flak guns nearby wink at him from every direction. He pulls up into a climbing spiral, an unorthodox, crazy-looking maneuver. The engine shudders from a hit and either shrapnel or engine debris flies into Rudel's leg, slashing through it and leaving it dangling by a few shreds of skin from his upper thigh. It is his good leg, not the one covered in plaster.

The left wing is on fire. He collects what is left of his wits—not much. He is in mortal agony. The pain blinds him, or else shock from the extreme loss of blood, something blinds him, he flies by instinct alone. He feels his living conscious soul draining down from the inside of his head into his torso and about to spurt out from his leg. His tail gunner actually saves his life, saves both their lives, by jolting Rudel awake every few seconds, speaking with a strange and steady calm as they come in for the crash-landing: "Pull up. Pull up. Watch those trees there. Pull up. Pull up."

Rudel sees only a blur of meaningless shapes. "What's the terrain like?" he manages to say.

"Bad. Hummocky," replies his gunner Gadermann.[6]

But Rudel can go no further. For several minutes he has been on the verge of blacking out from the pain. That draining sensation again . . . With his plastered leg he taps the rudder bar; just this tiny jolt causes him to shriek with such agony that he nearly loses control of the plane.

They go down. . . .

There had probably never been a more destructive war between two nations. Chroniclers have made different attempts to put it into words. A war of extermination between different species of insects. A fight to the death between beings from neighboring planets. In one of his franker declarations, Stalin once said that the devastation in the Soviet Union was akin to the aftermath of an atomic war.

The historian Barbara Tuchmann has made a telling observation about these kinds of statements. She was referring to the horrors of certain medieval wars, but the same idea could be applied to any tragic period in human history. The gist of her thinking was that the horrors of any given era are generally magnified tenfold by the later chroniclers of that era.

In short, even during the most terrible times, quiet often lies upon the land, the normal quiet of daylight and the weather, of people eating, sleeping, talking, attending to daily concerns. Even a climate of fear or terror must become somewhat dissipated within the ongoingness of the hours and days, of the weeks and months.

Some villages in Russia, even deep behind the German lines, were never entered by German soldiers. The Germans never had enough men to garrison them all, even to patrol them all. There were too many, and the wilderness around them was vast. A village may have been burned to the ground, all its inhabitants massacred during some brutal anti-partisan operation. Yet perhaps up to that one, horrible moment, these same villagers may have lived with scarcely any contact with the Nazi occupiers. Other villagers in even more inaccessible areas may never have seen them at all.

In 1945 Scherhorn's men are likely passing through some of these remote Russian villages, where German soldiers have never before set foot during these years of "atomic war." Possibly the inhabitants do not even recognize his men as German soldiers. Perhaps Scherhorn himself relies on this confusion to disguise their movements, though of course he is not always able to do so. But in 1945 the war, at least inside Russia, is over. Who are these bedraggled-looking armed men passing through this remote community in the Byelorussian forests? Partisans? Foreigners serving in the Red Army? The Red Army comprises a host of different peoples, different tongues; many soldiers speak little or no Russian.

But inevitably Scherhorn's men will be recognized at different points along their trek, and so their pursuers will close in once again . . .

SKORZENY

Commandos at Schwedt, Commandos in the Depths of Russia

At the end of January Himmler ordered Skorzeny to go to Schwedt, another German bridgehead on the east bank of the Oder between Altdamm and Kustrin, and take charge there.

It was an unusual demand. Skorzeny was the war's most famous commando leader. Along with German paratroopers, he and his men had rescued Mussolini from the daunting crag of the Gran Sasso in 1943. Gliders had carried the paratroopers and commandos onto the mountaintop, crashlanding on a steep slope scarcely larger than a football field. A Fieseler Storch had also been able to land there, barely, without wrecking itself.

The Storch was needed so Skorzeny could fly out with Mussolini after the assault troops had driven off the Italian guards and rescued the erstwhile dictator. The Gran Sasso was 7000 feet up in the Abruzzi Mountains of central Italy. The Storch turned around in order to take off from the steeply-inclined landing area. At the end of the runway (which looked less like a runway than a boulder-strewn ski jump) was a sheer drop of nearly 2000 feet. The pilot of the tiny plane was worried that just the additional weight of Skorzeny and his captive would be enough to drop them all onto the rocks far below. He wanted to leave Skorzeny behind and carry out Mussolini alone.

Skorzeny considered, staring down the slope which at the end of a preposterously short distance dropped off into the abyss. Mussolini was not a small man and Skorzeny was a giant. At six feet seven inches, he would have been among the largest combat soldiers of any nation.

On the other hand, Skorzeny had been ordered to hand Mussolini over to Hitler in person. He was not about to let the Italian dictator out of his sight. So they both boarded the plane. The cabin was barely large enough to accommodate them. Like everyone else involved in this mission, the pilot had volunteered. No doubt he now regretted this choice. At maximum throttle the plane rolled forward—or rather skidded down—along the uneven slope, rocking from wing to wing.

The Storch had hardly picked up any speed when it plummeted over the edge. It continued to drop nose-down, like a brick, for almost a thousand feet. Well, they were all going to die—so much for that. But somehow the pilot managed to pull the stick back, maybe catch an updraft, something—it was outside anything he had experienced or could imagine. The plane pulled out and they flew off through the mountains.

In civilian life Skorzeny had been an engineer. He was drafted at the somewhat advanced age of twenty nine, still undergoing training when Hitler invaded France in 1940. Like millions of other Germans, Skorzeny was in a fine mood when the lightning campaign ended with France's surrender. It seemed impossible that Britain would be able to continue the fight, which meant that the war for all practical purposes was over and done with. Skorzeny had seen no combat and was looking forward to returning to civilian life, where he had been happy and successful.

To his dismay Britain would neither surrender nor come to terms, and he found himself looking at an indefinite tour of duty in the infantry. He didn't much care for military life and the infantry in particular did not appeal to him, so he applied for transfer to the air force with the idea of becoming a pilot. By this time he was thirty and the Luftwaffe said he was too old.

He applied to join the Leibstandarte regiment of the Waffen SS. He did not seem to have any political motivation in doing this. More likely he was hoping that service with an elite unit would be less plodding and regimented than the hide-bound ways of the regular army. The Waffen SS was always having to compete with the army for manpower and Skorzeny was a remarkable physical specimen, to say nothing of being blessed with high intelligence; so they accepted him.

By early 1943 he had been fighting in Russia with SS Leibstandarte for almost two years, reaching the SS rank of Untersturmfuhrer, equivalent to a lieutenant. He had a good service record but had not particularly distinguished himself, though at least he found the more egalitarian, less traditionally military atmosphere in the Waffen SS more suited to his nature.

He was then given temporary duty back in Germany while

recovering from an illness. Through an odd chain of circumstances he soon found himself placed at the head of a group of commandos, which at first was anything but the elite unit that one might normally picture. The German military was not fond of commando warfare, but the sensational and rather embarrassing exploits of British commandos in France and Norway had inclined the Germans to come up with some kind of competing unit of their own. At first no one even had much of an idea what these men might be used for. Then suddenly the Allies invaded Italy and the Italian government changed sides overnight, deposing and imprisoning Mussolini in the process.

With his rescue of the dictator from the Gran Sasso, the name of the previously unknown Skorzeny became publicized throughout the world. More exploits would follow.

As the Third Reich entered upon its final months, Skorzeny remained as active as ever. In November of 1944 he had formulated a plan to depose Admiral Horthy, leader of Germany's Hungarian allies. Hitler feared that the sensible Horthy was either about to withdraw from the war or perhaps even go over to the Russians. By now Skorzeny had found his true calling; he had become a bold, imperturbable, buccaneering sort of leader who always took the most direct route to an objective. His men raided a castle outside Budapest and kidnapped Horthy's son; the admiral relinquished control of the government and followed his son into internment in Germany. His place as the leader of Hungary was taken by the crackpot fascist butcher Ferencz Szalaszi.

Most recently Skorzeny's commandos had parachuted behind American lines during the Battle of the Bulge, wearing GI uniforms and throwing the Allied High Command into a state of utter confusion. The English-speaking SS men created a panic out of all proportion to their tiny numbers. Suddenly every GI wandering behind the lines was suspected of being a German spy. Rumors about these SS infiltrators got out of control, finally escalating to fears that Skorzeny himself was on his way to Paris to assassinate General Eisenhower. Skorzeny had never had any such idea in mind, but for weeks afterward he was gratified by the chaos produced by dropping a few parachutists equipped with a handful of American slang expressions. In most cases, that had been about the extent of their knowledge of English.

* * *

He was probably the most famous German soldier below the rank of general. Now it was January of 1945, and in order to more properly exercise control over the German forces of Schwedt, SS Reichsfuhrer Himmler promoted him to the Waffen SS equivalent of general. But to Skorzeny this surprising promotion was no more than window dressing, and it was over a month before he bothered to fill out all the necessary papers authorizing his new rank. He had already risen from unknown lieutenant to captain to colonel in only two years; he had long lost all interest in such minor matters as military rank.

Without a doubt he could have held any rank at all and still exercised full control over the Schwedt bridgehead on the Oder. He was a charismatic figure with the ability to get his men to willingly, even eagerly, undertake the most hair-raising kinds of missions.

But these men had always been hand-picked volunteers, no different from commando units anywhere else in the world. And only a company or two were on hand to accompany Skorzeny to Schwedt. All the rest of his soldiers in the bridgehead were the miscellaneous dregs and scrapings of Himmler's ragtag Army Group Vistula, demoralized stragglers, untrained Volksturm units who had been wearing civilian clothes only a few weeks previously, Luftwaffe personnel with no experience in ground warfare—the entire haphazard collection of humanity which was now defending the Reich not only at Schwedt but at scores of other towns and cities.

Skorzeny had no experience dealing with such a motley and dispirited group. Nor did he have any experience commanding large forces on the ground in normal combat actions. But, typically, he seemed not at all perturbed by this. He simply extrapolated from his experience as a platoon leader in Russia or else used his own ingenuity. He was one of the war's great natural leaders.

He set about organizing all the forces under his control—ultimately about 15,000 men—in order to properly establish a defense against the oncoming Soviets. Skorzeny was a uniquely unflappable sort of individual. Men like him are often reported to have "ice water in their veins"; true enough, as far as it goes, but this cliche does little to express his ability to convey his inner calm and matter-of-fact confidence to those around him. While heroes are often worshipped by their cults of admirers, they sometimes tend to make other people nervous; the very awe they inspire tends to be off-putting and somewhat unreal to soldiers and civilians who have lived too long in a climate of fear, misery, mud, anguish, and governmental pomposity. At six foot seven, two heads taller than almost anyone he might come into contact with, and with an old duelling scar prominent on his right cheekbone, Skorzeny was undeniably an imposing presence. Yet he had a genuine and unpretentious magnetism which seemed to disarm any potential resentment or anxiety among those under his command. Nowhere would these personal qualities become more important than at Schwedt, where he turned a disorganized group of soldiers and civilians into an effective fighting force in a matter of weeks.

As this force had no real cohesion, his first order of business was to set about training his Volksturm and Luftwaffe men to fight and stand together as a unit. He kept his best NCOs and officers inside the town to take charge of this task. He sent other of his veteran commandos on long forays behind the Russian lines, scouting enemy strength and bringing in prisoners in order to gain information about Russian assault plans. These forays also included raids behind the German lines. Skorzeny needed supplies, especially heavy weapons, which Himmler had neglected to send along with him to the front lines. From a depot that had been abandoned in the face of the Soviet advance, his men retrieved a number of 75mm anti-tank guns. Even more daringly, or perhaps impudently, they took a short excursion down to Frankfurt-on-Oder and liberated a large number of MG 42 machine guns from a depot there.

Frankfurt was nearly surrounded, and to retrieve these weapons through normal bureaucratic channels would surely have been stonewalled by the supply authorities. The German military machine was frequently hamstrung by the maze of paperwork and special authorizations needed to release critical supplies of any kind to the combat troops. Even while facing the greatest threat in German history, officers in charge of supply dumps were notorious for refusing to relinquish weapons, gasoline, or food stocks without the proper paperwork; in a chaotic situation, German fighting men often found themselves exasperated by this peculiarly German bureaucratic rigidity. And having been trained and brought up in this kind of mindset themselves, they usually did not have the nerve to take what they needed by more direct means—that is, by stealing it. But in most ways Skorzeny was the antithesis of the typical German military mind (or civilian mind, for that matter). He did not so much have contempt for authority as an inherent disregard for it; it was not necessary for him to be worked into a state of anger or mutiny to defy his superiors. He simply did this as a matter of course.

In a like vein he tossed a number of inane or inspirational directives from Himmler into the waste basket. Most of them had to do with defending the outlying villages around Schwedt to the last man, or making some meaningless show of offensive action. Skorzeny knew that his men did not yet have the unit cohesion, nor the strength in materiel, to conduct any kind of counterattack. It would simply be throwing them into the meat-grinder—"Verheizen," as it was called elsewhere. The habit of counterattack was deeply ingrained in the German Army, even more so because this tactic had so often been successful in Russia. But an effective counterattack required a body of tough, experienced troops, men who were used to intimately working with each other in a crisis. And too often in 1945 these men were no longer available; the majority of them were already dead. It was much easier to train inexperienced troops to fight from defensive positions.

Skorzeny's defiance of authority was somewhat different from Rudel's—who was probably the Third Reich's other most renowned soldier below general rank. Rudel reports being unnerved by his own acts of defiance; he was driven to disobey by his addiction to flying and by his single-minded determination to help save his nation. He was a much greater celebrity than Skorzeny and seems to have been something of a prima donna, used to the adoration of the German public from Hitler down to the man in the street. He accomplishments were not in the order of teamwork but the exploits of a single man; he was revered by his comrades for these reasons, but for these same reasons he was probably never as well-liked by his men as Skorzeny was.

Skorzeny was also a celebrity—his rescue of Mussolini had caught the attention of the world—but the very nature of commando warfare necessitated that he be less in the public eye; his fame was always more mysterious than Rudel's. Rudel's deep personal drive was admirable, but there always seemed something egocentric about it. He was high-strung and somewhat self-preoccupied, almost in the manner of film stars or celebrity athletes.

Skorzeny was the kind of man who rose above, or simply ignored, his own fame. He was both the unquestioned leader and an equal among his own men, rather in the style of the leader of a band of outlaws. His fellow commandos never felt themselves operating in Skorzeny's shadow; rather he seemed to bring out the best in them as individuals, and many of them carried out missions during the war that were as bold and imaginative as his own exploits.

It is hard to imagine Skorzeny being distressed by his disobedience of Himmler or of anyone else; he was one of those rare people who seem nearly immune to stress. In a situation where panic and anxiety were nearly as threatening as the enemy, his calm seems to have infected not only his veteran commandos but also the civilian soldiers of the Volksturm.

But he was not a miracle worker. No one in Germany could make such claims in 1945. His task was made considerably easier by the fact that Schwedt was, at least for the moment, somewhat off the beaten path for the oncoming Soviets. About equidistant from Altdamm in the north and Kustrin in the south, Skorzeny's bridgehead did not face the overwhelming force marshaled against these two more important targets. Furthermore, the first probes of his defenses around Schwedt were made by Rumanian troops; fighting against their former allies, they did not quite share the Russians' crazed enthusiasm for killing Germans. These factors gave Skorzeny the critical few weeks he needed to create a coherent fighting force. Still, this was no mean accomplishment. He had no established units of divisional or even regimental strength. Under a less effective commander, the 15,000 men at his disposal could easily have degenerated into a mob that might have disintegrated at the first concerted attack.

Rumanian-crewed T-34s arrived on the scene ahead of the massive artillery trains the Russians were assembling elsewhere. The Volksturm soldiers quickly acquired the knack of using the panzerfaust to keep the tanks at bay. Frequently the T-34s were able to roam for miles inside the bridgehead, but so long as the defenders did not panic this was not an insurmountable problem. Without adequate infantry or artillery support, the tanks were vulnerable even to rear-echelon troops.

A scene from the Deutsche Wochenshau in February shows Skorzeny awarding the Tank Destruction Badge (Panzervernichtung Abzeichen) to a cook in a snowy clearing in the

416

bridgehead. With his massive height the commando leader appears out-of-scale in front of the middle-aged Volksturmers assembled there. His voice carries clearly, but it does not have the grating stridency that one often hears in the voices of other German officers addressing their men at this point in the war.

The cook who looks to be about forty, shakes hands with Skorzeny, then turns to the camera to give a brief account of his deed:

> I was busy making the soup when my comrade rushed in the door, crying, "Run, run, the Russians are here!" I said, "Calm down a bit, it can't be as bad as all that." I found myself a panzerfaust and went out to have a look. As the T-34 approached I was able to get off a shot. Peng! Up it went. I had a pistol in my other hand and was able to take the crew prisoner when they crawled out.[1]

Karinhall was not far from Schwedt, and one day Goering came by to have a look at things. He nodded approvingly at Skorzeny's work and strolled around the front lines handing out cigars and brandy to the troops, much like his performance at Stargard on the eve of Sonnenwende. A clownish fat man maybe, but not lacking in bravery. He joked nonchalantly with the men while artillery shells landed close by, then drove back to his hunting lodge an hour away.

Himmler showed no inclination to put in a personal appearance. He had little rapport or connections with army generals; this was one of the main reasons why he had picked Skorzeny to take charge at Schwedt. But Himmler was becoming annoyed that Skorzeny was conducting his defense with little of the fanaticism that he expected from an SS officer leading a last-ditch stand.

As the enemy strength mounted, a few outlying villages were abandoned. Himmler telephoned Skorzeny and demanded to know who the officer responsible was and had Skorzeny had him shot yet? He was curtly told that no one had been shot or would be shot. There was no further explanation.

Summoned to Himmler's headquarters to account for his rudeness, Skorzeny arrived four hours late, explaining that he had been dealing with a Russian attack. For a few moments the SS

Reichsfuhrer gave a rather poor imitation of a Hitler-style tantrum, raging about court-martials and mutiny.

Skorzeny declared that the villages had been abandoned on his own orders, in order to maintain a shorter, more defensible line without uselessly sacrificing his troops. He went on to say that he was getting fed up with receiving these unrealistic orders from Himmler and would prefer some material support instead.

Skorzeny was able to express even anger in a matter-of-fact way. Himmler calmed down, invited him to have some dinner, and after receiving a more detailed account of Skorzeny's needs promised to send a battery of Sturmgeschutzen to Schwedt.

They were needed there. Several Russian divisions had arrived to reinforce the Rumanians. The fighting mounted in intensity and the bridgehead began to shrink. Skorzeny toured the lines, urging his men to hold; there could be no more withdrawals. Yet he still carried himself in a serene manner. "Everything will be all right," he told his officers. "I plan to grow old and grey at Schwedt."[2]

Then, quite abruptly, he carried out the only act of brutality he is known to have committed. As was the case elsewhere, the Volksturm units were technically under the command of the local Nazi party boss. From the start Skorzeny had let this man know who was in charge here; he would have none of the divisiveness among the Volksturm which the swine Koch had used to harrass General Lasch in Konigsberg. The party boss at Schwedt was informed that if he wanted to keep command of his men he would have to do so by serving in the front lines.

By an odd coincidence, the battle was now at its height around a small village also known as Konigsberg. The party boss fled, saying the town had fallen to the Soviets. Skorzeny had just come back from the front and he knew the fighting had not subsided at Konigsberg and that the Volksturm units were still holding on there. He promptly court-martialed the Nazi official for desertion in the face of the enemy. Then he had him hung in the town square.

It must have been highly enlightening for the defenders to see one of the so-called "golden pheasants" dangling from the end of a rope. In Silesia General Schorner was hanging teenage boys, just as other SS squads and field police units were doing in Danzig and Altdamm and along the Seelowe Heights. So far as is known, this was the only execution for cowardice to take place at Schwedt. The "golden pheasants," as the Nazi civilian bosses were nicknamed, were, with only a few exceptions, heartily disliked by just about everyone. How amusing to see a colleague of the swine Koch and other wretched self-serving gauleiters choking his life out in the town square.

All the same, the act was out of character for Skorzeny, even considering the circumstances. But after so many years of war, it seemed that almost everyone bore a deep resentment against someone else, requiring only an instant's provocation to explode into rage and retribution. Some hated SS and Waffen SS men indiscriminately, some hated the military in general, some hated Hitler and the other leaders, some hated the other leaders but not Hitler, some took out their anger against young army deserters, and more than a few were learning to hate the Russians as they had never hated them before. Would Skorzeny have executed this pitiful man if he had been other than the local party boss? Perhaps not, though there is no way to know for sure. He had run like a rabbit and been hung for it.

This time Martin Bormann called up to complain. He was Hitler's personal secretary, as well as chief civilian administrator for all Nazi party affairs. The swine of swine, as it were, among all the "golden pheasant" breed. Contempt tends to bring out such mixed metaphors. Bormann informed Skorzeny that only a Nazi party tribunal had the authority to try senior members of the party. The conversation was again rather brief. Skorzeny replied that the man had been tried not as a party member but as a soldier. The battle around Konigsberg continued in all its fury.

The Lost Legion

During his assignment as an infantry commander in the Schwedt bridgehead, Skorzeny had more than enough problems to keep him occupied during all his waking hours. Yet during this time there was another situation that remained very much on his mind—a strange and far-removed struggle for survival over which he, to his dismay, had no control whatsoever.

The events in question had to do with yet another commando operation taking place in the depths of Russia—certainly an unlikely place for any German fighting men to be at this late date, with Zhukov's tanks already so close to Berlin. Skorzeny had organized this operation several months previously, and even now it was still going on, a long, drawn-out, and agonizing affair about which he received radio reports only at rare intervals; otherwise he remained in the dark.

It was perhaps just as well that he was so deeply engrossed in keeping the Rumanians and Russians at bay around Schwedt, but even so he must have found himself looking to the eastern horizon at odd hours of the day and night, worrying about the men who were lost out there a thousand miles behind enemy lines. Over the years he had formed close personal bonds with many of them; his style of leadership had always been conducive to such an atmosphere. In interviews after the war he would often refer to them as "mein schoenes Manner," a phrase which in English emerges as "my dear men" or "my beautiful men." But these words in German connote deeper nuances of fellowship which cannot be easily translated.

More specifically, a number of Skorzeny's commandos at this time were lost somewhere in the swamps and forests of Byelorussia, north of the city of Minsk. They had been sent out the previous fall on a daring, and as usual, probably suicidal rescue mission. It was in this area during the summer of 1944 that the Soviets had smashed Army Group Center, dealing the German military the greatest defeat in its history and expelling the invaders once and for all from the soil of old Russia. For months afterward, half-starving groups of Landsers had trekked through the enemy-infested wilderness, struggling to reach the German lines which by then had been pushed back into Poland hundreds of miles to the west. Only small handfuls of these men, called "Ruck-kampfer," came through this long march alive. Most were hunted down and killed at unknown locations in the forests by partisans or units detached from the advancing Red Army.

By September the very last—or so it was thought—of these human scarecrows had filtered back into German-held territory, to be greeted with amazement by comrades who had given them up for dead months before. But then strange radio messages began coming in over the German frequencies. Apparently a large group of survivors, as many as 2000 men, were still hiding out in the Byelorussian swamps over two hundred miles to the east, engaged in a struggle for survival that would last nearly to war's end. These men, and the commandos sent out by Skorzeny to rescue them, would comprise the last fighting remnants of the great invasion launched in 1941.

Hiding out, lost, disoriented, in a region of vast wilderness, these men under a certain Captain Scherhorn were unable to provide exact information as to their own whereabouts. Thus Skorzeny sent out four teams that were parachuted at different points across the general area, hoping that at least one of them could make contact with the so-called "lost legion." The commandos were equipped with Russian uniforms and identity papers and given close-cropped haircuts in the Red Army style. Some were Russian-speaking ethnic Germans from the Baltic states, while others were actual Russian POWs recruited from General Vlasov's anti-Stalinist "Liberation Army." (This "army" was a rather modest formation which the Germans maintained more for propaganda purposes than actual fighting, though eventually they did see combat in the Kustrin area.) The remaining commandos were German, resourceful veterans of Skorzeny's earlier missions.

Group A took off into the twilight of an October evening. After parachuting into the forests, they were able to send only the following radio message: "Drop zone spotted by the enemy. Machine guns firing."

That was all.

Group B was then sent out. These men sent no messages at all, apparently vanishing without a trace.

Skorzeny must have agonized over whether to fly any more men out on this hopeless mission. Yet already he felt a certain admiration for the unknown Captain Scherhorn, whose soldiers had survived for so long in their own seemingly hopeless predicament.

After five long nights of waiting the radio operator at Skorzeny's headquarters suddenly removed his headphones and declared excitedly that a message had come in from Group B. Not only were they all still alive, but they had made contact with Scherhorn's men. A wave of emotion passed through the place. Captain Scherhorn radioed a heart-felt message of thanks.

The men of Groups C and D were still charged with their own anxious adrenalin, their nerves stretched taut by the long days of waiting. Skorzeny must have debated the wisdom of sending them in now that contact with the lost soldiers had been made. But they were still anxious to go, and Scherhorn's people were in such bad shape that the addition of even a few more able-bodied men would be helpful. Groups C and D were sent out over the next two nights, but they never found Scherhorn's men. Both groups vanished without a trace.

Such disappearances were all too common, for both Allied and German commandos during the war.

Skorzeny could only focus his attention on the survivors. He had hoped that Scherhorn's men would be able to clear a landing strip in the forest and so be air-lifted to safety. But the problem was not to be solved so easily—these last survivors of the great Army Group Center were sick, starving, and dressed only in threadbare summer uniforms. Winter was fast approaching. They were on their last legs, too undernourished and exhausted to carry out such a laborious project. Before anything could be done they required food, ammunition, and medical supplies. Skorzeny set about scrounging everything he could find from the notoriously parsimonious Wehrmacht supply depots. After a great deal of wrangling, which also involved finding more transport planes for the numerous flights involved, he managed to send Scherhorn the vital stores he needed, as well as an engineer to manage construction of the airstrip and a doctor with equipment to set up a field hospital.

The long autumn weeks passed by. October of 1944 gave way to November. But over this time the rescue mission appeared to be taking shape. Scherhorn reported that his men were regaining their strength and that work was underway to clear a landing site. Then more bad news came in over the radio waves. The constant drone of aircraft overhead had attracted the attention of the Russians. The enemy began closing in on Scherhorn's lost outpost in the wilderness. By now it was almost December and the Red Army was established hundreds of miles to the west along the Vistula. Only smaller Soviet forces had been left behind to garrison the newly liberated areas of Byelorussia, but any concerted attack would be more than enough to wipe out Scherhorn's band. As the enemy patrols closed in, scattered firefights broke out around the perimeter of the as yet unfinished airstrip. It was a clear signal that larger forces would soon arrive on the scene.

After so many weeks of preparation and hard work it was a heart-breaking dilemma. What to do now? Most of the survivors were now healthy enough to walk, but where could they go? To escape to the west would mean breaking through the Russian army on the Vistula—a possibility for a small group of men but not for two thousand. Finally it was resolved that only one option remained open to Scherhorn's men.

Almost two hundred miles to the north lay a remote region covered with a number of large lakes, whose frozen surfaces could be used as landing strips by rescue aircraft. Somehow the lost legion would have to struggle across enemy territory to reach those lakes. This Captain Scherhorn, about whom little is known, must have been a man of some resolve. Rather than being discouraged by the prospect of such a dangerous trek in mid-winter, he radioed back an enthusiastic message of approval to Skorzeny. Skorzeny found himself wondering if he would ever be able to meet this man in person.

Thus began the second phase of the lost legion's long ordeal. They began groping their way slowly northward across the winter landscape, the beginning of a months-long odyssey that would continue into 1945 and would finally end in oblivion.

During these months Skorzeny would listen anxiously for the intermittent radio reports of their progress. In the meantime he was left to plan and carry out still other operations—the kidnapping of Admiral Horthy's son in November, dropping infiltrators behind Americans lines in December. And still, far to the east, Scherhorn's men struggled onward, trekking past the graves of Germans and Russians who had fought over this ground since 1941.

In January Skorzeny took over command of the Schwedt bridgehead at Himmler's bidding, thus engaging in his own personal struggle with the Russians. Beyond the embattled perimeter at Schwedt the snowy countryside stretched for a thousand miles, to some unknown point in Russia where Scherhorn's men were marching still. Skorzeny had all he could do to locate supplies and ammunition for his Volksturm units fighting in the bridgehead, yet he also had to battle authorities in Berlin to ensure that supplies continued to be flown out to Scherhorn's men. With the Soviet deluge now deep inside Germany, the powers that be were beginning to lose interest in this nearly forgotten group of stragglers. Fewer planes were available, and now they had to fly longer and longer distances as airfields were abandoned to the advancing Red Army. Skorzeny was beginning to lose hope, but he continued to radio encouraging messages to Scherhorn, who had become a kind of invisible personal acquaintance somewhere out there in the ether. And his own men, his commandos, were out there too.

Supplies that should have lasted them until they reached the lakes were used up as they were forced to halt and fight off ever larger groups of Soviet attackers in the snowy wastelands. That they had not all been wiped out long since was something of a miracle. Clearly no all-out effort had yet been made by any centralized Soviet authority. Most of these running battles must have been led by the commanders of small local garrisons, who would have had their own difficulties in attracting the interest of higher Soviet authorities preoccupied with the final invasion of Germany.

But above all Scherhorn's men must have continued to rely on the vast stretches of wilderness inside the Soviet Union to elude their pursuers. To avoid all contact with the civilian population on such a march would have been nearly impossible—and besides, there was the matter of food to be foraged to supplement the less and less frequent air drops. But many of the villages they passed through would have been too remote to house even a small Soviet garrison. Somehow, some way, they managed to keep going. No record of their flight survives, except for the radio messages sent to Skorzeny.

February 27th 1945. The Volksturmers still held an ever-shrinking perimeter around Schwedt. By this time supplies of any kind were almost impossible to get hold of; only one flight per week was being sent out to Scherhorn. On this date the seemingly impossible news from the lost legion finally arrived. They had made it to the frozen lakes. Not only that, but they had met up with the commandos of Group A—the men who had been given up for dead after sending out their one desperate radio message back in October.

Yet Skorzeny's elation was crushed almost as soon as this message was received. The lakes that Scherhorn had struggled to reach for three months lay in a nearly uninhabited region where the borders of Lithuania, Latvia, and Byelorussia converged, about two hundred miles east of the German forces still holding out in the Courland Peninsula. The latest reports indicated that for the moment they had eluded any pursuing Soviet forces, though clearly such a fortuitous situation could change within hours. The trekkers were exhausted and low on food and ammunition, but they had made it, and Scherhorn requested that the airlift be got underway with all possible haste.

Skorzeny immediately contacted transport authorities in Berlin to requisition the necessary planes. To fly out all of Scherhorn's survivors would require not one round trip but at least a dozen, and possibly more. Word came back from Berlin—there were no longer enough fuel stocks remaining to carry out such a large operation. No fuel, no planes—nothing. The supply flights were over; the rescue mission was over.

Skorzeny was well aware of the desperate fuel situation; perhaps he had already anticipated problems of this kind, but the shock of such a tragic finish to all these months was almost too much to bear. He got on the telephone intent on using all his powers of persuasion—he had, after all, managed to wrangle supplies from every imaginable source over the preceding months. But the answer was final and the answer was no. Left to his own resources, he might have managed to commandeer a certain amount of fuel from somewhere, from nearby airfields, or from God only knew where. But he realized in despair that whatever he might collect would never be enough to make all the flights needed to save Scherhorn's men.

And so they were lost. The perversity of the situation was spun out to its final detail—one more flight was made, not to carry men out, but to drop a few last supplies, including the Knight's Cross for Scherhorn and the leader of Commando Group B, who had made the first contact with Scherhorn and remained at his side ever since last October.

Nothing more was ever heard from these men. They were wiped out, or starved to death in the forests, or, perhaps most likely, were taken prisoner and shipped off to camps in Siberia, there to die years after the war in forgotten anguish.

Only one ray of hope emerged from this long and tragic episode. The final group of men to be sent out, the men of Group D, never met up with Scherhorn and were presumed lost. But six weeks after being parachuted into Byelorussia they made it back to the German lines in East Prussia, every man surviving and in good health. Their enemy uniforms and fluency in Russian had provided perfect cover; they related a few almost comical episodes of feasting and drinking with Red Army units along the way.

Thus for the divergent fates of different groups of men.

The war went on, the violence in the east raging unabated through the final months and weeks. As for Skorzeny, his commando skills were soon in demand again. He was relieved of command at Schwedt, where Russian attacks had failed to make any further headway. On March 7th 1945, the Americans captured the bridge over the Rhine at Remagen. Hitler wanted Skorzeny to organize a team of frogmen and demolish the span. The commando leader went back to work.

The Lost Legion: Postscript

The story of the Lost Legion has a kind of epic fascination, with all its elements of drama, tragedy, and isolation in the wilderness. What a nuisance it is then, to have to confess that this story may not be true—not entirely true anyway. For other sources suggest that Skorzeny and his commandos may have been taken in by an elaborate Russian counterintelligence hoax.

This alternative version carries a somewhat irksome air of authenticity—irksome not only because it deflates the terrible drama of Scherhorn's ordeal, but also because the details provided by this other source, though fairly convincing, are not specific enough to establish the entire truth of the story.

Let us start over again from the beginning and see how this other version stands up to Skorzeny's account.

The source in question is a Luftwaffe veteran named Peter Stahl, a former member of the mysterious special operations Geschwader known as KG 200 (and author of the book KG 200). This Geschwader carried out a number of bizarre missions in both the East and the West during the last two years of the war. According to Stahl, planes and pilots of KG 200 were used to drop supplies to Scherhorn's men during those long winter months of 1944-45.

Unfortunately Stahl's account is highly confusing, obliging the reader to sort through a muddle of information which Stahl does not present in any clear fashion. First of all he states, or at least implies, that several agencies besides Skorzeny's commando group were involved in this mission, operating independently of each other. This should come as no surprise to anyone familiar with the overlapping and Byzantine command structures that had always been one of the peculiar features of Hitler's Germany, particularly in an operation in which the Luftwaffe, intelligence agencies, and the SS were (in theory at least) working together.

Stahl suggests that KG 200 was not placed under Skorzeny's command during these months, but remained subordinate only to the Luftwaffe. It is not entirely clear whether he means that KG 200 was merely placed at Skorzeny's disposal at this time, while not technically being under his command, or if the planes and pilots used to carry Skorzeny's commandos into Russia came from some different source altogether. It seems ludicrous to think that such a delicate and dangerous mission was not carried out under a single unified command, though not inconceivable, given the strange rivalries between various German military organizations. Ultimately (that is to say after several close readings of his story) Stahl seems to be saying that while Skorzeny had command of the four original commando flights, in which his men were parachuted into Byelorussia, all subsequent flights and supply drops were conducted by the Luftwaffe and KG 200.

Stahl does state that the existence of Scherhorn's legion was not a hoax. The first radio messages from Scherhorn in the autumn of 1944 were scrutinized with a good deal of suspicion; a series of "control questions" were then radioed back to him to ensure that the whole business was not a Russian trick. Furthermore, when Skorzeny's commandos finally linked up with Scherhorn, they also responded appropriately to control questions to establish beyond a doubt that the Lost Legion truly existed.

Where then does the idea of a hoax enter into all this?

Stahl's account implies, though still without any degree of clarity, that at some point Scherhorn's men were wiped out or captured by the Russians, and that all subsequent messages then became a part of a Soviet intelligence game. But the critical question of just when this deception began is left unanswered.

In Skorzeny's account, the last radio contact with Scherhorn occurred in late February or early March of 1945, after the legion's long trek to the frozen lakes from which they hoped to be airlifted to safety. Yet Stahl relates that two Arado Ar 232 transport planes were sent out to Scherhorn as late as April 20th. (What a strange situation—the Russians had just broken through at the Seelowe Heights and were already entering Berlin at the same moment two German planes were flying deep into Russia.) Neither of these planes made it to the target. The first had to abort shortly after takeoff due to mechanical problems; the second was finally forced to return due to severe storms over Poland or Byelorussia.

The radio traffic from Scherhorn, after he was informed of this setback, took on an increasingly suspicious tone; control questions and other instructions sent out from Germany were not responded to appropriately. It seemed that Russian agents were now operating the radio transmitters.

Conceivably all these events could be made to jibe fairly easily with Skorzeny's own account. If Scherhorn's people were killed or captured at the beginning of March, then it certainly makes sense that a Soviet intelligence operation could have been responsible for all the radio messages sent after that date. But at this point Stahl throws everything into confusion by declaring that the rescue operation had been nothing but a Russian double-cross for "perhaps as long as six months,"[3] that is to say almost from the very moment Skorzeny's commandos were originally flown in. "One could now assume with near certainty that the whole Operation Scherhorn was nothing but an enemy trick."[4]

In retrospect these statements do not make a great deal of sense. Stahl himself confirms that the Lost Legion did actually exist, and that not only Skorzeny's commandos but also other specialist personnel dropped later by KG 200 did link up with Scherhorn. But at what point did the Russians wipe them out and begin sending out false radio signals? Could this have happened as far back as December 1944 (or even earlier), before Scherhorn's men began their winter odyssey to the frozen lakes region? Or did the hoax only come into play after their arrival at the lakes?

It seems that these questions can only be placed alongside other unsolved puzzles from the chaos of the war's last days. As a final note, Stahl labels Skorzeny as "not the most reliable of sources"—fair enough, perhaps. Stahl's account, on the other hand, seems not so much unreliable as muddled almost to the point of being incomprehensible. Though perhaps not accurate on every single point, the greater coherence and wealth of detail in Skorzeny's version probably points to a better picture of what actually happened to Scherhorn and his men.

Rall was one of the top fighter pilots. Nearly 300 kills, up there with Hartmann and Nowotny and a few others. Shot down in Russia in 1941—a broken back, semi-paralyzed for months afterward. Then he returned to action. Later in the war his thumb was shot off, but he kept on flying.

He flew a Me 109 and remembered escorting Rudel's Stukas at different times on missions over the Soviet Union. After the war both of them were held prisoner by the Americans and later by the British, sharing the same cell for several months while their captors interrogated them about the tactics of German pilots.

He found that living in close confinement with the famed Stuka pilot was beginning to get on his nerves. Interviewed by a journalist many years later, Rall said:

"Living very close together you get acquainted, and you come to understand the thinking of such a man. But I had known him before then. Anyhow, I was very surprised by this egocentric man; the greatest in his own mind, that sort of fellow. It was a little disgusting to me."[1]

A PLEA FOR THE SALVATION OF THE NATION

Rudel Speaks from His Hospital Bed

Skorzeny's commandos were fighting everywhere now. There were those manning the bridgehead at Schwedt, there were those wandering with the Lost Legion in Russia. While he picked a team to make the frogman assault on the Remagen bridge, other small groups of Skorzeny's commandos were scattered across eastern Germany, filling in gaps in the defensive lines, fighting alongside regular infantry formations to hold back the Soviets. Many were overrun and killed in these battles. Some would be sent to the Kustrin area in the Oder valley, where by mid-April they would be all but annihilated.

In the midst of these events, perhaps just after being relieved of his assignment at Schwedt, Skorzeny found time to visit Hans Rudel in a Berlin hospital. The meeting smacked of a newsreel publicity stunt, but the newsreels were not present. In any case Skorzeny would hardly have bothered to make such a side-trip unless he had personal reasons for doing so. It is not clear if he had ever met Rudel before; they would have had little opportunity to run into each other, except perhaps during some chance meeting at Hitler's headquarters. He may only have desired to wish the Stuka pilot well. How these two renowed personalities took to each other can only be guessed. In his memoirs Rudel states only in passing, "Skorzeny dropped by to visit me for an hour's chat."[2]

As can be imagined, Rudel was not in the best of shape. His leg was gone, and he had lost many quarts of blood. Even so, he could think of nothing except finding someone to manufacture an artificial leg for him so he could begin flying again. The newsreels did not follow Skorzeny to his bedside, but they were there on one other occasion, only a day or two after the surgeon had amputated the few tendons and shreds of skin connecting Rudel's shattered leg to his body.

Typically, Rudel was annoyed that the surgeon had not somehow managed to save his hopelessly mangled leg. But he accepted the loss soon enough, still determined that it would not stop him from flying. The newsreel cameras show him chatting with the surgeon, Rudel blithely mentioning his hopes of soon getting back into the cockpit of his Stuka. The surgeon, no doubt thinking this preposterous, humors him with equally blithe reassurances. A smiling young woman arrives at the bedside bearing flowers for the Herr Oberst, wishing him well. She seems a little star-struck, chattering hurriedly in a shyly flirtatious manner. She is followed by an oily-looking man in a black uniform, who holds out a microphone and interviews Rudel for the nation.

Rudel tries to sit up, but is only able to lift his head a little higher on the pillow. His face has a pallid shine to it and his normally wavy brown hair looks damp and slicked-down with fever. Still, one would not guess that beneath the sheets he has only one leg remaining. He gives the interviewer a brief account of how he was shot down a few days earlier. His voice seems a little subdued from fatigue, though possibly this is also due to the fact that he has been interviewed so many times in the past.

He then turns his head from the interviewer and speaks directly into the camera in a tightly-framed closeup. He speaks a little more clearly now, in a calm and straightforward tone:

> Since being wounded I have been sorely troubled, at this moment of crisis in the war, that I am unable to fly and must leave my comrades—my squadron—to carry on flying alone.
>
> At this time, while I can neither fly nor carry out other duties except in this severely limited condition, I find there is nothing to do but grit my teeth, to endure this sacrifice, knowing that our people will have fought bravely to the end, will have gritted their own teeth until the final victory has been won.[3]

These words sound rather banal, and Rudel in his exhausted state is unable to put much passion into them. Most likely he is simply repeating a few lines given to him by the newsreel people, and his face bears the diffident expression of a man who feels wearily obligated to cooperate with the press, just as he has done so many times in the past, though with less and less en- thusiasm as time goes on. There is something about Rudel tiredly speaking these words that calls to mind countless other twen- tieth century celebrities who have been borrowed by government propaganda agencies to exhort their fellow citizens—yet who often manage to sound as if they are reciting no more than a perfunctory, meaningless list of phrases. In the last decades of this century we have become used to this dismal media phe- nomenon; somehow one also suspects that German civilians in 1945 would have felt more than a little cynical about it.

Rudel's speech from his hospital bed ties in neatly with the next newsreel segment, in which citizens of Berlin are shown building primitive defensive works around the city, laboriously carting around huge blocks of stone and other debris to erect barriers against the Bolshevik invaders. The commentator de- clares: "These brave folk will continue to grit their teeth for Oberst Rudel!"[4] The newsreel comes to an end.

Rudel's hospital room was located in the depths of the great flak tower standing beside the Berlin Zoo. In architectural terms, Berlin had never been a very distinguished city; hailing from Vi- enna, Skorzeny referred to it as a "hideous brickpile." So perhaps it was fitting that this grim and enormous flak tower was one of the most visible features of the Berlin skyline. Also referred to as the Zoo Bunker, it rose twenty stories high and was built from the same reinforced concrete and steel beams found in the great bunkers of the Atlantic Wall. More than just a gun tower, it had emergency accommodations capable of housing several thou- sand people, with hospital equipment and communication cen- ters. It was the strongest above-ground structure in Berlin.

Adjacent to it sprawled the many acres of the famous Berlin Zoo. Rudel, surprising everyone but himself, made a fast recov- ery, even though his stump had not fully healed and still dealt him a great deal of pain. He had trouble finding a maker of ar- tificial limbs who would fit him with a new leg while his stump was not yet healed. He had no patience for such a delay, and at length persuaded a manufacturer to fit him with an artificial leg on a "purely experimental basis."

So now he could walk again, with the assistance of crutches. Most of the time he hobbled around without the plastic leg, which grated painfully against his raw stump. He really only needed the new leg when he was flying; in the meantime he remained intent on getting healthy as soon as possible. Pretty young visitors flocked to his bedside, but Rudel was in love with his wife. He did allow a certain Sister Gudrun to escort him on one of his first attempts to walk outside, hobbling for a while through the zoo next to the flak tower.

It was mid-March by now and spring weather had come early to Berlin. They stopped in front of the monkey cage and Rudel decided to have some fun with one of the apes. "Of course I do just what one should not do and I push both my crutches through the bars with the idea of tickling his tail." The bored-looking primate was stimulated by this game and immediately pulled the crutches into the cage. Rudel pulled back, balancing precariously on his good leg. The creature was stronger than it looked and the two them were suddenly locked in a tug of war, while Sister Gudrun hung on to Rudel to keep him from falling over.

While they struggled the air raid sirens began to wail over Berlin. At last the monkey wrenched the rubber caps off the tips of the crutches, contenting himself with inspecting and devouring these items while Rudel pulled free. The short battle had left him gasping and weak. It was a long, painstaking hobble back to the shelter of the bunker, with people running for their lives all around him. He and the good sister made it back to safety just as the first bombs were falling.

He continued to get his strength up by walking around outside between air raids, though staying away from the monkey cage. Whenever he wore the artificial leg it chafed painfully against his stump, but he made no complaint. At the end of March he pronounced himself ready to join his squadron again. Hitler summoned him to the Reichskanzellerei to say goodbye, clearly pleased by this young soldier's incredible devotion to duty. The Fuhrer's grounding edict was still in effect, but this time Hitler didn't even bother to mention it. As a cripple, Rudel would at last have to be satisfied with leading his men from behind a desk.

His squadron had been transferred once again, back to General Schorner's command in Silesia. Rudel thought highly of Schorner; the hangman's reputation brought no reproach from him. After saying goodbye to his tail gunner Gadermann, still recovering from the crashlanding at Lebus, Rudel telephoned Berlin's Templehof Airport to have a Stuka made ready for him.

He flew off to his squadron's airfield in the Sudeten Mountains and resumed combat flying the day after his arrival.

Impenetrable darkness. No moon. No stars. The dankness of mist. The rumble of motors everywhere, advancing in blindness. Exhaust flames from the tanks dazzle the men's eyes before they can adjust to really see anything. They keep going. As yet there is no gunfire, or only a little.

The battalion commander's Kubelwagen bogs down in a crater. He shouts angrily at some men nearby, but they cannot get him free. Finally he hails one of the King Tigers and climbs on board. Even such a large tank has little room inside for an extra man. The battalion commander raises his head through the loader's hatch and watches from there, while the tank commander stays in position in the commander's hatch. Still it is barely possible for either of them to see anything ahead. Down in the hull the driver can see absolutely nothing through his periscope. Tensely he listens to instructions from the tank commander over the intercom. The 68 ton vehicle keeps on rumbling slowly ahead at five or six miles per hour.

THE LAST ATTACK

Climax on the Oder

By the end of March Himmler had been in command of Army Group Vistula for over two months. His only accomplishments of note had been to enlist the services of energetic warriors like Skorzeny and Rudel. An army or army group can still function to some degree with an incompetent commander, so long as he is not a meddler and surrounds himself with good staff officers. To some extent, Himmler had done exactly this; he tended to let his staff tell him what to do, then issued the appropriate orders. But he was beginning to lose interest in this role, and between sleeping late at his headquarters and taking rest cures at the clinic of his personal doctor, he was becoming difficult for his subordinates to locate when they needed him.

In effect, Army Group Vistula was leaderless. As Chief of Staff, General Wenck could have resolved this problem by taking care of operational matters. But he had been in the hospital for over a month, recovering from the skull fracture received in his crash along the autobahn. His successor to this post, General Krebs, was a competent officer but he did not possess Wenck's qualities of leadership and drive; thus he was not the ideal man to compensate for Himmler's ineptitude.

All the same, with the redundancy of command that tends to proliferate at higher military levels (and this had always been especially true in the German army), this leadership void may not have been as serious as it would appear. Certainly the Soviets did little to take advantage of the situation. Generals Busse and von Manteuffel, in charge of the 9th and 3rd Panzer Armies which comprised Army Group Vistula (Steiner's 11th SS Army having been dissolved almost as soon as it was created), were both capable commanders, well able to take up the slack left by Himmler's inactivity. Without an overly aggressive chief looking over their shoulders, they were able to devote themselves to the tasks that most needed doing—reorganizing their shattered forces and consolidating their defenses.

For Busse's 9th Army, facing Zhukov's bridgeheads across the Oder between Frankfurt and Kustrin, this was an especially critical task. 9th Army had been ripped apart by the Vistula offensive in January, and it had taken Busse all these precious weeks to reassemble any kind of effective fighting force. Some of these reinforcements had been frittered away by his counterattacks against the Oder bridgeheads during February, but these had had little success and by March Busse had largely gone over to the defensive, intending to create an impregnable barrier along the Seelowe Heights that would keep Zhukov's forces bottled up in the valley below.

Yet even now during the last week of March another counterattack was still in the offing, as it almost always was in the German scheme of things. It was destined to be the last of the war—the last death ride, the last hideous shambles.

Busse was apprehensive. He knew his divisions, especially his few panzer divisions, would be unlikely to accomplish anything decisive. They had, after all, accomplished very little during the first attacks against Zhukov's bridgeheads in February. Busse did not have to deal with Himmler breathing down his neck, but as always Hitler was another matter entirely. Hitler had been preoccupied with Sonnenwende in February and operations in Hungary earlier in March, but one final attempt to smash Zhukov's bridgeheads along the Oder never remained far from his thinking.

Unfortunately, his thinking was becoming more cloudy and overwrought. He remained fixated on the idea that the German military with its dwindling resources could strike major blows on every front; he remained relentlessly offensive-minded. Thus had Dietrich's 6th SS Army been thrown away in Hungary, accomplishing absolutely nothing; thus was Dietrich's army destined never to appear against Zhukov on the Oder.

That left only Busse's 9th Army in position here. On the map, Zhukov's two bridgeheads looked vulnerable. But Hitler had always been too fond of reading the course of events from what he saw on the map, like a sculptor seeing the finished statue inside the stone. Matters of logistics and materiel—Busse's relative weakness, Zhukov's overwhelming strength—never made as much impression on him as they should have.

While Zhukov had established two major crossings on the west bank of the Oder, the Germans still held two bridgeheads of their own on the east bank, the northerly one in the old fortress city of Kustrin and one further south across the river from Frankfurt.

At this time Kustrin was almost entirely surrounded and was fighting for its life, but the fighting around the more southerly German bridgehead had been much less severe. On the map it appeared that an attack launched from the Frankfurt bridgehead would stand an excellent chance of slashing north towards Kustrin, which was less than twenty miles away. Surely Busse's panzer divisions could get at least that far? And if this were done, then the southernmost of Zhukov's two bridgeheads would be entirely cut off on the west bank of the Oder. On the map there appeared a classic invitation to encircle and destroy the most advanced Soviet spearheads aimed at Berlin.

But by this time Hitler had at his disposal for this task only a handful of understrength panzer and panzer grenadier divisions, while Zhukov had corps and armies available—not only in the bridgeheads themselves but also stacked up to the rear on the east bank. Even Hitler had to realize that the odds against him were growing longer and longer, but by nature he seemed unable to resist any opportunity to attack, and for him such opportunities were always more clear-cut on the map than in the field.

Hitler could have resigned himself to a defensive battle, waiting for the Russians to strike Busse's heavily defended positions along the Seelowe Heights. But this would have been out of character for him. And by now probably all of these considerations had become more or less moot points; German resources, either to strike one last blow or to establish a defense in depth, were just about used up. Hitler stayed true to his nature and ordered Busse to attack.

What followed was a foredoomed, last-gasp act of defiance rather than a genuine military operation.

Himmler Steps Down

The actors played out their roles with a certain resignation, sensing that the fate of this business was already pre-destined (as it almost certainly was.) The players went stoically through their paces as in a Greek tragedy where every phrase uttered, every step taken, had already been familiar for generations both to themselves and to the audience. The drama would have lacked some of the emotional force of those ancient tragedies, perhaps, because all the players were very tired and only too well aware of the uselessness of their acts.

Guderian took the first step, which was to see once and for all that Himmler was relieved from command of Army Group Vistula. When an attack is to be mounted the presence of a capable commander is always more critical. Without consulting Hitler, Guderian drove up to Himmler's headquarters at Prenzlau, wanting to ensure in person that this imbecilic business was finished for good. The staff officers declared that Himmler was taking another rest cure at his doctor's sanatorium in a nearby town. Guderian drove on through the quiet north German forests. There was an endless uniformity to the firs and pines, only occasionally broken by a few deciduous trees sprouting their first green buds. This region was another part of old rural Germany as yet untouched by war.

Guderian found Himmler at the sanatorium, apparently suffering from a cold. Probably it was embarrassment at his inadequacy rather than stress or illness which had caused Himmler to seek refuge from his military duties. Guderian did not seek to embarrass the man further, having already done a pretty good job of this during the heated conference at Hitler's headquarters a month earlier. In addition, Guderian was suffering from such deep fatigue that he felt little desire to raise his voice. He simply talked sensibly to Himmler, probably intuiting that the SS Reichsfuhrer was ready, perhaps even hoping, for a visit like this.

It was too much responsibility for one man to tend to all the labyrinthine affairs of the SS and at the same time command an army group. Guderian made no mention of incompetence; it was no longer necessary to pin this addled little man to the wall.

Himmler appeared relieved, though still making a few perfunctory gestures and pronouncements in order to hide it. But he was still worried about how to get Hitler to let him off the hook. He did not have the nerve to go to the Fuhrer and admit failure to his face. Hitler had never personally raged at Himmler before, but the SS leader seemed to fear that this might be the moment for it. He had witnessed some of these terrible outbursts over these last months. With Hitler being so high-strung, seemingly ready to turn on anyone, would Himmler find himself stripped not only of military command but also of any of his vast personal power over the SS? Well, who knew what Hitler would do or say; Himmler only knew for sure that he didn't want to face it. Beneath his meek and by now rather pitiful demeanor, the wheels of cunning and survival were still turning within his mind at all hours of the day.

"I can't go to him and tell him this," said Himmler.

"That's all right. I'll take care of it," said Guderian. "So you'll agree to step down then, if I break the news to him?"[1]

Himmler agreed. In his heart he was still faithful to and fearful of his great leader. On the other hand, things were getting quite precarious these days, and he had begun formulating plans to come to terms with the Western Allies behind Hitler's back. For the moment he said nothing of this. Guderian drove back to Berlin.

Hitler also seemed too exhausted and preoccupied to raise a fuss. Both he and Guderian were beginning to function like automatons, utterly worn down from having to deal with each other and with everything else. Hitler's body was coming more and more to resemble a withered shell, palsied and frail, within which the relentless life energies continued to flare, but in a more erratic and intermittent fashion. Guderian's face and neck were flushed continuously with an alarming red glow, leading his colleagues to fear he was dangerously close to a stroke or heart attack. Only a few years earlier Guderian had been a youthful, robust-looking general with a more than average zest for life. Stress was causing Hitler's body to fade away; with Guderian, it was causing his body to bulge from every fiber.

Guderian didn't know how the Fuhrer would take the news about Himmler, but he had no intention of getting into another shouting match. He could feel the vessels and sinews inside himself stretched with tension like a myriad of fuses. Since the Sonnenwende fiasco he had been somewhat less confrontational, if only because the stress raging inside his body had become physically unbearable; it took an effort to think clearly anymore. But he continued to seethe in silence; especially the utter futility of the Spring Awakening offensive in Hungary had led him to grit his teeth to keep from lashing out at Hitler.

So disposing of Himmler in such a peremptory fashion was certainly asking for trouble. He would just have to stay calm. He had a feeling that, even if Hitler started raving and refused to accept the Reichsfuhrer's resignation, somehow Himmler's removal was already a fait accompli. Guderian sensed that he had seen the last of the commander of Army Group Vistula.

He was right. In the Reichskanzellerei Hitler could only bring himself to mumble a few reproachful comments. It was outrageous for Guderian to take such steps on his own initiative. Looking too weary to initiate anything, Guderian underplayed his role and calmly stressed Himmler's own desire to be removed. Hitler shook his head, muttering to himself, not bothering to raise his voice.

It was done. The SS Reichsfuhrer would be relieved of military command. He could go back to tending his vast empire of murder, slave labor profiteering, and intrigue.

Hitler couldn't think of any suitable candidate to replace Himmler at this juncture. Army generals . . . he had had his fill of the entire lot of them. Guderian suggested General Heinrici, then commanding 1st Panzer Army, part of Schorner's army group in the out-of-the-way foothills of southeastern Silesia.

Heinrici was a deeply religious man, who had aroused Hitler's ire earlier in the war by expressing disdain for some of the anti-religious aspects of the Nazi cult. But the incident had been fairly trivial, and by 1945 Hitler would probably have had difficulty placing Heinrici's face. He listened to Guderian's recommendation of this general who supposedly had steady nerves in a crisis and had held his front together on several occasions during the grim retreats of the last few years. Then he agreed to the choice, and Heinrici became the last commander of the misbegotten Army Group Vistula.

But it was too late to make any difference. Busse's attack against Zhukov's bridgeheads had been delayed long enough and Hitler wanted it to go forward immediately. Summoned from Silesia to Berlin, Heinrici arrived on March 22nd and found he would have only a few days to meet with Busse and deal with all the arrangements and requirements to be taken care of before 9th Army's offensive.

This really left him with no time to accomplish anything at all. He could only trust that Busse had made thorough enough preparations on his own.

Busse had done so, but he still had little enthusiasm for this operation. Upon hearing the details, neither did Heinrici, who was briefed first by the weary Guderian in his command bunker at Zossen outside Berlin. The attack was to originate from the southern German bridgehead across the Oder from Frankfurt. There was only one bridge across the river at this point, which would have to carry all the traffic for all five of the divisions slated for this operation. It would be next to impossible for such an immensely long column of vehicles to make the crossing to the east bank in secret, and without the element of surprise the attack could not succeed. Furthermore, the assault units would be operating on their own on the Russian side of the river; if the attack failed they would have no means of retreating and might easily be annihilated by the enemy's overwhelming numerical strength.

Heinrici absorbed all this coolly. He asked Guderian if Hitler had set a firm date for the attack.

"The day after tomorrow," said Guderian.[2]

Heinrici was shocked and perplexed. For all the time he would have to prepare, Army Group Vistula might as well still be without a commander. The resigned, almost absent-minded tone with which Guderian mentioned the start-time was also distressing. Heinrici remembered the energetic Guderian of old, always on top of every situation, his mind as sharp and incisive as a surgical instrument. He was also struck by the ugly blood-flushed hue on Guderian's face.

The OKH chief was reaching the end of his rope. Already for months Guderian's other colleagues and subordinates had been thinking the same thing.

Heinrici drove on to Prenzlau to officially take the reins of command out of Himmler's hands. The same drive Guderian had made a few days before, the same moorlands and endless ranks of tall pines, the same villages.

Himmler had returned from his doctor's care and was actually at his headquarters in the mansion of a large old estate when Heinrici arrived. The SS Reichsfuhrer seemed to be having a few second thoughts about his unceremonious demotion; or at any rate he insisted on rambling on for a while before turning over his office, wearing down the already tired Heinrici with a barrage of semi-coherent details about the operations of Army Group Vistula to date.

Heinrici was an old general who looked like an old general— a short, grey-haired, bespectacled, uninspired but tough and competent man. He had been raised in a devout Protestant family and had adhered to his religious convictions throughout the brief tumultuous history of the Third Reich. His attitude towards the leadership, towards Nazi pomp and pageantry, vacillated between contempt and indifference.

He was still too preocupied trying to sort out his own thoughts to feel much contempt for Himmler; he only wished the man would finish talking and be gone so he could get on with his job.

Himmler droned on; as a speaker, he possessed the ability to lull people to sleep. At last the telephone rang. General Busse was at the other end of the line and he recited the following news. Zhukov's armies on the Oder front had just attacked and cut off Kustrin; in doing so, the two Soviet bridgeheads had linked up to form one massive platform on the west bank of the river. The SS Reichsfuhrer listened to all this and then handed the phone over to Heinrici, saying,

"All right, you're in command now. Please give the appropriate orders."[3]

Heinrici took the receiver and told Busse to counterattack the next morning. These were the first words he had spoken to the man who would be his most important subordinate for the coming final battles.

Before departing, Himmler off-handedly mentioned that he had taken steps to initiate peace talks with the Western Allies. Heinrici, dazed by this casual reference to high treason, said nothing. Then Himmler took his leave and Heinrici simply banished the man from his mind, telephoning General Busse again and talking long into the night.

March 23rd: First Attempt to Re-Open the Kustrin Corridor

Busse did not wait for the next day but launched a counterattack that same night. This counterattack had nothing to do with the long-planned operation coming out of Frankfurt—it was rather an immediate response to an emergency that for the German High Command could not have come at a worse time. The situation was as follows:

Kustrin, and a long narrow corridor leading west from Kustrin, lay between the two Russian bridgeheads on the Oder. For months now Zhukov had been ordering local attacks against this corridor in order to sever it and join his two bridgeheads together, thus to create a single massive platform from which to launch the final assault on Berlin.

It was a minor miracle that these local battles to shut off the Kustrin corridor had not succeeded weeks earlier. Mistakes had been made. The Soviets had suffered severe casualties in fruitless assaults against Fortress Kustrin itself, which was a considerably harder nut to crack than the long corridor. The garrison inside the city consisted in large part of SS police and SS paratrooper battalions, who fought like mad dogs in the face of insurmountable odds.

It should also be said that the constant pressure from Busse's divisions had obliged the Soviets to spend so much time defending their footholds on the west bank that it had been difficult to mount a concerted attack against the corridor. At last on March 22nd, with Busse's local attacks having largely petered out over the preceding weeks, Zhukov flung the full weight of his assaults against the flanks of the corridor, collapsing it that same day. Kustrin was now completely cut off, rendered impotent as a strategic position. It was of no more use to the Germans than Konigsberg, equally isolated two hundred miles to the east.

The most serious result of all this was that now Hitler's offensive coming out of Frankfurt would lose any operational importance it might have had. There was no point in Busse's panzer divisions attacking to reach a city isolated behind Russian lines. The corridor from Kustrin to the west had to be kept open in order to complete the encirclement of Zhukov's southern bridgehead; otherwise Busse's strike from Frankfurt might as well be advancing into empty space.

Busse, needing hardly any prompting from Heinrici's orders over the telephone, attempted to re-open the corridor at once. German doctrine held that an immediate counterattack after a Russian advance stood the best chance of success, catching the enemy in a disorganized state before he had a chance to solidify his gains and establish his defenses.

Indeed it was the only thing to do, but the forces available were simply not adequate. A night attack by two panzer grenadier divisions, spearheaded by the King Tigers of SS Panzer Abteilung 502, was a predictable failure. The SS tank crews had none of the advantages of other night attacks which had succeeded over the past few months, and they knew it. The essential factor—the element of surprise—would be non-existent. The Soviets were obviously aware of the critical importance of the corridor and would be expecting an instant German reaction to re-open it. From the moment Zhukov's attack succeeding in isolating Kustrin, PAK batteries and machine gun nests were set up to block the German counterattack; squadrons of T-34s were kept standing by on alert status.

In addition, a night attack necessitated a clearly mapped-out route of advance; otherwise the SS panzers would wind up milling about in confusion in the dark. The crews knew this too, and they knew that the terrain in front of them had been so thoroughly ravaged by shellfire over the preceding months that it would present a labyrinth of craters and unforeseen obstacles. The old veterans had a good feel for whether operations were likely to succeed or degenerate into a mess. But they had their orders, and they advanced into the corridor shortly after midnight on March 23rd.

As their crews had foreseen, the King Tigers became disorganized in the dark, losing sight of each other while navigating here and there to negotiate the torn-up and marshy countryside. In the impenetrable darkness they were sheltered from the Russian anti-tank nests, but they were also driving blind and many vehicles wound up stuck in bomb craters or invisible piles of rubble. A few worked their way free, but as dawn broke the attack had not achieved any real forward impetus; the critical moments of first light were wasted as the widely scattered tanks and infantry attempted to make contact with each other and re-assemble their formations.

By then it was too late. Soviet artillery fire rained down. PAK batteries were swung into action in such great numbers that the King Tigers still mobile were hit from every direction. A fruitless duel ensued: one anti-tank gun after another was blown to pieces, but others remained to fire in their places and the Tigers were either knocked out or too severely damaged to continue. The infantry support was scattered and chewed-up everywhere by the terrible deluge of Russian artillery and machine gun fire.

A long column of T-34s now entered the fray, bringing the usual results when faced head-to-head with German armor. Russian tanks were much easier to see than PAK nests, and the handful of King Tigers still in action annihilated the whole column at long range, leaving the stinking smoke to drift over the battlefield. But it made not the slightest difference; the attack was hopelessly stalled.

The King Tigers withdrew, many with tracks so badly shot-up they were lucky to reach the rear before becoming immobilized. The SS crews considered themselves fortunate to have gotten out of this fiasco alive. They passed other vehicles which had gotten stuck during the night only a short distance from the start-lines, recovery crews frantically working to repair them or pull them free. These men would be working at great personal risk far into the following night, going out into the battlefield to retrieve King Tigers disabled at the farthest points of the advance.

The Last Attack

So Kustrin remained isolated, and the main offensive from Frankfurt was still scheduled to go forward on March 27th. Conferring with Heinrici in Berlin, Hitler also wanted the attack against the Kustrin Corridor to continue. Heinrici declared it would be a waste of men, fuel, and ammunition, all of which were already in short supply for the strike force assembling at Frankfurt. The discussion degenerated into a kind of circular futility—unless the corridor were first re-opened, the attack from Frankfurt was liable to be a headlong march into disaster. Privately, Heinrici could only agree with this; if it were up to him, the Frankfurt attack would be called off as well. With fewer and fewer viable options, he would have preferred to continue Busse's work and concentrate on erecting a defensive curtain around Zhukov's bridgehead.

But he knew the uselessness of arguing about this with Hitler. The Frankfurt offensive would go forward as planned, regardless of how badly the situation on the Oder had deteriorated in the meantime.

Then apparently at the last moment Hitler again changed his mind. Whether this was due to Heinrici's arguments or his own realization of the futility of the situation, the Fuhrer relegated his long-awaited last-ditch attack out of Frankfurt to the dustbin.

The code name for this assault, "Operation Boomerang," reflects rather aptly on its premature demise. But Hitler still wanted to attack somewhere. Apparently all the key parties involved—Hitler, Guderian, Heinrici, and Busse—spent several days either in conference or sending numerous communiques to each other, in which they heatedly wrangled over operational details until a new plan emerged which really satisfied no one.

Though relieved to see the Frankfurt plan scrapped, Heinrici at last found himself agreeing to mount a second attack to re-open the corridor and relieve Kustrin. Neither he nor Busse had any enthusiasm for this idea, which seemingly had no better prospects for success than the first attack on March 23rd. And even if it did succeed, there would be little to be gained from it; without the other pincer arm coming up from Frankfurt there would be no opportunity to encircle and destroy any substantial number of Zhukov's forces.

In what must have been a mood of consummate frustration, Heinrici could reflect that at worst this second attack to re-open the corridor would simply fail; whereas Hitler's earlier proposal of sallying out of the Frankfurt bridgehead would probably have turned into an unmitigated disaster. But thoughts such as these offered little consolation to the new commander of Army Group Vistula. Everyone involved in these last-minute decisions—Heinrici, Busse, Guderian, Hitler—found themselves growing increasingly short-tempered and pessimistic, a mood which would result in a final cataclysmic confrontation between all parties a few days later.

But first the attack had to go forth. It would be the Third Reich's last major offensive effort of the war. The second attack to re-open the Kustrin corridor got underway on March 27th. The assault formations for 9th Army were as follows:

20th Panzer Grenadier Division
25th Panzer Grenadier Division
Fuhrer Panzer Grenadier Division
Panzer Division "Muncheberg"
Kampfgruppe "1001 Nights"
SS Panzer Abteilung 502

Notably absent from this assemblage was the Kurmark Panzer Grenadier Division, which had entered the fray in early February as one of the Reich's strongest remaining armored units, but which was by now nearly bled-out after the ceaseless fighting around the Reitwein Spur. Kurmark was still in position along this ridge; from the heights General Langkeit's exhausted grenadiers would have an excellent view of this final offensive crossing the valley floor just to the north.

20th Panzer Grenadier and Fuhrer Grenadier had just been transferred to the Oder Front from General Schorner's command in Silesia. By now the men of General Mader's Fuhrer Grenadier Division must have felt themselves part of a travelling circus. They had counterattacked in Pomerania as part of Sonnenwende in February; they had counterattacked at Lauban in Silesia in early March; now they would counterattack again across the devastated marshlands of the Oder Valley.

25th Panzer Grenadier had already had its fill of the fighting around the Kustrin Corridor in February. They had only recently been pulled out of the line and sent down to Frankfurt as one of the spearheads for "Operation Boomerang." With this operation now discarded, they were hastily turned around and marched back north to their earlier combat zone.

Though bearing a quaint name reminiscent of some Grimm Brothers fairy tale, Panzer Division "Muncheberg" was a powerful force comprising both Panther and Tiger detachments. This unit under General Mummert had been held in 9th Army reserve until early March and was probably the most formidable remaining armored division along the Oder. The even more quaintly named Kampfgruppe "1001 Nights" was an armored detachment equipped with about fifty Hetzers—excellent vehicles when deployed in ambush, but with their thin armor they were ill-suited to an all-out attack.

We have already followed the King Tigers of SS Panzer Abteilung 502 as they spearheaded the first attack on March 23rd. By March 27th they were ready—more or less—for this next attempt, their maintenance crews having worked themselves into a state of exhaustion over the few intervening days, towing back damaged tanks from the battlefield under enemy fire and then staying awake almost around the clock to render them combatworthy again.

Once again a night attack was in order, although this time the jump-off was pushed back from midnight to 0300 hours. Ostensibly the assault groups would still be sheltered by an initial interval of darkness, though hopefully with a shorter period before daybreak they would not lose cohesion as they had done on March 23rd.

But in fact the entire sorry affair on March 27th was almost an exact replay of the fiasco four days earlier. Though the German assault force was considerably stronger, so by this time were the Soviet defenses all around the approaches to the corridor. The difficulties that beset SS Panzer Abteilung 502 right from the start were so much the same that only upon close reading of combat reports from this unit is it possible to distinguish the first attack from the second.

Once again the King Tigers were hindered by having to negotiate the torn-up ground in the dark—"the bright flames from our exhaust pipes tended to blind us rather than illuminate our path."[4] Once again the heavy tanks were slowed to a crawl by the maze of bomb craters, barbed wire entanglements, and above all dense mine belts; one by one the King Tigers either bogged down or were disabled by the mines the Soviets had laid everywhere during the preceding days. As dawn broke the accompanying infantry—soldiers from the 20th Panzer Grenadier Division—were again observed to be scattered in confused groups after advancing in the dark.

As the rising sun burned away the early mist they were hammered mercilessly by Russian artillery and machine gun fire. The shelling was so overwhelming that combat reports from 20th Panzer Grenadier describe large groups of men breaking down entirely and fleeing in panic towards the rear. Eyewitness reports from the SS King Tigers in fact give a somewhat more charitable description of the scene:

> Enemy machine guns forced the charging lines to the ground. Death defying groups of infantrymen rose up again, charged into the raging fire and tried to reach the enemy trenches, only to collapse to the ground upon being hit one after the other. MGs hammered incessantly from the barbed wire.
>
> Defensive fire from enemy artillery blanketed the sector of the attack. The assault companies sought cover in the endless numbers of craters. Suddenly the vast brown fields appeared empty and abandoned, a

landscape of craters plowed over time and again by the shells.[5]

The SS panzer crews also witnessed a suicidal charge by a phalanx of 20th Panzer Grenadier's armored halftracks. The infantry was hopelessly stalled by dense belts of barbed wire, massacred where they stood or where they lay; the King Tigers just behind were likewise stalled by the densely seeded mines. The halftracks then came charging at high speed through this inferno, laying smoke to cover their advance, disregarding the mines and forcing an opening in the barbed wire by plowing right over it. The infantry and a few of the King Tigers followed in their wake, only to be stalled again as relentless Soviet fire poured in from both flanks of this momentary breakthrough.

It was probably around this time that the infantry lost hope and began falling back in disorder. The King Tigers remained out on the battlefield throughout the afternoon, shooting up Soviet PAK batteries and being shot up in return, as well as knocking out a few T-34s that appeared almost superfluously in the distance. At one point five King Tigers were jumbled up within a few yards of each other, all disabled by mines. In every respect the day seemed no more than a nightmarish flashback to the events of March 23rd. To cap it off the recovery crews (one begins to develop a great deal of sympathy for these men) again drove their trucks and prime movers out into the combat zone, there to undergo the arduous and maddening ordeal of towing the immobilized 68-ton tanks to the rear under heavy fire.

A horrifying and confusing account of this battle comes from Werner Adamczyk, the gun layer last seen retreating from the Vistula with 20th Panzer Grenadier Division back in January, after being nearly buried alive by Russian barrage fire.

Most of these retreating divisions had been incorporated into Schorner's Army Group Center in Silesia. It will be recalled that 1st Ukrainian Front under General Konev had crossed the Oder in this area and pushed westward to the Neisse, where the Germans were able to establish a new defensive line that would hold firm until the end of April. Adamczyk and 20th Panzer Grenadier were initially assigned to this sector along the Neisse, where the front remained relatively quiet in places. 20th Panzer Grenadier, however, was then transferred to Busse's 9th Army during the last week of March, there to participate in the failed attack against Kustrin described above.

The timing of this move from the Neisse to the Kustrin area makes Adamczyk's own recollections very difficult to follow. In addition, he was about to undergo his single worst experience of the war, which may account for much of the confusion in his memory.

The question is whether this nightmarish episode took place somewhere along the Neisse or during the Kustrin attack on March 27th. Adamczyk remembers being taken from his artillery battery to join the depleted ranks of the infantry in the forward trenches. He was not happy with this move; the infantry always had the worst of everything. He recalls that at some point near the end of March he was caught in the middle of an enormous Russian artillery barrage, the worst since his earlier ordeal along the Vistula.

> I saw whole bodies flying through the air. A shell hit right in front of me. The trench caved in and buried the periscope. I managed to crawl out of the mess, but I did not know where to go. Some armored troop carriers were coming up and I saw the infantry jumping on them, then they left in a hurry back to the rear.[6]

Adamczyk abandoned his demolished position and began fleeing in terror. Impenetrable smoke lay everywhere and he lost all sense of direction. He stumbled and rolled to the bottom of a large crater, landing upon a corpse embedded in the muck. He had been running in such panic that he now found himself exhausted; several times he tried to crawl out of the crater, but was too spent to get to the top. At last he settled back down at the bottom with the dead man, his mind numbed by apathy and fatigue.

After a while he noticed that the barrage had lifted. He finally managed to get out of the shellhole and began walking in a stupor towards the rear. He saw what he took to be a German battery firing in the distance and headed in that direction. For about half a mile he passed through the worst carnage he had ever seen, bodies littered in every direction and shattered vehicles belching out smoke and flame.

> I came to the conclusion that this must be an illusion. I must be dead now; yes, this must be how it is when one is dead.
> Some strange feeling of weightlessness came over me. I did not feel my feet anymore, yet I was still moving towards the firing battery. A shock such as I had never experienced before went through me. "This cannot be real anymore, what am I going to do?" I was screaming inside.[7]

Adamczyk was in a state of shock; intense shelling had had this effect on him and countless other men throughout the war. But I have never come across any other account in which the victim was so traumatized that he experienced the delusion that he was actually dead. There may have been others who experienced this sensation momentarily, but for Adamczyk the episode went on for a much longer time. He recalls walking on and on towards the distant German battery; only upon reaching it does he somehow snap out of his spell, though he seems unable to recall the exact moment when this happened. The next he knew he was swept up in a further chaotic retreat deep into the German rear, much like the flight from the Vistula two months before.

I have placed this incident at the time of 20th Panzer Grenadier's horrendous attack and subsequent flight in front of Kustrin on March 27th. So many of the details remembered by Adamczyk match other accounts of this debacle—especially the divisional history's description of men fleeing in panic from the Russian shellfire—that the conclusion seems fairly obvious.

But in the minds of men who lived through those days, nothing is ever so clear-cut. In Adamczyk's description the Russians were all on the far side of the river (he admits not remembering whether it was the Oder or the Neisse); whereas obviously Zhukov's bridgeheads at Kustrin were already on the German side of the river. He also says that after retreating from the shellfire, his unit boarded onto trucks and drove north for some hours, and only then did he (and presumably the rest of 20th Panzer Grenadier) arrive in the Kustrin area.

Clearly, the implication is that Adamczyk's delusion of death occurred during some battle along the Neisse, before the transfer to Kustrin. And indeed it is possible that all this happened in the way that he remembered it, though other accounts of his division's movements would seem to contradict him. As already mentioned, the German front along the Neisse remained stable till almost the end of the war; at least during March, there were no panic-stricken retreats from this river line. It seems more likely that Adamczyk's memory for dates and places has become blurred for this period—not surprisingly, in light of the terrible shock he had just suffered. On the other hand, nothing is more common than contradictory reports from amidst the "fog of battle"; it is conceivable that what he was describing was no more than a local Russian barrage along the Neisse, which from his own point of view became magnified into one of the worst battles of the war. In the end there is no way to know for sure exactly where this incident took place, no more than one can know for sure how Heinz Landau managed to so easily slip in and out of the holocaust at Budapest. But all the most vivid details point to the Kustrin battle.

In the sectors of the other attacking divisions, the events of March 27th varied only little from the scenes described above. The Fuhrer Grenadier Division, supported by one of Muncheberg's panzer battalions, made only slight progress into the Kustrin corridor before being pinned down; then General Mader's men somehow found the wherewithal to resume the attack in the late afternoon, advancing another few hundred yards through muddy woods and wrecked hamlets before darkness fell. That was as far as they got, still nowhere near the Oder.

Muncheberg's other panzer battalion, together with the Hetzers of Kampfgruppe "1001 Nights," was on the far left or northern wing of the attack. "1001 Nights" took nearly one hundred percent casualties, advancing bravely for several miles through a curtain of annihilation. The Hetzers were placed in the inane position of having to drive one by one by through a railroad underpass, a maneuver which lasted until after sunrise and created a traffic jam which the Russian PAK gunners and artillery observers must have enjoyed enormously.

After negotiating the underpass the tank destroyers formed into smaller groups and resumed the attack, but by then it was too late. By afternoon 25 out of 49 Hetzers had been knocked out, most likely permanently; with their thin armor plate almost all of these casualties would probably have been smoking unsalvageable wrecks. These were appalling losses for a German armored unit to suffer over the course of one day. "1001 Nights," which also comprised three companies of supporting infantry, suffered over 400 killed and wounded from an original complement of about 500 men.

So ended the last German attack of the war. The panzers and panzer grenadiers had started from forward positions beneath the Seelowe Heights, and at best had gained only a few hundred yards of ground in the direction of the corridor. The Soviets had lost nothing whatsoever of any importance.

Aftermath—the Last Confrontation between Guderian and Hitler

If anything the second Kustrin attack fared even worse than the first. By this time Zhukov's single unified bridgehead bore not the slightest resemblance to the scattered and precarious footholds of early February. The ice had long since melted and countless numbers of infantry, tanks, and PAK batteries had crossed the Oder via numerous pontoon bridges. Many of the massed heavy artillery batteries still remained behind on the east bank, but they were easily capable of unleashing a hurricane of fire on any target within the Oder valley or on the Seelowe Heights beyond. By the end of March Zhukov had had enough time to make his bridgehead nearly impregnable. The concentrations of men and weapons inside these few square miles would surely have equalled the concentrations inside the Kursk bulge in 1943, which had been Zhukov's previous masterpiece of deeply-echeloned defense.

And as at Kursk, these deep echelons of men and weapons formed a two-edged sword, blunting German attacks nearly in their tracks while simultaneously providing a platform for Zhukov's own massive offensive. And now there could be little doubt that the long wait for this final Soviet offensive would be over with very soon.

* * *

The wretched battlefield drama of March 27th was followed the next day by a heated personal drama at Fuhrer headquarters.

Guderian was there, along with the usual OKW team of Keitel and Jodl and other lesser personalities among the staff generals.

General Busse was also there, summoned from the front by Hitler to account for 9th Army's miserable performance the day before.

General Heinrici was not present, but he had already vented his disgust in an earlier phone call to Guderian. If Heinrici had any particular claim to fame, it was for maintaining a calm and stoic demeanor in the face of a crisis; this trait was well-remembered by officers who had served under him during a number of defensive battles in Russia. But now Heinrici could no longer contain himself.

Having served as commander of Army Group Vistula for less than a week, he had found operational control over matters eluding his grasp with almost every passing hour, with scarcely a single opportunity to set his own house in order. He had just seen the best divisions of his most important resource, 9th Army, squandered in an attack that had gone against all his better instincts. He couldn't stand it and lashed out abusively at Guderian. Guderian, to his credit, appears to have listened patiently to Heinrici's outburst; the two were old colleagues who had known and liked each other for a long time. Clearly he had no difficulty putting himself in Heinrici's place and understanding the other man's frustration. In fact during the hours immediately after the attack Guderian had defended both Heinrici and Busse against another tirade from Hitler, who naturally wanted to blame the whole fiasco on the two front-line generals. This exchange would be only the prelude to the still more heated conference the following day, to which Busse himself had been summoned so he could face Hitler's wrath in person.

This meeting, on March 28th in the Reichskanzellerei, would be Guderian's last confrontation with Adolf Hitler.

It was a quiet early spring afternoon in the shocking rubble of the German capital city. Busse arrived from the front to make his report; he and Guderian entered the conference room together. As so many other generals had discovered in the past, making a report actually meant listening to Hitler's constant interruptions and abusive monologues. Though not a mild-mannered sort, Busse was a reliable National Socialist who had not lost his respect for the Fuhrer. For the most part he listened in silence as Hitler delivered nonsensical accusations about Busse's inadequate use of supporting artillery and the poor fighting spirit of 9th Army. Rather it was Guderian who found himself no longer able to endure listening to these absurdities.

He now interrupted Hitler and began defending Busse in the most vociferous terms. Busse had indeed used every last artillery shell allotted to him for the attack; it was not his fault that ammunition stocks had dwindled to such pathetic levels, and for Hitler to claim otherwise was insufferable. Reports vary as to the actual decibel level of Guderian's outburst at this moment. He was clearly quite angry, and some accounts describe him as being "nearly purple with rage," so much so that some of those present feared he and Hitler were on the verge of coming to blows.[8] Guderian bitterly called Hitler to account, not only for his criticism of Busse but for all of his obstinate and senseless decisions over the past few months: the idiocy of maintaining Army Group Kurland in its useless corner of Latvia, the idiocy of refusing to establish a defense in depth behind the Vistula Front, the idiocy of throwing almost half of the Reich's remaining tanks away in Hungary, on and on.

Hitler reacted with an apoplectic fury, the apotheosis of all the "foaming at the mouth" stereotypes so often used to describe him in later years. He matched Guderian's tirade with an even more violent tirade of his own, spewing out such an incoherent raft of accusations that those present could barely follow what he was saying, seeming at one point on the verge of flinging himself upon Guderian.

This may (or may not) be an exaggerated description of what was already a highly dramatic scene. In his memoirs Guderian states only that he firmly repeated the same things he had said in Busse's defense the day before. But other accounts now mention General Krebs having to lead Guderian out of the room for twenty minutes in order to give him a chance to calm down and regain his composure. Guderian's "purple" complexion may well have been an indication of his fury, though his colleagues had seen this same ugly hue on his face for months now, a constant reminder of his serious heart troubles.

Hitler's tone, when at length Guderian re-entered the room, was curiously subdued—again, somewhat in the manner of a man in the throes of a violent domestic argument who suddenly regains his composure in front of his embarrassed guests.

He rather calmly suggested that Guderian take a six-week leave of absence from his post in order to give his heart a rest. Some authorities have interpreted these remarks as Hitler's way of dismissing Guderian for good; after all, by the time another six weeks had passed the war would be over. But Hitler had no way of knowing this. As far as he was concerned, even while defeat was looming larger than ever, the war might still drag on indefinitely, and he was still as determined as ever to make sure that it did.

By now he may have been thoroughly weary of this endlessly confrontational relationship with his chief of staff. But certainly his concern for Guderian's health was also genuine; the man's heart problems were as visible to Hitler as to any of Guderian's other colleagues.

In fact Hitler had already asked Guderian to take a leave of absence a week before the present meeting; at that point Guderian had refused, declaring that no suitable general was available to replace him. This attitude may have seemed the height of arrogance, but what Guderian actually had in mind was that the best available candidates—in his view either General Wenck or General Krebs—were both recovering from serious injury, Wenck from his automobile accident and Krebs from wounds suffered during an air raid on March 15th. At that time Guderian had told Hitler he would take his leave of absence when one or the other of these men had recovered enough to return to duty. Rather than pressing the issue, Hitler had accepted the compromise.

But all this had come to pass a week earlier. When Hitler asked Guderian to step down a second time on March 28th, the exhausted general put up no further arguments. By this time General Wenck was almost fully recovered, and the same was true for General Krebs—who as we saw a moment ago was now well enough to attend this turbulent conference. As it turned out, Krebs would be the one to succeed Guderian as OKH chief of staff.

For Guderian it was all over, though even now neither he nor his supreme commander was fully aware of this. The conference was not yet finished, but Guderian apparently felt his presence was no longer required and made to leave the room. He had opened the door and was about to walk out when Hitler called him back and requested that he stay until the meeting was concluded. Guderian's state of mind at this point can hardly be imagined, though perhaps a kind of dazed exhaustion may have succeeded his inner turmoil. He returned to his seat and listened in silence while the conference—as these meetings always seemed to do—dragged on interminably. Hitler refrained from any further criticism of General Busse, and a few times asked Guderian to comment on certain matters, with Guderian responding tiredly and quietly. When the fateful conference ended a few hours later his only reaction was one of relief.

Hitler's parting words to this volatile and adversarial general were the following:

"Please do your best to get your health back. The next six weeks will be critical. Then I will have urgent need of you. In the meantime, where do you think you will go?"[9]

Again, a great deal of irony has been read into these final remarks, perhaps with some justification. The more cynical view has Hitler simply wishing to be kept informed of Guderian's whereabouts, no doubt with the suspicion that Guderian might suddenly disappear or even start fomenting another conspiracy if he were not closely watched. No one will ever know Hitler's exact thoughts at this moment, but on the other hand it seems equally likely that he was speaking quite sincerely. Certainly it is possible that he had pondered firing Guderian once and for all. But he had been provoked by the general again and again, and at this point Hitler had no reason not to dismiss him for good if such was his desire. Instead, he declared that he would need him again, and if the war had dragged on longer than it did Guderian may well have found himself back at Hitler's side. The Fuhrer's peculiar attitude of respect for Guderian—which at times seemed almost to reach an atmosphere of intimacy—persisted.

The two men would never see each other again. As to where Guderian intended to take his rest cure, he could only offer the sardonic reply that it would have to be someplace not likely to be overrun by the enemy within the next 48 hours.

He left the building and stepped out into late afternoon sunshine. Perhaps he already intuited that this leave of absence would indeed become permanent. He drove through the sunny and unimaginable ruins of the city that to date had been bombed more continuously than any city in history. He met his wife at their residence in the suburb of Zossen. He told her he had been dismissed and they embraced each other with relief. The two of them headed south for the mountains.

WEEKS IN APRIL, YEARS IN MAY

The Fate of Berlin is Sealed on the Seelowe Heights; Brief Summary of a Horrible Battle

Fortress Kustrin, now cut off behind Russian lines, fell at last on March 30th. In April there remained only for the Soviets to attack, destroy Berlin and end the war.

Zhukov began his great offensive against 9th Army on the Seelowe Heights on April 16th. A titanic pre-dawn barrage surpassed in intensity the deluge of shells along the Vistula in January. It was the greatest assemblage of artillery power in the history of warfare.

The barrage—which could easily be heard as far away as Berlin—was spectacular and terrifying but not entirely effective. Since the failed attempt to relieve Kustrin on March 27th, General Heinrici had had time to more effectively deploy Army Group Vistula. In particular he had ordered Busse's 9th Army to withdraw between one and two miles from their forward positions in the Oder Valley. Thus much of the annihilating force of Zhukov's rockets and artillery shells fell on empty trenches.

It was a good move, the first indication that the Russian breakout from the Oder was not going to resemble their earlier breakout from the Vistula. The barrage did not entirely miss its target, and German defenders resorted to different phrases to describe such incredible shelling; the most common comparison was with being caught in the middle of an earthquake. But Zhukov's hoped-for results of total devastation and demoralization of the enemy did not follow this time. Instead, the four days that followed along the Seelowe Heights evolved into one of the bloodiest and hardest-fought battles of the war.

The desperate drama of this conflict was obscured somewhat by the seeming inevitability of its outcome. With a more than 5:1 advantage in men and a nearly 10:1 advantage in weapons, it appeared a foregone conclusion that Zhukov would push through 9th Army's defenses—as indeed he did on April 19th. But German resistance was well-organized and ferocious, and Soviet casualties in the "death valley" below the heights were astronomical. The four day period from April 16th to 19th saw as great a blood-letting for the Russians as any other similar stretch of time during the last two years of the war.

By the end of the first day, Soviet gains were so minimal and casualties so high that General Busse was able to record "a great defensive success" (Abwehrerfolg) in the combat log of 9th Army.[1] Such a phrase may have reflected an unreal mood of optimism at this point in the war; on the other hand, it was no more than a simple statement of the truth, at least for the moment. Apart from the high ground they already held on the Reitwein Spur, the Soviets had been entirely confined to the flat terrain down in the valley. Enormous waves of attacking infantry had been vaporized by the massed concentration of German guns firing from the Seelowe Heights. For a Western nation, a day of such carnage would probably have been remembered as a national tragedy—as July 1st 1916 is remembered in Great Britain to commemorate the first day of the Battle of the Somme. And indeed, Soviet losses during this entire four-day period would closely rival British losses during the first four days of the Somme battle. Photographs of the densely compacted waves of Soviet infantry advancing across the mud and smoke of the Oder Valley would also recall similar grim scenes from the First World War.

The Russians, of course, had long had a more fatalistic outlook regarding human loss. Nonetheless Zhukov, who had an excellent view of the carnage from an observation post atop the Reitwein Spur, was displeased and deeply worried by the results of the first day. In his anxiety he had compounded his difficulties by releasing his tank armies too early. As always the squadrons of T-34s had been held in reserve, waiting for the critical moment when the attacking formations of infantry, Stalin tanks, and self-propelled assault guns had forged a breach in the German lines. Late-war Soviet operations had used this tactic successfully again and again, but the offensive of April 16th would not proceed so smoothly.

The assault formations were unable to gain a foothold anywhere on the Seelowe Heights, much less forge an actual breach through which the T-34s could pour into the German rear. Frustrated by the lack of progress, Zhukov released the tank armies anyway, hoping they might simply bludgeon their way through. But they did not. Traffic snarls developed within the horribly compacted masses of men and vehicles in the Oder Valley; under urgent orders to move forward, the tank crews at times simply plowed through their own infantry, crushing more than a few who could not get out of the way. Even these brutal methods could not completely untangle these traffic jams. When the T-34s did finally advance within range of the German guns, Soviet armored losses escalated as quickly as those of the infantry. The German tank crews and PAK gunners on the heights were placed in a peculiar position during these four violent days. They knew they were fighting with their backs to the wall, and that almost certainly the Russians would eventually overwhelm them and wipe them out. But in the meantime they experienced hours of strange elation, during which they picked off Soviet tanks one after the other as if in a shooting gallery. At different points during the battle entire columns—as many as fifty T-34s at once—were annihilated within less than an hour by King Tigers or 88mm flak batteries set up in ambush positions.

The battle on the ground was matched by savage aerial combat overhead. Every available German plane, tanked up with almost the last gallons of fuel remaining to the Luftwaffe, flew nonstop sorties over the Oder Valley, either strafing Zhukov's troops or attacking the pontoon bridges across the river. British and American troops on the Western Front, who had seen almost no German aircraft in the skies for months on end, would have been shocked by this aerial display. One Special Operations Unit had even been trained in a deliberate imitation of Japanese kamikaze tactics; a few of these suicide pilots succeeded in crashing their planes into the Soviet bridges.

Also on the scene were some of the bizarre "Mistel" weapons, in which pilots in fighter planes rode piggyback on unmanned JU-88 bombers loaded with high explosives. The engines of both planes were used to get this weird assembly off the ground, with the fighter riding atop a tall metal gantry bolted to the back of the bomber. Once over the target, the pilot released the bomber and used remote control to guide it down against the bridges, sometimes with devastating results, though on the whole these awkward-looking craft (called "Father and Son" by Landsers watching them in action from the Seelowe Heights) were not very accurate.

Not surprisingly, the Red Air Force was even more active above the battlefield, strafing and bombing the terrible wall of German guns atop the heights. The close support provided by Stormoviks and A-20s would prove to be critical over the next few days, but before then the massed batteries of 88mm's effectively brought Zhukov's waves of men and tanks to a dead stop. Throughout the first day and well into the second, the Germans appeared to be on the verge of winning what was supposed to have been the war's final battle.

In its way, the difficult earlier decision to abandon the German counterattack from the Frankfurt bridgehead was now paying dividends. Almost certainly the five panzer and panzer grenadier divisions slated for that operation would have been annihilated somewhere in Zhukov's rear areas by the overwhelming material superiority of his forces. Unable to retreat to safety across the Oder, the strike force for "Operation Boomerang" would have been erased from the German order of battle.

The alternate plan of attacking from the west bank towards Kustrin on March 27th had satisfied no one, and with good reason. But at least the German armored units involved in that fiasco had been able to withdraw once the attack had failed; despite high losses, all of these divisions and battle groups had survived to fight another day. On April 16th, all of them were still available to defend the Seelowe Heights, inflicting their own considerable havoc on the Soviet attackers. Fighting from ambush positions instead of charging headlong into enemy mine belts and barrage fire, many German armored units suffered remarkably low casualties on April 16th. One battalion of King Tigers lost only two men killed, while exacting the huge toll already mentioned against the Russian armor advancing across the valley floor.

Zhukov's long-awaited final offensive found itself butting against a stone wall. With 9th Army so badly depleted after months of combat in the Oder Valley, savage resistance must have come as a rude shock to the Soviet commanders.

At this point one might begin to wonder about the German tactic of launching unrelenting counterattacks against the Soviet invasion in 1945. How much stronger would this defensive curtain along the Seelowe Heights have been if so many powerful units had not been squandered over the preceding months? So many tanks and men had already been thrown away, in Pomerania in February, in Hungary in March, and in the Oder Valley during all the preceding months of stalemate. With the exception of General Schorner's operations in Silesia, these continual counterattacks had led to minimal gains and crucial losses, losses which could never be made good again.

The same pattern had developed on the Western Front. Perhaps the most significant result of the Ardennes attack back in December had been the loss of so much German armor without any real strategic benefit. Prior to the Battle of the Bulge, the Germans had conducted a highly successful static defense against the Western Allies throughout the autumn of 1944. American attempts to breach the Siegfried Line in October and November had failed again and again; subsequently these costly and demoralizing battles have received only scant attention from American histories of the war in Europe. Conceivably, if Hitler had not launched the Ardennes counterattack, such a static defense might have continued to exact high casualties from the Western Allies and stalled their march into Germany long into 1945.[2]

But again it is safe to say that the wisest strategy always becomes clearer with the advantage of hindsight. To argue the pros and cons of German military operations during the final months of the war must necessarily evolve into a complex debate involving a multitude of factors. On the Eastern Front in particular the Third Reich was essentially facing a no-win situation—Germany no longer had the resources to conduct an adequate static defense all the way from Hungary to the Baltic. The collapse of the Vistula Front in January had demonstrated this beyond a doubt. All the same, one cannot help but ponder the few instances when strong defensive barriers led to severe maulings of Soviet attacks. The great offensives against the Courland Peninsula would last until the end of the war without budging the Germans from their defenses there.

Likewise, these opening phases of Zhukov's final assault against Berlin saw almost no significant gains. But Zhukov's reputation as a general who knew how to win the key battles was not without foundation. His armies might suffer enormous, even obscene, numbers of dead and wounded, but he invariably made certain that he had enough reserves on hand to hammer the enemy into submission. His assault on the Seelowe Heights was the epitome of this kind of fighting.

The second day, April 17th, followed much the same pattern as the first. The Soviets managed to oust 9th Army from a number of wrecked villages on the valley floor; slowly they battled their way across the numerous bitterly defended dykes and canals that threaded the marshland; by day's end they had gained footholds here and there at the base of the heights. But still they had not broken through; still the divisions of 9th Army held out atop the high ground. General Busse recorded another "Abwehrerfolg" in his diary at the end of the second day. Perhaps he felt no need to record the obvious drawback to this situation—it was already clear enough that too many more days of such "defensive successes" would result in his under-manned divisions being ground down to nothing. Germany had no meaningful reserves left; Germany really had nothing left at all. The decisive final battle for Berlin would not be fought inside the capital itself; it would take place here and only here, along the Seelowe Heights.

On the other side, Zhukov's mood of worry and frustration intensified. His subordinate commanders—notably the obstreperous Chuikov—were becoming disillusioned about the supposedly well-laid plans for the attack. In Moscow, Stalin was also worried and angry; reports indicate that after the first day he refused to communicate further with Zhukov, choosing to wait for news of success—or failure—behind an unnerving wall of silence.

But there is no point in trying to keep the reader in suspense when the outcome is known to all. The depleted units of 9th Army could not hold out indefinitely against the most densely concentrated assembly of armed force the world had ever seen. No more than the Spartans could have held out in Thermopylae against Xerxes. On the third day the repeated sledgehammer blows began to crumble the German front. The first two days had been fought in windy and overcast weather. On the third day, April 18th, fine spring sunshine fell across the whole battlefield, though probably much diffused by the rolling clouds of smoke and debris. The first sign of collapse came from the northern wing, at the boundary line between Busse's 9th Army and von Manteuffel's 3rd Panzer Army defending the lower reaches of the Oder. Here the remnants of the 5th Jaeger Division—whom we last saw at the beginning of March, retreating from the mainland to Wollin Island at the mouth of the Oder—were in position, along with several other recently scraped-together divisions and Volksturm units. The Soviets broke through the defenses of the badly undermanned jaeger companies at the village of Wriezen, threatening to envelop the northern rear areas of 9th Army.

At the same time, the Soviets at last made headway onto the Seelowe Heights in the center of the line, directly west of Kustrin. Here the 9th Parachute Division, the last of the elite Fallschirmjaeger units to be created, had been nearly wiped out over the preceding two days, defending the low ground at the base of the heights almost to the last man. Several companies of Skorzeny's commandos had been assigned to join the paratroopers, suffering the same terrible casualties.

These various groups of commandos and airborne soldiers comprised some of the most determined fighting men Germany still possessed, but unfortunately a parachute division was intrinsically lacking in heavy weapons. Despite support from the gun batteries lined along the heights, it was impossible to stop the Russians, who had marshaled their greatest strength in this area, from breaking through. 9th Parachute's commander General Brauer was then sacked after a phone call from none other than Herman Goering, who still perceived the parachutists as belonging to the Luftwaffe and thus saw fit to meddle with General Heinrici's chain of command. Brauer's executive officer Colonel Herrmann was put in charge of the survivors; in a devastated farmhouse at the base of the heights this man consoled Brauer over his unwarranted removal. The general listened in silence.

Yet having gained the high ground, the Russians continued to take staggering losses. Soviet armored columns finally crossed the Seelowe Heights, the crews of the T-34s no doubt smelling the moment of the decisive breakthrough. But it was not yet to be. They were now on the road to Berlin with no further natural obstacles in their path, but just behind the crest of the heights the last German armored reserves were again waiting in ambush.

Perhaps overconfident, thinking victory was within their grasp (as indeed it was, though most of these Russian tank crews would be dead within minutes), the T-34s surged westward along the highway almost as if on parade. Waiting for them near the village of Reichenberg were the Danes and Norwegians of the

SS Nordland Division, supported by the King Tigers of SS Panzer Abteilung 503. These two units had been fighting side by side ever since the relief of Arnswalde during Operation Sonnen-wende in February; they had been transferred to 9th Army from 3rd Panzer Army only days earlier. Their arrival proved fortuitous for the Germans and deadly for the Russians. Out of seventy odd T-34s rolling along the highway towards Reichenberg, nearly fifty were destroyed in another brief episode of mayhem and hysteria. Losses among the Danes, Norwegians, and the German King Tiger crews were negligible.

A nearly identical ambush was laid a few miles to the south, where a T-34 column belonging to Chuikov's 8th Guards Army had just crested the heights and was jammed up "head to toe" along another main road leading to the west, this time near the village of Diederhof.[3] A battle group comprising armored elements of Muncheberg, 20th Panzer Grenadier, and SS Panzer Abteilung 502 was able to exact revenge for their losses suffered during the earlier bloody attacks against Kustrin. Soviet infantry was riding on the decks of Chuikov's long column of T-34s, looking to be the first into Berlin. The German ambushers opened fire and shredded men and tanks in another short, horrible encounter, forcing Chuikov to order a hasty retreat back to the reverse slope of the heights.

This was at least the third instance in as many days in which Soviet tanks had advanced into such devastating traps. But these were to be the last "defensive successes," and they had little significance now. Zhukov's forces were atop the Seelowe Heights and this terrible battle of attrition had bled 9th Army to the bone. Soviet losses had been far higher, but they could be replaced; for 9th Army, the only remaining replacements were a few bus-loads of cannon fodder sent out from Berlin.

By afternoon of April 18th Soviet infantry and tanks in seemingly endless numbers were climbing the heights at other points where German tanks were now too few to drive them back. The Russians were exhausted and the critical breakout would not take place until the fourth day of the attack; but the battle was essentially over as evening fell on the third day. The road to Berlin was open and would not be barred again.

* * *

We turn now to the survivors of this month of April, along the Oder Front, and along all the other fronts from Vienna to Pillau. Here are their accounts of the end.

Heinz Landau on the Seelowe Heights

Heinz Landau, the Rumanian Saxon, was able to rejoin the SS Wiking Division after his mysterious escape from Budapest. Wiking itself only barely escaped encirclement after the Fruhlingserwachen debacle, breaking out of the town of Stuhlweissenberg and heading west in the chaotic retreat to the Austrian border. Like all the other Waffen SS divisions in Hungary, Wiking's fighting strength had by now nearly disintegrated. The remnants would fight on around Vienna and the Tyrolean Alps, but for some unexplained reason Landau and a few other Wiking comrades were despatched to Berlin for re-assignment. His wartime career continued to follow its own highly idiosyncratic path.

Enroute to Berlin he witnessed a ghastly bombing raid by the American 8th Air Force. Landau's train had just pulled into Regensberg station in Bavaria when the bombs began to fall. A hospital train on a nearby siding was blown to pieces. When the raid was over he emerged from shelter to see an endless debris field of severed limbs and torsoes, heads, and viscera. Landau found himself covered head to toe with gore splattered from these human remains. After so many years on the Eastern Front, this brief visit by the Americans had produced the most frightful carnage he would see during the war.

He continued to Berlin on foot, passing several nights in peasant cottages in the mountains, still untouched by the war. He hitched rides in army vehicles, walked the rest of the time, and at last caught a train which brought him into Berlin on the night of April 19th.

The next day he was on his way to the Seelowe Heights inferno, aboard a truck fueled by a mixture of wood and sawdust. He had been placed in command of a ragtag unit with green recruits ranging in age from fourteen to sixty. Landau didn't know whether to laugh or cry.

Some of these men were from RAD battalions, like those that had fought with General Raegenar's division at the beginning of the Oder Valley battles. Others were from Volksturm units, others were the miscellaneous survivors of various Army and SS units. Landau's group was part of Uberfallkommando Speer, or Special Ambush Group Speer. The task of this grandiosely named formation of 350 barely trained men was to stalk Russian tanks with panzerfausts. Apparently this group was named after Reich Armaments Minister Albert Speer, though the connection is obscure, perhaps having to do with the men culled from Speer's various organizations of laborers. Speer himself was never in command of this or any other military unit.

Attached to the Speer group was a sub-unit known as Sonderkommando Dora, which consisted of SS men equipped with panzerfausts and riding on bicycles back and forth along the Seelowe Heights, dismounting to ambush Soviet tanks wherever they saw them. After the war Guderian said about this strange formation: "They were brave men. Too bad about what happened to them." They were wiped out, of course.[4] And scurrying about on their bicycles with panzerfausts strapped to their backs, they must have presented a pathetically comical sight. But no matter their appearance—anyone carrying a panzerfaust was a deadly foe, and these men were determined and did manage to kill a large number of Russian tanks.

Meanwhile Landau and his men were unloaded a few miles behind the battle lines. They then marched up the more gradual western slope of the Seelowe Heights, reaching the crest and gazing down the steep eastern face at the valley below. (Landau refers to the east face as an "escarpment," which may give some idea of its suitability as a natural barrier.)

Although he remembers arriving in Berlin on April 19th, in all likelihood the date was a day or two earlier. The great battle was all but over by the 19th, whereas Landau's account from this point would suggest that he reached the heights while they were still in German hands.

His story continues with the usual sickening carnage in the face of hopeless odds. He was ordered to take his mostly teenaged crew into positions at the base of the escarpment, where the advancing Soviet tanks would come within the limited range of their panzerfausts. A group of paratroopers, most likely from the previously mentioned 9th Parachute Division, was already manning the trenches here. At one time among the Wehrmacht's elite fighting forces, the ranks of the Fallschirmjaeger had also been transformed by war's end; Landau saw only the scared faces of teenagers who looked little different from his own men. The Russian onslaught was not long in coming:

> I was watching the Ivans approaching from the top of our position, and it sent shivers down my spine. Tanks of assorted sizes but mostly T-34s in vast numbers, probably outnumbering our guns. How does one describe the sight of the Russian army on the move? I for one do not know. Even an army of ants is an understatement.[5]

This statement, and others like it from numerous eyewitnesses, would seem to belie some of the recent revisionist views about improved Red Army tactics later in the war. Perhaps Soviet tactics had improved in some respects since 1941, especially their ability to effectively coordinate large forces of tanks, infantry, and artillery. But this only meant that their attacks were no longer the hopelessly chaotic affairs they had been in the early years. Better organized or not, the Russian tanks and infantry still advanced in massed formations that invited massed slaughter from any concerted defense.

So it was in front of Landau's position at the base of the heights:

> Russian losses were colossal. I honestly do not think any other European nation could have survived this sort of carnage, but Ivan with his millions still managed to replace his losses instantly with twice the number lost. It reminded me of stories long since forgotten of many-headed Hydras, Dragons, two heads growing for each one severed.[6]

His reference to the mythical Hydra was echoed by many German veterans, who used this same term to describe the seemingly endless cycle of slaughter and rebirth that they saw in Red Army attacks.

Most of the carnage was inflicted by the 88mm flak batteries lining the heights above Landau and his men. He looked up to see "these hundreds of guns with barrels depressed at lower angles than I would have thought possible," firing down at the Russians swarming across the valley floor.[7] The whole area was littered with the smoking wrecks of T-34s, but, as mentioned by Landau a moment ago, the Soviets seemed to have more tanks than the Germans had guns to destroy them with.

A group of six Stukas arrived overhead, deposited their earth-shattering loads, then flew off again. Landau assumed they were from Rudel's squadron; German infantry always assumed Hans Rudel was flying overhead whenever they saw Stukas in action. But the one-legged pilot had not returned to the Oder Front after being shot down in February. In April he was flying his last sorties over General Schorner's front in Silesia.

The Soviet assault continued. The constant presence of the Luftwaffe during the first two days of the battle had dropped off severely by now, due to the German fuel crisis more than aircraft losses; whereas the Red Air Force was now overhead hour after hour, no longer hampered by the muddy winter conditions at their Polish air fields.

The Stormovik "Butcher" continued to live up to its nickname, with unending flights of these aircraft pounding Landau's position and the flak batteries on the high ground. While having a field day firing against Russian tanks, the 88mm's had little defense against these strafing attacks, nor against the hurricane of fire still being unleashed by the Russian artillery on the east bank of the river. One by one the deadly German guns were knocked out.

At the base of the escarpment Landau's men crawled forward to ambush T-34s with their panzerfausts, managing to knock out a few but dying "like flies" under fire from the enemy artillery and the Russian infantry escorting the tanks. There were no medics to be seen anywhere and Landau assigned some of his youngsters to bandage the wounded, only to find they were even less prepared to administer first-aid than to fire their weapons. The screams of their horribly mutilated comrades had reduced them to a helpless state of shock. Thus Landau and his few veteran NCOs had to spend much of the day tending to the wounded instead of fighting,

bandaging hideous wounds on a fourteen or fifteen year old, either screaming with pain or terror or biting his teeth together to the breaking point. It was among the most depressing tasks any of us had ever faced.[8]

The Russian tanks and infantry had still not broken through their lines. But apparently the German defenses had been over-run elsewhere to the north and south. A flak gunner descended the escarpment to inform Landau they were outflanked. The gun-ners spiked the few guns still remaining, then headed for the rear. Landau's pitiful group of about thirty survivors did likewise, climbing the hellish escarpment and straggling west in the di-rection of Berlin.

They hid or fled, encountering other German soldiers hiding or fleeing, sometimes fighting; at some point they met up with a group of Hitler Youth wearing shorts who were defending a farm-house. God save us, thought Landau. The Russians dogged their heels. An old Wiking comrade was wounded and dragged to shel-ter in the barn next to the farmhouse. Landau and a few men ran outside to fend off a group of Russian infantry. By the time he returned to the barn he found that his comrade had already been discovered by the enemy—impaled against a hay bale with a pitchfork.

Other old veterans who had survived the ordeal on the heights were shot down and killed during the retreat. They pressed on through a region of forests and beautiful lakes on the outskirts of Berlin. The passage of time began to blur. Hours passed in a daze. Darkness fell. Near midnight their flight came to an end amid surroundings that could only be described as surreal.

They had stumbled into a neighborhood of vacation chalets bordering a moonlit lake—weekend getaways for wealthy Ber-liners. But they were so exhausted that the strangeness of the scene made hardly any impression on them. They broke into one of these places and collapsed on beds and sofas, on the floor. The sounds of combat had faded away and they tried to sleep, but it was a while before they could relax with their shattered nerves. They lit cigarettes, instinctively cupping the flames in their palms, as if enemy eyes might still be watching them through the picture windows. Landau normally smoked a pipe, but it had been shot out of his mouth, along with several of his front teeth, during the fighting back at the escarpment. After their nerves had settled a bit he found a grammophone and put on a record. Other men broke into the liquor cabinet and they whiled the night away drinking and listening to the "beautiful, melancholy female voice" of a popular singer.

> Nun ist alles, alles zu Ende
> nun ist alles, alles vorbei . . .
> bei Dir war es immer so schoen
> warum muss ich nun von Dir gehn warum?

> Now everything, everything is ended
> Now everything, everything has gone by . . .
> With you it was always so sweet
> Why must I leave you, oh why?[9]

Peter Neumann in Vienna

Peter Neumann, one of Landau's fellow officers in SS Wiking, appeared only briefly in these pages. But his psychotic lust for killing Russians, "to drown in a lake of Russian blood," makes him hard to forget, and so we will tell the end of his story as well.

After the retreat from Hungary, Neumann remained in Vienna with most of the other Wiking survivors. The Soviets began their final assault on the city during the first week of April. Ironically, all the most famous Waffen SS divisions would make their last stand here in Vienna, rather than in Berlin. By this time nothing was left of any of them save for a few skeletal formations. Mixed battlegroups were formed—Wikingers fighting alongside troopers from Das Reich, eighteen year olds from Hitler Jugend fighting beside Leibstandarte men.

Neumann adds credence to the mood of disgust among the Leibstandarte troopers, once they received word of Hitler stripping them of their unit cuffbands. He recounts meeting a group of these men gathered around a charcoal brazier somewhere in the Austrian capital, voicing their indignation over this business in the crudest of terms.

They tell Neumann the same crazy story that seems to have originated with Jochen Peiper on the muddy Hungarian steppe: a used latrine bucket had been filled with medals and Leibstandarte cuffbands and sent to Hitler. Someone tells him that this filthy gift had also included the severed arm of some SS trooper.

Embellished by such hilarious details, the story was clearly beginning to take on a life of its own. Doubtless few of the SS men cared about the exact truth of any of this any longer. But it is obvious that rumors about the strange incident had spread like wildfire through their ranks.

They soon had other things to think about as the Russians began forcing their way into Vienna. Resistance by the shattered SS battlegroups was ferocious but sporadic. Russian combatants obliged to clear out these last-ditch pockets of resistance took their usual high casualties, but the divisions of the Red Army so vastly outnumbered the defenders that many Soviet soldiers saw little or no action, free to wander about drinking, celebrating, murdering and raping civilians. (This same pattern would evolve during the final days of fighting inside Berlin.)

According to Neumann, the Soviets had turned the health spa at Baden just outside Vienna into an enormous brothel, imprisoning Austrian women inside the buildings while soldiers lined up to take their turns outside. Indignant Soviet officers who tried to put a stop to this madness were turned back by the mutinous rumblings of a drunken mob. After the war many high-ranking Soviet officers would admit that the Red Army's notoriously strict code of discipline simply collapsed at moments like these. Probably Neumann only heard of this incident through the rumor-mill, but it was hardly more outrageous than other well-documented examples of Red Army behavior.

Meanwhile Neumann and his comrades were pushed back deeper into the network of canals that lined the inner city. The last days passed in a blur of nightmarish episodes. Russian soldiers infiltrated the tunnels of the subway system; grenade battles and hand to hand combat took place in the subterranean darkness, lit intermittently by the hideous glare of flamethrowers. The River Danube was clogged with the dead bodies of both sides, just as it had been at Budapest. Few SS prisoners were taken; most of those that did fall into enemy hands were simply lined up and shot. Neumann's group stripped the SS insignia and decorations from their uniforms and tossed these things into the Danube among the dead. Yet they fought on, and for the most part were bitterly resented by the Viennese civilian population, who had hoped to declare the capital an open city in order to avoid the fate of Budapest.

Neumann tells of Austrian civilians overtly shunning the SS

soldiers, offering them no food, no water, no shelter, at least not willingly. His account is clearly biased, colored by his own bitterness and rage, which he makes no attempt to hide whatsoever:

> I can't now help feeling that the Viennese would sell us to the enemy with pleasure and betray us remorselessly if we gave them the chance. . . . The Austrians are a race without character or will, superficial, pleasure-loving and frivolous, a nation that whines and trembles like a beaten girl.[10]

He witnesses pitiful old men of the Volksturm being lined up and shot for desertion. The executioners are SS, mostly German; the victims are almost all Austrian. Neumann seems to feel a moment of pity for these demoralized old men, drafted into their "quasi-military" units only a few weeks before. But his venom gets the better of him and he brushes any sympathetic thoughts aside. The executioners receive the order to fire—"a veritable massacre."

The incessant bombing, shelling, flame-throwing, and machine-gunning continues:

> I feel as though this din fills my whole being, destroying my will; it may drive me over the borderline of sanity if it goes on much longer.[11]

One might wonder if Neumann had already crossed that borderline long before. Many Waffen SS veterans have resented the term "fanatic" being automatically applied to them in the post-war accounts of the victors. Such a description would not really have fit Neumann himself during the early years; but by the same token, no one better epitomizes the die-hard fanatic than he during these last days.

At the very end he and a handful of others were hunted like rats through the inner city canals. Karl, a Wiking comrade who was also a life-long friend from Neumann's home town, was shot through the ankle; the bone was shattered and the man collapsed in agony in the middle of some deserted street. Their movements obscured by night darkness, Karl and Neumann crawled down into one of the canals, where they hid for hours beneath a bridge in the cold water.

Unable to stand, Karl sat on a large stone to keep his head above water. Overhead the Russians were everywhere, shooting at everything but mostly in celebration now. Eventually Karl declared he could go no further. Neumann spoke of the old days, reminding him of other hopeless traps they had escaped from in Russia . . . Cherkassy, where almost the whole Wiking Division had been wiped out the year before. But it was no use. Karl was sliding gradually down into the frigid water. Neumann put a bullet through his friend's head to spare him from being taken by the Russians.

He climbed out of the canal with the idea of massacring a group of Reds drinking around a bonfire nearby. He would be shot down instantly in return; for a moment the idea was appealing. He fingered the trigger of his Schmeisser, but then apparently had second thoughts. He went on through the darkness.

His story ends here. The details of his escape from Vienna, and where he took up residence after the war, remain a mystery, though he hints at some cruel time spent in a Soviet POW camp in Warsaw.

His final words display a strange ambiguity, coming out of the remorseless and bloodthirsty attitude that had consumed him during the last year of the war. It would be wrong to say he suddenly felt remorse for everything at the final moment, but a kind of terrible disgust, for himself, for all of it, seems to well up with these words:

> Why couldn't they have killed me?
> . . . Those nights, those interminable nights, spent in working out different ways to end it all. It is so impossible to die . . .
> In the ruins of Warsaw the burying of rotting flesh, the methodical clearing of the streets.
> The sneering brutality of the Soviet guards. Sometimes a sharp report. And again. For fun, this time.
> I'm out of luck. In spite of the rumors that the SS are to be ruthlessly exterminated. But they need men. Millions and millions of slaves.
> I look at my hands, my body, my clothes.
> Why couldn't they have killed me?[12]

Skorzeny in Vienna

Skorzeny's frogmen did not succeed in blowing up the Ludendorff Bridge over the Rhine at Remagen. Luftwaffe attacks finally rendered the span unusable, but by then the Americans were well-established on the east bank and ready to launch their final drive into Germany. They would meet little resistance.

Still later, in April, just before Zhukov's great offensive on the Oder, Hitler gave Skorzeny a new assignment. It would be his last of the war, and in fact he would never carry it out—though as usual rumors about his activities would give the Allies some highly exaggerated worries.

Hitler wanted Skorzeny to go to Bavaria and organize the "Werewolf Movement," a plan which called for partisan groups and surviving Army and SS divisions to establish lairs deep in the mountains of the Alps, creating an impregnable "Alpine Redoubt" which would continue to defy the enemy in the event that the rest of Germany was overrun.

The plan was no more than a fantasy, and Skorzeny's subsequent movements suggest he gave it only scant credence. Somehow Allied intelligence sources had already caught wind of this scheme; General Eisenhower, for one, took it quite seriously and diverted substantial American forces into Bavaria that would otherwise have kept heading for Berlin. There was an ominous ring to codenames like "Werewolf" and "Alpine Redoubt," but in reality this idea never amounted to more than a few memos lying on Hitler's planning table.

Skorzeny accepted the assignment but did not proceed with any great urgency. He left Berlin and drove south on a circuitous route that would include a lengthy detour into Vienna, the city of his birth.

He seemed to have nothing more in mind that a desire to see his home again before it fell to the Russians. What would he have thought about Peter Neumann's enraged tirade about his fellow Austrians? Perhaps Skorzeny would have been disgusted, or he might merely have shrugged it off as the ravings of a lunatic. Austrian divisions had been an integral part of the German army since the beginning of the war, fighting and dying on every front.

While Neumann and the SS die-hards continued to hold

out in a few isolated pockets, most of the rest of the city was quiet, as if lying in a stupor. Skorzeny entered Vienna at dusk, driving past demolished buildings, many still issuing palls of smoke; intermittently gunfire burst out both in the distance and nearby. With his usual nonchalance he drove on alongside the Danube, discovering his brother's house in ruins, discovering his mother's house in ruins; a neighbor informed him that she had fled the city a few days earlier.

He drove on in the direction of his own home. Despite the sporadic sounds of battle he could find no trace of the front lines, if they even existed. At a ramshackle barricade he was stopped by two policemen, who informed him with typical Viennese insouciance that they were the surviving garrison and that the "Russians were just over there somewhere," pointing down the street along which Skorzeny had just driven. Skorzeny, gratified to hear the dry humor of his countrymen, proceeded on to his own neighborhood and found his house undamaged. His wife had also been able to escape, leaving everything behind more or less as it had been before the war. Skorzeny passed a few moments looking around, gazing at familiar objects. Then he too left everything untouched for the Russians to do with as they pleased.

He paid a perfunctory visit to Baldur von Schirach, commander of what was left of the city's garrison, who was planning a counterattack that would encircle and destroy the Soviets. Skorzeny departed and drove off into the night, stopping at a village outside the city to send a message to Hitler, in which he stated simply that Vienna would probably fall the next day.

From here he resumed his journey towards the mountains of the "Alpine Redoubt." In Bavaria he found only war-weary civilians who had no interest in organizing a partisan movement. The die-hard troops that were to form the core of this fortress in the Alps were nowhere to be seen. He explored a few warehouses set up in caverns carved deep into the mountainsides. Supposedly they had been stocked with vast caches of weapons, ammunition, and other supplies. Skorzeny found them empty. He set up camp in a hut in the mountains to wait for the Americans and the end of the war.

Rudel in the Andes

After the war Rudel undertook many expeditions to the Andes and other remote mountain ranges. He had always been a passionate climber and he resumed this activity with enthusiasm. Mountain climbing may seem an inordinately difficult sport for a man with one leg, still more so than flying an airplane. But evidently the handicap did not do so much to deter him.

In April 1945 his squadron was stationed in a beautiful area of lakes and firs in the Sudeten Mountains that straddled Czechoslovakia and southern Silesia. A strange and almost overpowering sense of peace lay over this remote corner of the land, interrupted only by streams of American bombers flying overhead. But their targets were always somewhere else.

Most of the popular accounts of Rudel portray him as flying one of the new FW 190Ds during these last weeks, but in fact he piloted this aircraft on only one occasion. A group of schoolchildren was visiting the airfield, inspecting the planes with the enthusiasm of youngsters. Rudel decided to entertain them with a little aerial show. His Stuka was not as suited to acrobatic stunt-flying as the sleek FW 190, so he took off in one of the latter and performed a series of maneuvers in the skies above the children. His flight engineer had rigged the foot brake so Rudel could operate it by hand; otherwise he would have had difficulty flying the swift and responsive fighter.

A formation of American fighter-bombers (the hated Jabos, in German argot) flew overhead just as he was coming down to land. They were on their way to other targets, but Rudel's descent caught their attention and within moments the schoolday entertainment ended amidst bombs and strafing. The attackers flew off quickly; miraculously, none of the children had been hurt. Rudel had had to hop one-legged to shelter the instant he got out of his plane, an antic that must have resembled his flight from the Berlin Zoo after battling for possession of his crutches with the monkey. His disability seemed to lead him into more trouble on the ground than in the air.

The rest of the month passed in a jumble of equally peculiar episodes. He continued to lead his Stukas against Soviet tanks, destroying Stalins and T-34s up to the final hours of war. In the meantime he was ordered to fly back to Berlin on at least three more occasions to face Hitler; the Fuhrer ordered him to stop flying in combat, Rudel went back to his squadron and resumed flying in combat. Hitler felt as if he were dealing with an impudent child, saying as much to his entourage more than once. To get Rudel out of the cockpit Hitler gave him command (from a desk, hopefully) of a new jet bomber formation that would fly deep into the Soviet Union and destroy the heavy industry beyond the Urals. The assignment was as fantastical as the one he had just given Skorzeny in the Alpine Redoubt. Rudel turned it down, saying he felt duty-bound to keep on flying with his own men. Obviously this pig-headed young war hero was able to talk circles around his supreme commander; Guderian would surely have envied him.

On April 30th Hitler committed suicide in the depths of his bunker and Rudel no longer faced any interference from above. The Soviets invaded Czechoslovakia and he continued his tank-busting sorties into the first week of May, his unhealed stump bleeding all the while from chafing against his artificial leg. Obstacles on the ground still gave him more problems than those in the air. He was flying a Fieseler Storch to a briefing visit at Schorner's headquarters when the small craft experienced engine failure; Rudel wound up crashlanding the plane thirty feet up in a tree. After a few minutes Schorner drove up to ensure that Rudel was all right, then sent for the local fire brigade to help him climb down.

A few days later, a few last charred, blasted, smoking Stalins and T-34s later, Rudel and his Stuka pilots flew off to the west to surrender to the Americans.

Peiper in France

Skorzeny was put on trial for a number of his wartime activities. The charges were either outright fabrications or else highly dubious. (The latter focussed on his use of commandos disguised in enemy uniforms, a violation of the Geneva Convention—but Allied commandos had also used this same tactic on many occasions.) Skorzeny was one of the most notorious men in Europe and the Allies wanted to find him guilty of something. After two years' imprisonment and a harrowing, months-long trial, he was acquitted on all counts in September 1947.

The testimony of a handful of British commandos and secret agents about their own wartime activities was instrumental in saving him from the hangman's noose.

After his acquittal, Skorzeny spent nearly another year in a detention camp before becoming fed up with his treatment. In 1948 he escaped with the help of a few of his old commando friends. This time at least there was no great manhunt to track him down. Eventually he surfaced in Madrid, residing openly and leading an agreeable life until his death in 1975.

The famed panzer leader of SS Leibstandarte, Jochen Peiper, was also put on trial. The most serious indictment against him was responsibility for the murder of American prisoners by SS Leibstandarte at Malmedy during the Ardennes battle. Peiper's ordeal in prison was far more harrowing than Skorzeny's. On a number of occasions he and other SS comrades were marched from interrogation chambers to small rooms where hoods were fitted over their heads and nooses looped around their necks. They believed their American captors were about to execute them without even the benefit of a trial. The Americans simply wanted them to confess, and a few did so, even though most were innocent of the charges against them.

That SS troops perpetrated the Malmedy Massacre has been established beyond any reasonable doubt, but who actually ordered this act and participated in it, and what the exact circumstances were at the time, has always been fiercely debated. Though in combat quite nearby, Peiper was not actually present at Malmedy, nor did any evidence come to light that he had given orders for the murder of prisoners.[13]

Like Skorzeny he was a notorious figure, and the prosecution in what was essentially a kangaroo court was dead-set on finding him guilty of something.

Despite the extraordinary efforts of American defense attorney Colonel Everett, Peiper was condemned to death by hanging in July 1946. Condemned along with him were a handful of Leibstandarte men whose guilt in the massacre had actually been proven. The latter would eventually go to the gallows; Peiper's nightmare dragged on for another eleven years.

One of the most overlooked ironies of this period of American history was the determined effort by the Communist witchhunter Joseph McCarthy to get Peiper's sentence overturned.

Whether Senator McCarthy had any ulterior motives in this affair is not clear, but it is clear that he—and many others—sincerely believed in Peiper's innocence. During the same era in which he was destroying the careers and sometimes the lives of innocent Americans, he used his attack-dog style of debate to argue for Peiper's release. The unrelenting efforts of McCarthy and defense attorney Everett (a highly sympathetic figure whose alliance with McCarthy must have been a strange experience) resulted in Peiper's sentence being commuted to life imprisonment in 1952.

In 1957 a parole board recommended that he be freed, and he was subsequently released.

Peiper felt uncomfortable in post-war Germany and eventually settled in France, a country he had always liked. In July 1976 he was murdered in his home by French citizens who did not appreciate this former SS man living in their village.

We last saw Peiper through the eyes of SS Das Reich veteran Ernst Barkmann, leading his motley force of panzers in full retreat across the plains of western Hungary. Unlike Peter Neumann, Peiper did not get cornered and hunted down in Vienna. The shattered survivors of Sepp Dietrich's 6th SS Panzer Army were dispersed across Austria, with the lucky ones escaping the death throes in the capital. Apparently Peiper had lost none of his aptitude for sardonic wit—he declared that 6th SS Panzer Army was so-named because it had only six tanks remaining. It was only a slight exaggeration. Savage fighting against the Soviets in the Austrian Alps and Czechoslovakia continued through April. At war's end Peiper and his men moved west to surrender to the Americans, erroneously believing they would receive good treatment at their hands.

Despite the wretched fate that awaited him, he and other Waffen SS veterans were not wrong-headed in wanting to flee Soviet captivity. Because they had fought on the Western Front (if only for a comparatively short period of time in 1944), the men of SS Leibstandarte, SS Das Reich, SS Hitler Jugend, and SS Hohenstaufen were allowed to surrender to the Western Allies. Those not wanted for crimes at Malmedy or elsewhere were released within a year or so.

The men of SS Wiking and SS Totenkopf, who had fought solely on the Eastern Front since 1941, also tried to surrender to the Western Allies. The Americans accepted their surrender and then promptly handed all these men over to the Soviets. Some, especially officers from SS Totenkopf, were tried and executed. All the other veterans of these two divisions received sentences to labor camps in Siberia, generally ranging from ten to twenty five years. Few ever survived to return to Germany.

In 1972 Peiper moved into a small house he had built for himself and his family in Traves, a French village along the River Saone. He lived unobtrusively, though his identity was not a mystery. For the most part he incurred no wrath from his fellow villagers, who referred to him as "L'Allemand" (the German) and left him in peace. Even in his late fifties he still had much the same youthful appearance he had had during the war.

The war had been over for thirty years. Long hair and rock and roll prevailed in France as in Britain and the United States. I moved to France in August 1976, only a month after Peiper's murder (about which I knew nothing at the time, being youthful, preoccupied with my own experiences, and having little interest in current affairs). The younger French people I met seemed to regard the war as ancient history, as I did myself; the older people told stories occasionally, though few of them seemed to be living in the past either.

In Strasbourg I met an Alsatian who had served with the Waffen SS; he hinted at dark secrets from his past. I was vaguely aware that Alsace had been incorporated into Germany during the war, but I was more interested in drinking wine and studying the man's strange hard-bitten appearance than in paying close attention to his stories. My French was not so good either. Otherwise I might have learned from an eye-witness about the massacre of the entire village of Oradour-sur-Glane by troopers of SS Das Reich, among whom were many Alsatians, on their way to the Normandy front in June 1944. But, as with Peiper's murder, I learned nothing about any of this until years later. The man clearly wanted to talk, and seemed interested in meeting a young American, but I never saw him again after that one night in August 1976. If anyone was fully aware of Peiper's recent demise, it would have been he; perhaps he even feared for his own safety at the time. But all of this passed me by.

Neither Peiper nor any other men from SS Leibstandarte had been at Oradour. On the other hand, most people tend not to make fine distinctions about which men served with which SS divisions, perhaps understandably so. Compared with places like Poland, Yugoslavia, and the Soviet Union, France had not suffered extreme cruelty under the German occupation. Waffen SS divisions stationed there had gotten along reasonably well with French civilians—at least until guerrilla violence exploded on a large scale at the time of the Normandy invasion. As was so often the case in Russia and elsewhere, running battles with resistance groups had formed the prelude to SS Das Reich's massacre of the 500 odd residents of Oradour-sur-Glane, down to the last man, woman, and child.

But all of this was thirty years in the past. The butchery at Oradour had been a rare incident even at the time, horrible though it was. But some Frenchmen had longer memories than others; citizens of Yugoslavia or the Soviet Union would have no trouble understanding this.

Most of the villagers of Traves continued to leave Peiper in peace, the war receding still further into the past. But over time others began to resent his presence more and more, as if something loathesome had settled in their midst; and the more they thought about it the less they liked it.

Peiper's situation was not helped by a series of articles written about him by a Parisian journalist in 1976. He had never been anonymous, but previously his presence had been a vague and quiet thing. Now people who had had only hazy notions about his identity knew everything there was to know. It was not all bad; Peiper had already had his share of suffering in prison, waiting for years on end for the hangman to come to his cell, and most people in France knew this too. But somehow the continued residence of an SS man in a village only a hundred miles from Oradour grew more intolerable, an insult, an unextractable thorn in the minds of those who could not forget.

The distance to Oradour was not far, but by French standards it was not all that close by either. Traves was in another province, in another valley, by another river. In any case Peiper symbolized far more than Oradour; he represented the entire madness of the war, and above all the unforgettable madness of the organization known as the SS.

Peiper's house was burned to the ground by a Molotov cocktail at about 2 AM on July 15th 1976 that is, only hours after the end of Bastille Day, the French national holiday. The preceding evening a sympathetic gendarme had warned him to be on the lookout for trouble, but Peiper had gotten used to receiving threats against his life and did not appear worried. Later French investigators found his corpse inside the house, shrivelled to the size of a child, looking a good deal like men who had burned to death inside their tanks during the war. He had apparently fired shots at his attackers; rounds of expended ammunition lay beside the body.

In France the assassination was widely condemned; even former members of the resistance spoke out against it. The murderers were never found.

So died the author of some of the war's more memorable quips—bitterly sarcastic yet somehow lively remarks muttered in the heat of desperate combat. Leader of the Waffen SS panzer spearheads in the Battle of the Bulge. Leader of the "Blowtorch Battalion" in the Russian wastelands. Leader of the "submarine attack"—to use Peiper's words—into the Hungarian mud in 1945. The apocryphal sender of a shit-bucket filled with cuffbands to Adolf Hitler.

Probably his personality in life did not altogether correlate with the grimly amusing aura he left behind. Celebrity tends to exaggerate a man's ordinary presence in a room, in a village somewhere. He was not a brazenly matter-of-fact swashbuckler like Skorzeny; much of his humor seemed to be the product of severe stress in combat, which Skorzeny was more able to dismiss without any accompanying nervous commentary. Nor was he physically imposing; he was a small man with a somewhat oversized head. Peiper was strikingly handsome though; when the grime and haggardness of combat was not etched into his face, he somewhat resembled the American actor George Peppard in his younger days. In photos he is one of the most sympathetic appearing of all Waffen SS soldiers.

But what can one truly read in a photo? Or make out of all of this in the end? God only knows.

Even after all this has been said, Peiper's story would not be complete without the addition of one final complication. He has been portrayed as being unjustly condemned during the course of the victors' outraged demands for justice for Nazi crimes. True enough. But one unnerving fact about Peiper's career was not mentioned—or perhaps barely mentioned—at his trial. In 1939, before the beginning of his combat career, Peiper had served as an aide on the personal staff of Heinrich Himmler. He knew Himmler very well, far better than most Waffen SS soldiers ever did. He spent much of this time pleading with Himmler to transfer him to front-line duty; during this time he also became intimately aware of some of Himmler's more repulsive schemes for dealing with conquered peoples. Peiper was fully aware, for example, that thousands of Jews and Polish intellectuals were being hunted down and shot by the SS after the attack on Poland in 1939.

Again, what is one to make of all this? He wanted to fight as a soldier and at length Himmler agreed to transfer him to combat duty. There is no evidence that Peiper participated in these early "death squad" activities.

But the episode remains disturbing, or at least many would think it so. Sometimes one can only shake one's head, either in judgment or bewilderment.

Von Ruhland Escapes to the West

Only a few divisions fighting on the Eastern Front in 1945 would escape the long agony of Soviet captivity. 7th Panzer Division had seen uninterrupted service on the Eastern Front ever since 1941. In April 1945 the skeletal remains of this unit were shipped out from the West Prussian port of Hela, steaming towards freedom in the west.

But for almost all of these men, escape was only an illusion. Their long war with the Soviet Union was not over yet. Debarking at the port of Swinemunde, they were supposed to be transferred to Berlin, but the Russians had surrounded the capital before they could get there. The last soldiers of 7th Panzer were wiped out or taken prisoner by other Russian forces around the north German towns of Neustrelitz and Waren.

Paul von Ruhland's memories of his final days in combat are as blurred, frightening, and chaotic as any of his earlier experiences. He was trapped in a forest outside Neustrelitz with some other men, the Russians closing in from everywhere. The Germans were backed up against a swamp, but at the last moment one of von Ruhland's comrades discovered a long footbridge across the murky expanse. They fled for their lives in single file, bullets flying all around them. The footbridge was a rickety affair of loosely connected boards that went on for hundreds of yards; crossing it seemed to take forever. At intervals the boards had rotted away and some men fell into the swamp, drowning there or shot down by Russian bullets. Others were hauled out by their comrades and the mad flight continued. Von Ruhland was loaded down with ammunition containers and a spare machine gun barrel and nearly went down from exhaustion. At the end he felt the sudden presence of some supernatural force, the only thing that enabled him to keep going. He offered a prayer of thanks.

Still the fighting went on through the last April days. The Soviets destroyed the remains of 7th Panzer once and for all. By this time the advancing British and Americans had reached a point only a few miles to the west. But only scattered handfuls of men from this division succeeded in infiltrating the Russian lines and surrendering to the Western Allies. Paul von Ruhland was among them. All the rest were rounded up by the Russians for the beginning of the endless journey to Siberia, the final destination which von Ruhland had feared for so long.

Unlike the SS troopers of Wiking and Totenkopf, the few men of 7th Panzer who escaped to the west were not handed back over to the Soviets. Eventually von Ruhland emigrated and settled in Florida, where he lives today.

DeGrelle in Denmark and Spain

We last saw the Belgian fascist Leon DeGrelle leading the few hundred survivors of the Wallonian SS Division across the Oder bridge from Altdamm to Stettin, passing beneath the dangling corpses of three deserters.

DeGrelle's path would also take him though Neustrelitz and Waren, leading him to freedom—or so he hoped—in Denmark.

Before then the Walloons had passed a month of relative quiet in defensive works among the dunes at the mouth of the Oder, where von Manteuffel's 3rd Panzer Army was in position. Much of this force had been wrecked in Pomerania and the prolonged fighting in the rubble of the Altdamm Bridgehead. But the Russians concentrated their efforts to get across the Oder at points further south, against 9th Army around Frankfurt and Kustrin and against Schorner's army group in Silesia. Thus 3rd

Panzer Army had nearly a month to recuperate around Stettin, but little of practical value could be done during this time to overhaul such a several mauled force. In fact von Manteuffel's army was weakened further by the transfer of most of his remaining panzer units down to the Seelowe Heights in anticipation of Zhukov's offensive there.

When the 2nd Byelorussian Front of General Rokossovsky finally attacked across the lower Oder on April 20th, von Manteuffel's remaining divisions could only put up a brief and disorganized resistance. DeGrelle's SS Wallonian Division had received a few hundred more replacements; they were almost all lost in hopeless counterattacks against the Soviet crossing points among the dunes. Up to the very end these Belgian "crusaders" fought with a ferocity that drew notice from German and Russian combatants alike. Out of 650 men (the strength of the division was now that of a battalion), only 35 remained standing after six counterattacks against the Russian footholds in the dunes on April 21st.

These and other miscellaneous survivors from von Manteuffel's army, including policemen and a few Latvian companies, established another defensive position around the town of Bruessow about ten miles to the west. During the retreat from the Oder they passed a number of curious signposts that had been erected by SS General Felix Steiner, still serving under von Manteuffel after his own 11th SS Army had been dissolved. These signs were faced westward and intended for the eyes of the advancing Anglo-Americans. "Anti-Soviet Front," they declared in large lettering. Apparently Steiner, along with Hitler and a few other generals, clung to desperate hopes that the Western Allies would join forces with the German defenders at the last minute to hold back the Bolshevik hordes. Just how much faith Steiner or anyone else placed in these hopes, or in these strange signposts, is impossible to guess.

After three more days of brutal fighting, Rokossovsky's forces broke through the defenses at Bruessow on April 25th. The rout was on.

The Walloons no longer existed as a fighting force. DeGrelle fled in his trusty Kubelwagen, which was promptly strafed by Soviet aircraft. Frantically he repaired three blown-out tires and rattled onward, "while crazed pigs from some burning sties ran screaming in all directions."

He passed through Prenzlau, site of Himmler's headquarters during his command of Army Group Vistula. The entire town was burning and fell to the enemy within the hour. He drove on to the northwest, witnessing a volcano-like eruption from exploding ammunition dumps outside Neustrelitz. DeGrelle pushed on to Waren, the roads packed with fleeing refugees.

Now British Typhoons took over from the Russian Stormoviks, strafing the pitiful columns of civilians and retreating soldiers. On a side-trip to Berlin just before the final Soviet offensive (where he had seen Hitler for the last time) DeGrelle had managed to secure several thousand foreign workers' identity cards; he now distributed these among his Walloon survivors and some Flemish Belgians from the SS Langemarck Division. They began donning civilian clothes and mingling with the refugees, moving on in the direction of Hamburg, towards Montgomery's British and Canadian armies. DeGrelle and a handful of die-hards remained in uniform.

He drove on towards an old castle on the Baltic Sea, one of Himmler's residences; it was rumored that the SS Reichsfuhrer was there. An eerie scene greeted DeGrelle upon his arrival. The castle, a rambling place that looked like "the setting for a horror movie," was vacant except for a few confused SS guards. Himmler had fled; rumor had it that he was in Sweden, using this neutral power as a go-between to negotiate some last-minute deal for peace. Just beyond the castle DeGrelle saw the searchlights around Himmler's personal airstrip probing the night darkness in defiance of Allied air power, apparently keeping the field lit in anticipation of the Reichsfuhrer's return.

To DeGrelle's surprise Himmler did return the following morning, rushing about in a state of anxiety before driving off again. He spoke only briefly with DeGrelle, telling him to wait for his return in the village next to the castle.

DeGrelle spent the day in a blacksmith's house, sitting in a chair on the doorstep. He fell to daydreaming, interrupted only by the roar of trucks fleeing to the west or the roar of enemy fighter-bombers passing overhead. In the evening he walked across some ploughed fields and sat on a rock at the edge of the Baltic Sea. From time to time he would see German planes far out in the distance, skimming the waves to escape detection.

At nightfall he returned to the blacksmith's house. At 2 AM

he was roused by a messenger from Himmler, who informed DeGrelle that Adolf Hitler was dead.

DeGrelle has been described in very different ways by his critics and his admirers. Those who have come to his defense point out that he was no Nazi stooge, but rather an ardent nationalist who wanted to maintain Belgium's independence within Hitler's new National Socialist empire. His strongest motivation for creating a Wallonian combat legion, apart from his desire to fight the Communists, was to enhance his people in Hitler's eyes by showing the Fuhrer their strong martial spirit. Admirable enough, perhaps. On the other hand, DeGrelle's own words show incontrovertibly where his deepest sympathies lay. In the end, his reaction to the news of Hitler's death says more about him than any other single thing. He wrote the following, not in the heat of passion at war's end, but many years later:

> I spent the rest of the night thinking about Hitler.
> I saw him again, a simple, sensitive heart, full of genius and power. His people had loved him and followed him until the end. During the entire war, no blow had shaken the admirable fidelity of the German masses to a man whose honesty, unselfishness, public spirit, and sense of Germanic greatness they all knew.[14]

He also wrote:

> He disappeared in an apotheosis of vanquished gods, amid an uproar like the end of the world, which seemed to burst forth in a Wagnerian chorus. To end thus was to be resuscitated already in the imagination of the peoples with a superhuman intensity, cast in an epic which would never be extinguished.[15]

This latter passage, at least, has an undeniable element of truth in it, though most people would consider Hitler's "role" in this epic in a far different light from what DeGrelle had in mind. As for the former passage, it would be difficult to find a more pompous and banal description of Hitler. His genius and power, his sense of German greatness (in whatever form it took) were all certainly present, as was the devotion of many Germans to the very end and beyond the end. The rest of it stands as a checklist of the most preposterous lies, written by a man who in many ways was gifted and creative.

It would be fitting if DeGrelle's testament to Hitler should also stand as a testament to DeGrelle himself.

The mourning Belgian left the castle at dawn and drove on westward, catching sight of Himmler in his own car on two other occasions as the two men struggled on through the endless crowds of refugees. The last time was during a bombing raid on the great naval base at Kiel, only a few miles from the Danish border. Here Himmler told DeGrelle he would not flee to Denmark but planned to meet his end on German soil.

The SS Reichsfuhrer would be true to his word. He drove off again at the head of an entourage of SS vehicles and was captured by the British a few days later.

Himmler's manner of meeting his end on his native soil was rather ignominious, however. He abandoned his entourage and assumed the identity of a policeman named Heinrich Hitzinger, who had been condemned to death by a Nazi party tribunal. He completed the disguise by removing his spectacles and donning a black eyepatch. All the same, his captors recognized him almost at once and put him in a special cell. Himmler committed suicide by taking a cyanide capsule he had kept hidden on his person.

By an apt and rather sickening twist of fate, he had been captured only a few miles from the site of the first concentration camp to be shown at length to the outside world. This was Bergen-Belsen, entered by the British on April 25th. The soldiers were followed by film crews who spent the following days making the first extensive documentary record of what these places had really been.

Images from Bergen-Belsen struck viewers around the world with an unparallelled visceral force; the first viewing of these films was arguably one of the most singular emotional moments in the history of the human race. And Bergen-Belsen was not even an extermination camp. There were no artfully designed crematoria here, no gas chambers cleverly disguised as shower rooms. There were only great rotting heaps of corpses spread across thousands of acres, corpses scattered across the ground, piled up above the ground, or piled up to the rim in deep pits dug into the ground. Almost all had died of typhus or starvation. Interviews with the first British soldiers wandering through this place showed men who—like the surviving inmates themselves—were barely able to speak.

This great overseer of all this, Heinrich Himmler, took his life in a prison cell in Luneberg, twenty miles from Bergen-Belsen.

A thousand miles to the east in Poland, the Russians had already stumbled upon the true extermination camps months earlier, in the wake of the Vistula offensive—at Auschwitz, at Treblinka, at Maidenek, at Belzec. Scenes from these places did not have quite the same overwhelming impact, if only because Himmler had seen fit to raze them to the ground before the German retreat. The inmates had then been marched off to other camps or to die of starvation along the roads. (Many of the inmates at Bergen-Belsen had been transferred there from Auschwitz and other camps in the East.)

At smaller places like Sobibor, site of the only successful mass escape from a Nazi camp, it was not immediately clear what had happened there, or at least the full extent of the killing was not immediately clear. Auschwitz, on the other hand, covered an area as large as a city, and no edict from Himmler no matter how thoroughly carried out could hide the true purpose of this great factory. It is not clear how much detailed news of these places—filmed or otherwise—was released to the Soviet public. More than enough, no doubt.

The Soviets of course had their own special camps, scattered the length and breadth of their own country. The most notorious of these were along the Kolyma River, above the Arctic Circle in eastern Siberia, one of the coldest and most desolate regions on earth. German prisoners were already acquainted with these places, as were millions of the Soviet Union's own citizens. These Russian hell-holes were built in true Russian style—mostly small, isolated in vast wilderness, shabby, primitive, utterly wretched, filled with shallow graves. It has been maintained that more people died in these camps than in the German ones; but neither they nor probably anything else could ever evoke the overpowering grotesqueness of the Nazi factories.

After his last meeting with Himmler, Leon DeGrelle crossed the border into Denmark at the beginning of May. A few days later he was on board a HE 111 with barely enough fuel to carry him south to Spain.

There he lived in exile for the remainder of his life—fascist dog and author of one of the great memoirs about the war on the Eastern Front. In all likelihood he would have run into Otto Skorzeny now and again, though neither of the two has said as much publicly. Their war experiences and their anti-Communist feelings would provide them with a certain common ground, but in other respects their fates were quite different. Skorzeny was not a wanted man and was able to travel abroad as he pleased, leading by all accounts a robust and prosperous life. DeGrelle faced imprisonment and possibly a death sentence for treason at the hands of the Belgian government. Members of his family were harrassed and thrown into prison, and he was doomed to live as an exile for his remaining fifty years.

8th Panzer in the Moravian Gate

After the recapture of Lauban on March 6th, 8th Panzer was transferred to General Heinrici's 1st Panzer Army in the rolling foothills of southeastern Silesia. Heinrici was soon promoted to become the last commander of Army Group Vistula. His place was taken by General Walter Nehring, he of "Nehring's wandering cauldron," and architect of several of General Schorner's recent victories in the Oder-Neisse triangle.

In this remote hill country at the feet of the Carpathian Mountains 1st Panzer Army had conducted a dogged defense for several months. Heinrici's reputation as a master of defensive warfare was not unwarranted. Under General Nehring the forces in this area continued to resist stubbornly and retreat very slowly. After the initial breakout from the Vistula in January, the Soviets had made only about thirty miles of further progress towards the Carpathians. During the second half of March, General Konev launched a major offensive to clear the Germans from this long balcony along his southern flank. The Russians took high casualties and again made little headway, but the attack had other benefits. Panzer divisions which were sorely needed elsewhere, 8th Panzer among them, were diverted here to defend the Reich's last remaining deposits of coal and natural gas.

While Konev's armies had made only small gains attacking

from the north, other Soviet offensives on the southern flank of the Carpathians suddenly put 1st Panzer Army in a dangerously overextended position. After the collapse of the Hungarian front, the Russians attacked across the Hron River on March 25th and advanced rapidly westward along the north bank of the Danube. They were soon in possession of the southern approaches to the Moravian Gate, the long pass through the mountains that led directly to 1st Panzer Army's rear areas. This natural line of communication was also the only remaining link between the forces fighting on German soil and the shattered Army Group South around Vienna.

On April 15th, the day before Zhukov's offensive against the Seelowe Heights, General Schorner ordered 1st Panzer Army to attack south through the pass to re-establish contact with Army Group South. Almost nothing came of this effort, as none of the available divisions had the strength to mount offensive operations. The attack, such as it was, was spearheaded by 8th Panzer Division and its dozen or so remaining Panthers. The first enemy trenches were overrun and the Russian infantry scattered in all directions (probably the last thing they expected at this point was a surprise appearance by German armor). But the Soviets recovered quickly, and the following day 8th Panzer was surrounded by overwhelming force in the southern neck of the pass between Olmutz and Brunn.

The Panthers and panzer grenadiers set up a hedgehog position and held out for three days. The panzer crews still displayed a strong fighting spirit. With fuel and ammunition nearly gone, a small group of Panthers broke through the encirclement and reached the lines of 6th Infantry Division. Here they refueled and took on as much ammunition and other supplies as possible; they then had the gall to turn around and break back into the pocket, thus enabling the remains of the trapped division to keep on fighting.

The Russians were not amused and broadcast the following message over loudspeakers set up around 8th Panzer's perimeter:

> Siehst du, deutscher Kamerad, jetzt hast du kein Benzin mehr, und heute abend drucken wir Dich wie eine Zitronne zusammen. (Now see here, German

friend, you have no fuel left and come this evening we're going to squeeze you like a lemon.[16])

It was true that the bold sally had brought only a little fuel back into the pocket; it seemed to have been more an act of defiance than anything else. But the besieged men were at least able to hold out for another two days. At last they managed to break out to the north, suffering the bloody losses that invariably resulted from these desperate escape attempts, and re-established contact with 1st Panzer Army.

The situation stabilized and only desultory fighting occurred until news of final capitulation arrived on May 8th.

8th Panzer commander General Hax ordered his men to head west by whatever means and surrender to the Americans. Hax made it through; so did Hauptmann Sell and Lt. Wiswedel, who had spent the war in the East leading the panzer grenadiers in their armored halftracks. But as with 7th Panzer in northern Germany, many soldiers of 8th Panzer were unable to escape through the Russian lines. Most of them were trapped and surrendered somewhere in the pass or in the rolling hills. The events of these last days passed in the shadow of one of the few high peaks of the Carpathian chain, the 8,000 foot high Franz-Joseph Spitz, still covered in snow as the end came for the last groups of men scattered through the plains and foothills below.

> . . . and the mass of officers, NCOs, and enlisted men, including Russian Hilfswillige faithful to the last, took the first steps on the march into captivity, from which years later only a very few would ever return . . .[17]

So many combat histories of German divisions fighting in the East end with these or similar words, a dirge echoing across the final pages of the chronicles of 8th Panzer Division, 7th Panzer Division, 83rd Infantry Division, 215th Infantry Division, Grossdeutschland Division, and countless others. In 1941 8th Panzer had been part of the attack on Tikhvin in northern Russia, where the forests of the taiga stretched unbroken all the way to Siberia and the Pacific Ocean. It was the closest any German advance would ever come to the vast and infamous region of labor camps above the Arctic Circle. The men of this division would not see those forests again until the long march into Soviet captivity four years later.

Schorner in Czechoslovakia

General Schorner was a die-hard, but he also had strong survival instincts.

On May 7th, the day before the official announcement of capitulation, he broadcast an order to all men serving in his Army Group Center, absolving them of further responsibilities and granting them permission to move westward towards the American lines.

Schorner himself lost no time in grasping this opportunity. Rather than doing whatever he could to lead his divisions to safety, he simply fled.

He informed his chief of staff, General von Natzmer, of his intentions, declaring that the Soviets were eager to get their hands on him and he was not about to let that happen. Somehow he had managed to collect a large amount of cash and stuffed it into a briefcase. He offered some of this money to von Natzmer should he also wish to escape. Von Natzmer was taken aback and coldly replied that every man in Army Group Center would be fighting for his life over the next few days; it was Schorner's duty to help lead them out to the west. Not so, declared Schorner. His orders had just granted every man individual freedom of action and he was merely availing himself of that same opportunity.

He got in his car and drove off at high speed. It was the same touring car in which he had earlier escorted Joseph Goebbels to Lauban, the same car in which he had spent much of the preceding months driving back and forth through the rear areas of his army group, looking for deserters to hang. In disgust von Natzmer followed in his own car, thinking he might still appeal to Schorner's sense of honor and persuade him to change his mind.

At this time Army Group Center was spread across southern Silesia and northern Czechoslovakia. By now the Russians had finally crossed the Neisse River, advancing westward into the province of Saxony. Yet even during these final days, after Hitler's death and the fall of Berlin, some of Schorner's panzer groups continued to attack the flanks of the Russian spearheads, destroying large numbers of tanks in Saxony just as they had done in Silesia. A Polish brigade fighting with the Red Army lost almost fifty Stalin tanks in a melee with Panthers and Mk IVs of the Brandenburg Division in the last days of April.

Schorner drove recklessly into the Slovakian countryside and von Natzmer lost sight of him. He arrived at Saaz, where Schorner had told him a Fieseler Storch would be standing by. Schorner was there but the aircraft was not, and Russian tanks were firing on the airfield. The two generals, accompanied by a few staff officers, drove off again; von Natzmer no longer knew where Schorner was heading. But he must have made alternate arrangements at the last moment; outside the village of Podhorsan a Fieseler Storch was waiting in a meadow.

At some point during the drive Schorner had changed into the lederhosen and suspenders of a Bavarian peasant; he had also gotten himself completely drunk. Von Natzmer got out of his car to remonstrate with him again. Two of Schorner's commands, 1st Panzer Army and 17th Army, were no longer in radio contact and had not received the breakout order. The Storch was needed so Schorner, or someone at least, could fly to the headquarters of these armies and deliver the orders in person. Schorner was too drunk to listen; the powerfully built general stormed around in his leather shorts, berating the confused sentries guarding the plane. He then climbed on board and flew off into the west.

The plane crash-landed in Austria and Schorner disappeared for ten days. At length some civilians recognized him and reported him to some German Army officers who had already surrendered. They located Schorner and took him into custody, handing him over to the Americans. (The fact that these officers did not simply allow Schorner to continue his escape says a great deal about his popularity among German soldiers.) The Americans then handed Schorner over to the Russians, who later tried him for war crimes and sent him to prison in Siberia for ten years.

He was released in 1955 and returned to his native Bavaria. His reputation as a hangman in 1945 had not been forgotten. The relatives of thousands of German soldiers who had been executed at his orders clamored for his arrest. He was tried and convicted of manslaughter, spending another four and a half years inside a West German prison.

After facing the retribution of both the Russians and his countrymen, he was released in 1963 and died ten years later.

Schorner had been the Third Reich's most successful general in 1945. One could even argue that he had been the Third Reich's only successful general in 1945. He had organized the only counterattacks that had had any sustained success, meaningless though they were in the long run. He did have his admirers, among them Hans Rudel, and he was not the only one. Perhaps fanatically determined men have a tendency to sympathize with one another. On Schorner's long drives through Silesia he could be found hanging "shirkers" on the spot and later offering encouragement and gifts of food and chocolate to frontline soldiers, all on the same trip.

All the same, his later condemnation by both Russian and German courts was praised by many. And they might have been more satisfied to see him hang than serve his time in prison. On a few occasions, SS men who had not been convicted by the Allies at Nuremburg were later tried by German courts for various crimes, usually atrocities committed against civilians. Schorner was the only German general to be convicted for the widespread killing of his own soldiers.

On the Oder—Werner Adamczyk and Jan Montyn

Werner Adamczyk was in position with his artillery battery along the Seelowe Heights when Zhukov attacked on April 16th. For all the ferocity of that battle, Adamczyk's memories of it are not very detailed. His hallucinatory state of shock while fleeing from the Russian barrage during the Kustrin attack clearly left a much greater impression on him. It is almost as if the war ended for him at that point; he devotes only a few paragraphs to his experiences during the final battle in April.

He does remember that his guns were supplied with a great deal of ammunition at that time, substantiating reports that almost all of Germany's remaining stocks of shells were going to the Seelowe Heights, while fronts elsewhere had to make do with almost nothing. To him Zhukov's offensive was nothing but a ti-

tanic artillery duel fought between the two sides. In 1945 Adamczyk had already undergone two terrible ordeals under Russian
barrage fire—nearly buried alive along the Vistula in January, and
then reduced to a state of shock before Kustrin in March. What
more could he have to say?

He and the rest of 20th Panzer Grenadier Division retreated
towards Berlin, pausing a few times to set up firing positions in
the suburbs, then retreating again. His division, along with the
rest of the army, was disintegrating. Men began heading off on
their own, individually or in small groups, risking execution by
the field police or occasionally by their own officers and NCOs,
by anyone who was still determined to fight to the end.

Adamczyk and a few comrades commandeered a truck; one
of them was familiar with the autobahn network around Berlin
and so they circumvented the south side of the capital, then kept
on driving towards the American lines.

Other men of the division were no so lucky. Many were
wiped out in the suburb of Halle along the notorious "avenue of
death," a section of the autobahn where an immense traffic jam
of retreating men and vehicles was annihilated by yet another
Soviet barrage.

Adamczyk and 20th Panzer Grenadier had also participated
in the drive on Tikhvin in 1941. But he would not return to those
taiga forests as a prisoner of the Russians. West of Berlin he met
a group of black soldiers. He knew they could not be Russians
and prayed that these were the Americans. They were, and they
accepted his surrender.

Jan Montyn's experiences on the Oder Front also seem
somewhat anti-climactic, after what he had lived through in Courland and on the voyage home across the Baltic.

He was wounded by shellfire in January 1945 and shipped
out from Courland's port of Libau. The old transport vessel had
barely left the harbor when it was torpedoed by a Russian submarine. The sinking occurred during daylight hours and lifeboats
and rescue craft were able to bring most of the passengers back
to shore. Montyn was soon lying on a stretcher back on the dock
at Libau harbor, waiting apprehensively to be carried on board
another transport steamer. To be sunk once was bad enough,
but for Montyn this was the second time he had gone down in
the Baltic, and the first occasion had been far more terrifying.

Originally he had joined the Kriegsmarine, the German Navy, in the fall of 1944. One of the reasons he wound up fighting as an infantryman in the Courland trenches was that the torpedo boat he had been serving on had struck a mine far out to sea, sinking within minutes. Only a few square feet of the small craft's bow had remained above water, with Montyn and three other sailors clinging to it. Hour after hour they lived with the fear that the bow would go under, which would mean certain death in the freezing water. The air was also freezing and two of the men succumbed from exhaustion and exposure and lost their grip, sliding away to die in the sea. The others hung on, wondering when their turn would come. A rescue boat arrived after nightfall and took them back to shore in Pomerania. From here Montyn was transferred to the ground war in Courland.

He could not help but think back on these experiences while waiting on the Libau dock. At last he was carried on board another vessel for a second attempt to get back to Germany. This time the voyage passed uneventfully, but Montyn had been so traumatized by his two ordeals at sea that every creak of the ship's plates or odd beat from its engine filled him with dread. Though sick, exhausted, badly wounded, he lay awake with his eyes wide open for almost the entire three day voyage.

A few months later he was back in the trenches again, but the Oder Front was quieter and less frightening than the high dark latitudes of Courland. Montyn gives no indication of exactly where he was along the river, but it must have been some less active sector than Zhukov's bridgeheads below the Seelowe Heights. In some places the Oder Front was very quiet indeed. Along the forty mile stretch from Frankfurt south to the mouth of the Neisse River there was almost no fighting, with the two armies facing each across the river like border patrols in peacetime. Here at least there did exist that strange lull before the end that one reads about in many accounts of the final months.

Montyn passed his days quietly, enjoying the view across the river. To his amazement he was later joined by the one-armed captain who had been his commanding officer in Courland. The naval infantry unit to which they both belonged had nearly ceased to exist except on paper, but on paper it was now in position along the Oder and so there the captain was sent for further duty.

After a number of strange, almost enjoyable weeks, the end

came swiftly. Another day in April; another terrible barrage; another Soviet river crossing; another flight to the west by the shattered defenders.

Montyn also escaped to surrender to the Americans. He had fought with the German armed forces but he was not a German. Montyn was a Dutch citizen who had been dragooned into forced labor in a factory in Nazi-occupied Holland. Like many young men, he found this kind of life no different from slavery and was willing to take almost any alternative to get out of it. He might have joined the SS Nederland Division, which consisted almost entirely of Dutch volunteers fighting on the Eastern Front. But Montyn had no desire to be a member of the Waffen SS. He discovered he was eligible to join the Kriegsmarine and so took that option to escape from the factory.

This choice probably helped considerably in easing him back into civilian life after the war. He did not have to deal with the stigma of having served with the Waffen SS. He admits that besides the miserable conditions in the factory, it was also a youthful spirit of adventure that motivated him to get into the war, even if on the German side.

It was probably this same spirit which motivated him to join the Dutch contingent in the United Nations Police Force fighting in Korea, where he saw extensive combat in 1952.

Courland

The lonely and forgotten war zone. The sixth great Soviet offensive since the preceding fall had petered out at the beginning of April. It was the last Russian attack. During all these months the German and Latvian defenders had surrendered only a few miles of territory. Spring weather arrived among the lonely firs of this country. Warmer breezes blew in from the sea, bearing the stench of hundreds of thousands of unburied corpses.

By all accounts, though highly approximate as always, the Russians had lost over a quarter of a million men in these useless assaults. The defenders hoped to be evacuated by the German Navy, but it was not to be. Almost every ship of the Kriegsmarine had been diverted to help refugees escape from East and West Prussia. When the news of final capitulation arrived, a few last vessels carried a few lucky men out from the port of Libau. All the rest of Army Group Kurland—nearly 200,000 men—had no other choice but to surrender to the Soviets.

A few FW 190 pilots flew out with their last remaining fuel, the tiny cockpits jammed with one or two additional passengers—mechanics or other pilots. Some passed the long flight to the west lying down in total darkness, wedged into the narrow fuselage behind the cockpit after structural plates had been removed to make room for them.

Some of the Latvian soldiers did not surrender. They withdrew into the deep forests of the peninsula, fighting on as partisans against the Soviet occupation army, until the last of them were wiped out or betrayed by informers in 1947.

The reader will recall that the 15th Latvian SS Division had fought on German soil in Pomerania in 1945. After retreating to Wollin Island at the mouth of the Oder, this unit was dispersed. Some Latvians fought with Leon DeGrelle in April; some fought in and around Berlin. Some escaped to the west; others were captured by the Russians.

One battlegroup from this division escaped aboard a ship to Sweden, where they were interned until 1946. The Russians demanded that the Latvians be returned as prisoners of the Soviet Union. In a tragic episode condemned by many Swedish citizens, the Swedish government forced these Latvian survivors to board Russian ships in Stockholm harbor. The Cold War had just begun and many in Sweden feared imminent Soviet expansion into their country. Understandably, the Latvians feared for their lives once back in Russian hands. Some of these men attempted suicide by slitting their wrists; still alive, they were carried on stretchers aboard the Soviet vessels.

The ultimate fate of this Latvian contingent remains unknown.

Bix on the Frische Nehrung

The beaches of the Frische Nehrung were jammed with refugees, thousands upon thousands of them like bathers at a seaside resort—but a Dantesque resort maybe, as they were dressed in rags and nearly paralyzed with hunger and despair.

So it had been ever since January, when long columns of trekkers had crossed the ice from the mainland to reach the

Nehrung. During the long thaw in February and March they had kept on coming, with ugly holes marking the places where people and wagons had disappeared through the melting ice. When the great lagoon, the Frisches Haff, had reverted to open water they'd kept coming still, ferried over from Pillau, or fleeing from Danzig after Danzig fell to the Russians.

The Nehrung, this desolate and seemingly endless sandspit, was the very last unconquered territory of the Third Reich, in either the East or the West. Perhaps it was an appropriate setting for the last few acres of Hitler's empire, an empty sun-swept place extending from the mainland towards nothingness or infinity, lapped at by dull monotonous waves. One could imagine some dismal existentialist fable being staged here, Waiting for Godot, or Sartre's Nausee or The Flies.

They were waiting all right, the people there, all through April and into May, waiting for the ships of the Kriegsmarine to take them off. And the ships kept coming, they never ceased their journeys back and forth across the waters, but there were still more refugees than would be carried away. People lived and died; babies were born.

The Russians shelled and bombed the place, but otherwise showed little interest in it. The western approaches from Danzig had been cut off when German engineers blew the dykes and flooded the Vistula estuary at the end of March. At last at the end of April, after the tragic 83rd Infantry Division had been driven into the sea at Pillau, the Russians crossed over from Pillau to the eastern tip of the Nehrung.

Being only a mile wide, the sandspit was defensible for a while, even by just a handful of German troops. They established defensive positions numbered 1 through 10, holding off the Russians for a few days before giving up one position and retreating back to the next. So it went through the end of April and into May, Russian tanks charging at barriers in the dunes, grinding bodies and barbed wire into the sand and pushing slowly from east to west.

Hermann Bix had fallen back to the Nehrung from Danzig with 4th Panzer Division at the end of March. They had spent most of April in strange idleness, until the Russians finally crossed from Pillau on April 26th. Bix's Jagdpanther was still operational; and on May 6th it would have been one of the last German armored vehicles to engage in combat. He and his crew were holding the line at defensive position No. 7. Before them, spread across the sandspit from the Baltic beach to the lagoon beach, lay the hulks of Russian tanks knocked out during the final 48 hours of the war. The bodies of the crews lay shrivelled in the sand alongside, or burnt-up within the wrecks.

Just behind them more Soviet tanks were massing. Bix noticed some Russian infantry erecting an odd-looking barrier nearby, driftwood and gnarled dune trees heaped up in a pile. He could not grasp its purpose; then after a while he heard the noise of an engine growing louder as some vehicle, hidden from sight by the barricade, moved into position in front of his Jagdpanther. The Russian infantry pulled the branches aside as quickly as they had piled them up. Bix found himself staring into the mouth of a cannon as wide as a culvert. The 152mm gun had an enormous muzzle brake and was mounted on the Soviets' largest tank destroyer, an ISU-152 that German armored crews called the "Battering Ram" or "Tiger Killer." The Russians also called it the "Tiger Killer," or sometimes just "Beast" or "Animal."

As usual the German crew was quicker to fire. At close range the Jagdpanther's long 88mm seemed to inflict no damage whatsoever. The Russian fired, missing with the first two shots. The third shot blasted the long 88mm loose from its mantlet and laid Bix's crew nearly prostrate from concussion of the huge shell as it impacted on the frontal armor.

The Jagdpanther began backing away to escape while the radio operator called for help. The last two vehicles of Bix's platoon arrived on the scene. The first was likewise wrecked by the Russian gun. The last Jagdpanther maneuvered into a flanking position and destroyed the ISU-152 by firing into its thinner side armor.

Its immensely thick bow plate, where Bix's gunner had scored several direct hits moments earlier, was gouged as if by fingernails clawing through wet cement—but otherwise unharmed.

Bix and his men were taken off the Nehrung by a German cruiser on the night of May 8th, some hours after the announcement of capitulation. They were headed for the Hela Peninsula across Danzig Bay, another sandspit whose fate had resembled that of the Nehrung. But unbeknownst to them Hela had just surrendered to the Russians. They would have sailed into Soviet captivity if not for an encounter with two minesweepers that passed this news along. The vessels steamed out into the Baltic and headed west for Kiel, surrendering there to the British on May 14th.

Meanwhile the German Navy kept coming in to the Nehrung, and the last German soldiers kept fighting for days after war's end. The last ships departed on May 12th, bearing away all who were left.

Guderian

Guderian had suffered from a weak heart even before serving as the Army Chief of Staff in 1945. But clearly these months did a great deal to aggravate his condition; his tenacious personality was no help to him in this matter. After the war he lived quietly with his wife in West Germany, but he never fully recovered his health and died from heart disease in 1953.

Historians as well as his own acquaintances have often wondered why Guderian devoted so much energy to Hitler's cause during the last days of the Third Reich. He completed his memoirs just before his death, offering an explanation for what was to him a fairly simple matter.

Though not involved in the plot to assassinate Hitler in July 1944, he had been approached by some of the conspirators. Guderian remained aloof from this business, aware that a conspiracy was underway but not privy to the exact details of time or place. Essentially he thought the plan was misguided, fearing that Hitler's death would lead to an immediate disintegration of the army's will to fight on. In that case the Russians would overrun Germany in a matter of weeks, and to Guderian this possibility was simply not acceptable. By and large, Germans feel close ties to their native region or province; Guderian hailed from East Prussia, which he rightly feared would suffer the first and most terrible ravages of Soviet vengeance.

In a more fundamental sense he also felt it was his duty as a soldier to fight on for his nation during its greatest crisis. In particular he felt bound by the oath he and every other German soldier had sworn to Adolf Hitler. But this was and still remains a touchy subject. Obviously by 1944, and in some cases even earlier, many other German officers had fully rejected this oath without being troubled by their own consciences.

In his memoirs he speaks about the suspension of laws and basic rights in Nazi Germany, though interestingly he has little to say about these same conditions prevailing in the conquered nations, where the atmosphere of fear and repression was far worse than anything ever suffered by German citizens (excepting Jews, of course). But Guderian was not alone among German generals who wrote memoirs after the war focussing almost exclusively on military operations. Perhaps these men felt the criminality of their government had been so fully revealed by that time that they could not bring themselves to discuss it in a more personal vein. Still, this lack of reflection is unfortunate. No doubt their own consciences were still troubled to some degree, weighing their own personal responsibility for, or at least awareness of, the terrible events that had transpired.

This is not to say that all German generals felt a kind of shared guilt. Some, perhaps rightly, felt no more guilt than the average Landser. Ultimately the question of responsibility became so complex, and so loaded, that most of them seemed unable to bring themselves to speak about it.

In general historians have tended to regard Guderian as being above reproach, but perhaps a certain ambiguity will always surround him and the other highest-ranking officers who served Hitler to the end.

Landau in Berlin

Heinz Landau's book, GOODBYE TRANSYLVANIA, published in England in 1985, has received little publicity, but in many ways it is at least the equal of other more famous memoirs from the war.

His tone and writing style are nearly unique, highly emotional, biased, yet somehow very human in ways that do not often emerge from the accounts of other German soldiers, especially Waffen SS soldiers. His story is enlivened by a full repertoire of sarcastic German military slang, which perhaps better than anything expresses the day-to-day moods of ordinary soldiers. His descriptions of the complex and usually bitter politics in Eastern Europe provide a lot of insight into why different groups of people from those regions took their own highly divergent paths during the war. Landau's own biases, rather than diminishing his treatment of this subject, tend instead to make the whole situation more real to readers in another time and place.

He is not always fair, but neither is he blinded by the coldly idealistic hypocrisy which makes accounts by Leon DeGrelle and others of his ilk so often difficult to stomach.

Landau's book is quite short, in places rather sketchy. One wonders if a different editor or publisher might have kept after him to produce more detailed accounts of some of his experiences, especially from earlier in the war. For one of the book's peculiarities is that his memories of the fighting in 1945 are far more vivid than anything else—the terrible days in Budapest, at the Seelowe Heights, and finally in Berlin itself.

The strange idyll in the lakeside vacation home in the suburbs lasted only a single night. The next few days would pass inside Berlin in an unbearable crescendo of violence, dismemberment, and death.

Berlin, April 1945:

. . . a comrade decapitated by a shell, another shot through the heart, another with his legs blown off who begs Landau to put a bullet through his head. He squeezes Landau's hand, mutters, "Live long and hearty, Heinz." Then Landau shoots him.[18]

. . . a hand to hand struggle with a group of Russians in a pitch-dark cellar, slashing with knives and sharpened spades; torching a few last T-34s with panzerfausts in some city square, Landau knocked unconscious when a section of track from an exploding tank lands squarely on his back.

. . . a man from a Luftwaffe flak unit sitting in a doorway, his lower jaw dangling by a few strips of skin down onto his stomach; a boy with his genitals cut off by shrapnel who screams in such agony that one of Landau's friends knocks him out to silence him.

. . . the Russians attacking, attacking, though often in small groups now, showing an appreciation for squad tactics that Landau had rarely seen during the mass-slaughter of other battles. His mind becomes clouded with memories of the street fighting in Budapest, much of it identical to what he sees in Berlin, though he knows there will be no more hellish cities to fight in after this one.

. . . screams of civilians, an indescribable cacaphony of gunfire, shelling, and screaming. A woman being gang-raped by five Russians, who are promptly shot and beaten to death by Landau's men—they then discover the woman is a prostitute, who offers to service her rescuers as thanks for saving her life.

They decline and she shrugs.

They fight their way entirely through the city, into the western suburbs, from where they hope to break out and reach the American lines. But at last they are trapped inside a building and overwhelmed by a Russian attack. Landau tries to hide a 13 year old boy down in the cellar, but the boy is killed by shrapnel flying through a window. Landau is firing an MG 42 through the window when a blow to his helmet leaves him seeing stars and electrical short circuits within the darkness of his brain. When he finally comes to he finds he is a prisoner of the Russians.

Berlin has fallen. There was no concerted defense, only scattered groups like Landau's fighting with desperate ferocity. One of these other groups consisted of Frenchmen from SS Charlemagne, whose division had disintegrated in pathetic fashion in Pomerania in March. The survivors were eventually reformed into an understrength battalion, but in the ruins of Berlin they fought with a fury that overshadowed their earlier poor performance outside Hammerstein. One of the last Knight's Crosses of the war was awarded to a Frenchman from SS Charlemagne.

In area Berlin is the largest city in Europe. All of it has been blasted to rubble, leaving one of the most desolate cityscapes ever known to mankind. The citizens of the capital, as well as visitors after the war, will be haunted by these endless square miles of demolished buildings. The vacant hulks of these ruins will take on their own inscrutable aspect of architecture or design, an architecture of wreckage, yet in its way more monumental, more deeply evocative, than the living city that had preceded it or the re-born city that would come after it.

The Russians entering Berlin observed all this devastation with a great deal of satisfaction. Their tanks and artillery had collapsed many of these walls and buildings, but far more had been destroyed by the Anglo-American bomber campaign. In other words, when the Russians first entered Hitler's capital, they saw a city that had already been reduced to rubble; the fighting inside Berlin only added more rubble on top of it.

Thus the Russians looked with an admiring eye on this handiwork of British and American bombs. Up until this very moment, they had had almost no concept of the war being fought by the Western Allies (as likewise the Western Allies had had only limited notions of the titanic scale of the war on the Eastern Front).

The Russians, with some justification, believed they had borne far more than their share of the struggle against the Third Reich, and over the preceding years had tended to belittle the contributions of their allies in the west. But what they saw in Berlin caused them to change their opinions somewhat. For there was no place on earth like this city. Tokyo and other cities in Japan had been even more horribly devastated, it was true—but so much so that almost nothing remained of them but razed ground, dust-blown and empty under the sun, hardly more than vacant lots spread across thousands of acres. With less permanent piles of rubble lying about, and with their love for woodwork rather than stonework, the Japanese were actually able to rebuild their cities with surprising speed.

But the monumental aspect of the rubble in Berlin, the end-less stone eye-sockets of blown-out windows and doorways set in high, jagged walls of ancient masonry, was like nothing else. And almost all of this had been destroyed—or created—by the bomber fleets from the West. So the Russians wandered about, surveying the ruins and nodding in grudging approval, muttering, "Good. Good work. Well done. Very good. Very good."

Landau was dragged by the heels through the city by a group of Russian soldiers. Crowds of other Russians closed in, punching, kicking, clawing, gouging. From time to time his keepers let go of him and he was nearly beaten into the pavement. A female soldier straddled him and urinated over his prostrate body.

His guards then continued to drag him along until a Soviet pilot, his head wrapped in bandages, approached and pointed his pistol at Landau's temple. He told the "Nazi swine" to get down on his knees and beg for his life.

"Fuck your mother," replied Landau, who had learned a bit of Russian.[19] The Soviet pilot kicked him in the groin and Landau assumed the desired position. The guards intervened and a violent argument broke out. At length they convinced the pilot that they had responsibility for their captive and the journey continued. Landau was soaked with blood and urine and asked that he be allowed to clean off in a fountain. The guards picked him up and threw him in.

Along the way Russian soldiers were diverted from their attacks on the Waffen SS man whenever they happened to sight German women in the streets. Apart from obvious targets of hatred like Landau (and even he was not killed or tortured at this point), the Russian blood-lust seemed to have abated somewhat. There were fewer sadistic murders in Berlin than there had been in the eastern provinces a few months earlier. Perhaps disciplinary measures from higher authorities had curbed some of the soldiers' frenzy. The raping continued, however.

Many Red Army soldiers took possession of individual German women, caring for them, feeding them, raping them when they pleased, but otherwise acting as guardians and protecting them from being gang-raped by other wandering groups of soldiers. This strange situation came as a reprieve to many women in Berlin; often their captors would begin to act in a fairly kind manner, showing a kind of simple-minded concern for their welfare, the women meanwhile finding themselves simultaneously touched and revolted by the whole mad business. But anything was better than constant gang-rape. Women who were not taken under the protection of individual soldiers developed raw and unbearably painful vaginal wounds; more than a few were gradually raped to death.

Landau was taken to a place where he was interrogated, told off-handedly that he would be shot, and thrown into a cell. But instead of being executed he was sent off with thousands of other prisoners on a forced march that lasted for several months. They walked all the way through Germany, Poland, into the Soviet Union, receiving almost no food along the way, with the result that nearly half of Landau's group collapsed along the road to die of starvation. This treatment was identical to the Germans' enforced starvation of millions of Red Army prisoners earlier in the war.

These earlier German death-marches had culminated in their prisoners' arrival at death camps set up on the Russian steppes, places that would rival Auschwitz for the killing of human beings on a mass scale. The Russian prisoners were not exterminated by gas, but simply left to starve to death in empty compounds surrounded by barbed wire.

These human corrals of starvation constituted only one out of a number of motivations for the Russian orgy of vengeance in 1945. The voices of millions of Russians, all of which have been absent from this book, would easily rival or surpass Landau's own expressions of loathing for the people of the other side.

He survived to reach a POW camp near Gorki, east of Moscow. Conditions here were very bad, but at least the Germans were given enough food to avert the massive die-offs suffered by Russian prisoners in German camps. Thousands died nonetheless, most already in a critical state of weakness after the long march. Those still possessing some degree of physical fitness were better able to survive.

Landau himself was critically weak and would surely have died in long-term captivity. He escaped by means of a ruse. Non-German prisoners—mostly Rumanians and Hungarians, along with some of DeGrelle's Belgians and Frenchmen from the Charlemagne SS Division—were rounded up in order to be released back to their native lands. Having served with a German SS unit throughout the war, Landau was not eligible to join the Rumanian contingent, but he did so anyway, praying that the Soviet paperwork would be up to its usual shoddy standards and that no one would notice him. (He fell prey to a terrible fit of paranoia at this moment, for earlier in the war the Gestapo had conducted an extensive investigation into his personal file—Landau being a typically Jewish name—before releasing him from their clutches.) But the Russian investigators were not as thorough, in fact paying no attention to him, and he was able to walk out of the camp with the other Rumanians.

Writing about this years later, Landau makes the sardonic observation that many of the French and Belgian SS volunteers released at this same time would later join the French Foreign Legion to fight in Indo-China, singing the marching song of the Waffen SS as they paraded past the Soviet embassy in Saigon. (And indeed this happened. Not only Belgians and Frenchmen, but a number of German Waffen SS troopers would later join the Foreign Legion and spend many years fighting the Viet Cong.)

Landau, still fearing discovery, left his compatriots and began walking across the Soviet Union on his own. Russian peasants sometimes abused him, sometimes fed and sheltered him, sometimes doing both at the same time. A few times he was treated with great kindness and pity. "Why do some of us have to be so incredibly cruel while others are so unbelievably kind?"[20] But people were not always willing to give him food and he spent much of the journey on the verge of starvation, his body still weak from the beatings he'd received in Berlin, his mind lapsing into periods of semi-delirium which he would be unable to recall later. He walked, he got rides in farm carts or trucks, he walked again, he wandered in circles.

He reached Warsaw in December 1945, from where he was able to take a train to Berlin and then to Vienna. He had no desire to return to Rumania and disavowed his citizenship there, claiming that his family was of Austrian descent. The commander of a British garrison post treated him kindly and directed him to report to the Viennese police. The police were not so well-disposed upon hearing his story and promptly handed Landau back over to the Russians.

He then did time working at a Soviet labor camp in the Hungarian oil fields, before being informed that he would soon be transferred back into the Soviet Union. He would also receive an official sentence—something he had avoided previously—and could look forward to fifteen or twenty years in Siberia.

And so he had walked across half of Russia only to find himself on the verge of being sent back to his starting point.

Landau escaped again, using a ruse similar to the first one, and made his way back to Vienna where he threw himself upon the mercy of the British. After hearing his pleas they agreed to take him into protective custody—and so at last he was able to escape the endless nightmare of these years. Screaming nightmares would still haunt his sleep for years to come, but he was a free man now. The British released him and granted him permission to emigrate to England in 1947, where he married an Englishwoman and has remained to this day. His book is dedicated to "the British Army, for saving my sanity, possibly my life."[21]

EPILOGUE

83rd Infantry Division in Pillau

The last of the last. Not precisely so in chronological terms, but perhaps in some other sense.

The famous last stand, a mission doomed from the outset—episodes such as these have always had their own place in the annals of warfare. On the Eastern Front alone, from the beginning in 1941 to the very end, there were so many episodes of this kind that they can scarcely be counted—they formed much of the over-all pattern of that war. To Westerners, most of these last stands are not famous, most of them still unknown. But perhaps that will change over time.

83rd Infantry Division had had more than its share of these ordeals. The last stand of 277th Infantry Regiment at Velikiye Luki, the last stand of 257th Infantry Regiment at Graudenz. Less than twenty men had escaped from either one of these hell-holes. All the rest had been killed or else captured by the Russians, which usually became just a slower way of dying.

At Pillau at the end of April 1945 all of the 83rd's regiments, or what was left of them, would be destroyed. This would be no prolonged and agonizing siege like Velikiye Luki or Graudenz. 83rd Infantry Division would be driven into the sea beneath a rain of fire in less than 48 hours.

Armor and artillery—for both the Germans and the Russians—provided the twin conquering arms of military power on the Eastern Front. The infantry divisions provided the bodies, perhaps also the soul. It is probably no coincidence that all of the most moving and disturbing accounts of the war come from the infantrymen.

We last saw 83rd Infantry Division crossing Danzig Bay from Hela, arriving at Pillau to relieve the destroyed remnants of 32nd Infantry Division, 170th Infantry Division, the Grossdeutschland Division, and the nameless fragments of a few other units. These men were taken on board ships to be transported back to Hela, or to be ferried across the Pillau channel to the Frische Nehrung.

The 83rd was left alone to face the final Soviet onslaught against Pillau, which began in the early morning hours of April 25th. The Russians had amassed so much firepower across the two-mile wide neck of land at Pillau that there was hardly room to deploy it all.

On the left or western flank stood the 83rd's Infantry Regiment 251. Their sector started at the Baltic Sea beaches and extended through a pine plantation, planted years before to protect the town from the encroachment of the shoreline dunes. This scraggly forest provided little cover, having been mostly flattened during the battles of the preceding weeks. The regiment's front ended at the Jugendheim (Youth Hostel) and the aptly named Himmelreich (Kingdom of Heaven) Barracks.

In the middle, in front of Pillau proper, stood Infantry Regiment 412, incorporated into the 83rd from another division to replace Infantry Regiment 257, which had been left behind to die at Graudenz in February.

On the right stood Infantry Regiment 277, which had been re-formed early in 1945 after the original regiment had been annihilated at Velikiye Luki. Their sector began on the eastern side of the town and extended into a marshy area of reclaimed land that bordered the Pillau-Konigsberg Canal.

The left flank with its sand dunes and flattened pines was the hardest to defend; the Soviets rolled over the trenches of IR 251 almost immediately, surrounding individual companies who radioed frantically for help or permission to break out. Battalion commanders could not issue such orders on their own authority, but the surrounded men radioed that they would be wiped out within minutes; there was no time to contact regimental or divisional headquarters.

> The battalions sent the Solomon-like answer: "We will not judge local situations from where we are."[1]

An ambiguous sounding message, but the implications were clear enough. The trapped companies interpreted it as meaning freedom to act on their own and the survivors broke out of the fire-swept dunes into the town.

In the marshy areas along the right flank, Soviet pressure was less intense. IR 277 fell back towards the town to reinforce the defenses there.

There was nothing left standing in Pillau. The place was only a little larger than a village and had been bombed daily for months by the Red Air Force. Now every available Soviet artillery piece added to the devastation, until little remained but huge piles of brick and great clouds of suffocating dust. As there was almost nothing left to destroy, the defenders had no need to fear buildings collapsing on top of them; they fought on amidst the heaps of rubble, which for a while barred access of Soviet tanks into the town. The Russian infantry attacked led by standard bearers waving red flags, like a battle scene from another century. The Soviets had followed these flags into battle in a few other instances during the final days of the war; perhaps to them it symbolized the end of it all—victory—that is, for those who survived these last bloody attacks.

But they did not offer themselves as targets in a human wave. Once inside the ruins they dispersed into small groups, hunting down the shell-shocked defenders wherever they could find them, killing and being killed in a terrible dust-choked frenzy. Adding to the artillery fire were the Stormovik fighter-bombers, strafing at low level during every minute of the day until late afternoon, when the immense clouds of smoke and dust rising from Pillau grew so impenetrable that it was impossible to see the ground.

The defenders inside the town were outflanked to the west by the Soviets' rapid penetration of the dunes and pine plantation. By evening all three regimental command posts had pulled back and joined the divisional HQ in the citadel, which lay beside the concrete channel mole at the south end of Pillau. The citadel was almost the only structure still standing in the town; it was surrounded by a dry moat, behind which the defenders had gathered to make their last stand.

The citadel (or kremlin) was a common feature of towns in Russia. So it had been in Velikiye Luki, where the last survivors of the original IR 277 had fought on after the rest of that city had fallen. They were usually massive brick or stone structures surrounded by deep moats, dating from late medieval days. The citadel in this last German-held corner of East Prussia must have been something similar, though the shattered piles of masonry left behind by this battle would make it difficult to know for sure.

As darkness fell the holocaust of fire diminished somewhat. It was hard to say why. Perhaps the smoke was so dense that the Russians could no longer see to attack through it. Perhaps in a rare gesture of humanity—as much for his own men as for the defenders—the Soviet commander was allowing the remnants of the division a chance to surrender. But for whatever reason the Russians, by now only a few hundred yards from driving the defenders into the water, uncharacteristically suspended further assaults through the course of the night.

For the Germans this hiatus would lead to long hours of suspense which slowly grew more nerve-wracking than combat. Gradually the survivors began to assemble along the long concrete mole beside the channel that led out to the Baltic. Divisional commander General Heun had given the order to evacuate Pillau, if that was still possible. And indeed only the Russians' strange forbearance allowed it.

Only three of the "sea-snake" ferries were available to make the crossing to the Frische Nehrung. There was also one larger ship, destined for Hela, that was to be loaded with wounded men. For a while the boarding procedures were carried out in an orderly fashion, the defenders lining the mole waiting their turns to board with an agonized patience. Wounded were carried out from the citadel and the anxious crowds parted to let them through. The ship for Hela departed. Then the three "sea-snakes" departed for the Frische Nehrung, visible by the light of burning buildings only a mile away across the channel. Nervously the mass of men left behind waited for these small vessels to return.

Midnight came and went, the hours passed by, but the dark waters remained empty. Then they heard long bursts of machine gun fire from out in the channel. Rumors sparked the beginning of a breakdown in discipline. Had Russian patrol boats ambushed the ferries? The firing stopped and the waiting continued, the officers finding it harder and harder to maintain order as the ranks in the rear slowly pushed forward towards the mole. The mole was nothing but a long flat-topped finger of concrete extending into the sea. There was no cover on it anywhere and the men, illuminated by the light of countless fires from within the town, were standing in full view of the Russian guns. A few well-placed shellbursts would massacre everyone; even a few machine guns would do it.

The more one thinks about it, the stranger this whole episode becomes, especially in light of the Russians' frenzied lust for killing everywhere else in Germany. Despite all the smoke and darkness, it seems hard to believe that the Russians were unaware that an evacuation attempt was in progress. Had the Soviet commanders finally come to their senses, recognizing that the end of the war was perhaps only a few hours away? Were they showing mercy to their own long-suffering soldiers, refraining from further attacks, allowing them this respite at the very end after years of the most appalling losses any army had ever endured?

But these questions are only rhetoric. Whatever the real situation was, only the Russian commanders at Pillau would ever know it. Perhaps the Soviets were exhausted from the fighting earlier in the day, though by this point the ordering of further assaults would hardly have been necessary. The Russians were within hailing distance of the Germans. Massed firepower alone, delivered at such close range, would have obliterated the men along the mole.

And the waiting men knew this only too well. From time to time the quiet was broken by a few isolated Russian attacks, but these were carried out by small, almost insignificant groups of men, who seemed only to want to settle some last score with their enemy before the opportunity eluded them.

> The Soviets always seemed to find a man or two [eine paar Leute] willing to sacrifice themselves even in such a pointless situation.[2]

German machine gunners mowed them down. These were only brief interruptions in the silence, but even so the mood of the waiting men was brought that much closer to panic. Their nerves were already at the breaking point after enduring the worst shelling and bombing they had experienced in the war just a few hours earlier. And now this maddening silence . . .

At last a few more boats arrived. But these were only three fast patrol craft even smaller than the ferries. Now all discipline collapsed; as the three boats came alongside the mole the waiting crowds swarmed over them like rats. The first boat was over-filled almost to the point of sinking. Somehow, perhaps with the threat of force (the divisional history does not elaborate), the sailors convinced enough men to climb back on the mole to allow the boat to depart. But it was all becoming too much by now. As the boat began to pull away men jumped off the mole and swam after it, reaching up to grab hold of the low gunwales; they were all swept away into the water as the boat picked up speed, their cries vanishing out in the darkness.

So had desperate men clung to the wheels and wings of the very last transport planes to fly out of Stalingrad, falling to their deaths on frozen ground a thousand miles to the east of Pillau, two and a half years before.

520

The same terrible scenes were repeated with the next two boats. Then they were gone. The night passed by and no more came. Dawn came and still the Russians did not attack. Almost as if they could not endure the waiting anymore, the survivors mounted a last counterattack into the Russian lines, ostensibly to clear more room for the evacuation, but obviously it was all hopeless now. One last frenzy—and then the remnants of the division were swallowed up within a fire-storm of steel amongst the ruins. . . .

The sight of the Russian guns massed against them and the knowledge of their own utter helplessness was to be their last impression of Pillau. Their last attack was wiped out before they had scarcely taken a step forward.

The few who still remained on the mole fell into Russian hands and were marched away through the ruins of the burning city . . .[3]

Hells Gate!
The mole at Pillau where the remaining grenadiers of the 83rd Infantry Division made their last stand.

East and West in 1945—A Recapitulation

The German resistance against the Soviet invasion in 1945 can be seen in its entirety as one of history's most desperate and terrible last stands. The ferocity and costliness of these battles—for both sides—equalled in every respect the more famous battles on Russian soil earlier in the war.

Western histories tend to leave readers with the impression that the final months of the Third Reich were rather anti-climactic, and with good reason, if one focusses on events along the Western Front. After the Battle of the Bulge there were a few sporadic outbursts of heavy fighting—in the Reichswald, in Alsace. But by the end of February any kind of determined German defense in the West had ceased almost entirely. In retrospect, the importance of the capture of the Rhine Bridge at Remagen has been somewhat exaggerated, for over the next two weeks the British and Americans were able to cross the Rhine at other points along the whole length of the river, and most of these crossings faced little or no opposition. The contrast with the ferocious resistance put up against Zhukov's crossings of the Oder could not have been greater.

From here many British and American armored columns were able to advance into Germany almost as if on parade. Men continued to die in scattered ambushes laid by handfuls of SS or Hitler Youth die-hards. Small but fanatical bands of paratroopers, practically the only German units in the West to retain any kind of fighting spirit, continued to fiercely resist Montgomery's British-Canadian armies in small pockets along the lower Rhine. The few German tanks still operating in the West were occasionally able to shoot up confidently advancing columns of Sherman tanks. But all of these incidents were widely scattered, and on the whole Allied casualties were light, while hauls of German prisoners grew by the thousands every day.

In village after village, town after town, the Anglo-American forces passed windows and doorways draped with white flags, flags which seemed to indicate the welcoming of a liberating army as much as surrender. At the time, many soldiers interpreted all this as simply an expression of relief by German civilians that the war was over and that they had at last been freed from the oppression of Hitler's regime. No doubt they were relieved to see the war coming to an end, though as has been said before, German civilians had not really faced a great deal of persecution at the hands of their own government. What American and British soldiers may not have understood was just how much this welcome was based on an entirely different motivation—the overwhelming sense of relief that local populations must have felt to see their towns and villages falling to the Western Allies and not to the Russians.

The River Rhine was a long ways from Berlin, but in light of the rapid and almost unopposed nature of the Allied advance, there was a very real possibility that Eisenhower's armies could have reached Berlin before Zhukov's. Eisenhower's decision not to strike for the German capital with all possible speed has been much discussed over the last fifty years. Instead, he diverted much of his striking power towards what he considered purely military targets: the reduction of the so-called "Alpine Redoubt" in Bavaria, and the encirclement of the last cohesive German Army Group in the West in the Ruhr industrial area.

The former was nothing but an illusion (though perhaps an understandable one at the time); there was no "Alpine Redoubt," and thus there were no important military objectives in Bavaria. In the latter case, the substantial German forces still holding the Ruhr industrial area were not really what they appeared to be either. These armies under General Model consisted of demoralized, mostly second-rate divisions and fragments of units that had almost no remaining heavy weapons, fuel, or shells. Whatever tanks and artillery they had possessed had almost all been transferred to the Eastern Front to hold back the Soviets. Granted, if they had shown even a fraction of the determination to resist being displayed by their compatriots in eastern Germany, they might have posed serious difficulties for the Western Allies. But this did not happen. The Battle of the Ruhr Pocket (or "Kessel"—cauldron—to use the German term) consumed much of the month of April. But it was less of a battle than a vast maneuver of encirclement, at the end of which over 300,000 German troops surrendered, with most of them having barely put up a fight. General Model, who had taken charge of countless desperate situations on the Eastern Front, chose to commit suicide rather than surrender.

Thus had Eisenhower deployed his armies during the last weeks of the war. He can hardly be criticized for wanting to clear up potential threats along his flanks; the Russians were carrying out the same kinds of operations in Pomerania and Silesia. Eisenhower had also just undergone the highly sobering experience of throwing back Hitler's surprise attack in the Ardennes; he wanted to ensure that no similar surprises awaited him inside Germany. But there is much evidence to suggest that beneath these entirely genuine motives lay even deeper motives governing Eisenhower's maneuvers near the end of the war. In fact there is really no mystery to this subject; Eisenhower spoke quite frankly about where his deepest concerns lay.

With his armies pouring into Germany almost unopposed, Eisenhower must have realized that the chances of another enemy counterattack—or at least any kind of serious counterattack— were almost non-existent. Even should he err on the side of caution, the military power at his disposal was now so overwhelming that he had more than enough forces to strike directly and with all possible haste at Berlin.

But in many respects Eisenhower was one of history's most unusual supreme commanders. He was as much a diplomat as a general; he also had an overriding awareness of the human toll exacted by prolonged combat. He believed that if there was to be any last-ditch German resistance, that resistance would take place in Berlin, and Allied planners had forecast that any prolonged house-to-house fighting in this vast city might lead to as many as a hundred thousand casualties. Quite simply, Eisenhower did not want to see so many of his men killed for such an objective so near the end of the war. Whatever political importance Berlin might have would not be worth the human cost. If there was to be a blood-bath inside Hitler's capital, then let it fall to the Russians. (And indeed, even after shattering the German defense line on the Seelowe Heights, the Soviets would still suffer extremely heavy casualties mopping up the last disorganized pockets of resistance inside the city.)

One way or another, the war would be over and Nazi Germany would be defeated; to Eisenhower that single fact was more important than anything else. He was nearly alone in this kind of thinking. Roosevelt and Churchill, the Allied heads of state, as well as Eisenhower's subordinate commanders—Montgomery, Bradley, Patton—all voiced more enthusiasm for boring straight ahead and capturing the German capital. Roosevelt in particular was also concerned about the human cost, but a different supreme commander in Europe might easily have persuaded him to press on ahead regardless.

Yet Eisenhower was able to have his way. If he had struck more quickly for Berlin the later shape of the Cold War might have been very different, but during the last weeks of the war he seemed to develop a strange contempt for such political entanglements; casualties and bloodshed seemed more real to him than the inscrutable shape of the future. By the very nature of their jobs, military commanders tend not to make humanitarian concerns a top priority, especially during a period of total war. But Eisenhower was an unusual man.

In the introduction to this book, it was mentioned that the great majority of German panzer crews spent their entire careers fighting on the Eastern Front. As of February 15th 1945, the first day of the Sonnenwende counterattack, there were ten panzer and panzer grenadier divisions deployed on the Western Front, including Italy. On the Eastern Front, the total of panzer and panzer grenadier divisions was forty four.

The breakdown is as follows (asterisk indicates recent transfer from Western to Eastern Front):

Western Front—
2nd Panzer Division
9th Panzer Division
11th Panzer Division
116th Panzer Division
Panzer Lehr Division
3rd Panzer Grenadier Division
15th Panzer Grenadier Division
17th SS Panzer Grenadier Division "Goetz von Berlichingen"

Italian Front—
26th Panzer Division
29th Panzer Grenadier Division

Eastern Front—
1st Panzer Division
3rd Panzer Division
4th Panzer Division
5th Panzer Division
6th Panzer Division
7th Panzer Division
8th Panzer Division
12th Panzer Division

13th Panzer Division
14th Panzer Division
16th Panzer Division
17th Panzer Division
19th Panzer Division
20th Panzer Division
21st Panzer Division*
23rd Panzer Division
24th Panzer Division
25th Panzer Division

10th Panzer Grenadier Division
18th Panzer Grenadier Division
20th Panzer Grenadier Division
25th Panzer Grenadier Division

1st SS Panzer Division Leibstandarte*
2nd SS Panzer Division Das Reich*
3rd SS Panzer Division Totenkopf
4th SS Panzer Grenadier Division Polizei
5th SS Panzer Division Wiking
9th SS Panzer Division Hohenstaufen*
10th SS Panzer Division Frundsberg*
11th SS Panzer Grenadier Division Nordland (Scandinavian volunteers)
12th SS Panzer Division Hitler Jugend*
16th SS Panzer Grenadier Division Reichsfuhrer SS*
18th SS Panzer Grenadier Division Horst Wessel
23rd SS Panzer Grenadier Division Nederland (Dutch volunteers)

Grossdeutschland Panzer Grenadier Division
Fuhrer Panzer Grenadier Division*
Fuhrer Begleit Panzer Division*
Brandenburg Panzer Grenadier Division
Kurmark Panzer Grenadier Division
Muncheberg Panzer Division
Holstein Panzer Division
Feldherrnhalle Panzer Division
Hermann Goering Panzer Division
Hermann Goering Panzer Grenadier Division

All of these armored divisions were at varying levels of strength. The Waffen SS divisions slated for Operation Spring Awakening in Hungary had almost full complements of tanks. Also, a few of the brand new divisions, such as Muncheberg and Kurmark, were almost fully equipped. (Other brand new formations, ostensibly panzer units, had almost no tanks; I have not listed them above.) Almost all the other armored divisions, in both East and West, were seriously understrength. But the list above makes it clear why all the major armored battles in 1945 were fought on the Eastern Front.

I have not included the independent Tiger battalions, nor the various other independent formations fielding Sturmgeschutzen or other types of tank destroyers. But the deployment of these units also heavily favored the Eastern Front.

Perhaps never before had a nation, facing destruction on two different fronts, so completely abandoned resistance against one enemy in order to stake everything on resisting another enemy to the very last. Casualties had always been higher, far higher, on the Eastern Front. But the contrast between western and eastern Germany in 1945—for civilians as well as soldiers of opposing armies—was almost beyond description. Not surprisingly, German battle casualties for this period surpassed those suffered during any other comparable time span during the war against the Soviet Union. German losses in killed, wounded, and missing on the Eastern Front in 1945 were about two million—far more than had been lost at Stalingrad, or during the disastrous retreats in the summer of 1944.

Russian casualties were at a similar high level, nearly two and a half million dead and wounded. These also surpassed their losses during any other comparable time span—including the Battle of Stalingrad—since 1942. Only in 1941, with the horrendous defeats suffered during the opening phases of the war, were Soviet casualties higher than in 1945.

The death toll among civilians in eastern Germany in 1945 may never be known.

Possibly there has been no other last stand in history as violent or all-consuming as this one. One would have to look back at least as far as the era of the Mongol invasions, for which accurate tallies of human loss are hard to come by. But it is doubtful that any single nation inflicted such losses on the Mongol hordes before itself being wiped out.

The dramatic nature of this kind of last stand has always been part of military and historical lore. Yet the inherent drama of the last stand of the Third Reich has been overshadowed by the horror and tragedy of that war. The protagonist of such a drama was flawed, as all the protagonists of the world's great theatrical or mythical tragedies have been flawed. Of course, to describe the monstrous endeavors of the Nazi regime as merely tragic flaws seems ludicrous and grotesque. Yet it is this very grotesqueness which seems to prolong the world's unending fascination with this drama.

And of course the Soviets were far more, or far less, than the righteous avengers who prevailed in the last act of this tragedy. Perhaps it is not all that difficult to understand the Russians' berserk treatment of German civilians at the end of the war. As for Stalin's treatment of the citizens of his own nation, enough has been said about this subject over the years that there is probably little left to know.

Stalin did learn one thing from his great nemesis and rival Adolf Hitler. The Nazi death-camps aroused a great deal of interest in Stalin; as machines for extermination, they were so much more efficient than his own rickety empire of Arctic labor camps. In particular, the very thoroughness of the Nazi extermination of Europe's Jews fired Stalin's imagination, and he began to envisage similar means of disposing of all the surviving Jews inside the Soviet Union. The German holocaust had been laid bare before the eyes of the world— yet how much easier it would be to carry out such an operation within the hidden and inaccessible reaches of the Soviet Union.

Not much has ever been said about this particular legacy of Stalin's. The evidence for these plans remains controversial; perhaps more to the point, the evidence remains almost unknown, obscured by Stalin's cunning ability to carry out his plans beyond the view of the outside world. But the evidence is there, and merits deeper examination than it has received so far. The tradition of anti-Semitism and persecution in Russia was very old and very deep, still more so than in Germany. Stalin's paranoia and implacable methods of dealing with his paranoia knew no bounds. The evidence suggests that much of the machinery for this Russian holocaust was about to be set into motion when Stalin died in 1953. If so, then this final monstrosity died with him. With the advent of Nikita Krushchev's regime, the Soviet people entered what was for them a relatively enlightened era.

NOTES

CHAPTER 1—NO EXIT FROM COURLAND

1. Guderian, Heinz. PANZER LEADER. New York: Da Capo Press, 1996. p. 387.
2. Zeller, Konrad; Mehrle, Dr. Hans; Glauner, Theodore. WEG UND SCHICKSAL DER 215. WURTTEMBERGISCH-BADISCHEN INFANTERIE DIVISION 1936–1945. Friedberg: Podzun-Pallas Verlag. p. 159.
3. Haupt, Werner. KURLAND. Bad Nauheim: Podzun-Pallas Verlag, 1964. p. 85.
4. Zeller, Konrad. Ibid. p. 159.
5. Haupt, Werner. Ibid. p. 88.

Other Sources: Jan Montyn's account is taken from his memoir A LAMB TO SLAUGHTER. New York: Viking, 1986. For information about Latvia and Latvian soldiers in the Wehrmacht, see Silgailis, Arthur. LATVIAN LEGION. San Jose: Bender Publishing, 1986.

CHAPTER 2—BUDAPEST MERRY-GO-ROUND

1. Strassner, Peter. EUROPEAN VOLUNTEERS: HISTORY OF THE 5. SS PANZER DIVISION WIKING. Manitoba: JJ Federowicz Publishing, 1988. p. 195.
2. Rudel, Hans. STUKA PILOT. New York: Ballantine Books, 1958. p. 187.
3. A note on further possibilities. Even if successful, Wiking's thrust from Estregom would have brought only this one relatively small force into Budapest, the division by now being rather seriously depleted. But certainly the Wikings on the scene were not put off by the prospect. There seems to be no reason why Totenkopf, 711th Infantry Division, or other nearby units could not have been immediately sent in to reinforce Wiking once contact with the Budapest garrison had been made. Regarding this scenario, General Wohler is said to have offered the rather cryptic remark that Wiking's advance from Estregom was intended only as a kind of "Hussar's ride." Such an ambiguous phrase is open

to any number of conflicting interpretations—from a bold light-ning strike to a weak diversionary thrust designed only to confuse the enemy. Or could he have been implying that Wiking was too weak to sustain a viable relief corridor? Again, there is really no satisfactory explanation for this odd comment.

Meanwhile, reports from Hitler's headquarters suggest that he suddenly grew overly ambitious. The transfer of IV SS Corps to the Lake Balaton area on January 18th was intended not only to relieve Budapest from a different direction, but also to assist Wohler's army divisions in crushing an overextended Russian salient in this area. Only an extreme optimist could have expected to achieve these two goals simultaneously; to risk everything on this dubious op-portunity, while throwing away the gains Wiking had already made from Estregom, seems downright foolish.

Nonetheless, some accounts insist that the transfer of IV SS Corps to Lake Balaton very nearly worked: the Russian salient in this area barely escaped annihilation, and the new attempt to reach Budapest also nearly succeeded. But the operative word here is "nearly." By the time all this crazy shuffling around had come to pass an enormous amount of stamina and initiative had been demanded of Wiking and the Totenkopf men. Too much, no doubt.

For a good short account of these confusing operations, see McTaggart, Patrick. BUDAPEST 45: THE BITTER END. Com-mand Magazine, Issue No. 31.

4. Strassner. Ibid. p. 200.
5. Starssner. Ibid. p. 201.
6. Landwehr, Richard. "THE STALINGRAD OF THE WAFFEN SS," Siegrunen Issue No. 37: Bennington: International Graphics Co., 1985.

Other sources—Accounts of the SS Totenkopf around Budapest are taken from Karl Ullrich's WIE EIN FELS IM MEER/LIKE A ROCK IN THE SEA: HISTORY OF THE 3RD SS PANZER DIVI-SION TOTENKOPF. Osnabruck: Munin Verlag, 1987.

CHAPTER 3—A DELUGE OF SHELLS

1. Deutsche Wochenschau (German weekly Newsreel), January 1945.
2. Clark, Alan. BARBAROSSA. New York: Quill Press, 1985. p. 43.

3. Guderian, Heinz. Ibid. p. 387.

4. Ibid. p. 387.

5. The Vistula-Narew bridgehead, so recently vacated by IV SS Corps lay to the north of Warsaw. It too would be ripped apart by a separate Soviet thrust aimed at East Prussia and Danzig on the Baltic.

6. Adamczyk, Werner. FEUER! AN ARTILLERYMENS LIFE ON THE EASTERN FRONT. Wilmington: Broadfoot Publishing, 1992. p. 303.

7. Ibid. p. 349.

8. Ibid. p. 350.

9. Ibid. p. 352.

10. The word "Einzelkampfer" was a common part of the German military jargon, and can be loosely translated as "one man combat team." It is indicative of the German tradition of self-reliance and initiative down to the lowest levels of the enlisted ranks.

11. There is some confusion over the exact fate of Panzer Abteilung 424. One authority, Duffy in RED STORM ON THE REICH, mentions that "one fine battalion of Tiger tanks" (which could only have been 424, though he does not indicate the unit by name) was wiped out while refueling by a surprise air attack. Given the unprecedented number of losses involved, this would seem a reasonable explanation. But survivors of 424 have described the scene at Lissow in some detail and none of them makes any mention of an air attack. Possibly at some point in the ongoing chaos there was a surprise raid by the Red Air Force, at Lissow, at Kielce, or at some other place nearby. Such directly conflicting reports only provide another example of the kind of anomalies that can come out of the confusion of a rout.

See Duffy, Christopher. RED STORM ON THE REICH. New York: Antheneum, 1991. p. 70.

Probably the most detailed account of the last battle of Panzer Abteilung 424 can be found in Kleine und Kuhne. TIGER: THE HISTORY OF A LEGENDARY WEAPON, 1942–1945. Manitoba: JJ Fedorowicz Publishing, 1990. p. 145.

Other sources—For an early yet still definitive account of the Soviet invasion of Germany 1945, see Thorwald, Jurgen. FLIGHT IN THE WINTER. New York: Pantheon, 1951.

Account of the 72nd Infantry Division taken from DIE 72. INFANTERIE DIVISION 1939–1945. Friedberg: Podzun-Pallas Verlag.

Casualty figures and further information about Panzer Abteilung 424 in the Vistula battle may be found in Schneider, Wolfgang. TIGERS IN COMBAT, VOLUME 1. Manitoba: JJ Fedorowicz, 1994.

CHAPTER 4—STALIN

1. Sources—There are numerous, and often contradictory, accounts of Stalin's plans and concerns between the Vistula breakout and the subsequent deadlock on the Oder. The authorities which seem to offer the most incisive views are listed below.

Le Tissier, Tony. ZHUKOV AT THE ODER: THE DECISIVE BATTLE FOR BERLIN. Westport: Praeger, 1996.

Duffy, Christopher. Ibid.

Bullock, Alan. HITLER AND STALIN. New York: Alfred Knopf, 1992.

Glantz, David and House, Jonathan. WHEN TITANS CLASHED. University Press of Kansas, 1995.

CHAPTER 5—GROSSDEUTSCHLAND

1. Deutsche Wochenschau, July 1944.

Other sources—Much information about the Grossdeutschland Corps in 1945 can be gleaned from Spaeter, Helmut. PANZERKORPS GROSSDEUTSCHLAND. West Chester: Schiffer Publishing, 1990; and Scheibert, Horst. PANZER GRENADIER DIVISION GROSSDEUTSCHLAND. Carrollton: Squadron/Signal Publications, 1987.

CHAPTER 6—HITLER AND GUDERIAN

1. Guderian, Heinz. Ibid. p. 309.

Other sources—The best accounts of Hitler's relationship with Guderian (apart from Guderian's own memoirs) may be found in Thorwald. Ibid.; Duffy, Ibid.; and David Irving's HITLER'S WAR. Though widely praised for his day by day account of the war through Hitler's eyes, Irving, at least in my view, tends to go a bit overboard with revisionist ideas that downplay Hitler's shortcomings while parcelling out blame to Guderian (and nearly everyone else). See Irving, David. HITLER'S WAR. New York: Avon Books, 1990.

CHAPTER 7—SONNENWENDE

1. DeGrelle, Leon. CAMPAIGN IN RUSSIA. Costa Mesa: Institute for Historical Review, 1985. p. 284.
2. DeGrelle. Ibid. p. 284.
3. Many sources have recreated this well known conversation, with slight variations. See Thorwald. Ibid. p. 134.; Guderian. Ibid. p. 414.
4. DeGrelle. Ibid. p. 285.
5. Ibid. p. 285.
6. Ibid. p. 286.
7. Ibid. p. 280.
8. Ibid. p. 231.

Other sources—Leon DeGrelle's is perhaps the only highly detailed account of the short lived Sonnenwende offensive.

For more general information see Thorwald, Duffy and Guderian Ibid.

Fuhrer Begleit's bold dash into Arnswalde is taken from Spaeter. Ibid.

The failed attempt by SS Panzer Abteilung 503 to break through to Arnswalde just prior to the offensive is described in Fey, Willy. ARMOR BATTLES OF THE WAFFEN SS, 1943–45. Manitoba: JJ Federowicz, 1990. pp. 273–76.

CHAPTER 8—VILLAGES, REFUGEES, CHAOS

1. Von Garn, Arnulf. 252 INFANTERIE DIVISION 1939–1945. Friedberg: Podzun-Pallas. p. 151.
2. Silgailis. Ibid. p. 181.
3. Duffy. Ibid. p. 198.

Other sources—Silgailis in LATVIAN LEGION provides the most detailed account of this period. See also Michaelis, Rolf. DIE GRENADIER DIVISIONEN DER WAFFEN SS, VOL 1 (for Latvian SS) and VOL 3 (for Charlemagne SS Division). Erlangen: Michaelis Verlag, 1995.

CHAPTER 9—AFTERMATH OF SONNENWENDE

1. DeGrelle, Leon. Ibid. p. 292.
2. Ibid. p. 301.
3. Ibid. p. 303.
4. Ibid. p. 304.
5. Ibid. p. 306.
6. Duffy. Ibid. p. 237.

CHAPTER 10—THE HANGMAN TAKES COMMAND

1. Hassel, Sven. COMRADES OF WAR. Greenwich: Fawcett Books, 1963. p. 195.
2. Duffy. Ibid. p. 128.

Other sources—Thorwald also gives a good assessment of Schorner's ruthlessness.

CHAPTER 11—JOURNEYS BY RAIL

1. Haupt, Werner. DIE 8. PANZER DIVISION IM ZWEITEN WELTKRIEG. Friedberg: Podzun-Pallas Verlag, 1987. p. 394.
2. Carius, Otto. TIGERS IN THE MUD. Manitoba: JJ Fedorowicz, 1992. p. 130.
3. Kindel, Richard. DIE 8. PANZER DIVISION DER DEUTSCHEN WEHRMACHT. Privately published from the archives of the 8th Panzer Division, 1992. p. 338. (The quoted passages are taken from GEKAMPFT UND UBERLEBT {I FOUGHT AND I SURVIVED} an unpublished memoir by Lt. Dr. Wiswedel of the 8th Panzer Division. Portions of which are reproduced in Kindel's book.)
4. Ibid. p. 338.
5. Ibid. p. 338.
6. Ibid. p. 333. (Reproduction of front page of Der Wurfel, March 1945.)
7. Haupt, Werner. 8. PANZER DIVISION. Ibid. p. 397.

CHAPTER 12—LAUBAN

1. Haupt, Werner. 8. PANZER DIVISION. Ibid. p. 400.
2. Duffy. Ibid. p. 139.

3. Deutsche Wochenschau, March 1945.
4. Haupt, Werner. 8. PANZER DIVISION. Ibid. p. 401.
5. Ibid. p. 406.
6. Ibid. p. 276.

CHAPTER 13—HORROR

1. Thorwald. Ibid. pp. 36–38.
2. Grau, Karl Friedrich. SILESIAN INFERNO. Valley Forge: Land-post Press, 1984. Entries taken from the original German report regarding atrocities at Striegau taken from pp. 100–103.
3. Ibid. p. 104.

Other sources—Thorwald gives extensive coverage of Russian atrocities against German civilians, relying on numerous first hand accounts.

Duffy also discusses these massacres, though in a somewhat more general vein.

The work by Grau is not a narrative, but rather a compilation of first hand accounts taken from German civilians during this time. The result is a numbing compendium or horror, made almost unreadable by the sheer repetition of individual acts of atrocity.

CHAPTER 14—THE RUSSIANS

1. Thorwald. Ibid. p. 36.
2. Wallace, Robert. RISE OF RUSSIA. New York: Time-Life Books, 1967. p. 32.
3. Thorwald. Ibid. pp. 125–126.
4. Ibid. p. 54.

Other sources—There are a number of studies of the partisan warfare that raged behind German lines in Russia, though for some reason they tend to make only sparing use of first hand accounts. It is true that many of these accounts are quite grisly, but without them it is not possible to have a clear picture of the real nature of partisan warfare in Russia. See the following:

Cooper, Matthew. THE NAZI WAR AGAINST SOVIET PARTISANS. NewYork: Stein and Day, 1979.

Perro, Oskars. FORTRESS CHOLM, 1982. Memoir privately published in Canada by a Latvian Veteran. This is only one of many first hand accounts that more graphically describe partisan fighting.

Neumann, Peter. THE BLACK MARCH. New York: William Sloane, 1959. Contains several grim accounts of both partisan atrocities and brutal German retaliation.

Yerger, Mark. RIDING EAST. West Chester: Schiffer Publishing, 1996. Unit histories of the SS Cavalry Brigades which policed occupied Russia. Yerger refers to a number of German operational reports which employ euphemistic phrases to describe mass executions of partisans and/or Russian civilians.

For works by Russian authors about the combat experiences of soldiers in the Red Army, see the following:

Simonov, Konstantin. DAYS AND NIGHTS; also THE LIVING AND THE DEAD. Both available in numerous editions.

Grossman, Vassily. LIFE AND FATE. New York: Perennial Press, 1980.

Baklanov, Grigory. SOUTH OF THE MAIN BRIDGEHEAD. Philadelphia: Dufour Editions, 1963. This work is unique in providing a detailed and apparently authentic glimpse of Red Army soldiers during the war.

Kazakevich, E. SPRING ON THE ODER: Moscow: Foreign Languages Publishing House, 1953. In contrast to the above title this is some of the most banal and white-washed literature about the war. It depicts Russian soldiers during the Sonnenwende Operation in February 1945 in Pomerania and follows them through the final battles on the Oder.

CHAPTER 15—STALINGRAD BY THE DANUBE

1. Landua, Heinz. GOODBYE, TRANSYLVANIA. Derby, Breedon Books, 1985. p. 96.
2. Ibid. p. 28.
3. Ibid. p. 38.
4. Ibid. p. 95.
5. Ibid. p. 96.
6. Ibid. p. 97.
7. Ibid. p. 98.
8. Ibid. p. 98.
9. Ibid. p. 31.
10. Ibid. p. 64.

11. Neumann, Peter. Ibid. p. 246.
12. Landwehr, Richard. Ibid. p. 27.
13. Ibid. p. 27.

Other sources—Command Magazine, Issue No. 31, BUDAPEST 45; Deutsche Wochenschau, February 1945; Bayer, Hans. KAVALLERIE DIVISIONEN DER WAFFEN SS IM BILD. Osnabruck: Munin Verlag, 1982; Toland, John. THE LAST 100 DAYS. New York: Random House, 1966.

It should be noted that Heinz Landua's generally exceptional memoir does bear one similarity to the blander books written by Russian authors, in that he dwells extensively on the crimes of the enemy while seeming to minimize those committed by his own side. While providing an unusually graphic look at Soviet atrocities, he writes only sparingly about German brutality inside Russia; it is highly likely that Landua participated in some of these "punitive actions," as a member of one of the SS Cavalry Brigades. This tendency may partially explain why he devotes so much space to describing his experiences in 1945, when the most widespread Soviet atrocities occurred.

CHAPTER 16—MUD

1. Ziemke, Earl. STALINGRAD TO BERLIN: THE GERMAN DEFEAT IN THE EAST. Dorset House Publishers, 1979. p. 445.
2. Toland, John. Ibid. p. 188.
3. Perrett, Bryan. KNIGHTS OF THE BLACK CROSS. New York: St. Martins Press, 1986. p. 226.
4. Meyer, Kurt. GRENADIERS. Manitoba: JJ Fedorowicz Publishing, 1994. p. 190. (The footnote actually refers to an addendum to Kurt Meyer's book written by Hubert Meyer, concerning the events surrounding the cuffband incident. Hubert Meyer was with the 12th SS Hitlerjugend in Hungary at this time and declares that this version corresponds to the actual truth of the matter. For reference, version No. 1 in my own book is a summary of Hubert Meyer's account. Version No. 2, in which Balck and Stadler play a major role, has been more widely repeated and may be found in a number of sources. See next footnote.)
5. Williamson, Gordon. SS: THE BLOOD SOAKED SOIL. Osceola: Motorbooks Int., 1995. p. 183. (This is the source of version No. 2.)

6. Toland, John. Ibid. p. 338. (Again it should be emphasised that Peiper only talked about putting medals and cuffbands into a latrine bucket in a bitterly joking vein; the implication is that neither he nor his comrades actually went through with this. It is amazing how much hair splitting and rumour can arise out of such a trivial incident, but such is the stuff from which legends are made.)

7. Fey, Willi. Ibid. p. 267. (This conversation with Peiper was reported by Ernst Barkmann; I have taken the liberty of putting it into dialog.)

Other sources—Details of the advance of Panzer Abteilung 509 with Kampfgruppe Bradel can be found in Kleine and Kuhne, TIGER: HISTORY OF A LEGENDARY WEAPON. Manitoba: JJ Fedorowicz, 1989.

An account of the attack on the Hron Bridgehead by the 12th SS Hitlerjugend, along with its subsequent role in Operation Spring Awakening, can be found in Hubert Meyer's addendum to Kurt Meyer's GRENADIERS.

CHAPTER 17—FORTRESS GRAUDENZ

1. Tiemann, Richard. GESCHICHTE DER 83. INFANTERIE DIVISION 1939–1945. Friedberg: Podzun–Pallas Verlag, 1986. p. 282.
2. Ibid. p. 298.
3. Ibid. pp. 304–305.

Other sources—The story of the last survivors of IR 257 fleeing down the Vistula in rubber rafts can also be found in Thorwald, though he does not identify the unit by name.

CHAPTER 18—VERHEIZEN

1. Zeller et al. Ibid. p. 164.
2. Ibid. p. 164.
3. Ibid. p. 164.
4. Ibid. p. 165.

Other sources—The history of the 215th Infantry Division by Zeller et. al. is a photo album with pages of accompanying text briefly summarizing the division's campaigns. Tiemann's history of 83rd Infantry Division describes many of these same West Prussian battles around Gotenhafen and Oxhoft in much greater detail.

Duffy also gives good coverage to the Prussian battles.

Guy Sajer, who has left probably the most famous memoir of the Eastern Front, also gives a vivid description of this period in THE FORGOTTEN SOLDIER.

CHAPTER 19—BIX AND THE JAGDPANTHERS

Sources—I have taken most of the information for the story of Hermann Bix from Kurowski, Franz. PANZER ACES. Manitoba: JJ Fedorowicz, 1992.

Duffy also briefly mentions Bix's exploits in an addendum to his book covering German weapons and tactics.

CHAPTER 20—LESS HEROIC ADVENTURES

1. Von Ruhland, Paul John. AS THE WORLD CHURNS. New York: Vantage Press, 1986. pp. 140–141.
2. Yes, this was the same General von Saucken who had commanded the Grossdeutschland Corps. In March he was transferred to his native West Prussia to take command of 2nd Army.
3. Thorwald. Ibid. p. 150.
4. Duffy. Ibid. p. 229.

Other sources—Von Manteuffel, Hasso. DIE 7. PANZER DIVISION IM ZWEITEN WELTKRIEG. Friedberg: Podzun-Pallas Verlag, 1986.

CHAPTER 21—REDUCING THE TUMOR

1. Spaeter. Ibid. p. 159.
2. Ibid. p. 159.
3. Duffy. Ibid. p. 205.
4. Spaeter. Ibid. p. 159.

CHAPTER 22—HELL AND HIGH WATER

Sources—The Helferinnen are the subject of a short feature

shown with the Deutsche Wochenschau at various times during the war.

Thorwald's FLIGHT IN THE WINTER contains a detailed account of each of the "three great sinkings."

For a book length study of the Gustloff disaster, see Sellwood, A.V. THE DAMNED DON'T DROWN. Annapolis: Naval Institute Press, 1973.

CHAPTER 23—KONIGSBERG AND PILLAU

1. McTaggart, Patrick. SIEGE AND SURRENDER OF KONIGSBERG. World War II Magazine, March 1995. p. 32.
2. During these final months General Rendulic would be bounced all over the Eastern Front. In January he had briefly taken command of the Courland armies after General Schorner's departure; he then arrived in East Prussia to replace Reinhardt; he would later be transferred back to Courland to resume command there, before a final transfer to take command of Army Group South in Austria.
3. Duffy. Ibid. p. 165.
4. Kleine and Kuhne. Ibid. p. 179.
5. Duffy. Ibid. p. 215. Thorwald. Ibid. p. 91. (Lasch's final remarks vary slightly from author to author.)
6. Hamilton, Charles. LEADERS AND PERSONALITIES OF THE THIRD REICH, VOLUME 2. San Jose: R. James Bender Publishing, 1996. pp. 156–157, and Stewart, Emilie. SIGNATURES OF THE THIRD REICH. Brigantine: Privately published, 1996. p. 136.
7. Spaeter. Ibid. p. 159.
8. Ibid. p. 159.
9. Tieman, Reinhard. Ibid. p. 324.

Other sources—The most detailed accounts of the final battles around Konigsberg and the Samland can be found in Kleine and Kuhne, including Kerscher's defensive stand behind the "curtain."

CHAPTER 24—RUDEL

1. Rudel. Ibid. pp. 187–188.
2. Ibid. p. 197.
3. Ibid. p. 199.

4. Ibid. p. 200.

CHAPTER 25—DEATH VALLEY

1. Duffy. Ibid. p. 180.
2. Le Tissier. Ibid. p. 222.
3. Rudel. Ibid. p. 206.
4. Ibid. p. 206.
5. Ibid. p. 207.
6. Ibid. p. 208.

Other Sources—Le Tissier provides by far the most detailed coverage of this period along the Oder.

A contemporary sketch map of the Reitwein Spur may be found in Spaeter on page 174, giving an excellent perspective of the flat terrain surrounded by the Seelowe Heights.

The Deutsche Wochenschau of February 1945 features a segment with zebra striped Panthers counterattacking the Oder bridgeheads. The Panthers of Kurmark's I. Battalion were stationed in this area for several months; conceivably, however, the Panthers being filmed may have been part of the attack against the Kustrin Corridor by 21st Panzer Division on February 6th through 12th.

CHAPTER 26—SKORZENY

1. Deustche Wochenschau, February 1945.
2. Foley, Charles. COMMANDO EXTRAORDINARY. New York: Ballantine Books, 1957. p. 125.
3. Stahl, Peter. KG 200: THE TRUE STORY. London: Janes Publishing Co., Ltd., 1981. p. 93.
4. Ibid. p. 93.

Other Sources—For accounts of the collapse of the German Army Group Center in July 1944, and the ordeals of German soldiers stranded in enemy territory, see—Buchner, Alex. OSTFRONT 1944. West Chester: Schiffer Publishing, 1991; and Adair, Paul. HITLER'S GREATEST DEFEAT. London: Arms and Armour Press, 1994.

CHAPTER 27—A PLEA FOR THE SALVATION OF THE GERMAN NATION

1. Heaton, Colin. LUFTWAFFE ACE GUNTHER RALL REMEM-BERS. World War II Magazine, March 1995. p. 38.
2. Rudel. Ibid. p. 212.
3. Deustche Wochenschau, February 1945.
4. Ibid.

CHAPTER 28—THE LAST ATTACK

1. Various accounts of the conversations involving Guderian, Himmler, Heinrici, Hitler, etc. may be found in Thorwald; Guderian; Duffy; Toland, and others.
2. Ibid.
3. Ibid.
4. Fey. Ibid. p. 286.
5. Ibid. p. 287.
6. Adamczyk. Ibid. p. 362.
7. Ibid. pp. 362–363.
8. Reference footnote # 1
9. Guderian. Ibid. p. 429.

Other Sources—Again Le Tissier provides the best overall information about the Oder battles.

Fey provides lengthy first hand accounts by the Waffen SS King Tiger crews about the Kustrin attacks.

Duffy's account, which is very good in most respects, is marred by a curious bit of misinformation—he states on page 245 that the final attack against Kustrin on March 27th originated from the Frankfurt bridgehead, but Le Tissier's far more detailed account clearly indicates that this was not the case.

CHAPTER 29—WEEKS IN APRIL, YEARS IN MAY

1. Le Tissier. Ibid. p. 187.
2. An interesting comment regarding the Siegfried Line fighting has been made by the author of the combat history of the US 90th Infantry Division, John Colby. After participating in the final stages of the Battle of the Bulge, 90th Infantry Division did not see combat in the Siegfried Line until February 1945. By this

time relatively few of the hundreds of pillboxes and concrete blockhouses were occupied by German troops; even so it took several weeks of hard fighting for Colby's division to break through all these defensive barriers. The point he makes is that if the Siegfried Line had been as heavily defended in February as it had been in October and November—without so many German divisions thrown away in the Ardennes in the meantime—his division's attempts to crack this barrier could have been a nightmare.

See Colby, John. WAR FROM THE GROUND UP: THE 90TH DIVISION IN WW II. Austin: Nortex Press, 1991.

3. Le Tissier. Ibid. p. 218.

4. Lucas, James. WAR ON THE EASTERN FRONT. New York: Stein and Day, 1979. pp. 23–28.

5. Landau. Ibid. p. 108.

6. Ibid. p. 110.

7. Ibid. p. 108.

8. Ibid. p. 109.

9. Ibid. p. 112.

10. Neumann. Ibid. p. 258.

11. Ibid. p. 258.

12. Ibid. p. 275.

13. As with the cuffband incident in Hungary, Peiper's name will be forever associated with the massacre at Malmedy; both incidents have given rise to a seemingly endless number of versions and interpretations.

One point should be emphasized—the Malmedy Massacre was not the only instance of SS Leibstandarte men executing prisoners and Belgian civilians in the Ardennes battle. In particular, the killing of civilians seemed to stem from long-standing grudges and feuds between German and Belgian natives of this region—much of which had originally been German before being ceded to Belgium after World War I. The SS troopers took the view that many "non-Germanic" Belgian citizens were assisting the American forces and conducting guerrilla warfare. Perhaps there was some truth to this, but later scrutiny of these events indicates that these SS claims were highly exaggerated; in particular the execution of several hundred civilians around the village of Stavelot was no more than a ruthless murder of innocent hostages, in terrible scenes reminiscent of so many that had occurred during partisan warfare inside the Soviet Union.

Nonetheless, there remain some puzzling aspects to this affair. Why was it that only Peiper's Kampfgruppe, along with a few other SS Leibstandarte forces following behind him, left this trail of terror? SS Hitlerjugend and SS Das Reich were also heavily engaged in the Battle of the Bulge, and no accusations of massacres have been laid at their doors. If Peiper did not in fact order this campaign of terror—and the evidence for this remains maddeningly sketchy—why did his men behave so much more ruthlessly than the men of other SS units?

True, Peiper's force was the vanguard of the attack, and spent much of the battle operating in isolation deep in the American rear—a highly stressful situation which no doubt aggravated the SS penchant for ruthless reprisals against prisoners and civilians. But many eyewitness accounts also suggest that Peiper's men were out for blood right from the start.

The real issue though, at least in this book, remains Peiper himself. Realistically, it is unfair to blame a commanding officer when his men commit a spontaneous act of butchery when he himself is not present at the scene. This would seem to be the case for the incident at Malmedy. But when a commander's men commit such acts on numerous occasions in a short time span, the notion of his overall innocence in this business becomes more suspicious. While perhaps not issuing explicit orders, Peiper may well have tacitly condoned this kind of behavior to a far greater degree than he ever admitted to after the war. Even today his reputation among historians remains in a state of flux—while many have attempted to get at the "real facts" and clear his name, others continue to depict him as a typically ruthless product of the Waffen SS style of making war.

See: Kessler, Leo. SS PEIPER. Philomont: Eastern Front/Warfield Books, 1996.

Blumberg, Arnold. A WAVE OF TERROR. Command Magazine, Issue No. 41.

Weingartner, James. HITLER'S GUARD: THE STORY OF THE LEIBSTANDARTE SS ADOLF HITLER. Edwardsville: Southern Illinois University Press., 1974.

14. DeGrelle. Ibid. p. 327.
15. Ibid. p. 328.
16. Haupt. DIE 8. PANZER DIVISION. p. 409.
17. Ibid. p. 412.
18. Landau. Ibid. p. 123.

19. Ibid. p. 128.
20. Ibid. p. 154.
21. Ibid. See acknowledgements.

EPILOGUE

1. Tiemann. Ibid. p. 326.
2. Ibid. p. 329.
3. Ibid. p. 329.

ADDENDUM

Evidence suggests that Hitler and his Nazi party associates did consider the annihilation of the Russians, either in the form of deportation, slavery, or outright liquidation of large segments of the populace. Nazi plans for a subjugated Russian nation could by no means be called humane. The point is that German soldiers in Russia in 1941 did not behave like men of the Red Army in Germany in 1945—nor like the Japanese in China in 1938, another contemporary example. They did not engage in either spontaneous or premeditated orgies of murder, rape, and mutilation. (The exception posed by the SS Einsatzgruppen is discussed later in the chapter.) The German invasion of the Soviet Union was the most massive surprise attack in history by one nation upon another, replete with all the horror and devastation that such a campaign would entail. But ordinary German soldiers did not enter Russia intent on killing Russian civilians or for the annihilation of Slavic subhumans; this was not part of their pattern of behavior. Whatever sinister program Hitler and the Nazi leadership may ultimately have had in store for the Russian nation wasn't immediately implemented by the soldiers of the German Army.

Nevertheless the German Army was involved to some degree in the implementation and enforcement of Nazi occupation policies in the Soviet Union. German military leaders were aware of and, to varying degrees, involved with the cruelties of occupation policies. Clearly the all-consuming task of fighting the war was their chief concern, but they also shared responsibility for numerous repressive measures in the rear areas.

The simple element of Russian patriotism must also be added to this emotional cauldron, an element which Stalin cunningly utilized to deflect widespread fear and resentment of his own regime. And of course, given the mysterious and highly censored nature of Soviet society, there were millions of Russians who lived largely unaware of the extent of Stalin's criminality, or who did blame him personally for the abuses of the Soviet system. These citizens were easily motivated to fight with an ancient and deeply felt patriotism. The most diplomatic of conquerors would have faced enormous difficulties in subjugating the Soviet Union. The Germans possessed neither of these qualities. Many of the elements for a nightmarish circle of vengeance and counter-vengeance were already in place; more would soon be added.

BIBLIOGRAPHY

GENERAL

Bessell, Richard. *Life in the Third Reich*. London. Oxford University Press, 1985.

Carell, Paul. *Scorched Earth: The Russo-German War 1943–1944*. London. Harrap, 1970.

Clark, Alan. *Barbarossa: The Russo-German Conflict 1941–45*. New York. Quill Press, 1985.

Conquest, Robert. *The Kolyma*. New York. Viking, 1978.

Cooper, Matthew. *The Nazi War Against Soviet Partisans 1941–1944*. New York. Stein & Day, 1979.

Gander, Terry & Chamberlain, Peter. *Weapons of the Third Reich*. New York, Doubleday, 1979.

Glantz, David. *When Titans Clashed*. Lawrence. University of Kansas Press, 1996.

Goebbels, Joseph. *War Diaries 1942–1943*. New York. Doubleday, 1948.

Hamilton, Charles. *Leaders & Personalities of the Third Reich, Volume 2*. San Jose, R. James Bender Publishing, 1996.

Hardesty, Von. *Red Phoenix*. Washington. Smithsonian, 1984.

Haupt, Werner. *Das Buch der Infanterie*. Friedburg. Podzun Pallas.

Hohne, Heinz. *Order of the Death's Head, The Story of Hitler's SS*. London. Secker & Warburg, 1969.

Irving, David. *Hitler's War*. New York. Avon Books, 1990.

Kruuse, Jens. *War for an Afternoon*. New York. Random House, 1968.

Liddell-Hart, B.H. *The German Generals Talk*. New York. Morrow, 1948.

Lucas, James. *War on the Eastern Front: The German Soldier in Russia, 1941– 45*. New York. Stein & Day, 1979.

Madej, Victor. *Small Unit Actions on the Eastern Front*. Allentown, Valor Publishing, 1986.

Perrett, Bryan. *Knights of the Black Cross*. New York. St. Martins Press, 1986.

Sawodny, Wolfgang. *German Armored Trains in World War II*. West Chester. Schiffer Publishing Ltd., 1989.

Seaton, Albert. *The Russo-German War*. Westport. Praeger, 1971.

Stein, George. *The Waffen SS: Hitler's Elite Guard at War*. New York. Cornell University Press, 1966.

Stewart, Emilie Caldwell. *Signatures of the Third Reich*. Brigantine. Privately Published, 1996.

Thurston, Robert. *Life and Terror in Stalin's Russia*. Yale University Press, 1996.

Wallace, Robert. *Rise of Russia*. New York. Time-Life Books, 1967.

Ziemke, Earl. *Stalingrad to Berlin: The German Defeat in the East*. Washington. USGPO, 1968.

CAMPAIGN HISTORIES

Adair, Paul. *Hitler's Greatest Defeat: The Collapse of Army Group Center*. London, Arms & Armor Press, 1994.

Buchner, Alex. *Ostfront 1944: German Defensive Battles on the Russian Front 1944*. West Chester, Schiffer Publishing Ltd., 1991.

Duffy, Christopher. *Red Storm on the Reich: The Soviet March on Germany, 1945*. New York: Antheneum, 1991.

Elstob, Peter. *The Battle of the Reichswald*. New York. Ballantine Books, 1972.

Grau, Karl Friedrich. *Silesian Inferno: War Crimes of the Red Army on its March into Silesia in 1945*. Valley Forge. Landpost Press, 1984.

Haupt, Werner. *Kurland: Die Letze Front-Schicksal fur Zwei Armeen*. Bad Nauheim. Podzun Pallas, 1964.

Landwehr, Richard. *Budapest: The Stalingrad of the Waffen SS*. Siegrunen Magazine # 37, January-March 1985.

Landwehr, Richard. *Narva 1944: The Waffen SS and the Battle for Europe*. Silver Spring. Bibliophile Legion Books, 1981.

LeTissier, Tony. *Zhukov at the Oder: The Decisive Battle for Berlin*. Westport: Praeger, 1996.

Mc Taggart, Patrick. Konigsberg. World War II Magazine, March 1995.

Mc Taggart, Patrick. Budapest. Command Magazine # 31, November-December 1994.

Ruge, Friedrich. *The Soviets as Naval Opponents 1941–1945*. Annapolis, Naval Institute Press, 1979.

Ryan, Cornelius. *The Last Battle*. New York. Simon & Schuster, 1966.

Sellwood, A. V. *The Damned Don't Drown*. Annapolis, Naval Institute Press, 1973.

Thorwald, Jurgen. *Flight in Winter: Russia Conquers, January to May, 1945*. New York, Pantheon, 1951.

Toland, John. *The Last 100 Days*. New York. Random House, 1966.

Ziemke, Earl. *Berlin*. New York. Ballantine Books, 1972.

MEMOIRS and BIOGRAPHIES

Adamcyzk, Werner. *Feuer! An Artillerymens Life on the Eastern Front*. Wilmington: Broadfoot, 1992.

Anonymous. *A Woman in Berlin*. London. Secker and Warburg, 1955.

Blumberg, Arnold. Wave of Terror. Command Magazine # 41, January 1997.

Bullock, Alan. *Hitler and Stalin*. New York. Knopf, 1992.

Carius, Otto. *Tigers in the Mud*. Manitoba. JJ Fedorowicz Publishing, 1992.

DeGrelle, Leon. *Campaign in Russia: The Waffen SS in Russia*. Costa Mesa. Institute for Historical Review, 1985.

De la Maziere, Christian. *The Captive Dreamer*. New York. E.P. Dutton, 1972.

Foley, Charles. *Commando Extraordinary*. New York. Ballantine Books, 1957.

Galante, Pierre. *Voices From the Bunker*. New York. G. P. Putnam's & Sons, 1989.

Guderian, Heinz. *Panzer Leader*. New York. Da Capo Press, 1996.

Hitler, Adolph. Mein Kampf.

Kessler, Leo. *SS Peiper: The Life of SS Colonel Jochen Peiper*. Philomont. Eastern Front/Warfield Books Inc., 1995.

Kurowski, Franz. *Panzer Aces*. Manitoba. JJ Fedorowicz Publishing, 1992.

Landau, Heinz. *Goodbye Transylvania*. Derby. Breedon Books, 1985.

Meyer, Kurt. *Grenadiers*. Manitoba. JJ Fedorowicz Publishing, 1994.

Montyn, Jan. *A Lamb to Slaughter*. New York. Viking Press, 1986.

Neumann, Peter. *The Black March*. New York. Sloane, 1959.

Perros, Oskars. *Fortress Cholm*. Kurland Publishing, 1992.

Rall, Gunther. Interview World War II Magazine, March 1995.

Rudel, Hans. *Stuka Pilot*. New York. Ballantine Books, 1958.

Sajer, Guy. *The Forgotten Soldier*. New York. Harper & Row, 1971.

Virski, Fred. *My Life in the Red Army*. New York. MacMillan, 1949.

Von Ruhland, Paul. *As The World Churns*. New York. Vantage Press, 1986.

Wiswedel, A. *Gekampft und Uberlebt*. Braunschweig, 1984.

UNIT HISTORIES/ENGLISH LANGUAGE

Bender, Roger. *Uniforms and Traditions of the Waffen SS, Volumes 1–4*. San Jose, R. James Bender Publishing.

Colby, John. *War From the Ground Up: The 90th Division in WW II*. Austin. Nortex Press, 1991.

Fey, Willi. *Armor Battles of the Waffen SS, 1943–45*. Manitoba. JJ Fedorowicz Publishing, 1990.

Kuhne, Volkmar. *Tiger: History of a Legendary Weapon, 1942–45*. Manitoba. JJ Fedorowicz Publishing, 1989.

Landwehr, Richard. *Wallonian Legion*. Glendale. Sigruenen, 1992.

Lucas, James. *Storming Eagles: German Airborne Forces in World War Two*. London. Arms & Armor, 1988.

Meyer, Hubert. *History of the 12th SS Panzergrenadier Division Hitlerjugend*. Manitoba. JJ Fedorowicz Publishing, 1993.

Munoz, Anthony. *The Kaminski Brigade*. New York. Axis Europa, 1996.

Newland, Samuel. *Cossacks in the German Army*. London, Frank Cass, 1992.

Schneider, Wolfgang. *Tigers in Combat, Vol. 1*. Manitoba. JJ Fedorowicz Publishing. 1994.

Silgailis, Artur. *Latvian Legion*. San Jose. R. James Bender Publishing, 1986.

Stahl, Peter. *KG 200*. London. Janes Publishing, 1981.

Strassner, Peter. *European Volunteers: The 5th SS Panzer Division "Wiking."* Manitoba. JJ Fedorowicz Publishing, 1988.

Yerger, Mark. *Riding East: The SS Cavalry Divisions*. Atglen. Schiffer Publishing Ltd., 1996.

Sydnor, Charles. *Soldiers of Destruction: The SS Death's Head Division, 1933–1945*. Princeton. Princeton University Press, 1977.

UNIT HISTORIES/GERMAN LANGUAGE
GERMAN ARMY—INFANTRY DIVISIONS

5th Jager Division
35th Infantry Division
44th Infantry Division
61st Infantry Division
72nd Infantry Division
78th Infantry Division
83rd Infantry Division
205th Infantry Division
215th Infantry Division
252nd Infantry Division

GERMAN ARMY—PANZER DIVISIONS

1st Panzer Division
6th Panzer Division
7th Panzer Division/Text
8th Panzer Division/Photo
8th Panzer Division/Text
13th Panzer Division
16th Panzer Division
19th Panzer Division
Grossdeutschland Panzergrenadier Division. Spaeter
Grossdeutschland Panzerkorps. Spaeter
Grossdeutschland 1942–1944. Spaeter/Text

WAFFEN SS

Die Leibstandarte im Bild. Tiemann
Das Reich im Bild. Weidinger
Wie Ein Fels im Meer, Bande 1 & 2. Ulrich.
Die Guten Glaubens Waren.
Kavallerie Divisionen der Waffen SS im Bild
Grenadier Divisionen der Waffen SS, Bande 1, 2, & 3. Michaelis, Rolf.

NOVELIZED ACCOUNTS

Baklanov, Grigory. *South of the Main Offensive*. Philadelphia, Dufours, 1963.

Grossman, Vassily. *Life and Fate*. New York. Perrennial Press, 1980.

Hassel, Sven. *Legion of the Damned*. London. Allen Unwin, 1957; *Wheels of Terror*; *Comrades of War*. London. Sovenir Press, 1960.

Kazakevitch, E. *Spring on the Oder*. Moscow, 1953.

Rybalkov, A. *Dust and Ashes*.

Simonov, Konstantin. *Days and Nights*.

DEUTSCHE WOCHESCHAU—Newsreel excerpts from throughout the war.